BEHAVIORAL ADDICTIONS

Criteria, Evidence, and Treatment

BEHAVIORAL ADDICTIONS

Criteria, Evidence, and Treatment

Edited by

KENNETH PAUL ROSENBERG, M.D.

Cornell University Medical Center, Psychiatry Department, New York, NY, USA and UpperEastHealth.com

LAURA CURTISS FEDER, Psy.D.

Wellesley, MA, USA, www.drlaurafeder.com

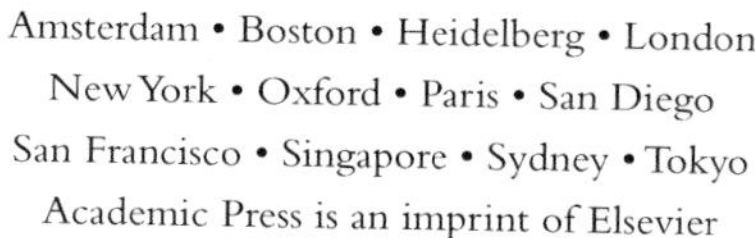
Amsterdam • Boston • Heidelberg • London
New York • Oxford • Paris • San Diego
San Francisco • Singapore • Sydney • Tokyo
Academic Press is an imprint of Elsevier

Academic Press is an imprint of Elsevier
32 Jamestown Road, London NW1 7BY, UK
225 Wyman Street, Waltham, MA 02451, USA
525 B Street, Suite 1800, San Diego, CA 92101-4495, USA

British Library Cataloguing-in-Publication Data
A catalogue record for this book is available from the British Library

Library of Congress Cataloging-in-Publication Data
A catalog record for this book is available from the Library of Congress

ISBN: 978-0-12-407724-9

For information on all Academic Press publications
visit our website at elsevierdirect.com

Typeset by TNQ Books and Journals
www.tnq.co.in

Printed and bound in United States of America

14 15 16 17 10 9 8 7 6 5 4 3 2 1

DEDICATION

For Claire and Alexander, Jonathan and Lilah

CONTENTS

FOREWORD

In *DSM-5* for the first time, the American Psychiatric Association added a non-substance addiction to the category of addictive disorders. In May 2013, Gambling Disorder was grouped in the section on Substance Use Disorders. Gambling appears in prior versions of the *DSM* as "Pathological Gambling" grouped with the impulse control disorders. Thus, the main effect of the 2013 revision was to change the name and the grouping. The criteria were modified slightly by the symptom threshold to four or more symptoms.

Recent research on gambling has revealed a clinical course similar to that of addictions, and recent brain imaging findings show that cues associated with gambling activate reward structures in the brain much the way addicting drugs do. The committee took the position that addiction is a disease of the reward system, and gambling activates brain reward structures that reinforce compulsive gambling behaviors. Thus, a behavior that activates the reward system can have the same effect as a drug.

The work group considered other behaviors as potential candidates for inclusion in *DSM* but maintained the consistent policy of requiring data in the peer-reviewed literature showing evidence for inclusion. Another behavior disorder, excessive Internet gaming, was seriously considered for inclusion because there are over 200 publications on "Internet Addiction." The papers, however, lack consistent diagnostic criteria. Most of the cases have been reported in Asian populations such as China, South Korea, and Japan. The group finally decided to add "Internet gaming disorder" in section 3 (Appendix) with a description of what future studies would be required to have this disorder later added to the main group. It is hoped that adding Internet gaming disorder to the Appendix of *DSM-5* will stimulate more research and perhaps result in its inclusion in the main body of the classification in a future revision.

Other behavior disorders were considered. They include sex addiction, food addiction, exercise addiction, and shopping addiction. The group adhered to the policy of not including any disorder that was not supported by multiple studies in peer-reviewed literature, although *Behavioral Addictions: Criteria, Evidence, and Treatment* addresses many of these disorders in great detail.

Thus, this volume on behavioral addictions is timely and should serve as a stimulus for more research. Data on prevalence in different populations, for example, would be helpful. Is there a gender effect? If so, what is the male:female ratio? Is there evidence of hereditary influence? What is the peak age of onset and range of age of those afflicted? What are the results of treatment? Do some patients simply outgrow the disorder?

For the clinician reading this book, it is my hope that Rosenberg and Feder's text will inform clinicians about the concepts of behavioral addiction and help clinicians assess and treat these patients with improved understanding of the behavioral principles involved.

Charles P. O'Brien, M.D., Ph.D.
Chair, DSM American Psychiatric Association
Task Force on Substance Abuse Disorders
Kenneth Appel Professor
Department of Psychiatry
University of Pennsylvania

PREFACE

In mental health and addiction treatment, the true pioneers have not been the medical experts or the providers, but the advocates and patients themselves. These men and women who came together in back rooms and 12-step meetings to declare that their behaviors constituted a medical illness that required treatment. In the 1930s, the pioneering movement was Alcoholics Anonymous. In the latter part of the 20th century, drug addicts and "pathological gamblers" (as they were then called) found a similar degree of solace, support, and healing from their peers, and founded groups such as Narcotics Anonymous and Gamblers Anonymous. Most recently, sex, love, shopping, food, and Internet "addicts" and advocates have also banded together and founded groups such as Overeaters Anonymous, Sex and Love Addicts Anonymous, and Debtors Anonymous. Much of the work here had been developed and inspired by these advocates in the community, and this book draws on and crystallizes their work in the first major text on the collective topic of behavioral addiction. Our aim is to move the body of literature forward by synthesizing existing opinions and research on the topic.

This book works to elevate the discussion about behavioral addictions into the medical and mental health lexicon with the science and theory that support it so patients can be taken more seriously and be less stigmatized as those with character flaws, personal weaknesses, or a lack of willpower and, rather, get the actual help and support they need in the form of documented and evidence-based treatment. Our text offers clinicians and researchers a basis for having informed discussions that will propel our field forward.

As an addiction psychiatrist and a clinical psychologist working together to edit this book (and formerly practicing together at *Upper East Health*, a multidisciplinary addiction treatment practice in Manhattan), we advocate and abide by a multidisciplinary and integrative treatment philosophy that is grounded in both research and theory. This book is an effort to bring together experts from various backgrounds and disciplines to address the topic of behavioral addiction, with an emphasis on treatment.

This book benefits from authors who are renowned clinicians and preeminent thinkers in their specialties. Most of our authors are trained in the basic sciences and are accomplished researchers. A few of the authors offer a perspective that could only belong to a trained outsider and observer. One author is an anthropologist. Another is an attorney trained in mental health law. One of our authors is an Indian spiritual leader with tens of millions of followers, co-writing the chapter with one of the book's editors.

We hope our readership includes clinicians (such as psychiatrists, psychologists, social workers, and mental health counselors) as well as nurses, physician assistants, doctors, clergy, and others in various helping and healing professions who work with those struggling with behavioral addiction. We also anticipate that some patients and their family members will peruse these pages. Some attorneys might find some of the information useful, as may those studying anthropology and sociology.

Each chapter works to provide the current research and data about how a particular behavioral addiction is defined and understood, including the clinical criteria, epidemiology, common comorbidities, and differential diagnoses and treatment recommendations. Clinical vignettes are then used to further illustrate the disorder.

Our text begins with introductory remarks about the inclusion of behavioral addictions into the psychiatric lexicon in the American Psychiatric Association's *Diagnostic and Statistical Manual of Mental Disorders,* Fifth Edition (*DSM-5*). We then present our own overview of the nature, phenomenology, and potential etiology of behavioral addictions. Given that some of the current behavioral addictions were originally classified as impulsive disorders or variants of obsessive-compulsive disorder, our next chapter explores the distinction and intersections between impulsive, compulsive, and addictive disorders. Gambling disorder, the most universally accepted behavioral addiction, is the first diagnostic category presented in the book. What follows are the chapters on particular behavioral addictions, roughly presented in order of popular acceptance. Certain behavioral addictions warrant more than one chapter. Abuses of the Internet are spelled out in three chapters: one on Internet addiction disorder, one on Internet gaming, and one on addictive social networking. Food addiction is explored in two chapters: one exploring the topic generally with a case example focusing on psychotherapy and one chapter on developments in the pharmacology of weight loss and food addiction, with a case example about medication choices. Sexual addiction is explored in two chapters: one on the overall disorder and a second on the delicate family issues that arise when one's partner or parent is revealed as a sex addict. More controversial diagnoses such as shopping, exercise, and love addiction are explored in scholarly and thorough chapters. Toward the end of the book, we include a chapter on meditation, mindfulness, spirituality, and yoga—Eastern techniques gaining popularity for treating addiction that are not addressed elsewhere in the book. In the final chapter, a mental health lawyer discusses what all this may mean in a court of law and gives suggestions for clinicians testifying as expert witnesses. We have chosen to focus on the addictions that currently have the most research support, and we have not included behaviors such as "workaholism" and excessive, unnecessary plastic surgery, which may be seen by some as addictions and which may be addressed in future editions. We have also not included chapters on disorders that fall more into the obsessive-compulsive and impulsive realm, such as trichotillomania and intermittent explosive disorder, but our authors do address the overlaps between obsessive, impulsive, and addictive disorders in Chapter 2 and elsewhere.

Our eclectic group of authors may hail from a range of disciplines and from around the globe, but all share an appreciation of the biopsychosocial addiction model. Hence, each chapter explains how biological, psychological, and sociocultural factors influence the development of the given disorder, and how they may inform treatment. Many chapters also address the overlapping factors of impulsivity and compulsivity, and among our authors, there is some debate about whether an orthogonal model of understanding these traits is more suitable than considering them to fall along a single spectrum.

Given where the field stands currently, we have edited a book that lives on the frontiers of science and clinical care. A book that is a collection of ideas and works to take the pulse of state-of-the-art behavioral addiction research, diagnosis, and treatment. Tentative concepts, speculative neuroscience, measured advocacy, healthy cynicism, and a commitment to clinical care are evident in every chapter. Consensus is not reached, as it does not currently exist, but the varying points of view—along with the data presented and the clinical vignettes presented throughout—provide a nuanced understanding of behavioral addictions as they are understood today.

We extend our gratitude to our publisher Nikki Levy at Elsevier Press for giving us the idea to write the book, and to our senior editorial project manager Barbara Makinster for her patience and trust in us. We also thank all of our authors who worked tirelessly. We thank those whose work informs these pages, but did not contribute, instead providing mentorship, support, and/or direction in the effort to solicit appropriate authors for these chapters: April Benson, Ph.D.; Donald Black, M.D.; Hilarie Cash,

Ph.D.; Robert Filewich; Allen Frances, M.D.; Richard Frances, M.D.; Martin Kafka, M.D.; Lorrin Koran, M.D.; Jean Petrucelli, Ph.D.; David Preven, M.D., Ph.D.; Bruce Roseman, M.D.; Todd Sacktor, M.D.; and Gail Zitin, M.Ed. Additionally, we thank the many researchers and developers who allowed reproduction of their behavioral addiction assessment scales in the appendices of our chapters. And most of all, we thank our patients, who continue to be generous with their life stories that are revealed in these pages, and who teach and inspire us with their dedication and determination to improve their lives.

Kenneth Paul Rosenberg, M.D. and Laura Curtiss Feder, Psy.D.

BIOGRAPHY

CO-EDITORS OF BEHAVIORAL ADDICTIONS: CRITERIA, EVIDENCE, AND TREATMENT

Kenneth Paul Rosenberg, MD, is a board-certified Addiction Psychiatrist and a Clinical Associate Professor in Psychiatry at the New York Presbyterian Hospital–Weill Cornell Medical College. He is Consulting Editor for the *Journal of Sex and Marital Therapy*, a Distinguished Fellow of the American Psychiatric Association, and has been recognized on the lists of *U.S. World & News Report* Best Doctors and *New York Magazine's* Top Addiction Psychiatrists. Dr. Rosenberg is Founder and Director of *Upper East Health Behavioral Medicine* in Manhattan, a psychiatric practice that provides treatment for individuals and families recovering from chemical and behavioral addictions. He has discussed addiction on national broadcasts of HBO, PBS, ABC, CNBC, and CNN and in the *New York Times, Washington Post, Huffington Post, Time Magazine,* and *People Magazine.* Dr. Rosenberg has produced educational films on mental health and addiction for HBO and PBS, and is a recipient of a George Foster Peabody Award.

Laura Curtiss Feder, PsyD, is a licensed clinical psychologist and mental health consultant in private practice in New York and Massachusetts. Her areas of specialty include treating addiction and compulsive behaviors, as well as program evaluation and college counseling. She has engaged in many years of clinical and research work in the fields of substance abuse and behavioral addiction. She has contributed to scholarly publications on the assessment and treatment of substance abuse and written for popular audiences on the emotional aspects of skin picking and acne on Birchbox's blog and in *100 Acne Tips & Solutions: The Clear Clinic Guide to Perfect Skin.* Dr. Feder holds her doctorate in clinical psychology from Rutgers, The State University of New Jersey, and completed postdoctoral fellowships at the William Alanson White Institute, including receiving a certificate in the treatment of eating disorders, compulsions, and addictions. To learn more about Dr. Feder, her research, consulting and clinical practice please see www.drlaurafeder.com.

FOREWORD

Charles P. O'Brien, MD, PhD, is the Vice Chair of Psychiatry at the University of Pennsylvania and the Director of the prestigious Center for Studies in Addiction. As a pre-eminent addiction researcher, Dr. O'Brien has made many important discoveries and contributions over the past 30 years that have become the standard of care in addiction treatment throughout the world, including developing medications to treat alcohol, opioid, and cocaine dependence; and increasing the understanding of the clinical aspects of addiction and the neurobiology of relapse.

CHAPTER 1: AN INTRODUCTION TO BEHAVIORAL ADDICTIONS

Kenneth Paul Rosenberg, MD (see above)
Laura Curtiss Feder, PsyD (see above)

CHAPTER 2: BEHAVIORAL ADDICTION: THE NEXUS OF IMPULSIVITY AND COMPULSIVITY

Natalie Leckie Cuzen, MA, is a Neuropsychologist and researcher at the University of Cape Town, with a background in addiction research in both adult and pediatric populations. She has also worked with individuals with obsessive-compulsive and substance use disorders in the United Kingdom.

Dan J. Stein, FRCPC, PhD, is Professor & Chair of the Department of Psychiatry at the University of Cape Town, and Director of the South African Medical Research Council (MRC) Unit on Anxiety & Stress Disorders. He has undertaken research on compulsive and impulsive disorders for many years and was Chair of the *DSM-5* subWorkgroup on obsessive-compulsive and related disorders.

CHAPTER 3: DIAGNOSIS AND TREATMENT OF GAMBLING DISORDER

Jon Grant, MD, JD, MPH, is a Professor of Psychiatry and Behavioral Neuroscience at the University of Chicago. Dr. Grant has written more than 200 peer-reviewed articles and book chapters on the phenomenology and pharmacological management of behavioral addictions and impulse control disorders, particularly pathological gambling, kleptomania, and grooming disorders.

Brian Odlaug, MPH, is a Visiting Researcher in the Department of Public Health, Faculty of Health & Medical Sciences at the University of Copenhagen, Denmark. He has authored or co-authored more than 120 peer-reviewed articles and book chapters on the phenomenology, treatment, and characteristics of mental illness, specializing in the areas of addiction, impulse control, and obsessive-compulsive disorder.

CHAPTER 4: PROBLEMATIC ONLINE GAMING

Orsolya Király, MA, earned her master's degrees in Marketing and Sociology at Babeş-Bolyai University, Cluj-Napoca, Romania. She is currently a researcher at the Doctoral School of Psychology, Eötvös Loránd University, Budapest, Hungary. Her research focus is the psychology of video games and she is particularly interested in the phenomenon of problematic gaming ("gaming addiction") and other behavioral addictions.

Katalin Nagygyörgy, MA, completed her master's degree in Psychology from the University of Szeged, Hungary, and is now a doctoral candidate at the Institute of Psychology, Eötvös Loránd University, Budapest, Hungary. Her focus of research is the psychology of online games and virtual environments, mainly the motivational background of problematic online gaming.

Mark D. Griffiths, PhD, CPsychol, FBPsS, FRSA, AcSS, is a Chartered Psychologist and Professor of Gambling Studies at the Nottingham Trent University (United Kingdom). He is internationally known for his work on behavioral addiction and has published more than 430 refereed research papers, 3 books, more than 100 book chapters, and has won 14 awards for his research.

Zsolt Demetrovics, PhD, is a Clinical Psychologist and Cultural Anthropologist and has a doctorate in addiction science. He is Professor of Psychology and Director of the Institute of Psychology at the Eötvös Loránd University, Budapest, Hungary. His primary research is focused on the epidemiology and psychological background of legal and illegal substance use and behavioral addictions.

CHAPTER 5: INTERNET ADDICTION DISORDER: OVERVIEW AND CONTROVERSIES

Aviv Weinstein, PhD, is a Psychologist and Senior Lecturer at the Behavioral Sciences Department at Ariel University and a Senior Research fellow at the Department of Nuclear Medicine at Tel Aviv Sourasky Medical Center in Israel. He has conducted brain imaging studies on the effects of drugs and video game playing on the brain and has published several reviews on behavioral addictions, particularly on Internet and video game addiction.

Laura Curtiss Feder, PsyD (see above)
Kenneth Paul Rosenberg, MD (see above)

Pinhas Dannon, MD, is a Psychiatrist and Head of the Psychiatric Rehabilitation Department at Beer Yaaqov Ness Ziona Center for Mental Health. He is also an Associate Professor at Sackler School of Medicine at Tel Aviv University in Israel and has a private practice specializing in the treatment of drug and behavioral addictions. He has published extensively on gambling, kleptomania, and other behavioral addictions.

CHAPTER 6: SOCIAL NETWORKING ADDICTION: AN OVERVIEW OF PRELIMINARY FINDINGS

Mark D. Griffiths, PhD, CPsychol, FBPsS, FRSA, AcSS (see above)

Daria J. Kuss, PhD, is a doctoral researcher at Nottingham Trent University interested in Internet culture and psychopathology. With her research, she intends to establish a comprehensive picture of Internet addiction by highlighting its clinical and societal relevance as discrete and prevalent disorder, and has published widely in the field.

Zsolt Demetrovics, PhD (see above)

CHAPTER 7: FOOD ADDICTION: EVIDENCE, EVALUATION, AND TREATMENT

Yvonne H. C. Yau, MSc, is a Postgraduate Associate at the Department of Psychiatry, Yale University School of Medicine. She has published several book chapters on obesity, binge-eating disorder, and food addiction.

Carrie D. Gottlieb, PhD, is a clinical psychologist in private practice in New York City focusing on the treatment of eating disorders and addictions. She is currently on the faculty of the William Alanson White Institute Eating Disorders, Compulsions, and Addictions Program.

Lindsay C. Krasna, MA, EdM, RD, CDN, is a Registered Dietitian and Certified Dietitian–Nutritionist, with graduate training in mental health counseling and addictions. She works in New York City as a Nutrition Counselor and specializes in eating disorders.

Marc N. Potenza, MD, PhD, is a Professor of Psychiatry, Child Study, and Neurobiology at Yale University. He is the Director of the Center of Excellence in Gambling Research and the Yale Program for Research on Impulsivity and Impulse Control Disorders. Dr. Potenza has published multiple research articles and book chapters on obesity, binge-eating disorder, and food addiction.

CHAPTER 8: NEW DIRECTIONS IN THE PHARMACOLOGICAL TREATMENT OF FOOD ADDICTION, OVEREATING, AND OBESITY

Amelia A. Davis, MD, is the Chief of the Adult Eating Disorders Recovery Center (EDRC) program in Psychiatry at the University of Florida. Dr. Davis specializes in evaluation and treatment of anorexia nervosa, bulimia nervosa, and other eating disorders.

Paula J. Edge, BA, has worked in the University of Florida Department of Psychiatry for 37 years and is the Editorial Program Assistant to Mark S. Gold, MD. From 2004 to the present, she has co-authored seven papers with Dr. Gold and other faculty.

Mark S. Gold, MD, is the Donald Dizney Eminent Scholar, Distinguished Alumni Professor, and Chairman of Psychiatry at the College of Medicine and McKnight Brain Institute, University of Florida in Gainesville, Florida. Dr. Gold is a national and internationally known addiction expert, who has been called "the most prolific and brilliant of the addiction experts writing today" by the *Journal of the American Medical Association*.

CHAPTER 9: SEX ADDICTION: AN OVERVIEW

Kenneth Paul Rosenberg, MD (see above)

Suzanne O'Connor, MA, was a Research Assistant and Project Coordinator for the International Institute for Trauma and Addiction Professionals (IITAP) for 8 years. She is finishing her doctorate in Clinical Psychology at Arizona School of Professional Psychology at Argosy University and is currently completing a predoctoral internship in Neuropsychology.

Patrick Carnes, PhD, is an author who has published widely on the topic of sexual addiction as well as related behavioral addiction issues for popular and professional audiences, beginning with *Out of the Shadows: Understanding Sexual Addiction* in 1992. Dr. Carnes is co-editor of *Sexual Addiction and Compulsivity: The Journal of Treatment and Prevention*. He developed a therapeutic technology based on his landmark study of the recoveries of roughly 1,000 sex addicts and opened the first inpatient facility treating sexual addiction in Minnesota prior to his position as Clinical Director for Sexual Disorder Services at The Meadows in Wickenburg, Arizona.

CHAPTER 10: THE TYRANNY OF LOVE: LOVE ADDICTION—AN ANTHROPOLOGIST'S VIEW

Helen Fisher, PhD, is a biological anthropologist at Rutgers University and Senior Research Fellow, The Kinsey Institute, Indiana University. She studies the evolution, brain systems (using fMRI), and biological patterns of romantic love, mate choice, marriage, adultery, and divorce. She has written five internationally bestselling books and publishes widely in academic journals. She lectures worldwide on the science of love, sex, and marriage, including lectures at the World Economic Forum (at Davos), the 2012 international meeting of the G-20, the National Academy of Sciences, the United Nations, The Economist, TED, Harvard Medical School, the Salk Institute, and The Aspen Institute. See her full CV at helenfisher.com.

CHAPTER 11: PICKING UP THE PIECES: HELPING PARTNERS AND FAMILY MEMBERS SURVIVE THE IMPACT OF SEX ADDICTION

Stefanie Carnes, PhD, CSAT-S, is the President of the International Institute for Trauma and Addiction Professionals. Her area of expertise is working with clients and families struggling with multiple addictions, such as sexual addiction, eating disorders, and chemical dependency. Dr. Carnes is the co-author of *Facing Heartbreak: Steps to Recovery for Partners of Sex Addicts.*

Mari A. Lee, LMFT, CSAT-S, is a Licensed Marriage and Family Therapist, a Certified Sex Addiction Therapist, and the founder of Growth Counseling Services in Glendora, California. Mari is an expert sex addiction therapist, and a popular national speaker on her ground-breaking work with spouses/partners. She co-authored *Facing Heartbreak: Steps to Recovery for Partners of Sex Addicts*. You can learn more about Mari's work at www.marileetherapy.com.

CHAPTER 12: COMPULSIVE BUYING DISORDER

Emma Racine, BA, is the Study Supervisor at the Compulsive, Impulsive, and Autism Spectrum Program at Albert Einstein College of Medicine and Montefiore Medical Center, Bronx, New York. She graduated magna cum laude from Hamilton College and is a member of the Phi Beta Kappa National Honors Society. She completed the post baccalaureate program in Psychology at Columbia University before beginning her work with Eric Hollander, MD.

Tara Kahn, BA, worked as the Study Supervisor at the Compulsive, Impulsive, and Autism Spectrum Program at Albert Einstein College of Medicine and Montefiore Medical Center, Bronx, New York, from 2012 to 2013. She has co-authored two other medical papers, one on panic and schizophrenia and the other on depression and autism. She graduated with honors from Wesleyan University and is currently pursuing a master's degree in Anthropology at Columbia University.

Eric Hollander, MD, is Clinical Professor of Psychiatry and Behavioral Sciences and Director of the Compulsive, Impulsive, and Autism Spectrum Program at Albert Einstein College of Medicine and Montefiore Medical Center, Bronx, New York. He is also Director of the Spectrum Neuroscience and Treatment Institute in New York, New York. Dr. Hollander served as the Chair of the Research Planning Agenda for *DSM-5* for Obsessive-Compulsive Spectrum Disorders and is a Member of the *DSM-5* Workgroup for Obsessive-Compulsive-Related Disorders; and Advisor for Behavioral Addictions and for the Anxiety, Post-Traumatic, and Obsessive-Compulsive chapter.

CHAPTER 13: EXERCISE ADDICTION

Krisztina Berczik, MA, is a PhD student at the Doctoral School of Psychology, Eötvös Loránd University, Budapest, Hungary. Her main research interest is exercise addiction. She is a clinical psychologist and is working at the Department of Clinical Psychology and Addiction at the Institute of Psychology, Eötvös Loránd University.

Mark D. Griffiths, PhD, CPsychol, FBPsS, FRSA, AcSS (see above)

Attila Szabo, PhD, completed his doctorate at the University of Montreal in Canada. Subsequently, he taught at Nottingham Trent University (UK) in the area of Psychology and Sport Sciences for nearly 9 years. Currently, he is Associate Professor and Deputy Director in the Institute for Health Promotion and Sport Sciences at Eötvös Loránd University.

Tamás Kurimay, MD, PhD, graduated from Semmelweis University Budapest in 1979. He is Head of the Saint John Hospital and North-Buda Integrated Hospitals, Psychiatric and Psychiatric Rehabilitation Department, Budapest, Hungary. He teaches at the Semmelweis University and Eötvös Loránd University. He has been published in more than 60 scientific publications and is author or co-author of more than 20 books and book chapters. His main interests are how to utilize and influence biopsychosocial systems, sports-related topics, and networks including families.

Róbert Urbán, PhD, is an Associate Professor of Health Psychology at the Institute of Psychology, Eötvös Loránd University, Budapest, Hungary. His main research fields are in health-related behaviors, with a special focus on smoking, psychometric analysis/scale development, and psychosocial epidemiology.

Zsolt Demetrovics, PhD (see above)

CHAPTER 14: MEDITATION AND SPIRITUALITY-BASED APPROACHES FOR ADDICTION

His Holiness Sri Sri Ravi Shankar is the founder of The Art of Living Foundation, which offers yoga and meditation-based self-development programs in 152 countries. He has published commentaries on many ancient yogic texts and is a well-respected authority on yoga and meditation. He has addressed many prestigious global forums such as the United Nations, the European Parliament, and World Economic Forum. He has also been honored by several governments and been awarded many honorary doctorates by universities around the world.

Kenneth Paul Rosenberg, MD (see above)

Anju Dhawan, MBBS, MD, is psychiatrist and working as Professor at the National Drug Dependence Treatment Centre of the All India Institute of Medical Sciences. She has conducted several research projects and has several publications in journals and books. Her areas of interest include the role of yoga in management of substance use disorders, service delivery in the public health perspective, opioid substitution treatment, and adolescent drug abuse.

Achar Vedamurthachar, PhD, completed a master's degree in Physiology and the Discovery channel broadcast a program based on his doctoral thesis work, "Biological Effects of Yogic Procedures during Alcohol Rehabilitation." He has done several research projects with the National Institute of Mental Health and Neuro Sciences, Bangalore, studying the effects of yoga (particularly Sudarshan Kriya Yoga) on different types of control groups. He has several publications and has also widely presented his work at conferences.

CHAPTER 15: BEHAVIORAL ADDICTION IN AMERICAN LAW: THE FUTURE AND THE EXPERT'S ROLE

Daniel H. Willick, JD, PhD practices health and mental health law in Los Angeles and teaches in the medical schools at the University of California, Los Angeles, and the University of Southern California. He represents physicians and medical groups, is a medical staff hearing officer, and is general counsel to the California Psychiatric Association. He has been a consultant to the University of California system on mental health law and has been involved in important cases concerning mental health confidentiality, including the Menendez brothers' murder case, the civil suit against O. J. Simpson for wrongful death, and the Clergy Abuse cases.

LIST OF CONTRIBUTORS

Krisztina Berczik
Department of Clinical Psychology and Addiction, Institute of Psychology, Eötvös Loránd University, Budapest, Hungary; Doctoral School of Psychology, Eötvös Loránd University, Budapest, Hungary

Patrick Carnes
The Meadows, Wickenburg, AZ, USA

Stefanie Carnes
International Institute for Trauma and Addiction Professionals, Carefree, AZ, USA

Natalie L. Cuzen
Department of Psychiatry and Mental Health, University of Cape Town, Cape Town, South Africa

Pinhas Dannon
Sackler School of Medicine and Beer Yaakov Ness Ziona Center for Mental Health, Israel

Amelia A. Davis
Department of Psychiatry, College of Medicine, University of Florida, Gainesville, FL, USA

Zsolt Demetrovics
Department of Clinical Psychology and Addiction, Institute of Psychology, Eötvös Loránd University, Budapest, Hungary

Anju Dhawan
National Drug Dependence Treatment Centre, AIIMS, New Delhi, India

Paula J. Edge
Department of Psychiatry, College of Medicine, University of Florida, Gainesville, FL, USA

Laura Curtiss Feder
Wellesley, MA, USA

Helen E. Fisher
Member, Center for Human Evolutionary Studies, Rutgers University, New Brunswick, New Jersey, USA and Senior Research Fellow, The Kinsey Institute, Indiana University, Bloomington, IN, USA

Mark S. Gold
Department of Psychiatry Chairman, College of Medicine and McKnight Brain Institute, University of Florida, Gainesville, FL, USA

Carrie D. Gottlieb
Private Practice and The William Alanson White Institute Eating Disorders, Compulsions, and Addictions Program, New York, NY, USA

Jon E. Grant
University of Chicago, Department of Psychiatry & Behavioral Neuroscience, Chicago, IL, USA

Mark D. Griffiths
International Gaming Research Unit, Psychology Division, Nottingham Trent University, Nottingham, UK

Eric Hollander
Albert Einstein College of Medicine and Montefiore Medical Center, Bronx NY, USA

Tara Kahn
Albert Einstein College of Medicine and Montefiore Medical Center, Bronx NY, USA

Orsolya Király
Department of Clinical Psychology and Addiction, Institute of Psychology, Eötvös Loránd University, Budapest, Hungary; Department of Clinical Psychology and Addiction, Doctoral School of Psychology, Eötvös Loránd University, Budapest, Hungary

Lindsay C. Krasna
New York, NY, USA

Tamás Kurimay
Institute for Health Promotion and Sport Sciences, Eötvös Loránd University, Budapest, Hungary

Daria J. Kuss
International Gaming Research Unit, Psychology Division, Nottingham Trent University, Nottingham, UK

Mari A. Lee
Growth Counseling Services, Glendora, CA, USA

Katalin Nagygyörgy
Department of Clinical Psychology and Addiction, Institute of Psychology, Eötvös Loránd University, Budapest, Hungary; Department of Clinical Psychology and Addiction, Doctoral School of Psychology, Eötvös Loránd University, Budapest, Hungary

Suzanne O'Connor
Arizona School of Professional Psychology at Argosy University, Phoenix, AZ, USA

Brian L. Odlaug
University of Copenhagen, Department of Public Health, Faculty of Health & Medical Sciences, Copenhagen, Denmark

Marc N. Potenza
Department of Psychiatry, Yale University School of Medicine, New Haven, CT, USA; Department of Child Study and Neurobiology, Yale University School of Medicine, New Haven, CT, USA

Emma Racine
Albert Einstein College of Medicine and Montefiore Medical Center, Bronx NY, USA

Sri Sri Ravi Shankar
The Art of Living Foundation, Ved Vignan Mahavidyapeeth, Bangalore, Karnataka, India

Kenneth Paul Rosenberg
Cornell University Medical Center, Psychiatry Department, New York, NY, USA and UpperEastHealth.com

Dan J. Stein
Department of Psychiatry and Mental Health, University of Cape Town, Cape Town, South Africa

Attila Szabó
Department of Psychiatry and Psychiatric Rehabilitation, Saint John Hospital, Budapest, Hungary

Róbert Urban
Department of Personality and Health Psychology, Institute of Psychology, Eötvös Loránd University, Budapest, Hungary

Achar Vedamurthachar
Centre for Addiction Medicine, National Institute of Mental Health and Neuro Sciences, Bangalore, Karnataka, India

Aviv Weinstein
Department of Behavioral Sciences, Faculty of Social Sciences and Humanities, Ariel University, Israel

Daniel H. Willick
Los Angeles, CA, USA

Yvonne H.C. Yau
Department of Psychiatry, Yale University School of Medicine, New Haven, CT, USA

CHAPTER 1

An Introduction to Behavioral Addictions

Kenneth Paul Rosenberg[1], Laura Curtiss Feder[2]
[1]Cornell University Medical Center, Psychiatry Department, New York, NY, USA and UpperEastHealth.com,
[2]Wellesley, MA, USA, www.drlaurafeder.com

THE HISTORY OF BEHAVIORAL ADDICTIONS

The concept of behavioral addictions is a new and revolutionary concept in American psychiatry. History is replete with sagas of disordered gambling and sex addiction. In ancient Greece, where organized gaming was part and parcel of daily life, Emperor Commodus possessed hedonistic and irresponsible gambling habits that may have contributed to the decline of the Roman Empire (Hekster, 2002). In the 1812 edition of the first American text on mental illness, Benjamin Rush, the founder of the American Psychiatric Association, called attention to the potentially pathological nature of excessive sexual desire (Rush, 1812). But it was not until 2010 that the Diagnostic and Statistical Manual Work Group for the *Diagnostic and Statistical Manual of Mental Disorders,* Fifth Edition (*DSM-5*), added the term *behavioral addictions* to the set of official psychiatric diagnoses. Their proposals documented a new era in the conceptualization of addictions. The work group argued that the phrase *addictions and related disorders* was a more appropriate descriptor than the old terms *substance abuse and dependence.* They argued that not all people who were dependent on substances were addicts (i.e., cancer patients requiring opiates) and that addiction was much more than physiological dependence. They reminded clinicians that cravings and the illicit and/or ego-dystonic behaviors commonly associated with addictions are more critical to making the diagnosis than mere dependency. In fact, the distinction between substance abuse and dependence was ultimately eliminated in the *DSM-5,* and criteria were provided for *substance use disorder* that no longer included a substance-related legal criterion, and focused on cravings and out-of-control behavior (American Psychiatric Association, 2013). More importantly, the work group noted that the emerging neuroscience supported a unified neurobiological theory of

Behavioral Addictions
http://dx.doi.org/10.1016/B978-0-12-407724-9.00001-X

addictions, regardless of the specific addictive substances, substrates, or activities, which now allowed for inclusion of behavioral as well as chemical addictions.

This line of thinking was evident with the inclusion of Gambling Disorder in the Non-Substance-Related Disorders category of Substance-Related and Addictive Disorders in the *DSM-5*, published in May of 2013—a shift from its previous categorization in "Impulse-Control Disorders Not Elsewhere Classified" in the *Diagnostic and Statistical Manual of Mental Disorders,* Fourth Edition, Text Revision (*DSM-IV-TR*) under the name Pathological Gambling (American Psychiatric Association, 2000).

Internet-related behavioral addictions were also at issue in the drafting of the *DSM-5*. A behavioral addiction called Internet Addiction Disorder was proposed based on the work of researchers like Ran Tao and colleagues (Tao et al., 2010). The proposed diagnosis shared key features with substance abuse, such as salience in one's emotional and cognitive processing, pursuit of the addictive behavior for the purpose of mood modification, the development of tolerance, the experience of withdrawal, tremendous conflict over the behavior, and relapse despite one's best intentions. Based on the current evidence available, the DSM work group on this topic determined that more research was needed on Internet addiction, but included Internet Gaming Disorder in the appendix to the manual, which is focused on conditions for further study (American Psychiatric Association, 2013). As Dr. Charles O'Brien noted in his Foreword to this book, other behavioral addiction subcategories, including sex addiction, exercise addiction, and shopping addiction, were considered for the substance-related and addictive disorders section of the *DSM-5* but were not included in this publication due to a lack of current peer-reviewed evidence to establish the diagnostic criteria to classify them as new mental disorders (American Psychiatric Association, 2013).

This book starts with a discussion of the overlapping factors of impulsivity and compulsivity in behavioral addictions, as illustrated by kleptomania (*DSM-5* classified as an impulse control disorder but also understood clinically as a behavioral addiction). The text then addresses gambling, Internet (i.e., online gaming, Internet addiction, and social networking addiction), food, sex, love, shopping (i.e., compulsive buying disorder), and exercise addictions. We have included a chapter that presents the evidence for spiritual approaches, from 12-step fellowships to meditation and breathing techniques derived from yoga. We conclude with a chapter on the legal implications of the new diagnoses. The authors define each behavioral addiction according to criteria specific to that disorder—more possible in some cases of behavioral addiction than others based on the current research and consensus—and then discuss the current epidemiological and theoretical literature and the contemporary "best practices" for assessment and treatment. Most of the chapters include case vignettes to bring these disorders to life.

DEFINING AND DETERMINING CRITERIA FOR A BEHAVIORAL ADDICTION

The American Psychiatric Association (2013), World Health Organization (2008), and American Society for Addiction Medicine (2010) have acknowledged the existence of behavioral addictions to varying degrees and with different, but similar, clinical criteria. Operationally, one of our authors, Mark Griffiths (2005) builds on other researchers' consensus to define a behavioral addiction by six core components: salience, mood modification, tolerance, withdrawal symptoms, conflict, and relapse. *Salience* means the behavior becomes the most important activity in a person's life and tends to dominate his or her thinking, feelings, and behavior. *Mood modification* refers to the emotional effect the behavior has on the individual which often serves as a coping strategy and is reported as the arousing "rush" or the numbing or the tranquilizing "escape" the behavior provides. *Tolerance* is the process whereby increasing amounts of the behavior are required to achieve the former mood-modifying effects, often meaning greater periods of time are spent engaging in the behavior, and/or there is a desired escalation in the intensity, recklessness, destructiveness, and ego-dystonic nature of the behavior. *Withdrawal symptoms* are the unpleasant feeling states and/or physical effects (e.g., the shakes, moodiness, irritability) that occur when the person is unable to engage in the behavior. *Conflict* references discord between the person and those around him or her (i.e., interpersonal conflict), conflicts with other activities (i.e., social life, work, hobbies, and interests) or from within the individual him- or herself (i.e., intrapsychic conflict and/or subjective feelings of loss of control) that are concerned with spending too much time engaging in the addictive behavior. *Relapse* addresses the tendency for repeated reversions to earlier patterns of excessive behavior to recur and for a common return to the most extreme patterns of excessive behavior soon after periods of control.

The chapters address the nuances of these factors, and the reader is directed to Chapter 6 about social networking for a particularly eloquent and complete outline of these factors. Additionally, Chapter 13 about exercise addiction works to differentiate neurobiological, psychological, and behavioral etiological theories with regard to this specific addiction, but in a way that is apt and useful for understanding a variety of behavioral addictions, particularly with regard to the authors' discussion of negative reinforcement of behaviors.

What makes a behavior—even a behavior in excess—qualify as an *addiction*? Even with alcohol and substance abuse, patients may be defined as suffering from abuse or addiction, yet tolerance and withdrawal are often lacking. Many behaviorally addicted patients defend their actions with the claim that they are simply healthy enthusiasts who have been unfairly labeled by others—doctors, parents, spouses, the police, etc. To complicate the issue further, behavioral addictions involve "normal" drives—highly rewarding and reinforcing drives toward sex, food, love, and money—which are only considered addictions when the behaviors reach a certain degree of excess and self-harm.

The self-help, 12-step fellowships emphasize the loss of control and unmanageability of the behavior and simplify the definition to "the use of a substance or activity, for the purpose of lessening pain or augmenting pleasure, by a person who has lost control over the rate, frequency, or duration of its use, and whose life has become progressively unmanageable as a result" (as quoted in Denizet-Lewis, 2009, p. 8). Our book's authors repeatedly make the point incisively, stating that "the difference between an excessive healthy enthusiasm and an addiction is that healthy enthusiasms add to life whereas addictions take away from it" (Griffiths, 2005, p. 195). The authors of Chapter 4 on problematic online gaming bring additional research findings into the discussion and delve further into the topic of how behavioral addictive processes are differentiated by tending to serve a compulsive drive to stem dissatisfaction from not engaging in the behavior versus enhance enthusiasm by engaging in the process.

Additionally, as we begin to hear more and more in the media about a particular politician or certain celebrity's unsavory behavior, questions such as "but does she or he have an *addiction*?" are interjected into the discourse. Yet excessive (or in some cases, embarrassing) behavior does not warrant the diagnosis of behavioral addiction, but rather the *individual's inability to curtail the activity despite the negative consequences* is what stands as the hallmark of the addiction process.

In summary, addictive behaviors and process addictions serve to produce pleasure, provide escape from emotional or physical discomfort, and are characterized by powerlessness (i.e., an inability to control the behavior) and unmanageability (i.e., significant negative consequences resulting from the behavior) (Goodman, 1990). This notion has been long supported in addiction research as well endorsed by self-help movements.

But expert opinion is not enough. Throughout the book, our authors critically examine the research and assessment scales that can be helpful for clinicians to utilize directly for diagnostic or research purposes as well as to inform their clinical interviewing and "detailed inquiry" with patients (Sullivan, 1954). While the scales may not be without caveats, as many suffer from a lack of consensus about the criteria that distinguish the given behavioral addiction, the assessments that are referenced in the chapters help the reader better understand the clinical criteria of the disorder and how to evaluate patients in research and practice. As explained in the chapter on sex addiction, addictions often co-occur, and act synergistically. Often, the patient can best be described as having an Addiction Interaction Disorder, a term coined by Carnes et al. (2005) and elaborated on in Chapter 9.

THEORIES AND EVIDENCE IN SUPPORT OF BEHAVIORAL ADDICTIONS

Biopsychosocial Model

We understand behavioral addiction through the lens of the *biopsychosocial model*—understanding the phenomenon as an interplay of factors: biological (i.e., genetic predispositions, the resulting effects of addiction in the brain), psychological (i.e., emotional, behavioral, and cognitive factors), and sociocultural (influences of one's family, friends, and broader culture). This model has been widely accepted in the chemical addiction field, as well as the burgeoning area of behavioral addictions (Donovan & Marlatt, 2005; Griffiths, 2005).

Neuroscience Research

Operationally, there are at least three neurobiological models for the addictive cycle, each emphasizing different aspects of brain function.

1. *The Reward/Executive Function model* is based on a theory that alterations in the mesolimbic system and medial frontal cortex perpetuate the addictive cycle. Activation of dopaminergic neurons in the Ventral Tegmental Area (VTA) projecting to the nucleus accumbens creates the drug high and initiates addiction. Repeated exposure to substrates of abuse enhances glutaminergic projections to the prefrontal cortex; alters neuroanatomy, gene expression, and synaptic transmissions; and forges

neural pathways that lead to addictive responses. This neuroplasticity found in the prefrontal cortex in rodents and correlative brain scans in humans explains the addict's relentless and self-destructive yearning, long after the initial rewards are experienced, when the intellect and reasoning of the prefrontal cortex should clearly recognize that the costs of the addiction far outweigh the benefits (O'Brien, Volkow, & Li, 2006).

2. The neuropsychological literature has provided us with models proposing that addiction results from vulnerabilities and malfunctions in the organism's decision-making process. Neuropsychologists Redish, Jensen, and Johnson (2008) developed an extensive computational model in which addictions develop when fast, reward-based networks replace slower, more discriminating networks. Their scholarly paper suggests that addicts are under the influence of dysfunctional, fast connections that have been learned and practiced. A related theory is derived from positive psychologist Mihály Csíkszentmihályi (1990) who coined the term *optimal flow*—a mental state of full immersion and energized focus. In the book *Flow: The Psychology of Optimal Experience*, Csíkszentmihályi proposes that certain "optimal flow" altered states are seen commonly in athletics and other endeavors associated with intense mental focus, wherein the individual becomes the captive of a certain order of psychic energy, fully and deeply immersed and engaged, so much so that the passing of time is nearly ignored. During the process of the addictive cycle—from the cravings, through the preparation, to the procurement of the substance or process of abuse—Carnes advances the concept that the patient be viewed as lost in a perverse and destructive form of "optimal flow" (as cited in Rosenberg, Carnes & O'Connor, 2013).

3. A third, related set of contemporary neurobiological theories involves *cellular memory*. Protein kinase M zeta (PKMzeta) is a molecule that is both necessary and sufficient for the maintenance of long-term potentiation (LTP) and long-term memory storage (Sacktor, 2011). PKMzeta activity in the accumbens core is a critical cellular substrate for the maintenance of memories of reward cues. Interfering with this memory molecule causes rats to "forget" long-term addiction-related cues. Environmental cues previously paired with morphine, cocaine, or high-fat food (but not opiate withdrawal symptoms) were abolished by inhibition of the protein kinase C isoform PKMzeta in the nucleus accumbens core of rats (Li et al., 2011). A memory-extinction procedure that decreases drug craving is associated with alternations in PKMZeta cellular activity (Xue et al., 2012).

The neuroscience of addiction is not without its detractors. Psychiatrist Sally Satel eloquently argues that the brain science is far from scientific (Satel & Lilienfeld, 2010). She argues that the fact that willpower and the threat of jail can deter—and even prevent—addictive behaviors casts the whole notion of a neurobiological model of addiction into question. Her point is well taken; however, in most nonpsychotic psychiatric conditions, such as depression or obsessive-compulsive disorder, the clinical manifestations can be temporarily restrained or overcome by leverage or threats, and a biological theory does not preclude influence from psychological and environmental factors. In fact, such external cues may help regulate the genetic and protein products associated with a psychiatric condition.

Proponents of behavioral addictions propose that these contemporary models of chemical addiction apply to addictive behaviors. Potenza (2006) and Tao et al. (2010) propose similar neurobiological models for problem gambling and Internet addictive disorder, respectively. In chromosomal linkage studies of problem gambling, Potenza (2006) found evidence for a reward deficiency model of lower normal activation of the mesolimbic structures among pathological gamblers, noted by abnormalities in the D2A1 allele of the D2 dopamine receptor gene. Grant and Odlaug further address problematic gambling in Chapter 3 of this book, whereas Internet addiction disorder and its related controversies are overviewed in Chapter 5.

In Chapter 9, the authors speculate about the neuroscience of sex addiction. Among the many studies cited, the authors note that Grant and Steinberg (2005) found compulsive sexual behavior occurred in 19.6% of 225 patients with problem gambling, suggesting similar biological and psychological processes are associated with both addictive behaviors. In 70.5% of those with co-occurring disorders, compulsive sexual behavior predated pathological gambling, suggesting that the sex addiction and problem gambling may share similar fundamental brain dysfunctions. A unitary hypothesis is further supported by the fact that patients treated with dopaminergic agents for idiopathic Parkinsonism commonly developed new onset pathological gambling and sexual compulsivity (Bostwick et al., 2009).

The neurobiology of food addiction is addressed in Chapters 7 and 8. Our authors elaborate on the contributions of Gearhardt et al. (2010), Wang, Ding, et al. (2004), and others who have proposed that hyperpalatable, hedonic, and reinforcing foods may cause addiction in vulnerable individuals. Gearhardt et al. (2010) cite that animals given intermittent access to sugar exhibit behavioral and neurobiological indicators of withdrawal and tolerance, and rats consuming high sugar and fat diets demonstrate reward dysfunction associated with drug addiction. The similarities between drug abuse and food addiction have been studied by Johnson and Kenny (2010) in obese rats. They found that obesity was associated with progressive deficits in neural reward response, similar to changes observed in cocaine or heroin abusers that are crucial in triggering the transition from casual to compulsive drug-taking. The authors found downregulation of striatal dopamine receptors in obese rats, similar to findings in chemically addicted humans, and concluded that overconsumption of palatable food triggers adaptive responses in brain reward circuits and drives the animal toward compulsive eating. In humans, diminished striatal dopamine receptor availability and striatal dysfunction have been associated with obesity (Wang et al., 2001) and weight gain (Stice et al., 2008).

In Chapter 13 on exercise addiction, the authors detail several prevailing biological theories on the impact of exercise: the *runner's high* hypothesis in which beta-endorphins are released after intense exercise; the *thermogenic regulation hypothesis,* which emphasizes the soothing increases in body temperature associated with exercise; and *the catecholamine hypothesis* in which exercise reduces the stress response. With these and other theories, the authors try to explain how exercise may shift from a healthy pastime into a harmful compulsion in vulnerable individuals.

In Chapter 10 on love addiction, the author explains how the biological drive for pair-bonding, associated with oxytocin and vasopressin release in the nucleus accumbens and ventral pallidum, respectively, may constitute a basis for romantic love. She details the evolutionary development of pair-bonding and the drive toward monogamy, mediated by dopamine. The author writes that romantic love has all the makings of a behavioral addiction and writes that it can be viewed as a "natural addiction that can have profound social, economic, psychological, and genetic consequences (both beneficial and adverse)." While successful love is seldom viewed as a problem, love gone awry, complicated by trauma, infidelity, divorce, and/or rejection, can lay the groundwork for dysfunctional neural networks and what the author calls "rejection addiction."

Psychological Underpinnings

Psychodynamic principles as well as ideas from motivational interviewing and cognitive behavioral theory inform the psychological underpinnings of behavioral addiction. While psychodynamic factors are referred to throughout and elaborated here, much of the current evidence-based treatment has been in the form of cognitive behavioral treatment (CBT) studies.

In Chapter 2, Cuzen and Stein continue these introductory remarks to elaborate how impulsivity and compulsivity help explain behavioral addiction, but note that the constructs are better understood as orthogonal, intersecting factors, rather than as opposite ends of an impulsive-compulsive spectrum. The authors illustrate this with a discussion of kleptomania as well as by outlining an "ABC model," citing various studies that illustrate how affect, behavioral addiction, and cognitive control are intertwined. They reference multiple studies in which affect, particularly negative affect and depression, are implicated in models of addiction, both to processes and substances.

Various motivational and personality factors are discussed throughout this volume on behavioral addictions (particularly in the chapters related to online and Internet-related disorders), which bring aspects of social and personality psychology into the discussion; however, the most attention is paid to impulsivity and compulsivity, as these traits are frequently implicated in theories of addiction (Brewer & Potenza, 2008). A number of authors in this volume suggest that high levels of impulsivity may catalyze the addictive process, promoting further behavior with immediate pleasurable, reinforcing rewards (e.g., hyperpalatable foods, sex, pleasure from gaming or gambling), despite one's awareness of later negative consequences. The addictive cycle is also fueled by the compulsion to continue engaging in the behavior—a compulsion that can serve to ward off the negative consequences and/or repercussions (e.g., negative affects of remorse or depression, craving), or to provide distraction from legal, relational, intrapsychic, occupational, or other consequences.

Although not all psychologists from psychodynamic or psychoanalytic backgrounds would debate the role of impulsivity and compulsivity in those with addiction, Dodes (2002) in *The Heart of Addiction* challenges these personality attributions, in turn expanding the dialogue. Dodes contends that it is not necessarily addicted individuals' impulsive traits that explain their behavior (as they can often delay efforts to engage in the addictive behavior beyond the point they were triggered), but rather that urges to engage in the behavior are better understood psychodynamically as "a consequence of inner conflict at a particular moment" (p. 101).

Essig (2012) is also a psychoanalyst who addresses such internal conflicts, in the context of Internet addiction and excessive gaming, but in ways that are more broadly applicable. He works to differentiate the symptom from the *meaning* of the symptom and describes behavioral addiction as a "failed solution" (Essig, 2012). He acknowledges the neurobiology as well as the psychodynamics, noting the rewarding effects of dopamine released during such activities, but also that by engaging in the excessive behavior, the individual responds with a flawed response to a psychological conflict. The author asserts that the behavioral addict is both trying to avoid something (e.g., negative affect) and is self-deluded into the belief that his or her addictive behavior (e.g., Internet use, online gaming) will completely fulfill his or her interpersonal needs—something Essig and his interpersonalist colleagues believe that only more genuine human interaction can truly provide. He describes this latter phenomenon as "simulation entrapment" (Essig, 2012, p. 1177) and also references the feelings of shame that often plague so many individuals struggling with behavioral addictions. Shame, in a dynamic sense, not only may be seen as a consequence of the addictive behavior, but also may suggest masochistic and self-defeating personality traits in some patients that are related to their ongoing addictive behaviors.

This line of thought opens up the idea of addiction—to substances and processes—as serving a maladaptive coping purpose to the individual and points to a central psychological theme of behavioral addiction referred to throughout this book: *affect dysregulation*.

A common theme across behavioral addictions is the comorbidity with mood and anxiety disorders as well as some personality disorders. Each chapter in the book works to address comorbidity within the given behavioral addiction, and Chapter 13 about compulsive buying disorder (CBD) also highlights the role low self-esteem can play in this behavioral addiction, a factor often seen across the range of disorders in this category. Although the overlap with regard to etiology remains unclear, affect dysregulation as a common psychological component is widely accepted in understandings of behavioral addiction. These patients' inability to modulate and/or contain their negative affect leads to seeking engagement in an addictive behavior to help them emotionally self-regulate. Essentially, people use their addictions to help decrease the intensity of their emotions or to rid themselves of their feelings altogether (McDougall, 2001).

Bromberg (2001) and other psychoanalysts explain that this difficulty with affective regulation leads to *dissociation* whereby the individual puts out of consciousness different aspects of him- or herself in the form of thoughts, feelings, and experiences, past and present. This is in line with the desire for escapism or numbing that often fuels the addictive process, and can be a result of various traumatic experiences from an individual's development.

Social Factors

An elaborate discussion of the various social, spiritual, and cultural factors that comprise this aspect of the biopsychosocial model are beyond the scope of this chapter's introductory remarks on behavioral addiction; however, it should be noted that these factors are always relevant for understanding behavioral addiction, and more so, for placing and understanding the individual patient within his or her sociocultural context.

Although this book is strengthened by a global set of authors based around the world, from Hungary to the United Kingdom to India to Israel to South Africa, and those in the United States, in America, in particular, behavioral addiction exists within a paradox. It is the land of plenty—inundated with availability of food, steeped in a culture of instant gratification, bombarded with advertising for all sorts of products—and a major producer of pornography; yet there is the backdrop of cultural morality influenced by the country's Puritan founders. Many of the authors throughout this book's pages, including those writing about food addiction, Internet addiction, and compulsive buying disorder allude to these dynamics. Denizet-Lewis (2009) in *America Anonymous* also highlights the cultural factors inherent to behavioral addictions, noting that whereas in France sex or food addiction are not widely accepted phenomena, in China a prevailing view is of Internet or video game addiction as a "moral failing demanding punitive action" (p. 9) that has resulted in labor camps and intense efforts to address these addictive behaviors, often without true treatment as a core goal.

The U.S. has been quicker to accept the idea of behavioral addiction, and incorporated the extensive 12-step recovery movement (further addressed in Chapter 14) into its fabric, but in America—and elsewhere—a lack of willpower or other character failing has often been pointed to as a culprit of behavioral addiction, further fueling the stigma and shame often associated with it (Coleman, 1992; Denizet-Lewis, 2009), rather than promoting a more nuanced understanding of the biopsychosocial forces at work in addictive behavior.

GUIDING PRINCIPLES FOR THE TREATMENT OF BEHAVIORAL ADDICTIONS

The guiding treatment principles that this book endorses for addressing behavioral addictions are inherently integrative. This is particularly highlighted in Chapter 7 about food addiction where a psychiatric researcher, an author with a public health background, a psychologist, and a nutritionist teamed up to address the research and treatment literature on the topic. It is our opinion that a targeted multimodal, multidisciplinary treatment that allows for individual, group, family (or conjoint) therapy (as elaborated in Chapter 11); medication management (when necessary); and adjunct treatments such as self-help groups or mindfulness-based techniques such as meditation (as elaborated in Chapter 14) will be the most cohesive and effective way to follow a biopsychosocial model and help patients recover from behavioral addictions.

Treatment can vary between an "abstinence-based" model (see Carnes, 2010; Carnes, Carnes & Bailey, 2011) or an approach that leans more on harm reduction (see Marlatt, 1998; Tatarsky, 2002). Defining abstinence is more complicated in behavioral addictions. Unlike chemical addiction in which the patient generally completely avoids the substances, in the case of behavioral addictions, each recovering patient may have his or her own particular set of behaviors that must be avoided (i.e., "bottom-line behaviors" as they are called in 12-step fellowships). For instance, just like the abstaining alcoholic needs to avoid ceremonial toasts, the abstinent sex addict may need to have the pornographic TV options blocked from his or her hotel room. On the other hand, abstinence for sex addicts does not mean avoiding sex (doing this altogether falls into the category of *sexual anorexia*); rather, it means avoiding the dysfunctional sexual activity. For many food addicts, abstinence may mean taking bread or other foods off the menu (and off the table, quite literally).

Harm reduction is typically viewed in the addiction field as a more perilous path, and may be the treatment contract when the patient refuses to abide by an abstinence-based model. From a harm reduction perspective, a patient trying to moderate his or her social networking addiction may access problematic sites but agrees to limit the time and frequency. A food addict may limit the consumption of triggering carbohydrates to once a week. More challenging for many clinicians would be a sex addict insisting upon continuing to visit prostitutes but doing so less frequently and after agreeing to take safety precautions. Treatment contracts and approaches are discussed throughout the book. Agreeing on the definition of what constitutes recovery *is* the art of psychotherapy, which must be individualized according to the needs of the patient and the comfort of the therapist.

With regard to the specifics of psychotherapy, motivational interviewing (Miller & Rollnick, 2002) is often helpful in individual or group formats in the early stages of addiction treatment, where high levels of ambivalence are common. This approach encourages the clinician to remain teamed up with the patient, and to "roll with resistance," to help the patient take more ownership and experience more empowerment with regard to his or her health decisions and recovery process, rather than being pushed into the position of defending him- or herself against punitive authority figures and/or those concerned others in the patient's life asking the patient to change. There are a variety of techniques in motivational interviewing, but often exploring the positive effects and the consequences of the behavior and highlighting discrepancies are key.

Cognitive behavioral therapy (CBT) is often the most advocated treatment for behavioral addiction because it is the most researched and evidence-based. This method involves therapist and patient discussing the maladaptive thoughts and behaviors in the context of the addictive behavior, coming up with competing strategies and linking them with deeper themes and core cognitions (see Ryan, 2013). Patients work to identify their patterns of abuse and addiction, avoid or better manage high-risk situations, and engage in alternative, more adaptive substitute behaviors. "Slips" are explored as learning experiences, and relapse prevention modules are also added once the behavior is in remission to shore up gains and prevent against future backslides (see Marlatt & Donovan, 2005). Dialectical behavioral therapy (see Linehan, 1993) is also often utilized or integrated with CBT. This is further discussed in Chapter 7 on food addiction.

Psychodynamic psychotherapy, particularly that from an interpersonal/relational orientation, addresses the patient's affect regulation issues as well as meaning of the symptoms, and as discussed previously, how they function as a "failed solution" for negotiating conflicts around genuinely relating to others (Essig, 2012). More specifically, in their introduction to *Hungers and Compulsions: The Psychodynamic Treatment of Eating Disorders*, Petrucelli and Stuart (2001) highlight the compulsive or addicted person's difficulty in self-regulation and how psychodynamic therapy offers for the therapeutic relationship to become a valuable tool that helps patients learn to shift from the world of their relating to the addictive process to the more interpersonal, relational realm—as vulnerable and challenging as that may be, as dissociation has been their method to avoid the challenges or pain of certain relationships and interpersonal experiences. By using "detailed inquiry" (Sullivan, 1954) into the addictive experience to understand the roots and meaning of it, the patient works through the symptoms and learns to develop new, more adaptive strategies and coping skills. It is important to stress that most, if not all, psychodynamic treatment for behavioral addictions should be integrative in nature, incorporating useful techniques from cognitive behavioral and relapse prevention therapy models (Connors, 2001).

Throughout the book, authors propose the use of psychiatric medications such as traditional antidepressants, anti-obsessive-compulsive medications, antipsychotics, mood stabilizers, anxiolytics, and attention deficit medications. In addition to the psychiatric medications that may treat associated psychiatric disorders, some of the authors propose the use of anti-addiction medications such as *N*-acetylcysteine (NAC), a glutamate-modulating agent that has also been found to be helpful in chemical addictive disorders. Our authors write that the most promising antibehavioral addiction medications may be the opiate antagonists naltrexone and nalmefene, which presumably act by interfering with reward center pathways, given in combinations with other anti-addiction drugs such as the $GABA_B$ agonist baclofen and the glutamate antagonist and anticonvulsant topiramate (Chapter 8 elaborates this topic specific to research on treatment for food addiction, overeating and obesity).

SOCIETAL AND LEGAL ISSUES

One of the concerns about legitimizing behavioral addictions as a psychiatric disorder is the fear of pardoning or excusing criminal behavior. In Chapter 15, an American attorney outlines such possibilities and proposes guidelines for the medical or mental health expert witness testifying in court about patients presumed to have behavioral addictions.

Still, some may worry that this book helps create new disorders that are nothing more than medical labels for bad behavior. Can stealing now be diagnosed as kleptomania? Irresponsibly accumulating debt diagnosed as compulsive buying? Financial recklessness diagnosed as gambling? Viewing child porn viewed as cybersex addiction? And so on. These considerations must be acknowledged. Practically speaking, at least in the sex-related addictions, the diagnoses tend to lengthen and toughen jail and prison sentences, as some of the stiffest prison sentences surround the crime of downloading child porn, with incarceration exceeding a decade in many cases—sentences that are often more severe than those for child molestation in the same jurisdiction. Hence, the evidence thus far suggests that, at least for sex addiction, a clinical diagnosis may not be helpful in avoiding incarceration.

While a sex addiction diagnosis, for example, is unlikely to pardon an offender, it can help safeguard society. Since the 1980s, Fred Berlin and his colleagues at Johns Hopkins, often treating incarcerated patients, have demonstrated that a sexual diagnosis and appropriate treatment are indicated for clinically ill sex offenders (Berlin, 1981).

But the point that as mental health professionals we may be pardoning or excusing criminal behavior is well taken. Surely, it is preferable for the philandering husband to call himself a sex addict and for the irresponsible shopper to call herself a compulsive buyer. The societal implications of the behavioral addiction diagnoses are—and should be—a matter for continual concern.

In sum, it is our hope that the existing body of research, this book, and the studies yet to come will further contribute to the understanding of behavioral addiction and foster rigorous research and treatments that will meet the thresholds of the scientific method and the medical model. Moreover, we hope that the patients will be served—those millions of people around the world often suffering in isolation, shame, and ignorance.

REFERENCES

American Psychiatric Association. (2000). *Diagnostic and statistical manual of mental disorders* (4th ed.). Washington, DC: Author.

American Psychiatric Association. (2013). *Diagnostic and statistical manual of mental disorders* (5th ed.). Washington, DC: Author.

American Society for Addiction Medicine. (2010). *Public policy statement on treatment for alcohol and other drug addiction*. Adopted: May 1, 1980, Revised: January 1, 2010.

Berlin, F. S., & Meinecke, C. F. (1981). Treatment of sex offenders with antiandrogenic medication: Conceptualization, review of treatment modalities and preliminary findings. *American Journal of Psychiatry*, *138*, 601–607.

Bostwick, J. M., Hecksel, K. A., Stevens, S. R., Bower, J. H., & Ahlskog, J. E. (2009). Frequency of new-onset pathologic compulsive gambling or hypersexuality after drug treatment of idiopathic Parkinson Disease. *Mayo Clinic Proceedings*, *84*, 310–316.

Brewer, J. A., & Potenza, M. N. (2008). The neurobiology and genetics of impulse control disorders: Relationships to drug addictions. *Biochemical Pharmacology*, *75*(1), 63–75.

Bromberg, P. M. (2001). Out of body, out of mind, out of danger: Some reflections on shame, dissociation and eating disorders. In J. Petrucelli & C. Stuart (Eds.), *Hungers and compulsions: The psychodynamic treatment of eating disorders and addictions* (pp. 65–80). New Jersey: Jason Aronson Inc.

Carnes, P. (2010). *Facing the shadow: Starting sexual and relationship recovery*. Carefree, AZ: Gentle Path Press.

Carnes, P., Carnes, S., & Bailey, J. (2011). *Facing addiction: Starting recovery from alcohol and drugs*. Carefree, AZ: Gentle Path Press.

Carnes, P., Murray, R., & Charpentier, L. (2005). Bargains with chaos: Sex addicts and addiction interaction disorder. *Sexual Addiction & Compulsivity*, *12*, 79–120.

Coleman, E. (1992). Is your patient suffering from compulsive sexual behavior? *Psychiatric Annals*, *22*(6), 320–325.

Connors, M. E. (2001). Integrative treatment of symptomatic disorders. *Psychoanalytic Psychology*, *18*(1), 74–91.

Csíkszentmihályi, M. (1990). *Flow: The psychology of optimal experience.* New York: Harper and Row.
Denizet-Lewis, B. (2009). *America anonymous: Eight addicts in search of a life.* New York, NY: Simon & Schuster Paperbacks.
Dodes, L. M. (2002). *The heart of addiction.* New York: HarperCollins Publishers.
Donovan, D. M., & Marlatt, G. A. (Eds.) (2005). *Assessment of addictive behaviors* (2nd ed.). New York, NY: The Guilford Press.
Essig, T. (2012). The addiction concept and technology: Diagnosis, metaphor, or something else? A psychodynamic point of view. *Journal of Clinical Psychology: In Session, 68*(11), 1175–1184.
Gearhardt, A. N., Grilo, C. M., DiLeone, R. J., Brownell, K. D., & Potenza, M. N. (2010). Can food be addictive? Public health and policy implications. *Addiction, 106,* 1208–1212.
Goodman, A. (1990). Addiction: definition and implications. *British Journal of Addiction, 85,* 1403–1408.
Grant, J. E., & Potenza, M. N. (2006). Compulsive aspects of impulse-control disorders. *Psychiatric Clinics of North America, 29,* 539–550.
Grant, J. E., & Steinberg, M. A. (2005). Compulsive sexual behavior and pathological gambling. *Sexual Addiction & Compulsivity, 12,* 235–244.
Griffiths, M. D. (2005). A 'components' model of addiction within a biopsychosocial framework. *Journal of Substance Use, 10,* 191–197.
Hekster, O. (2002). *Commodus: An emperor at the crossroads (Dutch monographs on ancient history and archaeology).* Amsterdam: Brill Academic Publishers.
Johnson, P. M., & Kenny, P. J. (2010). Dopamine D2 receptors in addiction-like reward dysfunction and compulsive eating in obese rats. *Nature, 13,* 635–641.
Li, Y. Q., Xue, Y. X., He, Y. Y., Li, F. Q., Xue, L. F., Xu, C. M., et al. (2011). Inhibition of PKM in nucleus accumbens core abolishes long-term drug reward memory. *Journal of Neuroscience, 31,* 5436–5446.
Linehan, M. M. (1993). *Skills training manual for treating borderline personality disorder.* New York, NY: The Guilford Press.
Marlatt, G. A. (Ed.). (1998). *Harm reduction: Pragmatic strategies for managing high risk behaviors.* New York, NY: The Guilford Press.
Marlatt, G. A., & Donovan, D. M. (2005). *Relapse prevention: Maintenance strategies in the treatment of addictive behaviors* (2nd ed.). New York, NY: The Guilford Press.
McDougall, J. (2001). The psychic economy of addiction. In J. Petrucelli & C. Stuart (Eds.), *Hungers and compulsions: The psychodynamic treatment of eating disorders and addictions* (pp. 3–26). New Jersey: Jason Aronson Inc.
Miller, W. R., & Rollnick, S. (2002). *Motivational interviewing: Preparing people for change* (2nd ed.). New York, NY: The Guilford Press.
O'Brien, C. P., Volkow, N., & Li, T.-K. (2006). What's in a word? Addiction versus dependence in DSM-V. *American Journal of Psychiatry, 163,* 764–765.
Petrucelli, J., & Stuart, C. (Eds.) (2001). Introduction. In *Hungers and compulsions: The psychodynamic treatment of eating disorders and addictions* (pp. xvii–xxix). New Jersey: Jason Aronson Inc.
Potenza, M. N. (2006). Should addictive disorders include non-substance related conditions? *Addiction, 101*(s1), 142–151.
Redish, A. D., Jensen, S., & Johnson, A. (2008). A unified framework for addiction: Vulnerabilities in the decision process. *Behavioral and Brain Sciences, 31,* 415–487.
Rosenberg, K. P., Carnes, P., & O'Connor, S. (2013). Evaluation and treatment of sex addiction. *Journal of Sex & Marital Therapy,* Published online: 21 Jun 2013.
Rush, B. (1812). *Medical inquiries and observations upon the diseases of the mind.* Philadelphia: Kimber & Richardson.
Ryan, F. (2013). *Cognitive therapy for addiction: Motivation and change.* Malden, MA: Wiley-Blackwell.

Sacktor, T. C. (2011). How does PKMzeta maintain long-term memory? *Nature Reviews Neuroscience, 12*, 9–15.
Satel, S., & Lilienfeld, S. O. (2010). Singing the brain disease blues. *AJOB Neuroscience, 1*(1), 46–54.
Stice, E., Spoor, S., Bohon, C., & Small, D. H. (2008). Relation between obesity and blunted striatal response to food is moderated by Taq1A A1 allele. *Nature, 322*, 449–452.
Sullivan, H. S. (1954). *The psychiatric interview*. New York, NY: W.W. Norton & Company.
Tao, R., Huang, X., Wang, J., Zhang, H., Zhang, Y., & Li, M. (2010). Proposed diagnostic criteria for Internet addiction. *Addiction, 105*, 556–564.
Tatarsky, A. (Ed.). (2002). *Harm reduction psychotherapy: A new treatment for drug and alcohol problems*. Northvale, NJ: Jason Aronson Inc.
Wang, E. T., Ding, Y.-C., Flodman, P., Kidd, J. R., Kidd, K. K., Grady, D. L., & Moyzis, R. K. (2004). The genetic architecture of selection at the human dopamine receptor D4 (DRD4) gene locus. *American Journal of Human Genetics, 74*, 931–944.
Wang, G. J., Volkow, N. D., Logan, J., Pappas, N. R., Wong, C. T., Zhu, W., Netusil, N., & Fowler, J. S. (2001). Brain dopamine and obesity. *Lancet, 357*, 354–357.
Wang, G. J., Volkow, N. D., Thanos, P. K., & Fowler, J. S. (2004). Similarity between obesity and drug addiction as assessed by neurofunctional imaging: A concept review. *Journal of Addictive Diseases, 23*(3), 39–53.
World Health Organization. (2008). *ICD-10: International statistical classification of diseases and related health problems* (10th Rev. ed.). New York, NY: Author.
Xue, Y. X., Luo, Y. X., Wu, P., Shi, H. S., Xue, L. F., Chen, C., et al. (2012). A memory retrieval-extinction procedure to prevent drug craving and relapse. *Science, 336*, 241–254.

CHAPTER 2

Behavioral Addiction: The Nexus of Impulsivity and Compulsivity

Natalie L. Cuzen, Dan J. Stein
Department of Psychiatry and Mental Health, University of Cape Town, Cape Town, South Africa

INTRODUCTION

The aim of this chapter is to present the constructs of impulsivity and compulsivity, and examine how these constructs relate to behavioral addictions. The discussion begins with a brief outline of what is understood by "impulsivity" and "compulsivity" and then proceeds to explore how the constructs may relate to each other. With this in mind, the authors introduce the concept of behavioral addiction, which falls on the border between impulsivity and compulsivity. Here, kleptomania (one of the behavioral addictions) is used to illustrate the overlap between impulsivity and compulsivity. Finally, a summary is presented of the current cognitive-affective clinical neuroscience literature in an ABC model of compulsive-impulsive behaviors, which has practical implications for the treatment of these conditions.

IMPULSIVITY AND COMPULSIVITY: WHAT'S IT ALL ABOUT?

Impulsivity is considered to be a multifaceted construct, and so it has many possible definitions (Robbins, Curran, & de Wit, 2012). Key elements of impulsivity include a maladaptive predisposition toward rapid reactions, reduced motor or response inhibition, automatic response to urges or impulses, delay aversion, insensitivity to delayed rewards, and lack of reflection when making decisions. These various impulsive actions are typically "poorly conceived, prematurely expressed, unduly risky, or inappropriate to the situation and…often result in undesirable outcomes" (Evenden, 1999, p. 1). Although healthy individuals may possess impulsive personality traits, excessive impulsivity is a key defining feature of many neuropsychiatric conditions, including attention deficit/hyperactivity disorder, substance use disorder, antisocial behavior, as well as many behavioral addictions, including pathological gambling and kleptomania (Dalley, Everit, & Robbins, 2011; Robbins, Gillan, Smith, de Wit, & Ersche, 2011).

Behavioral Addictions
http://dx.doi.org/10.1016/B978-0-12-407724-9.00002-1

Compulsivity, on the other hand, refers to persistent or perseverative behavior that is inappropriate to the situation and has no obvious relationship to an overall goal. These behaviors are often unpleasantly repetitive and performed in a habitual or stereotyped way (Chamberlain, Fineberg, Blackwell, Robbins, & Sahakian, 2006). Compulsive behaviors show striking persistence, typically enduring for long periods despite being harmful to the individual. Compulsivity is a hallmark of several psychiatric conditions and is observed most notably in obsessive-compulsive disorder (OCD). Other conditions with compulsive features include obsessive-compulsive and related disorders, eating disorders, substance dependence, as well as several impulse control disorders and behavioral addictions, such as compulsive Internet use. Similar to impulsivity, compulsivity may arise from failures in response inhibition or "top-down" control, an overstimulated drive state, or a combination of these factors (Grant, Brewer, & Potenza, 2006; Stein & Hollander, 1995).

Impulsivity and compulsivity share some common features: for instance, both are complex constructs that may be considered multifaceted (Fineberg et al., 2010), and both may share a relationship with various personality and cognitive dimensions including sensation seeking, risk taking, and decision making (Leeman & Potenza, 2012). On the other hand, impulsivity and compulsivity differ in several fundamental ways. For example, compulsive behaviors often occur without reference to the original goal of the behavior and in this way resemble habits. Furthermore, while impulsivity denotes rash action with the aim of achieving a reward (Patterson & Newman, 1993), compulsive behavior is typically performed with reduced regard for reward (although this is not always the case; e.g., compulsions to create symmetry may be rewarding when performed to satisfaction) (Everitt & Robbins, 2005; Fontenelle, Oostermeijer, Harrison, Pantelis, & Yücel, 2011).

HOW DO IMPULSIVITY AND COMPULSIVITY RELATE?

Traditionally, impulsivity and compulsivity are viewed as lying at opposite ends of a continuum of persistent and maladaptive traits and disorders, with conditions characterized by inadequate control, behavioral disinhibition, and risk seeking clustered at the "impulsive" end of the dimension, and conditions characterized by harm avoidance and risk aversion clustered at the "compulsive" end (Skodol & Oldham, 1996; Stein, Hollander, Simeon, & Cohen, 1994). A single dimension for impulsivity-compulsivity seems a reasonable heuristic given neurochemical and functional neuroanatomical differences between primary impulsive disorders on the one hand and primary compulsive disorders on the other hand. Specifically, primary impulsive disorders may be characterized by *decreased* serotonergic and frontal activity, whereas primary compulsive disorders may be characterized by *increased* serotonergic and frontal activity (Ebstein, Benjamin, & Belmaker, 2000). Nevertheless, closer inspection of the phenomenological and psychobiological data reveals several reasons why a unidimensional continuum is probably oversimplistic.

First, a unidimensional approach implicitly assumes that impulsivity is the polar opposite of compulsivity and that the two constructs are mutually exclusive (Yi, 2013). Clinical observation has shown this to be untrue: patients with primary impulsive psychopathology (e.g., pathological gambling) may demonstrate obsessive-compulsive features, whereas patients with primary compulsive psychopathology (e.g., OCD) may score high on impulsivity ratings, and/or have impulsive-aggressive symptoms or comorbid impulse control disorders (Stein & Lochner, 2006). Furthermore, a range of disorders, such as Tourette's disorder and trichotillomania, typically comprise both impulsive and compulsive features (Stein, 2000).

Second, overlapping impulsive and compulsive features may develop differently within the same disorder; specifically, impulsive and compulsive features may occur either simultaneously or at different times within the same disorder. Different trajectories of impulsivity and compulsivity within single disorders complicate how these disorders are understood by clinicians, as well as how they are treated (Grant & Potenza, 2006). Instead of considering the two constructs as polar opposites, an alternative and more realistic position is to consider impulsivity and compulsivity as orthogonal factors across a range of disorders, where either construct may be present to a greater or lesser degree independent of the other construct. When one considers impulsivity and compulsivity as orthogonal factors across disorders, it is important to keep in mind that there remains a great deal of individual variability in the extent to which patients diagnosed with the same illness may exhibit impulsive or compulsive features; for instance, some OCD patients may have high levels of compulsivity and impulsivity, and others low.

FROM IMPULSIVITY TO COMPULSIVITY IN SUBSTANCE USE DISORDER

Substance use disorder (SUD) provides an important window into debates about compulsivity and impulsivity. Current psychobiological models understand SUD as a transition between impulsive and compulsive behavior

(Dalley et al., 2011; Koob & Volkow, 2010). In SUD, impulsivity is at the root of a tendency to pursue short-term rewards (drugs) and is a powerful mechanism in the early stages of SUD (i.e., substance abuse) (Fernández-Serrano, Perales, Moreno-López, Pérez-García, & Verdejo-García, 2012; Verdejo-García, Lawrence, & Clark, 2008). Reward-based learning is responsible for repeated drug use early in the illness when drug use is a pleasurable, positively reinforcing experience.

With regular drug use over an extended period of time, these learning mechanisms become over-trained and so develop into compulsive habits. Two important features of habitual drug administration are (1) the behavior is driven by associations triggered by stimuli, and not by a clear goal/reward; and (2) the individual is unable to reverse the repetitive behavioral pattern, thus leading to compulsive drug use. In neurobiological terms, the transition from voluntary action in substance abuse to more habitual or compulsive modes in substance dependence seems to represent a shift in control over responding from prefrontal cortical to striatal control. This shift in control correlates clinically with a move away from positively reinforced behavior motivated by reward seeking in substance abuse, toward negatively reinforced behavior motivated by the avoidance of withdrawal symptoms in substance dependence (Everitt & Robbins, 2005).

In summary, impulsivity plays an important role in the early stage of SUD (substance abuse), while maladaptive learning processes and habit formation lead to the development of compulsive behavior in the later stage of SUD (substance dependence).

BEHAVIORAL ADDICTION: ON THE BORDER BETWEEN IMPULSIVITY AND COMPULSIVITY

Behavioral addictions arguably lie on the border between compulsivity and impulsivity. These conditions may be characterized by both compulsive and impulsive features, and so are sometimes called impulsive-compulsive disorders. As in the case of SUD, an argument can be made that impulsive traits are key to initiation of the behavior, which then develops compulsive characteristics (Dell'Osso, Altamura, Allen, Marazziti, & Hollander, 2006).

Kleptomania in some ways is a prototypical behavioral addiction, and so provides a window into the pros and cons of using a behavioral addiction framework to understand impulsivity and compulsivity. This discussion focuses on kleptomania, classified in the *Diagnostic and Statistical Manual of Mental Disorders,* Fourth Edition (*DSM-IV;* American

Psychiatric Association, 2000) as an impulse control disorder, and in the recent *DSM-5* (American Psychiatric Association, 2013) within the category of disruptive, impulse control, and conduct disorders. Although kleptomania retains its classification as an impulse control disorder in the latest revision to the *DSM*, the *DSM-5* marks the migration of pathological gambling from impulse control disorders (as it was classified in the *DSM-IV*) to the category of substance-related and addictive disorders. There are several possible reasons for the classification change for pathological gambling alongside no change for kleptomania. For instance, although pathological gambling shares features with impulse control disorders, little evidence exists on the association between pathological gambling and impulse control disorders (e.g., pyromania, intermittent explosive disorder, kleptomania) themselves (Petry, Blanco, Auriacombe, Borges, Bucholz, & Crowley, 2013). Furthermore, there is questionable evidence to support a classification of kleptomania within substance-related and addictive disorders, a point that will be explored later.

KLEPTOMANIA BEHAVIOR

Background

Kleptomania was first recognized in the late 1800s when it became apparent that in some cases of shoplifting, patients were unable to resist the temptation to commit the act, and so this behavior may, in some instances, be considered involuntary (Abelson, 1989). *Shoplifting* is defined as store theft, regardless of the motivation for the act. By contrast, *kleptomania* is a psychiatric diagnosis distinguished from shoplifting, and characterized by a recurrent failure to resist impulses to steal objects that are not necessarily needed for their personal use or monetary value (i.e., the individual often can afford to pay for the goods or has no use for the stolen goods) (Blanco et al., 2008; Dell'Osso et al., 2006). Kleptomania is characterized by an urge to perform an act that is pleasurable in the moment but subsequently leads to distress and dysfunction (Aboujaoude, Gamel, & Koran, 2004). While onset of the condition is typically in adolescence, mean age for presentation for treatment is far later—around 35 and 50 years for women and men, respectively (Talih, 2011).

The primary features of kleptomania, as outlined in the *DSM-5*, are (1) recurrent failure to resist impulses to steal objects that are not needed for personal use or for their monetary value; (2) increasing sense of tension immediately before committing the theft; (3) pleasure, gratification, or relief at the time of committing the theft; (4) the stealing is not committed to express anger or vengeance and is not in response to a delusion or a hallucination; and (5) the stealing is not better accounted for by conduct disorder, a manic episode, or antisocial personality disorder (*DSM-5;* American Psychiatric Association, 2013).

How Prevalent is Kleptomania?

Kleptomania accounts for about 5% of shoplifting cases in the United States; this translates annually to 100,000 arrests and a direct cost of roughly $500 million to the U.S. economy (Hollinger & Davis, 2003; McElroy, Pope, Hudson, Keck, & White, 1991). Compared to other impulse control disorders, kleptomania has received little attention in the scientific literature, and no epidemiological studies to date have focused on the condition. From available data, the prevalence rate of kleptomania is estimated to lie between 0.5% and 1% of the general population. It also appears that kleptomania has an increased prevalence in clinical samples. In a recent study of general psychiatric inpatients, 7.8% endorsed current symptoms for kleptomania, while 9.3% reported a lifetime history of kleptomania (Grant, Levine, Kim, & Potenza, 2005). The small discrepancy between current and lifetime rates for the disorder suggest that the course is frequently chronic if left untreated (Grant, 2006). In other studies of specific clinical groups, the rates for comorbid kleptomania in patients with primary depression, alcohol dependence, or pathological gambling were 3.7%, 3.8%, and 5%, respectively (Lejoyeux, Feuché, Loi, Solomon, & Adès, 1999; Lejoyeux, Arbaretaz, McLaughlin, & Ades, 2002; Specker, Carlson, Christenson, & Marcotte, 1995). Kleptomania shows a preponderance in females (between 63% and 81%), although this gender difference may be inflated due to the legal system's tendency to ascribe psychiatric explanations to female deviant behavior versus criminal explanations to male deviant behavior (Aboujaoude et al., 2004).

How is Kleptomania Like or Unlike an Addiction?

Kleptomania remains underinvestigated, and the pathophysiology of the condition is largely unknown (Talih, 2011). There are, however, a number of shared features between SUDs and various behavioral addictions, including kleptomania (Grant, 2006). The following features are common to SUDs and kleptomania: (1) an urge to engage in behavior despite associated negative consequences; (2) increasing tension until the behavior is performed; (3) immediate but short-lived reduction in tension following completion of the behavior; (4) gradual return of the urge to engage in the behavior following completion; (5) external cues (e.g., being in a location such as a retail store) unique to the behavior; (6) secondary conditioning by external or internal (e.g., feelings of dysphoria or boredom) cues; (7) hedonic feelings early in the condition (Marks, 1990). In addition to increased rates for kleptomania in SUDs mentioned in the previous section (i.e., 3.8% in alcohol dependence versus 0.5%–1% in the general population), lifetime rates of SUD are inflated in those with kleptomania (29%–50% in kleptomania cases versus 15% in the background population) (Kessler, Berglund, Demler, Jin, Merikangas, & Walters, 2005). SUDs are also comparatively common in first-degree relatives of individuals with kleptomania, suggesting possible shared vulnerability for the disorders (Grant & Potenza, 2004).

Some evidence of similar phenomenology and comorbidity patterns in kleptomania and SUDs may suggest a common mechanism across the two disorders, and support the inclusion of kleptomania within an addictive spectrum. However, other data call into question a close relationship between addictions and kleptomania. For instance, although one study reported evidence of "tolerance" to value of stolen items in kleptomania (value of stolen items increased over the course of the illness in most individuals), there is no evidence of physical tolerance or withdrawal in kleptomania. Second, and most importantly, the data supporting a link between kleptomania and addictions are rather limited, and so any theories of the overlap between these conditions must remain tentative pending more conclusive evidence.

How does Kleptomania Relate to Compulsive Buying Disorder?

Kleptomania shares a great deal of overlap with compulsive buying disorder (or shopping addiction, addressed in Chapter 12). The two conditions are clinically similar and share similar patterns of comorbidity with substance addictions, affective disorders, and obsessive-compulsive disorder (Black, 2007). In both kleptomania and compulsive buying disorder, initiation of the pathological behavior occurs in late adolescence or early adulthood, and both disorders show a preponderance in women (although this gender effect may be partially artifactual in both cases) (Talih, 2011). In clinical terms, both conditions are characterized by a preoccupation to acquire items that the person may not necessarily need. While individuals affected by either condition may find the behavior rewarding at the time, they often experience significant remorse or disrupted life functioning as a result of the behavior (Black, 2001). An important, but obvious, distinction between kleptomania and compulsive buying disorder is the fact that individuals with kleptomania steal (i.e., do not pay for) the relevant items, whereas those with compulsive buying disorder do pay for the goods. Interestingly, although kleptomania and compulsive buying disorder diverge at the point of payment, it appears that the act of stealing in the first case and the act of spending in the second case provide a similar thrill (i.e., positive reinforcement), which serves to encourage persistence of the behavior.

How is Kleptomania Like or Unlike OCD?

The irresistible and uncontrollable nature of the urge to shoplift in kleptomania is reminiscent of the frequently excessive, unnecessary, and unwanted rituals of obsessive-compulsive disorder (Grant, 2006). Furthermore, individuals with kleptomania often report hoarding symptoms similar to those seen in OCD (Grant & Kim, 2002). With regard to features that distinguish the two disorders, kleptomania is associated with high levels of sensation seeking and impulsivity, a craving state in anticipation of the behavior, and a hedonic experience during performance of the behavior. Although the ritualistic behavior may elicit pleasure in some cases, harm avoidance, as opposed to sensation seeking, is generally the driving force behind compulsive behavior in OCD (Hollander, 1993).

There is mixed evidence of comorbidity between OCD and kleptomania: some studies suggest high co-occurrence (45%–60%; McElroy et al., 1991; Presta, Marazziti, Dell'Osso, Pfanner, Pallanti, & Cassano, 2002), whereas others show little or no evidence of comorbidity (0%–6.5%; Baylé, Caci, Millet, Richa, & Olié, 2003; Grant, 2003a). Studies examining shared genetic vulnerability for the disorders are equally disparate: two uncontrolled studies reported an incidence of OCD in 7% to 25% of family members of individuals with kleptomania, while one study that did include a control group found no increased risk for OCD in relatives of individuals with kleptomania compared to controls. Similarly, although early reports suggested that kleptomania may demonstrate preferential response to selective serotonin reuptake inhibitors (SSRIs), a common treatment for OCD, more recent reports show conflicting results (Grant & Potenza, 2004). One possibility is that conflicting reports of treatment response in kleptomania may arise from heterogeneity in the disorder. The implication here may be that only some forms of kleptomania may be similar to (some types of) OCD, which would explain inconsistency seen in studies aiming to broadly identify commonalities between the two disorders (Grant, 2006). On the basis of the limited data currently available, however, there does not appear to be a clear support for a strong relationship between kleptomania and OCD.

To summarize, the notions of compulsivity (demonstrated in disorders such as OCD), impulsivity (seen in disorders such as intermittent explosive disorder), and compulsive-impulsive disorders (seen in both SUDs and behavior addictions) continue to be developed in the clinical literature and may well be relevant to describing a disorder such as kleptomania. There is also a growing cognitive-affective neuroscience literature, including animal laboratory research and human imaging research, which provides a window into the neurobiology and treatment of these constructs. The next section summarizes some of this clinical and scientific literature in a practical and useful ABC model of compulsive-impulsive behaviors using an illustrative case vignette of kleptomania.

AN ABC MODEL TO ASSESS AND MANAGE COMPULSIVE-IMPULSIVE DISORDERS

Understanding compulsive-impulsive behaviors from an A (affect)–B (behavioral addiction)–C (cognitive control) perspective is a helpful way to further characterize the conditions and inform treatment choice.

Case Vignette: Kleptomania

Anne is a 32-year-old woman who presented to a psychiatrist after having been involved in a court case where she was accused of shoplifting. The shop had decided not to prosecute, but Anne indicated to her psychiatrist that she did indeed have a problem with stealing from stores. She explained to her psychiatrist that she found it odd that she did not have a real need for the items (typically toiletries) that she stole, yet she found that the act of stealing somehow provided her with a real sense of gratification. She noted that the urge to steal came and went, but seemed particularly strong when she was going through stressful periods at work. At these times, she found herself visiting particular stores and experiencing a strong urge to take various cosmetic items. She would pick certain items in a ritualistic way and described a sense of rising tension leading up to and during the theft. She would then experience a wonderful sense of relief on exiting the store after having stolen the items. She stockpiled the toiletries and cosmetics in her bathroom as she accumulated far more than she could reasonably use. Although Anne had no other psychiatric problems, when pushed about mood symptoms, she noted that during stressful times at work, she would feel demoralized and would suffer some symptoms of depression such as loss of appetite and insomnia. Given Anne's few mood symptoms, her psychiatrist chose to not prescribe pharmacological treatment and instead referred her for cognitive-behavioral therapy.

Affect in Compulsive-Impulsive Behaviors

A number of studies have demonstrated that negative affect plays a key role in triggering compulsive-impulsive behavior (Di Nicola et al., 2010; Presta et al., 2002). This evidence is consistent with a long line of research showing that negative affect is inextricably linked to substance addiction—both at the initiation and maintenance stages (Kassel et al., 2007). Briefly, substances are frequently used to regulate mood, as indicated by stress-coping (Wills and Shiffman, 1985) and self-medication models (Khantzian, 1997). These models are supported by research indicating that depression frequently precedes substance use and may be considered a risk factor for drug initiation; further, other studies suggest a reciprocal relationship in which substance use and depression are mutually reinforcing (Brown, Lewinsohn, Seeley, & Wagner, 1996). Because addiction (substance or behavior) may be triggered by a desire to regulate negative affect, it is quite possible that a similar mechanism is relevant in compulsive-impulsive behaviors, suggesting that agents that improve affect regulation (e.g., SSRIs) may form a useful part of treatment in both substance addiction and compulsive-impulsive behaviors.

Addiction Biology in Compulsive-Impulsive Behaviors

Alterations in serotonin and dopamine systems may be relevant to our understanding of various compulsive-impulsive behaviors. First, neurobiological studies have reported alterations in the serotonergic system in individuals with disorders characterized by impaired impulse control, such as compulsive-impulsive behaviors. Here, such alterations may accompany impairment in prefrontal inhibition, which reduces ability to control desires, leading to impulsive action (Schlosser, Black, Repertinger, & Freet, 1994). Second, it is likely that the neurobiology of substance addiction is relevant in compulsive-impulsive behaviors. Substance addiction is linked to dopamine-related alteration in mesolimbic pathways linking the ventral tegmental area to the nucleus accumbens or ventral striatum. Specifically, alterations in the dopaminergic system (sometimes characterized as "reward deficiency syndrome") may produce heightened sensitivity to rewards, prompting reward-driven behavior and increasing risk for a range of substance addictions and compulsive-impulsive behaviors (Blum, Cull, Braverman, & Comings, 1996; Nestler and Aghajanian 1997). Functional neuroimaging studies have shown that images of appetizing food (Wang et al., 2004), gambling (Breiter, Aharon, Kahneman, Dale, & Shizgal, 2001), shopping (Knutson, Rick, Wimmer,

Prelec, & Loewenstein, 2007), and playing video games (Hoeft, Watson, Kesler, Bettinger, & Reiss, 2008) activate the anatomical regions (notably the mesolimbic system and extended amygdala) crucially activated by drug craving (Volkow & Fowler, 2000; Volkow, Wang, Fowler, Tomasi, & Baler, 2012). Other functional neuroimaging data provide additional support for these findings: diminished ventral striatal activation has been shown in both cocaine dependence and pathological gambling, suggesting that the mechanisms of chemical dependence and compulsive-impulsive behaviors may share similar pathways (Karim & Chaudri, 2012; Potenza, 2006). In simple neurobiological terms, if neurocircuitry can be altered by illicit drug exposure in substance addiction, then perhaps these same circuits may be similarly altered in compulsive-impulsive behaviors. The implication, then, is that similar pharmacological treatments could be applicable in both substance addiction and compulsive-impulsive behaviors (Holden, 2001). The neurobiological research and implications for treatment are discussed with regard to specific behavioral addictions throughout this volume.

At present, no medications are approved for the treatment of compulsive-impulsive behaviors. However, a few medications approved for use in substance addictions appear to provide effective treatment for compulsive-impulsive behaviors. Naltrexone, a mu-opioid receptor antagonist approved for treatment of opiate and alcohol use disorders, has shown efficacy in controlled clinical trials in pathological gambling and kleptomania, and has also shown some promise in open-label studies of compulsive sexual behavior, compulsive buying, Internet addiction, and pathological skin picking (Arnold, Auchenbach, & McElroy, 2001; Bostwick & Bucci, 2008; Grant, 2003b; Grant, Desai, & Potenza, 2009; Kim, Grant, Adson, & Shin, 2001). These studies suggest that the mu-opioid receptors may function similarly in substance addiction and compulsive-impulsive behaviors, possibly via modulation of dopaminergic tone in the mesolimbic pathway. Similarly, topiramate, a glutamate antagonist and anticonvulsant, has also shown promise in uncontrolled studies of both substance addiction and compulsive-impulsive behaviors, including alcohol, cigarette, and cocaine addiction, as well as pathological gambling, compulsive buying, and compulsive skin picking (Johnson, Swift, Addolorato, Ciraulo, & Myrick, 2005; Johnson et al., 2007; Kampman et al., 2004; Roncero, Rodriguez-Urrutia, Grau-Lopez, & Casas, 2009). Similar responsiveness to topiramate in both cases suggests that glutamatergic modulation of dopamine in the nucleus accumbens may also play a key role in both substance addiction and compulsive-impulsive behaviors.

Cognitive Control and Psychosocial Treatment of Compulsive-Impulsive Behaviors

Impulsivity is a hallmark of both substance addiction and compulsive-impulsive behaviors. In these conditions, impulsivity may arise due to dysregulation of prefrontal cortex circuitry (Jentsch & Taylor, 1999). A possible mechanism for such impulsivity is alteration in glutamate and dopamine functioning in the prefrontal cortex (as discussed in the preceding section), which compromises the transmission of inhibitory regulations, leading to increased impulsivity (Kalivas & O'Brien, 2008). Strengthening cognitive control is a key psychosocial strategy to counteract impulsivity in both substance addiction and compulsive-impulsive behaviors. Such psychosocial treatments generally rely on a relapse prevention model that promotes abstinence using a three-fold strategy: (1) identify patterns of abuse, (2) avoid or manage high-risk situations, and (3) select alternative, healthier behaviors. Specific psychosocial treatments using the relapse prevention model include motivational enhancement, cognitive behavioral therapies, and the 12-step self-help approaches. These strategies have proven to be effective in the treatment of a range of compulsive-impulsive behaviors, including kleptomania, pathological gambling, compulsive sexual behavior, pathological skin picking, and compulsive buying (Mitchell, Burgard, Faber, Crosby, & de Zwaan, 2006; Petry et al., 2006; Teng, Woods, & Twohig, 2006; Toneatto & Dragonetti, 2008).

CONCLUSIONS

Impulsivity and compulsivity are each key contributors to behavioral addiction. Specifically, impulsivity frequently plays a role in the initiation of behavioral addiction, while compulsivity supports the maintenance of the condition. Using kleptomania as a specific example of a behavioral addiction, this chapter has illustrated how impulsivity and compulsivity may overlap within the behavioral addictions as well as across other relevant conditions. A slowly growing body of research in behavioral addiction, combined with a well-established substance addiction literature, provides a foundation to manage impulsive and compulsive aspects of these conditions. An ABC model is provided, based partially on principles of substance addiction, as a framework to guide treatment of compulsive and impulsive disorders targeting key affective, behavioral addiction, and cognitive control clinical features of these conditions.

REFERENCES

Abelson, E. S. (1989). *When ladies go a-thieving: Middle-class shoplifters in the Victorian department store*. New York, NY: Oxford University.

Aboujaoude, E., Gamel, N., & Koran, L. M. (2004). Overview of kleptomania and phenomenological description of 40 patients. *Primary Care Companion to the Journal of Clinical Psychiatry*, *6*, 244–247.

American Psychiatric Association. (2000). *Diagnostic and statistical manual of mental disorders* (4th ed.). Washington, DC: Author.

American Psychiatric Association. (2013). *Diagnostic and statistical manual of mental disorders* (5th ed.). Washington, DC: Author.

Arnold, L. M., Auchenbach, M. B., & McElroy, S. L. (2001). Psychogenic excoriation. Clinical features, proposed diagnostic criteria, epidemiology and approaches to treatment. *CNS Drugs*, *15*, 351–359.

Baylé, F. J., Caci, H., Millet, B., Richa, S., & Olié, J. P. (2003). Psychopathology and comorbidity of psychiatric disorders in patients with kleptomania. *American Journal of Psychiatry*, *160*, 1509–1513.

Blanco, C., Grant, J., Petry, N., Simpson, H., Alegria, A., Liu, S. M., et al. (2008). Prevalence and correlates of shoplifting in the United States: Results from the National Epidemiologic Survey on Alcohol and Related Conditions (NESARC). *American Journal of Psychiatry*, *165*, 905–913.

Black, D. W. (2001). Compulsive buying disorder: Definition, assessment, epidemiology and clinical management. *CNS Drugs*, *15*, 17–27.

Black, D. W. (2007). A review of compulsive buying disorder. *World Psychiatry*, *6*, 14–18.

Blum, K., Cull, J. G., Braverman, E. R., & Comings, D. E. (1996). Reward deficiency syndrome. *American Scientist*, *84*, 132–145.

Bostwick, J. M., & Bucci, J. A. (2008). Internet sex addiction treated with naltrexone. *Mayo Clinic Proceedings*, *83*, 226–230.

Breiter, H. C., Aharon, I., Kahneman, D., Dale, A., & Shizgal, P. (2001). Functional imaging of neural responses to expectancy and experience of monetary gains and losses. *Neuron*, *30*, 619–639.

Brown, R. A., Lewinsohn, P. M., Seeley, J. R., & Wagner, E. F. (1996). Cigarette smoking, major depression, and other psychiatric disorders among adolescents. *Journal of the American Academy of Child & Adolescent Psychiatry*, *35*, 1602–1610.

Chamberlain, S. R., Fineberg, N. A., Blackwell, A. D., Robbins, T. W., & Sahakian, B. J. (2006). Motor inhibition and cognitive flexibility in obsessive-compulsive disorder and trichotillomania. *American Journal of Psychiatry*, *163*, 1282–1284.

Dalley, J. W., Everitt, B. J., & Robbins, T. W. (2011). Impulsivity, compulsivity, and top-down control. *Neuron*, *69*, 680–694.

Dell'Osso, B., Altamura, A. C., Allen, A., Marazziti, D., & Hollander, E. (2006). Epidemiologic and clinical updates on impulse control disorders: A critical review. *European Archives of Psychiatry and Clinical Neuroscience*, *256*, 464–475.

Di Nicola, M., Tedeschi, D., Mazza, M., Martinotti, G., Harnic, D., Catalano, V., et al. (2010). Behavioural addictions in bipolar disorder patients: Role of impulsivity and personality dimensions. *Journal of Affective Disorders*, *125*, 82–88.

Ebstein, R. P., Benjamin, J., & Belmaker, R. H. (2000). Personality and polymorphisms of genes involved in aminergic neurotransmission. *European Journal of Pharmacology*, *410*, 205–214.

Evenden, J. L. (1999). Varieties of impulsivity. *Psychopharmacology (Berl)*, *146*, 348–361.

Everitt, B. J., & Robbins, T. W. (2005). Neural systems of reinforcement for drug addiction: From actions to habits to compulsion. *Nature Neuroscience*, *8*, 1481–1489.

Fernández-Serrano, M. J., Perales, J. C., Moreno-López, L., Pérez-García, M., & Verdejo-García, A. (2012). Neuropsychological profiling of impulsivity and compulsivity in cocaine dependent individuals. *Psychopharmacology*, *219*, 673–683.

Fineberg, N. A., Potenza, M. N., Chamberlain, S. R., Berlin, H. A., Menzies, L., Bechara, A., et al. (2010). Probing compulsive and impulsive behaviors, from animal models to endophenotypes: A narrative review. *Neuropsychopharmacology*, *35*, 591–604.

Fontenelle, L. F., Oostermeijer, S., Harrison, B. J., Pantelis, C., & Yücel, M. (2011). Obsessive-compulsive disorder, impulse control disorders and drug addiction: Common features and potential treatments. *Drugs*, *71*, 827–840.

Grant, J. E. (2003a). Family history and psychiatric comorbidity in persons with kleptomania. *Comprehensive Psychiatry*, *44*, 437–441.

Grant, J. E. (2003b). Three cases of compulsive buying treated with naltrexone. *International Journal of Psychiatry in Clinical Practice*, 7, 223–225.

Grant, J. E. (2006). Understanding and treating kleptomania: New models and new treatments. *Israel Journal of Psychiatry and Related Sciences*, *43*, 81–87.

Grant, J. E., Brewer, J. A., & Potenza, M. N. (2006). The neurobiology of substance and behavioral addictions. *CNS Spectrums*, *11*, 924–930.

Grant, J. E., Desai, R. A., & Potenza, M. N. (2009). Relationship of nicotine dependence, subsyndromal and pathological gambling, and other psychiatric disorders: Data from the National Epidemiologic Survey on Alcohol and Related Conditions. *Journal of Clinical Psychiatry*, *70*, 334–343.

Grant, J. E., & Kim, S. W. (2002). Clinical characteristics and associated psychopathology in 22 patients with kleptomania. *Comprehensive Psychiatry*, *43*, 378–384.

Grant, J. E., Levine, L., Kim, D., & Potenza, M. N. (2005). Impulse control disorders in adult psychiatric inpatients. *American Journal of Psychiatry*, *162*, 2184–2188.

Grant, J. E., & Potenza, M. N. (2004). Impulse control disorders: Clinical characteristics and pharmacological management. *Annals of Clinical Psychiatry*, *16*, 27–34.

Grant, J. E., & Potenza, M. N. (2006). Compulsive aspects of impulse-control disorders. *The Psychiatric Clinics of North America*, *29*, 539–549.

Hoeft, F., Watson, C. L., Kesler, S. R., Bettinger, K. E., & Reiss, A. L. (2008). Gender differences in the mesocorticolimbic system during computer game-play. *Journal of Psychiatric Research*, *42*, 253–258.

Holden, C. (2001). Behavioral addictions: Do they exist? *Science*, *294*, 980–982.

Hollander, E. (1993). Obsessive-compulsive spectrum disorders: An overview. *Psychiatric Annals*, *23*, 355–358.

Hollinger, R. C., & Davis, J. L. (2003). *National retail security survey final report*. Gainesville, FL: Security Research Project.

Jentsch, J. D., & Taylor, J. R. (1999). Impulsivity resulting from frontostriatal dysfunction in drug abuse: Implications for the control of behavior by reward-related stimuli. *Psychopharmacology*, *146*, 373–390.

Johnson, B. A., Rosenthal, N., Capece, J. A., Wiegand, F., Mao, L., Beyers, K., et al. (2007). Topiramate for treating alcohol dependence. *Journal of the American Medical Association*, *298*, 1641–1651.

Johnson, B. A., Swift, R. M., Addolorato, G., Ciraulo, D. A., & Myrick, H. (2005). Safety and efficacy of GABAergic medications for treating alcoholism. *Alcoholism: Clinical and Experimental Research*, *29*, 248–254.

Kalivas, P. W., & O'Brien, C. (2008). Drug addictions as a pathology of staged neuroplasticity. *Neuropsychopharmacology*, *33*, 166–180.

Kampman, K. M., Pettinati, H., Lynch, K. G., Dackis, C., Sparkman, T., Weigley, C., et al. (2004). A pilot trial of topiramate for the treatment of cocaine dependence. *Drug and Alcohol Dependence*, *75*, 233–240.

Karim, R., & Chaudri, P. (2012). Behavioral addictions: An overview. *Journal of Psychoactive Drugs*, *44*, 5–17.

Kassel, J. D., Veilleux, J. C., Wardle, M. C., Yates, M. C., Greenstein, J. E., Evatt, D. P., et al. (2007). Negative affect and addiction. In M. Al'Absi (Ed.), *Stress and addiction: Biological and psychological mechanisms* (pp. 171–189). Burlington, MA: Academic Press.

Kessler, R. C., Berglund, P., Demler, O., Jin, R., Merikangas, K. R., & Walters, E. E. (2005). Lifetime prevalence and age-of-onset distributions of DSM-IV disorders in the National Comorbidity Survey Replication. *Archives of General Psychiatry, 62*, 593–602.

Khantzian, E. J. (1997). The self-medication hypothesis of substance use disorders: A reconsideration and recent applications. *Harvard Review of Psychiatry, 4*, 231–244.

Kim, S. W., Grant, J. E., Adson, D. E., & Shin, Y. C. (2001). Double-blind naltrexone and placebo comparison study in the treatment of pathological gambling. *Biological Psychiatry, 49*, 914–921.

Knutson, B., Rick, S., Wimmer, G. E., Prelec, D., & Loewenstein, G. (2007). Neural predictors of purchases. *Neuron, 53*, 147–156.

Koob, G. F., & Volkow, N. D. (2010). Neurocircuitry of addiction. *Neuropsychopharmacology, 35*, 217–238.

Leeman, R. F., & Potenza, M. N. (2012). Similarities and differences between pathological gambling and substance use disorders: A focus on impulsivity and compulsivity. *Psychopharmacology (Berl), 219*, 469–490.

Lejoyeux, M., Arbaretaz, M., McLaughlin, M., & Ades, J. (2002). Impulse control disorders and depression. *Journal of Nervous and Mental Disease, 190*, 310–314.

Lejoyeux, M., Feuché, N., Loi, S., Solomon, J., & Adès, J. (1999). Study of impulse-control disorders among alcohol-dependent patients. *Journal of Clinical Psychiatry, 60*, 302–305.

Marks, I. (1990). Behavioural (non–chemical) addictions. *British Journal of Addiction, 85*, 1389–1394.

McElroy, S. L., Pope, H. G., Hudson, J. I., Keck, P. E., & White, K. L. (1991). Kleptomania: A report of 20 cases. *American Journal of Psychiatry, 148*, 652–657.

Mitchell, J. E., Burgard, M., Faber, R., Crosby, R. D., & de Zwaan, M. (2006). Cognitive behavioral therapy for compulsive buying disorder. *Behaviour Research and Therapy, 44*, 1859–1865.

Nestler, E. J., & Aghajanian, G. K. (1997). Molecular and cellular basis of addiction. *Science, 278*, 58–63.

Patterson, M., & Newman, J. P. (1993). Reflectivity and learning from aversive events: Toward a psychological mechanism for the syndromes of disinhibition. *Psychological Review, 100*, 716–736.

Petry, N. M., Ammerman, Y., Bohl, J., Doersch, A., Gay, H., Kadden, R., et al. (2006). Cognitive-behavioral therapy for pathological gamblers. *Journal of Consulting and Clinical Psychology, 74*, 555–567.

Petry, N. M., Blanco, C., Auriacombe, M., Borges, G., Bucholz, K., & Crowley, T. J. (2013). An overview of and rationale for changes proposed for pathological gambling in DSM-5. *Journal of Gambling Studies*, [Epub ahead of print].

Potenza, M. N. (2006). Should addictive disorders include non–substance–related conditions? *Addiction, 101*, 142–151.

Presta, S., Marazziti, D., Dell'Osso, L., Pfanner, C., Pallanti, S., & Cassano, G. B. (2002). Kleptomania: Clinical features and comorbidity in an Italian sample. *Comprehensive Psychiatry, 43*, 7–12.

Robbins, T. W., Curran, H. V., & de Wit, H. (2012). Special issue on impulsivity and compulsivity. *Psychopharmacology, 219*, 251–252.

Robbins, T. W., Gillan, C. M., Smith, D. G., de Wit, S., & Ersche, K. D. (2011). Neurocognitive endophenotypes of impulsivity and compulsivity: Towards dimensional psychiatry. *Trends in Cognitive Sciences, 16*, 81–91.

Roncero, C., Rodriguez-Urrutia, A., Grau-Lopez, L., & Casas, M. (2009). Antiepileptic drugs in the control of the impulses disorders. *Actas Españolas de Psiquiatría, 37*, 205–212.

Schlosser, S., Black, D. W., Repertinger, S., & Freet, D. (1994). Compulsive buying: Demography, phenomenology, and comorbidity in 46 subjects. *General Hospital Psychiatry, 16*, 205–212.

Skodol, A. E., & Oldham, J. M. (1996). Phenomenology, differential diagnosis, and comorbidity of the obsessive–compulsive spectrum disorders. In J. M. Oldham & J. M. Ehaes (Eds.), *Impulsivity and compulsivity* (pp. 1–36). Washington, DC: American Psychiatric Press.

Specker, S. M., Carlson, G. A., Christenson, G. A., & Marcotte, M. (1995). Impulse control disorders and attention deficit disorder in pathological gamblers. *Annals of Clinical Psychiatry, 7*, 175–179.

Stein, D. J. (2000). Neurobiology of the obsessive-compulsive spectrum disorders. *Biological Psychiatry, 47*, 296–304.

Stein, D. J., Hollander, E., Simeon, D., & Cohen, L. (1994). Impulsivity scores in patients with obsessive-compulsive disorder. *Journal of Nervous and Mental Disease, 182*, 240–241.

Stein, D. J., & Hollander, E. (1995). Obsessive-compulsive spectrum disorders. *Journal of Clinical Psychiatry, 56*, 265–266.

Stein, D. J., & Lochner, C. (2006). Obsessive-compulsive spectrum disorders: A multidimensional approach. *Psychiatric Clinics of North America, 29*, 343–351.

Teng, E. J., Woods, D. W., & Twohig, M. P. (2006). Habit reversal as a treatment for chronic skin picking: A pilot investigation. *Behavior Modification, 30*, 411–422.

Talih, F. R. (2011). Kleptomania and potential exacerbating factors: A review and case report. *Innovations in Clinical Neuroscience, 8*, 35–39.

Toneatto, T., & Dragonetti, R. (2008). Effectiveness of community-based treatment for problem gambling: A quasi-experimental evaluation of cognitive-behavioral vs. twelve-step therapy. *American Journal on Addictions, 17*, 298–303.

Verdejo-García, A., Lawrence, A. J., & Clark, L. (2008). Impulsivity as a vulnerability marker for substance-use disorders: Review of findings from high-risk research, problem gamblers and genetic association studies. *Neuroscience & Biobehavioral Reviews, 32*, 777–810.

Volkow, N. D., & Fowler, J. S. (2000). Addiction, a disease of compulsion and drive: Involvement of the orbitofrontal cortex. *Cerebral Cortex, 10*, 318–325.

Volkow, N. D., Wang, G. J., Fowler, J. S., Tomasi, D., & Baler, R. (2012). Food and drug reward: Overlapping circuits in human obesity and addiction. In J. W. Dalley & C. S. Carter (Eds.), *Brain imaging in behavioral neuroscience* (pp. 1–24). Berlin, Heidelberg: Springer.

Wang, G. J., Volkow, N. D., Telang, F., Jayne, M., Ma, J., Rao, M., et al. (2004). Exposure to appetitive food stimuli markedly activates the human brain. *Neuroimage, 21*, 1790–1797.

Wills, T. A., & Shiffman, S. (1985). *Coping and substance use*. New York, NY: Academic Press.

Yi, S. (2013). Heterogeneity of compulsive buyers based on impulsivity and compulsivity dimensions: A latent profile analytic approach. *Psychiatry Research, 208*, 174–182.

CHAPTER 3

Diagnosis and Treatment of Gambling Disorder

Jon E. Grant[1], Brian L. Odlaug[2]
[1]University of Chicago, Department of Psychiatry & Behavioral Neuroscience, Chicago, IL, USA, [2]University of Copenhagen, Department of Public Health, Faculty of Health & Medical Sciences, Copenhagen, Denmark

INTRODUCTION

Gambling is a lucrative industry, with United States casinos reporting annual gross revenues of over $34 billion (American Gaming Association, 2012). The vast majority of individuals who gamble do so for recreation and report no significant financial consequences or any difficulties controlling their behavior. Some people (estimated to be 0.4%–5.3% worldwide; National Opinion Research Center, 1999; Petry, 2005; Shaffer, Hall, & Vander Bilt, 1999), however, develop a maladaptive form of gambling behavior associated with impaired functioning, reduced quality of life, and high rates of bankruptcy and divorce. This form of gambling behavior has been defined by the American Psychiatric Association in the fifth edition of the *Diagnostic and Statistical Manual of Mental Disorders* (*DSM-5*) as being a Gambling Disorder (APA, 2013). For individuals with Gambling Disorder, several promising therapeutic interventions have been developed (Stea & Hodgins, 2011).

Although recognized by both Emil Kraepelin (1856–1926) and Eugen Bleuler (1857–1939), disordered gambling behavior was first officially recognized in *DSM-III* as pathological gambling (Black & Grant, 2013). The condition has not received substantial empirical investigation until relatively recently. The disorder was categorized as one of the impulse-control disorders not elsewhere classified, along with disorders such as kleptomania, pyromania, and trichotillomania. In *DSM-5*, the disorder is included in the chapter on substance use disorders because of consistently high rates of comorbidity, similar presentations of some symptoms, and genetic and physiological overlap.

Prevalence rates for Gambling Disorder are based on national surveys across the globe. Past year rates of Gambling Disorder range from 0.2% in Norway, 5.3% in Hong Kong, and 0.4% to approximately 3% in the United States (Hodgins, Shea, & Grant, 2011). The variability in prevalence rates of Gambling Disorder are likely due to differences in survey methodology

Behavioral Addictions
http://dx.doi.org/10.1016/B978-0-12-407724-9.00003-3

(e.g., different screening tools, time frames, administration format, and response rates), as well as the availability and accessibility of gambling opportunities (Hodgins et al., 2011).

CLINICAL CHARACTERISTICS

Gambling Disorder usually begins in adolescence or early adulthood, with males tending to start at an earlier age (Ibáñez, Blanco, & Sáiz-Ruiz, 2002; Shaffer, Hall, & Vander Bilt, 1999). Although men seem to start gambling at earlier ages and have higher rates of Gambling Disorder, women, who constitute approximately 32% of individuals with Gambling Disorder in the United States, progress more quickly to a pathological state than do men (Grant, Odlaug, & Mooney, 2012).

Gambling Disorder is associated with significant impairment in a person's ability to function socially and occupationally (Soberay, Faragher, Barbash, Brookover, & Grimsley, 2013). Many individuals report intrusive thoughts and urges related to gambling that interfere with their ability to concentrate at home and at work (Grant & Kim 2001), work-related problems such as absenteeism and poor performance are common (National Opinion Research Center, 1999). Gambling Disorder is also frequently associated with marital problems, diminished intimacy and trust within the family (Grant & Kim, 2001), as well as greater rates of health problems (e.g., hypertension, obesity, insomnia) (Black, Shaw, McCormick, & Allen, 2012; Germain et al., 2011; Parhami, Siani, Rosenthal, & Fong, 2012). Finally, financial problems such as bankruptcy, defaulting on credit cards, mortgage foreclosures, and delinquent bank loans are commonplace among individuals seeking treatment for Gambling Disorder (Grant, Schreiber, Odlaug, & Kim, 2010; Ledgerwood, Weinstock, Morasco, & Petry, 2007).

Psychiatric comorbidity is the rule, not the exception, in Gambling Disorder (Chou & Afifi, 2011), and this comorbidity often needs to be treated either simultaneously or sequentially. Gambling Disorder has been associated with increased rates of co-occurring substance use (including nicotine dependence), depression, and anxiety disorders (Erbas & Buchner, 2012; Lorains, Cowlishaw, & Thomas, 2011). Research also suggests that Gambling Disorder is associated with high rates of suicide ideation and attempts (Ledgerwood & Petry, 2004; Wong, Chan, Conwell, Conner, & Yip, 2010). One question that is generally not addressed by these comorbidity studies, however, is whether the co-occurring disorder is secondary to the gambling, a trigger for the gambling, or an independent problem.

Clinicians need to screen for suicidal ideation and, if necessary, address it before working on the gambling problem. Drug and alcohol use may also negatively influence decision making, often worsen impulsivity, and prevent full compliance with gambling treatment. In the case of co-occurring depression or bipolar disorder, active depressive or manic symptoms may interfere with gambling treatment (e.g., not coming to appointments or doing homework). Thus, clinicians must assess for mood and substance use at the initial evaluation as well as during treatment. Mood and substance use may need to be addressed through other means such as hospitalization, medication intervention, detoxification, or residential treatment. Likewise, given the high prevalence of physical ailments in those with Gambling

Case Vignette: Michael

Michael is a 35-year-old, married man with a full-time job as an accountant. He has a limited psychiatric history but does acknowledge a history of alcohol abuse in his 20s and reports having been sober for the past 5 years. He reports that his father was an "alcoholic that never cleaned himself up." Recently, Michael has been experiencing increased stress and responsibility at work. When times became stressful at work years ago, he used to have a beer or two to calm his nerves. Now sober, Michael tries to exercise after work to work off his stress; however, he and his wife recently welcomed a baby to their family, and he reports not having the time to work out. After a particularly stressful week of work and thinking about the added financial responsibility he now bears, Michael sees a billboard for a casino nearby and decides to go. Sitting down at the slots, Michael plays for only an hour and wins $225. He goes home, feeling stress-free and happy. The next week, Michael finds himself thinking about gambling and decides to go to the casino again that Friday to play his "lucky" machine, but this time he loses $150. Believing this is just "bad luck," he decides to leave work early on the false pretense of a doctor's appointment to go to the casino again midweek. This time, he stays for 5 hours and loses $400, thinking that the machine will eventually "pay off". His gambling increases to an average of three times per week, and the losses start to build over the next 2 years. Given the late nights Michael is out, suspicious withdrawals from their bank account, and mounting credit card cash advances, his wife becomes suspicious that he is having an affair, resulting in late night arguments. Ever desperate for money, Michael starts to embezzle money from work to finance his gambling; however, he claims that he has every intention of putting the money back after he recoups his losses at the slots. He reports uncontrollable urges to gamble and admits that he frequently contemplates suicide while driving home after a gambling episode. It is under these conditions that Michael presents to a clinic for help.

Disorder, clinicians should encourage the client to seek medical care for the screening and treatment of chronic health conditions.

CLINICAL ASSESSMENT

In the *DSM-5,* Gambling Disorder, formerly listed with the "Impulse Control Disorders Not Elsewhere Classified," has been relocated to the chapter on substance use disorders. Prevalence surveys indicate that only a small proportion of the individuals who are suffering from Gambling Disorders seek formal treatment. This new placement of Gambling Disorder in the addiction chapter may improve recognition of the disorder and increase requests for treatment services, especially among substance abusers at high risk for gambling problems.

The name of the disorder has been changed from "Pathological Gambling" to "Gambling Disorder," mainly to reduce stigma attached to the word *pathological.* In addition, the number of core symptoms required for the diagnosis has been reduced from 5 of 10 symptoms to 4 of 9 (the previous criterion "has committed illegal acts..." has been eliminated). As published by the American Psychiatric Association (2013), the *DSM-5* Gambling Disorder diagnosis criteria include 4 of the following 9 symptoms:

1. Preoccupation with gambling
2. Need to gamble with more money (tolerance)
3. Tried to cut back or quit gambling
4. Restless and/or irritable when unable to gamble
5. Gambles to escape mood
6. Returns to gambling in an attempt to win money back ("chasing losses")
7. Lies to others about extent of behavior
8. Lost a significant relationship or opportunity due to gambling
9. Others have needed to relieve financial stressors caused by the gambling.

The assessment of individuals with probable Gambling Disorder begins with the identification of all mental health concerns that may be potentially causing and/or contributing to the gambling (e.g., gambling within context of a manic episode, excessive gambling only when under the influence of substances). In the case of comorbid conditions, the clinician must determine whether to treat the conditions simultaneously, in parallel, or sequentially (Najavits, 2003). The evaluation also must include a detailed understanding of the extent of the gambling, the repercussions of the problem on the individual's life (e.g., financial, social, psychological, and familial), the individual's readiness for change, and the individual's sense of control over the gambling.

SCREENING/DIAGNOSTIC INSTRUMENTS

Multiple, well-validated instruments (self-report as well as clinician-administered) can be used to diagnose Gambling Disorder (see Table 3.1). The choice should be based on ease of use for the patient and the information that the instrument can provide the clinician (for a review of diagnostic and screening instruments, see Stinchfield, Govoni, & Frisch, 2007). See Table 3.1 for summary of the assessment tools.

Table 3.1 Screening and Diagnostic Instruments for Pathological Gambling

Source	Instrument	Brief Description
Self-Report		
Lesieur & Blume, 1987	*South Oaks Gambling Screen (SOGS)*	A 20-item, self-report screening instrument based on lifetime gambling activity (although a more recent version of the SOGS examines the past 3 months of behavior) with a score of ≥5 indicating probable pathological gambling.
Toneatto, 2008	*Gamblers Anonymous 20 questions (GA-20)*	A score of ≥7 indicates that the respondent is a problem gambler.
Shaffer, LaBrie, Scanlan, & Cummings, 1994	*Massachusetts Gambling Screen (MAGS)*	A 14-item (only 7 of which are scored) self-report screen for problem gambling among adolescents and adults that classifies respondents into nonproblem, in-transition, or pathological gamblers using a weighted score.
Johnson et al., 1988	*Lie/Bet Questionnaire*	A 2-item screen that can be used in a self-report format: (1) "Have you ever had to lie to people important to you about how much you gambled?" and (2) "Have you ever felt the need to bet more and more money?"
Sullivan, 1999	*Early Intervention Gambling Health Test (EIGHT)*	Screening instrument designed for use in general practitioner settings where a score of ≥4 indicates possible pathological gambling.

Continued

Table 3.1 Screening and Diagnostic Instruments for Pathological Gambling—cont'd

Source	Instrument	Brief Description
Clinician-Administered		
Grant, Steinberg, Kim, Rounsaville, & Potenza, 2004	*Structured Clinical Interview for Pathological Gambling*	*DSM-IV*-based diagnostic interview that assesses both the 10 inclusion criteria and the exclusionary criterion of "not better accounted for by a Manic Episode."
Winters, Specker, & Stinchfield, 2002	*Diagnostic Interview for Gambling Schedule*	Structured interview that includes 20 diagnostic symptom items (lifetime and past-year), gambling treatment history, age of onset of gambling, and family and social functioning.
National Opinion Research Center	*National Opinion Research Center DSM-IV Screen for Gambling Problems*	A 17-question interview based on the *DSM-IV* diagnostic criteria that classifies respondents as low-risk gambler, at-risk gambler, problem gambler, or pathological gambler.

Given that the diagnostic instruments used to diagnose Gambling Disorder were based and validated using the *DSM-IV* criteria for pathological gambling, however, these instruments will need to be modified for current diagnostic purposes. For example, because the diagnostic interviews listed are based on *DSM-IV,* the clinician will need to exclude the illegal acts question from the total number of required criteria to properly diagnose the person with *DSM-5* Gambling Disorder. As in our case example of Michael, illegal behaviors such as embezzlement are still important to screen for but not a diagnostic criterion for *DSM-5*. Furthermore, self-report measures should be followed by an in-person assessment to exclude gambling behavior that results only in the context of alcohol/drug use or during hypomanic or manic episodes.

TREATMENT OPTIONS

Despite the significant personal costs associated with Gambling Disorder, research indicates that only a small proportion of the individuals who are suffering from Gambling Disorder seek formal treatment (Slutske et al., 2009; Suurvali, Hodgins, Toneatto, & Cunningham, 2011). In fact, Suurvali and colleagues (2008) found that less than 6% of problem gamblers actually seek formal treatment. A desire to handle the problem on their own, lack of knowledge about where to receive treatment, and feelings of shame have been identified as contributing to this low rate of treatment seeking (Suurvali, Cordingley, Hodgins, & Cunningham, 2009).

Although the phenomenon of natural recovery from problem gambling occurs in an estimated 35% of individuals (Slutske, 2006), most problem gamblers report a chronic course, with symptom severity fluctuating over time (Petry, 2005). Therefore, the majority of individuals with Gambling Disorder will not improve on their own, and this underscores the need for evidence-based treatments. Fortunately, research supports a number of potentially effective treatment options for someone with Gambling Disorder.

Current treatments for Gambling Disorder involve a number of different options: inpatient treatment, intensive outpatient treatment, individual and group cognitive behavioral therapy, and pharmacotherapy; however, not all options have equally persuasive evidence supporting their use (Hodgins, Stea, & Grant, 2011; Pallesen, Mitsem, Kvale, Johnsen, & Molde, 2005; Odlaug, Stinchfield, Golberstein, & Grant, 2012). There is no current evidence supporting the use of residential programs for Gambling Disorder. Such an option may be useful perhaps when co-occurring substance use disorders necessitate detoxification. Instead, the evidence supports the use of outpatient treatment for Gambling Disorder. Although there is currently no agreed-upon standard of care for Gambling Disorder, the most widely studied treatment has been some form of cognitive behavioral therapy (CBT) or the use of opioid antagonists.

PSYCHOTHERAPY

A variety of psychosocial treatments have been examined in the treatment of Gambling Disorder, including cognitive behavior therapy, cue exposure, motivational interviewing, and family therapies. Perhaps the most commonly studied approach has been some form of cognitive and behavioral approaches. Cognitive strategies have traditionally included cognitive restructuring, psychoeducation, understanding of gambling urges, and irrational cognition awareness training. Behavioral approaches focus on developing alternate activities to compete with gambling-specific reinforcers as well as the identification of gambling triggers.

Cognitive/Cognitive Behavioral Therapy

Controlled studies have examined the effect of cognitive restructuring in Gambling Disorder. One study (n = 40) used a combination of individual cognitive therapy and relapse prevention strategies (Sylvain, Ladouceur, & Boisvert, 1997). At 12 months, the treatment group showed significant reductions in gambling frequency and an increase in self-perceived control over their gambling behavior. The same cognitive therapy techniques combined with relapse prevention were compared with a 3-month wait-list control in a group of 88 pathological gamblers. The treatment group experienced symptom improvement at 3 months and maintained it at the 12-month follow-up (Ladouceur et al., 2001). A version of cognitive therapy modified for groups (2 hours weekly) has also been tested in 71 subjects with Gambling Disorder against a wait-list control condition (Ladouceur et al., 2003). After 10 sessions, 88% of those in group CBT no longer met pathological gambling criteria, compared with 20% in the wait-list condition. At the 24-month follow-up, 68% of the original group's CBT subjects still did not meet the criteria. Although both individual and group cognitive therapies have shown promise in treating Gambling Disorder, rates of treatment discontinuation were high in these studies (up to 47%).

The most common and the most rigorously designed trials have evaluated a combined CBT model. A randomized study of CBT in gamblers who play slot machines assigned subjects to one of four groups: (1) individual stimulus control and *in vivo* exposure with response prevention; (2) group cognitive restructuring; (3) a combination of (1) and (2); or (4) a wait-list control (Echeburúa, Baez, & Fernández-Montalvo, 1996). At 12-month follow-up, rates of abstinence or minimal gambling were higher in the individual treatment subjects (69%) compared with the cognitive restructuring (38%) and combined treatment (38%) groups. The same investigators also assessed individual and group relapse prevention for subjects completing a 6-week individual treatment program. At 12 months, 86% of those receiving individual relapse prevention and 78% of those in group relapse prevention had not relapsed, compared with 52% of those who received no follow-up treatment (Echeburúa, Fernández-Montalvo, & Baez, 2001).

Milton and colleagues (2002) compared CBT with CBT combined with interventions designed to improve treatment compliance in 40 subjects receiving eight sessions of manualized individual therapy. The interventions included positive reinforcement, identifying barriers to change, and applying problem-solving skills. Only 35% of the CBT-alone group completed treatment compared with 65% of the CBT-plus-interventions group. At 9-month follow-up, there was no difference in outcomes between treatments (Milton, Crino, Hunt, & Prosser, 2002).

Melville and colleagues (2004) reported two studies that used a system targeting three topics (understanding randomness, problem solving, and relapse prevention) to improve outcome. In the first study, 13 subjects were assigned to either 8 weeks of group CBT, group CBT with the topic-enhanced treatment, or a wait list. In the second study, 19 subjects were assigned to a topic-enhanced group or a wait-list group for 8 weeks. For those subjects who were in the topic-targeting CBT group, significant improvement was maintained both post-treatment and at a 6-month follow-up (Melville, Davis, Matzenbacher, & Clayborne, 2004).

Another study examined an eight-session manualized form of CBT, randomizing 231 subjects to weekly sessions with an individual counselor, therapy in the form of a workbook, or referral to Gamblers Anonymous (Petry et al., 2006). Although all groups reduced their gambling, subjects assigned to individual therapy or to the self-help workbook reduced gambling behaviors more than those referred to Gamblers Anonymous (Petry et al., 2006).

In a pilot study examining cognitive motivational behavior therapy (CMBT), a method that combines gambling-specific CBT with motivational interviewing techniques to aid in resolving treatment ambivalence and improve retention rates, 9 subjects received manualized treatment and were compared with a control group of 12 who received treatment as usual (TAU). All 9 subjects (100%) in the CMBT group completed treatment versus only 8 (66.7%) in the TAU group. Significant improvements were observed at the 12-month follow-up of the CMBT group (Wulfert, Blanchard, Freidenberg, & Martell, 2006).

A study using short-term group CBT for 14 subjects found that 85.7% of the treatment group experienced significant improvements in gambling symptoms post-treatment compared to 42.9% of a wait-list control group (Myrseth, Litlerè, Støylen, & Pallesen, 2009). The other dependent variable, money spent gambling over the past week, however, failed to indicate any significant group differences with 28.6% of both the CBT and wait-list control groups experiencing improvement.

Although not a controlled study, one recent study of 471 gamblers examined the delivery of CBT using an 8-week Internet-based program. After the treatment program, significant changes were found in gambling-related problems, gambling urges, impaired control of gambling, and gambling-related cognitive erroneous thoughts (Castrén et al., 2013).

Although the results of these studies are promising, research shows that there is a fairly pronounced "placebo" effect when treating Gambling Disorder. This effect may explain why the short-term results of these studies appear more encouraging than the longer-term benefits. A recent Cochrane review (Cowlishaw et al., 2012) examined 14 studies (n = 1245), 11 of which compared CBT with wait lists or Gamblers Anonymous referrals. CBT at 0 to 3 months post-treatment showed medium to large beneficial effects of therapy. Studies examining longer-term benefits (i.e., 9 to 12 months follow-up) from CBT, however, demonstrated smaller effects that were not significant. The review concluded that there is efficacy of CBT in reducing gambling behavior immediately following therapy, but the durability of therapeutic gain is unknown.

Cue-Exposure

Cue-exposure, based on classical conditioning, is a well-validated form of CBT used in the treatment of fear-based problems (Foa & Kozak, 1986) and has the goal of extinguishing a learned response through repeated exposure to a conditioned stimulus in the absence of the consequence. There is evidence that cue reactivity to relevant stimuli appears to be an important factor in relapse to addiction, particularly in the context of negative mood (Cooney, Litt, Morse, Bauer, & Gaupp, 1997). Cue-exposure studies conducted with Gambling Disorder (Kushner et al., 2007; McConaghy, Blaszczynski, & Frankova, 1991) have reported positive findings to date, yet with only a few randomized controlled trials.

The first randomized study compared imaginal desensitization (i.e., subjects were taught relaxation and then instructed to imagine experiencing and resisting triggers to gambling) with traditional aversion therapy (McConaghy, Armstrong, Blaszczynski, & Allcock, 1983). Both therapies had positive effects, but the imaginal desensitization group was more successful in reducing gambling urges and behavior. In a second study, 20 inpatient subjects were randomized to receive either imaginal desensitization or imaginal relaxation in 14 sessions over a 1-week period. Both groups improved post-treatment, but the therapeutic gains were not maintained by either group at a 12-month follow-up (McConaghy, Armstrong, Blaszczynski, & Allcock, 1988). In a larger study, 120 subjects were randomly assigned to aversion therapy, imaginal desensitization, *in vivo* desensitization, or imaginal relaxation. Subjects assigned to imaginal desensitization reported better outcomes at 1 month and up to 9 years later (McConaghy, Blaszczynski, & Frankova, 1991).

Using imaginal desensitization and combining cue-exposure with negative mood induction, Grant and colleagues (2009) examined 68 gamblers assigned to six sessions of treatment or Gamblers Anonymous. The negative mood induction involved focusing on the negative consequences of the problem behavior while the urge to engage in gambling is active. Idiosyncratic scripts were developed for each gambler, including gambling-related cues with the intention of activating each gambler's urge via imagination (repeatedly listening to the script recorded). The scripts emphasized internal events including thoughts and emotions experienced before, during, and after a gambling episode (e.g., euphoria before and during gambling and dysphoria and agitation after gambling). In the study, the pleasurable aspects of the script (i.e., anticipation of gambling and initial excitement) were then followed by the negative consequences of gambling unique to each gambler (negative mood induction). Grant and colleagues found that 64% of participants receiving imaginal exposure plus the negative mood induction as part of a six-session CBT program were able to maintain abstinence for 1 month, as opposed to only 17% of those randomly assigned to Gambler's Anonymous. For the CBT with imaginal exposure plus negative mood induction group, among those participants who responded to therapy after six sessions, 77% maintained their response for 6 months (Grant, Donahue, Odlaug, & Kim, 2011).

Motivational Interviewing

Motivational interviewing is empathic and uses the strengths of the client to enhance self-efficacy regarding changes in behavior. Motivational interviewing has been used in combination with CBT or on its own as a brief intervention or in a group format. A recent Cochrane review of gambling treatment (Cowlishaw et al., 2012) found that there is preliminary evidence for some benefits from motivational interviewing in the treatment of Gambling Disorder. The review cautioned, however, that the findings are based on limited studies.

In one study, Dickerson, Hinchy, and England (1990) randomly assigned 29 subjects to either a workbook or to a workbook plus a single in-depth interview. The workbook included CBT and motivational-enhancement techniques. Both groups reported significant reductions in gambling at a 6-month follow-up.

Hodgins and colleagues (2001) assigned 102 gamblers to a CBT workbook, a workbook plus a telephone motivational-enhancement intervention, or a wait list. Rates of abstinence at 6-month follow-up did not differ between the groups, although the frequency of gambling and amount of money lost gambling were lower in the motivational-intervention group. Compared with the workbook alone, the motivational intervention and workbook together reduced gambling throughout a 2-year follow-up period; notably, 77% of the entire follow-up sample was rated as improved at the 2-year assessment (Hodgins, Currie, el-Guebaly, & Peden, 2004).

Another study compared a single-session motivational-interviewing module plus a self-help workbook with the workbook and speaking with an interviewer about gambling for 30 minutes (Diskin & Hodgins, 2009). At 12-month follow-up, those who received the motivation interviewing plus workbook gambled less and spent less money than the workbook-alone group (Diskin & Hodgins, 2009).

Motivational interviewing has been used in a group format as well. Oei and colleagues (2010) randomized 102 gamblers to receive 6 weeks of individual or group CBT with motivational interviewing. At post-treatment and a 6-month follow-up, those completing the individual CBT program had better sustained outcomes in regard to gambling severity compared to the group CBT and wait-list control groups (although group CBT produced significant results versus the wait-list control group as well) (Oei, Raylu, & Casey, 2010).

Two self-directed motivational interventions were compared with a 6-week wait-list control and a workbook-only control in 314 pathological gamblers. Brief motivational treatment involved a telephone motivational interview and a mailed self-help workbook. Brief motivational booster treatment involved a telephone motivational interview, a workbook, and six booster telephone calls over a 9-month period. Both the brief and the brief booster treatment participants reported less gambling at 6 weeks than those assigned to the control groups. Brief and brief booster treatment participants gambled significantly less often over the first 6 months of the follow-up than workbook-only participants. Participants in the brief booster treatment group, however, showed no greater improvement than brief treatment participants (Hodgins, Currie, Currie, & Fick, 2009).

A similar combination of motivation interviewing and CBT was adapted to a web-based format (Carlbring & Smit, 2008) in which a therapist provides telephone support for individuals using online recovery materials. A wait-list control was compared with the 8-week Internet-based CBT program with minimal therapist contact via e-mail and weekly telephone calls of less than 15 minutes. The Internet-based intervention resulted in favorable changes in gambling, anxiety, depression, and quality of life. Follow-ups in the treatment group at 6, 18, and 36 months indicated that treatment effects were sustained.

A total of 150 primarily self-recruited patients with current gambling problems or pathological gambling were randomized to four individual sessions of motivational interviewing, eight sessions of CBT group therapy, or a no-treatment wait-list control. Treatment showed superiority in some areas over the no-treatment control in the short term, but no differences were found between motivational interviewing and group CBT at any point in time. Instead, both interventions produced significant within-group decreases on most outcome measures up to the 12-month follow-up (Carlbring, Jonsson, Josephson, & Forsberg, 2010).

A randomized controlled study found that a 10-minute session of behavioral advice, one session of motivational enhancement therapy, or one session of motivational enhancement therapy plus three sessions of CBT were all equally effective in reducing gambling among a sample of 117 college students with either problem or pathological gambling (Petry, Weinstock, Morasco, & Ledgerwood, 2009). Two small trials have shown that the addition of motivational interviewing to CBT reduces treatment attrition and improves outcomes (Diskin & Hodgins, 2009; Wulfert, Blanchard, & Freidenberg, 2006). Generally speaking, dropout rates from psychosocial treatment are high, so interventions that lead patients to complete treatment are potentially very valuable.

Family Therapy

Families of gamblers often feel intense dissatisfaction and a lack of trust over the deception often associated with Gambling Disorder (Mazzoleni, Gorenstein, Fuentes, & Tavares, 2009). Gambler's Anonymous for families, also known as GAM-ANON and modeled after AL-ANON for substance addiction, was established as a program for the families and friends of compulsive gamblers to understand and cope with these feelings and the interpersonal damage caused by problem gambling (Vander Bilt & Franklin, 2003). In a small study assessing the impact of family involvement (n = 43) in GAM-ANON in relation to gambling relapse for a spouse/significant other involved in Gambler's Anonymous, Zion, Tracy, and Abell (1991) found no association between GAM-ANON involvement and client relapse.

A self-help workbook of the Community Reinforcement and Family Therapy (CRAFT) model, adapted for gambling, has been evaluated in two randomized controlled trials (Hodgins, Toneatto, Makarchuk, Skinner, & Vincent, 2007; Makarchuk, Hodgins, & Peden, 2002). In CRAFT, family members are trained to use behavioral principles to reinforce nongambling behavior in individuals who are not addressing their gambling problem. Although positive effects for family members and their gambling relatives were found in both trials, the studies found that behavioral principles were too complex for family members to implement without the support of a therapist (Hodgins et al., 2007).

A coping skill-training program developed for alcohol problems has also been evaluated for gambling. The program consists of 10 weekly individual sessions to teach more effective coping skills. A small (n = 23) randomized controlled trial comparing the coping skills program to a delayed-treatment condition showed that partners of gamblers improved their ability to manage feelings of depression and anxiety. Partner gambling during that period decreased in both conditions but did not differ between them, nor did partner help seeking differ (Rychtarik & McGillicuddy, 2006).

PHARMACOTHERAPY

Despite a relatively high population prevalence, there are currently no approved medications in the United States or globally for Gambling Disorder; however, the double-blind, placebo-controlled trials that have been conducted suggest that certain medications may be beneficial in treating the urges, thoughts, and behaviors associated with Gambling Disorder.

Opioid Antagonists

The most studied and efficacious class of medications for Gambling Disorder to date is opioid antagonists. Opioid antagonists, like naltrexone (FDA approved for the treatment of alcohol dependence and opiate dependence) and nalmefene, block mu opioid receptors and modulate dopaminergic transmission in the mesocorticolimbic pathway. The first double-blind, placebo-controlled study of naltrexone was 11 weeks and included 45 individuals with Gambling Disorder. At the end of treatment, 75% of the naltrexone subjects and 24% of placebo subjects had significant improvement in their gambling urges, thoughts, and gambling behavior. Furthermore, individual subject analysis revealed that gamblers who had more intense urges to gamble at study intake had a more robust response to naltrexone. The mean efficacious dose noted in this trial was 188 mg/day, higher than the FDA-approved indicated dose for alcohol and opiate dependence.

A longer, 18-week trial in a larger number (n = 77) of patients with Gambling Disorder in which patients were randomized to receive either naltrexone or placebo found that naltrexone subjects reported significantly greater reductions in gambling urges, thoughts, and behavior compared to the placebo group. Naltrexone was also efficacious in helping subjects abstain from gambling, as nearly 40% of naltrexone subjects compared to 10.5% of placebo subjects reported gambling abstinence for at least 1 month at the end of the study (Grant, Kim, & Hartman, 2008).

Nalmefene has also shown promise in the treatment of Gambling Disorder in two, large multicenter, double-blind, placebo-controlled studies in the United States. In the first study, 207 subjects with Gambling Disorder received either nalmefene at varying doses or placebo over a course of 16 weeks. At the conclusion of the treatment period, researchers found that 59% of those assigned to nalmefene demonstrated significant reductions in gambling urges, thoughts, and behavior compared to only 34% receiving placebo, a statistically significant difference (Grant, Potenza, et al., 2006). In the second trial of 233 individuals with Gambling Disorder, researchers found no significant between-group differences for the nalmefene and placebo groups. A post hoc analysis, however, revealed that subjects titrated to the optimal 40 mg/d dose for at least 1 week had significantly greater reductions in gambling severity compared to the placebo group (Grant, Odlaug, Potenza, Hollander, & Kim, 2010).

These studies of opioid antagonists offer clinicians and patients the most promising pharmacotherapeutic treatment option at this time.

Glutamatergic Agents

N-acetylcysteine (NAC), a glutamate-modulating agent that has also been found to be helpful for other addictive disorders such as cocaine, tobacco, and cannabis abuse (Berk, Malhi, Gray, & Dean, 2013), has also shown promise for Gambling Disorder (Grant, Kim, & Odlaug, 2007). In an 8-week trial of 27 subjects with Gambling Disorder, subjects were administered NAC for the entire treatment period. Subjects classified as responders at the end of the 8-week trial (59% of subjects) were randomly assigned to receive an additional double-blind trial of NAC or matching placebo. Researchers found that 83% of the NAC group, compared to only 28.6% of the placebo group, were classified as responders at the end of the 6-week double-blind trial period (Grant, Kim, & Odlaug, 2007).

Antidepressants

Low levels of the serotonin metabolite 5-hydroxyindole acetic acid (5-HIAA) and blunted serotonergic response within the ventromedial prefrontal cortex (vmPFC) have been found to be associated with impulsive behaviors and, as a result, antidepressant medications have been examined as potential treatments for Gambling Disorder.

Sertraline has been examined in one study, in which 60 subjects were randomly assigned to receive either sertraline or placebo over a period of 6 months. At the end of the treatment period, no significant differences were noted between those on sertraline and those taking placebo (Saiz-Ruiz et al., 2005).

Mixed results have been found for the two double-blind trials of paroxetine in the treatment of Gambling Disorder. In the first study, 53 patients with Gambling Disorder were randomized to receive paroxetine or placebo over a period of 8 weeks. This study found that paroxetine significantly improved gambling symptoms for 61% of patients compared to only 23% of those assigned to placebo (Kim, Grant, Adson, Shin, & Zaninelli, 2002). A larger (n = 76) and longer (16-week) study, however, failed to note significant differences between placebo and paroxetine (Grant et al., 2003).

Like paroxetine, which has been examined in two separate placebo-controlled trials, fluvoxamine has also demonstrated mixed results in two studies. The first study included 15 subjects randomly assigned to fluvoxamine or placebo over a 16-week study, finding it significantly superior to placebo (Hollander et al., 2000), while the second, larger (n = 32) and longer (6-month) parallel-arm study failed to demonstrate any significant between-group differences (Blanco, Petkova, Ibáñez, & Sáiz-Ruiz, 2002).

Other studies have included a 12-week open-label study with an 8-week double-blind discontinuation of the antidepressant escitalopram for 13 patients with co-occurring Gambling Disorder and anxiety disorders (Grant & Potenza, 2006). Nearly half (6 of 13) of the subjects were considered responders in terms of reduction in both gambling and anxiety symptoms at the end of the open-label phase and were subsequently randomized to continue escitalopram (n = 3) treatment or receive placebo (n = 3). Further, the escitalopram group maintained their improvement while gambling and anxiety symptoms returned for those assigned to placebo.

The dopaminergic and noradrenergic antidepressant bupropion has also been examined in one placebo-controlled study for Gambling Disorder. In this study, 39 subjects with Gambling Disorder were randomized to receive bupropion or placebo over a 12-week treatment period. No significant differences were noted between groups at treatment endpoint, and treatment discontinuation was quite high (44%) (Black et al., 2007).

Despite their being the most widely studied class of medication for the treatment of Gambling Disorder, the literature does not currently support the use of antidepressant medications as a first-line treatment for Gambling Disorder.

Lithium and Anti-epileptics

A 10-week, double-blind, placebo-controlled study of sustained-release lithium carbonate was used in a trial of 40 subjects with bipolar spectrum disorders and Gambling Disorder. Researchers found that lithium (mean level, 0.87 meq/liter) reduced gambling thoughts and urges associated with Gambling Disorder; however, no significant differences were found in gambling episodes per week, time spent per gambling episode, or the amount of money lost (Hollander, Pallanti, Allen, Sood, & Baldini Rossi, 2005).

Berlin and colleagues randomized 42 patients with Gambling Disorder to 14 weeks of topiramate or placebo. At the end of the treatment period, no significant differences were found between groups (Berlin et al., 2013).

Atypical Antipsychotics

Negative results in treating Gambling Disorder have been found in two separate double-blind, placebo-controlled trials for the atypical antipsychotic *olanzapine* (Fong, Kalechstein, Bernhard, Rosenthal, & Rugle, 2008; McElroy, Nelson, Welge, Kaehler, & Keck, 2008). The first trial was conducted over a period of 7 weeks in a sample of 21 video-poker-playing Gambling Disorder patients. Researchers found no significant differences in gambling urges or behavior between the olanzapine and placebo groups (Fong, Kalechstein, Bernhard, Rosenthal, & Rugle, 2008). The second double-blind study involved a longer, 12-week treatment period with a larger (n = 42) patient sample; however, as with the Fong et al. (2008) study, researchers found no significant differences between groups (McEloy et al., 2008). Given the negative outcome of both of these studies and with the high adverse event profile associated with the use of atypical antipsychotics, they are not considered to be a first-line treatment for Gambling Disorder.

Case Vignette: Michael in Treatment

As noted previously, Michael is a 35-year-old male with the onset of a gambling problem in the past 2 years. Michael is screened with the Structured Clinical Interview for Pathological Gambling and meets 8 of the 10 *DSM-IV* criteria listed (which would be 7 out of 9 for *DSM-5* because illegal behavior has been taken out of the *DSM-5* criteria set for Gambling Disorder). When the clinician is assessing the available treatment options for Michael, two elements of his gambling and psychiatric history should promote the clinician to use a combination of medication and therapy. First, Michael has a personal and family history of alcohol abuse. Research has shown that pathological gamblers with a family history of alcohol abuse or dependence respond preferentially to opioid antagonists such as naltrexone (Grant, Kim, & Hartman, 2008). Further, the intense urges to gamble that Michael endorses are targeted by this class of medication. Second, and like many pathological gamblers, Michael reports cognitive distortions (chasing losses, having a "lucky" machine, feeling that the machine has to "pay off" soon, etc.) that could be treated with cognitive therapies. Further, and given the significantly psychosocial stressors that Michael is facing, cognitive behavioral therapy, perhaps followed by family therapy with his wife, may be helpful in getting his gambling under control. Finally, given the illegality of Michael's actions at work, it is important that the clinician encourage Michael to seek legal advice but equally as important that the clinician not try to manage any of Michael's legal affairs.

Additional resources beyond the peer-reviewed literature noted in the reference list include the following:

- National Center for Responsible Gaming (NCRG) and their associated Centers of Excellence at the University of Chicago (Dr. Jon Grant) and Yale University (Dr. Marc Potenza). More information is available at http://www.ncrg.org/.
- Ontario Problem Gambling Research Centre. More information is available at http://www.gamblingresearch.org/.

CONCLUSIONS

Although no universally agreed-upon standard psychotherapeutic treatment or pharmacological interventions have been established for Gambling Disorder, available evidence suggests that various successful interventions exist. Given that both medications and psychotherapy do not work for all gambling disordered individuals, many questions remain regarding what is the best treatment for any individual.

For instance, are there predictors—clinical, genetic, and so on—that can be identified in order to triage patients for more targeted treatments? Grant and colleagues (2008) found that patients with Gambling Disorder who had a family history of alcoholism responded significantly more preferentially to opiate antagonist treatment. This is important from the perspective of engaging patients in treatment because treatment seeking and maintenance of response are both low in Gambling Disorder patients. Further identification and dissemination of such predictors may encourage more individuals in the community with problematic gambling to seek treatment.

Second and similarly, what form of CBT has the greatest treatment success, and for how many sessions should patients be expected to engage in treatment? Whereas some studies have indicated that as many as 20 sessions are necessary to treat Gambling Disorder, brief interventions have also been equally as efficacious in other studies. Identifying which aspects of CBT are more effective and which patients would be ideal for shorter (i.e., brief interventions) versus longer (formalized, multisession CBT) interventions would likely engage more patients in treatment while lowering provider costs.

Another important question that remains is regarding the role of co-occurring psychiatric or physical health problems often seen in Gambling Disorder. After all, psychiatric comorbidity is the norm, not the exception, in Gambling Disorder, but the impact of carrying a comorbid illness on treatment outcome and symptom severity varies widely. In terms of treatment efficacy, for example, nicotine dependence has been shown to adversely impact treatment outcome in some studies (Grant, Donahue, Odlaug, & Kim, 2011) yet not in others (Odlaug, Stinchfield, Golberstein, & Grant, 2013). The same can be said for patients with Gambling Disorder who also have a substance use disorder (Champine & Petry, 2010; Hodgins & el-Guebaly, 2000). Assessing the true impact of comorbidity on treatment engagement, success, and maintenance of treatment gains is of vital importance and comprises a relatively nascent area of research in Gambling Disorders.

The final and most controversial question in Gambling Disorder is the question of whether abstinence should be the primary treatment goal for all Gambling Disorder patients. Rather, should controlled or reduced gambling be a treatment option offered to certain patients? Research in alcohol dependence has illustrated a growing acceptance of reducing alcohol consumption at national levels in Europe as the World Health Organization encourages the concept of *harm reduction* as a central goal of treatment (WHO, 2001). Consequently, offering flexibility (i.e., abstinence, decreased gambling, more control) to individuals with Gambling Disorder presenting for treatment would hypothetically increase treatment-seeking behaviors while simultaneously decreasing attrition. Ladouceur and colleagues (2009) reported that 66% of individuals involved in a 14-sesssion CBT paradigm treatment for Gambling Disorder changed their goal from controlled gambling to abstinence over the course of the 12-week treatment (Ladouceur, Lachance, & Fournier, 2009). Drop-out and treatment efficacy, however, was similar in both the controlled and abstinent-only treatment groups. This begs the question of whether certain patients, perhaps those with a more mild to moderate gambling severity, would be better suited for controlled or reduced gambling while more a more severe Gambling Disorder symptomology (including significant comorbidity) would be better suited for abstinence. Further research is needed to explore these and the many other questions that remain in order to advance our understanding of Gambling Disorder and improve the quality and timeliness of treatments.

REFERENCES

American Gaming Association. (2012). *Gaming revenue, 10-year trends*. Retrieved February 15, 2011 from http://www.americangaming.org/industry-resources/research/fact-sheets/gaming-revenue-10-year-trends.

American Psychiatric Association. (2013). *Diagnostic and statistical manual of mental disorders* (5th ed.). Washington, DC: Author.

Berk, M., Malhi, G. S., Gray, L. J., & Dean, O. M. (2013). The promise of N-acetylcysteine in neuropsychiatry. *Trends in Pharmacological Sciences*, *34*, 167–177.

Berlin, H. A., Braun, A., Simeon, D., Koran, L. M., Potenza, M. N., McElroy, S. L., et al. (2013). A double-blind, placebo-controlled trial of topiramate for pathological gambling. *World Journal of Biological Psychiatry*, *14*, 121–128.

Black, D. W., Arndt, S., Coryell, W. H., Argo, T., Forbush, K. T., Shaw, M. C., et al. (2007). Bupropion in the treatment of pathological gambling: A randomized, double-blind, placebo-controlled, flexible-dose study. *Journal of Clinical Psychopharmacology*, *27*, 143–150.

Black, D. W., & Grant, J. E. (2013). *DSM-5 guidebook: The essential companion to the Diagnostic and Statistical Manual of Mental Disorders*. Washington, DC: APPI.

Black, D. W., Shaw, M., McCormick, B., & Allen, J. (2012). Pathological gambling: Relationship to obesity, self-reported chronic medical conditions, poor lifestyle choices, and impaired quality of life. *Comprehensive Psychiatry*, *54*, 97–104.

Blanco, C., Petkova, E., Ibáñez, A., & Sáiz-Ruiz, J. (2002). A pilot placebo-controlled study of fluvoxamine for pathological gambling. *Annals of Clinical Psychiatry*, *14*, 9–15.

Carlbring, P., Jonsson, J., Josephson, H., & Forsberg, L. (2010). Motivational interviewing versus cognitive behavioral group therapy in the treatment of problem and pathological gambling: A randomized controlled trial. *Cognitive Behaviour Therapy*, *39*, 92–103.

Carlbring, P., & Smit, F. (2008). Randomized trial of Internet-delivered self-help with telephone support for pathological gamblers. *Journal of Consulting and Clinical Psychology*, *76*, 1090–1094.

Castrén, S., Pankakoski, M., Tamminen, M., Lipsanen, J., Ladouceur, R., & Lahti, T. (2013). Internet-based CBT intervention for gamblers in Finland: Experiences from the field. *Scandinavian Journal of Psychology, 54,* 230–235.

Champine, R. B., & Petry, N. M. (2010). Pathological gamblers respond equally well to cognitive-behavioral therapy regardless of other mental health treatment status. *American Journal on Addictions, 19,* 550–556.

Chou, K. L., & Afifi, T. O. (2011). Disordered (pathologic or problem) gambling and axis I psychiatric disorders: Results from the National Epidemiologic Survey on Alcohol and Related Conditions. *American Journal of Epidemiology, 173,* 1289–1297.

Cooney, L., Litt, M. D., Morse, P. A., Bauer, L. O., & Gaupp, L. (1997). Alcohol cue reactivity, negative-mood reactivity, and relapse in treated alcoholic men. *Journal of Abnormal Psychology, 106,* 243–250.

Cowlishaw, S., Merkouris, S., Dowling, N., Anderson, C., Jackson, A., & Thomas, S. (2012). Psychological therapies for pathological and problem gambling. *Cochrane Database System Reviews,* 11:CD008937.

Dickerson, M., Hinchy, J., & England, S. L. (1990). Minimal treatments and problem gamblers: A preliminary investigation. *Journal of Gambling Studies, 6,* 87–102.

Diskin, K. M., & Hodgins, D. C. (2009). A randomized controlled trial of a single session motivational intervention for concerned gamblers. *Behaviour Research and Therapy, 47,* 382–388.

Echeburúa, E., Baez, C., & Fernández-Montalvo, J. (1996). Comparative effectiveness of three therapeutic modalities in psychological treatment of pathological gambling: Long term outcome. *Behavioural and Cognitive Psychotherapy, 24,* 51–72.

Echeburúa, E., Fernández-Montalvo, J., & Baez, C. (2001). Predictors of therapeutic failure in slot-machine pathological gamblers following behavioural treatment. *Behavioural and Cognitive Psychotherapy, 29,* 379–383.

Erbas, B., & Buchner, U. G. (2012). Pathological gambling: prevalence, diagnosis, comorbidity, and intervention in Germany. *Deutsches Arzteblatt International, 109,* 173–179.

Foa, E. B., & Kozak, M. J. (1986). Emotional processing of fear: Exposure to corrective information. *Psychological Bulletin, 99,* 20–35.

Fong, T., Kalechstein, A., Bernhard, B., Rosenthal, R., & Rugle, L. (2008). A double-blind, placebo-controlled trial of olanzapine for the treatment of video poker pathological gamblers. *Pharmacology, Biochemistry, and Behavior, 89,* 298–303.

Germain, C., Vahanian, A., Basquin, A., Richoux-Benhaim, C., Embouazza, H., & Lejoyeux, M. (2011). Brief report: Coronary heart disease: An unknown association to pathological gambling. *Frontiers in Psychiatry, 2,* 11.

Grant, J. E., Donahue, C. B., Odlaug, B. L., & Kim, S. W. (2011). A 6-month follow-up of imaginal desensitization plus motivational interviewing in the treatment of pathological gambling. *Annals of Clinical Psychiatry, 23,* 3–10.

Grant, J. E., Donahue, C. B., Odlaug, B. L., Kim, S. W., Miller, M. J., & Petry, N. M. (2009). Imaginal desensitisation plus motivational interviewing for pathological gambling: Randomised controlled trial. *British Journal of Psychiatry, 195,* 266–267.

Grant, J. E., & Kim, S. W. (2001). Demographic and clinical characteristics of 131 adult pathological gamblers. *Journal of Clinical Psychiatry, 62,* 957–962.

Grant, J. E., Kim, S. W., & Hartman, B. (2008). A double-blind, placebo-controlled study of the opiate antagonist naltrexone in the treatment of pathological gambling urges. *Journal of Clinical Psychiatry, 69,* 783–789.

Grant, J. E., Kim, S.W., & Odlaug, B. L. (2007). N-acetyl cysteine, a glutamate-modulating agent, in the treatment of pathological gambling: A pilot study. *Biological Psychiatry, 62,* 652–657.

Grant, J. E., Kim, S. W., Potenza, M. N., Blanco, C., Ibanez, A., Stevens, L., et al. (2003). Paroxetine treatment of pathological gambling: A multi-centre randomized controlled trial. *International Clinical Psychopharmacology, 18,* 243–249.

Grant, J. E., Odlaug, B. L., & Mooney, M. (2012). Telescoping phenomenon in pathological gambling: Association with gender and comorbidities. *Journal of Nervous & Mental Disease, 200*, 996–998.

Grant, J. E., Odlaug, B. L., Potenza, M. N., Hollander, E., & Kim, S. W. (2010). Nalmefene in the treatment of pathological gambling: Multicentre, double-blind, placebo-controlled study. *British Journal of Psychiatry, 197*, 330–331.

Grant, J. E., & Potenza, M. N. (2006). Escitalopram treatment of pathological gambling with co-occurring anxiety: An open-label pilot study with double-blind discontinuation. *International Clinical Psychopharmacology, 21*, 203–209.

Grant, J. E., & Potenza, M. N. (2007). Commentary: Illegal behavior and pathological gambling. *Journal of the American Academy of Psychiatry and the Law, 35*, 302–305.

Grant, J. E., Potenza, M. N., Hollander, E., Cunningham-Williams, R., Nurminen, T., Smits, G., et al. (2006). Multicenter investigation of the opioid antagonist nalmefene in the treatment of pathological gambling. *American Journal of Psychiatry, 163*, 303–312.

Grant, J. E., Schreiber, L. R. N., Odlaug, B. L., & Kim, S. W. (2010). Pathological gambling and bankruptcy. *Comprehensive Psychiatry, 51*, 115–120.

Grant, J. E., Steinberg, M. A., Kim, S. W., Rounsaville, B. J., & Potenza, M. N. (2004). Preliminary validity and reliability testing of a structured clinical interview for pathological gambling. *Psychiatry Research, 128*, 79–88.

Hodgins, D. C., Currie, S., & el-Guebaly, N. (2001). Motivational enhancement and self-help treatments for problem gambling. *Journal of Consulting and Clinical Psychology, 69*, 50–57.

Hodgins, D. C., Currie, S., el-Guebaly, N., & Diskin, K. M. (2007). Does providing extended-release prevention bibliotherapy to problem gamblers improve outcome? *Journal of Gambling Studies, 23*, 41–54.

Hodgins, D. C., Currie, S., el-Guebaly, N., & Peden, N. (2004). Brief motivational treatment for problem gambling: a 24-month follow-up. *Psychology of Addictive Behaviors, 18*, 293–296.

Hodgins, D. C., Currie, S. R., Currie, G., & Fick, G. H. (2009). Randomized trial of brief motivational treatments for pathological gamblers: More is not necessarily better. *Journal of Consulting and Clinical Psychology, 77*, 950–960.

Hodgins, D. C., & el-Guebaly, N. (2000). Natural and treatment-assisted recovery from gambling problems: A comparison of resolved and active gamblers. *Addiction, 95*, 777–785.

Hodgins, D. C., Stea, J. N., & Grant, J. E. (2011). Gambling disorders. *Lancet, 378*, 1874–1884.

Hodgins, D. C., Toneatto, T., Makarchuk, K., Skinner, W., & Vincent, S. (2007). Minimal treatment approaches for concerned significant others of problem gamblers: A randomized controlled trial. *Journal of Gambling Studies, 23*, 215–230.

Hollander, E., DeCaria, C. M., Finkell, J. N., Begaz, T., Wong, C. M., & Cartwright, C. (2000). A randomized double-blind fluvoxamine/placebo crossover trial in pathologic gambling. *Biological Psychiatry, 47*, 813–817.

Hollander, E., Pallanti, S., Allen, A., Sood, E., & Baldini Rossi, N. (2005). Does sustained-release lithium reduce impulsive gambling and affective instability versus placebo in pathological gamblers with bipolar spectrum disorders? *American Journal of Psychiatry, 162*, 137–145.

Ibáñez, A., Blanco, C., & Sáiz-Ruiz, J. (2002). Neurobiology and genetics of pathological gambling. *Psychiatric Annals, 32*, 181–185.

Johnson, E. E., Hammer, R., Nora, R. M., Tan, B., Eistenstein, N., & Englehart, C. (1988). The lie/bet questionnaire for screening pathological gamblers. *Psychological Reports, 80*, 83–88.

Kim, S. W., Grant, J. E., Adson, D. E., Shin, Y. C., & Zaninelli, R. (2002). A double-blind placebo-controlled study of the efficacy and safety of paroxetine in the treatment of pathological gambling. *Journal of Clinical Psychiatry, 63*, 501–507.

Kushner, M. G., Abrams, K., Donahue, C., Thuras, P., Frost, R., & Kim, S. W. (2007). Urge to gamble in problem gamblers exposed to a casino environment. *Journal of Gambling Studies, 23*, 121–132.

Ladouceur, R., Lachance, S., & Fournier, P. M. (2009). Is control a viable goal in the treatment of pathological gambling? *Behaviour Research and Therapy, 47*, 189–197.

Ladouceur, R., Sylvain, C., Boutin, C., Lachance, S., Doucet, C., & Leblond, J. (2003). Group therapy for pathological gamblers: A cognitive approach. *Behaviour Research and Therapy, 41*, 587–596.

Ladouceur, R., Sylvain, C., Boutin, C., Lachance, S., Doucet, C., Leblond, J., et al. (2001). Cognitive treatment of pathological gambling. *Journal of Nervous and Mental Disease, 189*, 774–780.

Ledgerwood, D. M., & Petry, N. M. (2004). Gambling and suicidality in treatment-seeking pathological gamblers. *Journal of Nervous and Mental Disease, 192*, 711–714.

Ledgerwood, D. M., Weinstock, J., Morasco, B. J., & Petry, N. M. (2007). Clinical features and treatment prognosis of pathological gamblers with and without recent gambling-related illegal behavior. *Journal of the American Academy of Psychiatry and the Law, 35*, 294–301.

Lesieur, H. R., & Blume, S. B. (1987). The South Oaks Gambling Screen (SOGS): A new instrument for the identification of pathological gamblers. *American Journal of Psychiatry, 144*(9), 1184–1188.

Lorains, F. K., Cowlishaw, S., & Thomas, S. A. (2011). Prevalence of comorbid disorders in problem and pathological gambling: Systematic review and meta-analysis of population surveys. *Addiction, 106*, 490–498.

Makarchuk, K., Hodgins, D. C., & Peden, N. (2002). Development of a brief intervention for concerned significant others of problem gamblers. *Addictive Disorders and Their Treatment, 1*, 126–134.

Mazzoleni, M. H., Gorenstein, C., Fuentes, D., & Tavares, H. (2009). Wives of pathological gamblers: Personality traits, depressive symptoms and social adjustment. *Revista Brasileira Psiquiatria, 31*, 332–337.

McConaghy, N., Armstrong, M. S., Blaszczynski, A., & Allcock, C. (1983). Controlled comparison of aversive therapy and imaginal desensitization in compulsive gambling. *British Journal of Psychiatry, 142*, 366–372.

McConaghy, N., Armstrong, M. S., Blaszczynski, A., & Allcock, C. (1988). Behavior completion versus stimulus control in compulsive gambling: Implications for behavioral assessment. *Behavior Modification, 12*, 371–384.

McConaghy, N., Blaszczynski, A., & Frankova, A. (1991). Comparison of imaginal desensitization with other behavioural treatments of pathological gambling: A two- to nine-year follow-up. *British Journal of Psychiatry, 159*, 390–393.

McElroy, S. L., Nelson, E. B., Welge, J. A., Kaehler, L., & Keck, P. E., Jr. (2008). Olanzapine in the treatment of pathological gambling: A negative randomized placebo-controlled trial. *Journal of Clinical Psychiatry, 69*, 433–440.

Melville, C. L., Davis, C. S., Matzenbacher, D. L., & Clayborne, J. (2004). Node-link-mapping-enhanced group treatment for pathological gambling. *Addictive Behavior, 29*, 73–87.

Milton, S., Crino, R., Hunt, C., & Prosser, E. (2002). The effect of compliance-improving interventions on the cognitive-behavioural treatment of pathological gambling. *Journal of Gambling Studies, 18*, 207–229.

Myrseth, H., Litlerè, I., Støylen, I. J., & Pallesen, S. (2009). A controlled study of the effect of cognitive-behavioural group therapy for pathological gamblers. *Nordic Journal of Psychiatry, 63*, 22–31.

National Opinion Research Center. (1999). *Gambling Impact and Behavior Study: Report to the National Gambling Impact Study Commission*. Chicago: National Opinion Research Center at the University of Chicago. Available at http://www.norc.uchicago.edu/new/gamb-fin.htm.

Najavits, L. M. (2003). How to design an effective treatment outcome study. *Journal of Gambling Studies, 19*, 317–337.

Odlaug, B. L., Stinchfield, R., Golberstein, E., & Grant, J. E. (2013). The relationship of tobacco use with gambling problem severity and gambling treatment outcome. *Psychology of Addictive Behaviors, 27*(3), 696–704.

Oei, T. P., Raylu, N., & Casey, L. M. (2010). Effectiveness of group and individual formats of a combined motivational interviewing and cognitive behavioral treatment program for problem gambling: A randomized controlled trial. *Behavioural & Cognitive Psychotherapy, 38*, 233–238.

Pallesen, S., Mitsem, M., Kvale, G., Johnsen, B. H., & Molde, H. (2005). Outcome of psychological treatments of pathological gambling: A review and meta-analysis. *Addiction, 100*, 1412–1422.

Parhami, I., Siani, A., Rosenthal, R. J., & Fong, T. W. (2012). Pathological gambling, problem gambling and sleep complaints: An analysis of the National Comorbidity Survey: Replication (NCS-R). *Journal of Gambling Studies, 29*(2), 241–253.

Petry, N. M. (2005). *Pathological gambling: Etiology, comorbidity, and treatment.* Washington, DC: American Psychological Association.

Petry, N. M., Ammerman, Y., Bohl, J., Doersch, A., Gay, H., Kadden, R., et al. (2006). Cognitive-behavioral therapy for pathological gamblers. *Journal of Consulting and Clinical Psychology, 74*, 555–567.

Petry, N. M., Weinstock, J., Morasco, B. J., & Ledgerwood, D. M. (2009). Brief motivational interventions for college student problem gamblers. *Addiction, 104*, 1569–1578.

Rychtarik, R. G., & McGillicuddy, N. B. (2006). Preliminary evaluation of a coping skills training program for those with a pathological-gambling partner. *Journal of Gambling Studies, 22*, 165–178.

Saiz-Ruiz, J., Blanco, C., Ibáñez, A., Masramon, X., Gómez, M. M., Madrigal., M., et al. (2005). Sertraline treatment of pathological gambling: A pilot study. *Journal of Clinical Psychiatry, 66*, 28–33.

Shaffer, H. J., Hall, M. N., & Vander Bilt, J. (1999). Estimating the prevalence of disordered gambling behavior in the United States and Canada: A research synthesis. *American Journal of Public Health, 89*, 1369–1376.

Shaffer, H. J., LaBrie, R., Scanlan, K. M., & Cummings, T. N. (1994). Pathological gambling among adolescents: Massachusetts gambling screen (MAGS). *Journal of Gambling Studies, 10*, 339–362.

Slutske, W. S. (2006). Natural recovery and treatment-seeking in pathological gambling: Results of two U.S. national surveys. *American Journal of Psychiatry, 163*, 297–302.

Slutske, W. S., Meier, M. H., Zhu, G., Statham, D. J., Blaszczynski, A., & Martin, N. G. (2009). The Australian Twin Study of Gambling (OZ-GAM): Rationale, sample description, predictors of participation, and a first look at sources of individual differences in gambling involvement. *Twin Research and Human Genetics, 12*, 63–78.

Soberay, A., Faragher, J. M., Barbash, M., Brookover, A., & Grimsley, P. (2013). Pathological gambling, co-occurring disorders, clinical presentation, and treatment outcomes at a University-based counseling clinic. *Journal of Gambling Studies*, [Epub ahead of print].

Stea, J. N., & Hodgins, D. C. (2011). A critical review of treatment approaches for gambling disorders. *Current Drug Abuse Reviews, 4*, 67–80.

Stinchfield, R., Govoni, R., & Frisch, G. R. (2007). Assessment of problem and pathological gambling. In G. Smith, D. Hodgins & R. Williams (Eds.), *Research & measurement issues in gambling studies* (pp. 207–231). San Diego: Elsevier Press.

Sullivan, S. (1999). *Development of the "EIGHT" problem gambling screen.* Unpublished doctoral thesis. Auckland University, Auckland, New Zealand (Philson RefW4 S952–1999).

Suurvali, H., Cordingley, J., Hodgins, D. C., & Cunningham, J. (2009). Barriers to seeking help for gambling problems: A review of the empirical literature. *Journal of Gambling Studies, 25*, 407–424.

Suurvali, H., Hodgins, D., Toneatto, T., & Cunningham, J. (2008). Treatment seeking among Ontario problem gamblers: Results of a population survey. *Psychiatric Services, 59*, 1343–1346.

Suurvali, H., Hodgins, D. C., Toneatto, T., & Cunningham, J. A. (2011). Hesitation to seek gambling-related treatment among Ontario problem gamblers. *Journal of Addiction Medicine*, *6*(1), 39–49.

Sylvain, C., Ladouceur, R., & Boisvert, J. M. (1997). Cognitive and behavioral treatment of pathological gambling: A controlled study. *Journal of Consulting and Clinical Psychology*, *65*, 727–732.

Toneatto, T. (2008). Reliability and validity of the Gamblers Anonymous Twenty Questions. *Journal of Psychopathology and Behavioural Assessment*, *30*(1), 71–78.

Vander Bilt, J., & Franklin, J. (2003). Gambling in a familial context. In H. J. Shaffer, M. N. Hall, J. Vander Bilt & E. M. George (Eds.), *Futures at stake: Youth, gambling, & society* (pp. 100–125). Reno, NV: University of Nevada Press.

Winters, K. C., Specker, S., & Stinchfield, R. (2002). Measuring pathological gambling with the Diagnostic Interview for Gambling Severity (DIGS). In J. J. Marotta, J. A. Cornelius & W. R. Eadington (Eds.), *The downside: Problem and pathological gambling* (pp. 143–148). Reno, NV: University of Nevada. (Reno.

Wong, P. W., Chan, W. S., Conwell, Y., Conner, K. R., & Yip, P. S. (2010). A psychological autopsy study of pathological gamblers who died by suicide. *Journal of Affective Disorders*, *120*, 213–216.

World Health Organization. The world health report 2001—Mental health: New understanding, new hope. Retrieved February 2013 from http://www.who.int/whr/2001/en/.

Wulfert, E., Blanchard, E. B., Freidenberg, B. M., & Martell, R. S. (2006). Retaining pathological gamblers in cognitive behavior therapy through motivational enhancement. *Behavior Modification*, *30*, 315–340.

Zion, M. M., Tracy, E., & Abell, N. (1991). Examining the relationship between spousal involvement in GAM-ANON and relapse behaviors in pathological gamblers. *Journal of Gambling Studies*, 7, 117–131.

Problematic Online Gaming

Orsolya Király[1,2], Katalin Nagygyörgy[1,2], Mark D. Griffiths[3], Zsolt Demetrovics[1]

[1]Department of Clinical Psychology and Addiction, Institute of Psychology, Eötvös Loránd University, Budapest, Hungary, [2]Department of Clinical Psychology and Addiction, Doctoral School of Psychology, Eötvös Loránd University, Budapest, Hungary, [3]Nottingham Trent University, Psychology Division, Nottingham, United Kingdom

HISTORY AND TYPOLOGY OF ONLINE GAMES

Since their appearance in the 1990s, online video games have become widely popular and accessible. Nowadays, they are one of the most widespread recreational activities irrespective of culture, age, and gender. Parallel with this, dangers of problematic use have begun to arise. Video games can be played on many different platforms, such as personal computers (PCs), video game consoles, handheld game consoles, or smartphones—all of which can be played via access to the Internet. In this chapter, these games are referred to simply as *online games,* although several different names (e.g., *online video games, Internet video games*) can be found in the literature. Another important point to be made is that online gaming differs from online gambling, because there is no money staked during these games in an attempt to win further money.

Video games can be divided into two main groups—online and offline video games—a distinction that can significantly influence player behavior. Offline games are usually (but not always) played alone, they have a well-defined start and finish point, and the goals of the game can usually be achieved by the players themselves without external help from any other player. However, online games are typically played simultaneously by players who can communicate with one another in real time, cooperating or competing at will. Because of their inherent structural characteristics, these games do not usually have a predetermined end point. Furthermore, new tasks and quests are frequently added by the game developers and/or game operators. Subsequently, there is no real loss, and tasks can be repeated several times. Some goals can be achieved alone or together with other players, while others can be completed only by players working together in highly cooperative groups. Competing with fellow players is also possible and leads to immediate social comparison (Griffiths, 2010b; Kim & Kim, 2010;

Behavioral Addictions
http://dx.doi.org/10.1016/B978-0-12-407724-9.00004-5

Williams, Ducheneaut, Xiong, & Yee, 2006). Consequently, online games are distinguished from offline games mostly by their social nature (Charlton & Danforth, 2007; Choi & Kim, 2004; Kim & Kim, 2010). Although in some games the aforementioned characteristics blend, most of them can clearly be specified as offline or online games. Due to these characteristics, the popularity of these game types can differ greatly. De Prato et al. (2010) indicate that 70% of gamers prefer online as opposed to offline games.

Online gamers spend more time gaming than those who play offline games, mostly because of the social nature of these games. They find online games more pleasant and satisfying than offline games and sometimes prefer playing games to real-life activities (Ng & Wiemer-Hastings, 2005). These motives may also account for the findings showing that online games trigger the appearance of problematic use more often than offline games do (Griffiths, Davies, & Chappell, 2004; Griffiths & Meredith, 2009; Rehbein, Psych, Kleimann, Mediasci, & Mossle, 2010).

The first prototypical online games were the text-based virtual worlds called multi-user domains (referred to as MUDs) that appeared in the 1970s (Bartle, 2003). These were persistent[1] digital worlds where several players could "be present" and interact with each other at the same time (using their own imagination instead of graphics). This new environment created so many new possibilities (e.g., real-time chat, interaction between the players, parallel activities, cooperation, competition, social comparison) that the popularity of MUDs continued to increase as the number of Internet users rose. During the same period, table-top role-playing games (RPGs) appeared in which players threw dice to determine the outcomes of moving small figures around a player-drawn map. In both types of game (MUDs and RPGs), players created characters with attributes and skills to help them fight together through dungeons filled with dangerous beasts to acquire magical items (Barnett & Coulson, 2010).

Out of these text-based virtual worlds and table-top role-playing games arose the surprisingly complex (two- and three-dimensional) graphical virtual worlds, known today as MMOGs (massively multiplayer online games), or MMOs for short. The *massively* component indicates that hundreds or even thousands of players can be present in the same virtual game world at any given moment. The *multiplayer* word refers to the fact that people play simultaneously in the same online world, not in an individual copy of it, while the word *online* indicates that the game can be played only

1 *Persistence* refers here to the fact that these digital worlds not only are generated when some players enter the game but exist continually independently of the players' actual presence.

through a platform with an Internet connection (Barnett & Coulson, 2010). The three mosaic words also hint at the degree of complexity. For the time being, MMOGs are the most complex games and offer persistent virtual spaces for the hundreds of thousands of players that inhabit them. Multiplayer online games (MOGs) are arguably simpler. These are also played by groups of players together, but do not offer synchronic spaces, and the number of players is highly limited (e.g., 4–16 players). An online game (OG) simply refers to the fact that such games are played in an Internet-based environment, and the multiplayer mode is not a condition.

MMOs vary in terms of content, challenges, and setting, but all MMOs share six technical and design characteristics that collectively differentiate them from other types of games: persistence, physicality, avatar-mediated play, vertical game play, perpetuity, and social interaction (Chan & Vorderer, 2006). *Persistence* refers to the fact that the game world exists and changes even when a player is not actively playing (i.e., he or she is away from the keyboard), and as a result the game world may have been altered between two gaming sessions. *Physicality* means that the game models a more or less realistic world with a consistent set of physical rules, so for example a player's character will die when falling into a precipice. The player's character, or avatar, allows for *avatar-mediated play*, in which the player uses his or her character to interact with the game world and other players. *Vertical game play* and *perpetuity* refer to the fact that MMOs—unlike single-player games—cannot be completed; they can be played almost endlessly. After attaining the highest level, players may still remain in the game world and complete more challenges or just participate in the social activities. Even though players can play alone, *social interaction*, cooperation, and rivalry between the players form an essential part in an individual's game play (Chan & Vorderer, 2006), and provide the opportunity to make friends, overcoming physical distance and other limitations by way of a variety of specialized communication channels.

MMOs can be divided in three major groups and an "other" category (Nagygyörgy et al., 2012; Rice, 2006):

1. *Massively multiplayer online role-playing games* (MMORPGs) and their variations: As in traditional role-playing games, players control an avatar that becomes their virtual game self. Players choose a profession that determines their role and abilities. Through fulfilling different tasks or missions in the game, the avatars develop (a vertical development called "leveling up") and acquire precious objects that lead to the differentiation in status between avatars.

2. *Massively multiplayer online first person shooters* (MMOFPSs) and their variations: These are skill-demanding action games, in which the player controls a single avatar from a first-person perspective. They mostly rely on reaction time and attention abilities and offer several ways of cooperation and competition—on an individual or group level—between the players.
3. *Massively multiplayer online real-time strategy* (MMORTSs) games and their variations: As opposed to the first two game types, here the players typically oversee large troops and/or territories in a virtual world, engage in battles, or conclude alliances with other players. Through successful management, players establish status in the game world and gain esteem from other players.
4. *Other online games*: This category includes all the other online games, such as sport and racing games, music/rhythm games, multiplayer online social games, or turn-based strategy games. Because this is a mixed category, all the specific and idiosyncratic characteristics cannot be outlined. Compared to the other three game types, these games attract fewer players, but at the same time the proportion of female players is much higher (Nagygyörgy, Urbán et al., 2012).

Recent research has shown that 79% of online gamers have a clear gaming preference which might suggest that specific games fulfill specific psychological needs (Nagygyörgy, Urbán et al., 2012).

DEFINING PROBLEMATIC ONLINE GAMING

Despite the increasing amount of empirical research into problematic online gaming, the phenomenon sadly lacks a consensual definition (Blaszczynski, 2008; Griffiths & Meredith, 2009; Wood, 2007). One group of researchers consider video games as the starting point for examining the characteristics of this specific pathology (Charlton & Danforth, 2007; Griffiths, 2005a; Griffiths & Meredith, 2009; Peters & Malesky, 2008), whereas others consider the Internet as the main platform that unites different addictive Internet activities, including online games (Van Rooij, Schoenmakers, Vermulst, Van den Eijnden, & Van de Mheen, 2011; Young, 2009b). Recent studies make an effort to integrate both approaches (Demetrovics et al., 2012; Kim & Kim, 2010). Therefore, problematic online gaming can be seen either as a specific type of video game addiction, as a variant of Internet addiction, or as an independent diagnosis. In the following, each of these approaches is discussed.

Griffiths (2005a) notes that although each addiction has several particular and idiosyncratic characteristics, they have more commonalities than differences that may reflect a common etiology of addictive behavior. On the grounds of his "components" model of addiction, within a biopsychosocial framework (2005a), he considers online game addiction a specific type of video game addiction that can be categorized as a nonfinancial type of pathological gambling (Griffiths, 2005b). Griffiths (2010a) developed the components of his video game addiction theory by modifying Brown's (1991, 1993) six addiction criteria. These are (1) *salience*: This is when video gaming becomes the most important activity in the person's life and dominates his or her thinking (i.e., preoccupations and cognitive distortions), feelings (i.e., cravings), and behavior (i.e., deterioration of socialized behavior). (2) *Mood modification*: This is the subjective experience that people report as a consequence of engaging in video game play (i.e., they experience an arousing "buzz" or a "high" or, paradoxically, a tranquilizing and/or distressing feel of "escape" or "numbing"). (3) *Tolerance*: This is the process whereby increasing amounts of video game play are required to achieve the former effects, meaning that for persons engaged in video game playing, they gradually build up the amount of time they spend online engaged in the behavior. (4) *Withdrawal symptoms*: These are the unpleasant feeling states or physical effects that occur when video gaming is discontinued or suddenly reduced, for example, the shakes, moodiness, irritability. (5) *Conflict*: This refers to the conflicts between the video game player and those around him or her (i.e., interpersonal conflict), conflicts with other activities (e.g., job, schoolwork, social life, hobbies and interests), or conflicts from within the individual him- or herself (i.e., intrapsychic conflict and/or subjective feelings of loss of control) that are concerned with spending too much time engaged in video game play. (6) *Relapse*: This is the tendency for repeated reversions to earlier patterns of video game play to recur and for even the most extreme patterns typical at the height of excessive video game play to be quickly restored after periods of abstinence or control. Charlton and Danforth (2007, 2010) analyzed the six criteria presented here and found that tolerance, mood modification, and cognitive salience were indicators of high engagement, while the other components—withdrawal symptoms, conflict, relapse, and behavioral salience—played a central role in the development of addiction.

Porter et al. (2010) do not differentiate between problematic video game use and problematic online game use. They conceptualized problematic video game use as excessive use of one or more video games resulting in a preoccupation with and a loss of control over playing video games, and various negative psychosocial and/or physical consequences. Their criteria for problematic video game use did not include other features usually associated with dependence or addiction, such as tolerance and physical symptoms of withdrawal, because in their opinion there is no clear evidence that problem video game use is associated with these phenomena.

Although Internet Addiction Disorder (IAD) had been a candidate for *DSM-5* inclusion, it was rejected due to lack of scientific justification. However, online gaming addiction, as a specific type of IAD, had been better documented and thus, included in Section III (an appendix of disorders for further study) of the *DSM-5* under the name of Internet Gaming Disorder (American Psychiatric Association, 2013b).

The most well-known representative of the approach that considers online games a specific subtype of Internet activities is Young (1998a), who developed her theoretical framework for problematic online gaming from her Internet addiction criteria, which were based on the *Diagnostic and Statistical Manual of Mental Disorders,* Fourth Edition (*DSM-IV*) criteria for pathological gambling (American Psychiatric Association, 1994). Her theory states that online game addicts gradually lose control over their game play; that is, they are unable to decrease the amount of time spent playing while immersing themselves increasingly in this particular recreational activity and eventually develop problems in their real life (Young, 2009b). The idea that Internet/online video game addiction can be assessed by the combination of an Internet addiction score and the amount of time spent gaming (Han, Hwang, & Renshaw, 2010; Van Rooij et al., 2011) is also reflective of this approach.

Problematic Online Gaming as an Independent Diagnosis

Integrative approaches try to take into consideration both aforementioned approaches. For instance, Kim and Kim (2010) claim that neither the first nor the second approach can adequately capture the unique features of online games such as MMORPGs, therefore, it is absolutely necessary to create an integrated approach. They argue that "Internet users are no more addicted to the Internet than alcoholics are addicted to bottles" (p. 389), which means that the Internet is just one channel through which people may access whatever content they want (e.g., gambling, shopping, chatting, sex), and therefore users of the Internet may be addicted to the particular content or services that the Internet provides rather than the channel itself. On the other hand, online games differ from traditional stand-alone games, such as offline video games, in important aspects such as the social dimension or the role-playing dimension that allow interaction with other real players. Their multidimensional Problematic Online Game Use (POGU) model reflects this integrated approach fairly well. It had been developed theoretically on the basis of several studies and theories such as those of Armstrong, Phillips, and Saling (2000), Brown (1991, 1993), Caplan (2002), Charlton and Danforth (2007), Griffiths (1998), Lee and Ahn (2002), and Young (1999) and resulted in five underlying dimensions: euphoria, health problems, conflict, failure of self-control, and preference of virtual relationship. Demetrovics et al. (2012) also support the integrative approach and stress the need to include all types of online games in addiction models to make comparisons between genres and gamer populations possible [such as those who play online real-time strategy (RTS) games and online first-person shooter (FPS) games in addition to the widely researched MMORPG players]. According to their model, six dimensions cover the phenomenon of problematic online gaming: preoccupation, overuse, immersion, social isolation, interpersonal conflicts, and withdrawal.

Problematic Online Gaming as a Behavioral Addiction

Examining the empirical evidence, one can argue that online game addiction can be defined as one type of behavioral addiction (Demetrovics & Griffiths, 2012; Grant, Potenza, Weinstein, & Gorelick, 2010), a specific group of mental and behavioral disorders that had not been present yet in *DSM-IV* (American Psychiatric Association, 1994) or *ICD-10* (World Health Organization, 1994) but has recently been included in *DSM-5* (American Psychiatric Association, 2013a) as the second part of the "Substance-Related and Addictive Disorders" section. At present, the sole behavior in this new category on behavioral addictions is problematic gambling disorder. However, *Internet gaming disorder* has also been included in *DSM-5*'s Section III (American Psychiatric Association, 2013b), with a list of proposed diagnostic criteria similar to factors discussed throughout this chapter, to encourage research to determine whether this particular condition should be added to the manual as a disorder in the future.

Nevertheless, the authors of this chapter propose to use the name *problematic online gaming*. This term describes both the quintessence of the phenomenon (i.e., not only that the behavior is excessive, but gaming-related problems are also expected to be present), while avoiding the notion of dependency or disorder. The reason is that the precise future definition and diagnostic criteria need to be clarified and agreed upon on the basis of *DSM-5*.

SYMPTOMATOLOGY AND CONSEQUENCES

In the case of problematic online gaming, symptoms and consequences overlap to a significant extent and are therefore discussed together in this section. In the clinical understanding, problematic online gamers spend most of their time playing online games (or in many cases, one single online game) (e.g., Chappell, Eatough, Davies, & Griffiths, 2006; Griffiths, 2008; Porter et al., 2010). Although the amount of time spent on gaming is not predictive on its own (Griffiths, 2005a, 2010b), problematic gamers typically play much more than casual gamers (e.g., Gentile, 2009; Grusser, Thalemann, & Griffiths, 2007; Hussain & Griffiths, 2009). When they cannot play, they think, fantasize, and/or daydream about gaming instead of doing their usual daily activities. They may even dream about games and game playing (Griffiths, 2008; Porter et al., 2010). The activity gains a compulsive quality; namely, the player misses gaming, and as the feeling gets more intense and inner tension arises, the player gets restless, irritable, and moody (Chappell et al., 2006; Griffiths, 2008; Grusser et al., 2007; Hussain & Griffiths, 2009).

In the most extreme cases, the increasing inner tension may turn into aggressive behavior. To decrease this unpleasant feeling, the gamer continues to play on and on (due to tolerance) in ever-increasing amounts (Griffiths, 2008; Hussain & Griffiths, 2009). Such individuals are typically unable to control the activity, and recognize that it causes problems in their lives (Hussain & Griffiths, 2009; Porter et al., 2010). Should they manage to quit, they typically restart the activity sometime later (i.e., relapse) with the same intensity (Chappell et al., 2006; Griffiths, 2008; Hussain & Griffiths, 2009). Problematic gamers gradually lose interest in other recreational activities and start neglecting their everyday obligations, which leads to poorer educational and/or professional performance (Chappell et al., 2006; Gentile, 2009; Griffiths, 2008; Kim & Kim, 2010; Peng & Liu, 2010). The game becomes the absolute priority that usually leads to interpersonal and intrapersonal conflicts. As a result, their real-life relationships may deteriorate and/or come to an end (Chappell et al., 2006; Griffiths, 2008; Peng & Liu, 2010; Porter et al., 2010), and these players can become lonely (Kim & Kim, 2010; Lemmens, Valkenburg, & Peter, 2011; Van Rooij et al., 2011). To avoid conflicts, some players lie about their online activities and/or about the amount of time spent on gaming (Griffiths & Meredith, 2009; Young, 2009b).

In addition to psychological symptoms, somatic symptoms can also be observed in the case of problematic online gamers. These extend from ignoring basic biological needs such as eating, sleeping, and personal hygiene (Griffiths & Meredith, 2009; Peng & Liu, 2010; Porter et al., 2010) to different health problems such as gaining or losing weight, dry or strained eyes, headaches, back aches, carpal tunnel syndrome, repetitive strain injuries (RSIs), and general fatigue or exhaustion (Griffiths & Meredith, 2009; Peng & Liu, 2010; Porter et al., 2010).

Disease Process

Case studies and interviews (Allison, von Wahlde, Shockley, & Gabbard, 2006; Chappell et al., 2006; Griffiths, 2010a; Young, 2010) note that problematic online gaming—like other addictions or problematic behaviors—evolves gradually. Young (2010) calls the development of addiction a "downward spiral." At the initiation of the behavior, gaming is only a pleasant recreational activity, but slowly the player gets more and more involved until the activity becomes problematic. In Young's (2009b) opinion, the addiction process begins with a preoccupation with gaming. Gamers think about the game while they are offline when they should be concentrating on other things. This intensifies with time and slowly leads to a point when the game becomes the only priority that replaces all other recreational activities and everyday duties. At this time, other symptoms such as tolerance, withdrawal, and intrapersonal/interpersonal conflicts are present as well. To date, the duration of problematic use has been researched by a single longitudinal study. Gentile and his colleagues (2011) found that the problematic behavior existed 2 years later with the majority of children (84%) still being considered problematic gamers after the initial data collection. In the 2-year research period, only 1% of children became problematic gamers; therefore, the authors presume that problematic gaming might not be "simply a 'phase' that most children go through" (Gentile et al., 2011: pp. e325).

Regarding recovery, certain cases (Chappell et al., 2006; Young, 2010) suggest that—like other addictions—problematic online gamers reach a nadir when players become conscious of the problem itself and decide to change it. In such cases, they either seek external (e.g., professional) help or try to recover by themselves. However, given the potentially addictive nature of the problem, relapse appears to be quite frequent in these cases (Chappell et al., 2006; Young, 2010).

ASSESSMENT

The literature relating to the assessment of problematic online gaming shows there are many measures. Consequently, the aforementioned differences and uncertainties in definition must be continually kept in mind. The majority of researchers apply a theoretical approach. In several cases they have created new measures by modifying scales originally developed for the measurement of other behavioral addictions, but without careful psychometric analysis. For instance, the 20-item Internet Addiction Test/Scale (IAT/IAS) developed by Young (1998a, 1999) to measure Internet addiction has been taken as a basis for assessing online gaming addiction in a wide range of studies (Billieux et al., 2011; Jeong & Kim, 2011; Kim, Namkoong, Ku, & Kim, 2008; Kim et al., 2010; King, Delfabbro, & Griffiths, 2010a; Snodgrass, Lacy, Dengah, & Fagan, 2011; Wang & Chu, 2007; Whang, Heo, & Hur, 2004) even though the psychometric properties of the original scale were ambiguous (Demetrovics, Szeredi, & Rózsa, 2008; Koronczai et al., 2011). In other cases, researchers have assessed problematic online gaming by the combination of Internet addiction scores and weekly hours spent on Internet video gaming (Han et al., 2010; Van Rooij et al., 2011). This chapter's authors also consider this approach problematic because players do not necessarily view online gaming as an Internet activity but rather as "gaming." This may result in a lower Internet addiction score than is the actual case.

Other researchers propose not distinguishing problematic online gaming from problematic video gaming because the content is important, not the channel. In this approach, criteria for pathological gambling are often used as a starting point (Charlton & Danforth, 2007; Gentile, 2009; Gentile et al., 2011; Lemmens, Valkenburg, & Peter, 2009; Lemmens et al., 2011; Porter et al., 2010).

In addition to the previously discussed approaches, there are also measures that are based on the integrative approach, namely where both the special characteristics of video games and features of the channel (i.e., the Internet) are taken into consideration [i.e., Problematic Online Game Use Scale (POGU) (Kim & Kim, 2010), Online Game Addiction Diagnostic Scale (Lee & Han, 2007), Problematic Online Gaming Questionnaire (POGQ) (Demetrovics et al., 2012) and its short form (Pápay et al., 2013), which is reproduced in Appendix 4-1 of this chapter]. Of all the measures discussed, the POGU (Kim & Kim, 2010), the Game Addiction Diagnostic Scale (Lee & Han, 2007), and the POGQ (Demetrovics et al., 2012) and its short form (Pápay et al., 2013) show robust psychometric characteristics (see Table 4.1).

Table 4.1 Measures of Problematic Online Gaming

Source (Reference)	Measure	Definition of Problematic Online Gaming	Number of Items	Factors	Research Subjects, Method	Reliability/ Validity
Young (2009a)	Obsessive Online Gamer - Diagnostic Questionnaire	Internet-based approach	8	No data	No data	No data
Charlton and Danforth (2007, 2010)	Addiction–Engagement Questionnaire	Video game approach	29/24	**1.** Addiction **2.** Engagement	442 persons (2007); 388 persons (2010), online survey	EFA* (2007), Cronbach alpha (2010)
Gentile (2009)	Pathological-Gaming Scale	Video game approach	11	No data	1,178 American youth ages 8 to 18, national representative sample, online survey	Convergent and divergent validity analysis
Lemmens et al. (2009)	Game Addiction Scale for Adolescents	Video game approach	7	1 factor	Two independent samples of Dutch adolescents (N_1 = 352 and N_2 = 369), pen-and-pencil survey	EFA, convergent and criterion validity analysis
Porter et al. (2010)	Video Game Use Questionnaire, VGUQ	Video game approach	33	1 factor	1945 persons, online survey	No data

Continued

Table 4.1 Measures of Problematic Online Gaming—cont'd

Source (Reference)	Measure	Definition of Problematic Online Gaming	Number of Items	Factors	Research Subjects, Method	Reliability/Validity
Kim and Kim (2010)	Problematic Online Game Use Scale (POGU)	Integrative approach	20	**1.** Euphoria **2.** Health problem **3.** Conflict **4.** Failure of self-control **5.** Preference of virtual relationship	1,422 5th graders, 199 8th graders, and 393 11th graders from South Korea (pen-and-pencil survey)	EFA, CFA,★★ reliability analysis, convergent and discriminant validity analysis
Lee and Han (2007)	Online game addiction diagnostic scale	Integrative approach	30	**1.** Psychological dependence **2.** Daily life disorder **3.** Interpersonal relationship toward online **4.** Tolerance **5.** Negative behavior and emotions **6.** Mental disorder **7.** Physical disorder	2,317 South Korean elementary school students (pen-and-paper survey)	EFA, criterion validity analysis

Zhou and Li (2009)	Online Game Addiction Index (OGAI)	Integrative approach	12	**1.** Control disorder **2.** Conflict **3.** Injury	195 students (age 18–24 years) (in-home surveys)	EFA
Demetrovics et al. (2012)	Problematic Online Gaming Questionnaire (POGQ)	Integrative approach	18	**1.** Preoccupation **2.** Overuse **3.** Immersion **4.** Social isolation **5.** Interpersonal conflicts **6.** Withdrawal	3,415 online gamers (mean age 21 years, SD 5.9 years), online survey	EFA, CFA
Pápay et al. (2012)	Problematic Online Gaming Questionnaire Short Form (POGQ-SF)	Integrative approach	12	**1.** Preoccupation **2.** Overuse **3.** Immersion **4.** Social isolation **5.** Interpersonal conflicts **6.** Withdrawal	2,774 9th–10th graders in Hungarian secondary general and secondary vocational schools (mean age 16.4 years, SD 0.9), national representative sample	CFA, criterion validity

*EFA= Exploratory Factor Analysis
**CFA = Confirmatory Factor Analysis

EPIDEMIOLOGY

Prevalence and Demographics of the Online Gamer Population

At present, it is quite difficult to estimate the prevalence of problematic online gaming due to the lack of a clear definition, the application of measures without proper psychometric characteristics, and studies using different samples and different research methodologies. Large sample studies generally report prevalence values below 10%. A study conducted in the United States on a national representative sample of teenagers (Gentile, 2009) as well as a large sample of Singaporean children (Gentile et al., 2011) reported a problematic game use of approximately 9%. Results of another representative study in Germany showed that 3% of the male and 0.3% of the female students were diagnosed as dependent on video games, while another 4.7% of male and 0.5% of female students were at risk of becoming dependent (Rehbein et al., 2010). On a large Hungarian online gamer sample, 3.4% of gamers belonged to the high-risk group of problematic gaming and another 15.2% to the medium-risk group (Demetrovics et al., 2012). A proportion of 4.6% of Hungarian adolescents (approximately 16 years old) belonging to a national sample were classified as high-risk users (Pápay et al., 2013) (see Table 4.2).

According to an online survey examining all types of online gamers (Nagygyörgy, Urbán et al., 2012) (n = 4374), the mean age was 21 years, and participants were mostly male (91%) and single (66%). Their average weekly game time varied between less than 7 hours (10%) and more than 42 hours (also 10%) with most of the gamers playing 15–27 hours weekly (35%). Furthermore, 16% of all gamers were playing professionally (i.e., they participate in competitions and earn money if they win). The majority of the sample (79%) had a clear gaming preference; namely, they played one single game type (e.g., MMORPG/MMORTS/MMOFPS/other online games) most of the time.

Data regarding the three main game types give a more nuanced view. The proportion of female gamers is the lowest in the case of massively multiplayer online first-person shooter (MMOFPS) games (1%–2%; Jansz & Tanis, 2007; Nagygyörgy, Urbán et al., 2012) and the highest between massively multiplayer online role-playing game (MMORPG) users (15%–30%; Cole & Griffiths, 2007; Nagygyörgy, Urbán et al., 2012; Yee, 2006a). MMOFPS users are the youngest (18–19.8 years; Jansz & Tanis, 2007; Nagygyörgy, Urbán et al., 2012), while both massively multiplayer online real-time strategy (MMORTS; 22 years; Nagygyörgy, Urbán et al., 2012) and MMORPG

Table 4.2 Prevalence of Problematic Online Gaming

Author(s) (reference)	Location	Research Subjects [Mean Age (M), Standard Deviation (SD)]	Method	Measure	Criteria of Problematic Use	Life-Prevalence Value
Yee (2006)	USA, Canada	3,166 persons, MMORPG gamers	Online survey	Direct question ("Do you consider yourself addicted to MMORPGs?" yes/no question)	Yes to the direct question	50%
Grüsser, Thalemann, and Griffiths (2007)	Germany	7,069 gamers (M: 21.1 years, SD: 6.4)	Online survey	6 criteria of key symptoms of a dependence syndrome as outlined in WHO's *ICD-10*	3 or more criteria fulfilled	11.9%
Gentile (2009)	USA	1,178 persons (adolescents age 8–18 years)	National representative survey (online)	Pathological Video-Game Use	6 or more yes answers	8.5%
Porter et al. (2010)	USA, Canada, Europe, Australia, New Zealand, Asia, Central and South America	1,945 persons, gamers older than 14 years	Online survey	Video Game Use Questionnaire, (VGUQ), 10 criteria: 3 (preoccupation), 7 (adverse consequences), yes/no answers	2 or more criteria (preoccupation) + 3 or more criteria (adverse consequences)	8%

Continued

Table 4.2 Prevalence of Problematic Online Gaming—cont'd

Author(s) (reference)	Location	Research Subjects [Mean Age (M), Standard Deviation (SD)]	Method	Measure	Criteria of Problematic Use	Life-Prevalence Value
Van Rooij et al. (2011)	Netherlands	4,559 persons (M: 14.4 years, SD: 1.2) (T1) and 3,740 persons (M: 14.3 years SD: 1.0) (T2)	pen-and-pencil survey	Compulsive Internet Use Scale (CIUS) + weekly hours online gaming	Latent profile analysis	1.6% (T1), 1.5% (T2) ~ 1.5%
Gentile et al. (2011)	Singapore	3,034 persons elementary and secondary school students	2 years longitudinal study, pen-and-paper survey	Pathological Video-Game Use	5 or more yes answer	7.6%–9.9%
Lemmens, Valkenburg, and Peters (2011)	Netherlands	543 adolescent gamers (M: 13.9 years, SD: 1.4)	Longitudinal pen-and pencil survey	Game Addiction Scale	Score of 3 or higher	6% (T1), 4% (T2)
Rehbein et al. (2010)	Germany	15,168 ninth graders (15.3 years, SD: 0.69)	Nationally representative survey	Video Game Dependency Scale (KFN-CSAS-II)	Score higher than 42 dependent players; score between 35 and 41: players at risk	Dependent: boys 3%, girls 0.3%; at risk: boys 4.7%, girls 0.5%

Thomas and Martin (2010)	Australia	2,031 persons (705 university students, 1,326 secondary and college students)	Pen-and-paper survey	Adaptation of YDQ (Young's Diagnostic Questionnaire) to computer games	Score of 5 or higher	5%
Jeong and Kim (2011)	South Korea	600 persons (12–18 years)	Nationally representative pen-and-pencil survey	Young's Internet Addiction Test (IAT) modified by replacing the word *Internet* with *gaming*	Score above 80	2.2%
Demetrovics et al. (2012)	Hungary	3,415 persons, online gamers (M: 21 years, SD: 5.9)	Online survey	POGQ	Latent profile analysis	High-risk problematic online gamers: 3.4%; medium risk of problematic use: 15.2%
Pápay et al. (2012)	Hungary	5,045 students from secondary general and secondary vocational schools (M: 16.4, SD: 0.9)	Nationally representative survey (pen-and-pencil)	POGQ-SF	Latent profile analysis	4.6%

players (21–27 years; Nagygyörgy, Urbán et al., 2012; Yee, 2006a) are significantly older. Among the three main groups, MMORPG gamers spend the most time playing (Nagygyörgy et al., 2013). Because MMORPGs are the most researched games, there is additional information regarding such players that is still unknown in the case of other game types. For instance, half of MMORPG players work full time, 22.2% are students, and 14.8% are homemakers (89.9% of whom were female). Furthermore, 36% of the gamers are married, and 22% of them have children (Yee, 2006a, 2006d). Overall, the demographic composition of MMORPG users is quite varied and probably more diverse than the composition of MMORTS and MMOFPS users, although this needs to be empirically established.

Comorbidity

Problematic online gamers are twice as likely to be diagnosed with some kind of attention deficit disorder (ADD or ADHD) than gamers who play recreationally (Batthyany, Muller, Benker, & Wolfling, 2009; Bioulac, Arfi, & Bouvard, 2008; Chan & Rabinowitz, 2006; Gentile et al., 2011; Han et al., 2009). Depression is also a comorbid clinical disorder that appears in several studies (Gentile et al., 2011; Peng & Liu, 2010). In the case of MMORPG players, depressive symptoms (e.g., sadness, hopelessness, crying spells, insomnia, concentration problems) are related to habitual computer game playing at night (between 10 p.m. and 6 a.m.; Lemola et al., 2011). So far, it is unclear whether problematic online gaming is the reason for or the consequence of other psychiatric symptoms (Gentile, 2009). Although longitudinal data suggest that pathological gamers exhibit higher levels of depression, anxiety and social phobia during the follow-up period than normal gamers, the causal relation might be reciprocal (Gentile et al., 2011).

ETIOLOGY

As with other addictions, problematic online gaming is the consequence of many different integrated factors. Here the main aspects of gaming that contribute to the appearance and maintenance of problematic behavior in the academic literature are presented.

Neurobiological Aspects

Brain imaging is the newest area of behavioral addictions research and, for this reason, it is still in its infancy. Early studies suggest that cue-induced gaming urge activates the same brain regions (i.e., dorsolateral prefrontal cortex, orbitofrontal cortex, parahippocampal gyrus, and thalamus) that are activated by gambling in the case of pathological gamblers and substance use in the case of substance use abusers (Han et al., 2011; Ko et al., 2009). Other results suggest that the effects of excessive online game playing on working memory may be similar to those observed in patients with substance dependence (Kim et al., 2012). Consequently, researchers assume that problematic online gaming might share the same neurobiological mechanism as pathological gambling and substance dependence (Kuss & Griffiths, 2012c). However, further research in this area is quite necessary and is almost certain to come.

Personality Aspects

Although it can be argued there is no such thing as an "addictive personality," some personality characteristics seem to favor the development of problematic game use. For instance, several studies examined the relationship between the Big Five personality traits and problematic gaming and found low emotional stability (Charlton & Danforth, 2010; Mehroof & Griffiths, 2010; Nagygyörgy, Mihalik, & Demetrovics, 2012; Peters & Malesky, 2008), low agreeableness (Charlton & Danforth, 2010; Peters & Malesky, 2008), and low extraversion (Charlton & Danforth, 2010) as being associated with the phenomenon. However, in relation to agreeableness and extraversion, the relationship does not seem to be as robust as with that of neuroticism. A possible explanation of these results could be that problematic gamers spend more time gaming to avoid real-life social situations that seem threatening because of low social abilities and/or low emotional stability. To such individuals, online environments may seem safe and be preferred to real-life situations. However, this is speculation on the authors' part, and empirical research is needed to investigate such a hypothesis.

In addition to personality traits, other characteristics have also been examined. A study examining social skills found that the quality of interpersonal relationships decreased and the amount of social anxiety increased as the amount of time spent playing online games increased (Lo, Wang, & Fang, 2005). Problematic gaming has been negatively correlated with offline social self-efficacy and positively correlated with online social self-efficacy (Jeong & Kim, 2011). This echoes with research showing problematic gamers finding it easier to meet people online and having fewer friends in real life than in games (Porter et al., 2010). Inadequate self-regulation (Seay & Kraut, 2007), low self-esteem (Ko, Yen, Chen, Chen, & Yen, 2005; Lemmens et al., 2011), low emotional intelligence (Herodotou, Kambouri, & Winters, 2011), above average state and trait anxiety (Mehroof & Griffiths,

2010), increased feeling of loneliness (Lemmens et al., 2011; Seay & Kraut, 2007), narcissistic personality (Kim et al., 2008), and aggression (Kim et al., 2008; Mehroof & Griffiths, 2010) have also been found to be correlated with problematic online gaming. Additional studies report that problematic online gamers have lower life satisfaction (Ko et al., 2005; Wang, Chen, Lin, & Wang, 2008) and decreased psychosocial well-being compared to other gamers (Lemmens et al., 2011).

Because all the findings from these studies are correlational in nature, causal relations are unknown. Thus, Lemmens et al.'s (2011) longitudinal study worked to address this issue. Their analyses indicated that diminished social competence, lower self-esteem, and increased loneliness predicted an increase in problematic gaming 6 months later. Thus, lower psychosocial well-being can be considered an antecedent of problematic gaming among adolescent gamers. The analyses further indicated that loneliness was also a consequence of problematic gaming. This suggests that displacement of real-world social interaction resulting from problematic game use may deteriorate existing relationships, which could explain the increase in adolescent gamers' feelings of loneliness.

Motivational Aspects

Empirical studies suggest that gaming motives also play an important role in the development and maintenance of problematic online gaming (Demetrovics et al., 2011; Kuss & Griffiths, 2012a, 2012b). Online gaming involves multiple reinforcements whereby different features might be differently rewarding to different people (what could be called "the kitchen sink approach" where game designers include a diverse range of gaming rewards in the hope that at least some of them will appeal to players; Griffiths, 2010a). The game developers' aim is to satisfy as many different psychological needs as possible, to motivate the widely heterogeneous gamer community to play continuously.

The first theoretical model of motivational aspects was developed by Bartle (1996), who examined early text-based virtual world (MUD) players. He proposed that MUD players can be classified in one of the following four motivational types: achievers, explorers, socializers, and killers. Achievers are motivated by fulfilling game-related goals, explorers try to find out as much as they can about the virtual world, socializers love to meet and befriend other players, and killers prefer to cause distress to others.

Bartle's theoretical model has been empirically tested by Yee (2006c) among MMORPG players. Using exploratory factor analysis, he identified 10 motivational components that belong to three main factors labeled as achievement, social, and immersion. The components belonging to the achievement factor are advancement, mechanics, and competition. Socializing, relationship, and teamwork are the subcomponents belonging to the social factor and discovery, whereas role-playing, customization, and escapism contribute to the immersion dimension. Another important finding is that the 10 listed motivational dimensions do not suppress but complement each other depending on the gaming situation. Yee (2006c) found that escapism and advancement subcomponents were associated with problematic usage measured by a variation of Young's (1998b) diagnostic questionnaire. The escapism motivation referred to the use of the online environment to avoid thinking about real-life problems, while advancement referred to the desire to gain power, progress rapidly, and accumulate in-game symbols of wealth or status. Yee's research had been replicated on a European group (French, English, and Italian; Dauriat et al., 2011) and a Hungarian online MMORPG sample (Nagygyörgy, Mihalik et al., 2012) and yielded similar results (i.e., escapism and achievement main factor showed the strongest association with problematic online gaming). These models are not suitable for comparing different types of online gamers; therefore, Demetrovics et al. (2011) developed an empirically based motivational measure called the Motives for Online Gaming Questionnaire (MOGQ) comprising seven factors (i.e., social, escapism, coping, fantasy, skill development, recreation, and competition) and makes the comparison between online gamers possible (see Appendix 4-2).

All the aforementioned questionnaires have the structural characteristics of online games (or particularly MMORPGs) as their starting point. A different approach is applied by Ryan et al. (2006), who suggested that, as largely individual difference frameworks, these categories or typologies largely reflect the structure and content of current games, rather than the fundamental or underlying motives and satisfactions that can initiate and sustain participation across all potential players and game types. By contrast, they argued that a true theory of motivation should not focus on behavioral classification constrained by the structure of particular games, but instead address the factors associated with enjoyment and persistence across players and genres, and how games that differ in controllability, structure, and content might appeal to basic human motivational propensities and psychological needs. Therefore, they applied the Cognitive Evaluation Theory (CET) used in the research of intrinsic motivation in the case of sports and other recreational activities which states that activities induce intrinsic motivation depending on their capacity of satisfying the three basic human needs of autonomy, competence, and relatedness. The results support their conception that the enjoyment of video games and the desire to play again was significantly correlated with the level of autonomy, competence, and relatedness experienced in games (Przybylski, Ryan, & Rigby, 2009; Ryan et al., 2006). However, a connection between the three basic human needs and problematic online gaming has not yet been explored.

Wan and Chiou (2006) developed a different approach. Their starting point was Maslow's hierarchy of human needs. Their results showed that the psychological needs of players of online games were closer to the two-factor theory that depicts satisfaction and dissatisfaction dimensions than to different one-dimensional approaches applied in other empirical studies. The lower hierarchy of human needs refers to "dissatisfactory needs" that includes physical needs, safety needs, belongingness, and self-esteem. The higher hierarchy of human needs means "satisfactory needs" that comprises self-actualization and self-transcendence. Addicted players' need-gratification was similar to the feature of dissatisfactory factor. That is, the absence of playing online games is more likely to generate a sense of dissatisfaction; the addicts' compulsive use of online games appears to stem from the relief of dissatisfaction rather than the pursuit of satisfaction. In contrast, online games tend to provide nonaddicted players with a sense of satisfaction rather than a sense of dissatisfaction. This result is in line with the results of Wang and Chu (2007), who differentiated harmonious and obsessive passion in online gaming and found that only obsessive passion (the state when the player is controlled by his player activity instead of controlling it himself) was related to problematic online gaming. Although players with harmonious passion enjoy and feel cheerful about gaming, players with obsessive passion feel fanatic over it and become angry or anxious when they cannot play. A case study of Griffiths (2010b) also demonstrated two excessive gamers: a healthy enthusiast who played for joy and recreation and a game addict who played to avoid his life problems and to ease the irresistible urge to play again.

The Role of Structural Characteristics in Problematic Online Gaming

In the gambling literature, a number of authors have examined the role of structural characteristics of different gambling activities (i.e., slot machines) because they appear to be important in the acquisition, development, and maintenance of problem gambling behavior (Griffiths, 1993, 1999; Parke & Griffiths, 2007). A similar exploration regarding the structural characteristics of online games has also been suggested (King et al., 2010a; King, Delfabbro, & Griffiths, 2010b). In an early study, Wood et al. (2004) found that a high degree of realism (i.e., realistic sound, graphics, and setting), a rapid absorption rate, character development, the ability to customize the game, multiplayer features, winning and losing features, and the ability to save the game at regular intervals[2] were seen by most gamers as essential characteristics of video games.

King et al. (2010b) tried to enlarge and systematize Wood et al.'s (2004) list according to the gambling literature. They created a theoretical model that contained five main groups:

- *Social features* that refer to the socializing aspects of video games, such as how players can communicate with other players, and the features that create a cooperative and competitive community of players.
- *Manipulation and control features* that refer to the ways in which a player can interact with and control in-game properties using a physical control scheme.
- *Narrative and identity features* that refer to the ways in which players can take on another identity in the game (as a fictional character or a construction of the self).
- *Reward and punishment features* that refer to the ways in which players are reinforced for skillful play (i.e., winning) and punished for losing.
- *Presentation features* that refer to the aesthetic qualities of a video game, such as how the game looks and sounds to players.

In a follow-up empirical study, reward and punishment features, such as earning points, finding rare game items, and fast loading times, were rated by players among the most enjoyable and important aspects of video game playing. Problem video game players reported significantly higher enjoyment of features such as managing in-game resources, earning points, getting 100% in the game, and mastering the game than nonproblem players, which are features that typically take up more playing time than other features. In addition, the problem group identified

[2] In Wood et al.'s study the possibility to save the game regularly clearly refers to the structural characteristics of offline video games. However, in the case of online games, this feature is present by default because one's account preserves the current state of the player's development. When players leave the game and then re-enter it later, they are usually able to continue playing from the same point where they had logged out.

features such as "leveling up," earning meta-game rewards (e.g., "Achievements"), and fast loading times as having a significantly greater impact on their playing behavior than other players (King, Delfabbro, & Griffiths, 2011).

The relationship between reward and punishment features and problematic use has also been stressed in theoretical literature. For instance, this is what Shavaun Scott (2007) refers to when she calls the MMORPGs "the most incredibly complex Skinner boxes that anyone could ever imagine" (for further information on the topic, see Clark & Scott, 2009, pp. 84–89). Similar to the case of slot machines, online game developers apply the principle of the partial reinforcement effect (PRE) to keep players playing. PRE is a critical psychological ingredient of gaming addiction whereby the reinforcement is instant but intermittent (i.e., people keep responding in the absence of reinforcement hoping that another reward is just around the corner). Magnitude of reinforcement (e.g., a high points score for doing something in-game) is also important. Large rewards lead to fast responding and greater resistance to extinction—in short to increased "addiction" (Griffiths, 2010a). The effectiveness of operant conditioning is responsible for those situations when gamers keep playing or even increase their gaming time in spite of the fact that they do not enjoy the activity any more (Yee, 2006b). Such states may easily lead to the appearance of problematic gaming.

The Amount of Gaming Time and Its Relation to Problematic Online Gaming

Although several studies have reported a strong correlation between the amount of time spent on gaming and problematic use (e.g., Dauriat et al., 2011; Gentile, 2009; Grusser et al., 2007; Hsu, Wen, & Wu, 2009; Porter et al., 2010), excessive game play is not a sufficient condition of addiction or problematic gaming (despite the common colloquial use of the word *addiction*). According to Griffiths (2005a, pp. 195), "the difference between an excessive healthy enthusiasm and an addiction is that healthy enthusiasms add to life whereas addictions take away from it"; that is, additional negative consequences should be present to make the behavior classified as problematic or an "addiction." However, knowing that the development of the problematic gaming behavior is always a process, special attention must be given to excessive gamers because they appear to be at higher risk than normal gamers to developing problematic behavior.

PREVENTION AND TREATMENT

Prevention

Articles on the topic of prevention (Griffiths, 2003, 2008; Griffiths & Meredith, 2009) recommend that family members and/or friends initiate direct conversation with excessive or problematic players by showing true interest toward the game, the gamer, and everything the gamer likes in the virtual environment. Often this is the only topic that the player is willing to talk about or talks about with pleasure, and thus, it facilitates communication and emotional attachment with the user. Getting familiar with the games also helps toward establishing the mutually acceptable rules regarding them. If the gamer is a child or a teenager, it is highly recommended that parents or other family members choose the games together with the child using the official ratings as a guide for age appropriateness (e.g., ESRB ratings). These should be suitable for children in terms of content (e.g., violent or adult content must be avoided) while at the same time providing entertainment. Parents should encourage their children to play together with real-life friends because this helps the developing of personal relationships. This way, communication and cooperation skills learned online can be transferred more easily to real-life situations.

It is also worth determining daily and weekly game time together and in mutual agreement with players themselves, because this way it is easier to ask them to abide by it. It is also important to follow the game manufacturers' recommendations regarding monitor brightness, distance from the monitor, the taking of short and frequent breaks if gaming for a long time, not playing in the case of fatigue, etc. It is also extremely important that the gamer pursues other recreational activities (e.g., sports) in addition to gaming. If gamers play suitable games for an appropriate amount of time, playing can have several positive effects such as increasing self-esteem; improving reflexes, reaction time, memory, logical and strategic thinking, social and communication skills; and more (Griffiths, 2008, 2010a).

Treatment

Treatment techniques are based on the ones applied successfully to other behavioral addictions but specified to the particular features of online games (Griffiths, 2008; Griffiths & Meredith, 2009). Several different types of online support forums deal with problematic online gaming and/or its treatment possibilities. Such forum types are (1) the ones run by the parents and other family members of problem gamers who mainly discuss the nature of the problem, share their experiences, and support each other; (2) the self-help forums where the gamers themselves discuss similar topics and support each other; (3) and the ones established and administered by professional organizations where they offer information regarding the problem in general, provide some kind of criteria for self-assessment, and provide professionals to contact (Griffiths, 2008; Griffiths & Meredith, 2009). Much of the advice on these forums is based on behavioral reward and punishment systems. A self-help On-Line Gamers Anonymous Organization offers a supportive, Internet-based treatment approach based heavily on the Minnesota Model system of the 12 steps used by such groups as Alcoholics Anonymous and Gamblers Anonymous (Griffiths, 2008; Griffiths & Meredith, 2009).

There are some specialty addiction clinics in a few countries (e.g., United States, China, South Korea, United Kingdom), but few details of the therapeutic programs have been published in the academic literature. Most of the treatment clinics use a diverse range of interventions. The programs mainly follow two approaches: the total abstinence model (e.g., Broadway Lodge treatment center in Somerset, UK) and the harm reduction model that promotes moderation and balance and does not require the patient to completely stop game playing or using the computer altogether (e.g., Woog Laboratories, California). In addition, there are individual therapists such as Young (Center for On-Line Addiction) and, before her death, Orzack (Computer Addiction Services), who use multimodal elements but do not necessarily advocate total abstinence or moderation (Griffiths, 2008). The aim of all treatment programs is to increase game addicts' prosocial skills through social activities and real-life activities that replace time spent gaming. They also provide some form of psychotherapy to address comorbid or underlying issues such as depression and anxiety. Treatment programs also integrate management skills (i.e., goal setting or time keeping) to help players control their behavior (Griffiths, 2008).

Among therapies, those applied to other behavioral addictions [e.g., behavioral therapy, cognitive behavioral therapy (CBT), motivational interviewing] are mostly used with further specification. For instance, CBT teaches individuals to identify and eventually solve their underlying problem(s) and then to learn coping skills to prevent relapse. Although efficient, it is unlikely that CBT can cure addictive playing on its own because the online gaming addiction is likely to have biopsychosocial antecedents that require multimodal treatment interventions.

Therefore, CBT may also be accompanied by (online or *in vivo*) support groups and/or medication. Finding alternative ways to satisfy underlying needs that had been relieved by the problematic behavior is also quite important in avoiding relapse (Griffiths, 2008). In Young's (2010) opinion, therapy should use time management techniques that help the client structure and regulate online gaming sessions, and strategies that help gamers to develop alternative activities that take them away from the computer (e.g., spend more time with family, engage in hobbies or exercise programs). According to Young (2007), online gamers typically suffer interpersonal difficulties such as introversion or social anxiety, which is, in part, why they turn to virtual relationships and games, an issue that should also be addressed during therapy.

Griffiths (2008) sums up that therapeutic techniques appear to be based on CBT, skill training, and humanistic techniques. CBT is used for underlying psychological conditions such as social phobia, anxiety, and depression. Skills training is used for activities such as managing time, finding other rewarding activities, and developing other core life skills. Interpersonal therapy is used for developing personal skills and social functioning, and lastly, couples or family therapy is used for addressing problems caused between partners and family as a result of online gaming behavior.

Other treatment approaches include military-style boot camps in China and South Korea that aim to treat online game addiction by using high-intensity physical activity in natural surroundings to get problem gamers back into real life and find a substitute for the excitement of the cyberworld (Fackler, 2007; Griffiths, 2008). Unfortunately, there is no empirical or anecdotal evidence as to whether such methods are successful in treating online gaming addiction.

Pharmacotherapy

Han et al. (2010; 2012) presented some successful case studies regarding pharmacotherapeutic treatment. After a 6-week (Han et al., 2010) and a 12-week (Han & Renshaw, 2012) period of bupropion sustained-release treatment, problematic gamers showed significant improvement both in decreased problem behavior and decreased depression scores. The researchers' pharmacological choice had been driven by the similarities in neurological activity of substance dependence and behavioral addictions such as pathological gambling (Han et al., 2011; Ko et al., 2009; Kuss & Griffiths, 2012).

Case Vignette: Jeremy

Jeremy was a 38-year-old accountant who had been married 13 years and had two children. Over a period of a year and a half, his online playing of *Everquest* and (subsequently *Everquest 2*) had gone from about 3 or 4 hours of playing every evening to playing up to 14 hours a day. He claimed that his marital relationship was breaking down, that he was spending little time with his children, and that he constantly called in sick to work so that he could spend the day playing online games. When playing online, he claimed, "Life's worries go out of the window." He had tried to quit playing on a number of occasions but could not go more than a few days before he experienced "an irresistible urge" to play again—even when his wife threatened to leave him.

He claimed that giving up online gaming was worse than giving up smoking and that he was "extremely moody, anxious, depressed and irritable" if he was unable to play online. Over the next few months, things got even worse for Jeremy. He was fired from his job for being too unreliable and generally unproductive as a direct result of his excessive gaming (although his employers were totally unaware of his gaming behavior). As a result of Jeremy's losing his job, his wife also left him. This led to Jeremy "playing all day, every day." It was a vicious cycle in that his excessive online gaming was causing all his problems, yet the only way he felt he could alleviate his mood state and escape his life's stresses was to play online games.

Jeremy's behavior fulfills many of the characteristic signs of more traditional addictions. For Jeremy, online gaming was the most important thing in his life; he used gaming as a way of consistently modifying his mood (i.e., to escape other things in his life); he built up tolerance to gaming over time (escalating his gaming from 3 to 4 hours a day up to 14 hours a day); he suffered withdrawal effects if unable to play online (e.g., feelings of intense moodiness, anxiety, depression, and irritability); there was conflict in his life as a result of playing online games excessively (losing his family and job because he just could not stop playing); and he experienced relapse as he could not go more than a few days without an irresistible urge to play again. In an effort to reconcile with his family, Jeremy eventually asked his general practitioner to refer him to a psychologist who specialized in cognitive-behavioral therapy. However, his wife has now divorced Jeremy and, as far as the authors are aware, CBT treatment is still ongoing.

REFERENCES

Allison, S. E., von Wahlde, L., Shockley, T., & Gabbard, G. O. (2006). The development of the self in the era of the Internet and role-playing fantasy games. *American Journal of Psychiatry*, *163*(3), 381–385.

American Psychiatric Association. (1994). *Diagnostic and statistical manual of mental disorders* (4th ed.). Washington, DC: Author.

American Psychiatric Association. (2013a). *Substance-related and addictive disorders*. Retrieved July 10, 2013, from http://www.dsm5.org/Documents/Substance%20Use%20Disorder%20Fact%20Sheet.pdf.

American Psychiatric Association. (2013b). *Internet gaming disorder.* Retrieved July 10, 2013, from http://www.dsm5.org/Documents/Internet%20Gaming%20Disorder%20Fact%20Sheet.pdf.

Armstrong, L., Phillips, J., & Saling, L. (2000). Potential determinants of heavier Internet usage. *International Journal of Human-Computer Studies, 53*, 537–550.

Barnett, J., & Coulson, M. (2010). Virtually real: A psychological perspective on massively multiplayer online games. *Review of General Psychology, 14*(2), 167–179.

Bartle, R. (1996). *Hearts, clubs, diamonds, spades: Players who suit MUDs*. Retrieved October 17, 2013, from http://www.mud.co.uk/richard/hcds.htm.

Bartle, R. (2003). *Designing virtual worlds*. Indianapolis: New Riders Press.

Batthyany, D., Muller, K. W., Benker, F., & Wolfling, K. (2009). Computer game playing: clinical characteristics of dependence and abuse among adolescents. *Wien Klinische Wochenschrift, 121*(15–16), 502–509.

Billieux, J., Chanal, J., Khazaal, Y., Rochat, L., Gay, P., Zullino, D., et al. (2011). Psychological predictors of problematic involvement in massively multiplayer online role-playing games: Illustration in a sample of male cybercafé players. *Psychopathology, 44*, 165–171.

Bioulac, S., Arfi, L., & Bouvard, M. P. (2008). Attention deficit/hyperactivity disorder and video games: A comparative study of hyperactive and control children. *European Psychiatry, 23*(2), 134–141.

Blaszczynski. (2008). Commentary: A response to "problems with the concept of video game 'addiction': Some case study examples." *International Journal of Mental Health and Addiction, 6*(2), 179–181.

Brown, R. I. F. (1991). Gaming, gambling and other addictive play. In J. H. Kerr & M. J. Apter (Eds.), *Adult play: A reversal theory approach* (pp. 101–118). Amsterdam: Swets & Zeitlinger.

Brown, R. I. F. (1993). Some contributions of the study of gambling to the study of other addictions. In W. R. Eadington & J. A. Cornelius (Eds.), *Gambling behavior and problem gambling* (pp. 241–272). Reno, NV: University of Nevada.

Caplan, S. E. (2002). Problematic Internet use and psychological well-being: Development of a theory-based cognitive-behavioral measurement instrument. *Computers in Human Behavior, 18*, 553–575.

Chan, E., & Vorderer, P. (2006). Massively multiplayer online games. In P. Vorderer & J. Bryant (Eds.), *Playing video games: Motives, responses, and consequences* (pp. 77–88). Hillsdale, NJ: Erlbaum.

Chan, P. A., & Rabinowitz, T. (2006). A cross-sectional analysis of video games and attention deficit hyperactivity disorder symptoms in adolescents. *Annals of General Psychiatry, 5*, 16.

Chappell, D., Eatough, V., Davies, M., & Griffiths, M. D. (2006). EverQuest—It's just a computer game right? An interpretative phenomenological analysis of online gaming addiction. *International Journal of Mental Health and Addiction, 4*(3), 205–216.

Charlton, J. P., & Danforth, I. D. W. (2007). Distinguishing addiction and high engagement in the context of online game playing. *Computers in Human Behavior, 23*(3), 1531–1548.

Charlton, J. P., & Danforth, I. D. W. (2010). Validating the distinction between computer addiction and engagement: Online game playing and personality. *Behaviour & Information Technology, 29*(6), 601–613.

Choi, D. S., & Kim, J. (2004). Why people continue to play online games: In search of critical design factors to increase customer loyalty to online contents. *Cyberpsychology & Behavior, 7*(1), 11–24.

Clark, N., & Scott, P. S. (2009). *Game addiction: The experience and the effects*. Jefferson, NC: McFarland & Company, Inc.

Cole, H., & Griffiths, M. D. (2007). Social interactions in massively multiplayer online role-playing gamers. *Cyberpsychology & Behavior, 10*(4), 575–583.

Dauriat, F. Z., Zermatten, A., Billieux, J., Thorens, G., Bondolfi, G., Zullino, D., et al. (2011). Motivations to play specifically predict excessive involvement in massively multiplayer online role-playing games: Evidence from an online survey. *European Addiction Research, 17*(4), 185–189.

De Prato, G., Feijóo, C., Nepelski, D., Bogdanowicz, M., & Simon, J. P. (2010). Born digital/grown digital: Assessing the future competitiveness of the EU video games software industry. *JRC Scientific and Technical Reports*, Publication office of the European Union.

Demetrovics, Z., & Griffiths, M. D. (2012). Behavioral addictions: Past, present and future. *Journal of Behavioral Addictions*, *1*(1), 1–2.

Demetrovics, Z., Szeredi, B., & Rózsa, S. (2008). The three-factor model of Internet addiction: The development of the Problematic Internet Use Questionnaire. *Behavior Research Methods*, *40*(2), 563–574.

Demetrovics, Z., Urban, R., Nagygyorgy, K., Farkas, J., Zilahy, D., Mervo, B., et al. (2011). Why do you play? The development of the motives for online gaming questionnaire (MOGQ). *Behav Res Methods*, *43*(3), 814–825.

Demetrovics, Z., Urbán, R., Nagygyörgy, K., Farkas, J., Griffiths, M. D., Pápay, O., et al. (2012). The development of the Problematic Online Gaming Questionnaire (POGQ). *PLoS ONE*, 7(5), e36417.

Fackler, M. (2007). *In Korea, a boot camp cure for web obsession*. Retrieved October 17, 2013, from New York Times http://www.nytimes.com/2007/11/18/technology/18rehab.html?pagewanted=1&ei=5087&em&en=ae5b633804a5ee6b&ex=1195621200.

Gentile, D. A. (2009). Pathological video-game use among youth ages 8 to 18: A national study. *Psychological Science*, *20*(5), 594–602.

Gentile, D. A., Choo, H., Liau, A., Sim, T., Li, D. D., Fung, D., et al. (2011). Pathological video game use among youths: A two-year longitudinal study. *Pediatrics*, *127*(2), 319–329.

Grant, J. E., Potenza, M. N., Weinstein, A., & Gorelick, D. A. (2010). Introduction to behavioral addictions. *American Journal of Drug and Alcohol Abuse*, *36*, 233–241.

Griffiths, M. D. (1993). Fruit machine gambling: The importance of structural characteristics. *Journal of Gambling Studies*, *9*(2), 101–120.

Griffiths, M. D. (1998). Internet addiction: Does it really exist? In J. Gackenbach (Ed.), *Psychology and the Internet: Intrapersonal, interpersonal, and transpersonal implications* (pp. 61–75). San Diego: Academic Press.

Griffiths, M. D. (1999). Gambling technologies: Prospects for problem gambling. *Journal of Gambling Studies*, *15*(3), 265–283.

Griffiths, M. D. (2003). Video games: Advice for teachers and parents. *Education and Health*, *21*, 48–49.

Griffiths, M. D. (2005a). A 'components' model of addiction within a biopsychosocial framework. *Journal of Substance Use*, *10*(4), 191–197.

Griffiths, M. D. (2005b). Relationship between gambling and video-game playing: A response to Johansson and Gotestam. *Psychological Reports*, *96*(3 Pt 1), 644–646.

Griffiths, M. D. (2008). Diagnosis and management of video game addiction. *New Directions in Addiction Treatment and Prevention*, *12*, 27–41.

Griffiths, M. D. (2010a). Online video gaming: What should educational psychologists know? *Educational Psychology in Practice*, *26*(1), 35–40.

Griffiths, M. D. (2010b). The role of context in online gaming excess and addiction: Some case study evidence. *International Journal of Mental Health and Addiction*, *8*(1), 119–125.

Griffiths, M. D., Davies, M. N. O., & Chappell, D. (2004). Online computer gaming: A comparison of adolescent and adult gamers. *Journal of Adolescence*, *27*(1), 87–96.

Griffiths, M. D., & Meredith, A. (2009). Videogame addiction and its treatment. *Journal of Contemporary Psychotherapy*, *39*(4), 247–253.

Grusser, S. M., Thalemann, R., & Griffiths, M. D. (2007). Excessive computer game playing: Evidence for addiction and aggression? *Cyberpsychology & Behavior*, *10*(2), 290–292.

Han, D. H., Bolo, N., Daniels, M. A., Arenella, L. S., Lyoo, K. I., & Renshaw, P. F. (2011). Brain activity and desire for Internet video game play. *Comprehensive Psychiatry*, *52*(1), 88–95.

Han, D. H., Hwang, J. W., & Renshaw, P. F. (2010). Bupropion sustained release treatment decreases craving for video games and cue-induced brain activity in patients with Internet video game addiction. *Experimental and Clinical Psychopharmacology*, *18*, 297–304.

Han, D. H., Lee, Y. S., Na, C., Ahn, J. Y., Chung, U. S., Daniels, M. A., et al. (2009). The effect of methylphenidate on Internet video game play in children with attention-deficit/hyperactivity disorder. *Comprehensive Psychiatry, 50*(3), 251–256.

Han, D. H., & Renshaw, P. F. (2012). Bupropion in the treatment of problematic online game play in patients with major depressive disorder. *Journal of Psychopharmacology, 26*(5), 689–696.

Herodotou, C., Kambouri, M., & Winters, N. (2011). The role of trait emotional intelligence in gamers' preferences for play and frequency of gaming. *Computers in Human Behavior, 27*(5), 1815–1819.

Hsu, S. H., Wen, M. H., & Wu, M. C. (2009). Exploring user experiences as predictors of MMORPG addiction. *Computers & Education, 53*(3), 990–999.

Hussain, Z., & Griffiths, M. D. (2009). Excessive use of massively-multi-player online role-playing games: A pilot study. *International Journal of Mental Health and Addiction*, 7, 563–571.

Jansz, J., & Tanis, M. (2007). Appeal of playing online first person shooter games. *Cyberpsychology and Behavior, 10*, 133–136.

Jeong, E. J., & Kim, D. H. (2011). Social activities, self-efficacy, game attitudes, and game addiction. *Cyberpsychology, Behavior and Social Networking, 14*(4), 213–221.

Kim, E. J., Namkoong, K., Ku, T., & Kim, S. J. (2008). The relationship between online game addiction and aggression, self-control and narcissistic personality traits. *European Psychiatry, 23*(3), 212–218.

Kim, J. W., Han, D. H., Park, D. B., Min, K. J., Na, C., Won, S. K., et al. (2010). The relationships between online game player biogenetic traits, playing time, and the genre of the game being played. *Psychiatry Investigation*, 7(1), 17–23.

Kim, M. G., & Kim, J. (2010). Cross-validation of reliability, convergent and discriminant validity for the problematic online game use scale. *Computers in Human Behavior, 26*(3), 389–398.

Kim, S. M., Han, D. H., Lee, Y. S., Kim, J. E., & Renshaw, P. F. (2012). Changes in brain activity in response to problem solving during the abstinence from online game play. *Journal of Behavioral Addictions, 1*(2), 41–49.

King, D., Delfabbro, P., & Griffiths, M. D. (2010a). The role of structural characteristics in problem video game playing: A review. *Cyberpsychology: Journal of Psychosocial Research on Cyberspace, 4*(1), article 6.

King, D., Delfabbro, P., & Griffiths, M. D. (2010b). Video game structural characteristics: A new psychological taxonomy. *International Journal of Mental Health and Addiction, 8*(1), 90–106.

King, D., Delfabbro, P., & Griffiths, M. D. (2011). The role of structural characteristics in problematic video game play: An empirical study. *International Journal of Mental Health and Addiction, 9*(3), 320–333.

Ko, C. H., Liu, G. C., Hsiao, S. M., Yen, J. Y., Yang, M. J., Lin, W. C., et al. (2009). Brain activities associated with gaming urge of online gaming addiction. *Journal of Psychiatric Research, 43*, 739–747.

Ko, C. H., Yen, J. Y., Chen, C. C., Chen, S. H., & Yen, C. F. (2005). Gender differences and related factors affecting online gaming addiction among Taiwanese adolescents. *Journal of Nervous and Mental Disease, 193*(4), 273–277.

Koronczai, B., Urban, R., Kokonyei, G., Paksi, B., Papp, K., Kun, B., et al. (2011). Confirmation of the three-factor model of problematic Internet use on off-line adolescent and adult samples. *Cyberpsychology, Behavior and Social Networking, 14*, 657–664.

Kuss, D. J., & Griffiths, M. D. (2012a). Internet gaming addiction: A systematic review of empirical research. *International Journal of Mental Health and Addiction, 10*(2), 278–296.

Kuss, D. J., & Griffiths, M. D. (2012b). Online gaming addiction in children and adolescents: A review of empirical research. *Journal of Behavioral Addictions, 1*(1), 3–22.

Kuss, D. J., & Griffiths, M. D. (2012c). Internet and gaming addiction: A systematic literature review of neuroimaging studies. *Brain Sciences, 2*, 347–374.

Lee, C., & Han, S. (2007). Development of the scale for diagnosing online game addiction. Mathematical Methods and Computational Techniques in Research and Education. In P. Dondon, V. Mladenov, S. Impedovo, C. Cepisca & J. Lloret (Eds.), *Mathematical Methods and Computational Techniques in Research and Education. Proceedings of the 9th WSEAS International Conference on Mathematical Methods and Computational Techniques in Electrical Engineering (MMACTEE '07)* (pp. 362–367). Arcachon: WSEAS Press.

Lee, H. C., & Ahn, C. Y. (2002). Development of the Internet game addiction diagnostic scale. *The Korean Journal of Health Psychology*, 7, 211–239.

Lemmens, J. S., Valkenburg, P. M., & Peter, J. (2009). Development and validation of a game addiction scale for adolescents. *Media Psychology*, *12*, 77–95.

Lemmens, J. S., Valkenburg, P. M., & Peter, J. (2011). Psychosocial causes and consequences of pathological gaming. *Computers in Human Behavior*, *27*(1), 144–152.

Lemola, S., Brand, S., Vogler, N., Perkinson-Gloor, N., Allemand, M., & Grob, A. (2011). Habitual computer game playing at night is related to depressive symptoms. *Personality and Individual Differences*, *51*(2), 117–122.

Lo, S. K., Wang, C. C., & Fang, W. C. (2005). Physical interpersonal relationships and social anxiety among online game players. *Cyberpsychology & Behavior*, *8*(1), 15–20.

Mehroof, M., & Griffiths, M. D. (2010). Online gaming addiction: The role of sensation seeking, self-control, neuroticism, aggression, state anxiety, and trait anxiety. *Cyberpsychology, Behavior and Social Networking*, *13*(3), 313–316.

Nagygyörgy, K., Mihalik, Á., & Demetrovics, Z. (2012). Az online játékok pszichológiai vonatkozásai. In E. Gabos (Ed.), *A média hatása a gyermekekre és fiatalokra VI* (pp. 242–248). Budapest: Nemzetközi Gyermekmentő Szolgálat Magyar Egyesülete.

Nagygyörgy, K., Pápay, O., Urbán, R., Farkas, J., Kun, B., Griffiths, M. D., & Demetrovics, Z. (2013). [Problematic online gaming: a review of the literature] [Hungarian]. *Psychiatria Hungarica*, *28*(2), 122–144.

Nagygyörgy, K., Urbán, R., Farkas, J., Griffiths, M., Zilahy, D., Kökönyei, G., et al. (2012). Typology and socio-demographic characteristics of massively multiplayer online game players. *International Journal of Human-Computer Interaction*, doi:10.1080/10447318.2012.702636.

Ng, B. D., & Wiemer-Hastings, P. (2005). Addiction to the Internet and online gaming. *Cyberpsychology & Behavior*, *8*(2), 110–113.

Pápay, O., Urbán, R., Griffiths, M. D., Nagygyörgy, K., Farkas, J., Elekes, Z., et al. (2013). Psychometric properties of the Problematic Online Gaming Questionnaire Short-Form (POGQ-SF) and prevalence of problematic online gaming in a national sample of adolescents. *Cyberpsychology, Behavior and Social Networking*, *16*, 340–348.

Parke, J., & Griffiths, M. D. (2007). The role of structural characteristics in gambling. In G. Smith, D. Hodgins & R. Williams (Eds.), *Research and measurement issues in gambling studies* (pp. 211–243). New York: Elsevier.

Peng, W., & Liu, M. (2010). Online gaming dependency: A preliminary study in China. *Cyberpsychology, Behavior and Social Networking*, *13*(3), 329–333.

Peters, C. S., & Malesky, L. A. (2008). Problematic usage among highly-engaged players of massively multiplayer online role playing games. *Cyberpsychology & Behavior*, *11*(4), 480–483.

Porter, G., Starcevic, V., Berle, D., & Fenech, P. (2010). Recognizing problem video game use. *Australian and New Zealand Journal of Psychiatry*, *44*, 120–128.

Przybylski, A. K., Ryan, R. M., & Rigby, C. S. (2009). The motivating role of violence in video games. *Personality and Social Psychology Bulletin*, *35*(2), 243–259.

Rehbein, F., Psych, G., Kleimann, M., Mediasci, G., & Mossle, T. (2010). Prevalence and risk factors of video game dependency in adolescence: Results of a German nationwide survey. *Cyberpsychology, Behavior and Social Networking*, *13*(3), 269–277.

Rice, R. A. (2006). *MMO Evolution*. Raleigh, NC: Lulu Press.

Ryan, R. M., Rigby, C. S., & Przybylski, A. (2006). The motivational pull of video games: A self-determination theory approach. *Motivation and Emotion*, *30*(4), 347–363.

Scott, S. (2007). *Electronic game addiction? Part 3 of 4. Interview with Shavaun Scott psychotherapist.* Retrieved July 10, 2013, from http://www.youtube.com/watch?v=QoDLN6gGd_g&list=PL9ECB0D59EF3A32C5.

Seay, A. F., & Kraut, R. E. (2007). Project massive: Self-regulation and problematic use of online gaming. In *Paper presented at the CHI 2007: Proceedings of the ACM Conference on Human Factors in Computing Systems*. CA, USA: San Jose.

Snodgrass, J. G., Lacy, M. G., Dengah, H. J. F., & Fagan, J. (2011). Enhancing one life rather than living two: Playing MMOs with offline friends. *Computers in Human Behavior, 27*(3), 1211–1222.

Van Rooij, A. J., Schoenmakers, T. M., Vermulst, A. A., Van den Eijnden, R. J., & Van de Mheen, D. (2011). Online video game addiction: Identification of addicted adolescent gamers. *Addiction, 106*(1), 205–212.

Wan, C. S., & Chiou, W. B. (2006). Psychological motives and online games addiction: A test of flow theory and humanistic needs theory for Taiwanese adolescents. *Cyberpsychology & Behavior, 9*(3), 317–324.

Wang, C. C., & Chu, Y. S. (2007). Harmonious passion and obsessive passion in playing online games. *Social Behavior and Personality, 35*(7), 997–1005.

Wang, E. S., Chen, L. S., Lin, J. Y., & Wang, M. C. (2008). The relationship between leisure satisfaction and life satisfaction of adolescents concerning online games. *Adolescence, 43*(169), 177–184.

Whang, L. S. M., Heo, S. J., & Hur, M. Y. (2004). The online game addiction as a luxury syndrome: An immersion of digital world as a consumption of digital product. *Cyberpsychology & Behavior*, 7(3), 318.

Williams, D., Ducheneaut, N., Xiong, L., & Yee, N. (2006). From tree house to barracks—The social life of guilds in World of Warcraft. *Games and Culture, 1*(4), 338–360.

Wood, R. T. A. (2007). The problem with the concept of video game "addiction": Some case examples. *International Journal of Mental Health & Addiction, 6*, 169–178.

Wood, R. T. A., Griffiths, M. D., Chappell, D., & Davies, M. N. O. (2004). The structural characteristics of video games: A psycho-structural analysis. *Cyberpsychology & Behavior*, 7(1), 1–10.

World Health Organization. (1994). *BNO-10: International Statistical Classification of Diseases and Health Related Problems*. Geneva, Switzerland: Author.

Yee, N. (2006a). The demographics, motivations and derived experiences of users of massively-multiuser online graphical environments. *PRESENCE: Teleoperators and Virtual Environments, 15*, 309–329.

Yee, N. (2006b). The labor of fun—How video games blur the boundaries of work and play. *Games and Culture, 1*(1), 68–71.

Yee, N. (2006c). Motivations for play in online games. *Cyberpsychology & Behavior, 9*(6), 772–775.

Yee, N. (2006d). The psychology of MMORPGs: Emotional investment, motivations, relationship formation, and problematic usage. In R. Schroeder & A. Axelsson (Eds.), *Avatars at work and play: Collaboration and interaction in shared virtual environments* (pp. 187–207). London: Springer.

Young, K. S. (1998a). *Caught in the Net: How to recognize the signs of Internet addiction and a winning strategy for recovery*. New York: Wiley.

Young, K. S. (1998b). Internet addiction: The emergence of a new clinical disorder. *Cyberpsychology and Behavior, 1*, 237–244.

Young, K. S. (1999). Internet addiction: Symptoms, evaluation, and treatment. In L. Vande Creek & T. Jackson (Eds.), *Innovations in clinical practice: A source book*. Sarasota, FL: Professional Resource Press. (pp. 17, 19–31).

Young, K. S. (2007). Cognitive behavioral therapy with Internet addicts: Treatment outcomes and implications. *Cyberpsychology & Behavior, 10*, 671–679.

Young, K. S. (2009a). *Are you an obsessive online gamer?*. Retrieved April 12, 2013, from http://www.netaddiction.com/index.php?option=com_content&view=article&id=80%3Agamer&catid=42%3Arecovery-resources&Itemid=84.

Young, K. S. (2009b). Understanding online gaming addiction and treatment issues for adolescents. *American Journal of Family Therapy*, *37*, 355–372.
Young, K. S. (2010). *When gaming becomes an obsession: Help for parents and their children to treat online gaming addiction*. Retrieved October 17, 2013, from http://www.netaddiction.com/articles/Online%20Gaming%20Treatment.pdf.
Zhou, Y., & Li, Z. (2009). Online game addiction among Chinese college students measurement and attribution. *Studies in Health Technology and Informatics*, *144*, 149–154.

APPENDIX 4-1. PROBLEMATIC ONLINE GAMING QUESTIONNAIRE (POGQ)

Please read the statements below regarding *online gaming*. The questionnaire REFERS TO ONLINE GAMES exclusively, but we use the expression "game" in each statement for simplicity's sake.

Please indicate on the scale from 1 to 5 to what extent, and how often, these statements apply to you!

	Never	Seldom	Occasionally	Often	Almost Always/ Always
1. When you are not gaming, how often do you think about playing a game or think about how would it feel to play at that moment?	1	2	3	4	5
2. How often do you play longer than originally planned?	1	2	3	4	5
3. How often do you feel depressed or irritable when not gaming only for these feelings to disappear when you start playing?	1	2	3	4	5
4. How often do you feel that you should reduce the amount of time you spend gaming?	1	2	3	4	5
5. How often do the people around you complain that you are gaming too much?	1	2	3	4	5
6. How often do you fail to meet up with a friend because you were gaming?	1	2	3	4	5
7. How often do you day-dream about gaming?	1	2	3	4	5

	Never	Seldom	Occasionally	Often	Almost Always/ Always
8. How often do you lose track of time when gaming?	1	2	3	4	5
9. How often do you get irritable, restless or anxious when you cannot play games as much as you want?	1	2	3	4	5
10. How often do you unsuccessfully try to reduce the time you spend on gaming?	1	2	3	4	5
11. How often do you argue with your parents and/or your partner because of gaming?	1	2	3	4	5
12. How often do you neglect other activities because you would rather game?	1	2	3	4	5
13. How often do you feel time stops while gaming?	1	2	3	4	5
14. How often do you get restless or irritable if you are unable to play games for a few days?	1	2	3	4	5
15. How often do you feel that gaming causes problems for you in your life?	1	2	3	4	5
16. How often do you choose gaming over going out with someone?	1	2	3	4	5
17. How often are you so immersed in gaming that you forget to eat?	1	2	3	4	5
18. How often do you get irritable or upset when you cannot play?	1	2	3	4	5

	Preoccu--pation	Immersion	With-drawal	Overuse	Interpersonal Conflicts	Social Isolation
POGQ-18	1, 7	2, 8, 13, 17	3, 9, 14, 18	4, 10, 15	5, 11	6, 12, 16
POGQ-12	1, 7	2, 8	3, 14	4, 10	5, 11	6, 12

Note: More details on scoring and interpretation can be found in Demetrovics et al. (2012) and Pápay et al. (2013).

APPENDIX 4-2. MOTIVES FOR ONLINE GAMING QUESTIONNAIRE (MOGQ)

People play online games for different reasons. Some reasons are listed below.

Please indicate how often you play online games for the reasons listed below by circling the appropriate response—almost never/never (1), some of the time (2), half of the time (3), most of the time (4), almost always/always (5). There is no right or wrong answer! We are only interested in your motives for gaming.

	I Play Online Games...	Almost Never/ Never	Some of the Time	Half of the Time	Most of the Time	Almost Always/ Always
1.	... because I can get to know new people	1	2	3	4	5
2.	... because gaming helps me to forget about daily hassles	1	2	3	4	5
3.	... because I enjoy competing with others	1	2	3	4	5
4.	... because gaming helps me get into a better mood	1	2	3	4	5
5.	... because gaming sharpens my senses	1	2	3	4	5
6.	... because I can do things that I am unable to do or I am not allowed to do in real life	1	2	3	4	5
7.	... for recreation	1	2	3	4	5
8.	... because I can meet many different people	1	2	3	4	5
9.	... because it makes me forget real life	1	2	3	4	5
10.	... because I like to win	1	2	3	4	5
11.	... because it helps me get rid of stress	1	2	3	4	5
12.	... because it improves my skills	1	2	3	4	5
13.	... to feel as if I was somebody else	1	2	3	4	5
14.	... because it is entertaining	1	2	3	4	5
15.	... because it is a good social experience	1	2	3	4	5

	I Play Online Games...	Almost Never/ Never	Some of the Time	Half of the Time	Most of the Time	Almost Always/ Always
16.	... because gaming helps me escape reality	1	2	3	4	5
17.	... because it is good to feel that I am better than others	1	2	3	4	5
18.	... because it helps me channel my aggression	1	2	3	4	5
19.	... because it improves my concentration	1	2	3	4	5
20.	... to be somebody else for a while	1	2	3	4	5
21.	... because I enjoy gaming	1	2	3	4	5
22.	... because gaming gives me company	1	2	3	4	5
23.	... to forget about unpleasant things or offenses	1	2	3	4	5
24.	... for the pleasure of defeating others	1	2	3	4	5
25.	... because it reduces tension	1	2	3	4	5
26.	... because it improves my coordination skills	1	2	3	4	5
27.	... because I can be in another world	1	2	3	4	5

Social	Escape	Competition	Coping	Skill Development	Fantasy	Recreation
1, 8, 15, 22	2, 9, 16, 23	3, 10, 17, 24	4, 11, 18, 25	5, 12, 19, 26	6, 13, 20, 27	7, 14, 21

Note: More details on scoring and interpretation can be found in Demetrovics et al. (2011).

Internet Addiction Disorder: Overview and Controversies

Aviv Weinstein[1], Laura Curtiss Feder[2], Kenneth Paul Rosenberg[3], Pinhas Dannon[4]

[1]Department of Behavioral Sciences, Faculty of Social Sciences and Humanities, Ariel University, Israel, [2]Wellesley, MA, USA, [3]Cornell University Medical Center, Psychiatry Department, New York, NY, USA and UpperEastHealth.com, [4]Sackler School of Medicine and Beer Yaakov Ness Ziona Center for Mental Health, Israel

INTRODUCTION: INTERNET ADDICTION DISORDER AND ITS TREATMENT

Problematic Internet use (PIU) or Internet Addiction Disorder (IAD) is characterized by excessive or poorly controlled preoccupations, urges, or behaviors regarding Internet use that lead to impairment or distress. Due to the increased use of the Internet over the past 15 years, IAD has attracted attention of researchers and clinicians in the field. Young (1998) and Griffiths (1998, 2000) were the first who defined IAD and have done extensive research. Internet addiction has also attracted increasing coverage in the popular media and among researchers, and this attention has paralleled the growth in computer use and Internet access (Shaw & Black, 2008). Phenomenologically, there appear to be at least three IAD subtypes: excessive gaming-gambling, sexual preoccupations (cybersex), and socializing or social networking, including e-mail and messaging. Internet addicts may use the Internet for extended periods, isolating themselves from other forms of social contact, and focus almost entirely on the Internet rather than broader life events. Adolescents with problematic Internet use showed dysfunctional coping strategies with problems in school and home and showed worse interpersonal relations (Milani, Osualdella, & Di Blasio, 2009). IAD can also be explained by a need to "escape from oneself," which may account for the excessive playing of Internet games (Kwon, Chung, & Lee, 2011).

There are multiple proposed explanations for IAD (Dell'Osso, Altamura, Allen, Marazziti, & Hollander, 2006). Some researchers have considered IAD as part of the Impulse-Control Disorder and/or Obsessive-Compulsive Disorder models. These models are supported by brain-imaging and

Behavioral Addictions
http://dx.doi.org/10.1016/B978-0-12-407724-9.00005-7

pharmacological (SSRI) treatment studies. IAD was also suggested to be included in the Behavioral Addiction spectrum because it shows the features of excessive use, despite adverse consequences, withdrawal phenomena, and tolerance that characterize many substance use disorders; however, there are few data bearing on these claims. The frequent appearance of IAD in the context of numerous comorbid conditions raises complex questions of causality.

DIAGNOSIS AND CLINICAL CRITERIA

Four components were originally suggested as essential to the diagnosis of IAD for *DSM-5* inclusion (Block, 2008): (1) excessive Internet use, often associated with a loss of sense of time or a neglect of basic drives; (2) withdrawal, including feelings of anger, tension, and/or depression when the computer is inaccessible; (3) tolerance, including the need for better computer equipment, more software, or more hours of use; and (4) adverse consequences, including arguments, lying, poor school or vocational achievement, social isolation, and fatigue.

A major survey was conducted to develop diagnostic criteria for IAD and to evaluate its validity and reliability in the general population (Tao et al., 2010). The diagnostic criteria consisted of a symptom criterion (seven clinical symptoms of IAD), a clinically significant impairment criterion (functional and psychosocial impairments), a course criterion (duration of addiction lasting at least 3 months, with at least 6 hours of nonessential Internet usage per day), and an exclusion criterion (exclusion of dependency attributed to psychotic disorders). IAD was initially proposed for inclusion in the 2013 *DSM-5* but was not yet recognized as a disorder; however, Internet Gaming Disorder was included in the *DSM-5* appendix of disorders for further consideration and study.

ASSESSMENT OF INTERNET ADDICTION

The questionnaires for diagnosis of IAD have used items from substance dependence questionnaires, as well as new items related to Internet addiction. The most commonly used questionnaire is Young's Internet Addiction Test (IAT) (Young, 1998), which can be found in full in the appendix of this chapter. The IAT has been validated (Barke, Nyenhuis, & Kröner-Herwig, 2012; Bernardi & Pallanti, 2009; Chong, Isa, Hashim, Pillai, & Harbajan Singh, 2012; Ghamari, Mohammadbeigi, Mohammadsalehi, &

Hashiani 2011; Han et al., 2009; Jelenchick, Becker, & Moreno, 2012; Korkeila, Kaarlas, Jaaskelainen, Vahlberg, & Taiminen, 2009; Widyanto & McMurran, 2004). The Internet Addiction Scale (IAS) was developed by Griffiths (1998) and was validated by Nichols and Nicki (2004) and Canan, Ataoglu, Nichols, Yildirim, and Ozturk (2010). Other questionnaires include the Chen Internet Addiction Scale (CIAS) (Yen et al., 2012), the Questionnaire of Experiences Related to Internet (Beranuy, Chamarro, Graner, & Carbonell, 2009), the Compulsive Internet Use Scale (CIUS) (Khazaal et al., 2012; Meerkerk, Van Den Eijnden, Vermulst, & Garretsen, 2009), the Problematic Internet Use Questionnaire (PIUQ) (Demetrovics, Szeredi, Rãzsa, 2008), and the Internet-Related Problem Scale (IRPS) (Widyanto, Griffiths, & Brunsden, 2011). These questionnaires have been reviewed by Beard (2005), who noted that these instruments have yielded preliminary research on IAD but are based on different theoretical underpinnings and do not agree on the underlying dimensions that make their utilization problematic.

PREVALENCE RATES

International prevalence rates for Internet addiction range globally from 1.5% to 8.2% (Petersen, Weymann, Schelb, Thiel, & Thomasius, 2009), and in the United States from 0.3% to 0.7% (Shaw & Black, 2008) to 4% (Christakis, Moreno, Jelenchick, Myaing, & Zhou., 2011) to 6% (Greenfield, 1999) and 25% among Southern U.S. university students (Forston, Scotti, Chen, Malone, & Del Ben, 2007); see Moreno, Jelenchick, Cox, Young, and Christakis (2011) for review. In Europe, rates vary between 3% in Germany (Woelfling, Buhler, Lemenager, Mairsen, & Mann, 2009), 5.4% and 5% in Italy (Pallanti, Bernardi, & Quercioli, 2006; Poli & Agrimi, 2012), 10.4% in Greece (Tsitsika et al., 2009), and 18.3% in the United Kingdom (Niemz, Griffiths, & Banyard, 2005). A major survey of 11 European countries found a prevalence rate of 4.4% (Durkee et al., 2012).

Internet addiction has been most studied in the Far East. In China, prevalence rates vary between 10.2% of moderate users and 0.6% of the severely addicted (Lam, Peng, Mai, & Jing, 2009), between 2.4% and 5.52% in Hunan province (Cao, Su, Liu, & Gao, 2007; Deng, Hu, Hu, Wang, & Sun, 2007) and 6.44% in Shaanxi Province (Ni, Yan, Chen, & Liu, 2009), 6.7% in Hong Kong (Fu, Chan, Wong, & Yip, 2010) and 8.8% in Shanghai (Xu et al., 2012). In Taiwan, 17.9% of students were addicted (Tsai et al., 2009). In South

Korean middle school students, 16% were potential at-risk users, and 3.1% were high-risk users (Seo, Kang, & Yom, 2009). Other studies in South Korea have found 1.6% (Kim et al., 2006), 3.5% (Whang, Lee, & Chang, 2003), 4.3% (Jang, Hwang, & Choi, 2008), 10.7% (Park, Kim, & Cho, 2008), and 20.3% (Ha et al., 2007) of adolescents with Internet addiction.

PSYCHIATRIC COMORBIDITY

Cross-sectional studies on samples of patients report high comorbidity of Internet addiction with psychiatric disorders such as affective disorders, anxiety disorders (e.g., generalized anxiety disorder, social anxiety disorder), and attention deficit hyperactivity disorder (ADHD).

See Table 5.1 for a list of studies showing Internet addiction comorbidity with other psychiatric disorders and symptoms. The table is divided between adult and adolescent studies.

The mental status of Internet addicts prior to addiction, including the pathological traits that may trigger IAD, was explored by Dong, Lu, Zhou, and Zhao (2011), who detected abnormal obsessive-compulsive measures in participants before they became addicted to the Internet. Cho et al. (2012) found a relationship between withdrawal and anxiety/depression and future Internet addiction among South Korean males. Finally, a review of 20 studies correlating problematic Internet use (PIU) and mental disorders found that 75% reported significant correlations of PIU with depression, 57% with anxiety, 100% with symptoms of ADHD, 60% with obsessive-compulsive symptoms, and 66% with hostility/aggression (Carli et al., 2013).

RELATIONSHIP OF INTERNET ADDICTION WITH DRUG AND ALCOHOL USE

Alcohol and drug use have been found to be associated with problematic Internet use. Cannabis use was associated with Internet addiction in Finland (Korkeila et al., 2009), and substance use among Greek adolescents was associated with problematic Internet use (Fisoun, Floros, Siomos, Geroukalis, & Navridis, 2012). Additionally, Internet addiction was associated with harmful use of alcohol among Taiwanese students (Yen, Ko, Yen, Chang, & Cheng, 2009). Parental problem drinking was also associated with Internet addiction through anxiety, depression, and aggression for boys and through family function and aggression for girls (Jang & Ji, 2012).

Table 5.1 Internet Addiction-Comorbidity with Other Psychiatric Disorders and Symptoms

Comorbid Clinical Diagnosis	Studies	Country
	Adults	
Depression Depressive mood disorder	te Wildt, Putzig, Zedler, Ohlmeier (2007)	Germany
	Morrison & Gore, (2010)	UK
	Liberatore, Rosario, Colón-De Martí, & Martínez (2011)	Puerto Rico
	Alavi et al., (2010)	Iran
	Cho, Sung, Shin, Lim, & Shin (2012)	South Korea
Anxiety	Kratzer & Hegerl (2008)	Germany
	Alavi et al., (2010)	Iran
	Cho et al., (2012)	South Korea
Alcohol abuse	Yen, Ko, Yen, Chen, & Chen (2009)	Taiwan
Alexithymia and child maltreatment	Yates, Gregor, & Haviland (2012)	U.S.
Impulse control disorders	Mazhari (2012)	Iran
Aggression	Alavi et al., (2010)	Iran
	Adolescents	
Personality disorders: hypomania, dysthymia, obsessive-compulsive, borderline personality disorder, and avoidant personality disorder	Bernardi & Pallanti (2009)	Italy
Alexithymia, dissociative experiences, impulse dysregulation	De Berardis et al. (2009)	Italy
Alexithymia	Dalbudak et al., (2013)	Turkey
Dissociative symptoms	Canan, Ataoglu, Ozcetin, & Icmeli (2012).	Turkey
Conduct disorder and hyperactivity	Kormas, Critselis, Janikian, Kafetzis, & Tsitsika (2011)	Greece
Depression	Tsitsika et al., (2011)	Greece
	Ha et al., (2007)	South Korea
	Kim et al., (2006)	South Korea
	Park, Park, Lee, Kwon, & Kim (2012)	South Korea
	Yen, Ko, Yen, Wu, & Yang (2007)	Taiwan
	Xiuqin et al., (2010)	China
	Cheung & Wong (2011)	Hong Kong
	Guo et al., (2012)*	Hong Kong
	Morrison & Gore (2010)	UK

Continued

Table 5.1 Internet Addiction-Comorbidity with Other Psychiatric Disorders and Symptoms—cont'd

Comorbid Clinical Diagnosis	Studies	Country
Social phobia	Yen et al., (2007) Wei, Chen, Huang, & Bai (2012)	Taiwan
Somatic pain	Wei et al., (2012)	Taiwan
ADHD	Yen et al., (2007) Yen, Yen, Chen, Tang, & Ko (2009)	Taiwan
OCD	Xiuqin et al., (2010)	China
Insomnia	Cheung & Wong (2011)	Hong Kong

*In children

THE PHENOMENOLOGY OF INTERNET ADDICTION

As addressed elsewhere in the book, many factors can contribute to Internet addiction. They include coping with stress (Grusser, Thalemann, Albrecht, & Thalemann, 2005); expanding social networks (Campbell, Cumming, & Hughes, 2006); exhibiting greater control and social anxiety (Kuss & Griffiths 2011; Lee & Stapinski 2012); coping with developmental challenges (Ko et al., 2006; Israelashvili, Kim, & Bukobza, 2012); and creating a virtual "ideal self" and escapism (Achab et al., 2011; Billieux et al., 2011; Li, Liau, & Khoo, 2011; Zanetta et al., 2011). Sex addiction may be another contributing factor, leading people to the Internet to pursue cybersex (Brand et al., 2011; Ross, Månsson, & Daneback, 2012; Southern, 2008). There is also some speculative research that there is a subset of problematic Internet users who rely on the Internet as part of their attempts of body image avoidance, including Rodgers, Melioli, Laconi, Bui, and Chabrol (2013), who found that Internet addiction symptoms and body-image avoidance were both significant predictors of disordered eating among women.

PERSONALITY AND PSYCHOSOCIAL FACTORS ASSOCIATED WITH IAD

Personality factors such as lack of perseverance (Mottram & Fleming, 2009), psychoticism (Tosun & Lajunen, 2009), and neuroticism, sensation seeking, and aggressiveness (Mehroof & Griffiths, 2010) have been found to be associated with Internet addiction. Sensation seeking among Chinese Internet users was reported by Shi, Chen, and Tian (2011). High harm avoidance (HA), novelty seeking (NS), reward dependence (RD), low self-directedness, and low cooperativeness were reported in South Korean studies by Ha et al. (2007) and June, Sohn, So, Yi, and Park (2007). In Taiwan, high NS, high HA, and low RD predicted a higher proportion of adolescents with IAD (Ko et al., 2006). However, one study, by Cho, Kim, Kim, Lee, and Kim (2008), found that low NS was associated with IAD.

Internet addiction has also been positively associated with interpersonal factors such as perceived discontentment with peer interactions (Liu & Kuo, 2007), and problems with parenting attitudes, family communication, family cohesion, and family violence (Park et al., 2008).

Additional psychosocial factors are also noted in the literature. IAD has been associated with low self-esteem (Fioravanti, Dèttore, & Casale, 2012; Stieger & Burger, 2010), family dissatisfaction and recent stressful events (Lam et al., 2009), and few social friends, poor relations with teachers and students, and conflicting family relationships (Wang et al., 2011). Internet addiction has also been correlated with poor connectedness to school, high family conflict, low family function, substance and alcohol use, and living in rural areas by Yen, Ko, Yen, Wu, and Yang (2007) and Yen, Ko, Yen, Chang, and Cheng (2009) and associated with depressive symptoms, higher impulsivity, lower satisfaction with academic performance, being male, and insecure attachment style by Lin, Ko, and Wu (2011). Shin, Kim, and Jang (2011) also found that anxious and avoidant attachment styles and depression and phobias were associated with IAD.

COGNITIVE FACTORS ASSOCIATED WITH PROBLEMATIC INTERNET USE

Several cognitive factors have been found to be associated with problematic Internet use. Sun et al. (2009) found that IAD was associated with deficits in reward-based decision making. Ko et al. (2010) found participants had no impairments in reward-based decision making, but those with IAD had higher novelty-seeking characteristics, as noted previously.

Studies suggest that impaired executive control ability is relevant to understanding IAD. Dong, Zhou, and Zhao (2011) measured event-related brain potentials during a color-word Stroop task and noted that Internet-addicted individuals showed longer reaction time and more response errors on the Stroop task and reduced medial frontal negativity, indicating impaired executive control ability. Zhou, Yuan, and Yao (2012) found that among individuals with Internet game addiction, cognitive bias and executive function constructs involving mental flexibility and response inhibition were worse among longer-term users. Park et al. (2011) also found impaired performance related to attention among individuals who had IAD for a longer period of time.

PHYSICAL AND MENTAL HEALTH HAZARDS

The known health hazards associated with Internet addiction appear related to sleep deprivation or disturbance. High school students with Internet addiction in South Korea showed 37.7% prevalence of excessive daytime sleepiness, compared to 13.9% and 7.4% in possible addicts and nonaddicts, respectively. The prevalence of insomnia, witnessed snoring, apnea, teeth grinding, and nightmares was also higher in Internet addicts compared with possible addicts and nonaddicts (Choi et al., 2009). An association between continued Internet use and psychotic-like experiences was described by Mittal, Dean, and Pelletier (2012).

Little is understood about the habit-forming nature of the Internet and its potential for abuse. As the Internet permeates life at home, school, and work, it can create marital, academic, and job-related problems (Yellowlees & Marks, 2007; Young, 2004, 2007). A study of a small sample of adult Italian Internet addicts showed that it was strongly disabling, especially for family life (Bernardi & Pallanti, 2009). The Italian study shows that dissociative symptoms were prominent and strongly related with measures of IAD severity, subjective disability, and OCD symptoms.

TREATMENT

Treatment for IAD is mainly based on interventions and strategies previously used in the treatment of substance use disorders. For a review of treatment of Internet addiction, see King, Delfabbro, Griffiths, and Gradisar (2011). A meta-analysis of pharmacological and psychological treatment studies of Internet addiction by Winkler, Dörsing, Rief, Shen, & Glombiewski (2013), based on 16 studies, suggests that psychological and pharmacological interventions were highly effective for decreasing the amount of time Internet addicts spent online, as well as targeting symptoms of depression and anxiety.

Psychosocial Approaches

Psychosocial approaches are the mainstay of current treatment research, with very little study of pharmacological treatment. There is preliminary evidence for success of an "initiated abstinence" program in 12–15-year-old students in Austria, Germany, and Italy (Kalke & Rashke, 2004) and for a counseling program in Hong Kong (Shek, Tang, & Lo, 2009). Preliminary results from a study of 114 patients receiving cognitive behavior therapy indicated that most clients were able to manage their presenting complaints by the eighth session, and symptom management was sustained at 6-month follow-up (Young, 2007).

A treatment study using group cognitive behavioral therapy (CBT) for Internet addiction in adolescents was reported by Du, Jiang, and Vance (2010). A total of 56 patients, who met Beard's diagnostic criteria for Internet addiction, aged 12–17 years, were divided randomly into an active treatment group (n = 32) and a clinical control group (n = 24). Participants in the active treatment group were treated with an eight-session multimodal school-based group CBT, whereas participants in the clinical control group received no intervention. Internet use, time management, and emotional, cognitive, and behavioral measures were assessed for both groups at baseline, immediately after the intervention and at 6-month follow-up by investigators blind to the participants' group status. Results showed that Internet use decreased in both groups while only the multimodal, school-based group CBT evidenced improved time management skills and better emotional, cognitive, and behavioral symptoms. The authors suggest that multimodal, school-based group CBT is effective for adolescents with Internet addiction, particularly in improving emotional state and regulation ability, and behavioral and self-management style. Marital and family therapy may also help in selected cases. Additionally, online self-help books and tapes are available. Lastly, self-imposed abstinence from computer use and Internet access may be necessary in some situations (Shaw & Black, 2008).

Pharmacological Treatment

Pharmacological studies for IAD treatment used agents that were previously used for treatment of disorders such as ADHD and OCD and mainly address the Online Gaming Addiction subtype of IAD. A pharmacological open-label treatment study using extended release methylphenidate in Korean children with Internet video game addiction and comorbid ADHD found that, after 8 weeks of treatment, measures of Internet use and Internet use duration were significantly reduced, and this improvement was positively correlated with improvement in measures of attention (Han et al., 2009).

Another study identified the comorbidity of impulsive-compulsive Internet use with OCD to examine whether selective serotonin reuptake inhibitors (SSRIs) such as escitalopram can be useful for treatment of

Internet addiction. A pharmacological open-label treatment study using escitalopram with impulsive-compulsive Internet users showed significant decrease in the number of hours spent on the Internet during the first phase of treatment but not later (Dell'Osso, Altamura, Hadley, Baker, & Hollander, 2007).

Finally, bupropion, a dopamine and norepinephrine inhibitor medication used for treating nicotine and substance dependence, was used for the treatment of Internet video game addiction (Han, Hwang, & Renshaw, 2010). After a 6-week period of bupropion SR, craving for Internet video game play, total game play time, and cue-induced brain activity were decreased in the Internet video game-addicted players. A later study by Han and Renshaw (2012) showed that bupropion reduced Internet addiction scores, mean time of online game playing, and Beck Depression Inventory (BDI) scores in a group with comorbid excessive online video game playing (EOP) and Major Depressive Disorder (MDD). For review of existing pharmacological treatment for IAD, see Camardese, De Risio, Di Nicola, Pizi, and Janiri (2012).

Other Treatments

A treatment study combining electro-acupuncture with psychological intervention on cognitive function and event-related potentials, in patients with Internet addiction (IA), was described by Zhu et al. (2012). After treatment, in all groups, the IA score was lowered significantly, and scores of short-term memory capacity and short-term memory span increased significantly while the decreased IA score in the comprehensive therapy group was more significant than that in the other two groups.

CONCLUSIONS

At least three subtypes of Internet addiction have been identified: excessive gaming, sexual preoccupations, and socializing (i.e., e-mail or text messaging). All the variants share the following four components: (1) excessive use, often associated with a loss of sense of time or a neglect of basic drives; (2) withdrawal, including feelings of anger, tension, and/or depression when the computer is inaccessible; (3) tolerance, including the need for better computer equipment, more software, or more hours of use; and (4) adverse consequences, including arguments, lying, poor achievement, social isolation, and fatigue. There is debate as to whether IAD stands as its own diagnosis or is more a product of other existing disorders such as anxiety, depression, ADHD, or impulse-control disorders. There is growing evidence that Internet addiction is a behavioral addiction, yet the patho-physiological mechanisms underlying Internet addiction remain under investigation. The few published treatment studies for IAD are based on interventions and strategies used in the treatment of substance use disorders adapted to this population. Although it is premature to recommend any evidence-based treatment of Internet addiction, preliminary studies suggest that psychological treatment such as cognitive behavior therapy and pharmacological interventions such as bupropion or SSRIs seem promising, and the field of behavioral addictions will benefit from current and future research in this area.

DECLARATION OF INTEREST

The authors report no conflicts of interest. The authors alone are responsible for the content and writing of the paper.

ACKNOWLEDGMENTS

Dr. Weinstein is supported by grants from the National Institute for Psychobiology in Israel and the Israeli anti-drug authority.

REFERENCES

Achab, S., Nicolier, M., Mauny, F., Monnin, J., Trojak, B., Vandel, P., et al. (2011). Massively multiplayer online role-playing games: Comparing characteristics of addict vs non-addict online recruited gamers in a French adult population. *BMC Psychiatry, 11*, 144.

Alavi, S. S., Alaghemandan, H., Maracy, M. R., Jannatifard, F., Eslami, M., & Ferdosi, M. (2010). Impact of addiction to Internet on a number of psychiatric symptoms in students of Isfahan universities, Iran, International. *Journal of Preventive Medicine, 3*(2), 122–127.

Barke, A., Nyenhuis, N., & Kröner-Herwig, B. (2012). The German version of the Internet addiction test: A validation study. *Cyberpsychology Behavior and Social Networking, 15*(10), 534–542.

Beard, K. W. (2005). Internet addiction: A review of current assessment techniques and potential assessment questions. *Cyberpsychology and Behavior, 8*(1), 7–14.

Beranuy, F. M., Chamarro, L. A., Graner, J. C., & Carbonell, S. X. (2009). [Validation of two brief scales for Internet addiction and mobile phone problem use.]. *Psicothema, 21*(3), 480–485 [Article in Spanish].

Bernardi, S., & Pallanti, S. (2009). Internet addiction: A descriptive clinical study focusing on comorbidities and dissociative symptoms. *Comprehensive Psychiatry, 50*(6), 510–516.

Billieux, J., Chanal, J., Khazaal, Y., Rochat, L., Gay, P., Zullino, D., et al. (2011). Psychological predictors of problematic involvement in massively multiplayer online role-playing games: Illustration in a sample of male cybercafé players. *Psychopathology, 44*(3), 165–171.

Block, J. J. (2008). Issues for DSM-V: Internet addiction. *American Journal of Psychiatry, 165*, 306–307.

Brand, M., Laier, C., Pawlikowski, M., Schächtle, U., Schöler, T., & Altstötter-Gleich, C. (2011). Watching pornographic pictures on the Internet: Role of sexual arousal ratings and psychological-psychiatric symptoms for using Internet sex sites excessively. *Cyberpsychology Behavior and Social Networking, 14*(6), 371–377.

Camardese, G., De Risio, L., Di Nicola, M., Pizi, G., & Janiri, L. (2012). A role for pharmacotherapy in the treatment of "Internet addiction.". *Clinical Neuropharmacology, 35*(6), 283–289.

Campbell, A. J., Cumming, S. R., & Hughes, I. (2006). Internet use by the socially fearful: Addiction or therapy? *Cyberpsychology and Behavior, 9*(1), 69–81.

Canan, F., Ataoglu, A., Nichols, L. A., Yildirim, T., & Ozturk, O. (2010). Evaluation of psychometric properties of the Internet addiction scale in a sample of Turkish high school students. *Cyberpsychology Behavior and Social Networking, 13*(3), 317–320.

Canan, F., Ataoglu, A., Ozcetin, A., & Icmeli, C. (2012). The association between Internet addiction and dissociation among Turkish college students. *Comprehensive Psychiatry, 53*(5), 422–426.

Cao, F., Su, L., Liu, T., & Gao, X. (2007). The relationship between impulsivity and Internet addiction in a sample of Chinese adolescents. *European Psychiatry, 22*(7), 466–471.

Carli, V., Durkee, T., Wasserman, D., Hadlaczky, G., Despalins, R., Kramarz, E., et al. (2013). The association between pathological Internet use and comorbid psychopathology: A systematic review. *Psychopathology, 46*(1), 1–13 doi: 10.1159/000337971.

Cheung, L. M., & Wong, W. S. (2011). The effects of insomnia and Internet addiction on depression in Hong Kong Chinese adolescents: An exploratory cross-sectional analysis. *Journal of Sleep Research, 20*(2), 311–317.

Cho, S. C., Kim, J. W., Kim, B. N., Lee, J. H., & Kim, E. H. (2008). Biogenetic temperament and character profiles and attention deficit hyperactivity disorder symptoms in Korean adolescents with problematic Internet use. *Cyberpsychology and Behavior, 11*(6), 735–737.

Cho, S. M., Sung, M. J., Shin, K. M., Lim, K. Y., & Shin, Y. M. (2012). Does psychopathology in childhood predict Internet addiction in male adolescents? *Child Psychiatry and Human Development, 44*(4), 549–555.

Choi, K., Son, H., Park, M., Han, J., Kim, K., Lee, B., et al. (2009). Internet overuse and excessive daytime sleepiness in adolescents. *Psychiatry and Clinical Neurosciences, 63*(4), 455–462.

Chong, G. N., Isa, S. M., Hashim, A. H., Pillai, S. K., & Harbajan Singh, M. K. (2012). Validity of the Malay version of the Internet addiction test: A study on a group of medical students in Malaysia. *Asia Pacific Journal of Public Health*, [Epub ahead of print].

Christakis, D. A., Moreno, M. M., Jelenchick, L., Myaing, M. T., & Zhou, C. (2011). Problematic Internet usage in US college students: A pilot study. *BMC Medicine, 22*(9), 77.

Dalbudak, E., Evren, C., Aldemir, S., Coskun, K. S., Ugurlu, H., & Yildirim, F. G. (2013). Relationship of Internet addiction severity with depression, anxiety, and alexithymia, temperament and character in university students. *Cyberpsychology Behavior and Social Networking, 16*(4), 272–278.

De Berardis, D., D'Albenzio, A., Gambi, F., Sepede, G., Valchera, A., Conti, C. M., et al. (2009). Alexithymia and its relationships with dissociative experiences and Internet addiction in a nonclinical sample. *Cyberpsychology and Behavior, 12*(1), 67–69.

Dell'Osso, B., Altamura, C., Allen, A., Marazziti, D., & Hollander, E. (2006). Epidemiological and clinical updates on impulse control disorders: A critical review. *European Archives of Psychiatry and Clinical Neurosciences, 256*, 464–475.

Dell'Osso, B., Altamura, A. C., Hadley, S. J., Baker, B. R., & Hollander, E. (2007). An open-label trial of escitalopram in the treatment of impulsive-compulsive Internet usage disorder. *European Neuropsychopharmacology, 16*, S82–S83.

Demetrovics, Z., Szeredi, B., & Rãzsa, S. (2008). The three-factor model of Internet addiction: The development of the Problematic Internet Use Questionnaire. *Behavior Research Methods, 40*(2), 563–574.

Deng, Y. X., Hu, M., Hu, G. Q., Wang, L. S., & Sun, Z. Q. (2007). An investigation on the prevalence of Internet addiction disorder in middle school students of Hunan province. *Zhonghua Liu Xing Bing Xue Za Zhi, 28*(5), 445–448 [Article in Chinese].

Dong, G., Lu, Q., Zhou, H., & Zhao, X. (2011). Precursor or sequela: Pathological disorders in people with Internet addiction disorder. *PLoS One, 6*(2), e14703 doi: 10.1371/journal.pone.0014703.

Dong, G., Zhou, H., & Zhao, X. (2011). Male Internet addicts show impaired executive control ability: Evidence from a color-word Stroop task. *Neuroscience Letters, 499*(2), 114–118.

Du, Y. S., Jiang, W., & Vance, A. (2010). Longer term effect of randomized, controlled group cognitive behavioural therapy for Internet addiction in adolescent students in Shanghai. *Australia and New Zealand Journal of Psychiatry, 44*(2), 129–134.

Durkee, T., Kaess, M., Carli, V., Parzer, P., Wasserman, C., Floderus, B., et al. (2012). Prevalence of pathological Internet use among adolescents in Europe: Demographic and social factors. *Addiction, 107*(12), 2210–2222.

Fioravanti, G., Dèttore, D., & Casale, S. (2012). Adolescent Internet addiction: Testing the association between self-esteem, the perception of Internet attributes, and preference for online social interactions. *Cyberpsychology Behavior and Social Networking, 15*(6), 318–323.

Fisoun, V., Floros, G., Siomos, K., Geroukalis, D., & Navridis, K. (2012). Internet addiction as an important predictor in early detection of adolescent drug use experience-implications for research and practice. *Journal of Addiction Medicine, 6*(1), 77–84.

Forston, B. L., Scotti, J. R., Chen, Y. C., Malone, J., & Del Ben, K. S. (2007). Internet use, abuse, and dependence among students at a southeastern regional university. *Journal of American College Health, 56*(2), 137–144.

Fu, K. W., Chan, W. S., Wong, P. W., & Yip, P. S. (2010). Internet addiction: Prevalence, discriminant validity and correlates among adolescents in Hong Kong. *British Journal of Psychiatry, 196*(6), 486–492.

Ghamari, F., Mohammadbeigi, A., Mohammadsalehi, N., & Hashiani, A. A. (2011). Internet addiction and modeling its risk factors in medical students, Iran. *Indian Journal of Psychological Medicine, 33*(2), 158–162.

Greenfield, D. N. (1999). Psychological characteristics of compulsive Internet use: A preliminary analysis. *Cyberpsychology and Behavior, 2*(5), 403–412.

Griffiths, M. (1998). Internet addiction: Does it really exist? In J. Gackenbach (Ed.), *Psychology and the Internet* (pp. 61–75). New York: Academic Press.

Griffiths, M. (2000). Internet addiction—Time to be taken seriously? *Addiction Research, 8*, 413–418.

Grusser, S. M., Thalemann, R., Albrecht, U., & Thalemann, C. N. (2005). [Excessive computer usage in adolescents—Results of a psychometric evaluation.]. *Wien Klinische Wochenschrift, 117*(5–6), 188–195 [Article in German].

Guo, J., Chen, L., Wang, X., Liu, Y., Chui, C. H., He, H., et al. (2012). The relationship between Internet addiction and depression among migrant children and left-behind children in China. *Cyberpsychology Behavior and Social Networking, 15*(11), 585–590.

Ha, J. H., Kim, S. Y., Bae, S. C., Bae, S., Kim, H., Sim, M., et al. (2007). Depression and Internet addiction in adolescents. *Psychopathology, 40*(6), 424–430.

Han, D., Lee, Y., Na, C., Ahn, J., Chung, U., Daniels, M., et al. (2009). The effect of methylphenidate on Internet video game play in children with attention-deficit/hyperactivity disorder. *Comprehensive Psychiatry, 50*(3), 251–256.

Han, D. H., Hwang, J. W., & Renshaw, P. F. (2010). Bupropion sustained release treatment decreases craving for video games and cue-induced brain activity in patients with Internet video game addiction. *Experimental and Clinical Psychopharmacology, 18*(4), 297–304.

Han, D. H., & Renshaw, P. F. (2012). Bupropion in the treatment of problematic online game play in patients with major depressive disorder. *Journal of Psychopharmacology, 26*(5), 689–696.

Israelashvili, M., Kim, T., & Bukobza, G. (2012). Adolescents' over-use of the cyber world—Internet addiction or identity exploration? *Journal of Adolescence, 35*(2), 417–424.

Jang, K. S., Hwang, S. Y., & Choi, J. Y. (2008). Internet addiction and psychiatric symptoms among Korean adolescents. *Journal of School Health, 78*(3), 165–171.

Jang, M. H., & Ji, E. S. (2012). Gender differences in associations between parental problem drinking and early adolescents' Internet addiction. *Journal of Specialists in Pediatric Nursing, 17*(4), 288–300.

Jelenchick, L. A., Becker, T., & Moreno, M. A. (2012). Assessing the psychometric properties of the Internet Addiction Test (IAT) in US college students. *Psychiatry Research, 196*(2–3), 296–301.

June, K. J., Sohn, S. Y., So, A. Y., Yi, G. M., & Park, S. H. (2007). [A study of factors that influence Internet addiction, smoking, and drinking in high school students. *Taehan Kanho Hakhoe Chi[, 37*(6), 872–882 [Article in Korean].

Kalke, J., & Raschke, P. (2004). Learning by doing: 'initiated abstinence', a school-based programme for the prevention of addiction. Results of an evaluation study. *European Addiction Research, 10*(2), 88–94.

Khazaal, Y., Chatton, A., Horn, A., Achab, S., Thorens, G., Zullino, D., et al. (2012). French validation of the compulsive Internet use scale (CIUS). *Psychiatric Quarterly, 83*(4), 397–405.

Kim, K., Ryu, E., Chon, M. Y., Yeun, E. J., Choi, S. Y., Seo, J. S., et al. (2006). Internet addiction in Korean adolescents and its relation to depression and suicidal ideation: A questionnaire survey. *International Journal of Nursing Studies, 43*(2), 185–192.

King, D. L., Delfabbro, P. H., Griffiths, M. D., & Gradisar, M. (2011). Assessing clinical trials of Internet addiction treatment: A systematic review and CONSORT evaluation. *Clinical Psychology Review, 31*(7), 1110–1116.

Ko, C. H., Hsiao, S., Liu, G. C., Yen, J. U., Yang, M. J., & Yen, C. F. (2010). The characteristics of decision making, potential to take risks, and personality of college students with Internet addiction. *Psychiatry Research, 170*(1–2), 121–125.

Ko, C. H., Yen, J. Y., Chen, C. C., Chen, S. H., Wu, K., & Yen, C. F. (2006). Tridimensional personality of adolescents with Internet addiction and substance use experience. *Canadian Journal of Psychiatry, 51*(14), 887–894.

Ko, C. H., Yen, J. Y., Yen, C. F., Chen, C. S., Weng, C. C., & Chen, C. C. (2008). The association between Internet addiction and problematic alcohol use in adolescents: The problem behavior model. *Cyberpsychology and Behavior, 11*(5), 571–576.

Korkeila, J., Kaarlas, S., Jaaskelainen, M., Vahlberg, T., & Taiminen, T. (2009). Attached to the web—Harmful use of the Internet and its correlates. *European Psychiatry, 25*, 236–241.

Kormas, G., Critselis, E., Janikian, M., Kafetzis, D., & Tsitsika, A. (2011). Risk factors and psychosocial characteristics of potential problematic and problematic Internet use among adolescents: A cross-sectional study. *BMC Public Health, 11*, 595.

Kratzer, S., & Hegerl, U. (2008). [Is "Internet Addiction" a disorder of its own? A study on subjects with excessive Internet use.]. *Psychiatriche Praxis, 35*(2), 80–83 [Article in German].

Kuss, D. J., & Griffiths, M. D. (2011). Online social networking and addiction—A review of the psychological literature. *International Journal of Environmental Research in Public Health, 8*(9), 3528–3552.

Kwon, J. H., Chung, C. S., & Lee, J. (2011). The effects of escape from self and interpersonal relationship on the pathological use of Internet games. *Community Mental Health Journal, 47*, 113–121.

Lam, L. T., Peng, Z. W., Mai, J. C., & Jing, J. (2009). Factors associated with Internet addiction among adolescents. *Cyberpsychology and Behavior, 12*(5), 551–555.

Lee, B. W., & Stapinski, L. A. (2012). Seeking safety on the Internet: Relationship between social anxiety and problematic Internet use. *Journal of Anxiety Disorders, 26*(1), 197–205.

Li, D., Liau, A., & Khoo, A. (2011). Examining the influence of actual-ideal self-discrepancies, depression, and escapism, on pathological gaming among massively multiplayer online adolescent gamers. *Cyberpsychology Behavior and Social Networking, 14*(9), 535–539.

Liberatore, K. A., Rosario, K., Colón-De Martí, L. N., & Martínez, K. G. (2011). Prevalence of Internet addiction in Latino adolescents with psychiatric diagnosis. *Cyberpsychology Behavior and Social Networking, 14*(6), 399–402.

Lin, M. P., Ko, H. C., & Wu, J. Y. (2011). Prevalence and psychosocial risk factors associated with Internet addiction in a nationally representative sample of college students in Taiwan. *Cyberpsychology Behavior and Social Networking, 14*(12), 741–746.

Liu, C. Y., & Kuo, F. Y. (2007). A study of Internet addiction through the lens of the interpersonal theory. *Cyberpsychology Behavior, 10*(6), 799–804.

Mazhari, S. (2012). Association between problematic Internet use and impulse control disorders among Iranian university students. *Cyberpsychology Behavior and Social Networking, 15*(5), 270–273.

Meerkerk, G. J., Van Den Eijnden, R. J., Vermulst, A. A., & Garretsen, H. F. (2009). The Compulsive Internet Use Scale (CIUS): Some psychometric properties. *Cyberpsychology and Behavior, 12*(1), 1–6.

Mehroof, M., & Griffiths, M. D. (2010). Online gaming addiction: The role of sensation seeking, self-control, neuroticism, aggression, state anxiety, and trait anxiety. *Cyberpsychology Behavior and Social Networking, 13*(3), 313–316.

Milani, L., Osualdella, D., & Di Blasio, P. (2009). Quality of interpersonal relationships and problematic Internet use in adolescence. *Cyberpsychology and Behavior, 12*(6), 681–684.

Mittal, V. A., Dean, D. J., & Pelletier, A. (2012). Internet addiction, reality substitution and longitudinal changes in psychotic-like experiences in young adults. *Early Intervention in Psychiatry*, 7(3), 261–269.

Moreno, M. A., Jelenchick, L., Cox, E., Young, H., & Christakis, D. A. (2011). Problematic Internet use among US youth: A systematic review. *Archives of Pediatric and Adolescent Medicine, 165*(9), 797–805.

Morrison, C. M., & Gore, H. (2010). The relationship between excessive Internet use and depression: A questionnaire-based study of 1,319 young people and adults. *Psychopathology, 43*(2), 121–126.

Mottram, A. J., & Fleming, M. J. (2009). Extraversion, impulsivity, and online group membership as predictors of problematic Internet use. *Cyberpsychology and Behavior, 12*(3), 319–321.

Ni, X., Yan, H., Chen, S., & Liu, Z. (2009). Factors influencing Internet addiction in a sample of freshmen university students in China. *Cyberpsychology and Behavior, 12*(3), 327–330.

Nichols, L. A., & Nicki, R. (2004). Development of a psychometrically sound Internet addiction scale: A preliminary step. *Psychology of Addictive Behaviors, 18*(4), 381–384.

Niemz, K., Griffiths, M., & Banyard, P. (2005). Prevalence of pathological Internet use among university students and correlations with self-esteem, the General Health Questionnaire (GHQ) and disinhibition. *Cyberpsychology and Behavior, 8*(6), 562–570.

Pallanti, S., Bernardi, S., & Quercioli, L. (2006). The Shorter PROMIS Questionnaire and the Internet Addiction Scale in the assessment of multiple addictions in a high-school population: Prevalence and related disability. *CNS Spectrum, 11*(12), 966–974.

Park, J. W., Park, K. H., Lee, I. J., Kwon, M., & Kim, D. J. (2012). Standardization study of Internet addiction improvement motivation scale. *Psychiatry Investigations, 9*(4), 373–378.

Park, M. H., Park, E. J., Choi, J., Chai, S., Lee, J. H., Lee, C., et al. (2011). Preliminary study of Internet addiction and cognitive function in adolescents based on IQ tests. *Psychiatry Research, 190*(2–3), 275–281.

Park, S. K., Kim, J. Y., & Cho, C. B. (2008). Prevalence of Internet addiction and correlations with family factors among South Korean adolescents. *Adolescence, 43*(172), 895–909.

Petersen, K. U., Weymann, N., Schelb, Y., Thiel, R., & Thomasius, R. (2009). Pathological Internet use—epidemiology, diagnostics, co-occurring disorders and treatment. *Fortschritte der Neurologie Psychiatrie*, 77(5), 263–271 [Article in German].

Poli, R., & Agrimi, E. (2012). Internet addiction disorder: Prevalence in an Italian student population. *Nordic Journal of Psychiatry*, *66*(1), 55–59.

Rodgers, R. F., Melioli, T., Laconi, S., Bui, E., & Chabrol, H. (2013). Internet addiction symptoms, disordered eating, and body image avoidance. *Cyberpsychology Behavior and Social Networking*, *16*(1), 56–60.

Ross, M. W., Månsson, S. A., & Daneback, K. (2012). Prevalence, severity, and correlates of problematic sexual Internet use in Swedish men and women. *Archives of Sexual Behavior*, *41*(2), 459–466.

Seo, M., Kang, H. S., & Yom, Y. H. (2009). Internet addiction and interpersonal problems in Korean adolescents. *Computers Informatics Nursing*, *27*(4), 226–233.

Shaw, M., & Black, D. W. (2008). Internet addiction: Definition, assessment, epidemiology and clinical management. *CNS Drugs*, *22*(5), 353–365.

Shek, D. T., Tang, V. M., & Lo, C. Y. (2009). Evaluation of an Internet addiction treatment program for Chinese adolescents in Hong Kong. *Adolescence*, *44*(174), 359–373.

Shi, J., Chen, Z., & Tian, M. (2011). Internet self-efficacy, the need for cognition, and sensation seeking as predictors of problematic use of the Internet. *Cyberpsychology Behavior and Social Networking*, *14*(4), 231–234.

Shin, S. E., Kim, N. S., & Jang, E. Y. (2011). Comparison of problematic Internet and alcohol use and attachment styles among industrial workers in Korea. *Cyberpsychology Behavior and Social Networking*, *14*(11), 665–672.

Southern, S. (2008). Treatment of compulsive cybersex behavior. *Psychiatric Clinics of North America*, *31*(4), 697–712.

Stieger, S., & Burger, C. (2010). Implicit and explicit self-esteem in the context of Internet addiction. *Cyberpsychology Behavior and Social Networking*, *13*(6), 681–688.

Sun, D. L., Chen, Z. J., Ma, N., Zhang, X. C., Fu, X. M., & Zhang, D. R. (2009). Decision-making and prepotent response inhibition functions in excessive Internet users. *CNS Spectrum*, *14*(2), 75–81.

Tao, R., Huang, X., Wang, J., Zhang, H., Zhang, Y., & Li, M. (2010). Proposed diagnostic criteria for Internet addiction. *Addiction*, *105*, 556–564.

te Wildt, B. T., Putzig, I., Zedler, M., & Ohlmeier, M. D. (2007). Internet dependency as a symptom of depressive mood disorders. *Psychiatrische Praxis*, *34*(Suppl. 3), S318–S322 [Article in German].

Tosun, L. P., & Lajunen, T. (2009). Why do young adults develop a passion for Internet activities? The associations among personality, revealing "true self" on the Internet, and passion for the Internet. *Cyberpsychology and Behavior*, *12*(4), 401–406.

Tsai, H. F., Cheng, S. H., Yeh, T. L., Shih, C. C., Chen, K. C., Yang, Y. C., et al. (2009). The risk factors of Internet addiction—A survey of university freshmen. *Psychiatry Research*, *167*(3), 294–299.

Tsitsika, A., Critselis, E., Kormas, G., Filippopoulou, A., Tounissidou, D., Freskou, A., et al. (2009). Internet use and misuse: A multivariate regression analysis of the predictive factors of Internet use among Greek adolescents. *European Journal of Pediatrics*, *168*(6), 655–665.

Tsitsika, A., Critselis, E., Louizou, A., Janikian, M., Freskou, A., Marangou, E., et al. (2011). Determinants of Internet addiction among adolescents: A case-control study. *Scientific World Journal*, *11*, 866–874.

Wang, H., Zhou, X., Lu, C., Wu, J., Deng, X., & Hong, L. (2011). Problematic Internet use in high school students in Guangdong Province, China. *PLoS One*, *6*(5), e19660.

Wei, H. T., Chen, M. H., Huang, P. C., & Bai, Y. M. (2012). The association between online gaming, social phobia, and depression: An Internet survey. *BMC Psychiatry*, *12*, 92.

Whang, L. S., Lee, S., & Chang, G. (2003). Internet over-users' psychological profiles: A behavior sampling analysis on Internet addiction. *Cyberpsychology and Behavior, 6*(2), 143–150.

Widyanto, L., Griffiths, M. D., & Brunsden, V. (2011). A psychometric comparison of the Internet Addiction Test, the Internet-Related Problem Scale, and self-diagnosis. *Cyberpsychology Behavior and Social Networking, 14*(3), 141–149.

Widyanto, L., & McMurran, M. (2004). The psychometric properties of the Internet addiction test. *Cyberpsychology and Behavior, 7*(4), 443–450.

Winkler, A., Dörsing, B., Rief, W., Shen, Y., & Glombiewski, J. A. (2013). Treatment of Internet addiction: A meta-analysis. *Clinical Psychology Review, 33*(2), 317–329.

Woelfling, K., Buhler, M., Lemenager, T., Mairsen, C., & Mann, K. (2009). Gambling and Internet addiction: Review and research agenda. *Der Nervenarzt, 80*(9), 1030–1039 [Article in German].

Xiuqin, H., Huimin, Z., Mengchen, L., Jinan, W., Ying, Z., & Ran, T. (2010). Mental health, personality, and parental rearing styles of adolescents with Internet addiction disorder. *Cyberpsychology Behavior and Social Networking, 13*(4), 401–406.

Xu, J., Shen, L. X., Yan, C. H., Hu, H., Yang, F., Wang, L., et al. (2012). Personal characteristics related to the risk of adolescent Internet addiction: A survey in Shanghai, China. *BMC Public Health, 12*(1), 1106.

Yates, T. M., Gregor, M. A., & Haviland, M. G. (2012). Child maltreatment, alexithymia, and problematic Internet use in young adulthood. *Cyberpsychology Behavior and Social Networking, 15*(4), 219–225.

Yellowlees, P. M., & Marks, S. (2007). Problematic Internet use or Internet addiction? *Computers in Human Behavior, 23*(3), 1447–1453.

Yen, C. F., Ko, C. H., Yen, J. Y., Chang, Y. P., & Cheng, C. P. (2009). Multi-dimensional discriminative factors for Internet addiction among adolescents regarding gender and age. *Psychiatry and Clinical Neurosciences, 63*(3), 357–364.

Yen, J. Y., Ko, C. H., Yen, C. F., Chen, C. S., & Chen, C. C. (2009). The association between harmful alcohol use and Internet addiction among college students: Comparison of personality. *Psychiatry and Clinical Neurosciences, 63*(2), 218–224.

Yen, J. Y., Ko, C. H., Yen, C. F., Wu, H. Y., & Yang, M. J. (2007). The comorbid psychiatric symptoms of Internet addiction: Attention deficit and hyperactivity disorder (ADHD), depression, social phobia, and hostility. *Journal of Adolescent Health, 41*(1), 93–98.

Yen, J. Y., Yen, C. F., Chen, C. S., Tang, T. C., & Ko, C. H. (2009). The association between adult ADHD symptoms and Internet addiction among college students: The gender difference. *Cyberpsychology Behavior, 12*(2), 187–191.

Young, K. S. (1998). *Caught in the Net*. New York: John Wiley & Sons. http://netaddiction.com/Internet-addiction-test/.

Young, K. S. (2004). Internet addiction: A new clinical phenomenon and its consequences. *American Behavioral Scientist, 48*(4), 402–415.

Young, K. S. (2007). Cognitive behavior therapy with Internet addicts: Treatment outcomes and implications. *Cyberpsychology Behavior, 10*(5), 671–679.

Zanetta, D. .F., Zermatten, A., Billieux, J., Thorens, G., Bondolfi, G., Zullino, D., et al. (2011). Motivations to play specifically predict excessive involvement in massively multiplayer online role-playing games: Evidence from an online survey. *European Addiction Research, 17*(4), 185–189.

Zhou, Z., Yuan, G., & Yao, J. (2012). Cognitive biases toward Internet game-related pictures and executive deficits in individuals with an Internet game addiction. *PLoS One*, 7(11), e48961.

Zhu, T. M., Li, H., Jin, R. J., Zheng, Z., Luo, Y., Ye, H., et al. (2012). Effects of electroacupuncture combined psycho-intervention on cognitive function and event-related potentials P300 and mismatch negativity in patients with Internet addiction. *Chinese Journal of Integrative Medicine, 18*(2), 146–151.

APPENDIX 5-1 INTERNET ADDICTION TEST (IAT)

Dr. Kimberly Young

The Internet Addiction Test (IAT) is a reliable and valid measure of addictive use of the Internet, developed by Dr. Kimberly Young. It consists of 20 items that measures mild, moderate, and severe level of Internet addiction.

To begin, answer the following questions by using this scale:

0	Does not apply
1	Rarely
2	Occasionally
3	Frequently
4	Often
5	Always

	Question	Scale					
1	How often do you find that you stay on-line longer than you intended?	1	2	3	4	5	0
2	How often do you neglect household chores to spend more time on-line?	1	2	3	4	5	0
3	How often do you prefer the excitement of the Internet to intimacy with your partner?	1	2	3	4	5	0
4	How often do you form new relationships with fellow on-line users?	1	2	3	4	5	0
5	How often do others in your life complain to you about the amount of time you spend on-line?	1	2	3	4	5	0
6	How often do your grades or school work suffer because of the amount of time you spend on-line?	1	2	3	4	5	0
7	How often do you check your e-mail before something else that you need to do?	1	2	3	4	5	0
8	How often does your job performance or productivity suffer because of the Internet?	1	2	3	4	5	0
9	How often do you become defensive or secretive when anyone asks you what you do on-line?	1	2	3	4	5	0
10	How often do you block out disturbing thoughts about your life with soothing thoughts of the Internet?	1	2	3	4	5	0
11	How often do you find yourself anticipating when you will go on-line again?	1	2	3	4	5	0
12	How often do you fear that life without the Internet would be boring, empty, and joyless?	1	2	3	4	5	0
13	How often do you snap, yell, or act annoyed if someone bothers you while you are on-line?	1	2	3	4	5	0
14	How often do you lose sleep due to late-night log-ins?	1	2	3	4	5	0
15	How often do you feel preoccupied with the Internet when off-line, or fantasize about being on-line?	1	2	3	4	5	0
16	How often do you find yourself saying "just a few more minutes" when on-line?	1	2	3	4	5	0
17	How often do you try to cut down the amount of time you spend on-line and fail?	1	2	3	4	5	0
18	How often do you try to hide how long you've been on-line?	1	2	3	4	5	0
19	How often do you choose to spend more time on-line over going out with others?	1	2	3	4	5	0
20	How often do you feel depressed, moody or nervous when you are off-line, which goes away once you are back on-line?	1	2	3	4	5	0

Total the scores for each item. The higher your score, the greater level of addiction is.

20–49 points:

You are an average online user. You may surf the Web a bit too long at times, but you have control over your usage.

50–79 points:

You are experiencing occasional or frequent problems because of the Internet. You should consider their full impact on your life.

80–100 points:

Your Internet usage is causing significant problems in your life. You should evaluate the impact of the Internet on your life and address the problems directly caused by your Internet usage.

Prepared and posted by Dayu Internet Overuse Solution, the solution for Internet overuse and online addiction. An online version is available at http://www.internetoveruse.com/?p=171

Social Networking Addiction: An Overview of Preliminary Findings

Mark D. Griffiths[1], Daria J. Kuss[1], Zsolt Demetrovics[2]
[1]International Gaming Research Unit, Psychology Division, Nottingham Trent University, Nottingham, UK,
[2]Department of Clinical Psychology and Addiction, Institute of Psychology, Eötvös Loránd University, Budapest, Hungary

BRIEF HISTORY OF SOCIAL NETWORKING

Social networking sites (SNSs) are virtual communities where users can create individual public profiles, interact with real-life friends, and meet other people based on shared interests (Kuss & Griffiths, 2011). According to Boyd and Ellison (2008), SNSs are web-based services that allow individuals to (1) construct a public or semipublic profile within a bounded system, (2) articulate a list of other users with whom they share a connection, and (3) view and traverse their list of connections and those made by others within the system.

In terms of SNS history, the first social networking site (i.e., *SixDegrees*) was launched in 1997, based on the idea that everybody is linked with everybody else via six degrees of separation (Boyd & Ellison, 2008), and initially referred to as the "small world problem" (Milgram, 1967). In 2004, the most successful current SNS (i.e., Facebook) was established as a closed virtual community for Harvard students. The site expanded very quickly, and Facebook currently has more than 1.19 billion users, of whom 50% log on daily (Protalinski, 2013).

SNS usage patterns from both consumer research and empirical research indicate that overall, regular SNS use has increased substantially over the last few years (Kuss & Griffiths, 2011). This supports the availability hypothesis that where there is increased access and opportunity to engage in an activity (in this case SNSs), there is an increase in the numbers of people who engage in the activity (Griffiths, 2003). Research also indicates that compared to the general population, teenagers and students make the most use of SNSs (Kuss & Griffiths, 2011).

SNSs are predominantly used for social purposes, mostly related to the maintenance of established offline networks, relative to individual ones

Behavioral Addictions
http://dx.doi.org/10.1016/B978-0-12-407724-9.00006-9

(Kuss & Griffiths, 2011). However, recent evidence suggests that individuals may feel compelled to maintain their online social networks in a way that may, in some circumstances, lead to using SNSs excessively. The maintenance of already established offline networks itself can therefore be seen as an attraction factor, which according to Sussman et al. (2011) is related to the etiology of specific addictions. For instance, a number of addictive behaviors (e.g., alcoholism, video game addiction) may be maintained and hard to break because of the social ties that the addict has with others that engage in the activity (Griffiths, 1996).

In addition to presenting the risks and downsides of social networking, it should also be noted that the phenomenon itself might have developed along basic evolutionary drives. Humans as social beings have always lived in a community throughout evolution (i.e., a small and closed community offering security). However, with greater rates of migration to cities, these small, traditional communities declined, and in recent decades a whole new, more individualized way of life has been formed. However, the need for a secure and predictable community life that has evolved over millions of years has not changed. For this reason, human beings who have lost their traditional small communities make various attempts to compensate for this loss and among these (in addition to sports, hobbies, and many other social activities), one can find social networking activities. SNSs provide a means of secure and predictable communal space, which is in many aspects similar to the communal spaces of traditional communities (such as modern pubs or bars), where one can meet familiar faces with whom there is a possibility to share experiences as well as to live the experience of being a part of the community.

Many organizational employers have claimed that social networking addiction may be a concern, particularly among young people. For instance, in a survey of 120 youth work managers and practitioners, Davies and Cranston (2008) reported that their participants feared that use of online social networking displaces other activities and face-to-face social interaction. When asked to identify specific risks relating to online social networking, 23% reported addiction as being a concern, with other risks being bullying (53%), disclosing personal information (35%), and sexual predators (22%).

In many areas of behavioral addiction, there has been debate about whether some excessive behaviors should even be considered as genuine addictions (e.g., video games, Internet use, sex, exercise) and the same debate holds for addiction to social networking. Griffiths (2005) has operationally defined addictive behavior as any behavior that features what he believes are the six core components of addiction (i.e., salience, mood modification, tolerance, withdrawal symptoms, conflict, and relapse). Griffiths argues that any behavior (e.g., social networking) that fulfills these six criteria can be operationally defined as an addiction. In relation to social networking, the six components are as follows:

- *Salience*—This occurs when social networking becomes the single most important activity in a person's life and dominates his or her thinking (preoccupations and cognitive distortions), feelings (cravings), and behavior (deterioration of socialized behavior). For instance, even if people are not actually engaged in social networking, they will be constantly thinking about the next time that they will be (i.e., a total preoccupation with social networking).
- *Mood modification*—This refers to the subjective experiences that people report as a consequence of social networking and can be seen as a coping strategy (i.e., they experience an arousing "buzz" or a "high" or, paradoxically, a tranquilizing feeling of "escape" or "numbing").
- *Tolerance*—This is the process whereby increasing amounts of social networking activity are required to achieve the former mood-modifying effects. This basically means that for people engaged in social networking, they gradually build up the amount of the time they spend social networking every day.
- *Withdrawal symptoms*—These are the unpleasant feeling states and/or physical effects (e.g., the shakes, moodiness, irritability) that occur when people are unable to engage in social networking because they are ill, on vacation, etc.
- *Conflict*—This refers to the conflicts between a person and those around that person (interpersonal conflict), conflicts with other activities (social life, hobbies, and interests), or from within the individual him- or herself (intrapsychic conflict and/or subjective feelings of loss of control) that are concerned with spending too much time social networking.
- *Relapse*—This is the tendency for repeated reversions to earlier patterns of excessive social networking to recur and for even the most extreme patterns typical of the height of excessive social networking to be quickly restored after periods of control.

It should also be noted that Griffiths (2010a) asserts that excessive use of an activity (e.g., social networking) does not necessarily equate with addiction, as he has published case studies of excessive Internet users (i.e., up to 14 hours a day) who have few negative consequences in their lives (i.e., the time spent engaged in an activity does not always mean that it is problematic and/or addictive). Furthermore, Griffiths has also pointed out on numerous occasions (e.g., 2000; Widyanto & Griffiths, 2006) that there is a fundamental difference between addictions *to* the Internet and addictions *on* the Internet.

ETIOLOGY AND THEORIES OF SOCIAL NETWORKING ADDICTION

Researchers have suggested that the excessive use of new technologies (and especially online social networking) may be particularly problematic to young people (Echeburua & de Corral, 2010). In accordance with the biopsychosocial framework for the etiology of addictions (Griffiths, 2005) and the syndrome model of addiction (Shaffer, et al., 2004), it is claimed that those people addicted to using SNSs experience symptoms similar to those experienced by individuals who suffer from addictions to substances or other behaviors (Echeburua & de Corral, 2010). This has significant implications for clinical practice because unlike treatment for other addictions, the goal of SNS addiction treatment cannot be total abstinence from using the Internet *per se,* as it is an integral element of today's professional and leisure culture (Kuss & Griffiths, 2011). Instead, the ultimate therapy aim is controlled use of the Internet and its respective functions, particularly social networking applications, and relapse prevention using strategies developed within cognitive-behavioral therapies (Echeburua & de Corral, 2010). Additionally, some researchers have hypothesized that young vulnerable people with narcissistic tendencies are particularly prone to engaging with SNSs in an addictive way (La Barbera, La Paglia, & Valsavoia, 2009). More specifically, the structural characteristics of these Internet applications, (i.e., their egocentric construction) appear to allow favorable self-disclosure that draws narcissists to use it.

To explain the formation of SNS addiction, Turel and Serenko (2012) summarized three overarching theoretical perspectives that may not be mutually exclusive:

- *Cognitive-behavioral model*—This model emphasizes that "abnormal" social networking arises from maladaptive cognitions and is amplified by various environmental factors, and eventually leads to compulsive and/or addictive social networking.
- *Social skill model*—This model emphasizes that "abnormal" social networking arises because people lack self-presentational skills and prefer virtual communication to face-to-face interactions, and it eventually leads to compulsive and/or addictive use of social networking.

- *Socio-cognitive model*—This model emphasizes that "abnormal" social networking arises due to the expectation of positive outcomes, combined with Internet self-efficacy and deficient Internet self-regulation, and it eventually leads to compulsive and/or addictive social networking behavior.

Based on these three models, Xu and Tan (2012) suggest that the transition from normal to problematic social networking use occurs when social networking is viewed by the individual as an important (or even exclusive) mechanism to relieve stress, loneliness, or depression. They contend that those who frequently engage in social networking are poor at socializing in real life. For these people, social media use provides such people continuous rewards (e.g. self-efficacy, satisfaction), and they end up engaging in the activity more and more, eventually leading to many problems (e.g., ignoring real-life relationships, work/educational conflicts). The resulting problems may then exacerbate individuals' undesirable moods. This then leads such individuals to engage in the social networking behavior even more as a way of relieving dysphoric mood states. Consequently, when social network users repeat this cyclical pattern of relieving undesirable moods with social media use, the level of psychological dependency on social networking increases.

The rapid rise of online social networking—particularly in relation to the increasing amounts of time people spend online—has led some to claim that excessive SNS use may be addictive to some individuals (Kuss & Griffiths, 2011). Online, individuals engage in a variety of activities, some of which have the potential to be addictive, including the potentially excessive use of SNSs. Rather than becoming addicted to the medium *per se,* a minority of Internet users may develop an addiction to specific online activities (Griffiths, 2000). Young (1999) has argued that there are five different types of Internet addiction, namely *computer addiction* (i.e., computer game addiction), *information overload* (i.e., Web surfing addiction), *net compulsions* (i.e., online gambling or online shopping addiction), *cybersexual addiction* (i.e., online pornography or online sex addiction), and *cyber-relationship addiction* (i.e., an addiction to online relationships).

Social networking addiction arguably falls into the cyber-relationship addiction category of Young's typology given that the primary purpose and main motivation to use SNSs is to establish and maintain both online and offline relationships. However, it is worth noting that if social networking addiction is a cyber-relationship addiction, then it does not include activities such as playing *Farmville* on Facebook (Griffiths, 2012b). In such typologies, playing *Farmville* would be classed by Griffiths (2010b) as a gaming addiction rather than "Facebook addiction." Any further development of the Facebook addiction scales (discussed later) need to take this distinction into account.

Kuss and Griffiths (2011) argue that from a clinical psychologist's perspective, it may be plausible to speak specifically of "Facebook Addiction Disorder" (or more generally "SNS Addiction Disorder") because addiction criteria, such as neglect of personal life, mental preoccupation, escapism, mood-modifying experiences, tolerance, and concealment of the addictive behavior, appear to be present in some people who use SNSs excessively.

A behavioral addiction such as SNS addiction may thus be seen from a biopsychosocial perspective (Demetrovics & Griffiths, 2012; Griffiths, 2005). Just as with substance-related addictions, it would appear that in some individuals, SNS addiction incorporates the experience of the "classic" addiction symptoms, namely mood modification (i.e., engagement in SNSs leads to a favorable change in emotional states), salience (i.e., behavioral, cognitive, and emotional preoccupation with the SNS usage), tolerance (i.e., ever increasing use of SNSs over time), withdrawal symptoms (i.e., experiencing unpleasant physical and emotional symptoms when SNS use is restricted or stopped), conflict (i.e., interpersonal and intrapsychic problems ensue because of SNS usage), and relapse (i.e., addicts quickly revert back to their excessive SNS usage after an abstinence period).

It is generally accepted that a combination of biological, psychological, and social factors contributes to the etiology of addictions (Griffiths, 2005; Shaffer, LaPlante, LaBrie, et al., 2004) that may also hold true for SNS addiction. From this it follows that SNS addiction shares a common underlying etiological framework with other substance-related and behavioral addictions. However, due to the fact that the engagement in SNSs is different in terms of the actual expression of (Internet) addiction (i.e., pathological use of SNSs rather than other Internet applications), the phenomenon may be worthy of individual consideration, particularly when considering the potentially detrimental effects of both substance-related and behavioral addictions on individuals who experience a variety of negative consequences because of their addiction (American Psychiatric Association, 2000).

EPIDEMIOLOGY: EMPIRICAL STUDIES OF SOCIAL NETWORKING ADDICTION

To date, research into social networking addiction has been relatively sparse. Empirical studies into the behavior fall into one of four types: (1) self-perception studies of social networking addiction, (2) studies of social networking addiction utilizing a social networking addiction scale, (3) studies examining the relationship between social networking and other online addictions, and (4) studies examining social networking addiction and interpersonal relationships. Each of these is very briefly examined in turn.

Self-Perception Studies of Social Networking Addiction

A study by Machold et al. (2012) examined general patterns of Internet usage among 474 young Irish teenagers (aged 11–16 years) and also attempted to identify potential online hazards, including overuse and addiction. Approximately three-quarters of the sample (72%) reported frequent social networking, with most of these being Facebook users (95%). A third of the sample (33%) felt they engaged in social networking too often.

Cha (2010) explored the factors that affect the use of SNSs and focused on two dimensions of SNS use: frequency (i.e., how often people use SNSs) and amount (i.e., how much time people spend on social networks). The study surveyed 251 college students (mean age 20.5 years) of which 98% used at least one SNS. Using regression analyses, Cha found that (1) sites with increased interpersonal utility, (2) perceived easy use, (3) having fewer privacy concerns, and (4) being a younger age predicted the frequency of SNS use. The time spent on SNSs was best predicted by (1) sites with increased interpersonal utility, (2) social networking as form of escape, and (3) having increased Internet experience. Therefore, the strongest determinant for both frequency and amount of SNS use was the interpersonal utility motive.

Cabral (2011) surveyed 313 social media users (most aged 16–30 years). Over 98% of the sample used Facebook and 34% used Twitter. Two-thirds of the sample (64%) spent between 30 and 90 minutes on social media a day (with 10% spending over 2 hours a day). Over half of the participants (59%) claimed they felt that they were addicted to social media. Other findings relating to potential indicators of addiction symptoms indicated that 39% spent more time on social media than intended (i.e., tolerance); 80% checked social media sites often/very often (i.e., salience); 23% claimed they sometimes felt stressed out, disconnected, or paranoid when unable to access social media sites (i.e., withdrawal); and 17% often tried to cut down the amount of social media use but failed (i.e., relapse).

Olowu and Seri (2012) carried out a study of social networking behavior among 884 Nigerian university students (aged 16–30 years). Results indicated that 304 participants (34%) claimed to use social networks very often. The majority (64%) strongly agreed that they had an inability to stop using social network sites, and 25% said they "very often" overspent time on SNSs. A significant minority (21%) said they were very often agitated if unable to use social networks, and a slightly larger number (27%) strongly agreed that they were addicted to social networking. All of the studies in this section have severe methodological weaknesses particularly as they rely on self-report data, small sample sizes, and convenience sampling. Furthermore, none of these self-perception studies actually measured social networking addiction because no assessment scale was actually used. Additionally, some of the studies (e.g., Oluwu & Seri, 2012) did not even carry out basic statistical significance testing.

Studies of Social Networking Addiction Utilizing a Social Networking Addiction Scale

Pelling and White (2009) surveyed 233 undergraduate university students (64% females, mean age = 19 years) using a prospective design in order to predict high-level use intentions and actual high-level usage of SNSs via an extended model of the theory of planned behavior (TPB). High-level usage was defined as using SNSs at least four times per day. TPB variables included measures of intention for usage, attitude, subjective norm, and perceived behavioral control (PBC). Furthermore, self-identity, belongingness, and past and potential future usage of SNSs were investigated. Results indicated that past behavior, subjective norm, attitude, and self-identity significantly predicted both behavioral intention as well as actual behavior. Those who identified themselves as SNS users and those who looked for a sense of belongingness on SNSs appeared to be at risk for developing an addiction to SNSs.

Wan (2009) assessed SNS addiction in a sample of 335 Chinese college students aged 19–28 years also using the Internet Addiction Test (Young, 1998) modified to specifically assess the addiction to a common Chinese SNS, namely *Xiaonei.com*. Users were classified as addicted when they endorsed five or more of the eight IAT items. Wan assessed loneliness, user gratifications (based on the results of a previous focus group interview), usage attributes, and patterns of SNS website use. The results indicated that of the total sample, 34% were classified as addicted. Moreover, loneliness significantly and positively correlated with frequency and session length of using *Xiaonei.com* as well as SNS addiction. Social activities (such as having online conversations) and relationship building (i.e., making lots of friends online) were found to predict SNS addiction.

Wilson, Fornasier, and White (2010) surveyed an Australian university student sample of 201 participants (76% female, mean age = 19 years) to assess personality factors via the short version of the NEO Personality Inventory (Costa & McCrae, 1992), time spent using SNSs, and an Addictive Tendencies Scale (based on both Ehrenberg, et al., [2008] and Walsh,

White, & Young, [2007]). The Addictive Tendencies Scale included three items measuring salience, loss of control, and withdrawal. The results of a multiple regression analysis indicated that high extraversion and low conscientiousness scores significantly predicted both addictive tendencies and the time spent using an SNS. The researchers suggested that the relationship between extraversion and addictive tendencies could be explained by the fact that using SNSs satisfies the extraverts' need to socialize. The findings with regards to lack of conscientiousness appear to be in line with previous research on the frequency of general Internet use in that people who score low on conscientiousness tend to use the Internet more frequently than those who score high on this personality trait (Landers & Lounsbury, 2004).

Alabi (2012) surveyed Facebook addiction among 1,000 Nigerian University undergraduates using stratified and purposive sampling. The study used an instrument devised by the authors, the Facebook Addiction Symptoms Scale (FASS) with good internal consistency and a Cronbach's Alpha of 0.73. The FASS is a 15-item scale modeled on the content categories of Young's (1998) Internet Addiction Scale. Respondents answer the statements on a four-point Likert scale from 1 (Not at all) to 4 (Very regular). The FASS contains three items each under the following five categories: (1) preference for social network site, (2) loss of control, (3) preoccupation, (4) negative life consequences, and (5) withdrawal. Results showed that 31% of the sample accessed their Facebook account every hour. The study also revealed a relatively low level of Facebook addiction (1.6%). However, Alabi suggested that the low level of Internet access generally in Nigeria may have had an impact on the results.

A study by Cam and Isbulan (2012) examined gender differences in Facebook addiction in 1,257 Turkish university students (739 females and 518 males; aged 20–24 years). The authors adapted Young's (1998) Internet Addiction Test and named the new instrument the Facebook Addiction Scale (FAS). The survey items were answered using a Likert-type scale with six response choices (Does not apply, Rarely, Occasionally, Frequently, Often, and Always). The reliability of the scale was calculated with a very high Cronbach's alpha (0.92), although the authors made no reference to a cut-off score for what constituted Facebook addiction. Results showed males scored significantly higher than females on the FAS.

Those who scored high on the FAS were more likely to (1) prefer the excitement of Facebook to intimacy with their romantic partner; (2) have others in their life complain to them about the amount of time they spend on Facebook; (3) educationally suffer because of the amount of time they spend on Facebook; (4) check their Facebook messages before doing other things; (5)

occupationally suffer because of their Facebook use; (6) become defensive or secretive when anyone asks them what they do on Facebook; (7) find themselves anticipating going on Facebook again; (8) feel preoccupied with Facebook when offline or fantasize about being on Facebook; (9) try to cut down the amount of time they spend on Facebook and fail; (10) try to hide how long they have been on Facebook; (11) choose to spend more time on Facebook over going out with others; and (12) feel depressed, moody, or nervous when they are offline, which disappears once they are back on Facebook.

Andraessen, Tosheim, BrunBerg, and Pallesen (2012) developed the Bergen Facebook Addiction Scale (BFAS) based on Griffiths' (2005) six addiction components. The scale was constructed and administered to 423 students together with several other standardized self-report scales (e.g., including measures that assessed personality, attitudes toward Facebook, the Addictive Tendencies Scale). The scale positively related to various personality traits (e.g., neuroticism, extraversion), and negatively related to others (e.g., conscientiousness). High scores on the new scale were also associated with going to bed very late and getting up very late. Respondents are required to give one of five responses (Very Rarely, Rarely, Sometimes, Often, or Very Often) to six statements (e.g., "You feel an urge to use Facebook more and more" and "You use Facebook so much that it has had a negative impact on your job/studies"). The authors suggest that scoring Often or Very Often on at least four of the six items may suggest that the respondent is addicted to Facebook.

A study by Cheak, Goh, and Chin (2012) examined the relationship between social networking dependency and mood modification among 343 Malaysian undergraduates (mainly aged between 20 and 24 years). Social networking addiction was measured using an adaptation of 19 items from the Internet-Related Problem Scale (Armstrong, Phillips, & Saling, 2000). Social networking dependency was assessed with 12 items modified from Morahan–Martin and Schumacher's (2000) Pathological Internet Use Scale. Results showed that 46% engaged in social networking on a daily basis. The top activities engaged in on SNSs were checking messages (68%), checking comments/testimonies (54%), and playing games (52%). Predictably, there was a large positive correlation between social networking dependency and social networking addiction (0.68). Mood modification also correlated positively with social networking addiction (0.56).

Floros and Siomos (2013) reported a cross-sectional study examining the relationship between adolescent social networking (SN) motives, parenting styles, and cognitions related to Internet Addiction Disorder (IAD) in a Greek high-school student sample (n = 1971; aged 12–19 years). Based on Davis's

(2001) model of IAD, the Online Cognitions Scale (OCS) was devised and shown to provide an accurate estimate of Internet addiction (Davis et al., 2002). The OCS contains 36 items on a seven-point Likert scale with results grouped in four factors: (1) social comfort, (2) loneliness/depression, (3) diminished impulse control, and (4) distraction. Results demonstrated SN participation was the most frequent online activity among the sample, and that keeping in touch with friends was the strongest reason for frequent SN participation. Results also included a validated model of a negative correlation between optimal parenting, motives for SN participation, and IAD. Results also showed that frequent adolescent SN users were older, started using the Internet before their peer group, used the Internet to escape from everyday life, and used the Internet impulsively. This combination of variables explained over a third of the variance (35%) in their theoretical model.

Turel and Serenko (2012) tested and validated the dual effect of enjoyment, with a data set of 194 American students (19–40 years of age [mean age 23 years] and all of whom were social networking website users) analyzed with structural equation modeling techniques. They hypothesized that Information Systems (IS) use habit is positively related to addiction to social networking websites. Facebook addiction was assessed using an adapted version of Charlton and Danforth's (2007) online gaming addiction scale. The addiction statements included such items as "I sometimes neglect important things because of my interest in this social networking website," "When I am not using this social networking website, I often feel agitated". Perceived enjoyment was found to be the key antecedent of habit. The results of the study provide support for the authors' hypothesis that perceived enjoyment is linked with two potentially diverging outcomes (i.e., a habit that can facilitate increased addiction levels on one hand, but high engagement on the other).

Sofiah, Zobidah, Bolong, and Osman (2011) examined Facebook addiction among 380 Malaysian female university students (aged 19–28 years). Facebook addiction was assessed using a self-devised 11-item scale. The higher the overall score, the more addicted the person is deemed to be. No cut-off scores were provided by the authors to determine classification as a Facebook addict. The results of the 11 statements in terms of those who answered Strongly Agree (followed by the mean score of the sample out of 7, and standard deviation) are presented here:

- "Facebook has become part of my daily routine." (19%; 5.5; 1.0)
- "I find that I stay on Facebook longer than I intended." (16%; 5.2; 1.2)
- "I feel out of touch when I haven't logged onto Facebook for a while." (13%; 5.0; 1.4)
- "I think life without Facebook would be boring." (14%; 4.7; 1.5)

- "I tend to spend more time on Facebook over going out with others." (5.5%; 4.0; 1.6)
- "I often spend time playing games with friends through Facebook." (5.5%; 3.7; 1.7)
- "I often think about Facebook when I am not using it." (4%; 3.5; 1.7)
- "I often lose sleep due to late-night login to Facebook." (4%; 3.4; 1.7)
- "I neglect everyday responsibilities to spend more time on Facebook." (3%; 3.3; 1.5)
- "My priority is to log on to Facebook rather than do other things." (3%; 3.1; 1.7)
- "My grades are getting lower because of the amount of time I spend on Facebook." (3%; 3.0; 1.6)

Based on the results, the authors identified five motives for Facebook use (i.e., social interaction, passing time, entertainment, companionship, and communication) and found that there was a significant relationship between these five motives for Facebook use and Facebook addiction. Through use of regression analyses, the most significant motivational predictor of Facebook addiction was using Facebook as a way of passing time, followed by using Facebook for entertainment and communication. The combination of these three motivational variables accounted for 24% of the variance.

A study by Wolniczak et al. (2013) examined the association between Facebook dependence and poor sleep quality in a sample of 418 undergraduate university students in Peru (mean age = 20 years). The authors assessed Facebook dependence by adapting the Internet Addiction Questionnaire (Echeburua, 1999). The adapted instrument comprised eight yes/no questions and focuses on worries, concerns, satisfaction, time of use and efforts to reduce Facebook use, control, and other activities due to Facebook use. The authors used a cut-off of 5 or more to establish the presence of dependence as previously reported by Echeburua (1999). They reported Facebook dependence in 8.6% of the sample, whereas poor sleep quality was present in 55%. The study reported a significant association between Facebook dependence and poor sleep quality, mainly explained by daytime dysfunction after adjusting for age, gender, and year of study.

Koc and Gulyagci (2013) explored Facebook addiction among 447 Turkish college students and examined associated behavioral, demographic, and psychological health predictors. A Facebook Addiction Scale (FAS) was developed to assess addictive Facebook usage comprising eight items related to the core components of addiction (e.g., cognitive and behavioral salience, conflict with other activities, euphoria, loss of control, withdrawal, and relapse/reinstatement). Results indicated that time spent on Facebook varied between 10 minutes and 70 hours a week with a mean of 7 hours a week. The mean FAS score was only 13.66 (SD = 5.92; range 8–37). This indicates that reported levels of Facebook addiction were low among Turkish students. Those with high FAS scores reported a negative impact on their education, and students who frequently used Facebook for social interaction reported higher levels of addiction. Through use of regression analysis, 22% of the variance in Facebook addiction was explained by four significant predictors (i.e., weekly time commitment, social motives, anxiety and insomnia, and severe depression), and all were positively associated with addictive usage. The results support a cognitive-behavioral model, which assumes the necessity of a pre-existing psychopathology as a source of online addiction.

These quantitative studies suffer from a variety of methodological limitations. They attempted to assess SNS addiction, but mere assessment of addiction tendencies does not suffice to demarcate real pathology. Most of the samples were generally small, specific, self-selected, convenient, and skewed with regards to young adults and female gender. This may have led to the very high addiction prevalence rates (up to 34%) reported in some studies because individuals from these sociodemographic groups are likely to be more heavy social networking users. Empirical studies need to ensure that they are assessing addiction rather than excessive use and/or preoccupation.

Studies Examining the Relationship between Social Networking and Other Online Addictions

Kittinger, Correia, and Irons (2012) examined how the use of Facebook relates to problematic Internet use among 281 American undergraduate students (mean age of 20 years). The authors used the 20-item Internet Addiction Test (IAT) (Young, 1998) to assess Internet addiction (see the Appendix in Chapter 5). Respondents rate each of the items on a 5-point Likert-type scale, ranging from 1 (rarely) to 5 (always). Scores ranging from 50 to 79 are considered as indicative of occasional or frequent problems due to Internet use, whereas scores at or above 80 are indicative of more significant problems. The authors reported that most of their participants fell below the recommended cut-off for problematic Internet use, although a sizable minority (15%) reported scores above 50. Those scoring above 50 on the IAT were significantly more likely to report specific problems related to their use of Facebook. IAT scores were significantly correlated with both daily use of

Facebook, and self-reports by participants that they felt addicted. Using regression analyses, including age, gender, amount of time spent online per day (including use of Facebook), the number of times Facebook accounts were accessed per day, and the minutes spent on Facebook per day accounted for 34% of the variance in IAT scores. Time spent online and the daily frequency of Facebook use were the most significant predictors. The authors concluded that the use of Facebook contributes to IAT scores, even after accounting for demographic variables and general patterns of Internet use.

Zhou (2010) assessed SNS game addiction via the IAT (Young, 1998) in 342 Chinese college students aged 18–22 years. In this study, SNS game addiction referred specifically to being addicted to the SNS game *Happy Farm*. Students were defined as addicted to using this SNS game when they endorsed a minimum of five (out of eight) items of the IAT. Using this cut-off, Zhou classified 24% of the participants as addicted. Zhou also investigated rewards of SNS game use, loneliness, leisure boredom, and self-esteem. The findings indicated that there was a weak positive correlation between loneliness and SNS game addiction and a moderate positive correlation between leisure boredom and SNS game addiction. The rewards of "inclusion" (in a social group) and "achievement" (in game), leisure boredom, and being male significantly predicted SNS game addiction.

Karaiskos, Tzavellas, Balta, and Paparrigopoulos (2010) reported the case of a 24-year old female who used SNSs to such an extent that her behavior significantly interfered with her professional and private life. Consequently, she was referred to a psychiatric clinic. She used Facebook excessively for at least 5 hours a day and was dismissed from her job because she continuously checked her SNS instead of working. Even during the clinical interview, she used her mobile phone to access Facebook. In addition to excessive use that led to significant impairment in a variety of areas in the woman's life, she developed anxiety symptoms as well as insomnia, which suggestively points to the clinical relevance of SNS addiction. Such extreme cases have led some researchers to conceptualize SNS addiction as Internet spectrum addiction disorder. This indicates that first, SNS addiction can be classified within the larger framework of Internet addictions, and second, that it is a specific Internet addiction, alongside other addictive Internet applications such as Internet gaming addiction (Kuss & Griffiths, 2012a), Internet gambling addiction (Kuss & Griffiths, 2012b), and Internet sex addiction (Griffiths, 2012a).

This particular qualitative case study illustrates that from a clinical perspective, SNS addiction is a mental health problem that may require professional treatment. Unlike the other quantitative studies outlined in this chapter, the case study emphasizes the significant individual impairment that is experienced by individuals that spans a variety of life domains, including their professional life as well as their psychosomatic condition. Future researchers are therefore advised not only to investigate SNS addiction in a quantitative way, but also to further our understanding of this new mental health problem by analyzing cases of individuals who suffer from excessive SNS usage.

Studies Examining Social Networking Addiction and Interpersonal Relationships

Elphinston and Noller (2011) carried out a study examining the relationship between Facebook intrusion, jealousy in romantic relationships, and relationship outcomes among 342 Australian undergraduate students (aged 18–25 years) involved in a romantic relationship. The authors' self-constructed measure—the eight-item Facebook Intrusion Questionnaire (FIQ)—was to all intents and purposes a measure of "Facebook addiction" because the eight statements were based on the core components of addiction (Griffiths, 2005). The authors claimed that a single-factor structure for the FIQ was supported (i.e., it was a unidimensional scale) and that the internal consistency of the measure was high. Results showed that Facebook intrusion was associated with relationship dissatisfaction (via jealous cognitions and surveillance behaviors), although time spent on Facebook was not. The authors argued that their findings highlighted the possibility of high levels of Facebook intrusion "spilling over" into romantic relationships and leading to jealousy and relationship dissatisfaction. Facebook intrusion was only moderately associated with time spent on Facebook and supports Griffiths' (2010a) assertions that online excessive use does not necessarily equate with addiction.

Porter, Mitchell, and Grace (2012) also examined the relationship between social media use, interpersonal relationship satisfaction, and addiction in 219 young adult social media users aged 18–25 years. They used Mitchell and Beard's (2010) Internet Dependency Scale (IDS) to measure time spent using social media and social media withdrawal. Results showed that participants would feel some withdrawal from social media after a certain period of time. The results did not support their hypothesis that there would be a negative correlation between social media use and relationship satisfaction. As with other survey studies highlighted in this chapter, the sample sizes for these two studies were small, specific, and they used self-selected convenience samples.

Social Networking Addiction versus Facebook Addiction

Griffiths (2012b) recently noted that for many researchers, Facebook addiction has become almost synonymous with social networking addiction. Facebook is just one of many websites where social networking can take place. Therefore, scales such as the BFAS (Andraessen et al., 2012), FAS (Cam & Isbulan, 2012), and the FIQ (Elphinston & Noller, 2011) have been developed relating to addiction to one particular commercial company's service (i.e., Facebook) rather than the whole activity itself (i.e., social networking). Griffiths argues that the real issue here concerns what people are actually addicted to and what the new Facebook addiction tools are measuring. These arguments are almost identical to those in areas such as Internet addiction (Widyanto & Griffiths, 2006) and mobile phone addiction (Choliz, 2010).

For instance, Facebook users can play games like *Farmville* (Griffiths, 2010b), can gamble on games like poker (Griffiths & Parke, 2010), can watch videos and films, and can engage in activities such as swapping photos or constantly updating their profile and/or messaging friends on the minutiae of their life (Griffiths, 2012b; Kuss & Griffiths, 2011). Therefore, "Facebook addiction" is not synonymous with "social networking addiction"; they are two fundamentally different things because Facebook has become a specific website where many different online activities can take place—and may serve different purposes to various users.

What this suggests is that the field needs a psychometrically validated scale that specifically assesses "social networking addiction" rather than Facebook use. In scales like the BFAS, social networking as an activity is not mentioned; therefore, the scale does not differentiate between someone addicted to *Farmville* or someone addicted to constantly messaging Facebook friends. However, the BFAS is arguably the most psychometrically robust scale, and it is based on the components model of addiction (Brown, 1993; Griffiths, 2005) that has been used to develop many other psychometrically valid scales to assess other behavioral addictions (e.g., online gaming addiction, exercise addiction, work addiction). Revalidation of the BFAS using the term *social networking* instead of *Facebook use* may prove worthwhile to researchers.

Case Vignette: Marina

Marina is a 19-year-old British woman. Till recently, she was a university student until she failed all her coursework and exams and was asked by her university to repeat the year with attendance. Her mother claims she is "addicted to Facebook" and that the reason she failed everything on her modern languages degree was that she spent all her time chatting with friends online via Facebook. She spends most of her waking day checking her Facebook account using her phone that she carries around all the time. She cannot get to sleep unless her phone is on her bedside table. She cannot leave the house without her mobile phone. Her mother claims "she seems to spend her whole life online" and that even when she is eating a meal with her family, she is constantly checking her phone to see what messages she has received. Marina has more than 1,000 "friends," the vast majority of which she has either never met or had only the briefest of social contact with.

Her mother claims that all of Marina's conversation is related to information and gossip on Facebook. She claims Marina's mood is "totally dictated" by whether people are commenting on her status updates and/or dependent on how people react to the things she says online. Marina first set up a Facebook account when she was 16 years old and only ever accessed her account on the family computer in her father's study. Over the next 2 years, the number of hours she spent on Facebook gradually increased to the extent that almost all her time after school was spent on the computer. There was one period when she was 17 years of age when her Facebook usage was at a minimum, and this was a 6-week period when both her parents made her review for her A-level exams. During this period, her mother said Marina was very frustrated, irritating, and moody. The mother thought this was because of the stress of Marina's exams but now thinks it was because her daughter's access to the computer was denied. As soon as the exams were over (and Marina was allowed back on the family PC), her Facebook usage increased greatly (with her mother claiming that she was on Facebook "all the time"). The end of the exam period coincided with Marina's 18th birthday, when she was given a smartphone. This was the point at which her Facebook usage escalated to the point at which she was on Facebook for hours and hours at a time.

At university, Marina's Facebook use appears to have taken up most of the day. Even when attending lectures, she would be on Facebook. The few relationships she had with boys at university fizzled out because she would rather spend time on Facebook than with the person she was supposed to be dating. After Marina failed all her exams, the only way she could console herself was by chatting with her friends on Facebook.

Marina appears to display the core components of addiction. Facebook appears to be the most important thing in Marina's life, and she is totally

Continued

Case Vignette: Marina—cont'd

preoccupied with it. She uses it as a way of modifying her mood, and her use appears to conflict with everything in her life (relationships, education, family life). She also appears to have displayed withdrawal symptoms during her exam revision period. Marina's parents were so worried about her constant Facebook use that they sought professional advice (including contacting the first author for help). Marina refuses to see a psychologist and says she is doing what her friends do. Should her parents ever manage to get her into treatment, interventions such as cognitive-behavioral therapy (along with motivational interviewing) would perhaps be the most effective treatment approach.

PREVENTION AND TREATMENT OF SOCIAL NETWORKING ADDICTION

To date, there have been no papers published on the treatment of addiction to social networking, although the treatment studies relating to Internet addiction would appear to be applicable. Echeburua and de Corral (2010) noted that in relation to social networking, prevention strategies in both home and school settings should be implemented on the basis of behavioral risk factors and demographic characteristics. They also noted that the goal of treatment for this type of addiction (unlike the case of other addictions) should be controlled use rather than total abstinence because it is not particularly feasible to stop people from accessing devices that have Internet access (i.e., their computer or mobile phone) in today's culture. They assert that the psychological treatment of choice would appear to be stimulus control and gradual exposure to the Internet, followed by a cognitive-behavioral intervention in relapse prevention. However, it is possible to cease engaging in social networking on the Internet while still engaging in other Internet-related activities (e.g., playing online games). Gupta, Arora, and Gupta (2013) claim that in relation to SNS addiction, corrective strategies include but are not limited to (1) content-control software, (2) counseling, and (3) cognitive-behavioral therapy. They advise treatment practitioners get their clients to follow these strategies to manage and treat SNS addiction:

- Recognize the signs of a Facebook addiction.
- Start questioning what you are doing on Facebook.
- Write down exactly how much time you spend on each site.
- Decide what is of value on Facebook.
- Give yourself a set time of the day to visit.

- Try giving up Facebook for a specific event to see how you fare.
- Turn off e-mail notifications.
- Target solutions to enable smarter, brighter usage of Facebook in the future.
- Be careful of the race to have as many friends as possible.
- Avoid being a Facebook automaton. Every time you feel like saying "I'll Facebook you," check yourself and rephrase that with "I'll see you" or "I'll call you." And mean it; doing so settles the catch-up time straightaway.
- Meditate as soon as the thought of Facebook arises.

There is a clear need for more and better information about social networking addiction and the most appropriate and effective treatment programs. Echeburua and de Corral (2010) also note that more research is required on the motivational enhancement for treatment and the types of brief intervention available in relation to the problematic use of the Internet (including social networking among young people).

CONCLUSIONS

The aim of this chapter was to present an overview of the emergent empirical research relating to social networking addiction. The scientific literature addressing the addictive qualities of social networks on the Internet is scarce, but an increasing number of studies of variable quality have been published over the last few years. It is recommended that researchers assess factors that are specific to SNS addiction, including the pragmatics, attraction, communication, and expectations of SNS use because they may predict the etiology of SNS addiction as based on the addiction specificity etiology framework (Sussman, et al., 2011). Due to the scarcity of research in this domain with a specific focus on SNS addiction specificity and comorbidity, further empirical research is necessary.

Whether social networking addiction exists is debatable depending on the definition of addiction used, but there is clearly evidence that a minority of social network users experience addiction-like symptoms as a consequence of their excessive use. Studies endorsing only a few potential addiction criteria are not sufficient for establishing clinically significant addiction status. Similarly, significant impairment and negative consequences that discriminate addiction from mere abuse were generally not assessed. Thus, future studies have great potential in addressing the emergent phenomenon of SNS addiction by means of applying better methodological designs, including more representative samples, and using more reliable and valid addiction scales so that current gaps in empirical knowledge can be filled.

Furthermore, research must address the presence of specific addiction symptoms beyond negative consequences. These should be based on the *DSM-5* criteria for substance dependence and/or pathological gambling (American Psychiatric Association, 2013) and the *ICD-10* criteria for a dependence syndrome (World Health Organization, 1992), including (1) tolerance; (2) withdrawal; (3) increased use; (4) loss of control; (5) extended recovery periods; (6) sacrificing social, occupational, and recreational activities; and (7) continued use despite negative consequences. These have been found to be adequate criteria for diagnosing behavioral addictions (Griffiths, 2005) and thus appear sufficient to be applied to SNS addiction. To be diagnosed with SNS addiction, at least three (but preferably more) of the aforementioned criteria should be met in the same 12-month period, and they must cause significant impairment to the individual.

In addition, specific attention needs to be paid to selecting larger samples that are representative of a broader population to increase the respective study's external validity. The generalizability of results is essential to demarcate populations at risk for developing addiction to SNSs. Similarly, it appears necessary to conduct further psychophysiological studies to assess the phenomenon from a biological perspective. Furthermore, clear-cut and validated addiction criteria need to be assessed. It is insufficient to limit studies into addiction to assessing just a few criteria. The differentiation of pathology from high frequency and problematic usage necessitates adopting frameworks that have been established by the international classification manuals. Moreover, in light of clinical evidence and practice, it appears essential to pay attention to the significant impairment that SNS addicts experience in a variety of life domains as a consequence of their abusive and/or addictive behaviors.

Similarly, the results of data based on self-reports are not sufficient for diagnosis because research suggests that they may be inaccurate (Bhandari & Wagner, 2004). Conceivably, self-reports may be supplemented with structured clinical interviews, and further case study evidence as well as supplementary reports from the users' significant others. Research into social networking addiction is needed specifically in relation to clinical applicability and criteria for diagnosis. Furthermore, research is needed to examine gender differences because there appears to be a higher prevalence of problems among females (as opposed to other problematic online behaviors such as gaming addiction, which is more prevalent among males; Kuss

& Griffiths, 2012a). Such observations strengthen the rationale for a clear-cut social networking addiction classification rather than an umbrella term of *Internet addiction*.

REFERENCES

Alabi, O. F. (2012). A survey of Facebook addiction level among selected Nigerian university undergraduates. *New Media and Mass Communication, 10*, 70–80.

American Psychiatric Association. (2000). *Diagnostic and statistical manual of mental disorders—Text revision* (4th ed.). Washington, DC: Author.

American Psychiatric Association. (2013). *Diagnostic and statistical manual of mental disorders—Text revision* (5th ed.). Washington, DC: Author.

Andraessen, C. S., Tosheim, T., BrunBerg, G. S., & Pallesen, S. (2012). Development of a Facebook addiction scale. *Psychological Reports, 110*, 501–517.

Armstrong, L., Phillips, J. G., & Saling, L. L. (2000). Potential determinants of heavier Internet usage. *International Journal of Human-Computer Studies, 53*, 537–550.

Bhandari, A., & Wagner, T. H. (2004). *Self-report utilization: Improving measurement and accuracy.* San Diego: US National Institutes of Health.

Boyd, D. M, & Ellison, N. B. (2008). Social network sites: Definition, history, and scholarship. *Journal of Computer-Mediated Communication, 13*, 210–230.

Cabral, J. (2011). Is Generation Y addicted to social media? *Elon Journal of Undergraduate Research in Communications, 2*(1), 5–13.

Cam, E., & Isbulan, O. (2012). A new addiction for teacher candidates: Social networks. *Turkish Online Journal of Educational Technology, 11*(3), 14–19.

Cha, J. (2010). Factors affecting the frequency and amount of social networking site use: Motivations, perceptions, and privacy concerns. *First Monday, 15*(12). Located at http://firstmonday.org/ojs/index.php/fm/article/viewArticle/2889/2685.

Charlton, J. P., & Danforth, I. D. W. (2007). Distinguishing addiction and high engagement in the context of online game playing. *Computers in Human Behavior, 23*, 1531–1548.

Cheak, A. P. C., Goh, G. G. G., & Chin, T. S. (2012). Online social networking addiction: Exploring its relationship with social networking dependency and mood modification among undergraduates in Malaysia. *Proceedings of the International Conference on Management, Economics and Finance*, 247–262. Sarawak, Malaysia: Global Research.

Choliz, M. (2010). Mobile phone addiction: A point of issue. *Addiction, 105*, 373–374.

Costa, P. T., & McCrae, R. R. (1992). *Revised NEO personality inventory (NEO-PI-R) and the NEO Five-Factor inventory (NEO-FFI): Professional manual.* Odessa, FL: Psychological Assessment Resources.

Davies, T., & Cranston, P. (2008). *Youth work and social networking: Interim report.* Leicester: National Youth Agency.

Davis, R. (2001). A cognitive–behavioral model of pathological Internet use. *Computers in Human Behavior, 17*, 187–195.

Davis, R.A., Flett, G.L., & Besser, A. (2002). Validation of a new scale for measuring problematic internet use: implications for pre-employment screening. *CyberPsychology and Behavior, 5*, 331–345.

Echeburua, E. (1999). *Adicciones...Sin drogas? Las nuevas adicciones: Juego, sexo, comida, compras, trabajo, Internet; Desclee-de-Brouwer, editor.* Bilbao, Espana.

Echeburua, E., & de Corral, P. (2010). Addiction to new technologies and to online social networking in young people: A new challenge. *Adicciones, 22*(2), 91–95.

Ehrenberg, A., Juckes, S., White, K. M., & Walsh, S. P. (2008). Personality and self-esteem as predictors of young people's technology use. *CyberPsychology & Behavior, 11*, 739–741.

Elphinston, R. A., & Noller, P. (2011). Time to face it! Facebook intrusion and the implications for romantic jealousy and relationship satisfaction. *Cyberpsychology, Behavior, and Social Networking, 14*, 631–635.
Floros, G., & Siomos, K. (2013). The relationship between optimal parenting, Internet addiction and motives for social networking in adolescence. *Psychiatry Research*. http://dx.doi.org/10.1016/j.psychres.2013.01.010.
Griffiths, M. D. (1996). Behavioural addictions: An issue for everybody? *Journal of Workplace Learning, 8*(3), 19–25.
Griffiths, M. D. (2000). Internet addiction—Time to be taken seriously? *Addiction Research, 8*, 413–418.
Griffiths, M. D. (2003). Internet gambling: Issues, concerns, and recommendations. *CyberPsychology & Behavior, 6*, 557–568.
Griffiths, M. D. (2005). A 'components' model of addiction within a biopsychosocial framework. *Journal of Substance Use, 10*, 191–197.
Griffiths, M. D. (2010a). The role of context in online gaming excess and addiction: Some case study evidence. *International Journal of Mental Health and Addiction, 8*, 119–125.
Griffiths, M. D. (2010b). Gaming in social networking sites: A growing concern? *World Online Gambling Law Report, 9*, 12–13.
Griffiths, M. D. (2012a). Internet sex addiction: A review of empirical research. *Addiction Research and Theory, 20*, 111–124.
Griffiths, M. D. (2012b). Facebook addiction: Concerns, criticisms and recommendations. *Psychological Reports, 110*(2), 518–520.
Griffiths, M. D., & Parke, J. (2010). Adolescent gambling on the Internet: A review. *International Journal of Adolescent Medicine and Health, 22*, 58–75.
Gupta, V. K., Arora, S., & Gupta, M. (2013). Computer-related illnesses and Facebook syndrome: What are they and how do we tackle them? *Medicine Update, 23*, 676–679.
Karaiskos, D., Tzavellas, E., Balta, G., & Paparrigopoulos, T. (2010). Social network addiction: A new clinical disorder? *European Psychiatry, 25*, 855.
Kittinger, R., Correia, C. J., & Irons, J. G. (2012). Relationship between Facebook use and problematic Internet use among college students. *Cyberpsychology, Behavior, and Social Networking, 15*, 324–327.
Koc, M., & Gulyagci, S. (2013). Facebook addiction among Turkish college students: The role of psychological health, demographic, and usage characteristics. *Cyberpsychology, Behavior, and Social Networking*. http://dx.doi.org/10.1089/cyber.2012.0249.
Kuss, D. J., & Griffiths, M. D. (2011). Addiction to social networks on the Internet: A literature review of empirical research. *International Journal of Environment and Public Health, 8*, 3528–3552.
Kuss, D. J., & Griffiths, M. D. (2012a). Online gaming addiction: A systematic review. *International Journal of Mental Health and Addiction, 10*, 278–296.
Kuss, D., & Griffiths, M. D. (2012b). Internet gambling behavior. In Z. Yan (Ed.), *Encyclopedia of Cyber Behavior* (pp. 735–753). Pennsylvania: IGI Global.
Landers, R. N., & Lounsbury, J. W. (2004). An investigation of Big Five and narrow personality traits in relation to Internet usage. *Computers in Human Behavior, 22*, 283–293.
Mitchell, K., & Beard, F. (2010). Measuring Internet dependence among college students: A replication and confirmatory analysis. *Southwestern Mass Communication Journal, 25*(2), 15–28.
Machold, C., Judge, G., Mavrinac, A., Elliott, J., Murphy, A. M., & Roche, E. (2012). Social networking patterns/hazards among teenagers. *Irish Medical Journal, 105*, 151–152.
Milgram, S. (1967). The small world problem. *Psychology Today, 2*, 60–67.
Morahan-Martin, J., & Schumacher, P. (2000). Incidence and the correlates of pathological Internet use among college students. *Computers in Human Behavior, 16*, 13–29.

Olowu, A. O., & Seri, F. O. (2012). A study of social network addiction among youths in Nigeria. *Journal of Social Science and Policy Review, 4*, 62–71.

Pelling, E. L., & White, K. M. (2009). The theory of planned behavior applied to young people's use of social networkting web sites. *CyberPsychology & Behavior, 12*, 755–759.

Porter, K., Mitchell, J., Grace, M., Shinosky, S., & Gordon, V. (2012). A study of the effects of social media use and addiction on relationship satisfaction. *Meta-Communicate, 2*(1). Located at http://journals.chapman.edu/ojs/index.php/mc/article/view/340.

Protalinski, E. (2013). Facebook passes 1.19 billion monthly active users, 874 million mobile users, and 728 million daily users. *The Next Web,* October 30. Located at http://thenextweb.com/facebook/2013/10/30/facebook-passes-1-19-billion-monthly-active-users-874-million-mobile-users-728-million-daily-users/

Shaffer, H. J., LaPlante, D. A., LaBrie, R. A., Kidman, R. C., Donato, A. N., & Stanton, M. V. (2004). Toward a syndrome model of addiction: Multiple expressions, common etiology. *Harvard Review of Psychiatry, 12*, 367–374.

Sofiah, S., Zobidah, O. S., Bolong, J. N., & Osman, M. (2011). Facebook addiction among female university students. *Public Administration and Social Policy Review, 2*, 95–109.

Sussman, S., Leventhal, A., Bluthenthal, R. N., Freimuth, M., Forster, M., & Ames, S. L. (2011). A framework for specificity of the addictions. *International Journal of Environmental Research and Public Health, 8*, 3399–3415.

Turel, O., & Serenko, A. (2012). The benefits and dangers of enjoyment with social networking websites. *European Journal of Information Systems, 21*, 512–528.

Walsh, S. P., White, K. M., & Young, R. M. (2007). In G. Goggin & L. Hjorth (Eds.), *Young and connected: Psychological influences of mobile phone use amongst Australian youth, Mobile Media 2007. Proceedings of an International Conference on Social and Cultural Aspects of Mobile Phones, Media, and Wireless Technologies, Sydney, 2007* (pp. 125–134). Sydney: University of Sydney.

Wan, C. (2009). *Gratifications & loneliness as predictors of campus-SNS websites addiction & usage pattern among Chinese college students*. Hong Kong: Chinese University of Hong Kong.

Widyanto, L., & Griffiths, M. D. (2006). Internet addiction: A critical review. *International Journal of Mental Health and Addiction, 4*, 31–51.

Wilson, K., Fornasier, S., & White, K. M. (2010). Psychological predictors of young adults' use of social networking sites. *Cyberpsychology, Behavior and Social Networking, 13*, 173–177.

Wolniczak, I., Caceres-DelAguila, J. A., Palma-Ardiles, G., Arroyo, K. J., Solıs-Visscher, R., et al. (2013). Association between Facebook dependence and poor sleep quality: A study in a sample of undergraduate students in Peru. *PLoS ONE 8(3)*, e59087. http://dx.doi.org/10.1371/journal.pone.0059087.

World Health Organization. (1992). *The ICD-10 classification of mental and behavioral disorders: Clinical descriptions and diagnostic guidelines*. Geneva, Switzerland: World Health Organization.

Xu, H., & Tan, B. C. Y. (2012). *Why do i keep checking Facebook: Effects of message characteristics on the formation of social network services addiction*. Located at http://elibrary.aisnet.org/Default.aspx?url=http://aisel.aisnet.org/cgi/viewcontent.cgi?article=1216&context=icis2012.

Young, K. S. (1998). Internet addiction: The emergence of a new clinical disorder. *CyberPsychology & Behavior, 3*, 237–244.

Young, K. S. (1999). Internet addiction: Evaluation and treatment. *Student British Medical Journal*, 7, 351–352.

Zhou, S. X. (2010). *Gratifications, loneliness, leisure boredom and self-esteem as predictors of SNS-game addiction and usage pattern among Chinese college students*. Hong Kong: Chinese University of Hong Kong.

CHAPTER 7

Food Addiction: Evidence, Evaluation, and Treatment

Yvonne H.C. Yau[1], Carrie D. Gottlieb[2], Lindsay C. Krasna[3], Marc N. Potenza[1,4]

[1]Department of Psychiatry, Yale University School of Medicine, New Haven, CT, USA, [2]Private Practice and The William Alanson White Institute Eating Disorders, Compulsions, and Addictions Program, New York, NY, USA, [3]New York, NY, USA, [4]Department of Child Study and Neurobiology, Yale University School of Medicine, New Haven, CT, USA

INTRODUCTION

The global obesity epidemic poses significant public health problems and has, in recent years, rapidly developed to be a leading risk for global deaths. Defined as "abnormal or excessive fat accumulation that may impair health" (World Health Organization, 2012, para. 1), it is estimated that up to 35.7% of the U.S. population meets the criteria for obesity (Ogden, Carroll, Kit, & Flegal, 2012). Although overweight status and obesity are more prevalent in industrialized societies, the obesity epidemic is not limited to these countries; in developing countries, it is estimated that over 115 million people suffer from obesity-related problems (World Health Organization, 2012). Globally, the World Health Organization, or WHO (World Health Organization, 2012), estimates that prevalence has more than doubled since 1980, with estimates from 2008 suggesting that at least 500 billion adults, 20 and older, were obese. In 2010, more than 40 million children under the age of 5 were overweight or obese. Epidemiological studies indicate that obesity is an important risk factor for or contributor to potentially life-threatening health problems including type II diabetes, cardiovascular disease, osteoarthritis, and certain cancers (Joranby, Pineda, & Gold, 2005; Mokdad, Marks, Stroup, & Gerberding, 2003; Must et al., 1999). Obesity-related problems are the second leading cause of preventable death in the United States (Danaei et al., 2009; Mokdad et al., 2004), and are responsible for more than 2.8 million deaths globally each year (World Health Organization, 2012).

There have been multiple and diverse attempts to provide treatment tools for individuals to lose weight and maintain a healthy body habitus; these have ranged from preventative interventions, such as weight-loss campaigns

Behavioral Addictions
http://dx.doi.org/10.1016/B978-0-12-407724-9.00007-0

promoting healthy food choices and regular exercise, to pharmaceutical interventions and surgeries including bariatric procedures. Unfortunately, most obesity treatments do not result in lasting weight loss with most patients regaining their lost weight within 5 years (Astrup, Meinert Larsen, & Harper, 2004; Geloneze, Mancini, & Coutinho, 2009; Maciejewski et al., 2011; Wadden, Butryn, & Byrne, 2004).

The difficulty in treating and decreasing the prevalence of obesity may reflect the heterogeneity of obesity as a syndrome (Karelis, St-Pierre, Conus, Rabasa-Lhoret, & Poehlman, 2004). Obesity may result from various factors, including social and environmental contributions, personal lifestyle choices, and eating behaviors (Adam & Epel, 2007). One conceptualization that has gained popularity in both scientific and popular media in recent years is that foods, particularly highly palatable ones, may be "addictive" in ways similar to drugs of abuse (Avena & Gold, 2011; Volkow, Wang, Fowler, Tomasi, & Baler, 2012). The general view expressed in these reports posits that food addiction, unlike other behavioral addictions such as pathological gambling, is similar to substance addiction in that there is a physical agent that has neurochemical effect(s) in the brain. An addictive "loss of control" over consumption of specific foods (especially "engineered" products introduced into the market in the past decades) could potentially account for the increasing obesity epidemic and, if this view is valid, it could have major implications for interventions and policy making. This chapter reviews the proposed definitions of food addiction, describes the present state of the evidence in this area, and discusses the implications of a food addiction framework in treating the obesity epidemic.

CRITERIA AND DEFINITION

Although research in the field is still in its infancy, there has been a significant increase in the number of academic publications relating to food addiction over the past decade (Gearhardt, Davis, Kuschner, & Brownell, 2011). During the same period, there has also arguably been a shift in perspectives toward the view that addiction should be considered as a syndrome with multiple opportunistic expressions and reframed as a maladaptive desire for pleasure and a loss of control over the behavior, irrespective of the source of the reward (e.g., substance use, gambling, food consumption; Potenza, 2006; Shaffer et al., 2004). The rewarding experience associated with eating can lead to eating in the absence of metabolic need. Recent research suggests drug-seeking behaviors in substance-dependent individuals and food-seeking behaviors in obese individuals demonstrate phenotypic parallels (i.e., share similar features) and engage similar neurocircuitry (Gearhardt, Corbin, & Brownell, 2009a; Volkow & O'Brien, 2007). This has consequently led to the conceptualization of "foods as drugs" (Davis & Carter, 2009).

However, the concept of "food addiction" represents a controversial issue and its validity remains considerably debated in the scientific community. Comparing food addiction with substance use disorders (SUDs) has been questioned for several reasons, including that food consumption, unlike drug usage, is a normative behavior that is necessary for survival. This controversy is exemplified by the lack of a formal definition and few attempts to determine the "addictive" properties of foods using rigorous scientific criteria. Some investigators argue that there currently exists conflicting evidence that is insufficient to support the notion of food addiction and counsel strongly against using this model to guide policy making (Ziauddeen, Farooqi, & Fletcher, 2012a, 2012b; Ziauddeen & Fletcher, 2013). Others argue that this construct may be particularly relevant to certain subgroups of obese individuals, such as those with binge-eating disorder (BED), and caution against prematurely dismissing the conceptualization (Avena, Gearhardt, Gold, Wang, & Potenza, 2012). While BED may have been formally diagnosed as an "Eating Disorder Not Otherwise Specified" in the *DSM-IV,* it was included in the *DSM-5* as a formal diagnostic entity (American Psychiatric Association, 2013). Although not labeled as such, several of the diagnostic criteria for BED approximate criteria for SUDs, including diminished control over eating (American Psychiatric Association, 2000, 2013). Over a quarter of clinicians report often or always using addiction-based therapies for BED (von Ranson & Robinson, 2006), further suggesting phenomenological and clinical similarities between BED and SUDs. Both food addiction and BED appear to be characterized by excess food consumption, which could result in elevated body mass indexes (BMIs; Gearhardt, White, & Potenza, 2011). A recent study reported that 57% of BED patients met criteria for food addiction (Gearhardt et al., 2012). Additionally, although factors related to binge-eating (i.e., negative affect, eating disorder psychopathology) did not predict binge-eating frequency, higher food addiction scores were related to more frequent binge-eating episodes (Gearhardt et al., 2012). Taken together, these data suggest that BED and food addiction may represent unique yet overlapping conditions. It is important to keep in mind that food addiction does not explain all of obesity and that for some individuals overeating is a relatively passive event that takes the form of liberal snacking, large portions, and physical inactivity (Avena, Bocarsly, Hoebel, & Gold, 2011; Marcus & Wildes, 2009).

To investigate the clinical utility of the construct of food addiction, researchers at Yale University recently developed a measure to operationalize and identify aspects of addiction to foods (particularly high-fat, high-sugar foods) through translating and adapting diagnostic criteria for substance dependence in the *DSM-IV-TR* to food consumption (Gearhardt, Corbin, & Brownell, 2009b). The 25-item self-report Yale Food Addiction Scale (YFAS; located in the Appendix of this chapter and available online at http://www.midss.ie/content/yale-food-addiction-scale-yfas) provides two scoring options: the first measures food addiction "features," and the second provides a food addiction "diagnosis" based on the *DSM-IV-TR* diagnostic for substance dependence. Preliminary data suggest that the YFAS exhibits good internal reliability and convergent validity with other measures of eating pathology, especially binge eating, and may therefore be a useful tool not only to identify potential candidates with addictive tendencies toward food for research purposes, but also to help clinicians better identify food-use-related disorders in their patients (Davis et al., 2011; Gearhardt et al., 2009b).

EPIDEMIOLOGY

Using the YFAS, Gearhardt, Corbin, and Brownell (2008) observed that the most common features were (1) repeated unsuccessful attempts to cut down [71.3%]; (2) continued use despite problems [28.3%]; and (3) large amounts of time spent to obtain food, eat, or recover from eating [24.0%]. These three features were also the most often endorsed in obese individuals with BED (Gearhardt et al., 2012). In a study by Merlo, Klingman, Malasanos, and Silverstein (2009), 15.2% of overweight children indicated they "often," "usually," or "always" think they are addicted to food. Moreover, food addiction features were correlated with overeating, uncontrolled eating, emotional eating, food preoccupation, overconcern with body size, and caloric awareness and control (Merlo et al., 2009). Among adults, 11.4% of normal-weight individuals met the YFAS criteria for food addiction (Gearhardt et al., 2009b). Prevalence estimates of food addiction diagnoses in obese individuals are two to three times greater than among lean individuals, with 25% to 27.5% of obese individuals meeting the YFAS criteria for food addiction (Davis et al., 2011; Meule, 2011). Currently, few studies have examined the prevalence of food addiction, and large-scale studies are lacking; as such, these prevalence estimates may best be considered as informative but preliminary.

EVIDENCE FOR FOOD ADDICTION

Insights into the Physiology of Food Consumption and Abuse

Although early discussions described mood-enhancing effects and cravings that food addiction may share with drug abuse (Rogers & Smit, 2000), evidence of their biological parallels is more recent. Facilitated by a robust substance addiction literature and driven largely by well-controlled animal studies, neurobiological research has gained increasing attention and has, to date, provided perhaps the strongest empirical evidence for food addiction.

Regular consumption of energy-dense food may be accompanied by concomitant neural changes, and there is now evidence that food and drugs of abuse may exploit similar pathways in the brain, including the dopaminergic and opioidergic systems (Koob & Volkow, 2010; Volkow et al., 2012). Although dopamine release is not equivocal to addictive properties, dopamine has been associated with reward sensitivity, conditioning, and control over both food and drugs of abuse. Increased dopamine release has been reported in response to food and food cues (Di Chiara & Imperato, 1988), both of which are crucial aspects of food intake (Volkow, Wang, & Baler, 2011). Repeated stimulation of the dopaminergic reward pathways is believed to trigger neurobiological adaptions that may promote increasingly compulsive behavior (Everitt et al., 2008). Further, administration of dopamine antagonists or lesions of the dopaminergic system may attenuate the responding for food and reduce the reward value of both high-sugar foods and drugs of abuse in rats (Avena & Hoebel, 2003; Colantuoni et al., 2002; Wise & Rompre, 1989).

As with substance addiction (Koob & Volkow, 2010), studies using [^{11}C]raclopride positron emission tomographic (PET) scanning have demonstrated that D2-like dopamine receptor availability is reduced in obese mice (Geiger et al., 2008; Huang et al., 2006) and humans (Wang, Volkow, Thanos, & Fowler, 2009). Among obese humans, D2-like dopamine receptor availability correlated negatively with BMI scores (Wang et al., 2001). Blocking D2-like dopamine receptors using antipsychotic medications may increase food intake and raise the risk for obesity (Allison et al., 1999). Importantly, decreases in striatal D2-like dopamine receptor availability have been linked to the development of addiction-like reward deficits and onset of compulsive food intake in obese rodents (Johnson & Kenny, 2010) and decreased metabolic activity in the orbitofrontal cortex (OFC) and anterior cingulate cortex (ACC) in obese humans (Volkow et al., 2001). Several areas of the dopaminergic mesolimbic pathway have also been implicated in feeding motivations (Rolls, 2004). Imaging studies in obese (versus lean) individuals have documented significantly increased activation of the ventral medial prefrontal cortex (vmPFC) and dorsolateral prefrontal cortex (dlPFC) upon exposure to food-related stimuli (Gautier et al., 2000; Miller et al., 2007). In contrast to cue-induction studies, ingestion of food has been associated with reduced activation of the brain reward system among obese individuals. Stice, Spoor, Bohon, Veldhuizen, and Small (2008) reported that obese (versus lean) adolescent girls showed diminished caudate activation in response to anticipated intake and actual consumption of hyperpalatable foods. The authors suggest that this may potentially reflect decreased dopamine receptor availability. Down-regulation of the dopaminergic mesolimbic pathway may motivate overeating to temporarily compensate for an understimulated reward system and may ultimately lead to food addiction.

In parallel, there is evidence that peripheral homeostatic regulators of energy balance such as leptin, insulin, orexin, and ghrelin also regulate behaviors that are nonhomeostatic and modulate the rewarding properties of food (Volkow, Wang, & Baler, 2011; Yau, Yip, & Potenza, in press). These neuropeptides may be involved with food intake regulation by interacting with the dopaminergic system through cognate receptors in ventral tegmental area (VTA) dopamine neurons, which project not only to the nucleus accumbens (NAc), but also to prefrontal and limbic regions, all of which are part of the brain reward system commonly implicated in substance abuse (Clark, 2012; Volkow et al., 2012).

Opioids have also been implicated in addictive behaviors, and neuroadaptations in the opioidergic system have been documented in SUDs such as cocaine (Zubieta et al., 1996) and alcohol dependence (Heinz et al., 2005). Similarly, endogenous opioid release has been implicated in food consumption (Kelley et al., 2002), especially foods with high sugar content, although the precise nature of their influences is unclear. The endogenous opioidergic system is thought to underlie the rewarding properties of drugs of abuse and hyperpalatable foods (Yeomans & Gray, 1997), and opioid receptor antagonists such as naltrexone can reduce the reinforcement value and craving for alcohol in dependent individuals (O'Malley, Krishnan-Sarin, Farren, Sinha, & Kreek, 2002). High doses of naloxone, another opioid receptor antagonist, increased sugar consumption and opiate-like withdrawal symptoms including elevated plus-maze anxiety, teeth chattering, and head shakes in sugar-binging rats following a period of abstinence (Avena, Bocarsly, Rada, Kim, & Hoebel, 2008; Avena, Rada, & Hoebel, 2009; Colantuoni et al., 2002). It is interesting to note that a recent study by Bocarsly, Berner, Hoebel, and Avena (2011) did not replicate these findings with high-fat diets. Rats on high-fat diets did not show signs of opiate-like withdrawal when precipitated by naloxone or during fasting. These negative findings suggest that although fat-rich food may impart addiction-like effects, the brain opioidergic system may be differently affected by the overeating of different nutrients, these findings highlight the importance of understanding the effects of specific nutrients.

New Clinical Evidence for Food Addiction

Obesity is a heterogeneous construct, and data suggest that certain subgroups, such as those with BED, may exhibit food addiction features more than others. BED is characterized by recurrent binge-eating episodes (i.e., bouts of unusually large food intake in relatively short periods of time, usually after abstinence or deprivation) without compensatory efforts at weight loss, such as purging. BED shares similar features with SUDs, including periodic poor control, overconsumption, and diminished ability or willingness to cut down on consumption (Avena, 2010; Davis & Carter, 2009; von Ranson & Cassin, 2007). BED may differ from other forms of obesity and eating disorders in various behavioral, body image, psychological, and psychiatric features (Allison et al., 1999; Grilo, Masheb, & White, 2010). Overweight BED (versus non-BED overweight and lean) subjects reported enhanced reward sensitivity and showed stronger medial OFC responses when presented with food cues (Schienle, Schäfer, Hermann, & Vaitl, 2009). Similarly, individuals with BED compared to BMI-matched non-BED obese and lean individuals show relatively diminished activity in the vmPFC, inferior frontal gyrus, and insula during the Stroop color-word interference task (Balodis, Molina, et al., 2013). The same research group also found that during another cognitive control task (the Monetary Incentive Delay task), BED obese (versus non-BED obese) individuals showed relatively diminished ventral striatal activity during anticipatory phases, whereas non-BED obese individuals showed heightened ventral striatal and vmPFC responses in comparison to lean individuals (Balodis, Kober, et al., 2013). Taken together, these results suggest people with BED may exhibit neural alterations in reward sensitivity and cognitive control with respect to those with obesity alone. It is important to consider that despite their similarities, BED and food addiction may represent unique yet overlapping conditions. For example, 43%–50% of those with BED did not meet the YFAS criteria for food addiction and roughly 30% of the food addiction group were not clinically significant binge eaters (Davis et al., 2011; Gearhardt et al., 2012).

Moreover, compared to patients not classified as having food addiction, the subset of BED patients who met food-addiction criteria had significantly higher levels of negative affect, greater emotional dysregulation, lower self-esteem, and more eating disorder psychopathology (Gearhardt et al., 2013). These findings suggest that similar to drug addictions, binging is one form of excessive intake, and not the only consumption pattern that may lead to poor control, overconsumption, and dependence.

Although there is growing biological support for "food addiction," there have been few rigorous explorations of behavioral indicators of dependence in humans. To date, only one neuroimaging study has directly assessed food addiction in humans (Gearhardt, Yokum, Orr, Stice, Corbin, & Brownell, 2011). Among lean and obese young females, activation in the ACC, medial OFC, and amygdala in response to anticipated receipt of food was positively correlated with food addiction scores. Furthermore, females with high (versus low) YFAS scores showed greater activation in the dlPFC and the caudate in response to anticipated receipt of food, but decreased activation in the OFC in response to receipt of food. Interestingly, no significant correlation was observed between YFAS score and BMI, suggesting that despite the frequent co-occurrence of food addiction and obesity, food-addiction-related neural functioning may occur across a range of body weights.

Potential Risk Factors for Food Addiction

High-sugar and High-fat Foods

Although almost all food is rewarding to consume, it is hypothesized that certain foods may possess more addictive qualities. Animal models of sugar dependence have received the most research attention and have yielded consistently positive results. Based on a diet-induced model of obesity, rats fed a high-sugar diet compared to those on an unrestricted diet showed decreased dopamine release in the NAc following 36 hours of food deprivation (Avena et al., 2008). Animals with prolonged exposure to high-sugar diets increased daily food intake over time, developed patterns of copious consumption, and displayed withdrawal symptoms when placed back on a normal unrestricted diet (Avena & Hoebel, 2003). Such work has been expanded and replicated with other diets including those that are highly palatable (Johnson & Kenny, 2010) and high-fat (Lutter & Nestler, 2009). For example, healthy human adults placed under a nutritionally adequate but monotonous diet, compared to those on an unrestricted diet, showed greater activation of the hippocampus, insula, and caudate in response to cues of foods they favored (Pelchat, Johnson, Chan, Valdez, & Ragland, 2004).

Obesity

Although food addiction can be present across a range of body weights (Gearhardt, Yokum, et al., 2011), the presence of obesity may moderate the risk for food addiction. Rats classified as prone to binge eating (versus binge-eating-resistant rats) consumed significantly more highly palatable and energy-dense (high-fat, high-sugar) food and tolerated significantly higher levels of foot shock for access to such foods (Oswald, Murdaugh, King, & Boggiano, 2011), suggesting the development of compulsivity (Everitt et al., 2008). Alsiö et al. (2010) found that rats fed a high-fat (versus unrestricted) diet showed decreased expression of D1 and D2 dopamine receptors in the VTA, NAc, and PFC following an 18-day withdrawal. Moreover, obesity-prone rats showed increased craving and anxiety compared to obesity-resistant rats during the second withdrawal week following discontinuation of the energy-dense diet (Pickering, Alsiö, Hulting, & Schiöth, 2009). In humans, obese individuals (versus controls) showed greater activation in regions associated with cue-related craving for substance addictions including the ACC, striatum, insula, and dlPFC in response to pictures of high-calorie food versus low-calorie food (Rothemund et al., 2007; Stice, Spoor, Ng, & Zald, 2009; Stoeckel et al., 2008). Obese (versus lean) individuals have also shown enhanced corticolimbic-striatal activation to favorite-food cues and stress cues in a guided imagery fMRI task (Jastreboff, Sinha, Lacadie, Small, Sherwin, & Potenza, 2013). In the same study, measures of insulin resistance correlated positively with regional brain activations to favorite-food, stress, and neutral-relaxing cues in obese but not lean individuals, and regional brain activations (particularly in the thalamus) mediated the relationships between insulin resistance and favorite-food-cue-induced craving in obese but not lean individuals. Collectively, these findings suggest obese/obesity-prone animals and humans may display neural changes, be hyper-responsive to food cues, and be more susceptible to addiction-like behaviors compared to their lean/obesity-resistant counterparts.

Personality Characteristics

Food addiction is associated with negative affect, mood disorders, emotion dysregulation, proneness to stress, and lower self-esteem scores (Davis et al., 2011; Gearhardt et al., 2012). Such findings suggest that individuals with food addiction may turn to excessive food consumption as a coping strategy for heightened emotional distress, similar to individuals with SUDs in whom depression and anxiety may serve as triggers for substance use (Holahan, Moos, Holahan, Cronkite, & Randall, 2001; Nunes & Rounsaville, 2006;

Thorberg & Lyvers, 2006). An individual's mental state may moderate responses to drugs. For example, negative affect and anxiety correlated positively with increases in brain dopamine levels and greater subjective feelings of happiness in response to the psychostimulant drug methylphenidate (Volkow et al., 1994). Whether such findings extend to hyperpalatable foods warrants further research. Also noteworthy is the relation between food addiction and high levels of impulsivity (Davis et al., 2011; Gearhardt et al., 2012). Strong links with impulsivity have been reported in drug and behavioral addictions (Brewer & Potenza, 2008). High impulsivity may promote behavioral actions with immediate rewards (e.g., consumption of drugs and hyperpalatable foods) despite knowledge of later negative consequences. Impulsivity may be especially problematic in our current food environment with the abundance of highly palatable and varied foods promoted and marketed by the food industry and distributed and packaged for maximal convenience. Interestingly, a study by Guerrieri, Nederkoorn, and Jansen (2008) found that impulsivity did not affect food consumption with a monotonous diet, but when variety was present, the high (versus low) impulsivity group consumed significantly more calories.

Family History/Genetic Influences

With regard to hereditary factors, some studies have shown that as much as 60% of the overall variance of risk for obesity can be attributed to genetic factors (Volkow & Wise, 2005). Furthermore, rates of obesity are 10-fold higher in people with an obese first-degree relative (Segal & Allison, 2002). Kampov-Polevoy, Garbutt, and Khalitov (2003) reported that individuals with a paternal history of alcohol dependence had increased preference for sweetness, suggesting similar genetic mechanisms could contribute to both alcohol and sugar addictions. However, the extent to which shared environmental factors may moderate the relationship between genetics and risk for food addiction warrants further research. In animal models, when pregnant rats maintained a highly palatable and energy-dense (high-fat, high-sugar) diet, their offspring showed an increased preference for sugar and fat in comparison to those with mothers on a control diet (Vucetic, Kimmel, Totoki, Hollenbeck, & Reyes, 2010). Additionally, dopamine and opioid receptor expression in reward-related brain regions including the NAc, PFC, and hypothalamus was increased (Vucetic et al., 2010).

Individuals may overeat to compensate for hypofunctioning of reward-related brain regions, and this may be more apparent in those with genetic polymorphisms proposed to attenuate the dopamine signaling in these regions.

The negative relation between striatal responses to food receipt and BMI (Stice, Spoor, Bohon, Veldhuizen, et al., 2008) was stronger among individuals with the Taq1A1 polymorphism of the dopamine D2 receptor (*DRD2*) gene, and the presence of these alleles predicted future increases in body mass (Stice, Yokum, Bohon, Marti, & Smolen, 2010). The same research group also found that the presence of the Taq1A1 allele moderated the negative relation between BMI and activation in the left caudate during receipt of milkshake versus a tasteless solution (Stice, Spoor, Bohon, & Small, 2008). Furthermore, obese individuals with BED (versus non-BED obese controls) had lower frequencies of the Taq1A1 allele of the dopamine receptor (*DRD2*) gene and higher frequencies of the G118 allele of the mu-opioid receptor gene (*OPRM1;* Davis et al., 2009). However, as the Taq1A1 allele of the dopamine receptor (*DRD2*) gene is in linkage disequilibrium with the *Ankk1* gene (one which maps more closely to addictive behaviors than does the Taq1A1 allele), it is possible that the findings may not link directly to *DRD2* (Dick et al., 2007). Genetic polymorphisms of the serotonin transporter (*5HTTLPR*) gene have also been implicated; adolescents with the short allelic variant showed higher BMI scores than those with the homozygous long variant and were more likely to be overweight (Sookoian et al., 2007).

It is important to note that at present, no genetic study has directly investigated food addiction. As such, the extent to which the aforementioned findings relate to food addiction remains unclear.

TREATMENT

As outlined in this chapter, there are parallels between substance and food addictions. Importantly, practical implications may be inferred from a food addiction model and may provide a helpful framework for the development of effective treatments for compulsive overeating. However, one unique challenge for food addiction is that food, unlike drugs of abuse, is indispensable for survival. For example, many addiction treatment programs endorse an abstinence policy that avoids the dangers of potential priming effects of drugs—a proposed key contributor to relapse (Shaham, Shalev, Lu, De Wit, & Stewart, 2003). Similar effects with food are much harder to achieve because consumption is necessary and long periods of abstinence may severely damage one's health. However, strategies promoting the avoidance of certain foods (e.g., hyperpalatable foods rich in sugar or fat) that may be seductive and not necessary for food health may help reduce the priming effects that trigger compulsive overeating.

While behavioral and pharmacological treatments for some substance addictions are relatively well established, treatments for food addiction are currently scant, and few systematic examinations of their efficacy have been conducted. The following review will target the treatments that may provide beneficial outcomes by addressing behavior modification. In addition, examples will be drawn from the relatively more extensive BED literature. However, it is important that these findings are not misconstrued as providing unconditional support for the efficacy of such treatments in food addiction because the two conditions are distinguishable (Gearhardt et al., 2012, 2013).

Pharmacologic Treatments

Multiple pharmacological treatments adapted from SUDs are currently either under development or in clinical trials. As mentioned previously, several preclinical studies have identified potential therapeutic targets such as dopamine and endogenous opioids that may help diminish food cravings, compulsive overeating, and binge eating. However, the implications for these findings in human populations have yet to be systematically examined, and their potential adverse effects in this population are unknown. There has been some support for the usage of selective serotonin reuptake inhibitors in targeting binge-eating, psychiatric, and weight-related features (Reas & Grilo, 2008), although the effectiveness and duration of these medications remain unclear (Devlin, Goldfein, Petkova, Liu, & Walsh, 2007; Guerdjikova et al., 2008; Leombruni et al., 2006, 2008). For a more detailed review of the pharmacological treatments for food addiction and obesity, see Chapter 8.

Psychotherapy

Cognitive Behavioral Therapy

Cognitive behavioral therapy (CBT) is a semistructured and problem-orientated psychotherapeutic technique concerned with processes that maintain compulsive behaviors; CBT has shown promising results with SUDs (Aharonovich, Nunes, & Hasin, 2003; Maude-Griffin et al., 1998; Waldron & Kaminer, 2004). CBT addresses dysfunctional emotions and maladaptive behaviors and cognitive processes through goal-oriented, explicit systematic procedures that aim to replace them with adaptive behaviors and cognitive processes. The particular therapeutic technique varies according to the particular type of patient or issue but typically involves keeping a diary of significant events and associated feelings, thoughts, and behaviors; recording cognitions, assumptions, evaluations, and beliefs that may be maladaptive; and trying new ways of behaving and reacting. To the authors' knowledge, no CBT program for food addiction currently exists, although CBT is a relatively well-established psychological treatment for BED (Wilson, Grilo, & Vitousek, 2007) and has been the subject of a recent narrative review (Mitchell, Devlin, de Zwaan, Crow, & Peterson, 2008) and several systematic reviews (Brownley, Berkman, Sedway, Lohr, & Bulik, 2007; Sysko & Walsh, 2008). Most clinicians (87%) report frequently using CBT techniques with patients suffering from eating-related disorders (von Ranson & Robinson, 2006), and CBT is often the "gold standard" to which other treatments are compared.

Adapted from Fairburn's (1981) CBT model for bulimia nervosa, the model for BED retains most of the original structure although there are indications that unhealthy and chaotic eating in BED is less restrictive than in bulimia nervosa (Masheb & Grilo, 2000, 2006) and that obesity is a frequently co-occurring problem. CBT for BED consists of three stages that span over 20 sessions (Fairburn, Wilson, & Schleimer, 1993). Stage one focuses on engaging with the patient to establish a therapeutic relationship and on educating the patient on the rationale underlying the CBT approach. Stage two emphasizes replacing binge eating with a stable pattern of regular eating and additionally broadens the focus to address all forms of dieting; body image concerns about shape and weight; and more general cognitive distortions including dichotomous reasoning, low self-esteem, and extreme perfectionism. The third and final stage aims to ensure that progress is maintained in the future through discussion of termination and future plans, including relapse plans.

Both group and individual CBT have been shown be to efficacious in reducing the numbers of binging days and binge episodes and improving psychopathological features of BED, including excessive concerns with body shape, eating, and weight among BED patients (Devlin et al., 2007; Munsch et al., 2007; Vocks et al., 2010; Wilson et al., 2007). However, these effects appear to be short-lived following treatment cessation (although there have been some positive findings [Hilbert et al., 2012]) and have little effect on body weight, which is typically raised in BED patients (Berkman et al., 2006; Vocks et al., 2010). Future research is needed to examine the efficacy of a CBT model in the context of food addiction.

Dialectic Behavior Therapy

Dialectical behavior therapy (DBT) was first developed by Marsha Linehan for the treatment of borderline personality disorder (BPD) and has been used to treat a variety of other mental health issues such as depression, substance abuse, and eating disorders (Lynch, Chapman, Rosenthal, Kuo, & Linehan, 2006). DBT proposes that individuals who struggle with BED may lack the skills necessary to cope with their affective states and, therefore, may use food as a means to avoid or escape from emotional distress (Wiser & Telch, 1999). DBT aims to teach patients more adaptive emotional regulation and distress tolerance skills so that the reliance on food and eating for these purposes is lessened or eliminated (Telch, Agras, & Lienham, 2000; Wiser & Telch, 1999).

DBT is a didactic therapy that is conducted in either group or individual therapy sessions. DBT for BED (DBT-BED) involves the following modules: mindfulness skills, emotional regulation, and distress tolerance. Mindfulness modules include skills geared toward enhancing one's awareness level of moment-to-moment experiences in an attempt to counteract tendencies to avoid emotions. Emotional awareness skills are aimed at decreasing emotional vulnerability by helping patients identify and understand their emotions. It involves identifying prompting events (i.e., who, what, where, and when), bodily sensations and body language, and the functions of emotions (Linehan, 1993). Often food journals and other types of logs are utilized as emotional awareness exercises. Distress tolerance skills teach patients to better tolerate painful affective states and decrease maladaptive coping skills. Linehan (1993) contends that "the ability to tolerate and accept distress is essential for mental health" (p. 96). Central to distress tolerance skills are acceptance strategies that teach patients how to stop fighting both emotionally and behaviorally against distressing situations, but rather to embrace or accept them. Traditional DBT also includes modules on interpersonal effectiveness; however, these are not included in DBT-BED (Telch et al., 2000).

To date, little research has been conducted regarding the efficacy of DBT-BED. Preliminary findings and pilot studies suggest that DBT-BED is effective in terms of decreasing binge-eating episodes (Safer, Robinson, & Jo, 2010). Specifically, DBT-BED is effective at enhancing patients' overall level of emotional regulation and may be superior to CBT in terms of abstinence from binge eating (Telch et al., 2000). More research concerning the efficacy of DBT-BED as a treatment, specifically in terms of retention in treatment and relapse rates, as well as comparing it to other forms of therapy, is needed. Despite the limited empirical data, DBT continues to be commonly used to treat patients with BED and food addiction.

Interpersonal Psychotherapy

Interpersonal psychotherapy (IPT) has been examined as an alternative psychotherapeutic treatment to CBT and is structured around both psychodynamic psychotherapy and contemporary CBT approaches. IPT typically focuses on the connection between current symptoms and interpersonal (i.e., relationship) problems and holds the assumption that the condition is maintained by interpersonal problems (Markowitz & Weissman, 2004). Thus, the treatment targets identifying and modifying social and interpersonal deficits rather than modifying features of BED directly. IPT is an empirically validated treatment for multiple psychiatric disorders, particularly depression and mood disorders (Weissman, 1994). However, IPT for SUDs has received less research attention despite suggested adaptations and usage (Brache, 2012; Markowitz & Weissman, 2004).

IPT is designed to occur over 12–16 sessions. Similar to CBT, there are three stages of treatment in IPT. The initial stage includes identifying the target diagnosis and interpersonal context in which it presents. The four primary types of interpersonal problems on which IPT focuses are "complicated bereavement" (e.g., death of loved ones), "role dispute" (e.g., struggle with a significant other), "role transition" (e.g., going through important life changes), and in the absence of any of these, the default focus is on "interpersonal deficits," which describes a variety of relational challenges including an absence of social interaction. During the second stage, the clinician and patient explore the nature of the current problem, interpersonal problems, and strategies of change. These strategies strive to achieve three goals: (1) acceptance of the need to stop addictive or compulsive behavior, (2) management of impulsivity and delaying immediate gratification, and (3) recognition of the context of overeating (Brache, 2012). The third and final stage primarily reviews the work done and reinforces the changes made.

IPT has demonstrated efficacy in the treatment of BED, with reported reductions in binge episodes ranging from 53% to 96% (Carter & Fairburn, 1998; Nauta, Hospers, Kok, & Jansen, 2000; Peterson et al., 1998; Ricca et al., 2001; Wilfley et al., 2002; Wilson, Wilfley, Agras, & Bryson, 2010). Randomized trials have found IPT to be equally as effective as CBT in initial reduction of binging, eating disorders, and psychiatric symptoms, although only slight decreases in body weight were observed (Hilbert et al., 2012; Wilfley et al., 2002; Wilson et al., 2010). These improvements were maintained following IPT cessation with approximately 60% of the patients remaining abstinent from binge eating at a 1-year (Wilfley et al., 2002) and 4-year follow-up (Hilbert et al., 2012). In addition, although low self-esteem and high eating-disorder psychopathology undermined the long-term efficacy of CBT and behavioral weight loss treatments, these factors did not diminish the influence of IPT (Wilson et al., 2010).

IPT represents an efficacious treatment for BED and associated psychopathology. When determining the treatment approach, clinicians and patients should together evaluate the advantage and disadvantages of utilizing IPT, CBT, and other therapeutic modalities. IPT may be more suitable for a subset of patients with low self-esteem and high eating-disorder psychopathology (Wilson et al., 2010). Given the association between these features and food addiction (Davis et al., 2011; Gearhardt et al., 2012, 2013), IPT may be particularly suitable for individuals suffering from food addiction and warrants future research.

Relational Psychotherapy

According to the relational therapeutic perspective, addictive behaviors may stem from an individual's need to avoid feeling emotional pain and an inability and/or reluctance to enter into meaningful interpersonal relationships (Stuart, 2001). Individuals with eating disorders specifically learn to relate to the world through food; food becomes the substitute for both emotions and meaningful relationships (Brisman, 2001). Relational psychotherapy is longer term in nature and less directive and didactic than many of the earlier mentioned treatments. It aims to shift a patient's focus from food toward relationships by helping patients to recognize dysfunctional relational patterns and enhancing emotional awareness (Petrucelli, 2004). Currently, the efficacy of relational psychotherapy for the treatment of food addiction and BED has yet to be tested. Further research into the treatment outcome of relational psychotherapy in the context of compulsive overeating is needed.

Family Therapy

Family therapy is conceptually similar to IPT and relational psychotherapy in that they target interpersonal relationships. However, family therapy specifically focuses on the relationship between family members and significant others, emphasizing that such relationships are important factors in psychological health and typically involving multiple family members in the treatment process. Multiple familial factors may moderate the relationships between addictive processes and their remediation; they include (1) familial disruption, stresses, and losses; (2) family members who engage in "enabling" behaviors that perpetuate addictive behaviors; and (3) poor child-rearing practices and lack of parental monitoring (Stanton & Shadish, 1997).

Therapists often employ a range of counseling and therapeutic techniques drawn from cognitive-behavioral, psychodynamic, attachment, and object-relations approaches (Lebow, 2005). Modest benefits have been reported for family therapy in substance abuse (Edwards & Steinglass, 1995; Liddle et al., 2001). Addressing and improving family dynamics may help in moderating binge eating and overconsumption of hyperpalatable foods and may have cross-generational benefits.

Self-help

Individuals seeking treatment for eating-related problems often display large variations in frequency and composition of symptoms. Many patients seeking treatment may not meet diagnostic criteria for BED, and it is common for patients to migrate between diagnoses (Fairburn, Cooper, & Shafran, 2003). Although psychotherapy has been found to be beneficial—particularly with regard to reducing binge-eating symptoms—this type of intervention is costly and may be unnecessarily intensive for some individuals (Fairburn et al., 1993). Self-help may facilitate the dissemination of treatment to a wider population of individuals who need it and can be distributed through various media such as in group format with videotapes (Peterson et al., 1998), self-help books (Kessler, 2009), by telephone (Wells, Garvin, Dohm, & Striegel-Moore, 1997), and on the Internet (Ljotsson et al., 2007).

Several investigations have found that cognitive-behavioral techniques administered in both pure and guided/assisted self-help formats can lead to marked reductions in binge-eating frequency and improvements in areas concerning self-concept, depression, and body-shape satisfaction among BED patients (Carter & Fairburn, 1998; Ghaderi & Scott, 2003; Grilo & Masheb, 2005; Loeb, Wilson, Gilbert, & Labouvie, 2000; Peterson et al., 1998; Wells et al., 1997), but as with psychotherapeutic techniques, self-help did not significantly alter body weight. Ljotsson et al. (2007) reported that these positive effects were maintained at a 6-month follow-up. Several popular self-help books have been written on the topic of "sugar addiction" (Bennett, 2007; DesMaisons, 2001), although their efficacy in the treatment of food addiction and prevention of relapse has yet to be systematically tested. Although traditional therapist-led group CBT for BED may be associated with better short-term outcomes including higher rates of binge-eating abstinence and greater reductions in binge-eating frequency (Grilo, 2007), group self-help intervention was comparable to therapist-led and therapist-assisted CBT at post-treatment (Peterson et al., 1998) and at 6- and 12-month follow-ups (Peterson, Mitchell, Crow, Crosby, & Wonderlich, 2009). Taken

together, the literature presents a compelling case that self-help is a feasible option for individuals with binge-eating problems. Delivering self-help could be considered a first-line intervention in a stepped care for the majority of individuals with overeating problems (Wilson, Vitousek, & Loeb, 2000), such as food addiction, allowing for effective allocation of resources catered to patient need.

Peer Support (12-Step Program)

One of the most popular treatment programs based on a food addiction model is Overeaters Anonymous (OA), a 12-step group self-help program for people with food-related problems such as, but not limited to, food addiction. OA promotes working toward or maintaining a healthy body weight. To identify potential members, a 15-item questionnaire consisting of questions such as "Do you eat when not hungry, or not eat when your body needs nourishment?" and "Do you give too much time and thought to food?" is conducted. Endorsing several of these items suggests that the individual may have, or be prone to have, compulsive eating or overeating problems (Overeaters Anonymous, 2013). Adopted from the 12-step program for substance abuse, the process involves admitting the loss of control over food; recognizing a higher power that can give strength; examining past errors (with the help of a sponsor or experienced member) and making amends; learning to live a new life with a new code of behavior; and helping and carrying the message to other compulsive overeaters (American Psychological Association, 2007; Overeaters Anonymous Inc. Staff, 1993). While 12-step programs for SUDs such as Alcoholics Anonymous stress absolute abstinence, abstinence in OA takes the form of limiting "trigger foods" (e.g., chocolate, cheese, fried goods) that may induce compulsive eating and/or irrational food behaviors. These long-recognized "trigger foods" in OA have strong parallels with the hyperpalatable foods discussed in the existing literature on food addiction.

Several qualitative studies have reported beneficial effects in managing eating disorder symptoms (Ronel & Libman, 2003; Westphal & Smith, 1996). However, systematic research into the therapeutic benefits from OA in terms of weight loss or physiological parameters (e.g., blood pressure, blood-sugar levels) are lacking. Thus, the efficacy of a 12-step program for food addiction remains unclear. As with substance addiction, food addiction may represent a chronic condition with periods of protracted abstinence (i.e., restriction of hyperpalatable foods) and periods of relapse (i.e., compulsive eating). Thus, it is likely that continuous care is required. Given that a large number of individuals turn to OA for treatment, future research into the efficacy of the 12-step system in the treatment of food addiction and other addictions is important.

Nutrition Counseling

Similar to the previous treatments discussed, scientific research on the efficacy of nutrition counseling for food addiction and BED remains sparse. Given shared nutritional and medical complications that may be associated with both BED and food addiction, nutrition interventions targeting BED may also hold promise for those struggling with a food addiction.

Nutrition professionals with an understanding of the psychology of eating, such as Registered Dietitians (RDs), can assess information relating to nutritional status, food beliefs, and eating behaviors and create tailored meal plans to support and facilitate healthy behavior change for those struggling with food addiction (Setnick, 2013; Waterhous & Jacob, 2011). RDs can help patients identify foods that may trigger compulsive eating, interpret food labels, and clarify portion sizes, which often become distorted for binge eaters (Herrin, 2003). Nutrition professionals can also work with patients to generate creative, nutritionally acceptable substitutes to hyperpalatable foods that will satisfy and accommodate taste preferences without triggering overeating (Peeke & Van Aalst, 2012).

As previously discussed, hyperpalatable (i.e., high-fat, high-sugar) foods have been posited as a potential risk factor for food addiction; diets excluding such foods may therefore be protective. According to the Food Addiction Research Education (2009), those struggling with food addiction should seek to avoid processed foods, artificial sweeteners, flour, gluten grains, and products with hydrogenated, partially hydrogenated and trans fats, and replace these potentially addictive foods with quality proteins, mono- and polyunsaturated fats, complex carbohydrates, and fruits and vegetables. Avoidance of caffeine and liquid calories has also been suggested to curb cravings. The recommendation to exclude hyperpalatable foods on a permanent versus temporary basis is a debated topic in the field, and more research is needed to establish the most effective approach to promote and sustain food addiction recovery (Setnick, 2013).

A meal plan can be a useful tool for individuals struggling with BED (Waterhous & Jacob, 2011), who, like those with a food addiction, may struggle with improper macronutrient (i.e., carbohydrates, protein, fat) balance, meal timing, and ability to honor or recognize satiety cues. A calorically adequate, individualized meal plan may add much needed structure for those with BED and food addiction (Setnick, 2013). Similar to those with food addiction, individuals with BED may make attempts to compensate for their overeating with periods of dietary restriction. However, physical and psychological states of deprivation created by dietary restriction may diminish an individual's ability to self-regulate around food, consequently exacerbating his or her propensity to ignore satiety signals and overeat at future meals. Furthermore, these overeating and/or binge episodes can intensify the guilt and shame that accompanies the eating patterns of those with food-addictive behaviors and can "reinforce the erroneous notion that restrictive eating is a solution" (Herrin, 2003, p. 156). A tailored food plan that promotes balanced macronutrient intake, proper portioning, and regular meal timing may help "recalibrate" the appetite of disordered eaters, realign dietary intake with an individual's specific nutritional needs, and reduce physiologically based urges to compulsively eat or binge (Herrin, 2003).

Based on the observation that once a triggering food has been eliminated, dysfunctional behaviors can surface around other foods, it has been suggested that nutrition treatment focusing on abstinence from unhealthy behaviors is more effective than avoiding any one particular food (Setnick, 2013). Behavioral modification strategies that may be helpful in reducing symptoms of food addiction include avoiding engaging in other activities while eating, discarding leftovers, making a grocery list, avoiding food shopping while hungry, eating single-serving foods, buying food that requires preparation, carrying limited money, eating meals with others, and brushing teeth after eating (Fairburn, 1995; Setnick, 2013). Practicing mindful eating techniques, stocking the kitchen with nontriggering foods, engaging in exercise, and getting adequate sleep have also been suggested by the Food Addiction Research Education (2009) as practical strategies.

Self-monitoring strategies can be used to bolster patients' self-awareness around food and have been shown to decrease the frequency of binge eating in BED (Herrin, 2003), suggesting their potential effectiveness in helping those battling food addiction. Food journaling, for example, is a self-monitoring tool commonly used in the treatment of eating disorders. This approach involves documenting daily food intake, hunger-fullness levels, and emotional states associated with eating. Food journaling may help patients differentiate between physical and emotional hunger and fullness by allowing them to later reflect on their feelings to gain a more comprehensive understanding of their affective state that may be overlooked in the moment of a binge or overeating episode (Herrin, 2003). For example, an individual who frequently reports guilt after eating certain foods may benefit from working with a therapist to investigate other sources of guilt unrelated to food and eating (Setnick, 2013). Finally, the very act of journaling may assist patients in independently identifying, coping with, and/or avoiding their personal triggers to overeat or binge.

Therapy Integration

Addictions remain challenging conditions to treat. Thus, an integrated treatment approach may be utilized by drawing on several modalities of therapy with an aim of creating a more comprehensive treatment model that focuses on addressing symptoms as well as underlying dynamics that contribute to and maintain the addictive behavior. For example, CBT, DBT, and relational psychotherapy may be blended together so that treatment focuses on reducing symptoms of food addiction and/or binge-eating episodes as well as exploring relational themes and attachment patterns (Gottlieb, 2013). Additionally, the inclusion of nutrition therapy, medication, medical monitoring, and intervention can also be important and mutually beneficial.

Many food-addicted individuals may report being at times able to get better control over their eating patterns, only to resort to dysfunctional behaviors at a later date, and this pattern may lead to "yo-yo" dieting and patterns of weight loss and regain. Underlying multiple theoretical orientations is the notion that food addictions, like other addictive and eating-disordered behaviors, serve as means by which an individual modulates affect (Conners, 2010; Whiteside et al., 2007). It is hypothesized that food temporarily "numbs" a negative emotion or creates a distraction away from a distressing affect. Consequently, combining multiple treatment strategies may help patients develop more adaptive coping skills so that they are better able to identify, manage, and tolerate their affective states.

Case Vignette: Patient F

F is a Caucasian female administrative assistant in her mid-40s who presented for therapy for treatment of binge-eating disorder as well as to gain better control over her mood and anxiety. At the start of therapy, F weighed approximately 245 lbs. at a height of 5′4″.

F reported a long history of food addiction, indicating that she struggled with her weight and binge eating since adolescence and expressed frustration in her inability to achieve and maintain weight loss. She reported a history of multiple treatment failures and described her eating behaviors as "out of control," indicating that she often ate when she felt overwhelmed by stress or anxiety and felt that she had little power to stop herself from engaging in binge-eating episodes, a feeling state often described by food-addicted patients. She gravitated toward carbohydrates and sugary foods when she would binge or overeat and

Continued

Case Vignette: Patient F—cont'd

added that often these behaviors would cluster over the course of a few consecutive days, which was typically followed by a pattern of more mindful eating. In this way, an on/off or black/white pattern emerged with food, one that is frequently observed in individuals with substance abuse and other addictions.

Food addiction, like other addictive behaviors, is a complex issue composed of the interplay of emotional and behavioral factors. Given this, an integrative treatment approach drawing on the treatment modalities of CBT, DBT, and relational psychotherapy was utilized to address F's symptoms. In addition, she attended a year-long hospital-based weight loss program, which included support group meetings as well as nutrition sessions. Her psychotherapy focused on the following areas: emotional awareness, distress tolerance, and other relational issues.

- Emotional awareness: F was continually asked to think about how she felt and was able to learn how food served to block or dissociate her from her affective states and, consequently, perpetuated her cycle of binge eating and emotional unawareness. F was asked to keep a thought journal and a food journal to help enhance her emotional and behavioral awareness outside therapy sessions.
- Emotional acceptance/ distress tolerance: When F was able to identify her emotions, tolerating these states created a great deal of anxiety for her as well as urges to eat/binge. Therapy worked to normalize these experiences and desires as well as to generate strategies to manage her feelings when they became overwhelming. Strategies such as calling a friend, taking a walk, and journaling were favorites of F's. In addition, the importance of "riding it out" with the belief that an emotion is a temporary state that will pass became important. This is a strategy often used with substance abuse patients and referred to as "urge surfing" (Lloyd, 2008).
- Relational issues: As treatment progressed, patterns in F's relationships began to emerge. She began to recognize an inability to say no and a habit of overextending herself. As a consequence, F often felt stressed, resentful, and lacked time for necessary self-care. Such behaviors occurred across settings, happening at work as well as with her friends and family members. Therapy focused on helping recognize this relational pattern and learning how to set better boundaries with those around her.

Conclusion

When F completed her year-long hospital-based weight loss program, she began to attend support groups set up for former program participants. F continued with her food and thought journaling. Binge-eating episodes were more isolated, and she was able to get back on track more quickly. F continued to lose weight, although her loss was slow and often intermittent, which was frustrating for F. She remains in therapy at the time of this publication, attending sessions every other week to help maintain her progress.

PREVENTION: PUBLIC HEALTH AND POLICY IMPLICATIONS

Addiction prevention is a long-term endeavor and requires joint effort from medical communities, industries, and government agencies. One of the most successful prevention interventions in public health in the last century was in promoting smoking cessation. Prevalence rates of adult smoking in the United States have dropped from 43% in 1972 to an all-time low of 20% in 2012 (Gallup, 2012). The dramatic decline has been largely attributed to the introduction and implementation of effective educational campaigns based on informing the public about the deleterious health effects of smoking and the campaign to alert the medical community to the importance of evaluating and treating smokers (Backinger et al., 2003). Tobacco-control policies, including smoking bans in public spaces, increased cigarette prices, and enactment and enforcement of laws restricting youth access to tobacco products, are also thought to have contributed to the decline.

The success of such interventions for substance (nicotine) addiction may be useful for designing effective campaigns to reduce rates of food addiction (Gearhardt, Grilo, DiLeone, Brownell, Potenza, 2011). Although other therapies are in the pipeline, the importance of exercise and nutrition should not be underestimated. Education regarding healthy eating, including scientific knowledge of the effects of different foods (particularly hyperpalatable foods), and the importance of regular exercise should be initiated from an early age to encourage children to develop life-long healthy eating habits. The engagement of pediatricians and family physicians might facilitate early detection and treatment of food addiction in childhood and adolescence. Medical communities should be cautious of prematurely dismissing food addiction and should be prepared to identify, evaluate, and treat it.

Banning tobacco companies from sponsoring sporting and entertainment events and selling or distributing items (e.g., hats and tee-shirts) with tobacco brands or logos has contributed importantly to reducing tobacco use (FDA, 2012d). In contrast, low-cost, nutrient poor, and calorie-dense hyperpalatable food are arguably the most frequently marketed products and are often designed to target children and adolescents (Powell, Szczypka, Chaloupka, & Braunschweig, 2007). Little attention has been given to how the engineering and marketing of hyperpalatable food may interact with possible risk factors to generate brain responses like those to drugs of abuse. Restricting advertisement of potentially addictive foods may be an important health strategy. Furthermore, the food industry should be encouraged to make healthy foods more attractive (e.g., by advertisements and price reductions); and, as with tobacco products, schools, workplaces, rest stops, and other public places should make efforts to remove junk foods from dispensing machines and cafeterias. These proposed reforms, however, have been lobbied against by the food industry (and arguably other bodies) that argues that individuals should be given the freedom to make their own food choices. The food industry has formed partnerships with health charities and health sector organizations; for example, UNICEF Canada, which promotes and supports nutritional programs in developing countries, has partnered with Cadbury chocolate bars (Freedhoff & Hebert, 2011). Through these partnerships, the food industry communicates that rather than the promotion and consumption of calorie-rich products, other factors such as inactivity may be the prime cause of obesity. For instance, Dr. Dean Ornish, president of the Preventative Medicine Research Institute, has headlined a Mars Inc. web page stating, "It's important to find a balance between what we eat and how much we exercise, and it's important to balance enjoying snack foods along with eating a variety of other types of foods" (Mars Inc., 2010).

One widely discussed and controversial control policy is the "soda tax" legislation aimed to discourage unhealthy diets by taxing sugar-sweetened beverages. As mentioned previously, researchers have demonstrated that high-sugar diets may be addictive (Avena, Bocarsly, & Hoebel, 2012). It is posited that sweetened beverages may be the single largest source of sugar (Brownell et al., 2009; Brownell & Frieden, 2009). Brownell and colleagues at the Yale Rudd Center for Food Policy and Obesity first introduced the concept in 2004 and suggest that every 10% increase in price could, on average, decrease consumption by 7.8% [others have reported impacts of smaller magnitude (Fletcher, Frisvold, & Tefft, 2010)] and could help raise revenue that could be directed toward bettering health care service (Brownell & Frieden, 2009; United States Department of Agriculture, 2010). This policy is now adopted by 40 states with small taxes imposed on sweetened beverages and snack foods (Brownell & Frieden, 2009). New York State has recently discussed the introduction of larger taxes, but this has been vigorously opposed by the beverage industry, and the proposed taxes were eventually abandoned. Interestingly, Mississippi, the state that had the nation's highest rate of obesity (34.9%) in 2011 (CDC, 2011), passed legislation on

March 21, 2013, banning local government from restricting food-serving size.

Other policies such as enforcing informative nutrition labeling on food products may also help in promoting balanced, healthy diets. Efforts have been made by the Food and Drug Administration (FDA) to enforce standardized labeling and ingredient and nutrient declaration with several acts, including the Nutrition Labeling and Education Act of 1990 (NLEA) and Dietary Supplement Health and Education Act of 1994 (DSHEA) having been passed in recent decades. However, companies do not consistently comply with these acts. In 2009, the FDA identified 17 food manufacturers with one or more products that violated the NLEA act (FDA, 2012b), and audits from 2011–2012 reported nearly 740 cases in which manufacturers were not compliant with "current good manufacturing practices" (FDA, 2012a, 2012c). Violations include unauthorized nutrient content claims, unauthorized health claims, and the unauthorized use of terms such as *healthy*. Moreover, companies often suggest and print serving sizes much smaller than what is actually consumed, and the recommended daily intake information is often calculated only for adult males. Various legal, legislative, and regulatory approaches including stricter enforcement and clearer labeling, such as front-of-package labeling, are needed. However, significant social, legal, financial, and public perception barriers have hindered these efforts.

CONCLUSION

Recent findings have strengthened the case for food addiction. Support for various components of a food addiction model comes from data documenting common neural features with SUDs including in pathways involved in reward sensitivity, conditioned learning, and cognitive control. In particular, certain foods (e.g., hyperpalatable foods rich in carbohydrates or fats, or their combination) may possess enhanced motivational properties in a manner analogous to drugs of abuse and may be more likely to lead to addictive eating patterns. These findings may serve to validate the perception of food addiction in patients and inform psychotherapeutic, psychoeducational, pharmacological, and other treatments for chronic food cravings, compulsive overeating, and/or binge eating.

Studying the relationship between food addiction and obesity, particularly exploring the behavioral and psychopathological responses to food consumption, offers useful information for maintaining weight loss and preventing obesity. Screening for food addiction using standardized self-reported measures such as the YFAS has the potential to identify people with eating difficulties that may compromise their weight management efforts. While the YFAS has been demonstrated to be a reliable and valid measure of food addiction (Davis et al., 2011; Gearhardt et al., 2009b), it has yet to be widely adopted, and food addiction often remains overlooked in clinical settings. Large-scale prevention and treatment programs for food addiction (like those for substance addiction) will require participation from the medical community; unfortunately, physicians, nurses, psychologists and other clinicians currently receive little or no training in the management of overeating behaviors.

It is premature to reject the concept of food addiction, and existing findings are compelling to warrant further epidemiological and clinical research. The development of empirically validated, efficacious, and tolerable treatments is needed. This process will likely be facilitated by an improved understanding of the mechanisms underlying food addiction and by identification of mediators and moderators of outcome. Future research should include a focus on food addiction in humans, and such research should involve the development of improved prevention, treatment, and policy efforts.

Additional resources beyond the peer-reviewed literature noted in the reference list include the following:

- Yale Rudd Center for Food Policy & Obesity. More information is available at http://www.yaleruddcenter.org/
- Obesity and Food Addiction Summit. More information is available at http://www.foodaddictionsummit.org/

REFERENCES

Adam, T. C., & Epel, E. S. (2007). Stress, eating and the reward system. *Physiology & Behavior, 91*(4), 449–458.

Aharonovich, E., Nunes, E., & Hasin, D. (2003). Cognitive impairment, retention and abstinence among cocaine abusers in cognitive-behavioral treatment. *Drug and Alcohol Dependence, 71*(2), 207–211.

Allison, D. B., Mentore, J. L., Heo, M., Chandler, L. P., Cappelleri, J. C., Infante, M. C., et al. (1999). Antipsychotic-induced weight gain: A comprehensive research synthesis. *American Journal of Psychiatry, 156*(11), 1686–1696.

Alsiö, J., Olszewski, P. K., Norbäck, A. H., Gunnarsson, Z. E. A., Levine, A. S., Pickering, C., et al. (2010). Dopamine D1 receptor gene expression decreases in the nucleus accumbens upon long-term exposure to palatable food and differs depending on diet-induced obesity phenotype in rats. *Neuroscience, 171*(3), 779–787.

American Psychiatric Association. (2000). *Diagnostic and statistical manual of mental disorders* (4th ed., text rev.). Washington, DC: Author.

American Psychiatric Association. (2013). *Diagnostic and statistical manual of mental disorders* (5th ed.). Washington, DC: Author.

American Psychological Association. (2007). *APA dictionary of psychology*. Washington, DC: Author.

Astrup, A., Meinert Larsen, D. T., & Harper, A. (2004). Atkins and other low-carbohydrate diets: Hoax or an effective tool for weight loss? *Lancet, 364*(9437), 897–899.

Avena, N. M. (2010). The study of food addiction using animal models of binge eating. *Appetite, 55*(3), 734–737.

Avena, N. M., Bocarsly, M. E., & Hoebel, B. G. (2012). Animal models of sugar and fat bingeing: Relationship to food addiction and increased body weight. In F. H. Kobeissy (Ed.), *Psychiatric disorders: Vol. 829*. (pp. 351–365). Humana Press.

Avena, N. M., Bocarsly, M. E., Hoebel, B. G., & Gold, M. S. (2011). Overlaps in the nosology of substance abuse and overeating: The translational implications of "food addiction". *Current Drug Abuse Reviews, 4*(3), 133–139.

Avena, N. M., Bocarsly, M. E., Rada, P., Kim, A., & Hoebel, B. G. (2008). After daily bingeing on a sucrose solution, food deprivation induces anxiety and accumbens dopamine/acetylcholine imbalance. *Physiology & Behavior, 94*(3), 309–315.

Avena, N. M., Gearhardt, A. N., Gold, M. S., Wang, G.-J., & Potenza, M. N. (2012). Tossing the baby out with the bathwater after a brief rinse? The potential downside of dismissing food addiction based on limited data. *Nature Reviews Neuroscience, 13*(7), 514–514.

Avena, N. M., & Gold, M. S. (2011). Variety and hyperpalatability: Are they promoting addictive overeating? *American Journal of Clinical Nutrition, 94*(2), 367–368.

Avena, N. M., & Hoebel, B. G. (2003). A diet promoting sugar dependency causes behavioral cross-sensitization to a low dose of amphetamine. *Neuroscience, 122*(1), 17–20.

Avena, N. M., Rada, P., & Hoebel, B. G. (2009). Sugar and fat bingeing have notable differences in addictive-like behavior. *Journal of Nutrition, 139*(3), 623–628.

Backinger, C. L., Fagan, P., Matthews, E., & Grana, R. (2003). Adolescent and young adult tobacco prevention and cessation: Current status and future directions. *Tobacco Control, 12*(Suppl. 4), IV46–53.

Balodis, I. M., Kober, H., Worhunsky, P. D., White, M. A., Stevens, M. C., Pearlson, G. D., et al. (2013). Monetary reward processing in obese individuals with and without binge eating disorder. *Biological Psychiatry, 73*(9), 877–886.

Balodis, I. M., Molina, N. D., Kober, H., Worhunsky, P. D., White, M. A., Sinha, R., et al. (2013). Divergent neural substrates of inhibitory control in binge eating disorder relative to other manifestations of obesity. *Obesity, 21*(2), 367–377.

Bennett, C. (2007). *Sugar shock!: How sweets and simple carbs can derail your life—and how you can get it back on track*. New York, NY: Penguin Group.

Berkman, N. D., Bulik, C. M., Brownley, K. A., Lohr, K. N., Sedway, J. A., Rooks, A., et al. (2006). Management of eating disorders. *Evidence Report Technology Assessment (Full Rep), 135*, 1–166.

Bocarsly, M. E., Berner, L. A., Hoebel, B. G., & Avena, N. M. (2011). Rats that binge eat fat-rich food do not show somatic signs or anxiety associated with opiate-like withdrawal: Implications for nutrient-specific food addiction behaviors. *Physiology & Behavior, 104*(5), 865–872.

Brache, K. (2012). Advancing interpersonal therapy for substance use disorders. *American Journal of Drug and Alcohol Abuse, 38*(4), 293–298.

Brewer, J. A., & Potenza, M. N. (2008). The neurobiology and genetics of impulse control disorders: Relationships to drug addictions. *Biochemical Pharmacology, 75*(1), 63–75.

Brisman, J. (2001). The instigation of dare: Broadening therapuetic horizons. In J. Petrucelli & C. Sturat (Eds.), *Hungers and compulsions: The psychodynamnic treatment of eating disorders and addictions* (pp. 53–64). Northvale, NJ: Jason Araonson Inc.

Brownell, K. D., Farley, T., Willett, W. C., Popkin, B. M., Chaloupka, F. J., Thompson, J. W., et al. (2009). The public health and economic benefits of taxing sugar-sweetened beverages. *New England Journal of Medicine, 361*(16), 1599–1605.

Brownell, K. D., & Frieden, T. R. (2009). Ounces of prevention—The public policy case for taxes on sugared beverages. *New England Journal of Medicine, 360*(18), 1805–1808.

Brownley, K. A., Berkman, N. D., Sedway, J. A., Lohr, K. N., & Bulik, C. M. (2007). Binge eating disorder treatment: A systematic review of randomized controlled trials. *Internaltion Journal of Eating Disorders, 40*(4), 337–348.

Carter, J. C., & Fairburn, C. G. (1998). Cognitive-behavioral self-help for binge eating disorder: A controlled effectiveness study. *Journal of Consulting and Clinical Psychology, 66*(4), 616–623.

CDC. (2011). Overweight and obesity. Retrieved March 21, 2013, from http://www.cdc.gov/obesity/data/adult.html.

Clark, A. M. (2012). Reward processing: A global brain phenomenon? *Journal of Neurophysiology, 109*(1), 1–4.

Colantuoni, C., Rada, P., McCarthy, J., Patten, C., Avena, N. M., Chadeayne, A., et al. (2002). Evidence that intermittent, excessive sugar intake causes endogenous opioid dependence. *Obesity Research, 10*(6), 478–488.

Conners, M. E. (2010). Symptom-focused dynamic psychotherapy. *Journal of Psychotherapy Integration, 20*, 37–45.

Danaei, G., Ding, E. L., Mozaffarian, D., Taylor, B., Rehm, J., Murray, C. J., et al. (2009). The preventable causes of death in the United States: Comparative risk assessment of dietary, lifestyle, and metabolic risk factors. *PLoS Med, 6*(4), e1000058.

Davis, C., & Carter, J. C. (2009). Compulsive overeating as an addiction disorder. A review of theory and evidence. *Appetite, 53*(1), 1–8.

Davis, C., Curtis, C., Levitan, R. D., Carter, J. C., Kaplan, A. S., & Kennedy, J. L. (2011). Evidence that 'food addiction' is a valid phenotype of obesity. *Appetite, 57*(3), 711–717.

Davis, C. A., Levitan, R. D., Reid, C., Carter, J. C., Kaplan, A. S., Patte, K. A., et al. (2009). Dopamine for "wanting" and opioids for "liking": A comparison of obese adults with and without binge eating. *Obesity, 17*(6), 1220–1225.

DesMaisons, K. (2001). *Your last diet!: The sugar addict's weight-loss plan*. Toronto, ON: Random House.

Devlin, M. J., Goldfein, J. A., Petkova, E., Liu, L., & Walsh, B. T. (2007). Cognitive behavioral therapy and fluoxetine for binge eating disorder: Two-year follow-up. *Obesity (Silver Spring), 15*(7), 1702–1709.

Di Chiara, G., & Imperato, A. (1988). Drugs abused by humans preferentially increase synaptic dopamine concentrations in the mesolimbic system of freely moving rats. *Proceedings of the National Academy of Science U S A, 85*(14), 5274–5278.

Dick, D. M., Wang, J. C., Plunkett, J., Aliev, F., Hinrichs, A., Bertelsen, S., et al. (2007). Family-based association analyses of alcohol dependence phenotypes across DRD2 and neighboring gene ANKK1. *Alcoholism: Clinical and Experimental Research, 31*(10), 1645–1653.

Edwards, M. E., & Steinglass, P. (1995). Family therapy treatment outcomes for alcoholism. *Journal of Marital and Family Therapy, 21*(4), 475–509.

Everitt, B. J., Belin, D., Economidou, D., Pelloux, Y., Dalley, J. W., & Robbins, T. W. (2008). Review. Neural mechanisms underlying the vulnerability to develop compulsive drug-seeking habits and addiction. *Philosophical Transactions of the Royal Society B: Biological Sciences, 363*(1507), 3125–3135.

Fairburn, C. (1981). A cognitive behavioural approach to the treatment of bulimia. *Psychological Medicine, 11*(4), 707–711.

Fairburn, C. (1995). *Overcoming binge eating*. New York: The Guilford Press.

Fairburn, C. G., Cooper, Z., & Shafran, R. (2003). Cognitive behaviour therapy for eating disorders: A "transdiagnostic" theory and treatment. *Behaviour Research and Therapy, 41*(5), 509–528.

Fairburn, C. G., Wilson, G. T., & Schleimer, K. (1993). *Binge eating: Nature, assessment, and treatment*. New York: Guilford Press.

FDA. (2012a). Current Good Manufacturing Practices (CGMPs)/Compliance. Retrieved March 20, 2013, from FDA http://www.fda.gov/Drugs/GuidanceComplianceRegulatoryInformation/Guidances/ucm064971.htm.

FDA. (2012b). Front-of-package labeling initiative questions & answers. Retrieved March 20, 2013, from http://www.fda.gov/Food/IngredientsPackagingLabeling/LabelingNutrition/ucm202734.htm.

FDA. (2012c). Inspections, compliance, enforcement, and criminal investigations. Retrieved March 20, 2013, from FDA http://www.fda.gov/ICECI/EnforcementActions/WarningLetters/2012/default.htm.

FDA. (2012d). Regulations restricting the sale and distribution of cigarettes and smokeless tobacco. Retrieved March 20, 2013, from http://www.fda.gov/TobaccoProducts/ProtectingKidsfromTobacco/RegsRestrictingSale/.

Fletcher, J. M., Frisvold, D., & Tefft, N. (2010). Can soft drink taxes reduce population weight? *Contemporary Economic Policy*, *28*(1), 23–35.

Food Addiction Research Education. (2009). How do I heal from a food addiction. Retrieved March 20, 2013, from http://foodaddictionresearch.org/question-and-answer/if-im-addicted-to-food-what-can-i-do.

Freedhoff, Y., & Hebert, P. C. (2011). Partnerships between health organizations and the food industry risk derailing public health nutrition. *Canadian Medical Association Journal*, *183*(3), 291–292.

Gallup. (2012, & July 9 2012). Gallup Poll social series: Consumption habit. Retrieved March 19, 2013, from http://www.gallup.com/file/poll/156842/Smoking_120822.pdf.

Gautier, J. F., Chen, K., Salbe, A. D., Bandy, D., Pratley, R. E., Heiman, M., et al. (2000). Differential brain responses to satiation in obese and lean men. *Diabetes*, *49*(5), 838–846.

Gearhardt, A., Davis, C., Kuschner, R., & Brownell, K. (2011). The addiction potential of hyperpalatable foods. *Current Drug Abuse Reviews*, *4*(3), 140.

Gearhardt, A., White, M., & Potenza, M. (2011). Binge eating disorder and food addiction. *Current Drug Abuse Reviews*, *4*(3), 201–207.

Gearhardt, A. N., Corbin, W. R., & Brownell, K. D. (2008). Instruction Sheet for the Yale Food Addiction Scale. Retrieved February 28, 2013, from http://www.yaleruddcenter.org/resources/upload/docs/what/addiction/FoodAddictionScaleInstructions09.pdf.

Gearhardt, A. N., Corbin, W. R., & Brownell, K. D. (2009a). Food addiction: An examination of the diagnostic criteria for dependence. *Journal of Addiction Medicine*, *3*(1), 1–7.

Gearhardt, A. N., Corbin, W. R., & Brownell, K. D. (2009b). Preliminary validation of the Yale Food Addiction Scale. *Appetite*, *52*(2), 430–436.

Gearhardt, A. N., Grilo, C. M., DiLeone, R. J., Brownell, K. D., & Potenza, M. N. (2011). Can food be addictive? Public health and policy implications. *Addiction*, *106*(7), 1208–1212.

Gearhardt, A. N., White, M. A., Masheb, R. M., & Grilo, C. M. (2013). An examination of food addiction in a racially diverse sample of obese patients with binge eating disorder in primary care settings. *Comprehensive Psychiatry*, *54*(5), 500–505.

Gearhardt, A. N., White, M. A., Masheb, R. M., Morgan, P. T., Crosby, R. D., & Grilo, C. M. (2012). An examination of the food addiction construct in obese patients with binge eating disorder. *International Journal of Eating Disorders*, *45*(5), 657–663.

Gearhardt, A. N., Yokum, S., Orr, P. T., Stice, E., Corbin, W. R., & Brownell, K. D. (2011). Neural correlates of food addiction. *Archives of General Psychiatry*, *68*(8), 808–816.

Geiger, B. M., Behr, G. G., Frank, L. E., Caldera-Siu, A. D., Beinfeld, M. C., Kokkotou, E. G., et al. (2008). Evidence for defective mesolimbic dopamine exocytosis in obesity-prone rats. *FASEB Journal*, *22*(8), 2740–2746.

Geloneze, B., Mancini, M. C., & Coutinho, W. (2009). Obesity: Knowledge, care, and commitment, but not yet cure. *Obesidade*, *53*(2), 117–119.

Ghaderi, A., & Scott, B. (2003). Pure and guided self-help for full and sub-threshold bulimia nervosa and binge eating disorder. *British Journal of Clinical Psychology*, *42*(3), 257–269.

Gottlieb, C. (In press). Come together: The blending of CBT, DBT, and interpersonal psychotherapy in the treatment of eating disorders. In J. Petrucelli (Ed.), Body-states: Interpersonal/relational perspectives on the treatment of eating disorders. New York/ London: Routledge.

Grilo, C. M. (2007). Guided self-help for binge-eating disorder. In J. D. Latner & G. T. Wilson (Eds.), *Self-help for obesity and eating disorders* (pp. 73–91). New York, NY: Guilford.

Grilo, C. M., & Masheb, R. M. (2005). A randomized controlled comparison of guided self-help cognitive behavioral therapy and behavioral weight loss for binge eating disorder. *Behavior Research and Therapy*, *43*(11), 1509–1525.

Grilo, C. M., Masheb, R. M., & White, M. A. (2010). Significance of overvaluation of shape/ weight in binge-eating disorder: Comparative study with overweight and bulimia nervosa. *Obesity*, *18*(3), 499–504.

Guerdjikova, A. I., McElroy, S. L., Kotwal, R., Welge, J. A., Nelson, E., Lake, K., et al. (2008). High-dose escitalopram in the treatment of binge-eating disorder with obesity: A placebo-controlled monotherapy trial. *Human Psychopharmacology: Clinical and Experimental*, *23*(1), 1–11.

Guerrieri, R., Nederkoorn, C., & Jansen, A. (2008). The interaction between impulsivity and a varied food environment: Its influence on food intake and overweight. *International Journal of Obesity*, *32*(4), 708–714.

Heinz, A., Reimold, M., Wrase, J., Hermann, D., Croissant, B., Mundle, G., et al. (2005). Correlation of stable elevations in striatal mu-opioid receptor availability in detoxified alcoholic patients with alcohol craving: A positron emission tomography study using carbon 11–labeled carfentanil. *Archives of General Psychiatry*, *62*(1), 57–64.

Herrin, M. (2003). *Nutrition counseling in the treatment of eating disorders*. New York: Routledge.

Hilbert, A., Bishop, M. E., Stein, R. I., Tanofsky-Kraff, M., Swenson, A. K., Welch, R. R., et al. (2012). Long-term efficacy of psychological treatments for binge eating disorder. *British Journal of Psychiatry*, *200*(3), 232–237.

Holahan, C. J., Moos, R. H., Holahan, C. K., Cronkite, R. C., & Randall, P. K. (2001). Drinking to cope, emotional distress and alcohol use and abuse: A ten-year model. *Journal of Studies on Alcohol*, *62*(2), 190–198.

Huang, X. F., Zavitsanou, K., Huang, X., Yu, Y., Wang, H., Chen, F., et al. (2006). Dopamine transporter and D2 receptor binding densities in mice prone or resistant to chronic high fat diet-induced obesity. *Behavioral Brain Research*, *175*(2), 415–419.

Jastreboff, A. M., Sinha, R., Lacadie, C., Small, D. M., Sherwin, R. S., & Potenza, M. N. (2013). Neural correlates of stress- and food cue-induced food craving in obesity: Association with insulin levels. *Diabetes Care*, *36*(2), 394–402.

Johnson, P. M., & Kenny, P. J. (2010). Dopamine D2 receptors in addiction-like reward dysfunction and compulsive eating in obese rats. *Nature Neurosciene*, *13*(5), 635–641.

Joranby, L., Pineda, K. F., & Gold, M. S. (2005). Addiction to food and brain reward systems. *Sexual Addiction & Compulsivity*, *12*(2–3), 201–217.

Kampov-Polevoy, A. B., Garbutt, J. C., & Khalitov, E. (2003). Family history of alcoholism and response to sweets. *Alcoholism: Clinical and Experimental Research*, *27*(11), 1743–1749.

Karelis, A. D., St-Pierre, D. H., Conus, F., Rabasa-Lhoret, R., & Poehlman, E. T. (2004). Metabolic and body composition factors in subgroups of obesity: What do we know? *Journal of Clinical Endocrinology & Metabolism*, *89*(6), 2569–2575.

Kelley, A. E., Bakshi, V. P., Haber, S. N., Steininger, T. L., Will, M. J., & Zhang, M. (2002). Opioid modulation of taste hedonics within the ventral striatum. *Physiological Behavior*, *76*(3), 365–377.

Kessler, D. A. (2009). *The end of overeating: Taking control of the insatiable American appetite*. New York, NY: Rodale.

Koob, G. F., & Volkow, N. D. (2010). Neurocircuitry of addiction. *Neuropsychopharmacology*, *35*(1), 217–238.

Lebow, J. L. (2005). *Handbook of clinical family therapy*. New Jersey: Wiley.
Leombruni, P., Piero, A., Brustolin, A., Mondelli, V., Levi, M., Campisi, S., et al. (2006). A 12 to 24 weeks pilot study of sertraline treatment in obese women binge eaters. *Human Psychopharmacology*, *21*(3), 181–188.
Leombruni, P., Piero, A., Lavagnino, L., Brustolin, A., Campisi, S., & Fassino, S. (2008). A randomized, double-blind trial comparing sertraline and fluoxetine 6-month treatment in obese patients with binge eating disorder. *Progress in Neuropsychopharmacology and Biological Psychiatry*, *32*(6), 1599–1605.
Liddle, H. A., Dakof, G. A., Parker, K., Diamond, G. S., Barrett, K., & Tejeda, M. (2001). Multidimensional family therapy for adolescent drug abuse: Results of a randomized clinical trial. *American Journal of Drug and Alcohol Abuse*, *27*(4), 651–688.
Linehan, M. M. (1993). *Cognitive behavioral treatment of boderline personality disorder*. New York: Guilford Press.
Ljotsson, B., Lundin, C., Mitsell, K., Carlbring, P., Ramklint, M., & Ghaderi, A. (2007). Remote treatment of bulimia nervosa and binge eating disorder: A randomized trial of Internet-assisted cognitive behavioural therapy. *Behaviour Research and Therapy*, *45*(4), 649–661.
Lloyd, A. (2008). *Cognitive behavior therapy: Applying empirically supported techniques in your practice* (2nd ed.). Hoboken, NJ: John Wiley & Sons Inc.
Loeb, K. L., Wilson, G. T., Gilbert, J. S., & Labouvie, E. (2000). Guided and unguided self-help for binge eating. *Behavorial Research Therapy*, *38*(3), 259–272.
Lutter, M., & Nestler, E. J. (2009). Homeostatic and hedonic signals interact in the regulation of food intake. *Journal of Nutrition*, *139*(3), 629–632.
Lynch, T. R., Chapman, A. L., Rosenthal, M. Z., Kuo, J. R., & Linehan, M. M. (2006). Mechanisms of change in dialectic behavior therapy: Theoretical and empirical observations. *Journal of Clinical Psychology*, *62*, 459–480.
Maciejewski, M. L., Livingston, E. H., Smith, V. A., Kavee, A. L., Kahwati, L. C., Henderson, W. G., et al. (2011). Survival among high-risk patients after bariatric surgery. *Journal of the American Medical Association*, *305*(23), 2419–2426.
Marcus, M. D., & Wildes, J. E. (2009). Obesity: Is it a mental disorder? *International Journal of Eating Disorders*, *42*(8), 739–753.
Markowitz, J. C., & Weissman, M. M. (2004). Interpersonal psychotherapy: Principles and applications. *World Psychiatry*, *3*(3), 136–139.
Mars Inc. (2010). Feeling good. Retrieved November 6, 2010, from http://marshealthyliving.com/feeling-good.
Masheb, R. M., & Grilo, C. M. (2000). Binge eating disorder: A need for additional diagnostic criteria. *Comprehensive Psychiatry*, *41*(3), 159–162.
Masheb, R. M., & Grilo, C. M. (2006). Eating patterns and breakfast consumption in obese patients with binge eating disorder. *Behavioral Research Therapy*, *44*(11), 1545–1553.
Maude-Griffin, P. M., Hohenstein, J. M., Humfleet, G. L., Reilly, P. M., Tusel, D. J., & Hall, S. M. (1998). Superior efficacy of cognitive-behavioral therapy for urban crack cocaine abusers: Main and matching effects. *Journal of Consulting and Clinical Psychology*, *66*(5), 832–837.
Merlo, L. J., Klingman, C., Malasanos, T. H., & Silverstein, J. H. (2009). Exploration of food addiction in pediatric patients: A preliminary investigation. *Journal of Addiction Medicine*, *3*(1), 26–32.
Meule, A. (2011). How prevalent is 'food addiction'? *Frontiers in Psychiatry*, *2*, 61.
Miller, J. L., James, G. A., Goldstone, A. P., Couch, J. A., He, G., Driscoll, D. J., et al. (2007). Enhanced activation of reward mediating prefrontal regions in response to food stimuli in Prader-Willi syndrome. *Journal of Neurology, Neurosurgery, & Psychiatry*, *78*(6), 615–619.
Mitchell, J. E., Devlin, M. J., de Zwaan, M., Crow, S. J., & Peterson, C. B. (2008). *Binge-eating disorder: Clinical foundations and treatment*. Cambridge, UK: Cambridge University Press.

Mokdad, A. H., Ford, E. S., Bowman, B. A., Dietz, W. H., Vinicor, F., Bales, V. S., et al. (2003). Prevalence of obesity, diabetes, and obesity-related health risk factors, 2001. *Journal of the American Medical Associatiion, 289*(1), 76–79.

Mokdad, A. H., Marks, J. S., Stroup, D. F., & Gerberding, J. L. (2004). Actual causes of death in the United States, 2000. *Journal of the American Medical Associatiion, 291*(10), 1238–1245.

Munsch, S., Biedert, E., Meyer, A., Michael, T., Schlup, B., Tuch, A., et al. (2007). A randomized comparison of cognitive behavioral therapy and behavioral weight loss treatment for overweight individuals with binge eating disorder. *International Journal of Eating Disorders, 40*(2), 102–113.

Must, A., Spadano, J., Coakley, E. H., Field, A. E., Colditz, G., & Dietz, W. H. (1999). The disease burden associated with overweight and obesity. *Journal of the American Medical Association, 282*(16), 1523–1529.

Nauta, H., Hospers, H., Kok, G., & Jansen, A. (2000). A comparison between a cognitive and a behavioral treatment for obese binge eaters and obese non-binge eaters. *Behavioral Therapy, 21*, 441–461.

Nunes, E. V., & Rounsaville, B. J. (2006). Comorbidity of substance use with depression and other mental disorders: from *Diagnostic and Statistical Manual of Mental Disorders*, (4th ed.). (DSM-IV) to DSM-V. *Addiction, 101*, 89–96.

O'Malley, S., Krishnan-Sarin, S., Farren, C., Sinha, R., & Kreek, M. (2002). Naltrexone decreases craving and alcohol self-administration in alcohol-dependent subjects and activates the hypothalamo–pituitary–adrenocortical axis. *Psychopharmacology (Berlin), 160*(1), 19–29.

Ogden, C. L., Carroll, M. D., Kit, B. K., & Flegal, K. M. (2012). *Prevalence of Obesity in the United States: National Center for Health Statistics, U.S.* Department of Health and Human Services.

Oswald, K. D., Murdaugh, D. L., King, V. L., & Boggiano, M. M. (2011). Motivation for palatable food despite consequences in an animal model of binge eating. *International Journal of Eating Disorders, 44*(3), 203–211.

Overeaters Anonymous. (2013). Is OA for You? Retrieved March 20, 2013, from http://www.oa.org/newcomers/is-oa-for-you/.

Overeaters Anonymous Inc. Staff. (1993). *The Twelve Steps and Twelve Traditions of Overeaters Anonymous*. Rio Rancho, NM: Overeaters Anonymous.

Peeke, P., & Van Aalst, M. (2012). *The hunger fix*. New York: Rodale.

Pelchat, M. L., Johnson, A., Chan, R., Valdez, J., & Ragland, J. D. (2004). Images of desire: Food-craving activation during fMRI. *NeuroImage, 23*(4), 1486–1493.

Peterson, C. B., Mitchell, J. E., Crow, S. J., Crosby, R. D., & Wonderlich, S. A. (2009). The efficacy of self-help group treatment and therapist-led group treatment for binge eating disorder. *American Journal of Psychiatry, 166*(12), 1347.

Peterson, C. B., Mitchell, J. E., Engbloom, S., Nugent, S., Mussell, M. P., et al. (1998). Group cognitive-behavioral treatment of binge eating disorder: A comparison of therapist-led versus self-help formats. *International Journal of Eating Disorders, 24*(2), 125–136.

Petrucelli, J. (2004). Treating eating disorders. In R. Coombs (Ed.), *Handbook of addictive disorders. A practical guide to diagnosis and treatment*. New Jersey: Wiley and Sons.

Pickering, C., Alsiö, J., Hulting, A. L., & Schiöth, H. B. (2009). Withdrawal from free-choice high-fat high-sugar diet induces craving only in obesity-prone animals. *Psychopharmacology (Berlin), 204*(3), 431–443.

Potenza, M. N. (2006). Should addictive disorders include non-substance-related conditions? *Addiction, 101*(1), 142–151.

Powell, L. M., Szczypka, G., Chaloupka, F. J., & Braunschweig, C. L. (2007). Nutritional content of television food advertisements seen by children and adolescents in the United States. *Pediatrics, 120*(3), 576–583.

Reas, D. L., & Grilo, C. M. (2008). Review and meta-analysis of pharmacotherapy for binge-eating disorder. *Obesity (Silver Spring), 16*(9), 2024–2038.

Ricca, V., Mannucci, E., Mezzani, B., Moretti, S., Di Bernardo, M., Bertelli, M., et al. (2001). Fluoxetine and fluvoxamine combined with individual cognitive-behaviour therapy in binge eating disorder: A one-year follow-up study. *Psychotherapy Psychosomatics*, *70*(6), 298–306.

Rogers, P. J., & Smit, H. J. (2000). Food craving and food "addiction": A critical review of the evidence from a biopsychosocial perspective. *Pharmacology Biochemistry and Behavior*, *66*(1), 3–14.

Rolls, E. T. (2004). The functions of the orbitofrontal cortex. *Brain Cognition*, *55*(1), 11–29.

Ronel, N., & Libman, G. (2003). Eating disorders and recovery: Lessons from Overeaters Anonymous. *Clinical Social Work Journal*, *31*(2), 155–171.

Rothemund, Y., Preuschhof, C., Bohner, G., Bauknecht, H. C., Klingebiel, R., Flor, H., et al. (2007). Differential activation of the dorsal striatum by high-calorie visual food stimuli in obese individuals. *NeuroImage*, *37*(2), 410–421.

Safer, D. L., Robinson, A. H., & Jo, B. (2010). Outcome from a randomized controlled trial of group therapy for binge eating disorder: Comparing dialectic behavior therapy adapted for binge eating to an active comparison group therapy. *Behavior Therapy*, *41*, 106–120.

Schienle, A., Schäfer, A., Hermann, A., & Vaitl, D. (2009). Binge-eating disorder: Reward sensitivity and brain activation to images of food. *Biological Psychiatry*, *65*(8), 654–661.

Segal, N. L., & Allison, D. B. (2002). Twins and virtual twins: Bases of relative body weight revisited. *International Journal of Obesity & Related Metabolic Disorders*, *26*(4), 437–441.

Setnick, J. (2013). Using addiction concepts to treatment overating. Retrieved March 21, 2013, from http://www.eatrightli.org/webinarregistration.html.

Shaffer, H. J., LaPlante, D. A., LaBrie, R., Kidman, R. C., Donato, A. N., & Stanton, M. V. (2004). Toward a syndrome model of addiction: Multiple expressions, common etiology. *Harvard Review of Psychiatry*, *12*, 367–374.

Shaham, Y., Shalev, U., Lu, L., De Wit, H., & Stewart, J. (2003). The reinstatement model of drug relapse: History, methodology and major findings. *Psychopharmacology (Berlin)*, *168*(1–2), 3–20.

Sookoian, S., Gemma, C., García, S. I., Gianotti, T. F., Dieuzeide, G., Roussos, A., et al. (2007). Short allele of serotonin transporter gene promoter is a risk factor for obesity in adolescents. *Obesity*, *15*(2), 271–276.

Stanton, M. D., & Shadish, W. R. (1997). Outcome, attrition, and family–couples treatment for drug abuse: A meta-analysis and review of the controlled, comparative studies. *Psychological Bulletin*, *122*(2), 170–191.

Stice, E., Spoor, S., Bohon, C., & Small, D. M. (2008). Relation between obesity and blunted striatal response to food is moderated by TaqIA A1 allele. *Science*, *322*(5900), 449–452.

Stice, E., Spoor, S., Bohon, C., Veldhuizen, M. G., & Small, D. M. (2008). Relation of reward from food intake and anticipated food intake to obesity: A functional magnetic resonance imaging study. *Journal of Abnormal Psychology*, *117*(4), 924–935.

Stice, E., Spoor, S., Ng, J., & Zald, D. H. (2009). Relation of obesity to consummatory and anticipatory food reward. *Physiology & Behavior*, *97*(5), 551–560.

Stice, E., Yokum, S., Bohon, C., Marti, N., & Smolen, A. (2010). Reward circuitry responsivity to food predicts future increases in body mass: Moderating effects of DRD2 and DRD4. *NeuroImage*, *50*(4), 1618–1625.

Stoeckel, L. E., Weller, R. E., Cook, E. W., 3rd, Twieg, D. B., Knowlton, R. C., & Cox, J. E. (2008). Widespread reward-system activation in obese women in response to pictures of high-calorie foods. *NeuroImage*, *41*(2), 636–647.

Stuart, C. (2001). Addictive economies: Intrapsychic and interpersonal discussion of McDougal's chapter. In J. Petrucelli & C. Sturat (Eds.), *Hungers and compulsions: The psychodynamnic treatment of eating disorders and addictions* (pp. 27–38). Northvale, NJ: Jason Araonson Inc.

Sysko, R., & Walsh, B. T. (2008). A critical evaluation of the efficacy of self-help interventions for the treatment of bulimia nervosa and binge-eating disorder. *International Journal of Eating Disorders*, *41*(2), 97–112.

Telch, C. F., Agras, W. S., & Lienham, M. M. (2000). Group dialectic behavior therapy for binge eating disorder: A preliminary, uncontrolled trial. *Behavior Therapy*, *31*, 569–582.

Thorberg, F. A., & Lyvers, M. (2006). Negative Mood Regulation (NMR) expectancies, mood, and affect intensity among clients in substance disorder treatment facilities. *Addictive Behaviors*, *31*(5), 811–820.

United States Department of Agriculture. (2010). *Taxing caloric sweetened beverages: Potential effects on beverage consumption, calorie intake, and obesity*. Washington, DC: USDA Economic Research Service.

Vocks, S., Tuschen-Caffier, B., Pietrowsky, R., Rustenbach, S. J., Kersting, A., & Herpertz, S. (2010). Meta-analysis of the effectiveness of psychological and pharmacological treatments for binge eating disorder. *International Journal of Eating Disorders*, *43*(3), 205–217.

Volkow, N. D., Chang, L., Wang, G. J., Fowler, J. S., Ding, Y. S., Sedler, M., et al. (2001). Low level of brain dopamine D2 receptors in methamphetamine abusers: Association with metabolism in the orbitofrontal cortex. *American Journal of Psychiatry*, *158*(12), 2015–2021.

Volkow, N. D., & O'Brien, C. P. (2007). Issues for DSM-V: Should obesity be included as a brain disorder? *American Journal of Psychiatry*, *164*(5), 708–710.

Volkow, N. D., Wang, G.-J., & Baler, R. D. (2011). Reward, dopamine and the control of food intake: Implications for obesity. *Trends in Cognitive Sciences*, *15*(1), 37–46.

Volkow, N. D., Wang, G. J., Fowler, J. S., Logan, J., Schlyer, D., Hitzemann, R., et al. (1994). Imaging endogenous dopamine competition with [11C]raclopride in the human brain. *Synapse*, *16*(4), 255–262.

Volkow, N. D., Wang, G. J., Fowler, J. S., Tomasi, D., & Baler, R. (2012). Food and drug reward: Overlapping circuits in human obesity and addiction. In C. S. Carter & J. W. Dalley (Eds.), *Brain Imaging in Behavioral Neuroscience: Vol. 11*. (pp. 1–24). Berlin Heidelberg: Springer.

Volkow, N. D., & Wise, R. A. (2005). How can drug addiction help us understand obesity? *Nature Neuroscience*, *8*(5), 555–560.

von Ranson, K. M., & Cassin, S. E. (2007). Eating disorders and addiction: Theory and evidence. *Eating Disorders and Weight Loss Research*, 1–37.

von Ranson, K. M., & Robinson, K. E. (2006). Who is providing what type of psychotherapy to eating disorder clients? A survey. *International Journal of Eating Disorders*, *39*(1), 27–34.

Vucetic, Z., Kimmel, J., Totoki, K., Hollenbeck, E., & Reyes, T. M. (2010). Maternal high-fat diet alters methylation and gene expression of dopamine and opioid-related genes. *Endocrinology*, *151*(10), 4756–4764.

Wadden, T. A., Butryn, M. L., & Byrne, K. J. (2004). Efficacy of lifestyle modification for long-term weight control. *Obesity Research*, *12*(Suppl), 151S–162S.

Waldron, H. B., & Kaminer, Y. (2004). On the learning curve: The emerging evidence supporting cognitive–behavioral therapies for adolescent substance abuse. *Addiction*, *99*, 93–105.

Wang, G.-J., Volkow, N. D., Logan, J., Pappas, N. R., Wong, C. T., Zhu, W., et al. (2001). Brain dopamine and obesity. *Lancet*, *357*(9253), 354–357.

Wang, G. J., Volkow, N. D., Thanos, P. K., & Fowler, J. S. (2009). Imaging of brain dopamine pathways: Implications for understanding obesity. *Journal of Addiction Medicine*, *3*(1), 8–18.

Waterhous, T., & Jacob, M. A. (2011). Nutrition intervention in the treatment of eating disorders. *Journal of the American Dietetic Association*, *111*(8), 1236–1241.

Weissman, M. J. C. (1994). Interpersonal psychotherapy: Current status. *Archives of General Psychiatry*, *51*(8), 599–606.

Wells, A. M., Garvin, V., Dohm, F.-A., & Striegel-Moore, R. H. (1997). Telephone-based guided self-help for binge eating disorder: A feasibility study. *International Journal of Eating Disorders*, *21*(4), 341–346.

Westphal, V. K., & Smith, J. E. (1996). Overeaters anonymous: Who goes and who succeeds? *Eating Disorders*, *4*(2), 160–170.

Whiteside, U., Chen, E., Neighbors, C., Hunter, D., Lo, T., & Larimer, M. (2007). Difficulties regulating emotions: Do binge eaters have fewer strategies to modulate and tolerate negative affect? *Eating Behaviors*, *8*, 162–169.

Wilfley, D. E., Welch, R. R., Stein, R. I., Spurrell, E. B., Cohen, L. R., Saelens, B. E., et al. (2002). A randomized comparison of group cognitive-behavioral therapy and group interpersonal psychotherapy for the treatment of overweight individuals with binge-eating disorder. *Archives of General Psychiatry*, *59*(8), 713–721.

Wilson, G. T., Grilo, C. M., & Vitousek, K. M. (2007). Psychological treatment of eating disorders. *American Psychologist*, *62*(3), 199–216.

Wilson, G. T., Vitousek, K. M., & Loeb, K. L. (2000). Stepped care treatment for eating disorders. *Journal of Consulting and Clinical Psychology*, *68*(4), 564–572.

Wilson, G. T., Wilfley, D. E., Agras, W. S., & Bryson, S. W. (2010). Psychological treatments of binge eating disorder. *Archives of General Psychiatry*, *67*(1), 94–101.

Wise, R. A., & Rompre, P. P. (1989). Brain dopamine and reward. *Annual Review of Psychology*, *40*, 191–225.

Wiser, S., & Telch, C. F. (1999). Dialectic behavior therapy for binge-eating disorder. *Journal of Clinical Psychology*, *55*, 755–768.

World Health Organization. (2012). Obesity and overweight. Retrieved January 29, 2012, from http://www.who.int/mediacentre/factsheets/fs311/en/.

Yau, Y., Yip, S., & Potenza, M. N. (in press). Understanding "behavioral addictions": Insights from research. In D. A. Fiellin, S. C. Miller & R. Saitz (Eds.), Principles of addiction medicine (5th ed.). Philadelphia, PA: Lippincott Williams & Wilkins.

Yeomans, M. R., & Gray, R. W. (1997). Effects of naltrexone on food intake and changes in subjective appetite during eating: Evidence for opioid involvement in the appetizer effect. *Physiology & Behavior*, *62*(1), 15–21.

Ziauddeen, H., Farooqi, I. S., & Fletcher, P. C. (2012a). Food addiction: Is there a baby in the bathwater? *Nature Review Neuroscience*, *13*(7), 514.

Ziauddeen, H., Farooqi, I. S., & Fletcher, P. C. (2012b). Obesity and the brain: How convincing is the addiction model? *Nature Review Neuroscience*, *13*(4), 279–286.

Ziauddeen, H., & Fletcher, P. C. (2013). Is food addiction a valid and useful concept? *Obesity Reviews*, *14*(1), 19–28.

Zubieta, J. K., Gorelick, D. A., Stauffer, R., Ravert, H. T., Dannals, R. F., & Frost, J. J. (1996). Increased mu opioid receptor binding detected by PET in cocaine-dependent men is associated with cocaine craving. *Nature Medicine*, *2*(11), 1225–1229.

APPENDIX 7-1*. YALE FOOD ADDICTION SCALE

Gearhardt, Corbin, & Brownell (2009)

This survey asks about your eating habits in the past year. People sometimes have difficulty controlling their intake of certain foods such as

- Sweets like ice cream, chocolate, doughnuts, cookies, cake, candy
- Starches like white bread, rolls, pasta, and rice
- Salty snacks like chips, pretzels, and crackers
- Fatty foods like steak, bacon, hamburgers, cheeseburgers, pizza, and French fries
- Sugary drinks like soda pop

* Contact: agearhar@umich.edu for scoring instructions

When the following questions ask about "CERTAIN FOODS" please think of ANY food similar to those listed in the food group or ANY OTHER foods you have had a problem with *in the past year.*

In the Past 12 Months	Never	Once a Month	2–4 Times a Month	2–3 Times a Week	4 or More Times or Daily
1. I find that when I start eating certain foods, I end up eating much more than planned.	0	1	2	3	4
2. I find myself continuing to consume certain foods even though I am no longer hungry.	0	1	2	3	4
3. I eat to the point where I feel physically ill.	0	1	2	3	4
4. Not eating certain types of food or cutting down on certain types of food is something I worry about.	0	1	2	3	4
5. I spend a lot of time feeling sluggish or fatigued from overeating.	0	1	2	3	4
6. I find myself constantly eating certain foods throughout the day.	0	1	2	3	4
7. I find that when certain foods are not available, I will go out of my way to obtain them. For example, I will drive to the store to purchase certain foods even though I have other options available to me at home.	0	1	2	3	4
8. There have been times when I consumed certain foods so often or in such large quantities that I started to eat food instead of working, spending time with my family or friends, or engaging in other important activities or recreational activities I enjoy.	0	1	2	3	4

In the Past 12 Months	Never	Once a Month	2–4 Times a Month	2–3 Times a Week	4 or More Times or Daily
9. There have been times when I consumed certain foods so often or in such large quantities that I spent time dealing with negative feelings from overeating instead of working, spending time with my family or friends, or engaging in other important activities or recreational activities I enjoy.	0	1	2	3	4
10. There have been times when I avoided professional or social situations where certain foods were available, because I was afraid I would overeat.	0	1	2	3	4
11. There have been times when I avoided professional or social situations because I was not able to consume certain foods there.	0	1	2	3	4
12. I have had withdrawal symptoms such as agitation, anxiety, or other physical symptoms when I cut down or stopped eating certain foods. (Please do NOT include withdrawal symptoms caused by cutting down on caffeinated beverages such as soda pop, coffee, tea, energy drinks, etc.)	0	1	2	3	4
13. I have consumed certain foods to prevent feelings of anxiety, agitation, or other physical symptoms that were developing. (Please do NOT include consumption of caffeinated beverages such as soda pop, coffee, tea, energy drinks, etc.)	0	1	2	3	4

Continued

—Cont'd

In the Past 12 Months	Never	Once a Month	2–4 Times a Month	2–3 Times a Week	4 or More Times or Daily
14. I have found that I have elevated desire for or urges to consume certain foods when I cut down or stop eating them.	0	1	2	3	4
15. My behavior with respect to food and eating causes significant distress.	0	1	2	3	4
16. I experience significant problems in my ability to function effectively (daily routine, job/school, social activities, family activities, health difficulties) because of food and eating.	0	1	2	3	4
In the Past 12 Months:	**No**	**Yes**			
17. My food consumption has caused significant psychological problems such as depression, anxiety, self-loathing, or guilt.	0	1			
18. My food consumption has caused significant physical problems or made a physical problem worse.	0	1			
19. I kept consuming the same types of food or the same amount of food even though I was having emotional and/or physical problems.	0	1			

In the Past 12 Months:	No	Yes			
20. Over time, I have found that I need to eat more and more to get the feeling I want, such as reduced negative emotions or increased pleasure.	0	1			
21. I have found that eating the same amount of food does not reduce my negative emotions or increase pleasurable feelings the way it used to.	0	1			
22. I want to cut down or stop eating certain kinds of food.	0	1			
23. I have tried to cut down or stop eating certain kinds of food.	0	1			
24. I have been successful at cutting down or not eating these kinds of food.	0	1			
25. How many times in the past year did you try to cut down or stop eating certain foods altogether?	1 time	2 times	3 times	4 times	5 or more times

Continued

—Cont'd

26. Please circle ALL of the following foods you have problems with:
    Ice cream
    White bread
    Chocolate
    Rolls
    Apples
    Lettuce
    Doughnuts
    Broccoli
    Cookies
    Rice
    Cake
    Crackers
    Candy
    Chips
    Pretzels
    Pizza
    French fries
    Soda pop
    Carrots
    Pasta
    Steak
    Strawberries
    Bananas
    Bacon
    Hamburgers
    Cheeseburgers
    None of the above
27. Please list any other foods that you have problems with that were not previously listed:

INSTRUCTION SHEET FOR THE YALE FOOD ADDICTION SCALE

(Gearhardt, Corbin, & Brownell, 2009)

Contact Information: ashley.gearhardt@yale.edu

The Yale Food Addiction Scale is a measure that has been developed to identify those who are most likely to be exhibiting markers of substance dependence with the consumption of high-fat/high-sugar foods.

Development

The scale questions fall under specific criteria that resemble the symptoms for substance dependence as stated in the *Diagnostic and Statistical Manual of Mental Disorders IV-TR* and operationalized in the Structured Clinical Interview for *DSM-IV* Axis I Disorders.

1. Substance taken in larger amount and for longer period than intended
   Questions #1, #2, #3
2. Persistent desire or repeated unsuccessful attempts to quit
   Questions #4, #22, # 24, #25
3. Much time/activity to obtain, use, recover
   Questions #5, #6, #7
4. Important social, occupational, or recreational activities given up or reduced
   Questions #8, #9, #10, #11
5. Use continues despite knowledge of adverse consequences (e.g., failure to fulfill role obligation, use when physically hazardous)
   Question #19
6. Tolerance (marked increase in amount; marked decrease in effect)
   Questions #20, #21
7. Characteristic withdrawal symptoms; substance taken to relieve withdrawal
   Questions #12, #13, #14
8. Use causes clinically significant impairment or distress
   Questions #15, #16

Cut-offs

The following cut-offs were developed for the continuous questions. 0 = criterion not met, 1 = criterion is met

The following questions are scored 0 = (0), 1 = (1): #19, #20, #21, #22

The following question is scored 0 = (1), 1 = (0): #24

The following questions are scored 0 = (0 thru 1), 1 = (2 thru 4): #8, #10, #11

The following questions are scored 0 = (0 thru 2), 1 = (3 & 4): #3, #5, #7, #9, #12, #13, #14, #15, #16

The following questions are scored 0 = (0 thru 3), 1 = (4): #1, #2, #4, #6

The following questions are scored 0 = (0 thru 4), 1 = (5): #25

The following questions are NOT scored, but are primers for other questions: #17, #18, #23

Scoring

After computing cut-offs, sum up the questions under each substance dependence criterion (e.g., Tolerance, Withdrawal, Clinical Significance, etc.). If the score for the criterion is > 1, then the criterion has been met and is scored as 1. If the score = 0, then the criteria has not been met.

Example

Tolerance: (#20 = 1) + (#21 = 0) = 1, Criterion Met

Withdrawal (#12 = 0) + (#13 = 0) + (#14 = 0) = 0, Criterion Not Met

Given up (#8 = 1) + (#9 = 0) + (#10 = 1) + (#11 = 1) = 3, Criterion Met and scored as 1

To score the continuous version of the scale, which resembles a symptom count without diagnosis, add up all of the scores for each of the criteria (e.g., Tolerance, Withdrawal, Use Despite Negative Consequence). Do NOT add clinical significance to the score.

This score should range from 0 to 7 (0 symptoms to 7 symptoms).

To score the dichotomous version, which resembles a diagnosis of substance dependence, compute a variable in which clinical significance must = 1 (items 15 or 16 =1), and the symptom count must be > 3. This should be either a 0 or 1 score (no diagnosis or diagnosis met).

Norms (Undergraduates)

Diagnosis of Food Dependence–11.6%
Median Symptom Count Score–1.0
Withdrawal–16.3%
Tolerance–13.5%
Continued Use Despite Problems–28.3%
Important Activities Given Up–10.3%
Large Amounts of Time Spent–24.0%
Loss of Control–21.7%
Have Tried Unsuccessfully to Cut Down or Worried About Cutting Down–71.3%
Clinically Significant Impairment–14%

CHAPTER 8

New Directions in the Pharmacological Treatment of Food Addiction, Overeating, and Obesity

Amelia A. Davis[1], Paula J. Edge[1], Mark S. Gold[2]
[1]Department of Psychiatry, College of Medicine, University of Florida, Gainesville, FL, USA,
[2]Department of Psychiatry Chairman, College of Medicine and McKnight Brain Institute, University of Florida, Gainesville, FL, USA

INTRODUCTION

Obesity is defined as a body mass index (BMI) greater than 30 kg/m^2. There are many different causes of obesity, including certain health conditions such as hypothyroidism, Cushing's syndrome, and polycystic ovarian syndrome (PCOS), as well as medication-induced, such as taking corticosteroids or antiepileptic medications. Other causes include stress and emotional factors that can lead to overeating, an inactive lifestyle, and genetics. In addition, about 3.5% of adult women and 2% of adult men suffer from binge eating disorder (BED; Hudson, Hiripi, Pope, & Kessler, 2007), a disorder included in the recent publication of the *Diagnostic and Statistical Manual of Mental Disorders,* Fifth Edition (*DSM-5*) that is characterized by eating rapidly; eating more than was intended; eating alone; and feelings of disgust, guilt, or depression secondary to these binges (APA, 2000).

Over the past three decades, the prevalence of obesity has increased throughout the world (Flegal, Carroll, Ogden, & Johnson, 2002; Silventoinen et al., 2004). Obesity remains a major public health priority in the United States and is increasingly becoming a pandemic affecting the rest of the globe. In the United States, the prevalence of obesity among children and adolescents has more than tripled from approximately 5% to 16.9% (Ogden, Carroll, Curtin, Lamb, & Flegal, 2010) and currently, greater than 50% of the population is either overweight or obese. Obesity in childhood and adolescence tends to be associated with adult obesity, and obesity places individuals at risk for certain diseases such as diabetes,

Behavioral Addictions
http://dx.doi.org/10.1016/B978-0-12-407724-9.00008-2

cardiovascular disease, and certain cancers ("Clinical guidelines on the identification, evaluation, and treatment of overweight and obesity in adults—the evidence report. National Institutes of Health," 1998). If obesity rates increase at current rates for two more decades, 51% of all U.S. adults will be obese by 2030 and all African-American women will be obese by 2034 (Wang, Beydoun, Liang, Caballero, & Kumanyika, 2008). Given these statistics, the rising obesity pandemic can no longer be ignored (see Figure 8.1).

Obese individuals do not bear the full cost of their condition; some costs are paid by taxpayers, employers, and coworkers. For example, it has been calculated that the medical costs of obesity in the United States in 2006 totaled $85.7 billion, of which $19.7 billion was paid by Medicare, $8.0 billion was paid by Medicaid, and $49.4 billion was paid by private sources such as health insurance (Finkelstein, Trogdon, Cohen, & Dietz, 2009). With the increasing prevalence of obesity, the medical costs associated with obesity will only continue to increase. Because of these important economic and health consequences, obesity is a vital area of research and one in which new and innovative approaches toward treatment and public policy must be developed to stop this global pandemic.

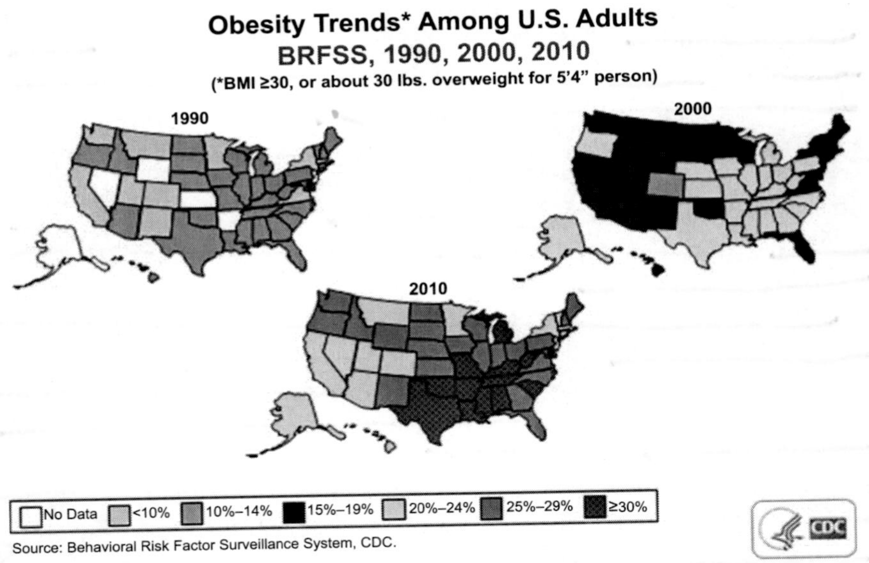

Figure 8.1 Obesity trends among U.S. adults in 1990, 2000, and 2010, from Behavioral Risk Factor Surveillance System, CDC.

THE DRIVE TO OVEREAT

Food is crucial to health, life, and even survival itself. Food, by providing the body with essential nutrients, helps ensure survival. Although this is obvious to most, food has important evolutionary significance. Our ancestral humans had to successfully meet the challenge of obtaining enough food to successfully mate and raise offspring. During pregnancy and lactation, fetuses and infants are literally eating off the mother, and the mother must assure an adequate nutrient supply for her young. Previously, evolution occurred in an environment in which food was scarcer than it is now. It then follows that humans developed mechanisms for overeating to make sure they overconsumed food when there was a plethora of food in order to stock up on food for times of famine. Food, which is energy, is stored in fat cells or adipose tissue to be used at a later time. From this perspective, one can see that in the past, there was an evolutionary advantage to overeating.

However, in today's world we have seen a sweetening in our food supply; an increase in energy-dense foods; increases in portion sizes; and Westernization of the world's diet secondary to globalization of modern food processing, marketing, and distribution techniques. All these factors have resulted in rapid massive changes in our food supply. Traditional weight-loss approaches have been remarkably ineffective, and we are in need of new innovative treatment approaches toward obesity, overeating, and food addiction. To help understand and develop some of the new treatment approaches toward these disorders, one needs to have a good foundation of knowledge, as discussed in the following sections.

FOOD ADDICTION

As discussed earlier, there are many causes of obesity, including medical conditions, certain types of medications, genetics, lifestyle considerations, as well as psychological components that can range from individuals overeating during times of stress to certain individuals having diagnosable BED. Some researchers hypothesize that some forms of obesity and related behaviors such as binge eating may manifest secondary to or along with a "food addiction." In some such circumstances, obesity is characterized by compulsive consumption of food, inability to restrain from further intake despite negative consequences, a desire to cut back, and increasing amounts of food needed to reach satiety. This is similar to the *DSM-IV-TR* (APA, 2000) criteria for substance dependence, which describes symptoms of preoccupation with substance, escalation of use, and continued use despite medical, psychological, or social consequences. For instance, an individual with alcohol dependence who continues to drink despite having cirrhosis of the liver might be analogous to a food addicted individual who continues to overeat or eat certain foods despite having diabetes mellitus or another serious medical condition that contraindicates such consumption.

As we have seen, overeating is a significant problem, especially in developed countries, as it can lead to obesity, which has significant adverse health consequences, including diabetes, cardiovascular disease, and certain cancers. One hypothesis for overeating is that processed foods with high concentrations of sugars, refined carbohydrates, and fat are addictive substances. Many people lose control over their ability to regulate such foods, similar to how people with substance use disorders are unable to regulate their behaviors toward certain substances. This is the food addiction hypothesis, and there is an increasing body of research that suggests that this loss of control toward these foods could account for the ever-increasing global epidemic of obesity (Ifland et al., 2009).

Food Addiction and Binge Eating Disorder

As discussed in the preceding chapter, the food addiction hypothesis is a fairly new concept, and unlike with obesity and binge eating disorder, there are currently no good estimates of the prevalence of food addiction in the population. Currently, the Yale Food Addiction Scale (YFAS) is likely the most widely used measure for examining food addiction (Gearhardt, Corbin, & Brownell, 2009b). In the initial validation study, food addiction was found to be related to emotional eating and predicted binge eating behaviors more than other measures of eating pathology in a sample of primarily normal weight undergraduates (Gearhardt et al., 2009b). This initial validation was extended by using the YFAS to measure food addiction in obese adults, which found higher levels of depression, binge eating, and trait impulsivity compared to a control group of obese adults who did not meet criteria for food addiction (Davis et al., 2011). While there was a large correlation between BED, a disorder characterized by compulsive overeating in which people consume huge amounts of food while feeling out of control to stop, 24% of participants who met criteria for food addiction did not meet criteria for BED, indicating that food addiction is distinct from binge eating (Davis et al., 2011). Similarly, in a sample of patients with BED, there was a relationship between those with food addiction and more depressed affect, poorer emotion regulation, lower self-esteem, and higher prevalence of mood disorders (Gearhardt, White, et al., 2012). Taken together, it appears that food addiction is a distinct construct from BED that overlaps BED and represents greater eating disorder psychopathology and associated pathology (Davis et al., 2011; Gearhardt, White, et al., 2012).

Obesity and Food Addiction

In addition, not all individuals who are overweight have food addiction or BED, which may mean that providers in the near future may be able to use better diagnostic tools to diagnose an individual with food addiction or compulsive eating to help further guide treatment. For instance, individuals who have food addiction may benefit from 12-step programs similar to individuals with substance use disorders. On the other hand, these diagnostic tools may also be used to help diagnose individuals who are normal weight and are at risk for obesity to help an individual avoid becoming obese in the future.

Assessing Food Addiction

The Yale Food Addiction Scale (YFAS) is a scale developed to measure the existence of substance dependence diagnostic criteria as applied to eating disorders (Gearhardt et al., 2009b). The content of the YFAS questions is based on substance dependence criteria in the *Diagnostic and Statistical Manual for Mental Disorders,* Fourth Edition Text Revision (*DSM-IV-TR*; APA, 2000). The *DSM-IV-TR* states that a diagnosis of dependence should be given when three or more of seven diagnostic criteria are experienced in a 12-month period and that this causes clinically significant impairment or distress (APA, 2000). Preliminary results from the YFAS indicate that the scale may be useful in diagnosing individuals with food addiction and provide support for the food addiction hypothesis.

Using the YFAS, 17.2% of participants in the study reported three or more of the seven diagnostic criteria, and 11.4% of participants met the full diagnostic criteria with inclusion of impairment or distress (Gearhardt et al., 2009b). Another study found that 15% of individuals met the YFAS-proposed diagnostic criteria among individuals with a body mass index (BMI) average of 36.1 kg/m^2 and of those not meeting criteria, 35% reported three or more symptoms in the absence of self-reported clinical distress or impairment (Eichen, Lent, Goldbacher, & Foster, 2013).

Although it is important to apply substance dependence criteria when applicable, it is also important to consider subclinical symptoms of addiction to food that would have major public health impact. Similarly to alcohol and nicotine, environmental factors have a major impact on the levels of clinical and subclinical problems related to substance use. This is true of food as well. Also, examining food addiction from a substance dependence perspective may be helpful for treatment options as well as helping guide public policy (Gearhardt, Corbin, & Brownell, 2009a). Individuals meeting criteria for food addiction as defined by YFAS do not account for all the individuals who are overweight or obese, but are a subset. If this subpopulation of individuals is addressed, there may be treatment approaches designed specifically to help individuals with food addiction versus those with BED versus those who are obese without food addiction or BED.

REWARD DEFICIENCY SYNDROME

There is growing research to support the food addiction model. In particular, the reward deficiency syndrome shows some similarities between drugs of abuse to addictions to gambling, sex, eating, and other impulsive and addictive behaviors. Dopamine is a neurotransmitter that has been commonly associated throughout the neuroscience literature with feelings of pleasure and happiness. It is produced in the nucleus accumbens in the mesolimbic system and is the brain reward site. In addition, low dopamine function is associated with addictive behaviors, and there is an abundance of literature that supports that low dopamine is associated with a high vulnerability to substance use and impulsive and addictive behaviors (Blum et al., 2000). "Sex, drugs and rock & roll" is not just a pop culture reference (Blum, Werner, et al., 2012). It is interesting that every known drug of abuse as well as gambling, sex, music, and eating is associated with neuronal release of dopamine in the brain reward site. In addition, the dopamine D2 receptor gene that regulates the synthesis of D2 receptors is associated with alcohol addiction as well as other addictions (Blum et al., 1990; Blum et al., 1996). While Dackis, Gold, et al. published the dopamine depletion hypothesis in 1985; Blum coined the term *reward deficiency syndrome* as an umbrella term for behaviors that result in a hypodopaminergic state that are associated with genetic antecedents and predispose to obsessive and impulsive behaviors (Blum et al., 1996). There is growing evidence that overeating is implicated in the reward deficiency syndrome (Blum & Gold, 2011; Blum, Liu, Shriner, & Gold, 2011; Blum, Oscar-Berman, et al., 2012).

FOOD REWARD SYSTEM

Neuroanatomy

Reward from food is processed by a complex neural system that includes the nucleus accumbens and ventral pallidum in the ventral striatum, the ventral tegmental area located in the midbrain and projecting through the mesolimbic dopamine system back to the nucleus accumbens, the prefrontal cortex, the hippocampus, and amygdala (see Figure 8.2), which is similar to that seen in the reward system for drugs of abuse (Kelley et al., 2002). In addition, for a person to give a rating of pleasure from palatable foods, humans appear also to use the prefrontal and cingulate cortex (Kringelbach & Berridge, 2010). Similar to individuals with alcohol, cocaine, and amphetamine addictions, individuals with a higher BMI were found to have decreased metabolic activity in prefrontal regions (Volkow et al., 1993, 2001, 2007, 2009).

In addition, the reward associated with food involves sensory inputs of taste, vision, olfaction, temperature, and texture that are first processed in the primary sensory cortices and primary somatosensory cortex and then the orbitofrontal cortex and amygdala (Rolls, 2007). Studies looking at obesity in girls found that obese girls had a greater activation in insula and gustatory somatosensory cortex in response to anticipated and actual consumption of food, and morbidly obese subjects were found to have higher metabolism in the gustatory somatosensory cortex (Wang et al., 2002).

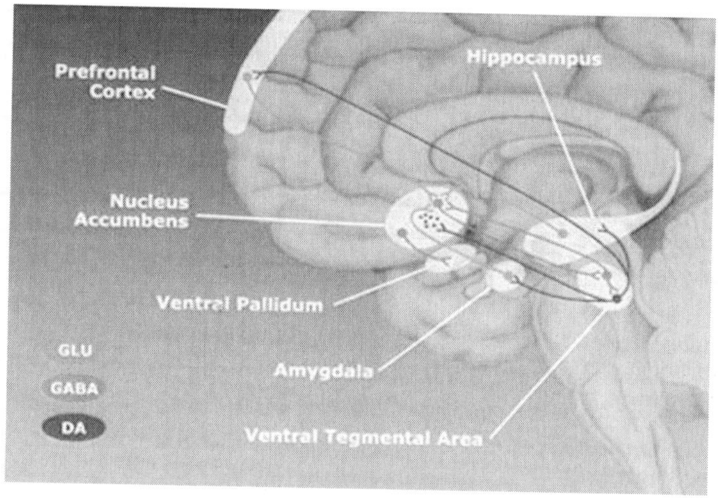

Figure 8.2 Neurocircuitry involved in food reward system.

These findings suggest that obese individuals are more sensitive to the sensory properties of food. This study only looked at obese individuals and did not differentiate the effects toward individuals with food addiction. Therefore, these individuals are not necessarily "addicted" to food, but this could be one of the variables contributing to their excess food consumption.

Neurochemistry

Dopamine and opioids are neurotransmitters that are associated with both the reward effects of drugs as well as with food. Dopamine has been shown to mediate the reinforcement of sugar and sucrose (Smith, 2004) and regulate pleasurable and motivating responses to food intake and stimuli (Volkow & Wise, 2005). Similar to individuals with drug addiction, obese individuals have reduced D2 receptor availability and dopamine transporter availability in the striatum that is inversely related to body mass index (BMI; Chen et al., 2008; Haltia et al., 2007; Stice, Spoor, Bohon, Veldhuizen, & Small, 2008).

Endogenous opioids are expressed throughout the limbic system, and palatable food increases endogenous opioid gene expression (Avena & Gold, 2011a; Chen et al., 2008). Furthermore, injection of mu-opioid agonists in the nucleus accumbens potentiates the intake of palatable food (Will, Franzblau, & Kelley, 2003). This is taken further in that opioid antagonists, such as naltrexone, reduce food ratings of pleasantness without affecting hunger (Woolley, Lee, & Fields, 2006). It is likely that the opioid system is involved with the liking of and may promote the intake of high-sugar and high-fat foods that are highly palatable (Avena & Gold, 2011c).

Leptin Insufficiency Syndrome

In addition to involvement in the dopamine reward system, food is also modulated by an interplay in the appetite-regulating network and the energy-regulating network in the hypothalamus (Avena & Gold, 2011c). Within the appetite-regulating network, there are different peptides including neuropeptide Y, agouti-related peptide, and gamma-aminobutyric acid in the arcuate nucleus that innervate the paraventricular nucleus and neighboring hypothalamic regions involved in propagating appetite (Kalra et al., 1999; Yeomans & Gray, 1997). The release of neuropeptide Y and other peptides involved in increasing appetite are under the direction of hormone signals such as anorexigenic leptin, which is secreted primarily by white adipose tissue and orexigenic gastric ghrelin (Kalra & Kalra, 2006; Yeomans & Gray, 1997).

Leptin appears to be involved in signaling to the hypothalamus episode appetitive drive and does so by suppressing ghrelin secretion from the stomach, counteracting the effects of ghrelin in the hypothalamic arcuate nucleus as well as repressing release of neuropeptide Y (Kalra & Kalra, 2006; Pu et al., 1999). In addition, leptin appears to be involved in regulating signals from the hypothalamus (Kalra, Bagnasco, Otukonyong, Dube, & Kalra, 2003), such as repressing insulin secretion from the pancreas; imposing euglycemia by an intricate control on glucose metabolism and disposal in liver, skeletal muscles, and adipose tissue; and promoting energy expenditure by activating nonshivering thermogenesis in brown adipose tissue (Bagnasco, Dube, Katz, Kalra, & Kalra, 2003; Otukonyong, Dube, Torto, Kalra, & Kalra, 2005).

Delivery of leptin peripherally in the blood resulted in little effect; however, when leptin was introduced intranasally and centrally in rats, there was a decrease in feeding, indicating that leptin gene therapy may be an avenue for new research for treatment of obesity (Kalra, 2009; Schwartz, Peskind, Raskind, Boyko, & Porte, 1996). In addition to suppression of hyperphagia in rats (Kalra, 2008), there was suppression of fat accrual, an upregulation of energy expenditure (Ueno, Inui, Kalra, & Kalra, 2006), and normalization of body weight, which prevented early mortality and normalized the life span of rats (Kalra, 2008).

Genetics

While gene therapy for treatment of obesity, overeating, and/or food addiction likely will not be developed for many years, understanding the genetics of obesity can help practitioners and researchers better understand these disorders and can provide evidence for a more biological basis of the disease process. Examining the genetics of obesity shows links between persons who have alcohol or drug addiction and obesity, suggesting there may be an addictive process contributing to some individuals who are overweight and supporting the food addiction hypothesis. Furthermore, understanding the genetic basis of obesity can reduce stigma associated with obesity, as it is recognized that there are influences that are beyond human control.

It is estimated that genetics and the "heritability" of obesity is between 40% and 70% within a specific environment (Kalra, 2009). This was found using concordance of obesity among monozygous and dizygous twins and adopted versus biological children and their parents. In addition, the D2 dopamine receptor gene (DRD2) that is associated with alcohol dependence (Boghossian, Ueno, Dube, Kalra, & Kalra, 2007) has also been associated with obesity (Blum et al., 1990).

Epigenetics

Other considerations are epigenetics, which may contribute to the obesity risk identified by twin and adoption studies. Epigenetics refers to the regulation of genomic functions like gene expression independent of DNA sequence, such as potentially reversible chemical modifications occurring on the DNA and/or histones leading to chromatin remodeling and histone modification, inducing alteration in gene expression (Noble et al., 1994). The environmental factors such as perinatal nutrition, maternal energy status, maternal endocrine status, and oxidative stress can affect methylation patterns on eating disorder specific genes, such as *FGF2*, *PTEN*, *CDKN1A*, and *ESR1* (Walters et al., 2010).

Maternal supplementation during gestation of dietary genistein in mice, at levels comparable with humans consuming high-soy diets, induced hypermethylation of six cytosine-guanine sites in *Agouti* gene, decreasing the expression of this gene and protecting offspring from obese phenotype (Henikoff & Matzke, 1997).

Other new research has shown that perinatal and prenatal exposure can affect development of obesity in the offspring by affecting later feeding behavior as well as the metabolic state of the offspring (Dolinoy, Weidman, Waterland, & Jirtle, 2006). Also, high maternal dietary intakes may stimulate specific food preference in children (Brion et al., 2010). Bocarsly et al. (2012) found that offspring of both sexes exposed to high fructose corn syrup (HFCS) or sucrose *in utero* had higher body weights in adulthood. Also female offspring showed sensitivity to alcohol (measured by increased alcohol intake), and male offspring had increased amphetamine-induced locomotor activity (Bocarsly et al., 2012). These data suggest that prenatal as well as pre-weaning exposure to fat- and sugar-rich diets not only increases body weight but also the response to nonfood substances of abuse.

It may well pay dividends to look at lessons learned from tobacco. We know that the risk of lifelong tobacco use and addiction is significantly increased by early exposure to tobacco via second-hand smoke, either *in utero* or in early life. This is also true for food. Preferences are set *in utero* and in early life and can become fixed and persistent going forward. One example is that today, intake of sugar-HFCS-sweetened beverages accounts for 10%–15% of calories consumed by children and adolescents and greatly surpasses their intake of milk. Just intake of one extra can of soda a day can increase the risk of obesity by 60% (Gold, 2013).

By understanding the multifactorial influences on obesity, overeating, and food addiction, one can begin to appreciate the need to reduce the stigma associated with being overweight. Obesity in Western culture is often associated with feelings of shame and guilt that are not therapeutic. Similarly, as in the treatment of drug dependence as well as mental health disorders, shame can be detrimental to clinical treatment because it spurs patients' reluctance to seek treatment and decreases treatment compliance (Keyes et al., 2010; Semple, Grant, & Patterson, 2005; Vartanian & Smyth, 2013). Also, providing education to patients regarding the contributing factors of obesity, overeating, and food addiction may help decrease the patients' shame of their condition. It is therefore important to foster an environment of acceptance when treating food-addicted patients (Puhl, Peterson, & Luedicke, 2012; Vartanian & Smyth, 2013). This should ideally be extended to the general public and media, as it is counterproductive to place blame on individuals who are obese, who overeat, and/or who are addicted to food (Vartanian & Smyth, 2013).

SURGICAL TREATMENTS OF OBESITY

Bariatric surgery (see Figure 8.3) is the only long-term weight loss therapy that produces weight losses of 15% or more of initial weight (Colquitt, Picot, Loveman, & Clegg, 2009). Current NIH guidelines recommend bariatric surgery as a treatment option for individuals with a BMI of greater than 40 kg/m^2 or greater than 35 kg/m^2 in the presence of comorbidities, including type 2 diabetes, hypertension, and sleep apnea (NHLBI, 2000).

Bariatric surgery consists of two different types of procedures: restrictive procedures, which induce early satiety by reducing gastric size, and malabsorptive procedures, which reduce gastrointestinal absorption by shortening the small intestine and decreasing nutrient absorption. Restrictive procedures include laparoscopic adjustable gastric banding, which has become increasingly popular since it received FDA approval in 2001 and is now the most commonly performed restrictive procedure worldwide (Schneider & Mun, 2005). In this procedure, an inflatable silicone band is placed around the fundus of the stomach, which can be adjusted by adding or removing saline from a subcutaneous port (Colquitt et al., 2009). Another restrictive procedure is the vertical sleeve gastrectomy, which is a relatively new procedure in which 75% of the stomach is removed (Colquitt et al., 2009).

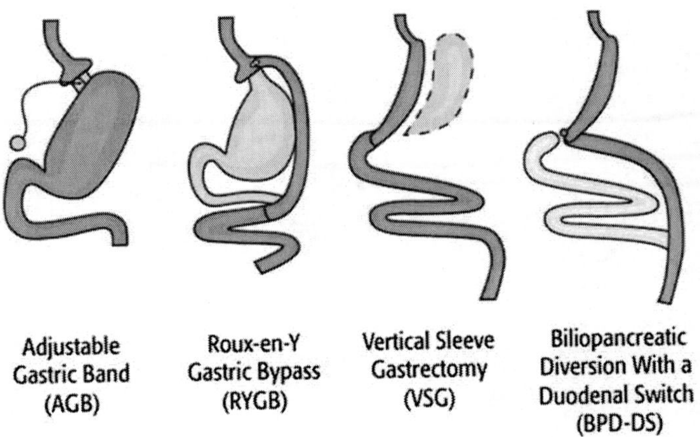

Figure 8.3 Bariatric surgical operations.

Malabsorption procedures include the biliopancreatic diversion, which involves a partial gastrectomy to create a 150–200 cc gastric sleeve, which is anastomosed (connected) to the distal 250 cm of small intestine (Colquitt et al., 2009). Although this procedure results in an impressive amount of weight loss, it is also associated with a significant number of complications and is generally reserved for patients with BMIs greater than 50 kg/m^2. It accounts for only 5% of bariatric procedures in the United States (Colquitt et al., 2009).

The Roux-en-Y gastric bypass is a combined restrictive and malabsorptive procedure that remains the most common bariatric procedure performed worldwide and is considered the gold standard treatment for extreme obesity. More than half of Roux-en-Y gastric bypass surgeries are now performed laparoscopically (Schneider & Mun, 2005).

The Downside of Bariatric Surgery

Although bariatric procedures do initially result in dramatic weight loss, they can also be expensive and have significant risks associated with them, including gastric dumping syndrome, malnutrition from impaired absorption, and increased risk of bone fractures (Nakamura et al., 2011; Vetter, Faulconbridge, Williams, & Wadden, 2012). In 2012, Conason and colleagues reported that patients may be at increased risk for substance use following bariatric surgery (Conason et al., 2012). These researchers found significant increases in smoking, drug use, and alcohol use. Additionally, they found increased risk for alcohol use in patients who underwent a

Roux-en-Y gastric bypass. Earlier, in 2010, Maluenda et al. reported that alcohol absorption was considerably modified after bariatric surgery (laparoscopic sleeve gastrectomy) with higher and longer blood alcohol values for equivalent amounts of alcohol (Maluenda et al., 2010). Avena and Gold suggested that post-bariatric sensitivity to alcohol may involve more than altered absorption and time to reach the brain (Avena & Gold, 2011b). They hypothesize that if food and alcohol compete for the same brain reinforcement sites, abstinence from one may make abuse of the other more likely (Avena & Gold, 2011b). All in all, there needs to be further research on the consequences (both positive and negative) of bariatric surgery and what light these procedures can shed onto better understanding food addiction.

PHARMACOTHERAPIES FOR TREATMENT OF OBESITY AND FOOD ADDICTION

Due to the counter-regulatory mechanisms that cause an increase in appetite and reduction in energy expenditure, weight loss with low-calorie diet, exercise, and behavior modification is often impossible; therefore, pharmacological treatment may be used adjunctively to help overweight patients battle obesity and associated comorbidities (Korner & Aronne, 2004). Compared to bariatric surgery, pharmacotherapy is indicated in individuals who are overweight or obese with a lower BMI. For bariatric surgery, an individual should have a BMI of greater than 40 kg/m^2 or greater than 35 kg/m^2 with comorbidities, while individuals who receive pharmacotherapy have a lower BMI cut-off, which is often a BMI of greater than 30 kg/m^2 or greater than 27 kg/m^2 with comorbidities. Therefore, pharmacotherapy may be used prior to bariatric surgery in less severe cases of obesity, although failure of medication management is not a requirement for an individual to receive bariatric surgery.

The history of pharmacological treatments for obesity and food addiction is dismal. As shown in Table 8.1, many approved drugs were later withdrawn due to poor safety profiles and relatively poor efficacy. First, amphetamines and appetite suppressants were prescribed and then later fat blockers. Even the drugs not withdrawn are approved only for short-term use under 12 weeks (with the exception of Orlistat, which tends to cause diarrhea). These medications also have long lists of side effects and contraindications.

Table 8.1 Anti-obesity Medications Prior to 2012

Drug	FDA Approved	Outcomes FDA Withdrawal Dates Highlighted
Pentermine	May 1959	Appetite suppressant; approved for short-term use (4–12 weeks) only.
Fenfluramine	June 1973	September 1997. The infamous fen-phen caused defects in heart valves (82) and pulmonary hypertension.
Dexfenfluramine	April 1996	September 1997. Redux had fewer heart valve defects (7) but caused brain damage in lab animals.
Orlistat	April 1999	Fat blocker; Available by script as Xenical or over the counter as Alli. Unpleasant side effects include excess gas, oily stools, and spotting. Weight loss 2.75 kg (6 lbs.) at 52 weeks.
Sibutramine	November 1997	October 2010. Appetite suppressant; users at higher risk of heart problems and stroke.
Rimonabant	Never approved by FDA in the US	June 2006 approved in Europe only. October 2010 recalled.
Diethylpropion	August 1959	Addictive. Anorectic with long list of side effects and interactions with foods and other medications.
Benzphetamine	October 1960	Addictive. Anorectic closely related to amphetamines; huge list of contraindications.
Phendimetrazine	September 1982	Addictive. Anorectic closely related to amphetamines; CNS stimulant puts stress on heart. Can cause vivid hallucinations.

2012: FDA Approved Anti-obesity Medications

The research supporting the link between the dopamine and opioid pathways with eating has helped open up new treatments for obesity and food addiction, by using drugs already proven successful in treatment of substance abuse. The current pharmacological options for treating obesity are expanding as the FDA approved two weight loss medications for treatment of obesity in 2012. These are the first new medications FDA approved for weight loss since 1999. While food addiction and obesity are far from synonymous, medications targeting obesity have relevant implications for the current and future treatment of food addiction.

Lorcaserin

Lorcaserin, marketed under the name of Belvig, was approved by the FDA May 10, 2012. It targets the serotonin 5HT2C receptor in the brain, which is thought to act by inducing satiety, thus suggesting its benefits in targeting food addiction. Lorcaserin should be taken 10 mg twice a day and was shown to have weight loss of 3.7% over placebo in three clinical trials that included over 8,000 overweight and obese patients and lasted from 52 to 104 weeks (Korner & Aronne, 2004). Overall, it was well tolerated. The most frequently reported adverse effects were upper respiratory infection, nasopharyngitis (inflammation of the nasal passages and upper pharynx), and headache. Echocardiographic safety data revealed no risk of valvulopathy (disease of the valves of the heart) in the clinical trials, which has resulted in the withdrawal of previous serotonergic weight loss medications, fenfluramine and dexfenfluramine, in 1997 due to associated cardiac effects (FDA, 2012). The FDA has also proposed a class IV schedule for the drug, making it a controlled substance, and the FDA recommends that people stop taking the drug if they do not lose 5% of their weight in 12 weeks because they are not likely to benefit and should not be exposed to the risks. The medication should be used with extreme caution when taken with serotonergic drugs such as SSRIs, SNRIs, MAOs, triptans, bupropion, dextromethorphan, and St. John's Wort due to risk of serotonin syndrome (Aronne, Brown, & Isoldi, 2007).

Qsymia

The other recently FDA-approved (July 17, 2012) weight loss medication is Qsymia, which is a combination of two FDA-approved drugs: phentermine, an appetite suppressant, and topiramate, commonly used to treat epilepsy and migraines. This medication is taken once a day, starting at the lowest dose of 3.75 mg phentermine/23 mg topiramate extended-release and then increasing to the recommended dose of 7.5 mg/46 mg. In some cases, patients may have their dose increased to the highest dose of 15 mg/92 mg (Korner & Aronne, 2004). Qysmia was tested in two clinical trials that included nearly 2,700 obese and overweight patients treated for up to 1 year. The weight loss ranged from 6.7% at the lowest dose to 8.9% at the recommended dose over those taking placebo. Sixty-two percent of patients at the lowest dose and 70% on the recommended dose lost at least 5% of their weight compared with 20% of the controls who received placebo (Aronne, Waitman, & Isoldi, 2008). If, after 12 weeks, a patient has not lost 3% of his or her weight on the recommended dose, the FDA recommends that treatment be discontinued or increased to the highest dose. If, after an additional 12 weeks, on the highest dose, a patient does not lose at least 5% of weight, Qysmia should be discontinued gradually. The most commonly reported side effects were dry mouth, tingling, altered taste, insomnia, and constipation (FDA, 2012).

Neither of these medications should be taken when pregnant because weight loss offers no benefit to pregnancy and is potentially harmful to the fetus. Qysmia is associated with fetal defects including cleft lip in infants exposed to Qysmia during the first trimester. In addition, these medications are only for patients with a BMI of greater than 30 kg/m^2 or 27 kg/m^2 with comorbidities, such as hypertension (elevated blood pressure), type 2 diabetes mellitus, or dyslipidemia (changes in cholesterol or fat level; Korner & Aronne, 2004).

IN THE PIPELINE

A number of new anti-obesity treatments that may have implications for food addiction treatment are in Phase 2 and Phase 3 trials (see Table 8.2). These include combinations such as raclopride and bupropion, which target dopamine; naltrexone, which targets the opioid system; and a baclofen/topiramate combination, which targets the GABAergic system. A good number of these medications or combinations thereof have proven successful in treating alcohol and drug addictions or other behavioral addictions such as problem gambling.

Contrave

Contrave is a combination of bupropion and naltrexone in a sustained-release formulation and is currently in the process of resubmission after the FDA declined to approve the medication in 2011, citing safety concerns at the time. Naltrexone is an opioid antagonist and is approved for treatment of alcohol and opioid addiction; it works by blocking opioid receptors in the brain. It has also shown efficacy in treatment of gambling disorder in addition to alcohol and opioid addiction (Grant, Kim, & Hartman, 2008; Grant, Odlaug, Potenza, Hollander, & Kim, 2010). Bupropion is currently approved to treat depression as well as smoking cessation and is thought to increase dopamine activity in specific receptors of the brain. Contrave

Table 8.2 New Treatments for Obesity

Brand/Generic (Manufacturer)	Status (Date)	New/Combined	Method of Action	Side Effects
Belvig/Lorcaserin (Arena)	FDA Approved 5/10/12	New class of selective serotonin 2C receptor agonists	Treatment stimulates receptors in hypothalamus, an area strongly associated with satiety.	Side effects reported were URI, nasopharyngitis, and headache.
Qsymia (Vivus)	FDA Approved 7/17/12	Combination of phentermine and topiramate (both drugs were used successfully in treating alcohol dependence)	Phentermine suppresses appetite, and topiramate decreases cravings by targeting the GABAergic system.	Side effects reported were dry mouth, tingling, altered taste, insomnia, and constipation.
Contrave (Orexigen)	CVOT in progress; potential approval in 2014	Combination of bupropion SR and naltrexone SR	Bupropion targets dopamine and reduces appetite by decreasing pleasure and interest in food and also increases energy expenditure; naltrexone targets the opioid system and decreases cravings.	Side effects reported were nausea, constipation, headache, vomiting, dizziness, insomnia, dry mouth, and diarrhea.
Tesofensine (NeuroSearch) Originally developed for Parkinson's and Alzheimer's but not efficacious and had side effect of weight loss	Phase 3 trials ongoing	Combined norepinephrine-serotonin-dopamine reuptake inhibitor	Tesofensine influences chemicals in the brain to suppress appetite and increase satiety.	Side effects reported were dry mouth, headache, nausea, insomnia, diarrhea, and constipation.
Empatic (Orexigen)	Phase 2 trials completed	Combined zonisamide SR and bupropion SR	Bupropion targets dopamine and reduces appetite by decreasing pleasure and interest in food. Also increases energy expenditure. Zonisamide decreases cravings.	Side effects reported were headache, insomnia, nausea, and hives.

achieved a 6.1% weight loss at both 28 weeks and 56 weeks of treatment, compared to 1.3% of placebo (Aronne et al., 2008; Orexigen Therapeutics, 2009b). Naltrexone may make certain foods less palatable, while bupropion may reduce appetite.

Tesofensine

Another medication, Tesofensine, is a combined norepinephrine-serotonin-dopamine reuptake inhibitor currently under way for Phase 3 trials. This drug was initially developed for treatment for Parkinson's disease and Alzheimer's dementia but was found to have limited effectiveness for these diseases; however, it had the reported side effect of weight loss. Phase 2 data demonstrated an average of 6.5%, 11.2%, and 12.6% among patients treated with 0.25 mg, 0.5 mg, and 1.0 mg of tesofensine, respectively, for 24 months. Patients treated with placebo lost an average of 2% of their body weight (Neurosearch, 2009). Common side effects include dry mouth, headache, nausea, insomnia, diarrhea, and constipation. Blood pressure and heart rate were increased by 1–3 mmHg and up to 8 bpm, respectively. This is a promising new drug that produces a weight loss twice that of currently approved anti-obesity drugs.

FDA-APPROVED MEDICATIONS THAT DO NOT HAVE FDA INDICATIONS FOR WEIGHT LOSS

Some medications are used as weight loss agents but do not have indications for weight loss. These medications have been approved by the FDA for indications other than weight loss, such as diabetes, but have shown efficacy as weight loss agents. These medications include metformin, exenatide, pramlintide, bupropion, and zonisamide.

Metformin

Metformin is an antihyperglycemic agent that acts by suppressing hepatic glucose production (Korner & Aronne, 2004). Metformin can reduce body weight and improve other cardio-metabolic risk factors but is not approved for weight loss. A meta-analysis of 31 randomized controlled trials of at least 8 weeks' duration found that in persons at risk for diabetes metformin decreased BMI 5.3%, fasting glucose by 4.5%, fasting insulin by 14.4%, triglycerides by 5.3%, low-density lipoprotein cholesterol by 5.6%, and increased high-density lipoprotein cholesterol by 5.0% compared to placebo or no treatment (FDA, 2012). The most frequently reported adverse effects are nausea, abdominal discomfort, diarrhea, flatulence, and bloating (Salpeter, Buckley, Kahn, & Salpeter, 2008). Lactic acidosis (too much acid in the blood) is a rare (1/100,000) but serious adverse effect (Aronne, 2007).

Glucagon-Like Peptide-1 Analogs

Exenatide and liraglutide are injectable antidiabetic medications that are glucagon-like peptide-1 analogs that increase insulin secretion and suppress glucose-dependent glucagon release (Neff & Aronne, 2007). Exenatide is FDA approved for patients with type 2 diabetes who have failed to achieve adequate glycemic control on oral antidiabetic medications. It improves glycemic control, slows gastric emptying, decreases food intake, enhances satiety, and reduces body weight when used to treat type 2 diabetes (Johns, 2007). In addition to improved hemoglobin A1C, the patients exhibited dose-dependent weight losses of 2.8 kg in the 10 μg group and 1.6 kg in the 5 μg group (Neff & Aronne, 2007). The most common side effects are nausea, diarrhea, and vomiting. Cases of hypoglycemia have been seen with exenatide treatment, but they usually occurred when co-administered with sulfonylurea, but not with metformin (Aronne, 2007).

Pramlintide

Pramlintide is a relatively new adjunct for diabetes, both type 1 and type 2, that is an injectable antihyperglycemic agent that mimics the pancreatic hormone amylin and in conjunction with insulin regulates postprandial glucose control. Amylin is a small peptide hormone that is released by the β-cells in the pancreas along with insulin (Neff & Aronne, 2007) and is completely absent in individuals with type 1 diabetes (Johns, 2007). While not FDA approved for weight loss, it has been shown to promote weight loss by increasing satiety and reducing food intake. A phase 2 multicenter trial in 204 non-insulin-treated obese subjects with or without type 2 diabetes showed weight loss of 3.7% and a reduction in waist circumference of 3.6 cm (Edelman, Maier, & Wilhelm, 2008). Also, about 31% of patients treated with pramlintide achieved a 5% reduction in weight, compared to only 2% of placebo-treated patients (Edelman et al., 2008). The most common side effects were nausea and injectable-related adverse effects. Mild hypoglycemic events, which resolved without medical intervention, were reported in 8% of the pramlintide-treated patients, and there were no reports of moderate or severe hypoglycemia (Edelman et al., 2008).

Empatic

Empatic is a combination of zonisamide SR, an antiepileptic therapy that increases monoamines, which are thought to suppress NPY/AgRP neurons, and bupropion SR, a medication approved for treatment of depression and smoking cessation and is thought to increase dopamine activity at specific receptors in the brain. This medication has undergone Phase 2 testing which demonstrated that patients who completed 24 weeks of treatment lost 9.9% of their baseline body weight compared to 1.7% in patients treated with placebo. The most commonly reported adverse events were headache, insomnia, and urticaria (Aronne et al., 2007; Oriexigen Therapeutics, 2009).

TREATMENT APPROACH BASED ON THE DRUG ABUSE MODEL

Combination of Baclofen and Naltrexone

New treatment approaches to target overeating use the model for drug abuse to develop pharmacotherapies that target food reinforcement or preference rather than appetite. Given the similarities observed between overeating and binge eating with drug use, Gold and Avena (2012) have looked at using baclofen, a $GABA_B$ agonist that can reduce the intake of some drugs of abuse, in combination with naltrexone, an opioid antagonist that reduces opiate relapse, bulimic eating, and alcohol relapse. In a study on binge eating in rats, there was a significant reduction in sugar, fat, and combination of fat-sugar intake in rats that were given baclofen/naltrexone combination in comparison with the control group. Baclofen plus naltrexone does not suppress appetite but causes weight loss by changing and reinforcing food preference. These data suggest the possibility of new treatment approaches to patients who are food addicted and/or overeat by using those medications used successfully in addictions treatment (Gold & Avena, 2013).

Impact on Public Policy

Food addiction has potentially important implications for affecting public policy. Unlike drug dependence, food addiction/foods that are high in sugar and fat are consumed at an early age, often in infancy. Can consumption of these foods at a young age change the development of children's brains, making them more susceptible to food addiction? This appears to be the case with drugs of abuse (i.e., that early age of onset of alcohol and drug use is associated with increased risk of drug dependence), and given the similarity described in this chapter regarding the similarities of the dopamine reward system in drug dependence and food addiction, then this would argue for the need of public policy to help protect the children from the risks of foods that are high in fat and sugar.

With the rising health care costs of obesity and medical conditions secondary to obesity, along with the increasing prevalence of obesity today, obesity is a financial burden that will likely be shared by everyone. Overall, it may be in the public's best interest to consider ways in which to encourage people to make healthy food choices and/or to develop programs that combat obesity and food addiction. Also, re-evaluation is needed of the current state of food marketing that often targets young children. This is similar to previous tobacco ads that tended to target children with cartoon characters. Food-addicted persons respond to an even higher level of food cues than their nonaddicted counterparts. Cues predictive of food availability are powerful modulators of appetite as well as food-seeking and ingestive behaviors (Brownell & Warner, 2009; Gearhardt, Bragg, et al., 2012; Gearhardt & Brownell, 2013).

Case Vignette: N.M.

N.M. is a 44-year-old married Caucasian female with a long history of issues relating to food. On initial presentation to the authors' weight management clinic, she was obese; her height was 5 feet 5.5 inches tall; and her weight was 188.5 pounds with a BMI of 30.9 kg/m^2. In addition to being obese, she had a history of reported polysubstance dependence in full sustained remission (alcohol, LSD, cocaine, cannabis, crystal meth), reporting that she had not used for 20 years and was never professionally treated for substance use (i.e., never went to drug rehabilitation program or took part in a 12-step program). The patient's family history was significant for alcohol dependence. At the time of initial evaluation, she was being treated in a psychiatric clinic for generalized anxiety disorder and major depressive disorder and was being prescribed fluoxetine, buproprion XL, and trazodone. She had a significant psychiatric history for inpatient hospitalizations as a teenager for depression, including one suicide attempt, and had tried multiple different psychotropic medications for treatment of depression, including venlafaxine, sertraline, paroxetine, lithium, escitalopram, and norpramin.

With regards to her weight, she reported that her weight had fluctuated throughout her life from her lowest adult weight of 118 pounds and BMI of 19.3 kg/m^2 when she was 21 years old to 280 pounds and a BMI of 46 kg/m^2. She had tried multiple weight loss programs including Weight Watchers, Overeaters

Continued

Case Vignette: N.M.—cont'd

Anonymous, and medication management such as taking phentermine in the past. She reported that she would lose the weight for a while but would end up gaining back the weight. Her chief health concerns included joint injuries, and she reported a history of surgeries on knee and shoulder that had limited her ability to exercise and thus contributed to her weight gain.

In addition to her concern about her weight, she also described having an unusual relationship with food. When she first presented, she reported binge eating daily and estimated eating up to 6,000 kilocalories in one binge that would sometimes be random and consist of food such as ketchup, sweet foods, or sometimes savory foods or foods like ice cream or fast foods that she normally did not eat. She reported eating despite feeling sick afterward and reported sometimes engaging in compensatory behaviors such as self-induced vomiting or excessive exercise following the binges (prior to her injuries). She also endorsed poor body image and reported binge eating to feel comfort when she was feeling depressed or sad. She also reported binge eating when she was not hungry and would binge eat in secret leading to subsequent guilt. She stated her teenage daughter appeared to have similar behavior, and she found her daughter hoarding food to the point that the patient would restrict what kind of food she had available in her house. Clearly, from her description, she meets the criteria for binge eating disorder and in the past may have had bulimia nervosa, although she denied any compensatory behaviors at this time.

In addition, she completed the Yale Food Addiction Scale (YFAS) and scored high enough to meet criteria for a food addiction in that she scored six out of seven criteria. She reported difficulty when she tried to cut back sweet, salty, or fatty foods and reported feelings of withdrawal if she removed these foods from her diet completely. The patient also reported that her food addiction affected her relationship with others in a similar way to how her alcohol dependence and polysubstance dependence affected her relationships with others in that she would engage in binge eating in secret instead of spending quality time with her teenage daughters and husband. She also reported challenges in her work as a nurse, as she felt more sluggish after eating a lot of food. She reported that food was now providing less comfort and help for her negative emotions than it did previously, and she has grown somewhat tolerant to the food. She also reported inability to eat a moderate amount of food despite having negative physical consequences of acid reflux and increased joint pain due to her excess body weight.

For treatment, in addition to attending Overeaters Anonymous meetings and obtaining a sponsor, she was started on topiramate 25 mg a day to help reduce her food cravings. This treatment appeared to help, although she reported some cognitive dulling as a side effect and elected to discontinue the medication. Phentermine was avoided for this patient, given its addictive potential and her history of substance use. Her fluoxetine was increased from 20 mg to 60 mg a day

Case Vignette: N.M.—cont'd

to help treat her binge eating disorder (with awareness that this can be a weight-gain-inducing medication). The patient's binge episodes subsequently decreased from once a day to less than once per week. Unfortunately, she continued to report thinking about food about 50%–70% of the time throughout the day, which she found very distressing. At that time, the clinic considered prescribing naltrexone, a medication used to treat alcohol and opiate addiction that when used in combination with bupropion is known as Contrave and may have a synergistic effect at promoting weight loss. Another option that was considered was prescribing baclofen with naltrexone, as baclofen is a $GABA_B$ agonist that has been shown to help with drugs of abuse as well as binge eating. It was thought that given her high YFAS score, as well as both her personal and family history of substance addiction, she has a food addiction in addition to binge eating disorder. At the time of this writing, she has declined using naltrexone, stating her preference to continue to work with her psychotherapist and continue her current medication regimen prior to adding an additional medication. However, this case illustrates the complexities of treating an individual with food addiction and demonstrates pharmacotherapies to consider when treating someone with obesity and binge eating disorder.

CONCLUSION

This chapter has addressed how overeating, obesity, and food addiction are multifactorial—a combination of genetics, environmental, and cultural factors, and comorbid psychiatric problems. From dopamine reward deficiency system to leptin deficiency system to serotonin and norepinephrine deficiency, new avenues of research offer novel ways in which to treat patients with food addiction and obesity. The food addiction hypothesis, a theory that certain highly palatable foods are addictive to certain individuals similarly to substance dependence, is a new and exciting foundation for research and treatment. Although food addiction and obesity are not mutually inclusive, there appears to be some overlap between the two as well as with binge eating disorder.

The traditional appetite suppressing drugs are effective for short-term weight loss but less effective for chronic, consistent weight loss that is maintained over time. Besides pharmacotherapy, bariatric surgery has been one of the most successful treatments for obesity for individuals with a BMI > 40 kg/m^2 or BMI > 35 kg/m^2 with medical complications, but there are risks and "down sides" to the procedure. Many new pharmacological treatments are currently being developed or have recently been released, including combination treatments, such as Qysmia, which is a combination of topiramate and low-dose phentermine, and Contrave, which is a combination of bupropion and naltrexone, an opioid antagonist and treatment for addiction. Another medication, tesofensine, is a combined norepinephrine-serotonin-dopamine reuptake, and lorcaserin targets the serotonin 5HT2C receptor in the brain, which is thought to act by inducing satiety.

Food addiction, overeating, and obesity provide an exciting avenue for new research and public health policy that will likely have an important impact on many individuals and future generations because obesity has become a global epidemic for which new treatments are continuing to be researched and developed.

REFERENCES

American Psychiatric Association. (2000). *Diagnostic and statistical manual of mental disorders* (4th ed. text rev.). Washington, DC: Author.

American Psychiatric Association. (2013). *Diagnostic and statistical manual of mental disorders* (5th ed.). Washington, DC: Author.

Aronne, L., Fujioka, K., Aroda, V., Chen, K., Halseth, A., Kesty, N. C., et al. (2007). Progressive reduction in body weight after treatment with the amylin analog pramlintide in obese subjects: A phase 2, randomized, placebo-controlled, dose-escalation study. [Clinical Trial, Phase II Multicenter Study Randomized Controlled Trial]. *Journal of Clinical Endocrinology and Metabolism, 92*(8), 2977–2983.

Aronne, L. J. (2007). Therapeutic options for modifying cardiometabolic risk factors. [Review]. *American Journal of Medicine, 120*(3 Suppl 1), S26–34.

Aronne, L. J., Brown, W. V., & Isoldi, K. K. (2007). Cardiovascular disease in obesity: A review of related risk factors and risk-reduction strategies. *Journal of Clinical Lipidology, 1*(6), 575–582.

Aronne, L. J., Waitman, J., & Isoldi, K. K. (2008). The pharmacotherapy of obesity. Retreived from http:///www.Endotext.Org/obesity/obesity15b/obesity15b.Htm.

Avena, N. M., & Gold, M. S. (2011a). Food and addiction—Sugars, fats and hedonic overeating. *Addiction, 106*(7), 1214–1215 discussion 1219–1220.

Avena, N. M., & Gold, M. S. (2011b). Sensitivity to alcohol in obese patients: A possible role for food addiction. *Journal of the American College of Surgeons, 213*(3), 451 author reply 451–452.

Avena, N. M., & Gold, M. S. (2011c). Variety and hyperpalatability: Are they promoting addictive overeating? *American Journal of Clinical Nutrition, 94*(2), 367–368.

Bagnasco, M., Dube, M. G., Katz, A., Kalra, P. S., & Kalra, S. P. (2003). Leptin expression in hypothalamic PVN reverses dietary obesity and hyperinsulinemia but stimulates ghrelin. [Research Support, U.S. Gov't, P.H.S.]. *Obesity Research, 11*(12), 1463–1470.

Blum, K., Braverman, E. R., Holder, J. M., Lubar, J. F., Monastra, V. J., Miller, D., et al. (2000). A biogenetic model for the diagnosis and treatment of impulsive, addictive, and compulsive behaviors. [Research Support, Non-U.S. Gov't Review]. *Journal of Psychoactive Drugs, 32*(Suppl. i–iv), 1–112 Reward deficiency syndrome.

Blum, K., & Gold, M. S. (2011). Neuro-chemical activation of brain reward meso-limbic circuitry is associated with relapse prevention and drug hunger: A hypothesis. *Medical Hypotheses, 76*(4), 576–584.

Blum, K., Liu, Y., Shriner, R., & Gold, M. S. (2011). Reward circuitry dopaminergic activation regulates food and drug craving behavior. *Current Pharmaceutical Design*, *17*(12), 1158–1167.

Blum, K., Noble, E. P., Sheridan, P. J., Montgomery, A., Ritchie, T., Jagadeeswaran, P., et al. (1990). Allelic association of human dopamine d2 receptor gene in alcoholism. *Journal of the American Medical Association*, *263*(15), 2055–2060.

Blum, K., Oscar-Berman, M., Bowirrat, A., Giordano, J., Madigan, M., Braverman, E. R., et al. (2012). Neuropsychiatric genetics of happiness, friendships, and politics: Hypothesizing homophily ("birds of a feather flock together") as a function of reward gene polymorphisms. *Journal of Genetic Syndrome & Gene Therapy*, *3*(112), doi: 10.4172/2157-7412.1000112.

Blum, K., Sheridan, P. J., Wood, R. C., Braverman, E. R., Chen, T. J., Cull, J. G., et al. (1996). The d2 dopamine receptor gene as a determinant of reward deficiency syndrome. *Journal of the Royal Soceity of Medicine*, *89*(7), 396–400.

Blum, K., Werner, T., Carnes, S., Carnes, P., Bowirrat, A., Giordano, J., et al. (2012). Sex, drugs, and rock 'n' roll: Hypothesizing common mesolimbic activation as a function of reward gene polymorphisms. [Research Support, N.I.H., Extramural Research Support, U.S. Gov't, Non-P.H.S. Research Support, U.S. Gov't, P.H.S. Review]. *Journal of Psychoactive Drugs*, *44*(1), 38–55.

Bocarsly, M. E., Barson, J. R., Hauca, J. M., Hoebel, B. G., Leibowitz, S. F., & Avena, N. M. (2012). Effects of perinatal exposure to palatable diets on body weight and sensitivity to drugs of abuse in rats. *Physiology & Behavior*, *107*, 568–575.

Boghossian, S., Ueno, N., Dube, M. G., Kalra, P., & Kalra, S. (2007). Leptin gene transfer in the hypothalamus enhances longevity in adult monogenic mutant mice in the absence of circulating leptin. [Research Support, N.I.H., Extramural]. *Neurobiology of Aging*, *28*(10), 1594–1604.

Brion, M. J., Ness, A. R., Rogers, I., Emmett, P., Cribb, V., Davey Smith, G., et al. (2010). Maternal macronutrient and energy intakes in pregnancy and offspring intake at 10 y: Exploring parental comparisons and prenatal effects. [Research Support, N.I.H., Extramural Research Support, Non-U.S. Gov't]. *American Journal of Clinical Nutrition*, *91*(3), 748–756.

Brownell, K. D., & Warner, K. E. (2009). The perils of ignoring history: Big tobacco played dirty and millions died. How similar is big food? *Milbank Quarterly*, *87*(1), 259–294.

Chen, P. S., Yang, Y. K., Yeh, T. L., Lee, I. H., Yao, W. J., Chiu, N. T., et al. (2008). Correlation between body mass index and striatal dopamine transporter availability in healthy volunteers—A spect study. [Research Support, Non-U.S. Gov't]. *Neuroimage*, *40*(1), 275–279.

Clinical guidelines on the identification, evaluation, and treatment of overweight and obesity in adults–the evidence report. National Institutes of Health. (1998). Consensus Development Conference, NIH Guideline Practice Guideline Review. *Obesity Research*, *6*(Suppl. 2), 51S–209S.

Colquitt, J. L., Picot, J., Loveman, E., & Clegg, A. J. (2009). Surgery for obesity. [Review]. *Cochrane Database of Systematic Reviews* (2), CD003641.

Conason, A., Teixeira, J., Hsu, C. H., Puma, L., Knafo, D., & Geliebter, A. (2012). Substance use following bariatric weight loss surgery. *Archives of Surgery*, 1–6.

Dackis, C. A., & Gold, M. S. (1985). New concepts in cocaine addiction: The dopamine depletion hypothesis. *Neuroscience and Biobehavioral Reviews*, *9*, 469–477.

Davis, C., Curtis, C., Levitan, R. D., Carter, J. C., Kaplan, A. S., & Kennedy, J. L. (2011). Evidence that 'food addiction' is a valid phenotype of obesity. *Appetite*, *57*(3), 711–717.

Dolinoy, D. C., Weidman, J. R., Waterland, R. A., & Jirtle, R. L. (2006). Maternal genistein alters coat color and protects Avy mouse offspring from obesity by modifying the fetal epigenome. [Research Support, N.I.H., Extramural Research Support, Non-U.S. Gov't]. *Environmental Health Perspectives*, *114*(4), 567–572.

Edelman, S., Maier, H., & Wilhelm, K. (2008). Pramlintide in the treatment of diabetes mellitus. [Review]. *BioDrugs: Clinical Immunotherapeutics, Biopharmaceuticals and Gene Therapy, 22*(6), 375–386.

Eichen, D. M., Lent, M. R., Goldbacher, E., & Foster, G. D. (2013). Exploration of "food addiction" in overweight and obese treatment-seeking adults. *Appetite, 67*, 22–24.

FDA. (2012). Medications target long-term weight control. Retrieved from http://www.Fda.Gov/forconsumers/consumerupdates/ucm312380.Htm.

Finkelstein, E. A., Trogdon, J. G., Cohen, J. W., & Dietz, W. (2009). Annual medical spending attributable to obesity: Payer- and service-specific estimates. [Research Support, Non-U.S. Gov't]. *Health Affairs, 28*(5), w822–831.

Flegal, K. M., Carroll, M. D., Ogden, C. L., & Johnson, C. L. (2002). Prevalence and trends in obesity among US adults, 1999–2000. *Journal of the American Medical Association, 288*(14), 1723–1727.

Gearhardt, A. N., Bragg, M. A., Pearl, R. L., Schvey, N. A., Roberto, C. A., & Brownell, K. D. (2012). Obesity and public policy. *Annual Review of Clinical Psychology, 8*, 405–430.

Gearhardt, A. N., & Brownell, K. D. (2013). The importance of understanding the impact of children's food marketing on the brain. [Comment Editorial]. *Journal of Pediatrics, 162*(4), 672–673.

Gearhardt, A. N., Corbin, W. R., & Brownell, K. D. (2009a). Food addiction: An examination of the diagnostic criteria for dependence. *Journal of Addiction Medicine, 3*(1), 1–7.

Gearhardt, A. N., Corbin, W. R., & Brownell, K. D. (2009b). Preliminary validation of the Yale Food Addiction Scale. *Appetite, 52*(2), 430–436.

Gearhardt, A. N., White, M. A., Masheb, R. M., Morgan, P. T., Crosby, R. D., & Grilo, C. M. (2012). An examination of the food addiction construct in obese patients with binge eating disorder. [Research Support, N.I.H., Extramural]. *International Journal of Eating Disorders, 45*(5), 657–663.

Gold, M. S. (2013). From cigarettes to obesity, public health at risk. In O. U. P. Blog & S. Harrington (Eds.), New York: Oxford University Press.

Gold, M. S., & Avena, N. M. (2012). *Effects of baclofen and naltrexone, alone and in combination, on binge eating in rats*. New Orleans, LA: Paper presented at the Society for Neuroscience Annual Meeting.

Gold, M. S., & Avena, N. M. (2013). Animal models lead the way to further understanding food addiction as well as providing evidence that drugs used successfully in addictions can be successful in treating overeating. [Letter]. *Biological Psychiatry*, doi: 10.1016/j.biopsych.2013.04.022.

Grant, J. E., Kim, S. W., & Hartman, B. K. (2008). A double-blind, placebo-controlled study of the opiate antagonist naltrexone in the treatment of pathological gambling urges. [Randomized Controlled Trial Research Support, N.I.H., Extramural]. *Journal of Clinical Psychiatry, 69*(5), 783–789.

Grant, J. E., Odlaug, B. L., Potenza, M. N., Hollander, E., & Kim, S. W. (2010). Nalmefene in the treatment of pathological gambling: Multicentre, double-blind, placebo-controlled study. [Multicenter Study Randomized Controlled Trial Research Support, Non-U.S. Gov't]. *British Journal of Psychiatry: The Journal of Mental Science, 197*(4), 330–331.

Haltia, L. T., Rinne, J. O., Merisaari, H., Maguire, R. P., Savontaus, E., Helin, S., et al. (2007). Effects of intravenous glucose on dopaminergic function in the human brain *in vivo*. [Clinical Trial Randomized Controlled Trial Research Support, Non-U.S. Gov't]. *Synapse, 61*(9), 748–756.

Henikoff, S., & Matzke, M. A. (1997). Exploring and explaining epigenetic effects. [Comment Editorial]. *Trends in Genetics, 13*(8), 293–295.

Hudson, J. I., Hiripi, E., Pope, H. G., Jr., & Kessler, R. C. (2007). The prevalence and correlates of eating disorders in the national comorbidity survey replication. [Research Support, N.I.H., Extramural Research Support, Non-U.S. Gov't]. *Biological Psychiatry, 61*(3), 348–358.

Ifland, J. R., Preuss, H. G., Marcus, M. T., Rourke, K. M., Taylor, W. C., Burau, K., et al. (2009). Refined food addiction: A classic substance use disorder. *Medical Hypotheses*, *72*(5), 518–526.

Johns, M. C. (2007). Therapies for diabetes: Pramlintide and exenatide. *American Family Physician*, *75*(12), 1831–1835.

Kalra, S. P. (2008). Central leptin insufficiency syndrome: An interactive etiology for obesity, metabolic and neural diseases and for designing new therapeutic interventions. [Research Support, N.I.H., Extramural Review]. *Peptides*, *29*(1), 127–138.

Kalra, S. P. (2009). Central leptin gene therapy ameliorates diabetes type 1 and 2 through two independent hypothalamic relays; a benefit beyond weight and appetite regulation. [Research Support, N.I.H., Extramural Review]. *Peptides*, *30*(10), 1957–1963.

Kalra, S. P., Bagnasco, M., Otukonyong, E. E., Dube, M. G., & Kalra, P. S. (2003). Rhythmic, reciprocal ghrelin and leptin signaling: New insight in the development of obesity. [Research Support, U.S. Gov't, P.H.S. Review]. *Regulatory Peptides*, *111*(1–3), 1–11.

Kalra, S. P., Dube, M. G., Pu, S., Xu, B., Horvath, T. L., & Kalra, P. S. (1999). Interacting appetite-regulating pathways in the hypothalamic regulation of body weight. [Research Support, U.S. Gov't, P.H.S. Review]. *Endocrine Reviews*, *20*(1), 68–100.

Kalra, S. P., & Kalra, P. S. (2006). Neuropeptide y: A conductor of the appetite-regulating orchestra in the hypothalamus. In A. J. Kastin (Ed.), *Handbook of biologically active peptides* (pp. 889–894). Amsterdam, The Netherlands: Elsevier Press.

Kelley, A. E., Bakshi, V. P., Haber, S. N., Steininger, T. L., Will, M. J., & Zhang, M. (2002). Opioid modulation of taste hedonics within the ventral striatum. [Research Support, U.S. Gov't, P.H.S. Review]. *Physiology & Behavior*, *76*(3), 365–377.

Keyes, K. M., Hatzenbuehler, M. L., McLaughlin, K. A., Link, B., Olfson, M., Grant, B. F., et al. (2010). Stigma and treatment for alcohol disorders in the United States. [Research Support, N.I.H., Extramural Research Support, Non-U.S. Gov't]. *American Journal of Epidemiology*, *172*(12), 1364–1372.

Korner, J., & Aronne, L. J. (2004). Pharmacological approaches to weight reduction: Therapeutic targets. [Research Support, U.S. Gov't, P.H.S. Review]. *Journal of Clinical Endocrinology and Metabolism*, *89*(6), 2616–2621.

Kringelbach, M. L., & Berridge, K. C. (2010). The functional neuroanatomy of pleasure and happiness. *Discovery Medicine*, *9*(49), 579–587.

Maluenda, F., Csendes, A., De Aretxabala, X., Poniachik, J., Salvo, K., Delgado, I., et al. (2010). Alcohol absorption modification after a laparoscopic sleeve gastrectomy due to obesity. *Obesity Surgery*, *20*(6), 744–748.

Nakamura, K. M., Haglind, E. G. C., Clowes, J. A., Achenbach, S. J., Atkinson, E. J., Melton, L. J., et al. (2011). Fracture risk after bariatric surgery. *Endocrine Reviews*, *32*, (03_Meeting Abstracts), OR44–45.

Neff, L. M., & Aronne, L. J. (2007). Pharmacotherapy for obesity. [Review]. *Current Atherosclerosis Reports*, *9*(6), 454–462.

Neurosearch. (2009). *Tesofensine*. Retrieved from http://neurosearch.Com/default.Aspx?Id+8265.

NHLBI.. (2000). *Obesity education initiative, the practical guide: Identification, evaluation, and treatment of overweight and obesity in adults*. Retrieved from http://www.Nhlbi.Nih.Gov/guidelines/obesity.

Noble, E. P., Noble, R. E., Ritchie, T., Syndulko, K., Bohlman, M. C., Noble, L. A., et al. (1994). D2 dopamine receptor gene and obesity. [Research Support, Non-U.S. Gov't]. *International Journal of Eating Disorders*, *15*(3), 205–217.

Ogden, C. L., Carroll, M. D., Curtin, L. R., Lamb, M. M., & Flegal, K. M. (2010). Prevalence of high body mass index in US children and adolescents, 2007–2008. *Journal of the American Medical Association*, *303*(3), 242–249.

Orexigen Therapeutics, Inc. (2009a). *Press Release, 07/20/09: Contrave obesity research phase 3 program meets co-primary and key secondary endpoints; exceeds FDA efficacy benchmark for obesity treatments*. http://ir,orexigen.com.

Oriexigen Therapeutics, Inc. (2009b). *Press Release, 09/30/09: Orexigen therapeutics phase 2b trial for empatic meets primary efficacy endpoint demonstrating significantly greater weight loss versus comparators in obese patients*. Retrieved from http://ir.orexigen.com.

Otukonyong, E. E., Dube, M. G., Torto, R., Kalra, P. S., & Kalra, S. P. (2005). Central leptin differentially modulates ultradian secretory patterns of insulin, leptin and ghrelin independent of effects on food intake and body weight. [Research Support, N.I.H., Extramural]. *Peptides*, *26*(12), 2559–2566.

Pu, S., Jain, M. R., Horvath, T. L., Diano, S., Kalra, P. S., & Kalra, S. P. (1999). Interactions between neuropeptide y and gamma-aminobutyric acid in stimulation of feeding: A morphological and pharmacological analysis. [Research Support, U.S. Gov't, P.H.S.]. *Endocrinology*, *140*(2), 933–940.

Puhl, R., Peterson, J. L., & Luedicke, J. (2012). Fighting obesity or obese persons? Public perceptions of obesity-related health messages. *International Journal of Obesity*, *37*(6), 774–782.

Rolls, E. T. (2007). Sensory processing in the brain related to the control of food intake. [Lectures Research Support, Non-U.S. Gov't]. *Proceedings of The Nutrition Society*, *66*(1), 96–112.

Salpeter, S. R., Buckley, N. S., Kahn, J. A., & Salpeter, E. E. (2008). Meta-analysis: Metformin treatment in persons at risk for diabetes mellitus. [Meta-Analysis Research Support, Non-U.S. Gov't Review]. *American Journal of Medicine*, *121*(2), 149–157.

Schneider, B. E., & Mun, E. C. (2005). Surgical management of morbid obesity. [Review]. *Diabetes Care*, *28*(2), 475–480.

Schwartz, M. W., Peskind, E., Raskind, M., Boyko, E. J., & Porte, D., Jr (1996). Cerebrospinal fluid leptin levels: Relationship to plasma levels and to adiposity in humans. [Comparative Study Research Support, U.S. Gov't, Non-P.H.S. Research Support, U.S. Gov't, P.H.S.]. *Nature Medicine*, *2*(5), 589–593.

Semple, S. J., Grant, I., & Patterson, T. L. (2005). Utilization of drug treatment programs by methamphetamine users: The role of social stigma. *American Journal on Addictions/American Academy of Psychiatrists in Alcoholism and Addictions*, *14*(4), 367–380.

Silventoinen, K., Sans, S., Tolonen, H., Monterde, D., Kuulasmaa, K., Kesteloot, H., et al. (2004). Trends in obesity and energy supply in the WHO Monica Project. [Multicenter Study Research Support, Non-U.S. Gov't Research Support, U.S. Gov't, P.H.S.]. *International Journal of Obesity and Related Metabolic Disorders: Journal of the International Association for the Study of Obesity*, *28*(5), 710–718.

Smith, G. P. (2004). Accumbens dopamine mediates the rewarding effect of orosensory stimulation by sucrose. *Appetite*, *43*(1), 11–13.

Stice, E., Spoor, S., Bohon, C., Veldhuizen, M. G., & Small, D. M. (2008). Relation of reward from food intake and anticipated food intake to obesity: A functional magnetic resonance imaging study. [Research Support, N.I.H., Extramural]. *Journal of Abnormal Psychology*, *117*(4), 924–935.

Ueno, N., Inui, A., Kalra, P. S., & Kalra, S. P. (2006). Leptin transgene expression in the hypothalamus enforces euglycemia in diabetic, insulin-deficient nonobese akita mice and leptin-deficient obese ob/ob mice. [Comparative Study Research Support, N.I.H., Extramural]. *Peptides*, *27*(9), 2332–2342.

Vartanian, L. R., & Smyth, J. M. (2013). Primum non nocere: Obesity stigma and public health. *Journal of Bioethical Inquiry*, *10*(1), 49–57.

Vetter, M. L., Faulconbridge, L. F., Williams, N. N., & Wadden, T. A. (2012). Surgical treatments for obesity. In K. D. Brownell & M. S. Gold (Eds.), *Food and addiction—A comprehensive handbook* (pp. 310–317). New York: Oxford University Press.

Volkow, N. D., Chang, L., Wang, G. J., Fowler, J. S., Ding, Y. S., Sedler, M., et al. (2001). Low level of brain dopamine d2 receptors in methamphetamine abusers: Association with metabolism in the orbitofrontal cortex. [Research Support, U.S. Gov't, Non-P.H.S. Research Support, U.S. Gov't, P.H.S.]. *American Journal of Psychiatry*, *158*(12), 2015–2021.

Volkow, N. D., Fowler, J. S., Wang, G. J., Hitzemann, R., Logan, J., Schlyer, D. J., et al. (1993). Decreased dopamine d2 receptor availability is associated with reduced frontal metabolism in cocaine abusers. [Comparative Study Research Support, U.S. Gov't, Non-P.H.S. Research Support, U.S. Gov't, P.H.S.]. *Synapse, 14*(2), 169–177.

Volkow, N. D., Wang, G. J., Telang, F., Fowler, J. S., Goldstein, R. Z., Alia-Klein, N., et al. (2009). Inverse association between BMI and prefrontal metabolic activity in healthy adults. [Research Support, N.I.H., Extramural Research Support, N.I.H., Intramural Research Support, U.S. Gov't, Non-P.H.S.]. *Obesity, 17*(1), 60–65.

Volkow, N. D., Wang, G. J., Telang, F., Fowler, J. S., Logan, J., Jayne, M., et al. (2007). Profound decreases in dopamine release in striatum in detoxified alcoholics: Possible orbitofrontal involvement. *Journal of Neuroscience, 27*(46), 12700–12706.

Volkow, N. D., & Wise, R. A. (2005). How can drug addiction help us understand obesity? [Review]. *Nature Neuroscience, 8*(5), 555–560.

Walters, R. G., Jacquemont, S., Valsesia, A., de Smith, A. J., Martinet, D., Andersson, J., et al. (2010). A new highly penetrant form of obesity due to deletions on chromosome 16p11.2. [Research Support, N.I.H., Extramural Research Support, Non-U.S. Gov't]. *Nature, 463*(7281), 671–675.

Wang, G. J., Volkow, N. D., Felder, C., Fowler, J. S., Levy, A. V., Pappas, N. R., et al. (2002). Enhanced resting activity of the oral somatosensory cortex in obese subjects. *Neuroreport, 13*(9), 1151–1155.

Wang, Y., Beydoun, M. A., Liang, L., Caballero, B., & Kumanyika, S. K. (2008). Will all Americans become overweight or obese? Estimating the progression and cost of the US obesity epidemic. *Obesity (Silver Spring), 16*(10), 2323–2330.

Will, M. J., Franzblau, E. B., & Kelley, A. E. (2003). Nucleus accumbens mu-opioids regulate intake of a high-fat diet via activation of a distributed brain network. [Research Support, U.S. Gov't, P.H.S.]. *Journal of Neuroscience, 23*(7), 2882–2888.

Woolley, J. D., Lee, B. S., & Fields, H. L. (2006). Nucleus accumbens opioids regulate flavor-based preferences in food consumption. [Research Support, Non-U.S. Gov't]. *Neuroscience, 143*(1), 309–317.

Yeomans, M. R., & Gray, R. W. (1997). Effects of naltrexone on food intake and changes in subjective appetite during eating: Evidence for opioid involvement in the appetizer effect. [Clinical Trial Randomized Controlled Trial Research Support, Non-U.S. Gov't]. *Physiology & Behavior, 62*(1), 15–21.

Sex Addiction: An Overview*

Kenneth Paul Rosenberg[1], Suzanne O'Connor[2], Patrick Carnes[3]
[1]Cornell University Medical Center, Psychiatry Department, New York, NY, USA and UpperEastHealth .com, [2]Arizona School of Professional Psychology at Argosy University, Phoenix, AZ, USA, [3]The Meadows, Wickenburg, AZ, USA

HISTORICAL CONTEXT

In his 1812 book, *Medical Inquiries and Observations Upon the Diseases of the Mind*, Benjamin Rush recounted a case of a man whose "excessive" sexual appetite caused him psychological distress to the point of requesting that he be medically rendered impotent (Rush, 1812). In 1886, German psychiatrist Dr. Richard von Krafft-Ebbing argued that Pathological Sexuality is a bona fide psychiatric illness. He wrote,

> *It (sex) permeates all (of the patient's) thoughts and feelings, allowing of no other aims in life, tumultuously, and in a rut-like fashion demanding gratification without granting the possibility of moral and righteous counter-presentations, and resolving itself into an impulsive, insatiable succession of sexual enjoyments.... This pathological sexuality is a dreadful scourge for its victim, for he is in constant danger of violating the laws of the state and of morality, of losing his honor, his freedom and even his life. (Krafft-Ebbing, 1886, 1965)*

Nearly a century later, British psychologist Dr. Jim Orford argued that Hypersexuality should be included into the spectrum of addictive disorders. In the *British Journal of Addictions*, Orford wrote,

> *It is argued that a theory of dependence must take into account forms of excessive appetitive behavior which do not have psychoactive drugs as their object. Excessive heterosexuality is an important but neglected example. Hypersexuality as an entity has been criticized on a number of grounds. These problems of concept and definition are paralleled in discussions of other excessive behaviors such as excessive drinking and excessive gambling. (1978)*

Though Orford argued for the theory of Hypersexual Dependence, he noted three problems with the dependence model of sex that were also noted by Carnes (1994) and are still relevant today: "(1) it is difficult to separate normal and abnormal sexual behavior; (2) it is difficult to determine

* This is a version of an article published in the *Journal of Sex & Marital Therapy*, DOI: 10.1080/0092623X.2012.701268. The accepted author version posted September 10, 2012, is available online at http://www.taylorandfrancis.com.

Behavioral Addictions
http://dx.doi.org/10.1016/B978-0-12-407724-9.00009-4

when loss of control occurs; and (3) it is difficult to assess the role of culture in this" (as cited in Carnes, 1994).

Caution in diagnosing Sex Addiction (SA) or related disorders is rightly justified because the research is incomplete. Furthermore, the vast majority of those who have multiple affairs, are promiscuous, or take part in novel expressions of sexuality are not sexually addicted. Levine (2010) performed a retrospective chart review to analyze the sexual patterns of 30 men who had been referred for problems with sexual addiction. He reported that only 25% of his case studies met the criteria of an addictive pattern.

PREVALENCE

Currently, the prevalence of SA is most often cited in between 3% and 6% of the general population (Carnes, 1991). The occurrence rates of SA vary in the literature depending on characteristics examined such as gender, sexual orientation, age, and the diagnostic criteria implemented in the study. In the clinical convenience sample of the American population by Kinsey, Pomeroy, and Martin (1948), male hypersexuality, defined as seven or more orgasms per week—a normal more consistent with normal sexuality today—identified hypersexuality in 7.6% of males between adolescence and age 30. Traeen, Spitznogle, and Beverfjord (2004) narrowed their research to pornography dependence in the adult Norwegian male population, and found that 1% of their sample masturbated to ejaculation twice or more per day while viewing pornography. A Swedish study of males and females in the general population found that 5%–10% of most sexually active respondents reported higher levels of co-occurring addictions, risk-taking behaviors, distress and psychiatric symptoms, suggesting a subgroup of the most sexually active who may have psychosocial impairments (Langstrom & Hanson, 2006).

SA-RELATED DIAGNOSES IN THE ICD AND DSM

Although psychological writings about excessive sexual behavior date back 200 years, the medical manuals have been slow to name diagnoses. Efforts to develop a diagnosis have met with understandable resistance because of the lack of scientific data. For instance, the *International Classification of Diseases* (*ICD-10,* World Health Organization, 2007) lists a diagnosis called "excessive sexual drive" and subdivides it into "nymphomania" for females and "satyriasis" for males. However, according to Vroege et al. (1998), members of the *ICD-10* task force were unable to come to consensus about the set of criteria for this category, as unlike the other sexual dysfunctions, there is a lack of explicit research criteria for excessive sexual drive. Vroege and colleagues argued that in future diagnostic systems, the sexual disorders should be subdivided by the phases of the sexual cycle. They stated that excessive sexual drive is largely a desire disorder, as opposed to an arousal or orgasm-based disorder, and that the current ICD nosology lacks sufficient scientific evidence.

In the American Psychiatric Association's *DSM-III-R* (American Psychiatric Association, 1987), the term *sexual addiction* fell under the diagnostic category of "Sexual Disorder Not Otherwise Specified." The term *sexual addiction* was removed from the fourth edition of the manual in 1997, primarily because of a lack of empirical research and consensus validating sexual behaviors as a bona fide behavioral addiction (Kafka, 2010). The place of sex addiction in the fifth and most recent version of the DSM is discussed later in this chapter.

Writing in the popular media, psychologist Dr. Patrick Carnes (1991) identified 10 clinical signs that individuals with SA most often endorse: Compulsive Behavior (94%), Loss of Control (93%), Efforts to Stop (88%), Loss of Time (94%), Preoccupation (77%), Inability to Fulfill Obligations (87%), Continuation Despite Consequences (85%), Escalation (74%), Social, Occupational and Recreational Losses (87%), and Withdrawal (98%). Carnes developed the Sexual Addiction Screening Test (SAST). When 13 was used as the cut-off score, 96.5% of respondents were correctly classified as sexually addicted when compared to diagnostic interviewing, while only 3.5% scoring 13 or above were undiagnosed (Carnes, 1991). Based on a convenience sample of 772 male sex addicts, 177 female sex addicts, and 141 controls, Carnes developed behavioral subtypes that were significantly higher in sex addicts than controls. Carnes identified Fantasy Sex (18%), Voyeurism (18%), Exhibitionism (15%), Seductive Role Sex (21%), Intrusive Sex (e.g., boundary violations; 17%), Anonymous Sex (18%), Trading Sex (12%), Paying for Sex (15%), Pain Exchange (16%), and Exploitive Sex (13%). Carnes noted that male sex addicts were significantly more likely than female sex addicts to engage in Voyeuristic Sex, Intrusive Sex, Exhibitionism, Anonymous Sex, Paying for Sex, and Exploitative Sex. Female sex addicts were more likely than male addicts to engage in Fantasy Sex, Seductive Role Sex, Trading Sex, and Pain Exchange and on par with addicted men in the areas of Exhibitionism and Intrusive Sex (Carnes, Nonemaker, & Skilling, 1991).

In psychiatry, there have been many efforts to formulate an SA-related diagnosis for clinical work and research. Psychiatrist Ariel Goodman (1998) proposed criteria for SA based on the prevailing diagnostic criteria for Substance Abuse Disorders such as tolerance, withdrawal, and interference with social and occupational functions (see Table 9.1).

Carnes (1983, 1991, 1994, 2005) proposed 10 diagnostic criteria for Sex Addiction, also adapting the principles of chemical addiction to sexual behavior (see Table 9.2).

To further investigate and validate the diagnosis, researchers began to develop testing instruments. Carnes accumulated data on more than 1,600 cases (1991); developed several self-report screening measures such as a 25-item Sexual Addiction Screening Test (SAST); and developed a brief screening test (Carnes et al., 2011) that was similar to the CAGE, a 4-item assessment for alcohol dependency used to assess whether or not the patient had been experiencing problems with Cutting down, someone Annoying

Table 9.1 Sexual Addiction Proposed Diagnostic Criteria*

A maladaptive pattern of sexual behavior, *leading to clinically significant impairment or distress,* as manifested by three (or more) of the following, occurring at any time in the same 12-month period:

(1) Tolerance, as defined by either of the following:
- **(a)** A need for markedly increased amount or intensity of the sexual behavior to achieve the desired effect.
- **(b)** Markedly diminished effect with continued involvement in the sexual behavior at the same level of intensity.

(2) Withdrawal, as manifested by either of the following:
- **(a)** Characteristic psychophysiological withdrawal syndrome of physiologically described changes and/or psychologically described changes upon discontinuation of the sexual behavior.
- **(b)** The same (or a closely related) sexual behavior is engaged in to relieve or avoid withdrawal symptoms.

(3) The sexual behavior is often engaged in over a longer period, in greater quantity, or at a higher level of intensity than was intended.

(4) There is a persistent desire or unsuccessful efforts to cut down or control the sexual behavior.

(5) A great deal of time is spent in activities necessary to prepare for the sexual behavior, to engage in the behavior, or to recover from its effects.

(6) Important social, occupational, or recreational activities are given up or reduced because of the sexual behavior.

(7) The sexual behavior continues despite knowledge of having a persistent or recurrent physical or psychological problem that is likely to have been caused or exacerbated by the behavior.

*Goodman, 1998, p. 233.

him about drinking, feeling Guilty about drinking, and needing an Eye-opener drink in the morning in order to deal with overnight withdrawal or hangover effects (Ewing, 1984).

Terms such as *compulsive sexual behavior* and *impulsive sexual disorder* were developed to describe SA-related behaviors, and measures such as the Sexual Compulsivity Scale were utilized for research. Coleman, Raymond, and McBean (2003) wrote that compulsive sexual disorders are characterized by sexual urges, behaviors, and thoughts that are both recurrent and intense. The symptoms cause significant distress across various other areas of functioning and cannot be better accounted for by a mental health disorder or medical condition.

Mick and Hollander (2006) suggested the term *Impulsive-Compulsive Sexual Behavior* for patients who demonstrated an impulsive component in initiating the cycle, and a compulsive component in the persistence of the dysfunctional behavior.

Table 9.2 Sexual Addiction Diagnostic Criteria*

A. A minimum of three criteria met during a 12-month period:

1) Recurrent failure to resist impulses to engage in specific sexual behavior.
2) Frequent engaging in these behaviors to a greater extent or longer duration than intended.
3) Persistent desire or unsuccessful efforts to stop, to reduce, or to control behaviors.
4) Inordinate amount of time spent in obtaining sex, being sexual, or recovering from sexual experiences.
5) Preoccupation with the behavior or preparatory activities.
6) Frequently engaging in the behavior when expected to fulfill occupational, academic, domestic, or social obligations.
7) Continuation of the behavior despite knowledge of having a persistent or recurrent social, financial, psychological, or physical problem that is caused or exacerbated by the behavior.
8) Need to increase intensity, frequency, number, or risk of behaviors to achieve the desired effect or diminished effect with continued behaviors at the same level of intensity, frequency, number, or risk.
9) Giving up or limiting social, occupational, or recreational activities because of behavior.
10) Distress, anxiety, restlessness, or irritability if unable to engage in the behaviors.

B. Has significant personal and social consequences (such as loss of partner, occupation, or legal implications).

*Proposed by Carnes (1991; 2005b).

In 2010 and 2011, two SA-related diagnoses were considered by the *Diagnostic and Statistical Manual of Mental Disorders,* Fifth Edition (*DSM-5*) Work Groups of the American Psychiatric Association. *Hypersexual Disorder* was studied by the Sexual and Gender Identity Disorder Working Group, and *Internet Addictive Disorder* was addressed by the Addiction and Related Disorders Working Group. Ultimately, both diagnoses were not included in the *DSM-5*.

Kafka (2010), writing on behalf of the Sexual and Gender Identity Disorder Working Group, proposed the diagnosis of Hypersexual Disorder (see Table 9.3). The diagnosis did not require dependence, tolerance, and withdrawal. Kafka's criteria incorporated other key aspects of addiction such as unsuccessful efforts to cut down, greater use than intended,

Table 9.3 Proposed Hypersexual Disorder Diagnostic Criteria*

A) Over a period of at least 6 consecutive months, recurrent and intense sexual fantasies, sexual urges, or sexual behaviors in association with four or more of the following five criteria:
- **1)** Excessive time consumed by sexual fantasies and urges, and by planning for and engaging in sexual behavior.
- **2)** Repetitively engaging in these sexual fantasies, urges, and behavior in response to dysphoric mood states (e.g., anxiety, depression, boredom, irritability).
- **3)** Repetitively engaging in sexual fantasies, urges, or behaviors in response to stressful life events.
- **4)** Repetitive but unsuccessful efforts to control or significantly reduce these sexual fantasies, urges, and behavior.
- **5)** Repetitively engaging in sexual behaviors while disregarding the risk for physical or emotional harm to self or others.

B) There is clinically significant personal distress or impairment in social occupational or other important areas of functioning associated with the frequency and intensity of the sexual fantasies, urges, and behaviors.

C) These sexual fantasies, urges, and behavior are not due to direct physiological effects of exogenous substances (e.g., drugs of abuse or medications) or to manic episodes.

D) The person is at least 18 years of age.

Specify if: Masturbation, Pornography, Sexual Behavior With Consenting Adults, Cybersex, Telephone Sex, Strip Clubs

Specify if in Remission: No Distress, Impairment, or Recurring Behavior and in an Uncontrolled Environment, and state duration of remission in months in a Controlled Environment.

*Proposed by Kafka (2010).

and serious social and occupational consequences. Ultimately, the *DSM-5* committee decided that there was not enough research to include Hypersexual Disorder as a diagnosis in the DSM-5.

SCREENING INSTRUMENTS FOR SA

In 2010, Carnes revised the Sexual Addiction Screening Test (SAST) to assess male homosexual and female heterosexual populations and include core addiction dimensions of (1) Preoccupation about sex, (2) Loss of Control despite problems, (3) Relationship Disturbances caused by sexual behavior, and (4) Affect disturbances such as anxiety and depression related to sexual behaviors. The instrument was studied in several populations such psychotherapy patients, college students, and veterans, and has demonstrated acceptable reliability with alphas in four studies ranging from 0.85 to 0.95 (Hook, Hook, Davis, Worthington, & Penberthy, 2010). The Sexual Addiction Screening Test - Revised (SAST-R) has 20 core items and subscales of 25 items and has shown reliability, with a cutoff of 6 (Carnes, Green, & Carnes, 2010). The SAST and SAST-R demonstrated good internal consistency and reliability and have been utilized by criminal justice, treatment centers, and educational programs.

Due to the length of the SAST-R (45 items), it was not considered suitable for certain clinical settings such as an emergency room. To meet the need for brevity in these types of settings, a screening instrument called PATHOS was developed to aid in the identification of those who may have sexual addiction. Similar to the CAGE (Ewing, 1984), this mnemonic six-item screener (extracted from the SAST-R) was found to have excellent to acceptable internal consistency (0.94–0.77) and using the cut-off score of 3, demonstrated respectable sensitivity and specificity ratings. See Table 9.4 for a list of PATHOS items.

Table 9.4 PATHOS Items

1) Do you often find yourself preoccupied with sexual thoughts? (Preoccupied)
2) Do you hide some of your sexual behavior from others? (Ashamed)
3) Have you ever sought help for sexual behavior you did not like? (Treatment)
4) Has anyone been hurt emotionally because of your sexual behavior? (Hurt)
5) Do you feel controlled by you sexual desire? (Out of control)
6) When you have sex, do you feel depressed afterwards? (Sad)

CYBERSEX

Aside from Problem Gambling, Internet Gaming Disorder will be added to the *DSM-5* appendix as a provisional behavioral addiction worthy of further research. Tao (2010) and others unsuccessfully argued for inclusion in the *DSM-5* of an Internet Addiction Disorder (IAD) that shares key features with substance abuse, such as salience (emotional and cognitive processing), mood modification, tolerance, withdrawal, conflict, and relapse. Tao (2010) proposed eight criteria for IAD: (1) preoccupation, (2) withdrawal, (3) tolerance, (4) unsuccessful efforts to control use, (5) continued use despite negative consequences, (6) loss of interest in non-Internet activities, (7) use to escape dysphoria, and (8) the deception of others such as family members and therapists. Of great interest to the SA community, IAD includes the subcategory of Cybersex Addiction. Since the 1990s, the SA community has been addressing the addictive potential of the Internet, particularly when it concerned pornographic material. In the SA literature, Cybersex is commonly referred as the "crack cocaine of sexual compulsivity" based on its ability to quickly engage the user and keep him focused on the material for extended periods of time (Cooper, Putnam, Planchon, & Boies, 1999). Vulnerable patients often report becoming lost in the trance of Internet pornography as they scroll through sites, holding off orgasm for hours at a time and spending a considerable amount of money on live chats—all this despite their intentions and promises to stop looking at Internet pornography.

COMORBIDITY IN SA-RELATED DISORDERS

Studies of the sexually disordered population reveal multiple disorders in the clinical population. Langstrom and Hanson's (2006) study of the general population in Sweden found that 5%–10% of most sexually active respondents reported higher levels of co-occurring addictions, risk-taking behaviors, and psychiatric symptoms. Co-occurring psychiatric disturbances and addictive disorders are common in the SA population.

SA has been associated with affect dysregulation (Samenow, 2010), depression and anxiety (Bancroft, 2009; Kaplan & Kruger, 2010), impulsivity (Miner, Raymond, Mueller, Lloyd, & Lim, 2009; Raymond, Coleman, & Miner, 2003), loneliness (Yoder, Virden, & Amin, 2005), low self-worth and insecure attachment styles (Earle & Earle, 1995; Zapf, Greiner, & Carroll, 2008), personal distress (Kafka & Henna, 1999; Kingston & Firestone, 2008), risk-taking behaviors such as substance abuse (Kaplan & Kruger, 2010; Sussman, 2007), and self-hatred and shame (Kaplan & Kruger, 2010; Kort, 2004; Reid, Harper, & Anderson, 2009).

Utilizing the Mood and Sexuality Questionnaire in studies of 919 heterosexual males (Bancroft, Janssen, Strong, Carnes, et al., 2003) and 662 gay men (Bancroft, Janssen, Strong, & Vukadinovic, 2003), it was found that only a minority of the sample reported greater interest in sexual thoughts or activities when depressed or feeling anxiety (15%–25%). The levels of distress in this minority population reflected levels of those that have problems with anxiety (Bancroft & Vukadinovic, 2004).

Employing the Sexual Addiction Screening Test (SAST) and the Experiences in Close Relationships-Revised (ECR-R), Zapf, Greiner, and Carroll (2008) examined attachment styles in sexually addicted adult males. The ECR-R measures adult romantic attachment styles on measures of anxiety and avoidance to produce four possible results of secure attachment style, preoccupied attachment style, fearful-avoidant attachment style, and dismissing-avoidant attachment style. Of the 52 participants examined, 32 were identified as sex addicts according to the SAST results, and 20 were defined as nonaddicts based on SAST results. Results of the study showed the ECR-R supported their hypothesis with 40% of the nonaddict population reporting a secure attachment style, while of the sexually addicted population only 8% reported a secure attachment style. In contrast, the sexually addicted population reported more frequently identifying with higher levels of avoidance and anxiety, and hence resulted in higher percentages in preoccupied, dismissing, and fearful-avoidant attachment styles than nonaddicts.

Reid and Carpenter (2009) investigated the differences between male hypersexual patients (n = 152) and normative group responses to the Minnesota Multiphasic Personality Inventory-2 (MMPI-2). Their findings showed "nearly all validity and clinical scales are higher for the hypersexual sample than they are for the norming sample." However, these elevations generally did not fall within the clinical range, and approximately one-third of the tested population had normal profiles. MMPI-2 clinical scales with the most frequent elevations for the hypersexual population included 7 (Psychasthenia) characterized by phobias, obsessions, compulsions, or excessive anxiety; 8 (Schizophrenia); 4 (Psychopathic deviate) characterized by general maladjustment, unwillingness to identify with social convention and norms, and impulse-control problems; and 2 (Depression), respectively. They further noted that within this study they did not find overall support for addictive tendencies or classifying the patients as obsessive or compulsive, but that their cluster analysis "provided evidence to support the idea that hypersexual patients are a diverse group of individuals" (p. 307). These findings are similar to Levine's (2010) retrospective multiple-case analysis that also calls into question the level of psychopathology among those with problematic sexual behaviors.

In a small convenience sample that included sexual offenders, comorbidity was studied in 88 men with paraphilias (i.e., socially deviant and aggressive forms of sexual impulsivity) and 32 men with paraphilia-related disorder (i.e., normophilic Hypersexuality). There were no differences in the comorbidity between paraphilic and normophilic groups in the categories of mood disorders (71.6%), dysthymic disorder (55%), anxiety disorders (38.3%), social phobia disorder (21.6%), psychoactive substance abuse (40.8%), alcohol abuse (30.0%), impulse disorder NOS (25%), and reckless driving (16.7%). However, Attention Deficit Disorder was significantly higher in paraphilia disorder (50%) than paraphilia-related disorder (16.7%) (Kafka & Hennen, 2002).

Among a sample of 1,603 sex addicts, 69% of heterosexual men, 79% of heterosexual women, and 80% of homosexual men reported a lifetime prevalence of other addictive and abusive behaviors, ranging from minor to serious. Forty percent of heterosexual men, 40% of heterosexual women, and 60% of homosexual men engaged in sexual acting out while simultaneously involved in other addictive or abusive behaviors such as substance abuse, gambling, or eating disorders (Carnes, Murray, & Charpentier, 2005).

In a study of pathological gamblers, Grant and Steinburg (2005) found that 19.6% of their subjects also met the criteria for Compulsive Sexual Behavior (CSB). Seventy percent of the subjects who met the criteria for both disorders reported that CSB had preceded their gambling problems.

ADDICTION INTERACTION DISORDER

Multiple addictions are so common in this population that in the SA community there is the term *Addiction Interaction Disorder,* which means that multiple addictive behaviors exist as part of a single illness (Carnes, Murray, & Charpentier, 2005). These behaviors interact as reinforcements and become part of one another. They, in effect, become packages in which the whole is greater than the sum of the parts. A common Addiction Interaction Disorder is the combination of cocaine abuse, alcohol abuse, and sexual behaviors that may occasionally rise to the level of SA (Rawson, Washton, Domier, & Reiber, 2002). At most substance abuse treatment centers, individuals seeking treatment for the combination of these behaviors would receive therapy only for substance abuse and dependence. As a core addictive process, the unaddressed SA will sometimes be the reason an individual relapses with substances and sex.

THE POSSIBLE NEUROSCIENCE OF SA

Changes in the phenomenology of addiction, now allowing for the inclusion of behavioral addictions, are founded on developments in neuroscience. Chapter 1 presented the prevalent theories of chemical addiction that may also support the existence of sex addiction and other behavioral addictions. The Reward/Executive–Function Theory supposes that alterations in the mesolimbic system and medial frontal cortex perpetuate the addictive cycle. Additionally, neuropsychological models propose that addiction results from vulnerabilities in the organism's decision-making process and focus. Finally, contemporary neurobiological theories explain addiction as involving cellular memory in the consolidation of memories at the synaptic level, known as long-term potentiation (LTP).

SA could conceivably develop through neurobiological mechanisms like those proposed for the protypical behavioral addiction, Problem Gambling (PG). Grant and Steinberg (2005) found compulsive sexual behavior occurred in 19.6% of patients with PG, suggesting similar biological and psychological processes are associated with both SA and PG. More importantly, in 70.5% of those with co-occurring disorders, compulsive sexual behavior predated pathological gambling, suggesting that the SA and PG may share similar fundamental brain dysregulations. A unitary hypothesis is supported by the fact that patients treated with dopaminergic agents for idiopathic Parkinsonism sometimes developed new onset pathological gambling and sexual compulsivity (Bostwick, Hecksel, Stevens, Bower, & Ahlskog, 2009). In addition, as discussed later, both PG and SA may be treated by the same investigational medication, naltrexone (Bostwick et al., 2009).

There is little convincing data that currently demonstrates a neurobiological pathway for SA. Pitchers et al. (2010) studied sexual behavior in rats exposed to amphetamines and found that sexual behavior enhanced the amphetamine locomotor response after 1 week of abstinence, supporting the notion that stimulants act synergistically with sexual behavior. After examining the rats' brains, they found morphological changes, increased dendritic spines in the shell and core of the nucleus accumbens, after 1 week, but not after 1 day, of sexual encounters. Hence, sexually induced morphological changes occur in response, or at least are enhanced, by abstinence, suggesting a mechanism for how sexual urges, or perhaps even sexual addiction, may become encoded in memory after abstinence.

Genetic data may ultimately help explain abnormalities in sexual desire. In humans, the heritability of sexually promiscuous behavior in both genders has been proposed to be 33% based on monozygotic and dyzygotic twin studies (Zietsch, Verweij, Bailey, Wright, & Martin, 2010). The effects of oxytocin and vasopressin may help explain fidelity and pair-bonding (Aragona et al., 2006; Carter, 1998; Depue & Morrone-Strupinsky, 2005; Fisher, Aron, Mashek, Li, & Brown, 2002; Insel & Young, 2001; Melis & Argiolas, 1995). Vasopressin 1a gene (AVPRIA) has been associated with marital satisfaction and pair-bonding in one study (Walum et al., 2008), but not another (Cherkas, Oelsner, Mak, Valdes, & Spector, 2004). Irregularities of the dopamine system may help explain excessive sexual behaviors. Genes mediating dopamine transmission, specifically the D4DR receptor, are thought to be associated with seeking novel stimulation, particularly when there are seven or more repeats in the allele (Chen, Burton, Greenberger, & Dmitrieva, 1999; Ding et al., 2002; Harpending & Cochran, 2002; Wang et al., 2004). Long alleles may predispose for Attention Deficit Hyperactivity Disorder (Li, Sham, Owen, & He, 2006), alcoholism (MacKillop, Menges, McGeary, & Lisman, 2007; Ray et al., 2008), financial risk taking (Dreber et al., 2009), disinhibition and impulsivity (Congdon, Lesch, & Canli, 2008), and initiating sexual activity (Eisenberg, 2007). Utilizing self-reports of sexual behavior history and buccal wash genotyping in 181 young adults, Garcia et al. (2010) found subjects with at least one 7-repeat allele (7R+) in D4DR were more likely to have had a one-night stand, yet found no significant differences in overall sexual infidelity.

The few brain imaging studies of "normal" human subjects during sexual arousal seem to implicate the same areas associated with chemical addictions and suggest that the frontal areas of the brain may exert control and exercise reason over the posterior reward centers (Georgiadis, 2012; Sescousse, Redouté, & Dreher, 2010). Brain scan studies of sexual dimorphism may help us understand the differences between males and females, particularly when it comes to sexual acting-out. For instance, one sexual activity-related PET study demonstrates that male arousal is more often associated with activation of the visual cortices of the brain—even when the subjects' eyes are closed (Georgiadis et al., 2010). Female arousal is associated with stronger activity in left dorsal fronto-parietal regions, including premotor areas and posterior parietal areas (Georgiadis et al., 2009). During orgasm, the male and female brain functioning appears similar with activation in the anterior lobe of the cerebellar vermis and deep cerebellar nuclei, and deactivations in the left ventromedial and orbitofrontal cortex. Although promising and intriguing, today's PET and fMRI studies do not yet provide any clinical guidance in treating sexual compulsivity.

In a preliminary study of 16 males, Miner et al. (2009) used the Compulsive Sexual Behavior Inventory, utilized an impulse-control task (computerized Go–No Go), and administered an MRI technique called diffusion tensor imaging to examine the potential of white matter disorganization in the frontal lobes of men with Compulsive Sexual Behavior (CSB). The neuroimaging scans were inconclusive and inconsistent with neuroanatomical correlates of impulse-control disorders (p. 146).

TREATMENT OF SEX ADDICTION

Psychotherapy

Regardless of the label given to these patients—compulsive, impulsive, hypersexual, or addicted—treatment generally consists of approaches that have been popularized for substance addiction such as group and individual therapy; motivational interviewing; cognitive-behavioral approaches to identify triggers; dialectical behavioral techniques to manage cravings; relapse prevention strategies; insight-oriented therapy to identify deeper causes; family therapy to resolve conflicts; exercise and nutrition; treatment of comorbid mental illness and addictions; referral to appropriate 12-step-based recovery groups; and psychopharmacology aimed at diminishing dysfunctional sexual behaviors, reducing cravings, improving the outcome during desired sexual experiences, and treating associated psychiatric disorders.

Throughout the United States, numerous inpatient and outpatient treatment centers use an addiction model to treat sexual compulsivity and addiction. The reader is referred to basic addiction texts such as *Clinical Textbook of Addictive Disorders,* Third Edition, by Frances, Miller, and Mack (2005) for an understanding of the approaches to addiction.

Carnes has developed a task-centered approach program with a series of operationalized workbooks appropriate for treating SA patients (Carnes, 2005). These workbooks provide homework assignments and readings for the first year of therapy.

What may surprise clinicians is that SA patients are generally not good at sex. They function poorly in the bedroom. Sex addicts feverishly pursue their dysfunctional sexual behaviors yet generally have sexual difficulties with intimate partners, healthy sexual encounters, and/or long-term partners. Therefore, in addition to addiction treatment, they need sex therapy. Premature ejaculation, erectile dysfunction, anorgasmia, and "sexual anorexia" (i.e., extended periods when the addict has no sexual activity) are common (Carnes, 1997). Masters, Johnson, and Kolodny (1988), Helen Singer Kaplan (1974), and others have developed Sex Therapy for sexual disorders; however, these behavioral interventions need to be modified when working with the sexually addicted client. Sex Therapy cannot commence until patients have their dysfunctional behaviors under control.

Another surprise for clinicians is how treating the sex addiction may worsen the marriage or relationship. Steinglass (1980) noted how in families in which there is alcoholism, alcohol may be the "glue" that enables the couple to meld, tolerate dysfunctional marriages, and/or avoid personal problems. Similarly, recovery from SA puts new demands on marital relationships. Significant others of sex addicts may suffer from sexual anorexia, sexual aversions, and/or sexual dysfunctions, explaining why partners have found it "acceptable" to live with the frequent lack of sexual intimacy. As discussed, SA patients themselves often have sexual disorders. Therefore, conjoint treatment is generally required to promote healthy relationships and satisfying sexual experiences during recovery.

12-Step Peer Support Groups

Peer-support groups are helpful. There are five self-help "fellowships" modeled after Alcoholics Anonymous: Sex Anonymous, Sexaholics Anonymous, Sex Addicts Anonymous, Sex and Love Addicts Anonymous, and Sexual Compulsives Anonymous. Partners and couples may attend S-Anon Family Groups, Co-Dependents of Sex Addicts, and Recovering Couples Anonymous. All these fellowships follow the Alcoholics Anonymous prototype of the 12 steps and 12 traditions, and recovery is viewed as a spiritual awakening, although spirituality can be idiosyncratic for different participants. Even within the same fellowship, individual groups vary according to the local culture, sexual orientation of the participants, and the group's approach to abstinence, celibacy, and masturbation. Therefore, the treating clinician needs to familiarize himself or herself with the local fellowship before making a recommendation to the patient.

Pharmacological Treatment

Pharmacologic treatment can be very helpful. Traditional medical treatment of associated anxiety and mood can be useful with the caveat that the clinician needs to be cognizant of the sexual side effects that may help or hinder the SA patient.

Citalopram has demonstrated a moderate and significant reduction in masturbation and pornography use (Muench, et al., 2007; Tosto, Talarico, Lenzi, & Bruno, 2008). Open-label trials and anecdotal reports support the use of medications that increase serotonin such as the selective serotonin reuptake inhibitor (SSRI) and serotonin/norepinephrine reuptake inhibitor (SNRI) antidepressants to reduce desire, arousal, and orgasm (Kafka, 2010). Antidepressants may be contraindicated if there is a history of adverse reactions or medication-induced mania.

Anti-anxiety agents other than SSRIs and SNRIs, may be helpful in SA patients whose sexual acting out is triggered by anxiety. Benzodiazepines need to be judiciously prescribed in the SA population because of their tendency toward multiple addictions, while the authors' clinical experience suggests nonaddictive anxiolytics such as buspirone may be useful. The treating clinician should know that theoretically, at least, the prodopaminergic buspirone may increase sexual desire.

Antipsychotics may be indicated when disturbed reality testing, thought disorders, or severe agitation are prominent clinical features. Antipsychotics may exert their benefit by reducing sexual desire, arousal, and orgasm.

SA patients often present with high-risk and high-intensity sexual behaviors, and patients may have a clinical presentation suggestive of bipolar disorder. Mood stabilizers and anti-impulsive medications such as lithium, valproic acid, carbamazepine, and lamotrigine may be useful, particularly when manic or impulsive features are prominent or when promiscuity is a major presenting feature. The mood stabilizers are also associated with sexual suppression and may therefore exert their benefit partly or entirely due to their sexual side effects.

Attention Deficit Hyperactivity Disorder (ADHD) is frequently associated with sexual risk taking. In particular, patients who become absorbed in Internet pornography and cybersex activities may demonstrate distractibility and search for novel stimuli, which are characteristic signs of ADHD. Stimulants, such as methylphenidate and dextroamphetamine, may be indicated for highly distractible and thrill-seeking individuals with ADHD (personal communication between Martin Kafka and Ken Rosenberg, February 2011), although the dopaminergic stimulants carry the risk of addiction and increasing sexual desire, a nonaddictive medication, such as atomoxetine, may be useful.

Naltrexone, commonly used in addiction psychiatry for chemical addiction, has been reported to be effective in reducing Problem Gambling and may be effective for some patients with SA. In a retrospective review of 19 adult males treated with naltrexone for compulsive sexual behavior, 89% indicated a reduction in Compulsive Sexual Behavior (CSB) symptoms (Raymond, Grant, & Coleman, 2010). A case report of an individual diagnosed with Internet Addiction Disorder also reported a decrease in symptoms when treated with naltrexone (Bostwick & Bucci, 2008). Grant and Potenza (2006) noted that the opiate antagonist nalmefene decreases sexual compulsivity to the same extent that the medication decreases compulsive gambling. Naltrexone, in general, decreases the hedonic experience of orgasm, and thereby may be helpful in reducing addictive behavior yet hurtful for healthy sexual relations (Holloway, 2012). The prescribing physician should also be aware of the fact that, theoretically, opiate antagonists are known to increase sex hormones such as testosterone and can thereby increase sexual urges (Bostwick et al., 2009).

Anti-androgens that can dramatically diminish all phases of the sexual response cycle may be indicated in extreme cases of sexual acting out (e.g., sentenced sex offenders). Guay (2009) proposed combination treatment of SSRIs and anti-androgenic treatments for refractory patients. Berlin and Meinecke (1981) have decades of experience in using anti-androgens for sexual offenders. However, their use remains controversial.

SA patients may require prosexual drugs to enhance sexual function. As noted, erectile dysfunction, impaired desire, sexual aversions, sexual anorexia, and anorgasmia are common among SA patients, particularly when they engage with long-standing partners or in stable relationships. If patients are closely monitored, erectogenics may be prescribed for primary, secondary, and/or situational erectile dysfunction.

Case Vignette: Clinical Examples

Patient 1

Patient 1 was a 21-year-old heterosexual college student referred by an inpatient rehabilitation facility after a 30-day inpatient stay focusing on Sex Addiction, with the presenting complaint, "I have erotized rage." During his pre-adolescence, the patient's Generalized Anxiety Disorder was treated with fluoxetine, and his Attention Deficit Hyperactivity Disorder was treated with methylphenidate. The patient has a family history of alcoholism, anxiety, and depression. His brother has a history of excessive porn use and crippling social anxiety.

While a college student, the patient had been discovered to be using his cellphone to record female students taking showers. His actions led to his prompt suspension from college and placement in rehab. For the 5 years prior, he masturbated to Internet pornography daily. For 3 years prior to the evaluation, he was using his cellphone to record his female peers in showers and later using these recordings as masturbatory material.

Although the patient was fairly popular with women, and he had long-term romantic and sexual relationships, the patient engaged in voyeurism on women who were inclined to reject him or who seemed unattainable.

At rehab, the patient determined that marijuana use was a problem and a trigger for compulsive sexual behaviors, and subsequently abstained from marijuana use but continued drinking alcohol with friends. As an outpatient, he participated in individual psychotherapy, family therapy, and group therapy for behavioral addictions. His extremely supportive family was engaged and coached in healthy behaviors that discouraged enabling of the patient's addiction. After months of self-reflection, the patient resumed sexual relations with women and abstained from unhealthy voyeuristic behaviors. However, many of sexual encounters occurred in the context of alcohol, including a few encounters that were solely the result of alcohol use. The patient recognized that while no longer engaged in voyeuristic behaviors, he was engaging in a self-soothing, ego-gratification-based sex that led to misguided and regretful entanglements. For the remaining year of treatment, he did not engage in any furtive, exploitative, and voyeuristic behaviors; returned to college; and, in psychotherapy, worked on having healthy relationships and positive sexual encounters.

Patient 2

Patient 2 was a married, 42-year-old businessman who was a father of one young child. He had spent the past decade deriving his sexual satisfaction at massage parlors and with prostitutes. He sought out paid sex at a minimum of once a week, up to three times a week, and would spend considerable time planning and anticipating his sexual rendezvous. He entered treatment after his wife of 17 years accidentally discovered his behavior through his e-mails. On the Sexual

Continued

Case Vignette: Clinical Examples—cont'd

Dependency Inventory, the patient endorsed 9 (out of 10) criteria for Sex Addiction and had a score of 16 (6 being the threshold for a likely Sex Addiction). The patient began weekly psychotherapy in which he and his therapist explored past traumas, family dynamics, and his sexual arousal template, and they engaged in cognitive behavioral assignments. The patient learned SKY Meditation Therapy (see Chapter 14 on meditation) and attended the local Sex and Love Addicts Anonymous (SLAA) group. The patient was prescribed fluoxetine 10 milligrams per day to decrease his anxiety, improve his mood, and reduce his compulsive sexuality. He had a sober and successful recovery and during his 2 years in treatment, only one slip in a massage parlor in which he was masturbated to orgasm. The most challenging part of his recovery was creating a healthy sexuality with his wife. For the duration of their marriage, they had rare sexual contacts. At the time of discharge from treatment, the patient had remained sober, but his wife, although eager for his recovery, was severely resistant to addressing their conjoint sexual problems. They were referred to a couple's therapist, and she was encouraged to seek her own individual treatment.

These clinical examples demonstrate common scenarios in the evaluation and treatment of Sex Addiction. Patients are often dually diagnosed but have a distinct Sex Addiction. Comprehensive treatment, with multimodal treatment, is required to address the biopsychosocial aspects of the addiction. Adjunct therapies such as Twelve Step Facilitation and Meditation training are helpful. If the patient is engaged in treatment, sobriety—defined as avoiding dysfunctional sexual behaviors—can be achieved. As with almost any addiction, the greatest challenge is changing the system—the family and subculture that fueled and supported the addictive behavior. In Sex Addiction, reprogramming the patient's arousal template and engaging the patient's family and/or partner are the hard-won components of long-term recovery and a satisfying life.

SUMMARY

The American Society of Addiction Medicine and the *International Classification of Diseases* believe that Sex Addiction exists (ASAM, 2010; World Health Organization, 2007). Psychiatric organizations, such as the American Psychiatric Association and the American Academy for Addiction Psychiatry, are more circumspect. While guild and professional organizations battle it out, many clinicians find that the addiction model applies to a subset of patients who may exist on a continuum that includes impulsive-compulsive sexual behaviors, hypersexual patterns, and, in its most compulsive form, Sex Addiction. It is anticipated that as psychiatric research improves our understanding, studies will support the existence of Sex Addiction and related disorders as painful and serious disorders.

There is no one-size-fits-all treatment approach, but rather health care providers are encouraged to practice good psychiatric, medical, and psychological care while focusing on the addictive cycle in order to restore the patient's mental, physical, and sexual health.

REFERENCES

American Psychiatric Association. (1987). *Diagnostic and statistical manual of mental disorders* Revised, p. 296. (3rd ed.). Washington, DC: Author.

Aragona, B. J., Liu, Y., Yu, Y. J., Curtis, J. T., Detwiler, J. M., Insel, T. R., et al. (2006). Nucleus accumbens dopamine differentially mediates the formation and maintenance of monogamous pair bonds. *Natural Neuroscience, 9*, 133–139.

ASAM Public Policy Statement on Treatment for Alcohol and Other Drug Addiction, Adopted: May 01, 1980, Revised: January 01, 2010.

Bancroft, J. (2009). *Human sexuality and its problems* (3rd ed.). New York: Elsevier.

Bancroft, J., Janssen, E., Strong, D., Carnes, L., Vukadinovic, Z., & Long, J. S. (2003). The relation between mood and sexuality in heterosexual men. *Archives of Sexual Behavior, 32*, 217–230.

Bancroft, J., Janssen, E., Strong, D., & Vukadinovic, Z. (2003). The relation between mood and sexuality in gay men. *Archives of Sexual Behavior, 32*, 231–242.

Bancroft, J., & Vukadinovic, Z. (2004). Sexual addiction, sexual compulsivity, sexual impulsivity, or what? Toward a theoretical model. *Journal of Sex Research, 41*(3), 225–234.

Berlin, F. S., & Meinecke, C. F. (1981). Treatment of sex offenders with antiandrogenic medication: Conceptualization, review of treatment modalities and preliminary findings. *American Journal of Psychiatry, 138*, 601–607.

Bostwick, J. M., & Bucci, J. A. (2008). Internet sex addiction treated with naltrexone. *Mayo Clinical Proceedings, 83*(2), 226–230.

Bostwick, J. M., Hecksel, K. A., Stevens, S. R., Bower, J. H., & Ahlskog, J. E. (2009). Frequency of new-onset pathologic compulsive gambling or hypersexuality after drug treatment of idiopathic Parkinson Disease. *Mayo Clinic Proceedings, 84*(4), 310–316.

Carnes, P. J. (1983). *Out of the shadows: Understanding sexual addiction*. Minneapolis, MN: CompCare Publishers.

Carnes, P. J. (1991). *Don't call it love: Recovering from sexual addiction*. New York: Bantam Books.

Carnes, P. J. (1994). *Contrary to love: Helping the sexual addict*. Center City, MN: Hazelden.

Carnes, P. J. (1997). *Sexual Anorexia: Overcoming sexual self-hatred*. Center City, MN: Hazelden.

Carnes, P. J. (2005). *Sexual Addiction: Chapter 18.4. Comprehensive Textbook of Psychiatry, Vol. 1. Sadock & Sadock*. Philadelphia, PA: Lippincott, Williams & Wilkins.

Carnes, P., Green, B., & Carnes, S. (2010). The same yet different: Refocusing the Sexual Addiction Screening Test (SAST) to reflect orientation and gender. *Sexual Addiction Compulsivity, 17*(1), 7–30.

Carnes, P. J., Green, B. A., Merlo, L. J., Polles, A., Carnes, S., & Gold, M. S. (2011). PATHOS: A brief screening application for assessing sexual addiction. *Journal of Addiction Medicine, 6*(1), 29–34.

Carnes, P., Murray, R., & Charpentier, L. (2005). Bargains with chaos: Sex addicts and addiction interaction disorder. *Sexual Addiction and Compulsivity: The Journal of Treatment and Prevention, 12*, 79–120.

Carnes, P. J., Nonemaker, D., & Skilling, N. (1991). Gender differences in normal and sexually-addicted populations. *American Journal of Preventative Psychiatry & Neurology, 3*(1), 16–23.

Carter, C. S. (1998). Neuroendocrine perspectives on social attachment and love. *Psychoneuroendocrinology, 23*, 779–818.

Chen, C. S., Burton, M., Greenberger, E., & Dmitrieva, J. (1999). Population migration and the variation of dopamine D4 receptor (DRD4) allele frequencies around the globe. *Evolution and Human Behavior, 20*, 309–324.

Cherkas, L. F., Oelsner, E. C., Mak, Y. T., Valdes, A., & Spector, T. D. (2004). Genetic influences on female infidelity and number of sexual partners in humans: A linkage and association study of the role of the vasopressin receptor gene (AVPR1A). *Twin Research*, 7(6), 649–658.

Coleman, E., Raymond, N., & McBean, A. (2003). Assessment and treatment of compulsive sexual behavior. *Minnesota Medicine, 86*(7), 42–47.

Congdon, E., Lesch, K. P., & Canli, T. (2008). Analysis of DRD4 and DAT polymorphisms and behavioral inhibition in healthy adults: Implication for impulsivity. *American Journal of Medical Genetics Part B: Neuropsychiatric Genetics, 147B*, 27–32.

Cooper, A., Putnam, D. A., Planchon, L. A., & Boies, S. C. (1999). Online sexual compulsivity: Getting tangled in the net. *Sexual Addiction & Compulsivity, 6*, 79–104.

Depue, R. A., & Morrone-Strupinsky, J. V. A. (2005). A neurobehavioral model of affiliative bonding: Implications for conceptualizing a human trait of affiliation. *Behavioral and Brain Science, 28*(3), 313–395.

Ding, Y., Chi, H., Grady, D. L., Morishima, A., Kidd, J. R., Kidd, K. K., et al. (2002). Evidence of positive selection acting at the human dopamine receptor D4 gene locus. *PNAS, 99*, 309–314.

Dreber, A., Apicella, C. L., Eisenberg, D. T. A., Garcia, J. R., Zamore, R. S., Lum, J. K., et al. (2009). The 7R polymorphism in the dopamine receptor D4 gene (DRD4) is associated with financial risk-taking in men. *Evolution and Human Behavior, 30*, 85–92.

Earle, R. H., & Earle, M. R. (1995). *Sex addiction: Case studies and management.* New York: Brunner/Mazel.

Eisenberg, D. T. A., Campbell, B., MacKillop, J., Modi, M., Dang, D., Lum, J. K., et al. (2007). Polymorphisms in the dopamine D4 and D2 receptor genes and reproductive and sexual behaviors. *Evolutionary Psychology, 5*(4), 696–715.

Ewing, J. A. (1984). Detecting alcoholism: The CAGE questionnaire,. *Journal of the American Medical Association, 252*, 1905–1907.

Fisher, H. E., Aron, A., Mashek, D., Li, H., & Brown, L. L. (2002). Defining the brain systems of lust, romantic attraction, and attachment. *Archives of Sexual Behavior, 31*(5), 413–419.

Frances, R. A., Miller, S. I., & Mack, A. H. (2005). *Clinical textbook of addictive disorders* (3rd ed.). New York, NY: Guilford Press.

Garcia, J. R., MacKillop, J., Aller, E. L., Merriwether, A. M., Wilson, D. S., & Lum, J. K. (2010). Associations between dopamine D4 receptor gene variation with both infidelity and sexual promiscuity. *PLoS One, 5*(11). Retrieved from http://www.plosone.org/article/info:doi/10.1371/journal.prone.0014162.

Georgiadis, J. R. (2012). Doing it... wild? On the role of the cerebral cortex in human sexual activity. *Socioaffective Neuroscience & Psychology, 2*, 17337.

Goodman, A. (1998). *Sexual addiction: An integrated approach.* Madison, CT: International Universities Press.

Grant, J. E., & Potenza, M. N. (2006). Compulsive aspects of impulse-control disorders. *Psychiatric Clinics of North America, 29*(2), 539–550.

Grant, J. E., & Steinberg, M. A. (2005). Compulsive sexual behavior and pathological gambling. *Sexual Addiction and Compulsivity, 12*, 235–244.

Guay, D. R. (2009). Drug treatment of paraphilic and nonparaphilic sexual disorders. *Clinical Therapy, 31*(1), 1–31.

Harpending, H., & Cochran, G. (2002). In our genes. *PNAS, 99*, 10–12.

Holloway, K. S. (2012). Opioid mediation of learned sexual behavior. *Socioaffective Neuroscience & Psychology, 2*, 14874.

Hook, J. N., Hook, J. P., Davis, D. E., Worthington, E. L., & Penberthy, J. L. (2010). Measuring sexual addiction and compulsivity: A critical review of instruments. *Journal of Sex & Marital Therapy, 36*, 227–260.

Insel, T. R., & Young, L. J. (2001). The neurobiology of attachment. *Nature Review Neuroscience, 2*(2), 129–136.

Kafka, M. P. (2010). Hypersexual disorder: A proposed diagnosis for DSM-V. *Archives of Sexual Behavior, 39*(2), 377–400.

Kafka, M. P., & Hennen, J. (1999). The paraphilia-related disorders: An empirical investigation of nonparaphilic hypersexuality disorders in outpatients males. *Journal of Sex & Marital Therapy, 25*, 305–319.

Kafka, M. P., & Hennen, J. (2002). A DSM-IV Axis I comorbidity study of males (N = 120) with paraphilias and paraphilia-related disorders. *Sexual Abuse: Journal of Research and Treatment, 14*, 349–366.

Kaplan, H. S. (1974). *New sex therapy: Active treatment of sexual dysfunctions.* New York: Random House.

Kaplan, M. S., & Krueger, R. B. (2010). Diagnosis, assessment, and treatment of hypersexuality. *Journal of Sex Research, 47*(2–3), 181–198.

Kingston, D. A., & Firestone, P. (2008). Problematic hypersexuality: A review of conceptualization and diagnosis. *Sexual Addiction & Compulsivity, 15*, 284–310.

Kinsey, A. C., Pomeroy, W. B., & Martin, C. E. (1948). *Sexual behavior in the human male.* Philadelphia, PA: W. B. Saunders.

Krafft-Ebing, R. von (1965). *Psychopathia sexualis.* New York: G. P. Putnam's Sons (Original work published 1886, *Neuroscience and Biobehavioral Reviews*, 19, 261–277).

Kort, J. (2004). Covert cultural sexual abuse of gay male teenagers contributing to etiology of sexual addiction. *Sexual Addiction & Compulsivity, 11*, 287–300.

Langstrom, N., & Hanson, R. K. (2006). High rates of sexual behavior in the general population: Correlates and predictors. *Archives of Sexual Behavior, 35*, 37–52.

Levine, S. B. (2010). What is sexual addiction? *Journal of Sex & Marital Therapy, 36*, 261–275.

Li, D., Sham, P. C., Owen, M. J., & He, L. (2006). Meta-analysis shows significant association between dopamine system genes and attention deficit hyperactivity disorder (ADHD). *Human Molecular Genetics, 15*(14), 2276–2284.

MacKillop, J., Menges, D. P., McGeary, J. E., & Lisman, S. A. (2007). Effects of craving and DRD4 VNTR genotype on the relative value of alcohol: An initial human laboratory study. *Behavioral and Brain Function, 3*, 11.

Masters, W. H., Johnson, V. E., & Kolodny, R. C. (1988). *Masters and Johnson on sex and human loving.* Boston: Little, Brown and Company.

Melis, M. R., & Argiolas, A. (1995). Dopamine and sexual behavior. *Neuroscience Biobehavioral Reviews, 19*(1), 19–38.

Mick, T. M., & Hollander, E. (2006). Impulsive-compulsive sexual behavior. *CNS Spectrum, 11*(12), 944–955.

Miner, M. H., Raymond, N., Mueller, B. A., Lloyd, M., & Lim, K. O. (2009). Preliminary investigation of the impulsive and neuroanatomical characteristics of compulsive sexual behavior. *Psychiatric Research: Neuroimaging, 174*, 146–151.

Muench, F., Morgenstern, J., Hollander, E., Irwin, T. W., O'Leary, A., Parsons, J. T., et al. (2007). The consequences of compulsive sexual behavior: The preliminary reliability and validity of the Compulsive Sexual Behavior Consequences Scale. *Sexual Addiction & Compulsivity, 14*, 207–220.

Orford, J. (1978). Hypersexuality: Implications for a theory of dependence. *British Journal of Addiction, 73*, 299–303.

Pitchers, K. K., Balfour, M. E., Lehman, M. N., Richtand, N. M., Yu, L., & Coolen, L. M. (2010). Neuroplasticity in the mesolimbic system induced by natural reward and subsequent reward abstinence. *Biological Psychiatry, 67*, 872–879.

Rawson, R. A., Washton, A., Domier, C. P., & Reiber, C. (2002). Drugs and sexual effects: Role of drug type and gender. *Journal of Substance Abuse Treatment, 22*(2), 103–108.

Ray, L. A., Bryan, A., MacKillop, J., McGeary, J., Hesterberg, K., & Hutchison, K. E. (2008). The dopamine D4 receptor (DRD4) gene exon III polymorphism, problematic alcohol use and novelty seeking: Direct and mediated genetic effects. *Addiction Biology, 14*, 238–244.

Raymond, N. C., Coleman, E., & Miner, M. H. (2003). Psychiatric comorbidity and compulsive-impulsive traits in compulsive sexual behavior. *Comprehensive Psychiatry, 44*, 370–380.

Raymond, N. C., Grant, J. E., & Coleman, E. (2010). Augmentation with naltrexone to treat compulsive sexual behavior: A case series. *Annals of Clinical Psychiatry, 22*(1), 56–62.

Reid, R. C., & Carpenter, B. N. (2009). Exploring relationships of psychopathology in hypersexual patients using the MMPI-2. *Journal of Sex & Marital Therapy, 35*, 294–310.

Reid, R. C., Harper, J. M., & Anderson, E. H. (2009). Coping strategies used by hypersexual patients to defend against the painful effects of shame. *Clinical Psychology and Psychotherapy, 16*, 125–138.

Rush, B. (1812). *Medical inquiries and observation upon the diseases of the mind*. Philadelphia, PA: Kimber & Richardson.

Samenow, C. P. (2010). Classifying problematic sexual behaviors—It's all in the name. *Sexual Addiction & Compulsivity, 17*, 3–6.

Sescousse, G., Redouté, J., & Dreher, J. C. (2010). The architecture of reward value coding in the human orbitofrontal cortex. *Journal of Neuroscience, 30*, 13095–13104.

Steinglass, P. (1980). A life history model of the alcoholic family. *Family Process, 19*(3), 211–226.

Sussman, S. (2007). Sexual addiction among teens: A review. *Sexual Addiction & Compulsivity, 14*, 257–278.

Tao, R., Huang, X., Wang, J., Zhang, H., Zhang, Y., & Li, M. (2010). Proposed diagnostic criteria for Internet addiction. *Addiction, 105*, 556–564.

Tosto, G., Talarico, G., Lenzi, G. L., & Bruno, G. (2008). Effect of citalopram in treating hypersexuality in an Alzheimer's disease case. *Neurological Science, 29*, 269–270.

Træen, B., Spitznogle, K., & Beverfjord, A. (2004). Attitudes and use of pornography in the Norwegian population 2002. *Journal of Sex Research, 41*, 193–200.

Vroege, J. A., Gijs, L., & Hengeveld, M. W. (1998). Classification of sexual dysfunctions: Towards DSM-V and ICD-11. *Comprehensive Psychiatry, 39*(6), 333–337.

Walum, H., Westberg, L., Henningsson, S., Neiderhiser, J. M., Reiss, D., Igl, W., et al. (2008). Genetic variation in the vasopressin receptor 1a gene (AVPR1A) associates with pair-bonding behavior in humans. *PNAS, 105*, 14153–14156.

Wang, E., Ding, Y., Flodman, P., Kidd, J. R., Kidd, K. K., Grady, D. L., et al. (2004). The genetic architecture of selection at the human dopamine receptor D4 (DRD4) gene locus. *American Journal of Human Genetics, 74*(5), 931–944.

World Health Organization. (2007). *International classification of diseases* (10th ed.). Geneva: Author.

Yoder, V. C., Virden, T. B., & Amin, K. (2005). Internet pornography and loneliness: An association? *Sexual Addiction and Compulsivity, 12*, 19–44.

Zapf, J. L., Greiner, J., & Carroll, J. (2008). Attachment styles and male sex addiction. *Sexual Addiction & Compulsivity, 15*, 158–175.

Zietsch, B. P., Verweij, K. J. H., Bailey, J. M., Wright, M. J., & Martin, N. G. (2010). Genetics and environmental influences on risky sexual behaviour and its relationship with personality. *Behavior Genetics, 40*(1), 12–21.

CHAPTER 10

The Tyranny of Love

Love Addiction—An Anthropologist's View

Helen E. Fisher

Member, Center for Human Evolutionary Studies, Rutgers University, New Brunswick, New Jersey, USA, and Senior Research Fellow, The Kinsey Institute, Indiana University, Bloomington, IN, USA

"When we want to read of the deeds of love, whither do we turn? To the murder column."

—George Bernard Shaw

Laymen and scientists have long regarded romantic love as part of the supernatural, or as an invention of the troubadours in 12th century France or as the result of cultural tradition. However, current data collected using brain scanning (functional magnetic resonance imaging or fMRI) indicate that feelings of intense romantic love engage regions of the brain's "reward system," specifically dopamine pathways associated with energy, focus, motivation, ecstasy, and craving, including primary regions associated with addiction (Acevedo et al., 2011; Aron et al., 2005; Bartels & Zeki, 2000, 2004; Fisher et al., 2003, 2005, 2010a; Ortigue et al., 2007; Xu et al., 2011). Moreover, men and women who are passionately in love show all the basic symptoms of addiction, including craving, tolerance, emotional and physical dependence, withdrawal, and relapse (see Fisher, 2004).

Because romantic love is regularly associated with a suite of traits linked with all addictions, several psychologists have come to believe that romantic love can potentially *become* an addiction (Griffin-Shelley, 1991; Halpern, 1982; Hunter et al., 1981; Mellody et al., 1992; Peele, 1975; Schaef, 1989; Tennov, 1979). However, many define addiction as a pathological, problematic disorder (Reynaud et al., 2010); and because romantic love is a positive experience under many circumstances (i.e., not harmful), researchers remain largely unwilling to officially categorize romantic love *as* an addiction.

But even when romantic love can't be regarded as harmful, it is associated with intense craving and anxiety and can impel the lover to believe, say, and do dangerous and inappropriate things. Moreover, all forms of

Behavioral Addictions
http://dx.doi.org/10.1016/B978-0-12-407724-9.00010-0

substance abuse, including alcohol, opioids, cocaine, amphetamines, cannabis, and tobacco, activate reward pathways (Breiter et al., 1997; Diana, 2013; Frascella et al., 2010; Koob & Volkow, 2010; Melis et al., 2005; Volkow et al., 2007), and several of these same reward pathways are also found to be activated among men and women who are happily in love, as well as those rejected in love (Acevedo et al., 2011; Aron et al., 2005; Bartels & Zeki, 2000, 2004; Fisher et al., 2003, 2005, 2010a; Ortigue et al., 2007; Xu et al., 2011). So regardless of its official diagnostic classification, I believe romantic love should be *treated* as an addiction (Fisher, 2004): a *positive* addiction when one's love is reciprocated, nontoxic, and appropriate (i.e., neither partner is married to someone else or has other inappropriate lifestyle issues); and a *negative* addiction when one's feelings of romantic love are inappropriate, toxic, not reciprocated, and/or formally rejected (Fisher, 2004).

This chapter maintains that romantic love is a *natural* addiction (Brown, in Frascella et al., 2010) that evolved from mammalian antecedents at the basal radiation of the hominid clade some 4.4 million years ago in conjunction with the evolution of serial social monogamy and clandestine adultery—hallmarks of the human reproductive strategy (Fisher, 1998, 2004, 2011). Its purpose was to motivate our forebears to focus their mating time and energy on a single partner at a time, thus initiating the formation of a pair bond to rear their young together as a team (Fisher, 1992, 1998, 2011; Fisher et al., 2006, 2011). The chapter discusses the traits associated with both positive and negative love addiction; it traces the evolution of love addictions to their likely origins; it proposes a theory for the biopsychological foundations of different types of love addiction; and it offers some scientifically based suggestions for treatment of individuals suffering from rejection addiction.

ROMANTIC LOVE AS A POSITIVE ADDICTION

Human romantic love, also known as passionate love, obsessive love, and "being in love," is a cross-cultural phenomenon. In a survey of 166 societies, Jankowiak and Fischer (1992) found evidence of romantic love in 147 of them. No negative evidence was found; in the 19 remaining cultures, anthropologists had failed to ask the appropriate questions. Jankowiak and Fischer concluded that romantic love constitutes a human universal or near universal phenomenon (Jankowiak & Fischer, 1992).

Romantic attraction is associated with a suite of psychological, behavioral, and physiological traits (Fisher, 1998; Harris, 1995; Hatfield et al.,

1988; Hatfield & Sprecher, 1986; Liebowitz, 1983; Tennov, 1979). This passion begins as the lover starts to regard the beloved as special and unique; the beloved takes on "special meaning." The lover focuses his or her attention on the beloved (saliency), as well as aggrandizes the beloved's better traits while overlooking or minimizing his or her flaws. The lover expresses increased energy (hypomania), as well as ecstasy when the love affair is going well, mood swings into despair (and anhedonia) when problems in the relationship arise, and often general anxiety about his or her role, how to please, and how to achieve this goal: a union with the beloved. Adversity and social barriers heighten romantic passion and craving (frustration attraction). The lover suffers when apart from the beloved (separation anxiety) and expresses one or more sympathetic nervous system reactions when with the beloved, including sweating, stammering, butterflies in the stomach, a pounding heart, and/or difficulty eating or sleeping: the lover is emotionally and physically dependent. Lovers also distort reality, change their priorities and daily habits to accommodate the beloved, experience personality changes (affect disturbance), and sometimes do inappropriate or dangerous things to remain in contact with or impress this special other.

Smitten humans also exhibit increased empathy for the beloved; many are willing to sacrifice, even die for him or her. They can become jealous if they suspect others are jeopardizing the budding partnership, as well as intensely socially and sexually possessive (mate guarding; Buss, 2000). Lovers also express intense sexual desire for the beloved; yet their yearning for emotional union tends to overshadow their craving for sexual union with him or her. Most characteristic, lovers thinks obsessively about the beloved (intrusive thinking). They may also compulsively follow, incessantly call, write, or unexpectedly appear, all in an effort to be with their beloved day and night. Paramount to this experience is intense motivation to win him or her. Romantic attraction is also involuntary and difficult to control.

Moreover, besotted men and women express all the four basic traits of addiction: craving, tolerance (intensification), withdrawal symptoms, and relapse. Like all addicts, they yearn for the beloved (craving) and feel a "rush" of exhilaration when thinking about him or her (intoxication). As their tolerance builds, lovers seek to interact with the beloved more and more frequently. If the beloved breaks off the relationship, lovers experience the common signs of drug withdrawal, too, including protest, crying spells, lethargy, anxiety, insomnia or hypersomnia, loss of appetite or binge eating, irritability, and chronic loneliness. Like most addicts, rejected lovers also often go to extremes, even sometimes doing degrading or physically dangerous things to win back the beloved. Lovers also relapse the way drug addicts do: long after the relationship is over, events, people, places, songs, or other external cues associated with their abandoning sweetheart can trigger memories and initiate renewed craving, obsessive thinking, and/or compulsive calling, writing, or showing up in hopes of rekindling the romance—despite what they suspect may lead to adverse consequences.

Several neuroimaging studies of romantic love indicate the physiological underpinnings of this universal or near-universal human experience (Acevedo et al., 2011; Aron et al., 2005; Bartels & Zeki, 2000, 2004; Fisher et al., 2003, 2005, 2010a; Ortigue et al., 2007; Xu et al., 2011). In our first experiment (Aron et al., 2005; Fisher et al., 2003, 2005), we used functional magnetic resonance imaging (fMRI) to study 10 women and 7 men who had recently fallen intensely and happily in love. All scored high on the Passionate Love Scale (Hatfield & Sprecher, 1986), a self-report questionnaire that measures the intensity of romantic feelings; all participants also reported that they spent more than 85% of their waking hours thinking of their beloved.

Participants alternately viewed a photograph of their sweetheart and a photograph of a familiar individual, interspersed with a distraction-attention task. Group activation occurred in several regions of the brain's reward system, including the ventral tegmental area (VTA) and caudate nucleus (Aron et al., 2005; Fisher et al., 2003, 2005), regions associated with pleasure, general arousal, focused attention, and motivation to pursue and acquire rewards and mediated primarily by dopamine system activity (Delgado et al., 2000; Elliot et al., 2003; Schultz, 2000), as well as the insula, a brain region associated with anxiety. Moreover, in a principal component analysis on these 17 men and women, we found evidence suggesting that activity in the nucleus accumbens and prefrontal cortex covaried (unpublished data). These regions of the reward system are directly associated with addiction in many studies of drugs of abuse (Breiter et al., 1997; Diana, 2013; Frascella et al., 2010; Koob & Volkow, 2010; Melis et al., 2005; Panksepp et al. 2002; Volkow et al., 2007).

Our second fMRI investigation studied 17 men and women in their 50s and 60s who were married an average of 21 years and reported that they still felt the "high" of early stage intense romantic love. This study also showed group activation in the VTA, the nucleus accumbens, and other regions of the reward system (Acevedo et al., 2011). Further, in another study of "in love" men and women, Bartels and Zeki (2000) compared the brain scans of their love-struck individuals with those who were experiencing euphoria following injections of cocaine or opioids; many of the same regions of the reward system also became active.

These data from several studies indicate that individuals who are happily in love express activity in neural regions associated with drug addiction.

ROMANTIC REJECTION AS A NEGATIVE ADDICTION

Cross-culturally, few men or women are able to avoid suffering from romantic rejection at some point over their lives. In one American college community, 93% of both sexes queried reported that they had been spurned by someone whom they passionately loved; 95% reported they had rejected someone who was deeply in love with them (Baumeister et al., 1993). Romantic rejection causes a profound sense of loss and negative affect. It can induce clinical depression and in extreme cases lead to suicide and/or homicide. Some broken-hearted lovers even die from heart attacks or strokes caused by their depression (Rosenthal, 2000).

To identify some of these neural systems associated with this natural loss state, my colleagues and I used fMRI to study 10 women and 5 men who had recently been rejected by a partner but reported that they were still intensely "in love" (Fisher et al., 2010a). The average length of time since the initial rejection and the participants' enrollment in the study was 63 days. All scored high on the Passionate Love Scale (Hatfield & Sprecher, 1986), a self-report questionnaire that measures the intensity of romantic feelings. All participants also said that they spent more than 85% of their waking hours thinking of the person who rejected them; and all yearned for their abandoning partner to return to the relationship.

Participants alternately viewed a photograph of their rejecting partner and a photograph of a familiar, emotionally neutral individual, interspersed with a distraction-attention task. Their responses while looking at their rejecter in the scanner included feelings of romantic passion, despair, joyous and painful memories, rumination about why this had happened, and mental assessments of their gains and losses from the experience. Brain activations coupled with romantic rejection occurred in several regions of the brain's reward system. Included were the VTA associated with feelings of intense romantic love; the ventral pallidum associated with feelings of attachment; the insular cortex and the anterior cingulate associated with physical pain, anxiety, and the distress associated with physical pain; and the nucleus accumbens and orbitofrontal/prefrontal cortex associated with assessing one's gains and losses, as well as craving and addiction (Fisher et al.,

2010a). As noted previously, activity in several of these brain regions has been correlated with craving in cocaine addicts and other drugs of abuse (Diana, 2013; Frascella et al., 2010; Koob & Volkow, 2010; Melis et al., 2005).

Romantic rejection has several biopsychological components that most likely contribute to the intensity of this *negative* natural addiction.

Protest

Psychiatrists divide romantic rejection into two general stages (Fisher, 2004; Lewis Amini & Lannon, 2000). During the *protest phase*, the deserted lover obsessively tries to win back the beloved. As *resignation/despair* sets in, the lover gives up hope and slips into despair.

During the *protest phase,* rejection addiction may become the most intense, because psychiatrists Lewis, Amini, and Lannon (2000) propose that the *protest phase* is associated with elevated activity of the dopamine system, as well as with the closely related norepinephrine system. Moreover, they assert that the *protest phase* of human romantic rejection stems from a basic mammalian mechanism that becomes active when *any* kind of social attachment is ruptured. The example they give is the puppy that is removed from its mother and put into the kitchen by itself. Immediately, it begins to pace, frantically leaping at the door, barking and whining in protest. Isolated baby rats emit ceaseless ultrasonic cries; they hardly sleep because their brain arousal is so intense (Panksepp, 1998). So these psychiatrists believe that changes in the activities of these catecholamines are an adaptive mechanism that evolved to increase alertness and stimulate abandoned baby mammals to protest, search, and call for help.

Accompanying this protest is stress, which also elevates dopamine system activity. When mammals first experience severe stress, among their bodily reactions is an increase in the activity of the central dopamine and norepinephrine systems and a suppression of central serotonin, known as the *stress response* (Kapit , Macey, & Meisami, 2000). So this stress response during the *protest phase* of romantic rejection could potentially sustain or intensify the addictive thoughts and behaviors of romantically rejected lovers.

Rejection may trigger another brain response likely to sustain or intensify rejection addiction, known as *frustration-attraction* (Fisher, 2004, p. 16). When lovers encounter barriers to their romantic feelings, their passion often intensifies: adversity heightens romantic love. Frustration-attraction most likely also has biological foundations. When a reward is delayed in coming, neurons of the brain's reward system sustain their activation (Schultz, 2000)—sustaining the activity of central dopamine and thus rejection addiction.

During the *protest phase* of rejection, both men and women can also exhibit *frustration aggression*, known to psychologists as *abandonment rage* (Meloy, 1998, 2001). Even when a rejecting partner departs with compassion and graciously honors his or her responsibilities as a friend or coparent, many rejected people often oscillate between feelings of heartbreak and fury. This response also has neural correlates. The primary rage system is closely connected to centers in the prefrontal cortex that anticipate rewards (Panksepp, 1998). As a result, Lewis, Amini, and Lannon (2000) propose that when a human or other mammal begins to realize that an expected reward is in jeopardy, even unattainable, these regions of the prefrontal cortex stimulate the amygdala and trigger rage (Panksepp, 1998). This rage response to unfulfilled expectations is well known in mammals. When a cat's brain circuits for reward are artificially stimulated, it expresses pleasure. When this pleasurable stimulation is withdrawn, it bites.

Romantic passion and abandonment rage have much in common. Both are associated with bodily and mental arousal; both produce obsessive thinking, focused attention, motivation and goal-directed behaviors; and both cause intense yearning—either for union with or fury at the beloved (Fisher, 2004; Meloy & Fisher, 2005). Moreover, love and rage can act in tandem. In a study of 124 dating couples, Ellis and Malamuth (2000) reported that romantic love and "anger/upset" react to different kinds of information. The lover's level of anger/upset oscillates in response to events that undermine the lover's goals, such as a mate's infidelity, lack of emotional commitment, and/or rejection. The lover's feelings of romantic love fluctuate, instead, in response to events that advance the lover's goals, such as a partner's visible social support during outings with relatives and friends or direct declaration of love and fidelity. Thus, romantic love and anger/upset can operate concurrently, adding complexity and intensity to the expression of rejection addiction.

Another biological system may add to the complex addictive response of the rejected lover: jealousy. Romantic jealousy is common cross-culturally (Buss, 2000; Meloy, 1998; Meloy & Fisher, 2005), and it regularly leads to intense possessiveness of a mating partner. This possessiveness is so common in other mammalian and avian species that ethologists refer to it as mate guarding (Buss, 2000). The biological correlates of human mate-possessiveness are unknown. Data from studies of prairie voles, a pair-bonding species, suggest that vasopressin is one of the neurochemical systems likely to be involved in mate guarding (Young et al., 1998). Undoubtedly, many brain systems contribute to human jealousy. Regardless, this complex neural system for jealousy and mate guarding most likely contributes to the obsessive thoughts and inappropriate behaviors of those suffering from rejection addiction.

In fact, the preceding suite of negative biologically based phenomena associated with rejection in love, including protest, the stress response, frustration attraction, abandonment rage, jealousy, and mate guarding—in conjunction with craving and withdrawal symptoms—most likely leads to the high worldwide incidence of crimes of passion (see Meloy, 1998; Meloy & Fisher, 2005). Like many addictions, romantic love can lead to violence and criminality. Like many addictions, it can also jeopardize one's health, because abandonment rage stresses the heart, raises blood pressure, and suppresses the immune system (Dozier, 2002).

Resignation/Despair

Eventually, the abandoned lover ceases his or her pursuit of the beloved. This second general phase of romantic rejection, *resignation/despair* (Lewis, Amini, & Lannon, 2000), is less likely to be an addiction, but instead, an artifact of addiction. During this stage, the abandoned lover slips into feelings of resignation, despair, lethargy, despondency, melancholy, and depression (Najib et al., 2004; Panksepp, 1998), known as the *despair response* (Fisher, 2004; Lewis, Amini, & Lannon 2000; Panksepp, 1998). In a study of 114 men and women who had been rejected by a partner within the past 8 weeks, 40% experienced clinically measurable depression (Mearns, 1991). People can also die of a broken heart, either from myocardial infarctions or cerebral vascular accidents caused by their depression (Nemeroff, 1998; Rosenthal, 2002).

This feeling of despair has been associated with several different brain networks, including reduced activity in the dopamine reward system. As a depressed mammal comes to believe a reward will never come, the dopamine-producing cells in the reward system decrease their activity (Schultz, 2000). Diminishing activity of central dopamine produces lethargy, despondency, and depression (Panksepp, 1998). Stress contributes to this despair response. Short-term stress activates the production of dopamine and norepinephrine. But as stress continues, it suppresses the activity of these catecholamines—producing depression (Kapit et al., 2000; Panksepp, 1998).

Humans express a constellation of powerful neural systems designed to enable men and women to doggedly pursue specific mating partners, protest desertion, and suffer profound emotional and physical responses at abandonment. Why has *Homo sapiens* evolved this intense positive addiction to a potential mating partner and this dangerous negative addiction to a rejecting mate?

EVOLUTION OF ROMANTIC ADDICTIONS

It is likely that the neural systems associated with feelings of intense *positive* romantic addiction to a beloved evolved in conjunction with the evolution of the human predisposition for pair bonding, serving as a mechanism to stimulate mate choice and motivate individuals to remain with a mate long enough to breed and rear their offspring through infancy as a team.

Pair bonding is a hallmark of humanity. Data from the Demographic Yearbooks of the United Nations on 97 societies canvassed in the 1980s indicate that approximately 93.1% of women and 91.8% of men in that decade married by age 49 (Fisher, 1989, 1992). Worldwide marriage rates have declined since then; but today 85% to 90% of men and women in the United States are projected to marry (Cherlin, 2009). Cross-culturally, most individuals are monogamous; they wed one person at a time. Polygyny (many females) is permitted in 84% of human societies; but in the vast majority of these cultures, only 5% to 10% of men actually have several wives simultaneously (Frayser, 1985; van den Berghe, 1979). Moreover, because polygyny in humans is regularly associated with rank and wealth, monogamy may have been even more prevalent in prehorticultural, unstratified societies (Daly & Wilson, 1983) when the neural systems for positive (and negative) love addictions most likely evolved. (Polyandry, or many males, is permitted in less than 0.5% of societies on record and is not considered a central aspect of our basic human reproductive strategy.)

Several data suggest that the human predisposition for pair bonding has a biological basis. The investigation of human attachment began with Bowlby (1969, 1973) and Ainsworth et al. (1978) who proposed that, to promote the survival of the young, primates have evolved an innate attachment system designed to motivate infants to seek comfort and safety from their primary caregiver, generally the mother. Since these early studies, extensive research has been done on the behaviors, feelings, and neural mechanisms associated with this attachment system in adult humans and other animals (Eisenberger et al. 2003; Fraley & Shaver, 2000; MacDonald & Leary, 2005; Panksepp, 2003a, 2003b; Tucker et al., 2005). Currently, researchers believe that this biologically based attachment system remains active throughout the human life course, serving as the foundation for attachment between pair-bonded spouses for the purpose of raising offspring (Hazan & Diamond, 2000; Hazan & Shaver, 1987). Hatfield refers to the human feelings associated with these attachment behaviors as *companionate love,* which she defines as "a feeling of happy togetherness with someone whose life has become deeply entwined with yours" (Hatfield et al., 1988, p. 191).

The human penchant to form a pair bond is rare among mammals; only 3% form pair bonds to rear their young (Mock & Fujioka, 1990; Wittenberger & Tilson, 1980). But pair bonding is common in avian species; some 90% of more than 8,000 avian species practice pair bonding to rear their young (Mock & Fujioka, 1990; Wittenberger & Tilson, 1980). And in all avian and mammalian species in which monogamy is the primary reproductive strategy, it is associated with a particular group of behaviors, including mutual territory defense and/or nest building, mutual feeding and grooming, maintenance of close proximity, affiliative behaviors, and shared parental chores. Moreover, these behaviors are associated primarily with oxytocin and vasopressin activity in the nucleus accumbens and ventral pallidum, respectively (Lim et al., 2004; Lim & Young, 2004). The most informative biological research has been collected on prairie voles. These individuals mate soon after puberty and maintain a monogamous relationship throughout their life course, raising a series of litters as a team. When prairie voles engage in sex, copulation triggers the activity of oxytocin in the nucleus accumbens among females and arginine vasopressin in the ventral pallidum among males, which then facilitates dopamine release in these reward regions and motivates females and males to prefer a particular mating partner, initiate pair bonding, and express attachment behaviors toward one another (Carter, 1992; Gingrich et al., 2000; Lim et al., 2004; Lim & Young, 2004).

These data are corroborated in other species. Promiscuous white-footed mice and promiscuous rhesus monkeys do not form pair bonds or express attachment behaviors toward a specific mate, and the males of these species do not express the same distribution of vasopressin receptors in the ventral pallidum (Bester-Meredith et al., 1999; Wang et al., 1997; Young, 1999; Young et al., 1998). Moreover, when scientists (Lim & Young, 2004; Pitkow et al., 2001) transgenically inserted the genetic variant in the vasopressin system associated with pair bonding in male prairie voles into the ventral pallidum of male meadow voles, an asocial promiscuous species, vasopressin receptors were upregulated; these males also began to fixate on a particular female and mate exclusively with her, even when other females were available (Lim et al., 2004). When this gene was inserted into nonmonogamous male mice, these creatures also began to exhibit attachment behaviors (Young et al., 1999). Activity in the ventral pallidum has also been linked with longer-term pair bonding in humans (Acevedo et al., 2011). Although the vasopressin gene(s) in *Homo sapiens* are not homologous to the one(s) found in prairie voles, humans do have similar alleles in this genetic region (Walum et al., 2008), suggesting that a related biological system plays a role in human pair bonding.

More important to this chapter, in our studies of individuals who are happily in love (Aron et al., 2005; Fisher et al., 2003, 2005), we found that those in longer partnerships (8–17 months as opposed to 1–8 months) began to show activity in the ventral pallidum (associated with feelings of attachment), while continuing to show activity in the VTA and caudate nucleus associated with passionate romantic love. Thus, with time, feelings of attachment begin to *accompany* feelings of romantic love. Working in conjunction, these two basic neural systems for romantic love and attachment may constitute the biological foundations of human pair bonding—and provide the context for the evolution of love addictions.

Pair bonding could have evolved at any point in hominid evolution, and with it, various love addictions. However, two lines of data suggest that the neural circuitry for human pair bonding may have evolved at the basal radiation of the hominid stock (Fisher, 1992, 2011), in tandem with the hominid adaptation to the woodland/savannah eco-niche some time prior to 4 million years BP. *Ardipithecus ramidus*, currently dated at 4.4 million years BP, displays several sexually dimorphic physical traits that have been linked with pair bonding in many species, so Lovejoy (2009) proposes that human monogamy had evolved by this time. Anthropologists have also remeasured *Australopithicus afarensis* fossils for skeletal variations, and they report that by 3.5 million years BP hominids exhibited roughly the same degree of sexual dimorphism in several physical traits that the sexes exhibit today. Thus, they have proposed that these hominids were "principally monogamous" (Reno et al., 2003, p. 1073).

The emergence of bipedalism may have been a primary factor in the evolution of the neural circuitry for hominid pair bonding (Fisher, 1992, 2011) and concomitant evolution of romantic love (and attachment) addictions. While foraging and scavenging in the woodland/savannah eco-niche, bipedal Ardipithecine females were most likely obliged to carry infants in their arms instead of on their backs, thus needing the protection and provisioning of a mate while they transported nursing young. Meanwhile,

Ardipithecine males may have had considerable difficulty protecting and providing for a harem of females in this open woodland/savannah eco-niche. But a male could defend and provision a single female with her infant as they walked near one another, within the vicinity of the larger community.

So the exigencies of bipedalism in conjunction with hominid expansion into the woodland/savannah eco-niche may have pushed Ardipithecines over the *monogamy threshold,* selecting for the neural systems for attachment to a pair-bonded partner. And along with the evolution of pair bonding and the neural systems for attachment may have emerged the brain system for intense positive romantic addiction—serving to motivate males and females to focus their mating energy on a single partner and remain together long enough to trigger feelings of attachment necessary to initiate and complete their coparenting duties of highly infantile young (Fisher, 1992, 2004, 2011).

Considerable data suggest that the human brain system for romantic love arose from mammalian antecedents. Like humans, all birds and mammals exhibit mate preferences; they focus their courtship energy on favored potential mates and disregard or avoid others (Fisher, 2004; Fisher et al., 2006). This phenomenon is so common that the ethological literature regularly uses several terms to describe it, including *female choice, mate preference, individual preference, favoritism, sexual choice, selective proceptivity* (Andersson, 1994), and *courtship attraction* (Fisher, 2004). Further, most of the basic traits associated with human romantic love are also characteristic of mammalian courtship attraction, including increased energy, focused attention, obsessive following, affiliative gestures, possessive mate guarding, goal-oriented behaviors, and motivation to win and keep a preferred mating partner for the duration of one's species-specific needs (Fisher, 2004; Fisher et al., 2002, 2006).

The brain system for human romantic love also shows similarities with mammalian neural systems for courtship attraction. When a female laboratory-maintained prairie vole is mated with a male, she forms a distinct preference for him, associated with a 50% increase of dopamine in the nucleus accumbens (Gingrich et al., 2000). When a dopamine antagonist is injected into the nucleus accumbens, the female no longer prefers this partner. And when a female is injected with a dopamine agonist, she begins to prefer the conspecific (member of the same species) who is present at the time of the infusion, even if she has not mated with this male (Gingrich et al., 2000; Wang et al., 1999). An increase in the activities of central dopamine is also associated with courtship attraction in female sheep (Fabre-Nys et al., 1997). In male rats, increased striatal dopamine release has also been shown in response to the presence of a receptive female rat (Montague et al., 2004; Robinson et al., 2002).

Because human romantic love shares many behavioral and biological characteristics with mammalian courtship attraction, it is likely that human romantic love is a developed form of this mammalian neural courtship mechanism (Fisher, 1998, 2004). However in most species, courtship attraction is brief, lasting only minutes, hours, days, or weeks; while in humans, intense, early-stage romantic love can last 12–18 months (Marazziti et al., 1999) or much longer (Acevedo et al., 2011). So activity in the mammalian neural system for courtship attraction may have become intensified and prolonged as hominid pair bonding evolved, becoming the positive romantic addiction experienced by happily-in-love men and women around the world today.

Two artifacts of human pair bonding, however, may have contributed to *negative* romantic addictions: the human predisposition for infidelity and the human predisposition for divorce. Both contribute to partnership instability and the likelihood of rejection addiction.

INFIDELITY INTENSIFIES REJECTION ADDICTION

Monogamy is only part of the human reproductive strategy. Infidelity is also widespread (Buunk & Dijkstra, 2006; Fisher, 1992; see also Tsapelas, Fisher, & Aron, 2010). The National Opinion Research Center in Chicago reports that some 25% of American men and 15% of American women philander at some point during marriage (Laumann et al.,1994). Other studies of American married couples indicate that 20%–40% of heterosexual married men and 20%–25% of heterosexual married women have an extramarital affair during their lifetime (Greeley, 1994; Laumann et al., 1994; Tafoya & Spitzberg 2007). Still others indicate that some 30%–50% of American married men and women are adulterous (Gangestad & Thornhill, 1997).

The *Oxford English Dictionary* defines adultery as sexual intercourse by a married person with someone other than one's spouse. But researchers have broadened this definition to include sexual infidelity (sexual exchange with no romantic involvement), romantic infidelity (romantic exchanges with no sexual involvement), and sexual and romantic involvement (Glass & Wright, 1992). When one considers these varieties of adultery, statistics vary. In a meta-analysis of 12 studies of infidelity among American married couples, Thompson (1983) reported that 31% of men and 16% of women had a sexual affair that entailed no emotional involvement; 13% of men and 21%

of women had been romantically but not sexually involved with someone other than their spouse; and 20% of men and women had engaged in an affair that included both a sexual and emotional connection. Currently, 70% of American dating couples report an incidence of infidelity in their partnership (Allen & Baucom, 2006). Infidelity was also widespread in former decades, as well as in all other human societies and all mammalian and avian pair-bonding species for which data are available (see Tsapelas, Fisher, & Aron, 2010; Westneat et al., 1990).

In fact, infidelity is so widespread and persistent in monogamous avian and mammalian species, including humans, that scientists now refer to monogamous species as practicing *social monogamy*, in which partners display the array of social and reproductive behaviors associated with pair bonding while not necessarily displaying sexual fidelity as well.

Myriad psychological, sociological, and economic variables play a role in the frequency and experience of infidelity (Tsapelas, Fisher, & Aron, 2010). Most relevant to this chapter, however, Glass and Wright (1985) report that among Americans who engage in infidelity, 56% of men and 34% of women rate their marriage as "happy" or "very happy." This suggests that infidelity has biological underpinnings. Genetic studies support this hypothesis.

Walum et al. (2008) investigated 552 couples biologically, psychologically, and socially. All were either married or co-habiting for 5 or more years. Men carrying a specific allele in the vasopressin system scored significantly lower on the Partner Bonding Scale, indicating less feelings of attachment to their spouse. Moreover, their questionnaire scores were dose dependent: those carrying two of these alleles showed the lowest scores for feelings of attachment, followed by those carrying only one allele, followed by those carrying no copies of this allele. Men carrying this gene also experienced more marital crises during the past year, including threat of divorce. These results were also dose-dependent; men with two copies of the allele were approximately twice as likely to have had a marital crisis as those who had inherited either one copy or no copies. Men with one or two copies were also significantly more likely to be involved in a partnership without being married. Last, the spouses of men with one or two copies of this allele in the vasopressin system scored significantly lower on questionnaires measuring marital satisfaction.

This study did not measure infidelity directly; instead, it measured several factors likely to contribute to infidelity. But animal studies show a similar correlation between genetic variations in the vasopressin system and partnership instability. Among prairie voles, polymorphisms in a similar gene in the vasopressin system contribute to the variability in the strength of the monogamous pair bond (Hammock & Young, 2002), including the degree to which individuals express sexual fidelity (Ophir, Wolff, & Phelps, 2008). In another recent study (of 181 young adult humans), Garcia et al. (2010) found a direct link between specific alleles in the dopamine system and a greater frequency of uncommitted sexual intercourse (i.e., one-night stands), as well as a higher frequency of sexual infidelity.

Another biological system may contribute to infidelity. In the now classic "sweaty tee-shirt" experiment, women sniffed the tee-shirts of several anonymous men and selected the t-shirts of those they felt were the sexiest. They disproportionately selected the shirts of men with different genes (from themselves) in a specific part of the immune system, the major histocompatibility complex (MHC; Wedekind et al., 1995). In a subsequent investigation, women married to men with similar genes (to themselves) in this part of the immune system were also more adulterous; and the more of these genes a woman shared with her spouse, the more extra-dyadic partners she engaged with sexually (Garver-Apgar et al., 2006).

Brain architecture may also contribute to infidelity. I have previous proposed that humanity has evolved three broad, basic, distinct yet interrelated brain systems for mating, reproduction, and parenting: the sex drive, romantic love, and feelings of deep attachment to a mating partner (Fisher, 1998). These three neural systems interact with one another and many other brain systems in myriad flexible, combinatorial patterns to provide the range of cognitions, emotions, motivations, and behaviors necessary to orchestrate our complex human reproductive strategy (Fisher, 2004; Fisher et al., 2002). Nevertheless, these three brain systems are not always well connected, making it possible for one to express feelings of attachment for one individual, *while* one feels intense romantic love toward another, *while* one feels the sex drive for still other extra-dyadic partners (Fisher, 2004). The relative biological independence of these three neural systems enables *Homo sapiens* to engage in social monogamy and clandestine infidelity simultaneously (Fisher, 2004). Thus, this brain architecture easily accommodates infidelity.

Because philandering is prevalent worldwide; because it is associated with a range of psychological and sociological factors; because it is correlated with several biological underpinnings; because promiscuity is the primary reproductive strategy among our closest primate relatives, bonobos and common chimps; and because infidelity occurs even in "happy" and "very happy" marriages today, it is likely that infidelity is a core aspect of our human reproductive strategy that evolved in tandem with hominid serial social monogamy for adaptive purposes.

Many scientists have offered hypotheses regarding the selective value of infidelity (see Buss, 1994). Among these, it has been proposed that in the ancestral woodland/savannah eco-niche, philandering males and females would have disproportionately reproduced, as well as reaped the reproductive benefits of genetically more varied offspring (Fisher, 1992; Tsapelas, Aron, & Fisher, 2010). Unfaithful females may also have garnered economic resources from extra-dyadic liaisons, as well as parenting support if their primary partner died or deserted them (Fisher, 1992). Hence, clandestine infidelity (in conjunction with serial and/or lifelong social monogamy) may have had reproductive payoffs for both ancestral males and females, selecting for the biological underpinnings of infidelity in both sexes today.

The human predisposition for philandering most likely intensifies the experience and the incidence of human love addictions because adultery leads to partnership instability and abandonment—the crucible for rejection.

DIVORCE INTENSIFIES REJECTION ADDICTION

Negative romantic addiction to a partner may also have intensified in conjunction with the human predisposition for divorce. Human monogamy is not always life long. Nearly half of all marriages in the United States end in divorce; in fact, by age 35, 10% of American women have had three or more husbands (Cherlin, 2009). Data collected between 1947 and 1989 from the Demographic Yearbooks of the United Nations on 58 societies, as well as a host of ethnographic studies, indicate that divorce and remarriage are also common cross-culturally and historically (Fisher, 1989, 1992).

These data indicate three cross-cultural divorce patterns. Divorce occurs most frequently among couples with one dependent child; among couples at the height of their reproductive and parenting years (ages 25–29); and among couples married a modal duration of 4 years (Fisher, 1989, 1992). Because 4 years is the common duration of birth spacing in hunting/gathering societies, and because many monogamous avian and mammalian species form pair bonds that last *only long enough to rear the young through infancy*, this human cross-cultural modal divorce peak may represent the remains of an ancestral hominid reproductive strategy to remain pair bonded at least long enough to raise a single child through infancy, about 4 years (Fisher, 1992). Ancestral hominids that practiced serial social monogamy in association with offspring weaning would have created more genetic variety in their lineages, a biologically adaptive phenomenon (Fisher, 1992). As a result, serial social monogamy (as opposed to lifelong monogamy) may have been common among hominids as they expanded into the woodland/savannah eco-niche prior to 4 million years BP (Fisher, 1992, 2011). This pair-bond instability may well have contributed to the evolution of the suite of traits now associated with negative romantic addictions.

BIOPSYCHOLOGICAL CONSEQUENCES OF REJECTION

It appears as if evolution has overdone the negative response to romantic abandonment. But romantically rejected individuals have wasted precious courtship time and metabolic energy; they have lost essential economic and financial resources; their social alliances have been jeopardized; their daily rituals and habits have been altered; they may have lost property; and they have most likely experienced damage to their personal happiness, self-esteem, and reputation (see Leary, 2001). Most important, rejected lovers of reproductive age are likely to have lost reproductive opportunities or even a parenting partner for the offspring they have already produced—forms of reduced future genetic viability. Romantic rejection has severe social, psychological, economic, and genetic consequences.

Due to these profound costs, rejected individuals have inherited strong neural survival systems dedicated to helping them renew or sustain a failing partnership that is crucial to their reproductive future (Fisher, 2004). The *protest* and *stress responses* and *frustration-attraction* may have evolved to motivate the lover to entice a rejecting love-object to resume the partnership. *Abandonment rage* may have evolved to escalate estrangement so the disappointed lover could begin the process of looking for a more suitable mating partner. *Anhedonia, despair,* and *resignation* may have evolved to enable the rejected lover to send clear, honest signals to relatives and friends that he or she needs social support in a time of intense psychological and physical pain (Hagen, 2011) as well as time to rest and plan his or her next strategy to fulfill reproductive and social goals. Indeed, mildly depressed people make clearer assessments of themselves and others (Watson & Andrews, 2002).

PERSONALITY AND LOVE ADDICTIONS

During the past several years, psychologists have linked personality variations with variations in immunity to specific physical and psychological illnesses (Cohen et al., 2003, 2006, 2012; Marsland et al., 2001, 2006; Segerstrom et al., 2010). I have proposed that humanity has evolved four broad, basic styles of thinking and behaving (Brown et al., 2013; Fisher, 2009; Fisher et al., 2010b), associated primarily with the neural systems for dopamine, serotonin, testosterone, and estrogen. Perhaps individuals with particular personality dispositions are also predisposed to express particular styles of *negative* romantic love addiction. Preliminary speculations are offered here.

The constellation of cognitive and behavioral traits associated in the biological literature with dopamine and closely related norepinephrine neural pathways include novelty-seeking, thrill and adventure seeking, impulsivity, susceptibility to boredom, abstract intellectual exploration, cognitive flexibility, openness to new experiences, curiosity, energy, verbal and nonlinguistic creativity, and idea generation. This trait constellation has been designated the Curious/Energetic temperament dimension and those primarily expressive of this trait constellation labeled *The Explorer* (Brown et al., 2013; Fisher, 2009; Fisher et al., 2010b). These men and women may be predisposed to a particular form of *negative* addiction: becoming *romance junkies* (i.e., Don Juanism). This phenomenon might entail a disproportionate inability to commit (despite one's intense feelings of love), extreme restlessness in longer relationships, a disproportionate tendency toward infidelity, and a tendency to abandon a partner as the relationship matures in order to seek the "high" of a new romance.

The constellation of behavioral and cognitive traits associated in the biological literature with the serotonin system in the brain include observing social norms (conventionality); adherence to plans, methods, and habits; harm avoidance; orderliness; sociability; self-control; conscientiousness; managerial skills (cooperation and reduced autonomous problem solving); precision; interest in details; figural and numeric creativity; and self-transcendence (religiosity). This trait constellation has been designated the Cautious/Social Norm Compliant temperament dimension, and those primarily expressive of this trait constellation have been labeled *The Builder* (Brown et al., 2013; Fisher, 2009; Fisher et al., 2010b). These individuals may be predisposed to a different form of *negative* romantic addiction: *attachment junkies*, thus being disproportionately controlling during a relationship, as well as predisposed to continue protesting, pursuing and pressuring a rejecting partner long after appropriate, sensible, or safe.

The constellation of cognitive and behavioral traits associated with the testosterone system in the brain include enhanced visual-spatial perception; mathematical/engineering/mechanical skills; music aptitudes; intensified focus; narrow but deep interests; less emotion recognition; less eye contact;

reduced empathy; compromised verbal fluency; less social sensitivity; heightened sensitivity to social dominance; the drive for rank; emotional containment; and enhanced confidence, forthrightness and assertiveness. This suite of traits has been designated the Analytical/Tough-minded temperament dimension and those primarily expressive of this trait constellation labeled *The Director* (Brown et al., 2013; Fisher, 2009, 2010b). Individuals disproportionately expressive of this suite of traits, predominantly men (Fisher, 2009; Brown et al., in press), may be predisposed to emotional flooding and concomitant abandonment rage, leading to a disproportionate incidence of domestic violence, narcissistic stalking, and impulsive physical violence, including impulsive suicide and/or homicide. Some data support this hypothesis: Men are two to three times more likely to commit suicide after being rejected (Hatfield & Rapson, 1996); and men are far more likely to stalk a rejecting partner, as well as batter or kill her (Meloy, Davis, & Lovette, 2001).

The cognitive and behavioral traits associated with the estrogen system include contextual/holistic/synthetic thinking, linguistic and people skills, agreeableness, cooperation, theory of mind (intuition), empathy, nurturing, generosity, trust, the drive to make social attachments, heightened memory for emotional experiences, and emotional expressiveness. Oxytocin, closely related to estrogen, is also associated with several prosocial traits, including trust, reading emotions in others, and theory of mind (intuition). This trait constellation has been designated the Prosocial/Empathetic temperament dimension, and those who primarily express this trait constellation labeled *The Negotiator* (Brown et al., 2013; Fisher, 2009; Fisher, et al., 2010b). Individuals who primarily express this group of traits, predominantly women (Fisher, 2009; Fisher et al., 2010b), may be disproportionately predisposed to obsessive, introspective (unproductive) analysis of the partnership, as well as more susceptible to clinical depression and attempted suicide in response to romantic rejection. Some data support these hypotheses. Rejected women report more severe feelings of depression (Mearns, 1991), as well as more chronic strain and rumination after being rejected (Nolen-Hoeksema et al., 1999). Women are also more likely to talk about their trauma, inadvertently retraumatizing themselves (Hatfield & Rapson, 1996).

Researchers have long proposed that different childhood experiences, specifically one's form of attachment to mother, play a significant role in one's reaction to romantic rejection. But further research may find that various love addictions, including inappropriate sexual jealousy and mate guarding, partner stalking, spouse abuse, love homicide, love suicide, and clinical depression, are linked with biologically based personality dimensions as well.

IMPLICATIONS FOR TREATMENT

Clinicians have a host of strategies for helping lovers with their issues, including their obsession for a particular relationship partner. This topic is, however, beyond the scope of this chapter. But data from anthropology and neuroscience can offer some perspective on the neural correlates of love addictions, as well as a few hypotheses regarding treatment.

Foremost, the preceding cross-cultural and neurochemical data show that lovers express a host of traits commonly attributed to all addictions: These include intensely focused attention (saliency), euphoria (intoxication), mood swings, intrusive/obsessive thinking, emotional and physical dependence, tolerance, distortion of reality, personality changes, the willingness to do inappropriate and dangerous things to obtain or sustain the love relationship, loss of self-control, and craving for emotional and sexual union with the love-object. Moreover, these data indicate that romantic love engages a constellation of dynamic brain systems associated with craving, reward, and motivation mediated by dopamine activity; and dopamine pathways are implicated in all addictions. These data clearly indicate that romantic love should be *treated* as an addiction, regardless of its official diagnostic classification (Fisher, 2004).

Perhaps there is little that psychiatrists, psychologists, therapists, clergy, and others in the helping professions will find necessary to do to advise individuals who are happily in love with an appropriate person, except to assure them that the anxiety, obsession, dependence, craving, and other traits associated with romantic passion are natural responses. They might also recommend that the ecstatic lover refrain from making life-changing decisions until some of this natural elixir becomes subdued with time, because while in the grip of a full-blown *positive* love addiction, an individual's neural regions linked with social judgment and negative assessment become deactivated (Bartels & Zeki, 2004), rendering the lover less equipped to make well-reasoned choices.

The data of anthropology and neuroscience may offer clinicians more insight, however, as they treat those with a rejection addiction. Perhaps most important, the neural data indicate that rejected lovers should remove all reasonable evidence of their abandoning sweetheart, such as cards, letters, songs, photos, and memorabilia, as well as avoid contact with their rejecting partner, because any form of reminder or contact is likely to sustain the activity of brain circuits associated with romantic passion and retard the healing process. Some rejecters feel morally blameless; others feel guilty (Baumeister, Wotman, & Stillwell 1993); but most do not know how to handle the rejected lover's grief or their own feelings about the ruptured tie (Baumeister & Dhavale, 2001). So although the rejecter may be friendly when the disappointed lover contacts him or her, most will be perplexed, annoyed, or angry at the intrusion (Baumeister, Wotman, & Stillwell, 1993).

Clinicians might also advise disappointed lovers to join a 12-step program, preferably Sex and Love Addicts Anonymous. Many of the basic slogans would apply to romantically rejected men and women. "One day at a time" suggests that the lover should refrain from contacting a departed sweetheart *today*. "If you don't want to slip, don't go into slippery places" suggests that the lover avoid people, places, music, and other artifacts of the partnership that trigger romantic craving. "It's the first drink that gets you drunk" could be interpreted to mean: don't make that first phone call, write that first e-mail, or drive past his or her house that first time, as this is likely to lead to more efforts to connect, and more disappointment and misery. And "Think the drink through" could be interpreted to suggest that before the love-addict initiates any form of contact, he or she should think past the positive memories to focus on the negative events associated with the abandoning partner.

Several biological compounds have been suggested as antidotes to some of the symptoms of rejection, including oxytocin agonists, prolactin agonists, and norepinephrine agonists (see Panksepp et al., 2002). However, currently various serotonin-enhancing antidepressant medications are most widely used to counteract the depression associated with romantic rejection. These medications help to relieve physical and psychic pain and obsession; some may also repair some of the physical damage that has occurred, by stimulating the growth of nerve cells in the hippocampus, the brain's memory center, thereby reversing some of the harm often caused by prolonged stress (Goode, Peterson, & Pollack, 2002; Stahl, 2000). But many of these drugs have adverse sexual side effects (see Andrews et al., 2012; Fisher & Thomson, 2007); many also create apathy, or "emotional blunting" (Frohlich & Meston, 2000; Rosenthal, 2002). These side effects may be worth enduring if the lover is highly dysfunctional. But as rejected lovers begin to heal, they need an active, healthy emotion system to accurately assess potential new mates, select an appropriate new partner, and build a stable new relationship (Fisher, 2004; Fisher & Thomson, 2007). Thus, data from neuroscience suggest that antidepressant medications, particularly selective serotonin reuptake inhibitors (SSRIs), should be used short term, unless the individual uses these drugs long term for other medical purposes.

From the perspective of neuroscience, talking therapy is also useful to alleviate the symptoms of rejection addiction. Our research shows that rejected lovers are activating brain regions associated with assessing one's gains and losses, indicating that these men and women are trying to learn from their situation while in the scanner (Fisher et al., 2010a). *The brain is primed to engage in guided talking therapy.* Moreover, psychotherapy can produce many of the same changes in brain function that antidepressant medications produce (Brody et al., 2001; Goleman, 1996; Rosenthal, 2002). In fact, in some instances, talking therapy can be just as effective at alleviating major depression (Brody et al., 2001; Goleman, 1996; Rosenthal, 2002).

In one study, scientists compared 24 untreated adults suffering from the apathy, melancholy, and hopelessness of major depression with 16 adults with no psychiatric problems. First, each person's brain was scanned, using fMRI. The depressed men and women showed abnormally increased activity in regions of the prefrontal cortex, caudate, and thalamus; the controls showed none of these neural responses. Then 10 of the despondent subjects were administered the antidepressant paroxetine, which elevates serotonin activity. The balance of depressed participants attended 12 psychotherapy sessions instead. Then all the depressed patients were scanned again. Following both forms of treatment, activity declined in those brain regions that had shown abnormal activation (Brody et al., 2001). Those who underwent the psychotherapy got a bonus, however; they registered significant new activity in regions of the insula that can inhibit feelings of depression (Brody et al., 2001). As is commonly practiced today, a combination of talking therapy and (short-term) appropriate antidepressant medication may be the most effective treatment for rejection addiction.

Data suggest that disappointed lovers should also stay busy, to distract themselves (Rosenthal, 2002; Thayer, 1996). This advice may be successful because any form of novelty activates the dopamine system in the brain to create energy and optimism. Physical exertion also elevates mood (Rosenthal, 2002) because it triggers dopamine activity in the nucleus accumbens, bestowing pleasure (Kolata, 2002). Exercise activates endorphin pathways as well, reducing pain and increasing calm. Last, strenuous physical exercise increases brain-derived neurotrophic factor (BDNF) in the hippocampus, the memory center, to protect and make new nerve cells. In fact, some psychiatrists believe that exercise (aerobic or anaerobic) can be as effective in healing depression as psychotherapy or antidepressant drugs (Rosenthal, 2002).

Sunlight stimulates the pineal gland in the brain to regulate bodily rhythms in ways that elevate mood (Rosenthal, 2002). Smiling utilizes facial muscles that activate nerve pathways in the brain that can stimulate feelings of pleasure (Carter, 1998). Meditation affects several neural systems, thereby decreasing anxiety and escalating focus and sustained attention (Davidson et al., 1976; see also Davidson and Begley, 2012). Perhaps most important, time heals. In our study of rejected men and women, the greater the number of days since rejection, the less the activity in a brain region associated with feelings of attachment (Fisher et al., 2010a).

As disappointed lovers remove the stimuli that fan their ardor, follow some advisories of a 12-step program, build new daily habits, meet new people, take up new interests, find the right medication and/or therapist, and wait out the long days and nights of intrusive thinking and craving, their addiction will eventually subside. The brain is built to heal itself, most likely a trait that initially evolved so that our forebears could resume their search for an appropriate breeding and parenting partner.

CONCLUSION

Researchers have long discussed whether the compulsive pursuit of nonsubstance rewards, such as gambling, food, and sex, can be classified as addictions (Carnes, 1983; Frascella et al., 2010). Gambling, food, and sex can lead to obsession, tolerance, emotional and physical dependence, withdrawals, relapse, and other traits common to substance abuse. Moreover, these nonsubstance rewards also produce specific activity in dopamine pathways of the reward system, similar to drugs of abuse (see Frascella et al., 2010). This research suggests that uncontrolled use of these nonsubstances is addiction. Romantic love is likely to be a similar addiction, with one exception. Unlike all other addictions (that afflict only a percentage of the population), some form of love addiction is likely to occur to almost every human being who lives now and in our human past; few avoid the pain of rejection either.

Romantic love appears to be a *natural* addiction, "a normal altered state" experienced by almost all humans (Brown, in Frascella et al., 2010, p. 295), that evolved during human evolution to motivate our ancestors to focus their mating energy on a specific partner, thereby conserving mating time and energy, initiating reproduction, triggering feelings of attachment and subsequent mutual parenting, and assuring the future of their DNA. It is a *positive* addiction when the relationship is reciprocated, nontoxic, and appropriate; but a harmful, negative addiction when unreciprocated, toxic, inappropriate, and/or formally rejected.

If the medical community comes to understand that romantic love is an evolved drive (Fisher, 2004) and a natural addiction that can have profound social, economic, psychological, and genetic consequences (both beneficial and adverse), clinicians and researchers might develop more effective procedures for dealing with this powerful and primordial neural mechanism. Despite its joys, there is tyranny to love.

REFERENCES

Acevedo, B., Aron, A., Fisher, H., & Brown, L. (2011). Neural correlates of long-term intense romantic love. *Social Cognitive and Affective Neuroscience,* doi: 10.1093/scan/nsq092.

Ainsworth, M. D. S., Blehar, M. C., Waters, E., & Wall, S. (1978). *Patterns of attachment: A spsychological study of the strange situation*. Hillsdale, NJ: Erlbaum.

Allen, E. S., & Baucom, D. H. (2006). Dating, marital, and hypothetical extra-dyadic involvements: How do they compare? *Journal of Sex Research*, *43*, 307–317.

Andersson, M. (1994). *Sexual selection*. Princeton, NJ: Princeton University Press.

Andrews, P.W., Thomson, J. A., Jr., Amstradter, A., & Neale, M. C. (2012). Primun non nocere: An evolutionary analysis of whether antidepressants do more harm than good. *Frontiers in Evolutionary Psychology*, doi: 10.3389/fpsyg.2012.0011.00117.

Aron, A., Fisher, H. E., Mashek, D. J., Strong, G., Li, H. F., & Brown, L. L. (2005). Reward, motivation, and emotion systems associated with early-stage intense romantic love: An fMRI study. *Journal of Neurophysiology*, *94*, 327–337.

Bartels, A., & Zeki, S. (2000). The neural basis of romantic love. *NeuroReport*, *11*, 3829–3834.

Bartels, A., & Zeki, S. (2004). The neural correlates of maternal and romantic love. *NeuroImage*, *21*, 1155–1166.

Baumeister, R. F., & Dhavale, D. (2001). Two sides of romantic rejection. In M. R. Leary (Ed.), *Interpersonal rejection* (pp. 55–71). New York: Oxford University Press.

Baumeister, R. F., Wotman, S. R., & Stillwell, A. M. (1993). Unrequited love: On heartbreak, anger, guilt, scriptlessness and humiliation. *Journal of Personality and Social Psychology*, *64*, 377–394.

Bester-Meredith, J. K., Young, L. J., & Marler, C. A. (1999). Species differences in paternal behavior and aggression in *Peromyscus* and their associations with vasopressin immunoreactivity and receptors. *Hormones and Behavior*, *36*, 25–38.

Bowlby, J. (1969). *Attachment and loss: Vol. 1. Attachment*. New York: Basic Books.

Bowlby, J. (1973). *Attachment and loss: Vol. 2. Separation*. New York: Basic Books.

Breiter, H. C., et al. (1997). Acute effects of cocaine on human brain activity and emotion. *Neuron*, *19*, 591–611.

Brody, A. L., et al. (2001). Regional brain metabolic changes in patients with major depression treated with either paroxetine or interpersonal therapy: Preliminary findings. *Archives of General Psychiatry*, *58*(7), 631–640.

Brown, L. L., Acevedo, B., & Fisher, H. E. (2013) Neural correlates of four broad temperament dimensions: testing predictions for a novel construct of personality. *PLoS One,* Nov 13, 2013, doi: 10.1371/journal.pone.0078734.

Buss, D. (1994). *The evolution of desire: Strategies of human mating*. New York: Basic Books.

Buss, D. (2000). *The dangerous passion: Why jealousy is as necessary as love and sex*. New York: The Free Press 2000.

Buunk, A. P., & Dijkstra, P. (2006). Temptation and threat: Extra-dyadic relations and jealousy. In A. L. Vangelisti & D. Perlman (Eds.), *The Cambridge handbook of personal relationships* (pp. 533–555). New York: Cambridge University Press.

Carnes, P. (1983). *Out of the shadows: Understanding sexual addiction*. Minneapolis: CompCare.

Carter, C. S. (1992). Oxytocin and sexual behavior. *Neuroscience and Biobehavioral Reviews, 1*(16), 131–144.

Carter, R. (1998). *Mapping the mind*. Los Angeles CA: University of California Press.

Cherlin, A. J. (2009). *The Marriage-Go-Round: The state of marriage and the family in America today*. New York: Alfred A. Knopf.

Cohen, S., Doyle, W. J., Turner, R., Alper, C. M., & Skoner, D. P. (2003). Sociability and susceptibility to the common cold. *Psychological Science, 14*, 389–395.

Cohen, S., Janicki-Deverts, D., Crittenden, C. N., & Sneed, R. S. (2012). Personality and human immunity. In S. Segerstrom (Ed.), *The Oxford handbook of psychoneuroimmunology* (pp. 146–169). New York: Oxford University Press.

Cohen, S., & Pressman, S. D. (2006). Positive affect and health. *Current Directions in Psychological Science, 15*, 122–125.

Daly, M., & Wilson, M. (1983). *Sex, evolution and behavior* (2nd ed.). Boston: Willard Grant.

Davidson, R. J., & Begley, S. (2012). *The emotional life of your brain*. New York: Penguin Group 279.

Davidson, R. J., Goleman, D. J., & Schwartz, G. E. (1976). Attentional and affective concomitants of meditation: A cross-sectional study. *Journal of Abnormal Psychology, 85*, 235–238.

Delgado, M. R., Nystrom, L. E., Fissel, C., Noll, D. C., & Fiez, J. A. (2000). Tracking the hemodynamic responses to reward and punishment in the striatum. *Journal of Neurophysiology, 84*, 3072–3077.

Diana, M. (2013). The addicted brain. *Frontiers in Psychiatry, 4*, 40.

Dozier, R. W. (2002). *Why we hate: Understanding, curbing, and eliminating hate in ourselves and our world*. New York: Contemporary Books.

Eisenberger, N. I., Lieberman, M. D., & Williams, K. D. (2003). Does rejection hurt? An FMRI study of social exclusion. *Science, 302*, 290–292.

Elliott, R., Newman, J. L., Longe, O. A., & Deakin, J. F. W. (2003). Differential response patterns in the striatum and orbitofrontal cortex to financial reward in humans: A parametric functional magnetic resonance imaging study. *Journal of Neuroscience, 23*(1), 303–307.

Ellis, B. J., & Malamuth, N. M. (2000). Love and anger in romantic relationships: A discrete systems model. *Journal of Personality, 68*, 525–556.

Fabre-Nys, C. (1997). Male faces and odors evoke differential patterns of neurochemical release in the mediobasal hypothalamus of the ewe during estrus: An insight into sexual motivation. *European Journal of Neuroscience, 9*, 1666–1677.

Fisher, H., Aron, A., & Brown, L. L. (2005). Romantic love: An MRI study of a neural mechanism for mate choice. *Journal of Comparative Neurology, 493*, 58–62.

Fisher, H., Aron, A., & Brown, L. L. (2006). Romantic love: A mammalian brain system for mate choice. *Philosophical Transactions of the Royal Society: Biological Sciences, 361*, 2173–2186.

Fisher, H., Aron, A., Mashek, D., Strong, G., Li, H., & Brown, L. L. (2002). Defining the brain systems of lust, romantic attraction and attachment. *Archives of Sexual Behavior, 31*, 413–419.

Fisher, H., Aron, A., Mashek, D., Strong, G., Li, H., & Brown, L. L. (2003). *Early stage intense romantic love activates cortical-basal-ganglia reward/motivation, emotion and attention systems: An fMRI study of a dynamic network that varies with relationship length, passion intensity and gender*. Poster presented at the Annual Meeting of the Society for Neuroscience: New Orleans, LA, November 11.

Fisher, H. E. (1989). Evolution of human serial pair-bonding. *American Journal of Physical Anthropology, 78*, 331–354.
Fisher, H. E. (1992). *Anatomy of love: The natural history of monogamy, adultery, and divorce*. New York: W. W. Norton.
Fisher, H. E. (1998). Lust, attraction, and attachment in mammalian reproduction. *Human Nature, 9*, 23–52.
Fisher, H. E. (2004). *Why we love: The nature and chemistry of romantic love*. New York: Henry Holt.
Fisher, H. E. (2009). *Why him? Why her?* New York: Henry Holt.
Fisher, H. E. (2011). Serial monogamy and clandestine adultery: Evolution and consequences of the dual human reproductive strategy. In S. C. Roberts (Ed.), *Applied evolutionary psychology* (pp. 96–111). New York, NY: Oxford University Press. doi: 10.1093/acprof:oso/9780199586073.001.0001.
Fisher, H. E., & Thomson, J. A., Jr (2007). Lust, romance, attachment: Do the side-effects of serotonin-enhancing antidepressants jeopardize romantic love, marriage and fertility? In S. M. Platek, J. P. Keenan & T. K. Shakelford (Eds.), *Evolutionary cognitive neuroscience* (pp. 245–283). Cambridge, MA: MIT Press.
Fisher, H. E., Brown, L. L., Aron, A., Strong, G., & Mashek, D. (2010a). Reward, addiction, and emotion regulation systems associated with rejection in love. *Journal of Neurophysiology, 104*, 51–60.
Fisher, H. E., Rich, J., Island, H. D., & Marchalik, D. (2010b). The second to fourth digit ratio: A measure of two hormonally-based temperament dimensions. *Personality and Individual Differences, 49*(7), 773–777.
Fraley, R. C., & Shaver, P. R. (2000). Adult romantic attachment: Theoretical developments, emerging controversies, and unanswered questions. *Review of General Psychology, 4*, 132–154.
Frascella, J., Potenza, M. N., Brown, L. L., & Childress, A. R. (2010). Shared brain vulnerabilities open the way for nonsubstance addictions: Carving addiction at a new joint? *Annals of the New York Academy of Science, 1187*, 294–315.
Frayser, S. (1985). *Varieties of sexual experience: An anthropological perspective of human sexuality*. New Haven: HRAF Press.
Frohlich, P. F., & Meston, C. M. (2000). Evidence that serotonin affects female sexual functioning via peripheral mechanisms. *Physiology and Behavior, 71*, 383–393.
Gangestad, S. W., & Thornhill, R. (1997). The evolutionary psychology of extrapair sex: The role of fluctuating asymmetry. *Evolution and Human Behavior, 18*(2), 69–88.
Garcia, R., MacKillop, J., Aller, E. L., Merriwether, A. M., & Sloan Wilson, D. (2010). Associations between dopamine D4 receptor gene variation with both infidelity and sexual promiscuity. *PLoS One, 5*(11), e14162.
Garver-Apgar, C. E., Gangestad, S. W., Thornhill, R., Miller, R. D., & Olp, J. J. (2006). Major histocompatibility complex alleles, sexual responsivity, and unfaithfulness in romantic couples. *Psychological Science, 17*(10), 830–835.
Gingrich, B., Liu, Y., Cascio, C. Z., & Insel, T. R. (2000). Dopamine D2 receptors in the nucleus accumbens are important for social attachment in female prairie voles (*Microtus ochrogaster*). *Behavioral Neuroscience, 114*, 173–183.
Glass, S., & Wright, T. (1985). Sex differences in type of extramarital involvement and marital dissatisfaction. *Sex Roles, 12*, 1101–1120.
Glass, S., & Wright, T. (1992). Justifications for extramarital relationships: The association between attitudes, behaviors, and gender. *Journal of Sex Research, 29*, 361–387.
Goleman, D. (1996, February 15). Psychotherapy found to produce changes in brain function similar to drugs. *New York Times*, B12.
Goode, E., Petersen, M., & Pollack, A. (2002, June 30). Antidepressants lift clouds, but lose "miracle drug" label. *New York Times,* section A, 1–16.

Greeley, A. (1994). Marital infidelity. *Society, 31,* 9–13.

Griffin-Shelley, E. (1991). *Sex and love: Addiction, treatment and recovery.* Westport, CT: Praeger.

Hagen, E. H. (2011). Evolutionary theories of depression: A critical review. *Canadian Journal of Psychiatry, 56,* 716–726.

Halpern, H. M. (1982). *How to break your addiction to a person.* New York: McGraw-Hill.

Hammock, E. A., & Young, L. J. (2002). Variation in the vasopressin V1a receptor promoter and expression: Implications for inter- and intraspecfiic variation in social behaviour. *European Journal of Neuroscience, 16,* 399–402.

Harris, H. (1995). Rethinking heterosexual relationships in Polynesia: A case study of Mangaia, Cook Island. In W. Jankowiak (Ed.), *Romantic passion: A universal experience?* (pp. 95–127). New York: Columbia University Press.

Hatfield, E. (1988). Passionate and companionate love. In R. J. Sternberg & M. L. Barnes (Eds.), *The psychology of love* (pp. 191–217). New Haven, CT: Yale University Press.

Hatfield, E., & Rapson, R. L. (1996). *Love and sex: Cross-cultural perspectives.* Needham Heights, MA: Allyn and Bacon.

Hatfield, E., & Sprecher, S. (1986). Measuring passionate love in intimate relationships. *Journal of Adolescence, 9,* 383–410.

Hazan, C., & Shaver, P. R. (1987). Romantic love conceptualized as an attachment process. *Journal of Personality and Social Psychology, 52,* 511–524.

Hazan, C., & Diamond, L. M. (2000). The place of attachment in human mating. *Review of General Psychology, 4,* 186–204.

Hunter, M. S., Nitschke, C., & Hogan, L. (1981). A scale to measure love addiction. *Psychological Reports, 48,* 582.

Jankowiak, W. R., & Fischer, E. F. (1992). A cross-cultural perspective on romantic love. *Ethnology, 31*(2), 149.

Kapit, W., Macey, R. I., & Meisami, E. (2000). *The physiology coloring book.* New York: Addison Wesley Longman Inc.

Kolata, G. (2002, May 21). Runner's high? Endorphins? Fiction, some scientist say. *New York Times,* pp. F1 & F6.

Koob, G. F., & Volkow, N. D. (2010). Neurocircuitry of addiction. *Neuropsychopharmacology, 35,* 217–238.

Laumann, E. O., Gagnon, J. H., Michael, R. T., & Michaels, S. (1994). *The social organization of sexuality: Sexual practices in the United States.* Chicago: University of Chicago Press.

Leary, M. R. (Ed.), (2001). *Interpersonal rejection.* New York: Oxford University Press.

Lewis, T., Amini, F., & Lannon, R. (2000). *A general theory of love.* New York: Random House.

Liebowitz, M. R. (1983). *The chemistry of love.* Boston: Little Brown.

Lim, M. M., Murphy, A. Z., & Young, L. J. (2004). Ventral striatopallidal oxytocin and vasopressin V1a receptors in the monogamous prairie vole (*Microtus ochrogaster*). *Journal of Comparative Neurology, 468,* 555–570.

Lim, M. M., & Young, L. J. (2004). Vasopressin-dependent neural circuits underlying pair bond formation in the monogamous prairie vole. *Neuroscience, 125,* 35–45.

Lovejoy, O. C. (2009). Reexamining human origins in light of Ardipithecus ramidus. *Science, 326*(5949), 74–78.

MacDonald, G., & Leary, M. R. (2005). Why does social exclusion hurt? The relationship between social and physical pain. *Psychological Bulletin, 131*(2), 202–223.

Marazziti, D., Akiskal, H. S., Rossi, A., & Cassano, G. B. (1999). Alteration of the platelet serotonin transporter in romantic love. *Psychological Medicine, 29,* 741–745.

Marsland, A. L., Cohen, S., Rabin, B. S., & Manuck, S. B. (2001). Associations between stress, trait negative affect, acute immune reactivity, and antibody response to hepatitis B injection in healthy young adults. *Health Psychology, 20,* 4–11.

Marsland, A. L., Cohen, S., Rabin, B. S., & Manuck, S. B. (2006). Trait positive affect and antibody response to hepatitis B vaccination. *Brain, Behavior, and Immunity, 20,* 261–269.

Mearns, J. (1991). Coping with a breakup: Negative mood regulation expectancies and depression following the end of a romantic relationship. *Journal of Personality and Social Psychology*, *60*, 327–334.

Melis, M., Spiga, S., & Diana, M. (2005). The dopamine hypothesis of drug addiction: Hypodopaminergic state. *International Review of Neurobiology*, *63*, 101–154.

Mellody, P., Miller, A. W., & Miller, J. K. (1992). *Facing love addiction*. New York: HarperCollins Publishers.

Meloy, J. R. (Ed.). (1998). *The psychology of stalking: Clinical and forensic perspectives*. San Diego, CA: Academic Press.

Meloy, J. R., & Fisher, H. E. (2005). Some thoughts on the neurobiology of stalking. *Journal of Forensic Sciences*, *50*(6), 1472–1480.

Meloy, J. R., Davis, B., & Lovette, J. (2001). Risk factors for violence among stalkers. *Journal of Threat Assessment*, *1*, 1–16.

Mock, D. W., & Fujioka, M. (1990). Monogamy and long-term bonding in vertebrates. *Trends in Ecology and Evolution*, *5*(2), 39–43.

Montague, P. R., McClure, S. M., Baldwin, P. R., Phillips, P. E., Budygin, E. A., Stuber, G. D., et al. (2004). Dynamic gain control of dopamine delivery in freely moving animals. *Journal of Neuroscience*, *24*, 1754–1759.

Murdock, G. P., & White, D. R. (1969). Standard cross-cultural sample. *Ethology*, *8*, 329–369.

Najib, A., Lorberbaum, J. P., Kose, S., Bohning, D. E., & George, M. S. (2004). Regional brain activity in women grieving a romantic relationship breakup. *American Journal of Psychiatry*, *161*(12), 2245–2256.

Nemeroff, C. B. (1998). The neurobiology of depression. *Scientific American*, *278*, 42–49.

Nolen-Hoeksema, S., Larson, J., & Grayson, C. (1999). Explaining the gender difference in depressive symptoms. *Journal of Personality and Social Psychology*, 77, 1061–1072.

Ophir, A. G., Wolff, J. O., & Phelps, S. M. (2008). Variation in the neural V1aR predicts sexual fidelity and space use among male prairie voles in semi-natural settings. *Proceedings of the National Academy of Sciences*, *105*, 1249–1254.

Ortigue, S., et al. (2007). The neural basis of love as a subliminal prime: An event-related functional magnetic resonance imaging study. *Journal of Cognitive Neuroscience*, *19*, 1218–1230.

Panksepp, J. (1998). *Affective neuroscience: The foundations of human and animal emotions*. New York: Oxford University Press.

Panksepp, J. (2003a). At the interface of the affective, behavioral, and cognitive neurosciences: Decoding the emotional feelings of the brain. *Brain and Cognition*, *52*, 4–14.

Panksepp, J. (2003b). Neuroscience. Feeling the pain of social loss. *Science*, *302*, 237–239.

Panksepp, J., Knutson, B., & Burgdorf, J. (2002). The role of brain emotional systems in addictions: A neuro-evolutionary perspective and new 'self-report' animal model. *Addiction*, *97*, 459–469.

Peele, S. (1975). *Love and addiction*. New York: Taplinger Publishing Company.

Pitkow, L. J., Sharer, C. A., Ren, X., Insel, T. R., Terwilliger, E. F., & Young, L. J. (2001). Facilitation of affiliation and pair-bond formation by vasopressin receptor gene transfer into the ventral forebrain of a monogamous vole. *Journal of Neuroscience*, *21*, 7392–7396.

Reno, P. L., Meindl, R. S., McCollum, M. A., & Lovejoy, C. O. (2003). Sexual dimorphism in *Australopithecus afarensis* was similar to that of modern humans. *Proceedings of the National Academy of Sciences*, *100*, 1073.

Reynaud, M., Karila, L., Blecha, L., & Benyamina, A. (2010). Is love passion an addictive disorder? *American Journal of Drug and Alcohol Abuse*, *36*(5), 261–267.

Robinson, D. L., Heien, M. L., & Wightman, R. M. (2002). Frequency of dopamine concentration transients increases in dorsal and ventral striatum of male rats during introduction of conspecifics. *Journal of Neuroscience*, *22*, 10477–10486.

Rosenthal, N. E. (2002). *The emotional revolution: How the new science of feelings can transform your life*. New York: Citadel Press Books.

Schaef, A. W. (1989). *Escape from intimacy: The pseudo-relationship addictions.* San Francisco: Harper & Row.

Schultz, W. (2000). Multiple reward signals in the brain. *Nature Reviews Neuroscience, 1,* 199–207.

Segerstrom, S. C., & Sephton, S. E. (2010). Optimistic expectancies and cell-mediated immunity: The role of positive affect. *Psychological Science, 21,* 448–455.

Stahl, S. M. (2000). *Essential psychopharmacology: Neuroscientific basis and practical applications.* New York: Cambridge University Press.

Tafoya, M. A., & Spitzberg, B. H. (2007). The dark side of infidelity: Its nature, prevalence, and communicative functions. In B. H. Spitzberg & W. R. Cupach (Eds.), *The dark side of interpersonal communication* (2nd ed.) (pp. 201–242). Mahwah, NJ: Lawrence Erlbaum Associates.

Tennov, D. (1979). *Love and limerence: The experience of being in love.* New York: Stein and Day.

Thayer, R. E. (1996). *The origin of everyday moods: Managing energy, tension and stress.* New York: Oxford University Press.

Thompson, A. P. (1983). Extramarital sex: A review of the research literature. *Journal of Sex Research, 19,* 1–22.

Tsapelas, I., Fisher, H. E., & Aron, A. (2010). Infidelity: Who, when, why. In W. R. Cupach & B. H. Spitzberg (Eds.), *The dark side of close relationships II* (pp. 175–196). New York: Routledge.

Tucker, D. M., Luu, P., & Derryberry, D. (2005). Love hurts: The evolution of empathic concern through the encephalization of nociceptive capacity. *Development and Psychopathology, 17,* 699–713.

Van den Berghe, P. L. (1979). *Human family systems: An evolutionary view.* Westport, CT: Greenwood Press.

Volkow, N. D., Fowler, S. J., Wang, G. J., Swanson, J. M., & Telang, F. (2007). Dopamine in drug abuse and addiction: Results of imaging studies and treatment implications. *Archives of Neurology, 64*(11), 1575–1579.

Walum, H., Westberg, L., Henningsson, S., Neiderhiser, J. M., Reiss, D., Igl, W., et al. (2008). Genetic variation in the vasopressin receptor 1a gene (AVPR1A) associates with pair bonding behavior in humans. *Proceedings of the National Academy of Sciences, 105*(37), 14153–14156.

Wang, Z., Toloczko, D., Young, L. J., Moody, K., Newman, J. D., & Insel, T. R. (1997). Vasopressin in the forebrain of common marmosets (*Calithrix jacchus*): Studies with *in situ* hybridization, immunocytochemistry and receptor autoradiography. *Brain Research, 768,* 147–156.

Wang, Z., Yu, G., Cascio, C., Liu, Y., Gingrich, B., & Insel, T. R. (1999). Dopamine D2 receptor-mediated regulation of partner preferences in female prairie voles (*Microtus ochrogaster*): A mechanism for pair bonding? *Behavioral Neuroscience, 113*(3), 602–611.

Watson, P. J., & Andrews, P. W. (2002). Toward a revised evolutionary adaptationist analysis of depression: The social navigation hypothesis. *Journal of Affective Disorders, 72,* 1–14.

Wedekind, C., et al. (1995). MHC-dependent mate preferences in humans. *Proceedings of the Royal Society of London, 260,* 245–249.

Westneat, D. F., Sherman, P. W., & Morton, M. L. (1990). The ecology and evolution of extra-pair copulations in birds. In D. M. Power (Ed.), *Current ornithology* (pp. 331–369). New York: Plenum Press.

Wittenberger, J. F., & Tilson, R. L. (1980). The evolution of monogamy: Hypotheses and evidence. *Annual Review of Ecology and Systematics, 11,* 197–232.

Xu, X., Aron, A., Brown, L. L., Cao, G., Feng, T., & Weng, X. (2011). Reward and motivation systems: A brain mapping study of early-stage intense romantic love in Chinese participants. *Human Brain Mapping, 32*(2), 249–257.

Young, L. J. (1999). Oxytocin and vasopressin receptors and species-typical social behaviors. *Hormones and Behavior, 36,* 212–221.

Young, L. J., Wang, Z., & Insel, T. R. (1998). Neuroendocrine bases of monogamy. *Trends in Neuroscience, 21,* 71–75.

CHAPTER 11

Picking Up the Pieces: Helping Partners and Family Members Survive the Impact of Sex Addiction

Stefanie Carnes[1], Mari A. Lee[2]
[1]International Institute for Trauma and Addiction Professionals, Carefree, AZ, USA, [2]Growth Counseling Services, Glendora, CA, USA

Discovering that your family member is a sex addict is a devastating experience that sends a shock wave throughout the family system. Partners feel betrayed, angry, and heartbroken. Children are left feeling confused, scared, and traumatized. Parents feel helpless and often wonder what they could have done to shield their child. Extended family may also experience consequences such as shame, grief, and despair upon learning about the addiction. Discovering sex addiction is not the same as learning about other types of addictions. Sex addiction is often misunderstood by society. Sometimes its existence is denied and seen as an excuse for promiscuous behavior. Others make erroneous assumptions that sex addiction is untreatable or that all sex addicts are pedophiles or sex offenders. These stigmatizing notions cause the families to bear an increased burden of shame that does not typically accompany other process addictions like gambling.

As discussed in Chapter 9, treating sexually addicted and compulsive patients is a clinically rigorous process that necessitates specialized training. Supporting the sexually addicted patient requires a multilayered approach that includes key assessments, specific clinical interventions, a focused treatment plan, and a community of therapeutic support. The most popular methods of treatment for sex addicts include 12-step support, the Carnes Thirty Task Recovery Model, mindfulness training, motivational interviewing, trauma treatment, and attachment-based approaches. Much attention has been given to the addict's treatment, developing support groups, and providing materials to assist the addict in achieving and maintaining a sexual health plan. Unfortunately, fewer resources have been developed for family members of addicts.

Behavioral Addictions
http://dx.doi.org/10.1016/B978-0-12-407724-9.00011-2

In this chapter we highlight some of the unique considerations involved in family therapy for sex addiction. This includes an overview of the partner's experience, along with clinical recommendations. Later in the chapter, the impact on children is also discussed. Unfortunately, there is a dearth of research literature that focuses on the family members' response to sex addiction and evidence-based treatments; however, the limited research available is included here. For an overview of relevant reading material, see the Appendix.

TREATING PARTNERS OF SEX ADDICTS: CLINICAL IMPLICATIONS

In the following sections, we examine the complex dynamics in working with partners of sex addicts. This information takes into consideration both male and females, gay and straight partners. For consistency, the authors use the term *partner* to refer to the spouse or significant other of a sex addict. We discuss the impact of discovery, the traumatic response, and clinical interventions. Recovery tasks, transference and countertransference issues are also addressed.

Discovery and the Trauma Response

With sex addiction, the obsession progressively escalates and becomes out of control. During that process, the number of secrets and lies the addict tells family members also escalates. Sex addicts usually have compartmentalized lives that often contain a myriad of devastating secrets. Discovering sex addiction is different from discovering an affair. Although there may be some similarities, the quantity and variety of the sexual behaviors can be numerous, varied, and extreme. Thus, the partner learns of a multitude of betrayals and lies, which may include a frightening amount of unknown information. These secrets can include distressing behaviors such as long-standing affairs of many years, out of wedlock children, financial devastation such that accounts have been emptied, sexually transmitted diseases (STDs), arrests and illegal activities, job loss, and other such discoveries. The resulting impact on the partner post-discovery or following disclosure most often includes a trauma response (the emotional, physical and spiritual response to the trauma). In one study, research learned that partners often experienced Post-traumatic stress disorder (PTSD) symptoms and signs of acute stress disorder post-discovery/disclosure of sex addiction (Steffens & Rennie, 2006). Discovery or disclosure of these clandestine behaviors can severely impact the partner on many levels (see Table 11.1).

Table 11.1 The Impact of Discovery or Disclosure on the Partner

Impact	Description
Cognitive impairment	The partner is unable to focus on daily tasks and has periods of forgetfulness; higher reasoning systems are impacted as he or she struggles to make sense of the information.
Emotional impact	The partner is left with an acute sense of anxiety, fear, rage, sadness, and depression, and/or is unable to regulate his or her emotional state. For a small minority of partners, this could escalate to the point of suicidal ideation or homicidal ruminations. Feelings of low self-worth, depression, and/or anxiety may ensue.
Professional/ academic impact	The partner is unable to perform work tasks or educational requirements, which may place his or her career in jeopardy and impact earning potential.
Spiritual impact	The partner feels abandoned by his or her higher power and/or is angry with God or his or her higher power, resulting in a negative impact on faith and hope. The partner may also be ashamed of the sexually addicted mate's behaviors and begin to withdraw from his or her spiritual community.
Sexual impact	The partner feels a lack of worth in sexual attractiveness; feels sexually betrayed and/or neglected by the addict; may feel competitive with the acting-out focus of the sex addict's behavior (e.g., pornography, strippers, sex workers, affair partners); and may experience a loss of libido, sexual functioning, and sensuality. Perhaps the partner has contracted an STD as a result of the addict's compulsive choices.
Physical impact	Stress often manifests in health-related issues such as loss of sleep, changes in appetite, migraines, aches and pains, intestinal distress, high blood pressure, heart palpitations, and other such physical maladies. Additionally, partners have been known to seek out cosmetic surgery procedures such as breast augmentation or penile enhancements.
Behavioral impact	Other impairments may include addictive behaviors such as binge drinking, online shopping sprees, overeating, eating disorders, excessive working out, excessive TV watching, or escapist behaviors such as reading romance novels, visiting online chat rooms, and participating in other such soothing behaviors.

STAGGERED DISCLOSURE AS A TRAUMA TO THE PARTNER

Untreated addicts may attempt damage control by limiting the amount of information they share with their partner about their acting out. They may give the partner only bits and pieces of the story over time, thus staggering their disclosure. This deceptive cycle may happen over months and sometimes years. In one study, researchers learned that this staggered disclosure process occurs in approximately 60%–70% of cases (Corley & Schneider, 2003). The addict's efforts to control damage actually backfire, as this process of repeated dishonesty destroys the trust in the relationship. Eventually, for the partner, the hope and investment in the relationship are often replaced by feelings of intense despair, rejection, anger, depression, and finally, emotional disconnection.

Staggered disclosure is a term first coined by Dr. Jennifer Schneider and Deborah Corley, both pioneering researchers on the impact of sex addiction on the partner. Corley and Schneider report,

> *It is tempting for the addict to attempt damage control by initially revealing only some of what he or she did.... A recurrent theme among partners is the damage of staggered disclosure by the addict. When the addict claimed at the time to reveal all the relevant facts but actually withheld the most difficult information for later disclosure, partners reported that it was difficult restoring trust. (Corley & Schneider, 2002, p. 66).*

Table 11.2 shows a more detailed outline of the process.

Through research, therapists who have experience in treating partners of sex addicts now understand the partner's acute emotional responses to discovery by viewing their emotional reactivity and subsequent behaviors as a post-traumatic stress response to the trauma of discovering their mate's sexual addiction (Carnes, 1991; Milrad, 1999; Steffens & Rennie, 2006). This discovery often leaves partners feeling as if their primary relationship is being threatened; thus, partners often exhibit a limbic response in early treatment—fight, flight, or freeze—as they experience and register their mate's sex addiction as danger; the threat feels immediate and impacts their safety and well-being. When viewed through a trauma lens, efforts to control can be seen as the fight response; withdrawing emotionally, as the freeze response; and threats to leave or reveal, as the flight response.

Other responses to this relational trauma include

- Emotional turmoil
- Fear that manifests as protective behaviors
- Obsessing about the trauma
- Avoidance of thinking about or discussing the trauma

Table 11.2 The Nine Stages of Deception*

Stage	Description
1 Suspicion	The partner gets a sinking feeling inside—something does not "feel" right
2 Confrontation	The partner confronts the sex addict with an accusation
3 Denial of Reality	The addict lies about his or her sexual behavior either overtly or covertly (not telling the partner about it or hiding it)
4 Investigation	As suspicion persists, the partner may begin snooping, following the addict, going through pockets, checking e-mail, searching through paperwork, interviewing friends, reviewing text messages, and other probing behaviors
5 Accusation	A hostile confrontation happens involving yelling, tears, and threats of terminating the relationship if the whole truth is not revealed immediately
6 Staggered Disclosure	The addict admits to a small bit of the truth, often padded in elaborate details, but denies any other sexual secrets while withholding information
7 Deception/Bullying	The addict lies, bullies, and gets angry as a way of controlling the partner
8 Ultimatum/Bargaining	The addict or the partner strikes a bargain through ultimatums for the addict to change once and for all
9 Promises	The addict makes false promises to stop the dance and the addictive behavior

*Reprinted with permission from Carnes, Lee, & Rodriguez (2012, p. 12).

- Intrusive thinking about the addiction or acting-out behaviors
- Sleeplessness/nightmares

Additionally, not all disclosures are created equal. Certain information or circumstances surrounding the disclosure can be more traumatic than others. The level of trauma experienced in the disclosure can be influenced by some of the following characteristics:

- Amount of deception
- Length of time of deception
- Amount of covert emotional abuse or manipulation experienced at the hands of the addict (sometimes referred to as "gaslighting")
- Type of acting out or offending behavior (the more severe or offensive the behavior, the higher increase in the trauma experience)
- The partner's exposure to the sexual acting out

- Public embarrassment
- Impact on the children
- Impact on finances

This level of trauma experienced by the partner needs to be considered when developing a treatment plan.

The feelings generated from the trauma are often extraordinarily difficult for the partner to manage. Most partners do not know how to emotionally regulate and move forward. Untreated partners often draw on defense mechanisms such as shaming and blaming, control and manipulation. As a result, they may appear labile or chaotic. Conversely, partners may also cope by disengaging and emotionally shutting down. The latter patients' affect may appear quite peaceful on the surface, but they are the "ducks" in therapy—appearing serene, while paddling furiously beneath the surface. Both states, whether activated or shut down, are ways in which partners dissociate from the pain and stress. Until these clients are in therapy and working with a skilled clinician who can facilitate a focused healing process, they will likely swing back and forth between hyperactivation and dissociation.

There is tremendous variation in traumatic responses from partners. Not only do they experience a wide range in terms of the level of trauma, but they also vary greatly in terms of their resilience and coping skills. Many partners are very high functioning and resilient; they manage to get through the crisis without experiencing trauma symptoms or even symptoms of an adjustment disorder. On the other end of the spectrum, some partners' emotional stability can deteriorate rapidly, causing them to experience suicidal or homicidal ideation, and therefore require hospitalization. It is critical for the therapist to conduct a thorough assessment of the partners' emotional stability, safety issues, and trauma responses.

Additionally, some partners, especially those who may be dealing with an Axis I or II diagnosis, may experience an exacerbation of their primary diagnosis symptoms. Psychiatric care or a higher level of intensive treatment may be indicated in these cases. Early on, a skilled clinician must conduct a careful assessment of the trauma response in these partners to avoid confusing PTSD for a diagnosis of borderline personality disorder, histrionic personality disorder, or bipolar disorder.

TREATMENT FOR THE PARTNER

Working with partners of sex addicts is a complex and multifaceted process. It typically involves stabilizing the crisis, establishing safety and support, and developing a comprehensive plan to help these partners cope with the emotional devastation of the betrayal. Frequently, when addicts have progressed in their own recovery process, it also involves intensive couples therapy and family therapy.

Crisis Management, Safety Assessment, and Early Treatment Planning Steps

Early in the treatment process the most important goal is crisis stabilization and a comprehensive assessment. Establishing safety is paramount. Additionally, it is critical to form a solid therapeutic alliance. Partners may initially present as resistant to therapy often because of shame, a desire to allocate all financial resources to the addict's treatment, or due to minimization of the impact of the addiction. The guidelines in Table 11.3 should be considered during assessment and early treatment planning:

During early treatment, many partners' therapists discuss the importance of making no big life changes or choices when the addict and partner are in their first 6 to 12 months of recovery. This provides the opportunity for the partner to see if the addict embraces recovery and engages in a therapeutic process. This includes such choices as

- Divorce
- Moving
- Change of job
- Cosmetic surgery
- Large purchases (e.g., house, car)

The exception to this is when the partner's physical or emotional safety is at risk, or there is a risk to children, dependent adults, or elderly family members in the home. In such cases, a clinical separation is advised, with both partners in their own individual therapy, couples therapy, and therapy for the children and family. Mandated reporting must be considered in the context of this scenario. As stated earlier, the work of treating sex addicts and partners is highly complex, so working with a team (therapist, sponsor, group, etc.) and having the proper credentials and experience are imperative for the therapist and the client.

Facilitated Disclosure

It is not uncommon during the course of treatment for partners to experience a facilitated disclosure process. When addicts demonstrate stability in their sexual sobriety and are stable in recovery, it is important for them to share information about any sexual behaviors that are still unknown to the partners. This is done in a therapeutic setting and only with couples who are committed to staying together and working on their relationship.

Table 11.3 Nine Assessment and Early Treatment Planning Guidelines

Steps	Activity
1	Conduct an initial comprehensive clinical assessment that includes the sex addict (if appropriate) or contact the addict's therapist. (Note: There is an exception to this if the partner has divorced the addict or is no longer in a relationship with the addict.)
2	Develop a specific safety plan that may include **a.** Attention and ongoing monitoring of suicidal ideation **b.** A medical checkup to rule out STDs **c.** A psychological or psychiatric assessment and medication support when indicated **d.** Non-negotiable boundaries for the partner's ongoing physical and sexual safety (i.e., a period of abstinence while the addict is in treatment, a clinical separation while the addict seeks treatment, or no sex without protection from sexually transmitted diseases)
3	Pay attention to homicidal and suicidal thoughts, including potential reporting duties (based on the Tarasoff decisions), as well as clearly sharing with the client what the therapist's reporting responsibilities are (which include protecting children from potential harm in the home).
4	Include a thorough biopsychosocial assessment during the intake process.
5	Initiate a complete trauma assessment.
6	Create a detailed treatment plan that includes specific goals and supporting materials such as **a.** Workbooks **b.** Weekly exercises **c.** Bibliotherapy **d.** DVDs, CDs, and other such tools
7	Recommend adjunctive therapies that may include **a.** A therapy support group for partners or spouses of sex addicts **b.** An EMDR or trauma specialist **c.** A 12-step support group for partners (such as S-Anon, COSA, and Al-Anon) **d.** Substance abuse treatment if the partner is soothing with alcohol, drugs, over-the-counter medications, or other process addictions **e.** Inpatient or intensive outpatient referral when a higher level of care is required
8	Initiate cognitive-behavioral therapy with exercises that help contain the early reactivity, provide containment, and assist affective regulation.
9	Provide psychoeducation about sex addiction. If the partner is currently with the addict and the addict is in recovery with a qualified therapist, discuss what the partner can expect from the addict's treatment process.

A facilitated disclosure should be conducted by trained therapists in a supportive therapeutic setting. Both partner and addict are prepared for the disclosure and have a support plan in place.

This disclosure process supports the addicts' individual recovery goals of rigorous honesty and accountability and facilitates the letting go of shame. For the partners, facilitated disclosure empowers them with the truth and allows them to make healthy choices based on the truth. For couples, it provides a foundation for honesty on which to rebuild the relationship. This truthful experience, while difficult, can actually paradoxically spark hope in the dyad's relationship.

A facilitated disclosure is often followed up with a partner "impact statement," in which partners share with addicts how difficult the addiction has been for them. This processing of the impact can be quite detailed and emotional. Additionally, addicts usually make amends or make an effort at "emotional restitution." This can be the birth of a long-term couples therapy process.

Long-Term Treatment Goals

When stability and therapeutic alliance have been established, the opportunity for deeper work for the partner can be pursued. It is not uncommon for partners to become more introspective after the initial crisis has subsided. At this point, therapy can progress into a more insight-oriented process. Some of the most common areas of clinical focus include

- Family of origin work
- Communication skills training
- Anger management
- Boundaries education and practice
- Grief and loss
- Possible codependency issues
- Educating the partner on trauma re-enactment (repeating past traumas), betrayal bonding (situations of incredible intensity or importance in which there is an exploitation of trust or power)
- Helping the partner understand healthy intimacy
- Working to heal the core wounding of the partner's sexual worth and value
- Establishing goals toward healthy sexuality

It is valuable to consider these insight-oriented approaches when working with partners. When treatment is narrowed solely to crisis management or using the cognitive behavioral model, the short-term result is that the partner's reactivity may be contained for a brief time period; however, the deeper wounding that impacts the partner's self-worth is often not addressed. A comprehensive treatment approach which utilizes interventions that are directed at both the logical left brain and the more emotional right brain aid with internal affect regulation and help improve relationship functioning and stability. If these issues are not addressed, it may result in continued negative interactions and trauma re-enactments with the addict and other individuals interacting with the system.

Potential Clinical Pitfalls

The Addict Relapses

Another area of clinical focus that the clinician and treatment team must be aware of is the potential for ongoing sexual acting out by the addict and what this may trigger in the partner. A focused approach to educating, preparing, and walking the partner through key aspects of the addict's recovery includes an ongoing evaluation of boundaries for the partner's self-protection and creating a couple's plan in case the addict relapses.

The Partner's Therapy Is Neglected

In some cases, when primary treatment is focused only on the addict, there may be an unintentional neglect of the partner's recovery. When this occurs, the unfortunate outcome is that the partner, who is often reeling in the emotional aftermath of discovery, is abandoned. Failing to provide appropriate recovery support for the partner may eventually destabilize the treatment efforts of the primary therapist, and the addict's own recovery efforts as the partner may transfer focus, control, emotional trauma, and hope onto the addict's recovery outcome. Thereby, the partner neglects his or her own trauma wounds and core issues that also need attention and healing.

Additionally, if the partner and addict seek out recovery support and/or couples therapy, the psychological impact on the partner can be exacerbated if his or her experience is minimized by the treating professional, is not addressed with a specific and appropriate treatment plan, or is ignored altogether while treatment is focused on supporting the addict's recovery.

The Partner's Trauma Response Is Pathologized

Further, if the partner's trauma responses are pathologized by the therapist or treatment team (i.e., the partner is encouraged to participate in pornography use, to explore an open marriage or relationship, or is labeled frigid or histrionic), this can further traumatize the partner and derail both the partner's and addict's treatment process. Thus, partners must have their own treatment plan to launch them toward a place of safety and support while they move through the complex journey of a partner's recovery.

Partner Suicidality

Additionally, many partners report feelings of abandonment, anxiety, depression, and other challenging emotional responses that surface upon discovery. And, depending on the behavior of the addict and other biological, psychological, and social factors in the partner's life that detract or impact his or her emotional well-being, these symptoms of stress and trauma may resurface or even increase in severity over time for the partner. In some cases, thoughts of suicide may haunt the partner's psyche. If the partner is ashamed to share with friends and family, and refuses, or is not offered treatment, the partner is left alone in isolation and often will focus on the addict's recovery and behaviors with a renewed intensity.

Treatment Providers Not Working Together

Additionally, for therapists who primarily treat sex addicts, understanding the partner component is essential to supporting the overall recovery process. Working in tandem with the partner's therapist in developing a cohesive treatment plan that complements and paces with each patient's recovery process is vital. Patients (both the addict and the partner) can feel pulled in opposite directions by therapists who are at odds with each other's treatment goals. This friction erodes the work of the sex addict and the partner. If the therapist treating the addict is not skilled in partners' treatment, a wise step is to learn about the trauma responses and manage clinical expectations regarding the partner's recovery. Alternatively, the same advice would be well heeded by therapists who generally work with the partner. The treatment team must be just that—a team that is consistent, cohesive, safe, and dependable.

Breaking through Partner Resistance: Reframing Therapeutic Support

When an addict and partner first meet with a therapist, it is not unusual for partners to initially present a resistance to their own therapy and support. Partners have just experienced a severe betrayal and may be reluctant to trust anyone by sharing their deep feelings. Furthermore, shame can also be a barrier for treatment. Some partners have a limited amount of financial resources and feel it is more important for the addict to get care. Some partners share feelings of resentment and rage, and attempt to avoid attending therapy, expressing that the responsibility of treatment falls on the addict's shoulders.

An initial bridge-building step toward the partners' "buy-in" to their own healing process is for the therapist to gently explore and potentially normalize parts of their resistance and to help reframe the concept of therapeutic support as a critical gift they are giving themselves. This both validates the partners' trauma and safely encourages the partners to seek recovery as something they are choosing to do for themselves—a gift that they deserve, rather than as a punishment for being in a relationship with a sex addict. This can be very empowering for partners who have formerly felt very little power over their own sense of safety in the world and in their relationships. Developing the therapeutic alliance is essential in the beginning stages of treatment. Many partners will engage in therapy if they feel they are being supported, assisted, and have a plan for recovery. Having information and resources immediately available for partners will help them trust you and establish your competence.

Transference Considerations in Treating Partners of Sex Addicts

When a treating clinician is working with partners of sex addicts, especially in the early stages of recovery, it is imperative that the clinician be able to provide safety and containment for the partners. An important part of this process is the therapist's expertise, experience, as well as the clinician's ability to attend to his or her own countertransference rather than assigning issues that could be a product of the therapist's psyche onto the clients.

The traumatic reactivity of the partners will often manifest in the treatment room in a variety of ways. Some possible examples include episodic rage; acute sadness; difficulty in regulating conflicting states; rigid thinking; suicidal and homicidal threats; ruminating on the addict's acting out; blaming and shaming of the addict and/or the addict's therapist and/or the partner's therapist, Twelve Step sponsor, or recovery support group; frequent attempts at contact with the therapist out of session; boundary crossing into the addict's recovery; attempts at triangulating the therapist into the toxic dance with the addict; attempts at controlling or abandoning the treatment plan; or attempts at controlling the addict's treatment plan and treatment team; and further emotional reactivity.

The dramatic ebb and flow of the partner's healing process can impact the stability of treatment; thus, the clinician must be aware of the potential of the client's transference without personalizing the reactivity, colluding with the rage toward the addict or the addict's treating therapist, misdiagnosing the patient, rushing to diagnose an Axis II personality disorder, or abandoning the patient. If the primary therapist feels overwhelmed by the partner or does not have an understanding of treating trauma, sex addiction, or working with partners of sex addicts, it is ethically imperative that the therapist seek peer consultation, supervision by a therapist who is certified in the work, refer out to an expert, or seek a higher level of care for the patient, if needed.

It is not uncommon for even highly skilled and experienced therapists to feel triggered by the partner's transference and volatility. Working within a community of support is wise in order to manage countertransference that may show up as

- Overcompensating by not holding solid clinical boundaries with contact out of session
- Colluding with the rage toward the addict
- Experiencing compassion fatigue
- Minimizing the partner's trauma
- Undermining the efforts of the addict's treatment
- Parenting the patient
- Overdiagnosing the patient
- Becoming complicit with the overmedicating of the patient

However, when the therapist is able to manage his or her own countertransference through recognizing and understanding the patient's trauma (and how or whether it dovetails with the therapist's history), feels confident in his or her work, and has a sound treatment plan in place, then the partner feels intrinsically confident in the competence of the therapist. It is then that the partner can move more deeply in healing the early roots of pain without becoming overwhelmed with traumatic triggers in response to the addict.

Eventually, with safe, focused treatment, recovering partners are able to emotionally stabilize, regulate reactivity, build insight, and engage in therapy tasks to support their healing process, and progress forward in their life—whether or not they choose to stay in the relationship with the recovering addict.

IMPACT OF SEX ADDICTION ON CHILDREN

It is not only the partner who is traumatized by the addict's sexual addiction. Children, too, are impacted. Just like partners of sex addicts, children may be traumatized in similar ways. Learning about sex addiction in a parent is often a developmentally inappropriate sexual experience for children, depending on their age. According to the *Diagnostic and Statistical Manual of Mental Disorders* (*DSM-IV-R*), developmentally inappropriate sexual experiences can be traumatic events causing PTSD symptoms. Developmentally inappropriate sexual information can be confusing for children, causing a myriad of feelings. Some examples of the most common emotional reactions and behaviors include

- Fear of being sexualized, especially if the sex addict is the opposite sex
- Internalizing the sexual shame of the addiction
- Fear of the sex addict being an offender or a pedophile
- Public embarrassment
- Anger or despair about keeping the family secret
- Confusion about sexuality or fear that they, too, may be a sex addict
- Loyalty to a parent (e.g., needing to protect the partner)
- Caretaking or codependency behaviors
- Parentification or becoming an emotional surrogate spouse
- Troubling behavioral problems
- Trauma repetition (becoming a sex addict or pairing with a sex addict)
- Addictive behavior

The majority of parents attempt to hide the addiction from their children. However, in a survey of children of sexual addicts (n = 89), Black, Dillon, and Carnes (2003) surveyed children whose parents had disclosed to them that one of the parents was a sex addict. The researchers found that 67% of the sample stated that they knew about the addiction before they were told and it was confirmed by a parent. However, for those who did not know, the disclosure was a negative experience.

The researchers offered instances when disclosure is clinically indicated such as when the child has been exposed to the addict's acting-out behavior(s), to protect the welfare of the children, or to break the generational cycle. Some families may find themselves in a "forced" disclosure situation. A forced disclosure occurs when the child is about to learn about the addiction via non-nurturing means, such as the media or as a result of the judicial system.

Corley and Schneider (2003) surveyed parents who had been faced with the dilemma of whether or not to disclose. Parents who chose not to disclose offered reasons such as fear of loss of a relationship with a partner or child, fear of hurting the child, fear of children's negative response to a parent, or the parent did not feel ready. Common descriptions of children's reactions to disclosure by parents vary and include

- Shock, disbelief
- Fear and sadness, tearfulness
- Anger
- Validation of their suspicions or knowledge
- Appearing to understand but blocking out information and being surprised when told again later
- Attempting to comfort parents
- Praising parents for seeking recovery

Similarly, children's descriptions of their reactions to disclosure can differ. Of 29 respondents who were asked if they were glad they were told, 20 responded affirmatively, but most reported they did not like the experience of disclosure and did not want the information to be true (Black et al., 2003). Examples include

- Anger—"I felt like I wanted to punch them. But I just sat there."
- Fear of financial ramifications—"My dad was going on about his being a sex addict and treatment and steps and other stuff that I couldn't care less about and the word *bankruptcy* came up because at the time we were being sued, and that really struck a chord with me. What did that mean for me? Would I lose my bike?"
- Fear of "sex addiction," that parent was a pervert or child molester—"I felt sick, horrified. What are other people going to think? Can I be left home alone with him?"
- Confusion about the impact on the family—"I can't be totally honest about anything anymore because I'm bound to keep his secret. So a good part of my life is a big fat lie now."
- Emotional compliance/caretaking behavior—"I felt twinges of guilt and a sense of needing to protect my dad."
- Immediate relief /validation—"I was not crazy. I had known all along!"

In many cases, children are just too young to understand the concept of sex addiction, but they know something is wrong and the parents feel an explanation needs to be made. In this case, the family may choose to do a "softened" disclosure that incorporates language that is developmentally appropriate for the children. For example, if the children know that the parents have been fighting, they might offer an explanation like "daddy lied to mommy." Or in the case when a child has been exposed to porn on the computer, an addict might disclose by saying something like "Daddy looked at pictures of people without their clothes on the computer; this is not within our value system, so we are going to change the computer so that those images don't come up anymore." This developmentally appropriate language makes more sense to a child. Even very young children are aware when parental relations are stressed. Admitting to the children that something is amiss but that one or both parents are working toward a resolution benefits the children by confirming their reality and reinforces their sense of security. Black et al. (2003) recommend a minimum of mid-adolescence before explaining to children that a parent is a "sex addict."

Despite the scarcity of research, it is clear the disclosure to children should be taken on a case-by-case basis. Parents should always be able to articulate why it is in the children's best interest to disclose. The most obvious reasons include the children already know or the children are going to find out (forced disclosure). For those that do not know and will not find out, it is likely best in those cases to wait until the children are adults and better prepared to understand sex addiction. Adult children can benefit from knowing the addiction history in their family and perhaps even deepening their relationship with their parents.

Timing of disclosure to children is also of great concern. The researchers found that the optimal situation for disclosure to children includes

- The addict is accountable/out of denial.
- The addict can convey hope.
- The addict can demonstrate that he or she as had some behavioral changes.
- The partner is having difficulty being an effective parent and needs to explain.
- The partner is past the initial shock and/or rage stage (Black et al., 2003).

Both parents should be in agreement and strategize about what is to be shared, and neither parent should take the role of the victim. The child should not be used as a confidante because this would only perpetuate a cycle of family secrets and shame. Finally, disclosure should come from the addict. The partner should be present during the disclosure when possible.

In summary, disclosure to children should be developmentally appropriate and should be done only when there are clear benefits to the children. Parents should expect to keep an open dialogue with their children surrounding the issue. Further, parents will want to prepare themselves to teach their children about healthy sexuality. Due to the fact that this is a traumatic event, children should be involved in a therapy process for their own support. The parent should eventually make amends to the children and be accountable for how this behavior has impacted his or her relationship with the children. Parents should reassure the children they are in a recovery process. Finally, ongoing personal therapy for the children can be pivotal to their adjustment to the information.

REFERENCES

Black, C., Dillon, D., & Carnes, S. (2003). Disclosure to children: Hearing the children experience. *Sexual Addiction & Compulsivity, 10*, 67–78.

Carnes, P. J. (1991). *Don't call it love*. New York: Bantum Books.

Carnes, S., Lee, M., & Rodriguez, A. (2012). *Facing heartbreak: Steps to recovery for partners of sex addicts*. Carefree, AZ: Gentle Path Press.

Corley, D., & Schneider, J. P. (2002). *Disclosing secrets: When, to whom, & how much to reveal*. Carefree, AZ: Gentle Path Press.

Corley, D., & Schneider, J. P. (2003). Sex addiction disclosure to children: The parent's perspective. *Sexual Addiction & Compulsivity, 10*, 291–324.

Milrad, R. (1999). Coaddictive recovery: Early recovery issues for spouses of sex addicts. *Sexual Addiction & Compulsivity, 6*, 125–136.

Steffens, B. A., & Rennie, R. L. (2006). The traumatic nature of disclosure for wives of sexual addicts. *Sexual Addiction & Compulsivity, 13*, 247–267.

APPENDIX 11-1 RECOMMENDED READING

Addiction

Carnes, P., Carnes, S., & Bailey, J. (2011). *Facing addiction: Starting recovery from alcohol and drugs*. Carefree, AZ: Gentle Path Press.

Nakken, C. (1998). *The addictive personality: Understanding the addictive process and compulsive behavior*. Center City, MN: Hazelden.

Betrayal

Carnes, P. (1997). *The betrayal bond*. Deerfield Beach, FL: HCI.

Corley, D., & Schneider, J. (2002). *Disclosing secrets*. Carefree, AZ: Gentle Path Press.

Laaser, D. (2008). *Shattered vows*. Grand Rapids: MI: Zondervan.

Schneider, J. (1988). *Back from betrayal*. Center City, MN: Hazelden.

Schneider, J., & Schneider, B. (2001). *Sex, lies and forgiveness*. Center City, MN: Hazelden.

Boundaries

Katherine, A. (1994). *Boundaries—Where you end and I begin: How to recognize and set healthy boundaries*. Center City, MN: Hazelden.

Katherine, A. (2000). *Where to draw the line: How to set healthy boundaries every day*. New York: Fireside Books.

Lerner, R. (1995). *Living in the comfort zone: The gift of boundaries in relationships*. Deerfield Beach, FL: HCI.

Couples Recovery

Katehakis, A. (2010). *Erotic intelligence: Igniting hot, healthy sex while in recovery from sex addiction*. Deerfield Beach, FL: HCI.

Family of Origin

Black, C. (2002). *Changing course: Healing from loss, abandonment and fear.* Center City, MN: Hazelden.

Black, C. (2002). *It will never happen to me.* Center City, MN: Hazelden.

Whitfield, C. (1987). *Healing the child within.* Deerfield Beach, FL: HCI.

Partners of Sex Addicts

Carnes, S. (2011). *Mending a shattered heart: A guide for partners of sex addicts.* Carefree, AZ: Gentle Path Press.

Carnes, S., Lee, M., & Rodriguez, A. (2012). *Facing heartbreak: Steps to recovery for partners of sex addicts.* Carefree, AZ: Gentle Path Press.

Shame

Bradshaw, J. (2005). *Healing the shame that binds you.* Deerfield Beach, FL: HCI.

CHAPTER 12

Compulsive Buying Disorder

Emma Racine, Tara Kahn, Eric Hollander
Albert Einstein College of Medicine and Montefiore Medical Center, Bronx, NY, USA

INTRODUCTION

Leading up to the publication of the *Diagnostic and Statistical Manual of Mental Disorders,* Fifth Edition (*DSM-5*) in May 2013, many researchers debated how exactly to classify impulse control disorders (ICDs). Are these unique and singular disorders that operate independently from one another? Or are they primarily secondary to and comorbid with other disorders? Do they overlap and have similar brain circuitry as other disorders? What would this mean for their classification? In the *Diagnostic and Statistical Manual of Mental Disorders,* Fourth Edition, Text Revision (*DSM-IV-TR*), ICDs were grouped into a category called "Impulse Control Disorders Not Otherwise Specified" (American Psychiatric Association, 2000), a title that suggests a vague understanding of many of these ICDs. Many of the disorders that fall under Impulse Control Disorders–NOS, however, are composed of symptoms that are specific and well understood. This begs the question of whether these ICDs were properly represented under the ICD-NOS category, or whether they would be better categorized under other categories that more accurately describe their nature. This chapter explores compulsive buying disorder (CBD) as one of these ICDs that does have particular presenting characteristics, as well as a disorder that *also* has clear overlap with behavioral addictions. This chapter seeks to understand the complexities of trying to classify a disorder like CBD that shares characteristics with different groups of disorders.

The four most commonly posited disorders to which CBD has been attributed are impulse control disorders, obsessive-compulsive and related disorders, behavioral and substance addictions, and mood disorders (Dittmar, 2005). As in the *DSM-IV-TR,* CBD is not explicitly classified under any specific group in the *DSM-5.* However, it is specifically referred to in the behavioral addictions section of the *DSM-5,* along with such subcategories as "sex addiction," and "exercise addiction," but it is not included as a diagnosis in *DSM-5* because at this time there is insufficient peer-reviewed evidence to establish the diagnostic criteria and course descriptions needed to identify these behaviors as a new mental disorder (American Psychiatric Association, 2013).

Behavioral Addictions
http://dx.doi.org/10.1016/B978-0-12-407724-9.00012-4

Because CBD is still in the early stages of being researched, and while many researchers agree that CBD is a singular manifestation under a broader umbrella of disorders, there is not complete agreement about which disorders these are. Although each of the four disorders listed previously certainly display overlap with CBD, the similarities to obsessive-compulsive related disorders (OCRDs) and behavioral and substance addictions merit further exploration. The overlap between CBD, OCRD, and addiction suggests that these disorders lie along an impulsive/compulsive spectrum, where ICDs and addiction lie closer to the impulsive side and OCD lies closer to the compulsive side of the spectrum (Potenza, Koran, & Pallanti, 2011). The similarities, differences, and convergences of addiction, ICD, and OCD are further elaborated upon by Cuzen and Stein in Chapter 2 of this book.

In general, ICDs are characterized by intense urges to act out a specific behavior, which is dependent on the respective ICD; in CBD, the behavior is to seek out occasions to actively purchase goods or services. The behaviors become repetitive, as the urges to perform them continue to arise even after the behavior has been acted out, hence the compulsive nature of the behavior. This pattern—wherein an individual is consumed by an urge, unable to resist it, and as a means to alleviate the impulse, acts out a behavior—is a cycle very similar to that of OCD, which is characterized by a difficulty or inability to defy an urge to act out a behavior. For those with CBD, their shopping habits develop an impulsive quality when they become unable to resist the urgent need to shop, as a way to decrease negative emotions they are feeling. Furthermore, as with OCD, oftentimes with ICDs, the engagement in a respective behavior is motivated less by the enjoyable experience of that behavior, and more by the anxiety reduction that it accomplishes. This particular dynamic is highly characteristic of OCD, in which individuals engage in ritualistic, compulsive behaviors as a means to diminish an urge (Potenza, Koran, & Pallanti, 2011).

This behavioral sequence is also similar to addictive disorders—both substance and behavioral—in which individuals describe an overwhelming urge to use drugs or act out a behavior, and an inability to resist that impulse (Potenza, Koran, & Pallanti, 2011). Their time becomes consumed with finding ways to indulge the impulse to acquire and consume drugs or act out a behavior. Similar to drug and behavioral addictions—particularly pathological gambling (PG)—individuals who develop abnormal shopping habits become preoccupied with shopping and spend a great deal of time planning their next shopping trip. As with drug use and PG, the act of making a purchase relieves negative emotions the individual was experiencing prior to the shopping trip. Additionally, similar to drug abusers and pathological gamblers, compulsive shoppers can develop a tolerance, wherein they need to spend more money to get the same rush or pleasure (Karim & Chaudhri, 2012). This is particularly reminiscent of drug abuse and PG, in which individuals need to consume more of the respective drug or gamble more money to experience a biological response to it (Karim & Chaudhri, 2012; Potenza, Koran, & Pallanti, 2011).

The similarities of CBD to ICDs, OCD, and addiction are important to consider when thinking about how CBD should be classified, and there are advantages and disadvantages to grouping CBD as either an ICD or as an addiction. In many ways, the presenting clinical characteristics of CBD would fit into the category of Unspecified Disruptive, Impulse Control and Conduct Disorder in the *DSM-5,* and perhaps can be best conceptualized, understood, and treated as belonging to this category. However, there is a considerable downside to classifying CBD as an ICD that should not be disregarded. With the publication of the *DSM-5,* various groups that were previously used to classify different disorders have been broken up into smaller categories. The disintegration of groups is not ideal for classifying CBD as an ICD, because as mentioned earlier, the ICD-NOS category is not representative of the specific symptomatology seen in CBD.

Similarly, while CBD has strong parallels to substance and behavioral addictions that arguably merit its classification as a behavioral addiction, there are some limitations to this grouping, specifically within the realm of treatment. While clinicians might be tempted to apply opiate antagonist and self-help treatments to a condition such as CBD, based on the treatment of other addictions, this should be done with caution as, in the authors' opinion, addiction treatments are not always adequate and are not uniformly successful across various addictive disorders. Up until this point, the treatments for addictions have not been overwhelmingly effective, and thus applying them to other similar disorders might not be the most advantageous approach.

It is evident that CBD has distinct overlap with both ICDs and addiction disorders and that there are benefits and difficulties to classifying it as one or the other. Perhaps the most pressing issue at hand with regards to categorizing CBD is that there is not currently enough peer-reviewed data to justify its classification in either category. Until more funds are allocated toward studying this complex disorder, the debate surrounding CBD's grouping will inevitably ensue.

The remainder of this chapter explores CBD as a singular disorder, and not necessarily as a variation of OCD and addiction. In examining CBD exclusively, this chapter helps shed light on its many complexities and highlights the work that still lies ahead in improving the understanding of CBD's relationship to other disorders.

DIAGNOSTIC CRITERIA OF COMPULSIVE BUYING DISORDER

Presenting Clinical Characteristics of CBD

CBD has a general onset in one's late teens or early 20s (Black, 2011). In addition to age, there are, Dittmar (2005) argues, three core characteristics of CBD that are seen in individuals suffering from the disorder: The act of buying is irrepressible (the urge); one's buying tendencies are uncontrollable (the behavior); and one's buying behavior continues regardless of the negative consequences it leads to (the repetitive nonconsequentialist nature of the activity). These three features of CBD, as well as the psychological driving forces of the disorder, are worth examining in more depth to fully appreciate a differential diagnosis of CBD.

Irrepressible Buying

In Western societies where shopping is a common pastime, it can be difficult to differentiate between those who simply shop often and those who find shopping irresistible. Black (2011) argues that this is a crucial distinction to make, however, when diagnosing an individual with CBD. CBD is not present simply when an individual shops excessively, even if it appears compulsive at certain points, which occurs often for people around the holidays. For CBD to be diagnosed, an individual must be engrossed in shopping in a compulsive way. He or she will spend *hours* shopping and spending each week, and the shopping activity is coupled with an intense urge to purchase one or multiple items. This unavoidable urge to shop and purchase is overpowering and irrepressible, and is precisely what leads to uncontrollable shopping behaviors (Black, 2011).

Uncontrollable Buying

For those with CBD, the irresistible feeling to shop manifests itself as the uncontrollable act of buying. As mentioned previously, most individuals with CBD have overwhelming urges to buy products, and it is nearly impossible for individuals to successfully resist these urges. It must be noted, however, that these urges and the actions that result from them do not exclusively occur during manic episodes and that ruling out bipolar disorder is particularly important when diagnosing CBD (Claes et al., 2011). Black (2011) cites Christenson et al.'s 1994 study, in which the researchers found that while individuals with CBD attempted to resist this strong urge to buy products, 74% of the time they were unsuccessful, and their attempt concluded in a purchase. Nataraajan and Goff (1992) further describe this urge-buying dynamic in their model, which stipulates that those who suffer from CBD not only have high urges to shop, but also have low impulse control. The strong urges to purchase goods, coupled with low impulse control, result in more uncontrolled purchases.

Negative Consequences of Buying

It is not surprising that uncontrollable impulse purchases lead to negative consequences in all different domains of individuals' lives, including financial, familial, and occupational. Individuals who engage in CBD also encounter legal troubles, most often bankruptcy and debt, although some also resort to stealing—notably embezzlement and shoplifting—when their funds are exhausted (Black, 2011). These adverse consequences of compulsive buying are just as important when arriving at a differential diagnosis of CBD as the irresistible and uncontrollable urges; life impairments must result from buying behavior for compulsive buying to be considered a disorder. These detrimental ramifications in one's life highlight the compulsive nature of one's buying behaviors. When an individual will continue to purchase items even after doing so causes her to lose her job, or destroys his marriage, strains her relationships with her children, or leads to his legal troubles, the compulsive nature of that behavior is clearly revealed: the buying behavior is part of an addictive process.

Psychological Forces Behind CBD

Some research has gone into the psychological factors underlying CBD to understand the kinds of people whose shopping habits develop an addictive and compulsive quality. Researchers have suggested that those with CBD tend to be more distractible, irritable, impatient, and less productive in their occupations (Schwartz, 2004). Using the Zuckerman Sensation-Seeking Scale, Lejoyeux, Tassain, Solomon, and Ades (1997) also found that compulsive buyers are predictably more impulsive, both in cognitive and motor domains (i.e., the compulsive buyers scored higher on experience-seeking than noncompulsive buyers). These individuals also value materialism more than those who do not suffer from CBD, and their self-esteem levels are generally lower than noncompulsive buyers (Black, 2011).

The finding that those with CBD have lower self-esteem is an important psychological trait that helps to explain the reasons behind why these individuals buy as much as they do. Black (2011) suggests that those with low self-esteem highly value materialism because they believe that it leads to greater happiness and a better sense of self-worth. They purchase various goods with the intent that these products will make them a better person and will improve their sense of self. The advertising industry can be particularly influential on these individuals, promising them a host of self-improvements if they buy the respective product being advertised (Benson, Dittmar, and Wolfsohn 2010). As Benson, Dittmar, and Wolfsohn (2010) put it, "Buy this product and you can become whatever idealized self you aspire to; fail to buy, and you are an outcast at life's feast" (p. 25).

Suggested Neurological Factors in CBD

The thought process that buying a product will make one feel better about oneself is further supported by the kinds of emotions reported during a buying spree. Compulsive buyers cited negative emotions—anxiety, anger, and negative thoughts of self, for example—as the impetus to a buying spree, that tend to be promptly followed, after a product has been purchased, by a variety of positive emotions, such as happiness and relief of negative emotions (Miltenberger et al., 2003). However, these pleasurable feelings are short-lived, for once the purchase is completed, the positive emotions dissipate and feelings of guilt, remorse, and shame set in (Karim & Chaudhri, 2012). This cycle of emotions, in which a negative sense of self is remedied by a buying spree, is a dangerous sequence that reinforces shopping as a solution to address the existence of negative emotions. While shopping becomes an escape from negative feelings about oneself, it lasts only temporarily, leading to a dangerous emotional cycle that often spins out of control, in which individuals are constantly trying to manage negative feelings through quick shopping fixes as opposed to coping with the larger issues that might be causing one to compulsively shop in the first place. This negative-positive-negative pattern contributes to buying habits becoming addictive and leading to detrimental consequences (Faber & O'Guinn, 1992).

This cycle is highly representative of the emotional patterns seen in addiction disorders, a parallel that illustrates CBD's similarities to both substance and behavioral addictions more broadly. As with addiction disorders, the decision to go out and actually purchase something over and over again, as opposed to choosing to window shop, suggests an impairment in the decision-making areas of the brain (Karim & Chaudhri, 2012). Shopping, like substances, can lead to a dopamine release, a common reaction in the brain to a pleasurable activity. If an individual begins to shop more and more frequently, hyperstimulation of this dopamine release system is likely to occur, which can cause lasting alterations to these dopamine reward pathways. This change is referred to as neuroadaptation, and it is a distinctive feature of addiction: while more dopamine is being released, there are fewer receptors for the dopamine to bind to, leading to a need for more of a substance or specific behavior to deliver the same intensity of positive feelings. It is when individuals are attempting to re-create that pleasurable experience that dysregulation of judgment occurs: one will continue to shop even after he or she does not have the funds to do so, as an attempt to match a previously experienced enjoyable emotion. In recent literature, data have suggested that, like substances, shopping—as well as some other behaviors including sex and gambling, among others—is capable of being hyperstimulating, which in turn leads to addiction-like patterns in behavior (Hartston, 2012). This neurobiological dynamic, coupled with the emotional cycle described earlier, heavily reinforces the comparable features of CBD and addiction disorders.

Diagnostic Scales

Researchers have developed a number of accepted scales to diagnose CBD in individuals who present some or all of the symptomatology described previously. To make the diagnostic process of CBD more straightforward, McElroy, Keck, Pope, Smith, and Strakowski (1994) developed a set of diagnostic criteria for CBD. These criteria include the following:

- The individual has a maladaptive preoccupation with buying.
- Preoccupations with buying, impulses, or behaviors cause marked distress, consume significant time and meaningfully interfere with the individual's social or occupational function or lead to financial problems.
- The excessive buying or shopping behavior does not occur exclusively in the context of periods of hypomania or mania.

Black (2000) builds off these diagnostic criteria and posits that certain screening questions should be asked of all individuals to ascertain whether or not the buying habits of an individual are problematic, regardless of what scale is employed. It must be emphasized, however, that these questions should be posed sensitively so as not to appear as too intrusive. General screening questions include inquiries such as "Do you feel overly preoccupied with shopping and spending?" and "Do you ever feel that your shopping behavior is excessive, inappropriate, or uncontrolled?" Black (2000) suggests that positive responses to these questions should be followed by more explicit inquiries regarding each respective point. In posing these initial questions, the clinician can assess whether the shopping behavior of an individual is in fact problematic and merits a more comprehensive analysis such as administering the scales described in following sections.

One should keep these criteria in mind before implementing a scale. Researchers rely on two scales most frequently to diagnose CBD: the scale developed by Valence, D'Astous, and Fortier (1988) and the scale developed by Faber and O'Guinn (1992) (Dittmar, 2005).

Compulsive Buying Measurement Scale by Valence, D'Astous, and Fortier

The Compulsive Buying Measurement Scale addresses both financial and psychological aspects of CBD, and is used predominantly in the United Kingdom, Europe, and Canada (Dittmar, 2005). In constructing their scale, the researchers identified four characteristics of compulsive buying—an inclination to spend money, experiencing an urge to spend, a feeling of guilt after purchasing something, and familial environment—and developed 16 items around those characteristics (Black, 2000). Sample items from this scale include questions such as "As soon as I enter a shopping center, I want to go in a shop and buy something" or "I sometimes feel that something inside pushes me to go shopping" (Dittmar, 2005). Pilot data from this scale suggested that the items based on familial environment were not effective in identifying CBD, and these were excluded from the revised scale (Black, 2000). The revised version, containing 16 items each rated on a four-point scale, was found to have high reliability and validity.

Compulsive Buying Scale (CBS) by Faber and O'Guinn

The Compulsive Buying Scale (CBS) developed by Faber and O'Guinn is the one most commonly used in the United States, and focuses primarily on financial control (Dittmar, 2005). The initial scale was composed of 29 items chosen from previous studies, each of which was rated on a five-point scale. These items included questions centered on spending habits, such as not having enough money left but still feeling the need to spend; motivations behind shopping; feelings surrounding a shopping experience, etc. Administering this instrument to a sample composed of 388 individuals who self-identified as compulsive buyers and 292 randomly selected controls, Faber and O'Guinn found that 7 of those items successfully identified 88% of the participants as having CBD. Statistical analyses have also demonstrated that the CBS has high reliability and validity, and is accurate in prevalence estimations (Black, 2000). This scale, composed of the 7 core items, is reproduced in Appendix 12-1.

Other Scales

Other scales and screeners have been developed to identify and diagnose CBD. Christenson, Faber, and Zwaan (1994) constructed the Minnesota Impulsive Disorder Interview (MIDI), a semistructured interview used to evaluate CBD and other impulse control disorders such as pathological gambling and kleptomania, among others. The section of the interview that focuses on CBD contains 4 primary questions and 5 secondary or follow-up questions. These questions can continue with a module of 82 expanded questions if the individual tests positive for CBD using the initial primary and secondary questions. The screener has not yet been tested for reliability and validity, but researchers report that inter-rater reliability is high, and that the screener is effective in identifying those with CBD, specifically in research environments (Black, 2000).

Monahan, Black, and Gabel (1996) developed another scale to assess CBD in research settings. The researchers modified the Yale-Brown Obsessive Compulsive Scale (YBOCS) to develop the YBOCS–Shopping Version (YBOCS-SV) to track improvement during clinical trials (Black, 2000). This scale was developed to target behaviors and thoughts surrounding CBD, including questions about how much time is spent thinking about shopping, whether the thoughts about shopping are problematically intrusive or distressing, resistance to those thoughts, and control over those thoughts. Similar to the original YBOCS, the YBOCS-SV is composed of 10 items, 5 of which address obsessions, and 5 of which address behaviors or compulsions (Monahan et al., 1996). Statistical analyses of the YBOCS-SV have demonstrated its reliability and validity, as well as its effectiveness in capturing improvement during clinical trials, as noted previously (Black, 2000).

EPIDEMIOLOGY OF COMPULSIVE BUYING DISORDER

Industrialized Countries

Although there is debate about how to categorize compulsive buying disorder, researchers have agreed on and established clear characteristics of the phenotype. CBD is most commonly found in developed Western countries, with prevalence estimates ranging from 1% to 10% of the adult population (Dittmar, 2005). It has been reported in developed countries all around the world, including the United States, the United Kingdom,

Australia, Canada, Germany, Holland, France, Mexico, South Korea, Spain, and Brazil (Black, 2011). Its occurrence in developed Western cultures is not coincidental, and some researchers have offered sociological explanations for the rise of CBD in these societies. Black (2011) posits that a great availability of goods to choose from, attainable credit, and free time have all led to the increase in the development of CBD among individuals.

Benson, Dittmar, and Wolfsohn (2010) take Black's argument a step further and explore the role the economy plays in the growth of CBD rates. Benson et al. call attention to the fact that the economic productivity of developed nations has evolved to the point at which more goods are produced than are actually needed. This abundance of manufactured, unnecessary goods has given rise to an advertising industry, the purpose of which is to successfully persuade people to believe that they need goods they do not *actually* need; this, in turn, has caused individuals to shop more. When advertising generates the belief in a need for a product, this translates—in susceptible individuals with insecure self-identities—into an acute desire, a powerful feeling, that these products will bring them greater happiness (Benson et al., 2010). The persuasive power of the advertising industry, coupled with the factors Black (2011) explicates, has led to a higher prevalence rate of CBD in developed countries than in poorer nations (Benson et al., 2010).

Gender

Although researchers have agreed that those affected by CBD range from 1% to 10% of the adult population, there remains disagreement about the patterns of people who are most likely to develop CBD. One popular trend researchers have explored in depth is that women are overly represented in CBD samples. Dittmar's (2005) study on predictive characteristics of CBD found that women are more likely to develop CBD than men (see Table 12.1).

Dittmar (2005) found that the difference in the prevalence of CBD between women and men correlated with differences in how women and men shop. Whereas women are more inclined to buy products that are associated with identity, appearance, and rooted in mood control, men are more impulsive and are more likely to buy consumer goods associated with functionality and independence (Mueller, Claes, et al., 2011). In other words, women were more drawn toward goods that were linked to favorable psychological states (e.g., higher moods and feeling better about oneself),

Table 12.1 Summary of Hierarchical Regression Analysis of Gender, Age, and Materialistic Values as Predictors of Compulsive Buying (Studies 2 and 3 Combined)†, ††

Variable	B	SE B	β
Step 2			
Personal spending money	-0.00	0.00	0.01
Gender	0.13	0.08	0.08(*)
Step 3			
Personal spending money	0.00	0.00	0.02
Gender	0.15	0.07	0.09*
Age group	-0.20	0.05	-0.21***
Step 4			
Personal spending money	-0.00	0.00	-0.03
Gender	0.16	0.07	0.10*
Age group	-0.14	0.04	-0.15***
Materialistic values	0.54	0.06	0.41***

Note R^2 = .01 at Step 2 ($p < .10$); ΔR^2 = .05 for Step 3 ($p < .001$): ΔR^2 = .17 for Step 4 ($p < .001$). (*)$P < .10$. *$p < .05$, **$p < 0.1$, ***$p < .001$.

† *Source:* Dittmar (2005, p. 486).

†† Reprinted from *British Journal of Psychology* with permission by John Wiley and Sons.

whereas men preferred items that they could use. For women, then, shopping is linked to positivity—an enjoyable activity that leads to immediate happiness (even if this feeling does not last). For men, shopping is associated with a more negative attitude, a chore that needs to get done but is not something they want to commit time to. Although this relationship is not invariate (and can change depending on who is buying what), generally it seems that shopping is a more pleasurable experience for women, and they are thus more susceptible to transition from normal to abnormal shopping habits (Dittmar, 2005).

Stark gender differences in the prevalence of CBD, however, are by no means universally accepted. A more equal pattern of CBD gender distribution has been offered by Koran, Faber, Aboujaoude, Large, and Serpe (2006) whose data from a national telephone survey suggest that 5.5% of men and 6.0% of women are affected by CBD. Researchers offer various explanations for the discrepancy in gender estimates, most emphasizing various mechanisms of reporting or ascertainment bias. Black (2011), for example, posits that these differences may be due to how women and men report their spending habits: women may more readily acknowledge their abnormal shopping habits than men. Furthermore, women may be more heavily represented in research samples on addictive shopping, as they are more likely to participate in studies than men. Similarly, Dell'Osso, Allen, Altamura,

Buoli, and Hollander (2008) suggest that women are more inclined, in general, to seek treatment than men, which may indirectly lead to the discovery of CBD even among women being treated for separate disorders, such as anxiety or depression.

Age

Individuals most commonly affected by CBD tend to be young—those in their early 20s (Black, 2011; see Table 12.2).

Dittmar et al. (2005) cited that the average age of compulsive buyers is estimated to be 8–11 years younger than ordinary buyers. Benson et al. (2010) support these findings, as they explain that in the United States, Canada, France, Germany, and the United Kingdom, individuals under 30 years old are the most likely age cohort to become compulsive buyers. Black (2011) hypothesizes that this correlation of young age and compulsive buying habits is rooted in newfound independence that young adults acquire when they reach their early 20s. He also proposes that this is the period when individuals are first offered credit (2011), which, Benson et al. (2010) argue, is a dangerous step because many young individuals have profligate borrowing attitudes that lead to high levels of debt. Benson et al. (2010) cite findings from a study conducted by the Higher Education Research Institute, which found that in the last 20 years, young individuals have placed a higher value on material objects and believe that through the acquisition of material goods, one will achieve greater happiness. This shift in mentality from earlier generations, who placed less value on material goods, coupled with the availability of credit in developed countries, has led to high debt among the younger generation, irresponsible spending habits, and compulsive buying habits (Benson et al., 2010).

Results from Dittmar's (2005) studies confirm these arguments and found that, across different ages, genders, educational backgrounds, and socioeconomic statuses, age consistently predicted compulsive buying habits, with younger individuals more commonly partaking in compulsive buying than older individuals (see Table 12.1). Dittmar (2005) explored these age patterns in more depth and conducted a study with adolescents to further evaluate the role age played in compulsive buying tendencies. She found that the percentage of adolescents that was rated as having abnormal buying tendencies was very high, a finding that should be monitored closely because these spending habits were suggestive of early potential compulsive buying symptoms (see Table 12.1; Dittmar, 2005).

Table 12.2 Studies Involving Persons with CBD**, ***

Investigator(s)	Location	Subjects, *n*	Age, Years, Mean	% Female	Age at Onset, Years, Mean	Duration of Illness, Years, Mean
O'Guinn and Faber (1989)	Los Angeles, CA	386	37	92	N/A	N/A
Scherhorn et al. (1990)	Germany	26	40	85	N/A	N/A
McElroy et al. (1994)	Cincinnati, OH	20	39	80	30	9
Christensen et al. (1994)	Minneapolis, MN	24	36	92	18	18
Schlosser et al. (1994)	Iowa City, IA	46	31	80	19	12
Black et al. (1998)	Iowa City, IA	33	40	94	N/A	N/A
Ninan et al. (2000)	Cincinnati, OH; Boston, MA	42	41	81	N/A	N/A
Koran et al. (2002)	Stanford, CA	24	44	92	22	22
Miltenberger et al. (2003)	Fargo, ND	19	N/A	100*	18	N/A
Mitchell et al. (2006)	Fargo, ND	39	45	100*	N/A	N/A
Muller et al. (2008)	Bavaria, Germany	60	41	85	27	14

*Indicate that the sample recruit was female.
** Source: Black (2011, p. 201).
*** Reprinted from The Oxford Handbook of Impulse Control Disorders with permission by Oxford University Press.

Socioeconomic Status

While the socioeconomic status of an individual would seem to play a role in whether an individual becomes a compulsive shopper—that is, one with more disposable income might be more likely to develop compulsive shopping habits—results from studies have indicated that socioeconomic status is not predictive of whether or not one becomes a compulsive shopper. Although it would seem that lower incomes would deter individuals from overspending, this has not been found to be the case, as confirmed by Dell'Osso et al. (2008), who reported that the percentage of individuals with annual incomes under $50,000 was disproportionately high among those who reported as having CBD tendencies.

Black (2011) also explains that income is not predictive of CBD and that individuals from all different socioeconomic backgrounds suffer from CBD. The spending habits may differ depending on income, where those from a higher socioeconomic bracket may compulsively buy material goods from a more expensive boutique, whereas those individuals with lower incomes may spend their money at less expensive stores, such as second-hand boutiques (Black, 2011). Dittmar (2005) reinforced Black's conclusions and found that education, occupation, income, and credit power were not significant predictors of CBD (see Table 12.3).

The researchers concluded that no significant link exists between the socioeconomic status of their participants and CBD.

Regardless of income, those who suffer from CBD face serious economic troubles. Dell'Osso et al. (2008) cite a 1994 study by Gary Christianson and his colleagues, in which researchers concluded that 58.3% of CBD patients accumulate significant debt, and 41.7% are unable to pay off their debts. Additionally, 8.3% of these patients faced financial legal issues, and another 8.3% had criminal legal issues. Furthermore, in the United States, research has indicated that with the rise in credit card availability in the last few years, there has been an increase in careless buying practices, the kind seen most commonly among individuals with CBD; these spending patterns are at least partially responsible for the rise in the number of individual bankruptcies seen in the last 10 years (Benson et al., 2010). These personal economic hardships, while highly problematic on both an individual and societal level, are helpful in contributing to the prevalence estimates of CBD among the adult population because these people generally seek out help when they run into difficulties. It is worth noting that there may exist an entire cohort of individuals who suffer from the disorder but never seek help for it because it does not create a financial burden on them.

Table 12.3 Summary of Hierarchical Regression Analysis of Gender, Age, and Materialistic Values as Predictors of Compulsive Buying (Study 1)†, ††

Variable	B	SE B	β
Step 3			
Education	-0.05	0.06	-0.05
Occupational SES	-0.00	0.06	-0.00
Personal income	0.07	0.07	0.09
Number of credit cards	-0.02	0.07	-0.02
Gender	0.76	0.17	0.26***
Step 4			
Education	-0.09	0.05	-0.10
Occupational SES	0.02	0.06	0.02
Personal income	0.09	0.06	0.11
Number of credit cards	0.03	0.07	0.02
Gender	0.73	0.17	0.25***
Age	-0.03	0.01	-0.27***
Step 5			
Education	-0.03	0.05	-0.04
Occupational SES	0.03	0.05	0.04
Personal income	0.12	0.06	0.14*
Number of credit cards	0.05	0.06	0.04
Gender	0.77	0.15	0.26***
Age	-0.02	0.01	-0.20***
Materialistic values	0.53	0.07	0.39***

Note $R^2 = .06$ at Step 3 ($p < .001$); $\Delta R^2 = .07$ for Step 4 ($p < .001$); $\Delta R^2 = .15$ for Step 5 ($p < .001$).
*$P < .05$, **$p < .01$, ***$p < .001$.
† *Source:* Dittmar (2005, p. 479).
†† Reprinted from *British Journal of Psychology* with permission by John Wiley and Sons.

Materialism

More than any of the predictive elements discussed previously, materialism, or the overriding devotion to the inherent value of material objects and their possession, has emerged as arguably the strongest predictor of CBD. Dittmar (2005) conducted three separate studies and found that, in all three studies, those individuals who valued materialism, and for whom materialism was an important component of their value system, were more prone to become compulsive buyers than those individuals who did not value materialism as heavily (see Table 12.1). Dittmar explains that this relationship is not surprising because those who place value on materialism see it as a means to an end: material goods will make them happy and will make their lives better. As a result, it is expected that these individuals would be more likely to develop buying habits that are psychologically driven and that are aimed at improving their lives (Dittmar, 2005).

Furthermore, those who do value materialism are inherently different from those who do not. Individuals who place great significance on the acquisition of material goods as a way to achieve life improvements tend to be generally less happy and more insecure (Benson et al., 2010). As a result, they are more susceptible to the messages put forth by advertisers and are more inclined to buy those products that advertisements state will make them happier or better people (Benson et al., 2010). By internalizing the promises of advertisements, these individuals strongly incorporate materialism into their value systems, which—as stated earlier—can quickly develop into psychologically incentivized spending.

COMORBIDITY

As with many psychiatric disorders, individuals with CBD often manifest a variety of comorbid psychiatric illnesses. In their study of comorbidities and CBD, Mueller, Mitchell, Black, et al. (2010) found that individuals with CBD had high rates of psychiatric comorbidities, including Axis I and Axis II disorders. Specifically, the researchers found that 90% of the 171 CBD participants had a lifetime history of an Axis I disorder, and 51% of the participants met the criteria for an Axis I disorder at the time the study was conducted (see Table 12.4; Mueller et al., 2010). Furthermore, 21% of the sample had a lifetime history of a behavioral addiction (Mueller et al., 2010). In a separate study conducted by Schlosser, Black, Repertinger, and Freet (1994), 60% of their participants were found to have a comorbid personality disorder.

Axis I

The most common Axis I disorders seen among individuals with CBD are mood disorders, anxiety disorders, and substance use disorders (Black, 2011). In the same 2010 study by Mueller et al., the researchers found that 74% of CBD participants had a lifetime comorbid mood disorder, 57% of the CBD sample had lifetime comorbid anxiety disorder, and 21% had a lifetime comorbid impulse control disorder (Mueller et al., 2010; see Table 12.5).

Based on these findings, the researchers divided the participants into two clusters with one-third of the participants identified as more severe compulsive shoppers. Analyses on these clusters suggest that those with more

Table 12.4 Lifetime Psychiatric Comorbidity*, **

Dx, lifetime	Total Sample		Cluster I (CB)		Cluster II (Severe CB)		Comparison Cluster I vs Cluster II
	N=171		*N*=107		*N*=64		
	N	%	*N*	%	*N*	%	*P* (Chi² Test)
Any Axis I disorder	153	89.5	90	84.1	63	98.4	0.003
Any lifetime affective disorder	127	74.3	73	68.2	54	84.4	0.019
MDD	107	62.6	61	57.0	46	71.9	
Bipolar I disorder	3	1.8	1	0.9	2	3.1	
Bipolar II disorder	5	2.9	1	0.9	4	6.2	
Any dependence	35	20.5	16	15.0	19	29.7	0.021
Alcohol	24	14.0	13	12.1	11	17.2	
Sedative	8	4.7	4	3.7	4	6.2	
Cannabis	11	6.4	3	2.8	8	12.5	
Stimulants	4	2.3	2	1.9	2	3.1	
Opioid	7	4.1	4	3.7	3	4.7	
Cocaine	3	1.8	2	1.9	1	1.6	
Hallucinogen	3	1.8	1	0.9	2	3.1	
Any anxiety disorder	98	57.3	52	48.6	46	71.9	0.003
Panic disorder	42	24.6	19	17.8	23	35.9	
Social phobia	48	28.1	26	24.3	22	34.4	
Specific phobia	33	19.3	14	13.1	19	29.7	
OCD	32	18.7	18	16.8	14	21.9	
PTSD	23	13.5	9	8.4	14	21.9	
Any eating disorder	34	19.9	17	15.9	17	26.6	0.091
Anorexia nervosa	4	2.3	1	0.9	3	4.7	
Bulimia nervosa	13	7.6	8	7.5	5	7.8	
Binge eating disorder	24	14.0	10	9.3	14	21.9	

Continued

Table 12-4 Lifetime Psychiatric Comorbidity*, **—Cont'd

Dx, lifetime	Total Sample		Cluster I (CB)		Cluster II (Severe CB)		Comparison Cluster I vs Cluster II
	N=171		*N*=107		*N*=64		
	N	%	*N*	%	*N*	%	*P* (Chi² Test)
	N=146		N=95		N=51		
	N	%	N	%	N	%	
Any impulse control disorder[a]	30	20.5	16	16.8	14	27.5	0.130
Kleptomania	9	6.2	3	3.2	6	11.8	
Intermittent explosive disorder	16	11.0	9	9.5	7	13.7	
Pathological gambling	8	5.5	4	4.2	4	7.8	
Pyromania	0	0	0	0	0	0	
Trichotillomania	3	2.1	2	2.1	1	2.0	

Note. Because of multiple comparisons and significance level was set up at $p<0.01$.
[a]Other than compulsive buying.
* *Source:* Mueller et al. (2010, p. 351).
** Reprinted from *Psychiatry Research* with permission.

Table 12.5 Current Psychiatric Comorbidity*, **

Dx, Current	Total Sample		Cluster I (CB)		Cluster II (Severe CB)		Comparison Cluster I vs Cluster II
	N=171		*N*=107		*N*=64		
	N	%	*N*	%	*N*	%	*P* (Chi^2 Test)
Any Axis I disorder	102	50.9	53	49.5	49	76.6	<0.001
Any affective disorder	56	32.7	27	25.2	29	45.3	0.007
MDD	26	15.2	12	11.2	14	21.9	
Bipolar I disorder	0	0	0	0	0	0	
Bipolar II disorder	2	1.2	0	0	2	3.1	
Dysthymia	32	18.7	15	14.0	17	26.6	
Any abuse/dependence	3	1.8	1	0.9	2	3.1	0.291
Alcohol	2	1.2	1	0.9	1	1.6	
Sedative	0	0	0	0	0	0	
Cannabis	0	0	0	0	0	0	
Stimulants	0	0	0	0	0	0	
Opioid	0	0	0	0	0	0	
Cocaine	0	0	0	0	0	0	
Hallucinogen	0	0	0	0	0	0	
Any anxiety disorder	76	44.4	37	34.6	39	60.9	0.001
Panic disorder	22	12.9	9	8.4	13	20.3	
Social phobia	39	22.8	18	16.8	21	32.3	
Specific phobia	29	17.0	12	11.2	17	26.6	
Genesalized anxiety disorder	26	15.2	9	8.4	17	26.6	
OCD	25	14.6	13	12.1	12	18.8	
PTSD	15	8.8	5	4.7	10	15.6	

Continued

Table 12.5 Current Psychiatric Comorbidity*, **—Cont'd

Dx, Current	Total Sample		Cluster I (CB)		Cluster II (Severe CB)		Comparison Cluster I vs Cluster II
	N=171		*N*=107		*N*=64		
	N	%	*N*	%	*N*	%	*P* (Chi² Test)
Any somatoform disorder	15	8.8	6	5.6	9	14.1	0.059
Somatization disorder	7	4.1	2	1.9	5	7.8	
Pain disorder	9	5.3	5	4.7	4	6.2	
Hypochondriasis	4	2.3	3	2.8	1	1.6	
Body dysmorphic disorder	2	1.2	0	0	2	3.1	
Any eating disorder	20	11.7	9	8.4	11	17.2	0.084
Anorexia nervosa	0	0	0	0	0	0	
Bulimia nervosa	5	2.9	3	2.8	2	3.1	
Binge eating disorder	16	9.4	6	5.6	10	15.6	
Any impulse control disorder (without CB)[a]	24	16.6	13	13.8	11	21.6	0.231
Kleptomania	7	4.8	2.1	3.2	5	9.8	
Intermittent explosive disorder	15	10.3	8	8.5	7	13.7	
Pathological gambling	4	2.8	2	2.1	2	3.9	
Pyromania	0	0	0	0	0	0	
Trichotillomania	3	2.1	2	2.1	1	2.0	

Note. Because of multiple comparisons and significance level was set up at $p<0.01$.
aOther than compulsive buying.
* *Source:* Mueller et al. (2010, p. 352).
** Reprinted from Psychiatry Research with permission.

extreme compulsive shopping habits have higher rates of psychiatric comorbidity (see Table 12.6).

This finding supports other results from Black, Monahan, Schlosser, and Repertinger (2001), who also concluded that those with more severe compulsive shopping habits also have higher rates of psychiatric comorbidity. Specifically, the researchers found that more severe compulsive buying habits correlated with higher levels of OCD, substance use disorders, depression, and pathological gambling (Black et al., 2001).

Axis II

In addition to Axis I disorders, Axis II disorders are also seen with regularity among individuals with CBD. Employing a structured interview and a self-report, Schlosser, Black, Repertinger, and Freet (1994) determined that 60% of their 46 CBD-person sample also had a personality disorder. Specifically, the researchers found that 22% suffered from obsessive-compulsive type, 15% suffered from borderline type, and 15% from avoidant type (Schlosser et al., 1994).

Behavioral Addictions

As mentioned previously, 21% of the participants in Mueller et al.'s 2010 study, presented with a lifetime diagnosis of a behavioral addiction, including kleptomania, intermittent explosive disorder, pathological gambling, pyromania, and trichotillomania (Mueller et al., 2010). Furthermore, results suggest that those with more severe compulsive buying had overall higher rates of these comorbid behavioral addictions than those participants with less severe CBD (Mueller et al., 2010).

Heredity

In addition to their suffering from an array of comorbid disorders, research has also suggested that the first-degree relatives of those with CBD also have many Axis I and Axis II disorders (Black, Repertinger, Gaffney, & Gabel, 1998). In their study on relatives of those with CBD, Black et al. reported that the first-degree relatives of those with CBD were much more likely to have Axis I and Axis II disorders than the relatives of control subjects. Eighteen percent of CBD relatives suffered from depression compared with 7% of relatives from the control sample, and 20% of CBD relatives were found to have alcoholism compared with 4% of control relatives (Black et al., 1998).

Table 12.6 Sample Distribution between Clusters*, **

	Total sample N=171		Cluster I (CB) N=107		Cluster II (Severe CB) N=64		Comparison Cluster I vs Cluster II
	N	**%**	***N***	**%**	***N***	**%**	**Chi² test**
Sites (n=2)							
US	107	62.6	72	67.3	35	54.7	ns
Germany	64	37.4	35	32.7	29	45.3	
Sites (n =4)							
Fargo	73	42.7	52	48.6	21	32.8	ns (P=0.042)
Minneapolis	14	8.2	11	10.3	3	4.7	
Iowa	20	11.7	9	8.4	11	17.2	
Erlangen	64	37.4	35	32.7	39	45.3	

* *Source:* Mueller et al. (2010, p. 351).
** Reprinted from *Psychiatry Research* with permission.

Although these data suggest that Axis I and Axis II disorders run in families, it is still not clear whether CBD is a hereditary disorder. Of note, however, is that this same study found that 9.5% of CBD relatives also had CBD, a result that suggests the disorder may be heritable in nature. Despite these findings, not enough research has been conducted to conclude that CBD is genetically inherited.

TREATMENT

It is not surprising, given the overlaps between CBD and impulse control disorder, obsessive-compulsive related disorder, behavioral addiction, and affective disorder, that no consensus has been established for one treatment for CBD (Benson & Gengler, 2004). Rather, various studies that have employed various treatments have offered positive results. The following sections highlight the several effective pharmacological and psychological treatments that have been successfully used with CBD patients.

Pharmacological Treatments

Different pharmacological treatments have been employed in the management of CBD. Depending on which comorbid disorders the patient experiences, different medications appear to work more effectively than others. In one study, CBD patients with comorbid bipolar disorder or depression responded well to medications that target mood disorders. A combination of mood stabilizers (including valproate, lithium, and various antipsychotics) as well as antidepressants (bupropion, norptripyline, and others) was reported to reduce the impulses seen in CBD and well as the actual buying behavior. A host of other medications commonly used for other disorders (such as antidepressants like trazadone, bupropion, sertraline, desipramine, nortriptyline, and fluoxetine) have also yielded improvements in patients with CBD; this has led some researchers to posit that in treating the comorbid mood disorders a CBD patient presents with, improvements in CBD symptomatology will ensue (Benson & Gengler, 2004).

In CBD patients without any comorbid disorders, Black, Monahan, and Gabel (1997) found that fluvoxamine, a selective serotonin reuptake inhibitor (SSRI) marketed in the United States for the treatment of OCD, was an effective treatment in lessening the preoccupation with shopping, the time spent shopping, and the time spent thinking about shopping. In their sample of 10 subjects, 9 were considered responders to fluvoxamine treatment, as measured by decreases in scores from the Yale-Brown Obsessive

Compulsive Scale–Shopping Version. Subjects reported that they were able to better control their impulsive thoughts about shopping and resist the intrusive urges to shop with more efficacy. Additionally, the patients were spending less money per week, and some were even able to begin to pay off their debts. What is of particular interest in this study is that when the patients discontinued the fluvoxamine, their intrusive thoughts and urges regarding shopping gradually returned.

In a follow-up study, Black, Gabel, Hansen, and Schlosser (2000) conducted a double-blind, placebo-controlled version of their original experiment and found that patients improved both in the fluvoxamine and the placebo groups. Further research using SSRIs to treat CBD has also yielded improvements for both patients on medication and on placebo, although some studies, in which the SSRI is discontinued in one cohort of participants and not in the other, indicate that those patients who remain on SSRIs are significantly less likely to relapse than those who discontinue SSRI treatments (Benson & Gengler, 2004). While it appears that SSRIs do help some CBD patients with obsessive and compulsive aspects of CBD—particularly intrusive thoughts and urges—the high placebo response rates suggest the need for further research, some of which is currently being conducted at the present time.

Additionally, one of authors (EH) of this chapter, in his clinical practice, has noted improvement in individual cases of CBD with the use of opiate antagonists (naltrexone), stimulants (long-acting forms of dextroamphetamine and methylphenidate), dopamine reuptake inhibitors (buproprion), and atypical antipsychotics, in addition to the mood stabilizers and SSRIs noted previously.

Psychological Treatments

In addition to pharmacological treatments, researchers and therapists also have seen improvements through the application of insight-driven psychological treatments. Different kinds of individual therapy, as well as group therapy, are effective in helping individuals cope with and manage CBD. These various treatments are explored in more detail in the following sections.

Psychodynamic Individual Therapy

The primary focus for individuals seeking treatment for CBD is to understand why it is that they engage in these shopping behaviors. For many individuals with CBD, an inadequate sense of self, low self-esteem, and negative perceptions of oneself are all issues that contribute to compulsive shopping habits. It is *through* compulsive buying that these individuals hope to ameliorate their self-image: by consuming material goods, these negative feelings are diminished and *temporarily* suppressed. Thus, for many individuals with CBD, their shopping habits constitute a coping mechanism that comforts them and reduces their anxiety by providing them with fleeting positive emotions about themselves (Benson & Gengler, 2004).

For therapists, then, the goal is to lead patients to a place where they can understand *why* it is they are seeking this comfort in the first place; in other words, to help them come to terms with their negative self-image and to start to rebuild a more positive sense of self-worth. For psychodynamic therapists, the answer to why a patient engages in these shopping behaviors lies in the familial history and relationships of the patient. These therapists concentrate on family circumstances and relational patterns as a way to understand why the patient has developed compulsive buying habits (Benson & Gengler, 2004). This kind of therapy also centers on why patients employ shopping to regulate negative feelings, such as depression. The goal of therapy, then, is to help individuals develop positive notions of self-identity that, in turn, provide them with more adaptive ways of self-regulating their emotions (Krueger, 1988).

Cognitive Behavioral Therapy

Cognitive behavioral therapy (CBT) has also resulted in some preliminary improvements for those with CBD. In a study by Mitchell, Burgard, Faber, Crosby, and Zwaan (2006), 21 participants completed a CBT-based treatment. Over the course of 10 weeks, participants attended 12 sessions and were instructed to complete readings and homework assignments before each therapy session. During the therapy sessions, various topics were addressed, including actual shopping behavior problems, financial management, emotions and feelings associated with buying behavior, self-esteem, and consequences. The researchers concluded that those who had received CBT treatment had markedly fewer compulsive buying episodes after treatment compared to before treatment, as measured by a host of assessment scores (see Table 12.7).

Group Therapy

Benson and Gengler (2004) write extensively on a model they have used with success to treat individuals with CBD in a group format. Group therapy for CBD, as with individual therapy, focuses on understanding one's shopping habits and the emotions that accompany those behaviors. Additionally, group therapy for CBD is also concerned with the development of

Table 12.7 Baseline Comparison between the Participants Randomized to CBT Group Therapy or the Waiting List Control Condition*, **

Variable	WLC mean (SD) (*n*=11)	CBT mean (SD) (*n* = 28)
Age	44.6 (11.2)	45.1 (10.2)
BDI	12.6 (8.7)	12.9 (7.9)
CBS	-4.1 (1.8)	-3.4 (1.6)
MCS (SF-36)	47.8 (13)	41.9(11.9)
Y-BOCS-SV	21.1 (7.2)	22.6 (7.2)
Compulsive buying episodes (4 weeks)	9.4(5.3)	10.7 (8.3)
Total amount spent (4 weeks)	651 (738.7)	722.5 (778.6)
Total time spent (hours/4 weeks)	7.7 (7.8)	11.3(11.5)

* *Source:* Mitchell et al. (2006, p. 1863).
** Reprinted from *Behaviour Research and Therapy* with permission.

a healthy relationship toward money so that individuals feel in control of their finances and are not overpowered by their urges and intrusive thoughts to shop. Group therapy offers an environment where patients are taught coping skills that help them foster a better relationship towards their finances. Perhaps the most significant skill taught in these groups is the mastery of strategies that enable individuals to reject shopping urges. These strategies can take many forms, including not bringing money to a store; bringing only a debit card or cash versus a credit card; allowing some time to pass before succumbing to the urge right away; and constructing spending plans (Benson & Gengler, 2004). Group therapy is effective in empowering individuals, by providing a secure space where they can equip themselves with, and develop, skill sets that offer them ownership over their behaviors.

Perhaps most importantly, group therapy for those with CBD offers a setting where individuals can interact with other people who fully understand what they are experiencing—their addiction, the urges they feel to shop, and the emotions that surround these impulses. In interacting with people who are living with the same disorder, patients feel less emotionally isolated, less guilty, and less embarrassed by their condition. Group therapy provides an environment where members can offer positive feedback to each other when someone feels low. The power of emotional support that group therapy can provide is demonstrably effective in the recovery of individuals with CBD (Benson & Gengler, 2004).

In addition, the authors have also noted that patients with CBD may respond to keeping busy with other meaningful activities, maintaining structure and routine activities, minimizing alcohol and drug use, maintaining an exercise regimen and good sleep hygiene, and decreasing access to money for shopping activities.

Case Vignette: Ms. C

Ms. C is a 24-year-old single white female who is a graduate student in psychiatric social work. She suffers from a longstanding history of an eating disorder characterized by recurrent binge eating, purging/vomiting, and restricted eating patterns. She has trichotillomania, pulling hair from the top of her head, as well as her eyebrows and eyelashes. After pulling and after binge eating, she feels that she looks hideous and can become housebound, stuck looking at herself in the mirror, and comparing herself to idealized women of beauty in fashion magazines. Ms. C has also had repeated episodes in which she has spent large amounts of money online for cosmetics, clothing, and fashion accessories. She has stolen credit cards from her parents to be able to continue buying these items online. She has engaged in recurrent fights with her mother about these buying episodes and the amount of debt that she has run up as a result of the buying episodes. She has had some benefit from CBT treatment targeting her binge eating, hair pulling, and preoccupation with body image but has not achieved remission for the compulsive shopping. She has mild mood swings that were exacerbated by SSRI treatment, and the compulsive shopping did not respond to SSRI treatment. She has not responded to stimulant medications with regards to the compulsive shopping. She did achieve a 50% decrease in the frequency and severity of her compulsive shopping episodes with the opiate antagonist naltrexone 50 mg/day. She has benefitted from staying busy in graduate school and from a regular exercise and nutritional regimen. She has also benefitted from not having access to credit cards.

NEXT STEPS AND FURTHER RESEARCH

Although a fair amount of preliminary data exists about CBD's epidemiology, etiology, diagnosis, and treatment, a great deal more research needs to be done to fully understand the complexities that define it. The etiology of CBD is not understood in its entirety, as signaled by the fact that researchers still maintain differing opinions about how the disorder should be classified. Future studies should thus concentrate on the potential hereditary nature of the disorder, as well as its connections to OCD, addiction, and other impulse control disorders. When these connections are understood more completely, preventative therapeutic measures, early interventions, and pharmacological treatments can be developed to decrease the number of individuals who suffer from CBD.

In this same vein, treatment advancements are needed as well. Although a more comprehensive understanding of the causes of CBD might itself lead to new and effective care, these advances in research do not need to occur before improving already existing treatments. The first step in advancing the application of currently existing treatments relies on changing how clinicians perceive CBD. Most importantly, CBD must be understood by clinicians to be a serious disorder: an appreciation that many clinicians do not yet currently share (Benson & Gengler, 2004). In the absence of a consistent pathological framing of this disorder, many people suffering from CBD do not actively seek out help. As is the case with many mental health disorders, those suffering from them often do not understand the origins of their behaviors and feel ashamed, in this case regarding their spending activities. The social constructs through which these behaviors are understood often reference moral or ethical frameworks that mistakenly attribute behaviors to character defects rather than to illness. Many with CBD may be concerned that they will not be viewed as having a legitimate disorder, but rather as being simply materialistic, as Benson and Gengler (2004) point out.

It is only through increased awareness, knowledge, and research that clinicians, researchers, patients and families can effectively understand the dynamics of CBD as well as other ICDs. In applying rigorous methods that aim to elucidate all the various aspects of CBD, researchers will be able to better categorize, conceptualize, diagnose, and ultimately treat this and other ICDs in the future.

REFERENCES

American Psychiatric Association. (2000). *Diagnostic and statistical manual of mental disorders* (4th ed.). Washington, DC: Author.

Benson, A. L., Dittmar, H., & Wolfsohn, R. (2010). Compulsive buying: Cultural contributors and consequences. In E. Aboujaoude & L. A. Koran (Eds.), *Impulse control disorders* (1st ed., pp. 23–33). Cambridge: Cambridge University Press, 2010. *Cambridge Books Online*. Retrieved from http://dx.doi.org/10.1017/CBO9780511711930.

Benson, A. L., & Gengler, M. (2004). Treating compulsive buying. In R. H. Coombs (Ed.), *Handbook of addictive disorders: A practical guide to diagnosis and treatment* (pp. 451–491). Hoboken, NJ: John Wiley & Sons, Inc.

Black, D. W. (2000). Assessment of compulsive buying. In A. Benson (Ed.), *I shop, therefore I am—Compulsive buying and the search for self* (pp. 191–216). New York: Aronson.

Black, D. W. (2011). Epidemiology and phenomenology of compulsive buying disorder. In J. E. Grant & M. E. Potenza (Eds.), *The Oxford handbook of impulse control disorders* (pp. 196–207). New York: Oxford University Press.

Black, D. W., Gabel, J., Hansen, J., & Schlosser, S. (2000). A double blind comparison of fluvoxamine versus placebo in the treatment of compulsive buying disorder. *Annals of Clinical Psychiatry*, *12*(4), 205–211.

Black, D. W., Monahan, P., & Gabel, J. (1997). Fluvoxamine in the treatment of compulsive buying. *Journal of Clinical Psychiatry*, *58*(4), 159–163.

Black, D.W., Monahan, P., Schlosser, S., & Repertinger, S. (2001). Compulsive buying severity: An analysis of compulsive buying scale results in 44 subjects. *Journal of Nervous & Mental Disease*, *189*(2), 123–126.

Black, D.W., Repertinger, S., Gaffney, G. R., & Gabel, J. (1998). Family history and psychiatric comorbidity in persons with compulsive buying: Preliminary findings. *American Journal of Psychiatry*, *155*(7), 960–963.

Christenson, G. A., Faber, R. J., & de Zwaan, M. (1994). Compulsive buying: Descriptive characteristics and psychiatric comorbidity. *Journal of Clinical Psychiatry*, *55*, 5–11.

Claes, L., Bijttebier, P., Van Den Eynde, F., Mitchell, J. E., Faber, R., de Zwaan, M., & Mueller, A. (2010). Emotional reactivity and self regulation in relation to compulsive buying. *Personality and Individual Differences*, *49*, 526–530.

Dell'Osso, B., Allen, A., Altamura, C., Buoli, M., & Hollander, E. (2008). Impulsive-compulsive buying disorder: Clinical overview. *Australian and New Zealand Journal of Psychiatry*, *42*, 259–266.

Dittmar, H. (2005). Compulsive buying—A growing concern? An examination of gender, age, and endorsement of materialistic values as predictors. *British Journal of Psychology*, *96*, 467–491.

Faber, R. J., & O'Guinn, T. (1992). Money changes everything: Compulsive buying from a biopsychosocial perspective. *American Behavioral Science*, *35*, 809–819.

Hartston, H. (2012). The case for compulsive shopping as an addiction. *Journal of Psychoactive Drugs*, *44*(1), 64–67.

Karim, R., D.O., & Chaudhri, P. (2012). Behavioral addictions: An overview. *Journal of Psychoactive Drugs*, *44*(1), 5–17.

Koran, L. M., Faber, R. J., Aboujaoude, E., Large, M. D., & Serpe, R. T. (2006). Estimated prevalence of compulsive buying behavior in the United States. *American Journal of Psychiatry*, *163*(10), 1806–1812.

Kruger, D. W. (1988). On compulsive shopping and spending: A psychodynamic inquiry. *American Journal of Psychotherapy*, *42*(4), 574–584.

Lejoyeux, M., Tassain, V., Solomon, J., & Ades, J. (1997). Study of compulsive buying in depressed patients. *Journal of Clinical Psychiatry*, *58*(4), 169–173.

McElroy, S. L., Keck, P. E., Pope, H. G., Smith, J. M., & Strakowski, S. M. (1994). Compulsive buying: A report of 20 cases. *Journal of Clinical Psychiatry*, *55*(6), 242–248.

Miltenberger, R. G., Redlin, J., Crosby, R., Stickney, M., Mitchell, J., Wonderlich, S., et al. (2003). Direct and retrospective assessment of factors contributing to compulsive buying. *Journal of Behavior Therapy and Experimental Psychiatry*, *34*(1), 1–9.

Mitchell, J. E., Burgard, M., Faber, R., Crosby, R. D., & de Zwaan, M. (2006). Cognitive behavioral therapy for compulsive buying disorder. *Behavior Research and Therapy*, *44*, 1859–1865.

Monahan, P., Black, D. W., & Gabel, J. (1996). Reliability and validity of a scale to measure change in persons with compulsive buying. *Psychiatry Research*, *64*, 59–67.

Mueller, A., Claes, L., Mitchell, J. E., Faber, R. J., Fischer, J., & de Zwaan, M. (2011). Does compulsive buying differ between male and female students? *Personality and Individual Differences*, *50*, 1309–1312.

Mueller, A., Mitchell, J. E., Black, D. W., Crosby, R. D., Berg, K., & de Zwaan, M. (2010). Latent profile analysis and comorbidity in a sample of individuals with compulsive buying disorder. *Psychiatry Research*, *178*, 348–353.

Nataraajan, R., & Goff, B. G. (1992). Manifestations of compulsiveness in the consumer-marketplace domain. *Psychology & Marketing*, *9*(1), 31–44.

Potenza, M. N., Koran, L. M., & Pallanti, S. (2001). Relationship between impulse control disorders and obsessive compulsive disorder. In E. Hollander, J. Zohar, P. J. Sirovatka & D. A. Regier (Eds.), *Obsessive compulsive spectrum disorders* (pp. 89–115). Arlington, VA: American Psychiatric Publishing, Inc.
Schlosser, S., Black, D. W., Repertinger, S., & Freet, D. (1994). Compulsive buying: Demography, phenomenology, and comorbidity in 46 subjects. *General Hospital Psychiatry*, *16*(3), 205–212.
Schwartz, B. (2004). *The paradox of choice*. New York: Harper Collins.

APPENDIX 12-1. COMPULSIVE BUYING SCALE*, **

1. Please indicate how much you agree or disagree with each of the statements below. Circle the number that corresponds with the answer that best indicates how you feel.

If I have any money left at the end of the pay period, I just have to spend it.

Strongly Agree	Somewhat Agree	Neither Agree or Disagree	Somewhat Disagree	Strongly Disagree
(1)	(2)	(3)	(4)	(5)

2. Please indicate how often you have done each of the following things by circling the number corresponding with the best answer for each question.

a. *Felt others would be horrified if they knew of my spending habits.*

Very Often	Often	Sometimes	Rarely	Never
(1)	(2)	(3)	(4)	(5)

b. *Bought things even though I couldn't afford them.*

Very Often	Often	Sometimes	Rarely	Never
(1)	(2)	(3)	(4)	(5)

* *Source:* Faber & O'Guinn (1992).
** Reprinted from *American Behavioral Science* with permission by University of Chicago Press.

c. *Wrote a check when I knew I didn't have enough money in the bank to cover it.*

Very Often	Often	Sometimes	Rarely	Never
(1)	(2)	(3)	(4)	(5)

d. *Bought myself something in order to make myself feel better.*

Very Often	Often	Sometimes	Rarely	Never
(1)	(2)	(3)	(4)	(5)

e. *Felt anxious or nervous on days I didn't go shopping.*

Very Often	Often	Sometimes	Rarely	Never
(1)	(2)	(3)	(4)	(5)

f. *Made only the minimum payments on my credit card.*

Very Often	Often	Sometimes	Rarely	Never
(1)	(2)	(3)	(4)	(5)

SCORING INSTRUCTIONS

Scoring equation = –9.69 + (Q1 × .33) + (Q2a × .34) + (Q2b × .50) + (Q2c × .47) + (Q2d × .33) + (Q2e × .38) + (Q2f × .31).

Substitute your score 1 to 5 on each question for its place in the equation. For example, if you marked question 1 as 2 (somewhat agree), use 2 in place of Q1 and multiply it by .33.

When you have answered each question, add your individual scores together and subtract 9.69 to determine your overall score.

If your overall score is a higher negative score than –1.34 (for example, –2.04), you would be classified as a compulsive buyer.

CHAPTER 13

Exercise Addiction

Krisztina Berczik[1,2], Mark D. Griffiths[3], Attila Szabó[4], Tamás Kurimay[5], Róbert Urban[6], Zsolt Demetrovics[1]

[1]Department of Clinical Psychology and Addiction, Institute of Psychology, Eötvös Loránd University, Budapest, Hungary, [2]Doctoral School of Psychology, Eötvös Loránd University, Budapest, Hungary, [3]Nottingham Trent University, Psychology Division, Nottingham, United Kingdom, [4]Department of Psychiatry and Psychiatric Rehabilitation, Saint John Hospital, Budapest, Hungary, [5]Institute for Health Promotion and Sport Sciences, Eötvös Loránd University, Budapest, Hungary, [6]Department of Personality and Health Psychology, Institute of Psychology, Eötvös Loránd University, Budapest, Hungary

THE HISTORY OF EXERCISE ADDICTION

Regular exercise can be conceptualized as a set of planned, structured, and repetitive complex movement activities carried out with sufficient frequency, intensity, and duration to be effective in health promotion, while also playing a significant role in disease prevention (Caspersen, Powell, & Christenson, 1985; Waddington, 2000). Research has demonstrated that regular physical exercise contributes to the maintenance of health (Blair et al., 1989; Paffenbarger, Hyde, Wing, & Hsieh, 1986; Royal College of Physicians, 1991; Stephens, 1988; United States Department of Health and Human Services, 1996). There is also consensus in the literature that the optimal level of habitual physical exercise has favorable effects on both the physical and mental well-being of the adult population (Folsom et al., 1985; Lamb, Roberts, & Brodie, 1990; Lotan, Merrick, & Carmeli, 2005; Warburton, Nicol, & Bredin, 2006), as well as on children's and teenagers' general well-being (Biddle, Gorely, & Stensel, 2004; Lotan et al., 2005; Piko, 2000; Piko & Keresztes, 2006).

However, since the 1970s, it has been recognized that there can also be negative consequences of excessive exercising (Berczik et al., 2012). Taking into consideration the favorable effects of exercise, Glasser (1976) introduced the concept of "positive addiction" into the psychological literature. Glasser attempted to pinpoint these beneficial effects of physical exercise and the positive dose-response relationship between exercise and health, in contrast to substance use and other addictions that bear a negative dose-response relationship in terms of behavioral outcomes. However, Morgan (1979) questioned Glasser's conceptualization because psychiatric case studies had shown that exaggerated exercise could lead not only to physical

Behavioral Addictions
http://dx.doi.org/10.1016/B978-0-12-407724-9.00013-6

injury, but also to the negligence of the most paramount everyday responsibilities such as work, personal relationships, and family life. In these extreme clinical cases, the overuse of exercise was conceptualized as a new form of addiction (Morgan, 1979). In a more recent review of behavioral addiction, Griffiths (1996) questioned the criteria for positive addiction and argued that Glasser's (1976) criteria bore little resemblance to the accepted signs or components of addictions.

Based on his observations, Morgan (1979) presented arguments that the most typical symptoms of addiction could also be applied to excessive exercising, primarily through the presence of withdrawal symptoms, detrimental social consequences, and several other negative effects such as disturbed psychological functioning. Because of these negative consequences, Morgan viewed exercise addiction as a behavioral dysfunction and negative addiction, in contrast to Glasser's concept of positive addiction. Although this connotation is still used occasionally in the literature, more uniform terminologies, such as *exercise addiction* have started to be used (e.g., Berczik et al., 2012). In addition to *exercise addiction*, several other terms are used as an alternative to this term. The most popular among these is perhaps *exercise dependence* (Cockerill & Riddington, 1996; Hausenblas & Symons Downs, 2002a). Nevertheless, some scholars refer to the condition as *obligatory exercising* (Pasman & Thompson, 1988) and *exercise abuse* (Davis, 2000), while in the media the condition is often described as *compulsive exercise* (Dalle Grave, Calugi, & Marchesini, 2008).

DEFINITION AND DIAGNOSIS

Exercise addiction has been conceptualized as a behavioral addiction (Demetrovics & Griffiths, 2012). However, it was not included in the current (fifth) edition of the *Diagnostic and Statistical Manual of Mental Disorders* (American Psychiatric Association, 2013) and has never been included in any of the earlier editions. The symptoms and consequences of exercise addiction have been characterized by six common components of addiction: salience, mood modification, tolerance, withdrawal symptoms, personal conflict, and relapse (Brown, 1993; Griffiths, 2005). However, it is important to clarify whether exaggerated exercise behavior is a primary problem in the affected person's life or emerges as a secondary problem in consequence to other psychological dysfunctions. In the former case, the dysfunction is classified as *primary exercise addiction*, while in the latter case it is termed as *secondary exercise addiction* because it co-occurs with another dysfunction, typically with eating disorders such as anorexia nervosa or bulimia nervosa (Bamber, Cockerill, & Carroll, 2000; Blaydon, Lindner, & Kerr, 2002; de Coverley Veale, 1987). In the former, the motive for overexercising is typically geared toward avoiding something negative (Szabo, 2010), although the affected individual may be totally unaware of his or her motivation. It typically occurs as a form of escape response to a source of disturbing, persistent, and/or uncontrollable stress. In these cases, for example, the person doesn't want to face conflicts in relation to his or her relationship or work and instead suppresses his or her anxiety by overexercising. However, in the latter, excessive exercise is used as a means of weight loss (in addition to very strict dieting). Thus, secondary exercise addiction has a different etiology than primary exercise addiction. Nevertheless, it should be highlighted that many symptoms and consequences of exercise addiction are similar whether exercise addiction is primary or secondary. The distinguishing feature between the two is that in primary exercise addiction the *exercise is the objective*, whereas in secondary exercise addiction *weight loss is the objective,* such that excessive exercise is one of the primary means in achieving the objective.

Bamber, Cockerill, Rodgers, and Carroll (2003) interviewed 56 regularly exercising adult women. Based on the qualitative analysis of the results, the authors identified three factors in the diagnostic criteria of secondary exercise addiction. Among these factors, only the presence of eating disorder symptoms differentiated secondary from primary exercise addiction. The other two factors (i.e., dysfunctional psychological, physical, or social behavior, and the presence of withdrawal symptoms) were nonspecific to secondary exercise addiction. However, Blaydon, Lindner, and Kerr (2004) attempted to further subclassify secondary exercise addiction based on the primary source of the problem, which in their view was related to either a form of the eating disorder or to an exaggerated preoccupation with body image. Although this appears to have face validity, to date, there is no empirical evidence for such speculation. Furthermore, based on qualitative research, Bamber, Cockerill, Rodgers, and Carroll (2000) found no evidence for primary exercise addiction. In fact, they believe that all problematic exercise behaviors are linked to eating disorders. However, this view remains critically challenged in the literature (Szabo, 2000, 2010), and there are documented case studies (e.g., Griffiths, 1997) in which no eating disorders were present at all.

Exercise addiction often has been identified on the basis of the presence of withdrawal symptoms. For example, Sachs (1981) defined addiction to running as "addiction of a psychological and/or physiological nature, upon a regular regimen of running, characterized by withdrawal symptoms after 24 to 36 hours without participation" (p. 118). This definition has frequently been used in the literature (e.g., Furst & Germone, 1993; Morris, 1989; Sachs & Pargman, 1984). However, withdrawal symptoms in exercise addiction are only one of the several other critical symptoms universally observable in behavioral addictions (Brown, 1993; Griffiths, 1997, 2005).

As discussed by a number of scholars (e.g., Griffiths, 1997, 2005; Szabo, 1995, 2010; Szabo, Frenkl, & Caputo, 1996), it is therefore incorrect to establish the presence of exercise addiction merely on the basis of withdrawal symptoms. Consequently, the type, frequency, and the intensity of withdrawal symptoms need to be examined, because negative psychological feelings are reported by almost all habitual exercisers (or hobby makers) at times when exercise is prevented for an unexpected reason (Szabo et al., 1996; Szabo, Frenkl, & Caputo, 1997). Indeed, Szabo et al. (1996) noted that even participants in physically "light effort" types of exercises, such as ten-pin bowling, report withdrawal symptoms when bowling is prevented for unforeseen reasons. However, the intensity of the symptoms reported by these individuals is less than that reported by aerobic dancers, weight-trainers, cross-trainers, and fencers (Szabo et al., 1996). Therefore, it is essential to understand that the presence of withdrawal symptoms alone is insufficient in the screening or diagnosis of exercise addiction. It is the *intensity* of these symptoms that is the crucial factor in separating committed and habitual exercisers from addicted exercisers. However, at this moment there is no final consensus on the diagnostic criteria of exercise addiction, and as mentioned before, this disorder is not yet included in the official diagnostic systems.

ASSESSMENT

Several instruments have been developed and adopted for the assessment of exercise addiction (Allegre, Souville, Therme, & Griffiths, 2006). Two relatively early scales, namely the Commitment to Running Scale (CRS; Carmack & Martens, 1979) and the Negative Addiction Scale (NAS; Hailey & Bailey, 1982), are no longer used because of theoretical and methodological shortcomings that have been discussed extensively elsewhere (e.g., Szabo et al., 1997). Among the psychometrically tested instruments, the Obligatory Exercise Questionnaire (OEQ; Ackard, Brehm, & Steffen, 2002;

Pasman & Thompson, 1988), the Exercise Dependence Scale (EDS; Hausenblas & Symons Downs, 2002b; Symons Downs, Hausenblas, & Nigg, 2004), and the Exercise Dependence Questionnaire (EDQ) (Ogden, Veale, & Summers, 1997) have proved to be both psychometrically valid and reliable instruments for gauging the symptoms and assessing the extent of exercise addiction (see Table 13.1).

The OEQ is a 20-item self-report questionnaire that assesses the urge for undertaking exercise. Participants rate each item on a 4-point Likert scale from "never" to "always." The questionnaire has three subscales: (1) emotional element of exercise, (2) exercise frequency and intensity, and (3) exercise preoccupation (Steffen & Brehm, 1999). The EDS (Hausenblas & Symons Downs, 2002b) conceptualizes exercise dependence on the basis of the *DSM-IV* criteria for substance abuse or addiction (American Psychiatric Association, 2000), and empirical research shows that it is able to differentiate between at-risk, dependent, and nondependent athletes, and also between physiological and nonphysiological addiction. The EDS has seven subscales: (1) tolerance, (2) withdrawal, (3) intention effect, (4) lack of control, (5) time, (6) reduction of other activities, and (7) continuance. EDS has been validated in many independent studies in several cultures (e.g., Costa, Cuzzocrea, Hausenblas, Larcan, & Oliva, 2012; Mónok et al., 2012; Symons Downs et al., 2004). The full EDS can be found in the appendix of this chapter.

In contrast to the EDS, the EDQ aims to measure compulsive exercise behavior as a multidimensional construct. It can be used in assessing compulsion in many different forms of physical activities. The questionnaire comprises the following eight subscales: (1) interference with social/family/work life, (2) positive reward, (3) withdrawal symptoms, (4) exercise for weight control, (5) insight into problem, (6) exercise for social reasons, (7) exercise for health reasons, and (8) stereotyped behavior.

To generate a quick and easily administrable tool for surface screening of exercise addiction, Terry, Szabo, and Griffiths (2004) developed the Exercise Addiction Inventory (EAI), a short six-item instrument aimed at identifying the risk of exercise addiction. The EAI assesses the six common symptoms of addictive behaviors: (1) salience, (2) mood modification, (3) tolerance, (4) withdrawal symptoms, (5) social conflict, and (6) relapse. The EAI has been psychometrically investigated and has relatively high internal consistency and convergent validity with the EDS (Griffiths, Szabo, & Terry, 2005; Terry et al., 2004). This assessment measure is also reprinted in this chapter's appendix.

Table 13.1 Instruments for Assessing Exercise Addiction

Instrument	Type	Number of Items	Number of Subscales	Areas Covered or Factors Identified	Theoretical Underpinnings	Empirical Underpinnings	Comments
Obligatory Exercise Questionnaire (OEQ) (Ackard et al., 2002; Pasman & Thompson, 1988)	4-point Likert scale	20	3	- Exercise fixation - Exercise frequency - Exercise commitment	Assesses psychological aspects of obligatory exercise	EFA	Assesses only certain aspects of exercise dependence
Exercise Dependence Scale (EDS) (Hausenblas & Symons Downs, 2002b)*	6-point Likert scale	21	7	- Tolerance - Withdrawal effects - Continuance - Lack of control - Reductions in other activities - Time - Intention	*DSM-IV*	CFA	
Exercise Dependence Questionnaire (EDQ) (Ogden et al., 1997)	7-point Likert scale	29	8	- Social-occupational interference - Positive reward - Withdrawal symptoms - Exercise for weight control - Insight into problem - Exercise for social reasons - Exercise for health reasons - Stereotyped behavior		EFA; Cronbach's alpha: 0.52–0.81	

Exercise Addiction Inventory (EAI) (Terry, Szabo, & Griffiths, 2004)*	5-point Likert scale	6	1	Salience, mood modification, tolerance, withdrawal symptoms, conflict, relapse	Based on Brown's (1993) general components of addictions	Cronbach's alpha = 0.84	
Bodybuilding Dependence Scale (BDS) (Smith & Hale, 2004; Smith, Hale, & Collins, 1998)	Likert scale	9	3	- Social dependence - Training dependence - Mastery dependence	-	EFA, CFA	Specific to body-building
Commitment to Exercise Scale (CES) (Davis, Brewer, & Ratusny, 1993)	Uses a continuum line with bipolar adjectives on either end OR 4-point Likert scale	8	2	- Pathological aspects of exercising - Obligatory aspects of exercising	- Assesses the psychological commitment one has to exercising - Takes a dimensional approach to exercise	EFA; Cronbach's alpha = 0.77	Correlations between the 2 factors = 0.42

Note: EFA = exploratory factor analysis; CFA = confirmatory factor analysis.
*Included in Appendix of this chapter.

There are several other instruments available for assessing exercise addiction. However, they are either rarely adopted in research or are aimed at a specific form of physical activity. For instance, the Bodybuilding Dependency Scale (BDS; Smith et al., 1998) was developed to specifically assess compulsive training in bodybuilding and has satisfactory reliability (Smith & Hale, 2005; Smith et al., 1998). It comprises three subscales: (1) social dependence (i.e., the need to be in the gym), (2) training dependence (i.e., compulsion to train), and (3) mastery dependence (i.e., the need to control training). A more general but seldom adopted instrument is the Exercise Beliefs Questionnaire (EBQ; Loumidisa & Wells, 1998) that gages individual thoughts and beliefs about exercise and is based on four factors: (1) social desirability, (2) physical appearance, (3) mental and emotional functioning, and (4) vulnerability to disease and aging. Empirical testing shows the instrument to have acceptable psychometric properties. Another tool is the Exercise Dependence Interview (EXDI) (Bamber, Cockerill, Rodgers, et al., 2000). This tool assesses not only compulsive exercising but also eating disorders. The EXDI gages excessive engagement in physical activity in the past 3 months prior to the date of assessment, the associated thoughts, and their association with eating behavior. It also determines the self-appraisal of exercise dependence and exercise habits. However, one of the major limitations of this measure is that no psychometric properties have been reported.

Another scale developed by Davis, Brewer, and Ratusny (1993)—the Commitment to Exercise Scale (CES)—examines the pathological aspects of exercising (e.g., continued training despite injuries) and compulsory activities (e.g., feeling guilty when exercise is not fulfilled). The CES has a satisfactory level of reliability. Finally, the Exercise Orientation Questionnaire (EOQ) (Yates, Edman, Crago, & Crowell, 2001) measures attitudes toward exercise and related behaviors. The EOQ comprises six factors: (1) self-control, (2) orientation to exercise, (3) self-loathing, (4) weight reduction, (5) competition, and (6) identity. It should be highlighted that among the instruments outlined, the most popular currently are the EDS and the EAI (due to its brevity and easy scoring). Research has shown that when employed together, these two instruments yield comparable results (Mónok et al., 2012).

EPIDEMIOLOGY

Studies of exercise addiction prevalence have been carried out almost exclusively on American and British samples of regular exercisers. In five studies carried out among university students, Hausenblas and Downs (2002b) reported that between 3.4% and 13.4% of their samples were at high risk of exercise addiction. Griffiths, Szabo, and Terry (2005) reported that 3.0% of a British sample of sport science and psychology students were identified as at risk of exercise addiction. These research-based estimates are in concordance with the argument that exercise addiction is *relatively* rare (de Coverley Veale, 1995; Szabo, 2000) especially when compared to other addictions (Sussman, Lisha, & Griffiths, 2011).

Among those who are also professionally connected to sports, the prevalence may be even higher. For example, Szabo and Griffiths (2007) found that 6.9% of British sport science students were at risk of exercise addiction. However, in other studies in which more intense exercisers were studied, much higher estimates have generally been found. Blaydon and Linder (2002) reported that 30.4% of triathletes could be diagnosed with primary exercise addiction, and a further 21.6% with secondary exercise addiction. In another study, 26% of 240 male and 25% of 84 female runners were classified as "obligatory exercisers" (Slay, Hayaki, Napolitano, & Brownell, 1998). Lejoyeux et al. (2008) found that 42% of clients of a Parisian fitness room were identified as exercise addicts. Recently, he reported lower rates of just under 30% (Lejoyeux, Guillot, Chalvin, Petit, & Lequen, 2012). However, one study that surveyed 95 "ultra-marathoners" (who typically run 100 km races) reported only three people (3.2%) as at risk for exercise addiction (Allegre, Therme, & Griffiths, 2007). Gender can also have a moderating effect on ideal-weight goals and exercise dependence symptoms (Cook, Hausenblas, & Rossi, 2013). However, it is evident that in addition to differences in the applied measures and criteria, these appreciable disparities in the estimates may be attributable to the sample selection, small sample size, and the sampling method. With the exception of the study by Lejoyeux et al. (2012) (that applied consecutive sampling), all the aforementioned studies used convenience sampling. To date, the only national representative study examining exercise addiction was carried out by Mónok et al. (2012). This study surveyed a Hungarian adult population aged 18–64 years (n = 2,710) and assessed exercise addiction using both the EAI and the EDS. Results showed that 6.2% (EDS) and 10.1% (EAI) of the population were characterized as nondependent-symptomatic exercisers, while the proportion of the people at risk for exercise dependence was 0.3% and 0.5%, respectively.

COMORBIDITY

As noted earlier, there is a strong association between exercise addiction and various forms of eating disorders (Sussman et al., 2011). Furthermore, depressive and anxiety problems are also often present among exercise-dependent persons. Several studies have reported that disordered eating behavior is often (if not always) accompanied by exaggerated levels of physical exercise. The reverse relationship has also been established. Individuals affected by exercise addiction often (but not always) show an excessive concern about their body image, weight, and control over their diet (Blaydon & Lindner, 2002; Klein et al., 2004; Lyons & Cromey, 1989; Sundgot-Borgen, 1994). This comorbidity makes it difficult to establish what the primary disorder is. This dilemma was empirically investigated by using trait and personality-oriented investigations. In an early, but widely cited controversial study, Yates, Leehey, and Shisslak (1983) concluded that addicted male long-distance runners resembled anorexic patients on a number of personality dispositions (e.g., introversion, inhibition of anger, high expectations, depression, and excessive use of denial) and labeled the similarity as the "anorexia-analogue" hypothesis.

To further test the hypothesis, Yates et al. (1983) examined the personality characteristics of 60 male obligatory exercisers and then compared their profiles to those of clinical patients diagnosed with anorexia nervosa. While the study did not lend support to the hypothesis, Yates and colleagues claimed that running and extreme dieting were both dangerous attempts to establish an identity, as either addicted to exercise or being anorexic. The study has been criticized for a number of shortcomings including the lack of supporting data, poor methodology, lack of relevance to the average runner, over-reliance on extreme cases or individuals, and exaggerating the similarities between the groups (Blumenthal, O'Toole, & Chang, 1984). Indeed, later investigations have failed to find similarities between the personality characteristics of people affected by exercise addiction and those suffering from eating disorders (e.g., Blumenthal et al., 1984; Coen & Ogles, 1993). Therefore, the anorexia analogue hypothesis has failed to secure empirical support. Numerous studies have further examined the relationship between exercise addiction and eating disorders (for a review, see Szabo, 2010), but no consensus has emerged. One reason for the inconsistent findings may be attributed to the fact that the extent of comorbidity could vary from case to case depending on personality predispositions, the underlying psychological problem that has led to exercise addiction, and/or the interaction of the two, as well as the form and severity of the eating disorder.

ETIOLOGY

Physiological Explanations

As a physiological explanation for exercise addiction, perhaps the oldest, most popular, and arguably most controversial among runners and many other exercisers—in light of the scientific evidence for it—is the "runners' high" hypothesis. It has long been reported that after intensive running, it is not fatigue or exhaustion that runners report but an intense feeling of euphoria. It has been described as a sensation of flying, characterized by effortless movements that have become the legendary goal referred to as "the zone" (Goldberg, 1988). The sensation has been ascribed to beta-endorphin activity in the brain. Research has shown that the human body produces endorphins that—similarly to morphine—may cause dependence (Farrell, Gates, Maksud, & Morgan, 1982). Exercise intensity and the duration of exercise are crucial factors in increasing peripheral beta-endorphin concentration. Indeed, exercise needs to be performed at above 60% of the individual's maximal oxygen uptake (VO_2 max; Goldfarb & Jamurtas, 1997). Furthermore, it needs to be sustained for at least 3 minutes to detect changes in beta-endorphin levels (Kjaer & Dela, 1996). The dilemma is that the changes observed in beta-endorphin levels were seen in the plasma and, therefore, it is a peripheral change. However, because of its chemical structure, beta-endorphins cannot cross the blood brain barrier (BBB), meaning that changes in plasma levels may not be accompanied by simultaneous changes in the brain.

In spite of this serious dilemma, some researchers believe that endogenous opiates in the plasma also act centrally and, therefore, may be used to trace central nervous system activity (Biddle & Mutrie, 1991). Currently, this hypothesis relies on the speculation that met-encephalin and dynorphin, two other endogenous opioids, possess a modification mechanism that could possibly transport them across the BBB (Sforzo, 1988). Unfortunately, direct measurement of changes in brain beta-endorphins involves dissecting the brain and performing radioimmunoassay on its slices. Similar studies with rats have revealed an increase in the opioid receptor binding sites after exercise (Sforzo, Seeger, Pert, Pert, & Dotson, 1986). Nevertheless, the evidence for the runners' high hypothesis and its mediation through changes in beta-endorphin levels in the brain remains inconclusive.

Another physiological explanation is based on Thompson and Blanton's (1987) research. The authors argue that regular exercise, especially aerobic exercise like running, if performed for a sustained period, results in lower basal heart rate, reflecting a training effect or the adaptation of the organism to exercise. The training effect is also accompanied by lower sympathetic activity at rest and, in parallel, lower levels of arousal, which may be experienced as lethargic or energy-lacking states. According to Thomson and Blanton, the lower arousal initiates the individual to do something about it (i.e., to increase arousal) for the sake of optimal functioning. For avid exercisers, the obvious way to increase the arousal level is via exercise. However, the effects of exercise are only temporary and, therefore, further bouts of exercise may be needed to achieve the optimal state of arousal. Moreover, not only the frequency but also the intensity of exercise may need to increase due to progressive training effect (i.e., tolerance).

The *thermogenic regulation hypothesis* is based on the physiological fact that intense physical activity increases body temperature. Warmth in the body may trigger a relaxing state with concomitant reduction in anxiety. Consequently, physical exercise reduces anxiety and aids in relaxation as a consequence of increased body temperature (De Vries, 1981; Morgan & O'Connor, 1988). Lower levels of state anxiety and higher states of relaxation act as positive reinforcers, or motivational incentives, for the continuation of exercise behavior. The pleasant psychological state experienced through the relaxing and anxiety-relieving effects of exercise conditions people to turn to exercise whenever they experience anxiety. Higher levels of anxiety may be associated with a greater need for exercise and more frequent and intense workouts. Therefore, in stressful situations, the frequency, duration, and the intensity of exercise may progressively increase (i.e., develop tolerance) to obtain a stronger antidote to stress and anxiety.

Empirical observations have shown that levels of circulating catecholamines increase following exercise. This led to the formulation of the *catecholamine hypothesis* (Cousineau et al., 1977). Catecholamines, among other functions, are involved in both the stress response and the sympathetic response to intense physical exercise. According to this hypothesis, brain catecholaminergic activity is altered through exercise. Knowing that central catecholamine levels are involved in regulating both mood and affect, and additionally play an important role in the reward system, the changes in brain catecholamine levels following exercise are an attractive explanation for the addictive nature of exercise. However, there is no conclusive evidence for this conjecture. Indeed, similarly to the beta-endorphin dilemma, it is unclear whether the peripheral changes in catecholamine levels have an effect on brain catecholamine levels or vice versa. Moreover, the dynamics of changes in brain catecholamine levels during exercise in humans are unknown because direct measurement in the human brain is not possible.

Psychological Explanations

Szabo (1995) proposed a *cognitive appraisal hypothesis* for understanding the etiology of exercise addiction. According to this theory, once the habitual exerciser uses exercise as a means of coping with stress, the affected individual learns to depend on (and need) exercise at times of stress. The individual is convinced that exercise is a healthy means of coping with stress, as recommended in both scholastic and public media sources. Therefore, the person uses rationalization to explain the exaggerated amounts of exercise, which slowly but progressively takes its toll on other obligations and normal daily activities. If unforeseen events prevent the person from exercising or require the person to reduce the amount of daily exercise, negative psychological feelings emerge. These appear in the form of irritability, guilt, anxiousness, sluggishness, etc. These collective feelings are thought to represent the withdrawal symptoms experienced due to a lack of exercise.

When exercise is used to cope with stress, apart from the negative psychological feelings, there is also a loss of the coping mechanism (i.e., exercise). Concomitantly, exercisers lose control over the stressful situation(s) that they typically deal with through exercise. The loss of the coping mechanism, followed by the loss of control over stress, generates an increased perception of vulnerability to stress that further amplifies the negative psychological feelings associated with the lack of exercise. The mounting pressure urges the individual to resume exercise even at the expense of the other obligations in his or her daily life. Obviously, while exercise provides an instant reduction in the negative psychological feelings, the ignorance or neglect of other social and work obligations can result in relationship conflict, detriments to work or education, or even loss of job, which together cause further stress. The addicted exerciser is then trapped in a vicious cycle needing more exercise to deal with the consistently increasing life stress, part of which is caused by exercise itself.

The *affect regulation hypothesis* suggests that exercise has a dual effect on mood (Hamer & Karageorghis, 2007). First, it increases positive *affect* and, therefore, contributes to an improved general *mood* state (defined as prolonged psychological feeling states lasting for several hours or even days). Second, it decreases negative affect or the temporary states of guilt, irritability, sluggishness, and anxiety associated with missed exercise or training sessions. Through this relief, exercise further contributes to improved general mood state (Hamer

& Karageorghis, 2007). However, the affect-regulating consequences of exercise are temporary, and the longer the interval between two exercise sessions, the experience of negative affect becomes more likely. In fact, after prolonged periods of abstention from exercise, these negative affective states become severe deprivation sensations and/or withdrawal symptoms that can be relieved only through further exercise. Therefore, as the cycle continues, further increasing amounts of exercise are needed to experience improvement in affect and general mood. Progressively, the inter-exercise rest periods decrease as a way of preventing the surfacing of withdrawal symptoms.

Etiology from a Behavioral Perspective

The incentive or motive for fulfilling planned exercise is an important distinguishing characteristic between addicted and nonaddicted exercisers. Indeed, people exercise for unique reasons. The reason is often an intangible reward such as feeling in shape, looking good, being with friends, staying healthy, building muscles, losing weight, etc. The personal experience of the anticipated reward strengthens the exercise behavior. Behaviorists postulate that all human behavior can be understood and explained through reinforcement and punishment. Paradoxically, exercise addiction may be seen as self-punishing behavior. It is a rare form of addiction in contrast to alcohol, tobacco, or drug use because it requires substantial physical effort and stubborn will power.

Individuals addicted to exercise may be motivated via negative reinforcement (e.g., to avoid withdrawal symptoms) as well as via positive reinforcement (e.g., to enjoy an aspect of exercise, to experience the runner's high [Pierce, Eastman, Tripathi, Olson, & Dewey, 1993; Szabo, 1995]). Exercise for negative reinforcement is not a characteristic of the committed exercisers who wish to improve and to enjoy their exercise (Szabo, 1995). Indeed, committed exercisers maintain their exercise for benefiting or gaining from their activity and, thus, their behavior is motivated via positive reinforcement. However, addicted exercisers *have to* exercise, or else something bad could happen to them. Their exercise may be a chore that needs to be fulfilled, or otherwise an unwanted event would occur such as the inability to cope with stress, or gaining weight, becoming moody, etc. Every time a person undertakes behavior to avoid something negative, bad, and/or unpleasant, the motive behind that behavior appears as a negative reinforcement.

In these situations, the person involved *has to do it* as opposed to *wants to do it*. Duncan (1974)—in relation to drug addiction—has suggested that addiction is almost identical with, and semantically just another name for, avoidance or escape behavior when the unpleasant or painful feeling is being negatively reinforced by drug taking. In this view, people addicted to exercise reach for a means—with which they have had past relief-inducing experience—that provides them with temporary escape from an ongoing state of stress or hassle with daily challenges. In Duncan's view, all addictions represent similar negatively reinforced behaviors. Duncan has also argued that negative reinforcement is a powerful means for sustaining highly frequent and persistent behaviors. Animals that can escape a noxious stimulus or event by pressing a bar will often do so to the point of ignoring other instinctual activities such as eating, sleeping, and sexual activity. Avoidance behaviors are highly resistant to extinction, and even when they appear to have been finally eliminated, they often reoccur spontaneously. For this reason, the relapse rate in addictions is high. In Duncan's view, the intensity, compulsiveness, and proneness to relapse that are important components of addictive behaviors result from the negative reinforcement of the behavior.

TREATMENT

Therapeutic guidelines for the treatment of exercise addiction have not yet been developed with the appropriate theoretical background and methodology. This is primarily due to the fact that this form of addiction does not appear as a distinct disorder in the standard diagnostic manuals currently in use (e.g., *DSM-IV-TR, DSM-5,* and *ICD-10*). Developing therapeutic guidelines for exercise addiction is also rendered more difficult by the fact that the incidence of this disorder is comparatively low, and sufferers rarely seek expert help. Another explanation for the difficulty involved in developing a therapeutic protocol may be the fact that—as discussed previously—opinions are divided on whether exercise addiction is a distinct pathology (Blaydon & Lindner, 2002) or rather a concomitant factor or manifestation of an eating disorder (Bamber, Cockerill, & Carroll, 2000). However, there is a very strong correlation between exercise addiction and eating disorders, based on the published data. As individuals suffering from the two conditions demonstrate similarities along a number of dimensions (Klein et al., 2004; Lyons & Cromey, 1989; Sundgot-Borgen, 1994; Yates et al., 1983), the guidelines for treating eating disorders may therefore offer some guidance for therapy for exercise addicts.

Two psychotherapeutic interventions have proven to be effective in the treatment of various types of substance and behavioral dependencies: motivational interviewing (Miller & Rollnick, 2002) and cognitive-behavioral therapy. Although there is a lack of clinical trials investigating their utility with exercise dependence, these two approaches may be effective when treating exercise addiction. Cognitive-behavioral therapy has also been proven to be among the most effective methods in treating eating disorders (Fernandez-Aranda et al., 1998; Hay & Bacaltchuk, 2001; Wilson, Fairburn, & Agras, 1997). Therefore, this approach may also be effective and beneficial in treating exercise addiction. The adaptation of the treatment of substance and behavioral dependencies may also be promising.

With exercise addiction, as with other conditions, an accurate diagnosis and differential diagnosis are critical to an appropriate therapeutic plan. It is important to be aware of co-occurring disorders, especially if it is an eating disorder, and both must be treated. If only exercise addiction is treated, a person may resort to increased bulimic or anorexic behavior in order to maintain low weight levels (Freimuth, Moniz, & Kim, 2011). The presence of other associated comorbid disorders (e.g., anxiety, depression) may serve to perpetuate a vicious cycle, thus potentially causing the person's condition to deteriorate further. It is also essential to distinguish exercise addiction from obsessive-compulsive disorder, and in terms of therapy, it is imperative for the clinician to determine whether or not excessive exercise is a response to obsession. Furthermore, it is important to ascertain whether or not a person who shows symptoms of exercise addiction is suffering from personality disorder. In such cases, therapy aimed at personality disorder may also be necessary to treat exercise addiction effectively.

When one is treating exercise addiction, abstinence from exercise may not be the required goal, because exercise has many benefits for health. A typical treatment goal may be to return to moderate and controlled exercise. In some cases, a different form of exercise may be recommended (Freimuth et al., 2011). Furthermore, one of the first steps is to motivate the client for treatment, for which motivational interviewing techniques can be quite useful (Miller & Rollnick, 2002). Clients must be aware that their excessive exercise can have negative consequences and should be modified in a more moderate and controlled direction. When the person is motivated for treatment, cognitive-behavioral therapy may be the next step. A main part of cognitive therapy is identifying and correcting (via cognitive restructuring) the person's negative automatic thoughts that result in maladaptive behaviors and negative emotions (Beck, 1976, 1995). For example, negative thoughts can involve the idea that the person is not able to do anything when not exercising (Johnston, Reilly, & Kremer, 2011) or the conception that exercise is the only way to reduce negative feelings.

Case Vignette: Joanna

Joanna is a 25-year-old, well-educated female, from a stable family background, who realized that she had a problem surrounding exercise. She describes herself as being in excellent physical condition except for an injury sustained to her arm during a Jiu-Jitsu session. Here, Joanna's behavior is described in terms of the main components of addiction (i.e., salience, tolerance, withdrawal, mood modification, conflict, loss of control, relapse, and negative consequences due to the behavior; Kurimay, Griffiths, Berczik, & Demetrovics, 2013).

- Salience: Jiu-Jitsu is the most important activity in Joanna's life. Even when not actually engaged in the activity, she is thinking about the next training session or competition. She estimates that she spends approximately 6 hours a day (and sometimes much more) involved in training (e.g., weight training, jogging, general exercise). At university, she missed one of her exams to attend a Jiu-Jitsu competition in another part of the country. She fell behind in her university coursework due to exercise because she claimed she could not find the time to study.
- Tolerance: Joanna started Jiu-Jitsu at an evening class once a week during her teenage years and built up slowly over a period of about 5 years. She now exercises every single day, and the lengths of the sessions have become longer and longer (suggesting tolerance). When not engaged in Jiu-Jitsu, she has to do some other form of exercise. This can be seen as a form of cross-tolerance.
- Withdrawal: Joanna claims she becomes highly agitated and irritable if she is unable to exercise. When her arm was bandaged because of an arm injury, she went for 3-hour jogs instead. She claims she also gets headaches and feels nauseous if she goes for more than a day without training or has to miss a scheduled session.
- Mood modification: Joanna experiences mood changes in a number of ways. She feels very high and "buzzed up" if she has done well in a Jiu-Jitsu competition (especially so if she wins). She also feels high if she has trained hard and for a long time.
- Conflict: Joanna's relationship with her long-term partner ended as a result of her exercise. She claimed she never spent much time with him and was not even bothered about their breakup. Her university work suffered because of the lack of time and concentration.
- Loss of control: Joanna claims she cannot stop herself engaging in exercise when she "gets the urge." Once she has started, she has to do a minimum of a few hours of exercise. She claims she has a total lack of concentration during lectures. She also claims she has an inability to study for exams unless she has done her exercise.

Continued

Case Vignette: Joanna—cont'd

- Relapse: Joanna can only go a few days with no exercise before her day-to-day living becomes absolutely unbearable. If she misses a Jiu-Jitsu competition, she is just as bothered. The thought that she could have won a medal but was not there is particularly painful for her. She has continually tried to stop and/or cut down but claims she cannot. She becomes highly anxious if she is unable to engage in exercise and then has to go out and train to make herself feel better. She is well aware that exercise has taken over her life but feels powerless to stop it.
- Negative consequences: Joanna spends money beyond her means to maintain her exercising habit (e.g., on entrance fees for weight training, swimming). She also spends a lot of time in between two towns and therefore has several dual memberships at various health clubs. She is financially in debt not just because she is a student, but also because she funds herself to attend Jiu-Jitsu competitions across the country. She has resorted to socially unacceptable means (e.g., stealing) to get money to fund herself. She is worried about her injured arm, which is never given enough time to heal properly before she gets the urge to take part in Jiu-Jitsu training and competitions again. Her doctor has advised her to give up the sport because he thinks she will do permanent damage to her arm. This is something she feels she is totally unable to do even if it means permanent damage.

There is little doubt that Joanna is addicted to exercise and that she displays all the core components of any bona fide behavioral addiction and scored 28 out of 30 on the EAI. Joanna displays no other comorbid addictions as she (a) believes any drugs (including alcohol and nicotine) would impair her physical performance) and (b) has little time in her life for other activities that can be classified as behavioral addictions because exercise takes up so much time in her life. Exercise is the most important thing in her life, and the number of hours engaged in physical activity per week has increased substantially over a 5-year period. She displays withdrawal symptoms when she does not exercise and experiences euphoric experiences related to various aspects of her exercising (e.g., training hard, winning competitions). She experiences conflict over exercise in many areas of her life and acknowledges she has a problem. Furthermore, she has lost friends, her relationship has broken down, her academic work has suffered, and she has considerable debt. She was advised to seek psychological help by those close to her, but she has not taken the advice. Given that Joanna (1) has very fixed beliefs about the psychological and physical benefits of exercise and (2) is so motivated by exercise and believes the advantages far outweigh the disadvantages, she is perhaps a case that would be best treated via a concurrent course of both motivational interviewing and cognitive-behavioral therapy.

In relation to targeted interventions, it is essential to clarify which effects led to the development of the addiction in a particular individual, and which factors and situations perpetuate the disorder. It is of key importance during therapy to establish the individual, dysfunctional meaning associated with the body and exercise and to correct both this and a potentially distorted body image through therapy. Furthermore, it is important to work with the person to develop adaptive, alternative behaviors and coping methods to replace excessive exercise. Contingency management, as a behavioral strategy, has also been recommended (Adams, 2009). Such individuals are tested regularly to make sure they are not engaging in the undesired behavior—in this case uncontrolled and excessive exercising. Such individuals get rewards when they pass the test and are penalized when they fail. Adaptive, alternative behaviors that substitute for excessive exercise are also rewarded. In more severe cases, it is necessary to identify and correct dysfunctional beliefs and maladaptive schemas that can contribute to and/or cause a disturbed relation to self, body, and exercise.

The use of education may also be an effective step in the treatment of exercise dependence (Adams, 2009). Adams and Kirkby (2001) claim that individuals with exercise dependence have a poor understanding of the negative health consequences of excessive exercising, and of the mechanism of exercise adaptation and the need for rest between exercise sessions. Qualitative studies also suggest that clients are insufficiently attuned to the adverse effects generated by their behavior (Johnston et al., 2011). Therefore, it is imperative that the patient is given clarification as to the real, harmful effects and complications that can accompany extreme exercise. Furthermore, the public promotion of healthy, appropriate exercise patterns may reduce the incidence of exercise dependence.

ACKNOWLEDGMENTS

Zsolt Demetrovics acknowledges financial support of the János Bolyai Research Fellowship awarded by the Hungarian Academy of Science. This work was supported by the Hungarian Scientific Research Fund (grant number: 83884).

REFERENCES

Ackard, D. M., Brehm, B. J., & Steffen, J. J. (2002). Exercise and eating disorders in college-aged women: Profiling excessive exercisers. *Eating Disorders, 10*(1), 31–47.

Adams, J. (2009). Understanding exercise dependence. *Journal of Contemporary Psychotherapy, 39*, 231–240.

Adams, J., & Kirkby, R. J. (2001). Exercise dependence and overtraining: The physiological and psychological consequences of excessive exercise. *Sports Medicine, Training and Rehabilitation, 10*, 199–222.

Allegre, B., Souville, M., Therme, P., & Griffiths, M. D. (2006). Definitions and measures of exercise dependence. *Addiction Research and Theory*, *14*, 631–646.

Allegre, B., Therme, P., & Griffiths, M. D. (2007). Individual factors and the context of physical activity in exercise dependence: A prospective study of 'ultra-marathoners.' *International Journal of Mental Health and Addiction*, *5*, 233–243.

American Psychiatric Association. (2000). *Diagnostic and statistical manual for mental disorders* (4th ed., text revision). Washington, DC: Author.

American Psychiatric Association. (2013). *Diagnostic and statistical manual of mental disorders* (5th ed.). Washington, DC: Author.

Bamber, D. J., Cockerill, I. M., & Carroll, D. (2000). The pathological status of exercise dependence. *British Journal of Sports Medicine*, *34*(2), 125–132.

Bamber, D. J., Cockerill, I. M., Rodgers, S., & Carroll, D. (2000). "It's exercise or nothing": A qualitative analysis of exercise dependence. *British Journal of Sports Medicine*, *34*(6), 423–430.

Bamber, D. J., Cockerill, I. M., Rodgers, S., & Carroll, D. (2003). Diagnostic criteria for exercise dependence in women. *British Journal of Sports Medicine*, *37*(5), 393–400.

Beck, A. T. (1976). *Cognitive therapy and the emotional disorders*. New York: International University Press.

Beck, J. S. (1995). *Cognitive therapy: Basics and beyond*. New York: Guilford Press.

Berczik, K., Szabo, A., Griffiths, M. D., Kurimay, T., Kun, B., Urban, R., et al. (2012). Exercise addiction: Symptoms, diagnosis, epidemiology, and etiology. *Substance Use and Misuse*, *47*(4), 403–417.

Biddle, S. J. H., Gorely, T., & Stensel, D. J. (2004). Health-enhancing physical activity and sedentary behaviour in children and adolescents. *Journal of Sports Sciences*, *22*(8), 679–701.

Biddle, S. J. H., & Mutrie, N. (1991). *Psychology of physical activity and exercise: A health-related persective*. London: Springer Verlag.

Blair, S. N., Kohl, H. W., 3rd, Paffenbarger, R. S., Jr., Clark, D. G., Cooper, K. H., & Gibbons, L. W. (1989). Physical fitness and all-cause mortality. A prospective study of healthy men and women. *JAMA*, *262*(17), 2395–2401.

Blaydon, M. J., & Lindner, K. J. (2002). Eating disorders and exercise dependence in triathletes. *Eating Disorders*, *10*(1), 49–60.

Blaydon, M. J., Lindner, K. J., & Kerr, J. H. (2002). Metamotivational characteristics of eating-disordered and exercise-dependent triathletes: An application of reversal theory. *Psychology of Sport and Exercise*, *3*(3), 223–236.

Blaydon, M. J., Lindner, K. J., & Kerr, J. H. (2004). Metamotivational characteristics of exercise dependence and eating disorders in highly active amateur sport participants. *Personality and Individual Differences*, *36*(6), 1419–1432.

Blumenthal, J. A., O'Toole, L. C., & Chang, J. L. (1984). Is running an analogue of anorexia nervosa? An empirical study of obligatory running and anorexia nervosa. *JAMA*, *252*(4), 520–523.

Brown, R. I. F. (1993). Some contributions of the study of gambling to the study of other addictions. In W. R. Eadington & J. A. Cornelius (Eds.), *Gambling behavior and problem gambling* (pp. 241–272). Reno: University of Nevada Press.

Carmack, M. A., & Martens, R. (1979). Measuring commitment to running: A survey of runners' attitudes and mental states. *Journal of Sport Psychology*, *1*, 25–42.

Caspersen, C. J., Powell, K. E., & Christenson, G. M. (1985). Physical activity, exercise, and physical fitness: Definitions and distinctions for health-related research. *Public Health Reports*, *100*(2), 126–131.

Cockerill, I. M., & Riddington, M. E. (1996). Exercise dependence and associated disorders: A review. *Counselling Psychology Quarterly*, *9*(2), 119–129.

Coen, S. P., & Ogles, B. M. (1993). Psychological characteristics of the obligatory runner: A critical examination of the anorexia analogue hypothesis. *Journal of Sport & Exercise Psychology*, *15*(3), 338–354.

Cook, B., Hausenblas, H., & Rossi, J. (2013). The moderating effect of gender on ideal-weight goals and exercise dependence symptoms. *Journal of Behavioral Addictions, 2,* (in press).

Costa, S., Cuzzocrea, F., Hausenblas, H. A., Larcan, R., & Oliva, P. (2012). Psychometric examination and factorial validity of the exercise dependence scale-revised in Italian exercisers. *Journal of Behavioral Addictions, 1*(4), 186–190.

Cousineau, D., Ferguson, R. J., de Champlain, J., Gauthier, P., Cote, P., & Bourassa, M. (1977). Catecholamines in coronary sinus during exercise in man before and after training. *Journal of Applied Physiology, 43*(5), 801–806.

Dalle Grave, R., Calugi, S., & Marchesini, G. (2008). Compulsive exercise to control shape or weight in eating disorders: Prevalence, associated features, and treatment outcome. *Comprehensive Psychiatry, 49*(4), 346–352.

Davis, C. (2000). Exercise abuse. *International Journal of Sport Psychology, 31,* 278–289.

Davis, C., Brewer, H., & Ratusny, D. (1993). Behavioral frequency and psychological commitment: Necessary concepts in the study of excessive exercising. *Journal of Behavioral Medicine, 16*(6), 611–628.

de Coverley Veale, D. M. (1987). Exercise dependence. *British Journal of Addiction, 82*(7), 735–740.

de Coverley Veale, D. M. (1995). Does primary exercise dependence really exist? In J. Annett, B. Cripps & H. Steinberg (Eds.), *Exercise addiction. Motivation and participation in sport and exercise* (pp. 1–5). Leicester, UK: The British Psychological Society.

De Vries, H. A. (1981). Tranquilizer effect of exercise: A critical review. *The Physician and Sportsmedicine, 9*(11), 47–53.

Demetrovics, Z., & Griffiths, M. D. (2012). Behavioral addictions: Past, present and future. *Journal of Behavioral Addictions, 1*(1), 1–2.

Duncan, D. F. (1974). Drug abuse as a coping mechanism. *American Journal of Psychiatry, 131*(6), 724.

Farrell, P. A., Gates, W. K., Maksud, M. G., & Morgan, W. P. (1982). Increases in plasma beta-endorphin/beta-lipotropin immunoreactivity after treadmill running in humans. *Journal of Applied Physiology, 52*(5), 1245–1249.

Fernandez-Aranda, F., Bel, M., Jimenez, S., Vinuales, M., Turon, J., & Vallejo, J. (1998). Outpatient group therapy for anorexia nervosa: A preliminary study. *Eating and Weight Disorders, 3,* 1–6.

Folsom, A. R., Caspersen, C. J., Taylor, H. L., Jacobs, D. R., Jr., Luepker, R. V., Gomez-Marin, O., et al. (1985). Leisure time physical activity and its relationship to coronary risk factors in a population-based sample. The Minnesota Heart Survey. *American Journal of Epidemiology, 121*(4), 570–579.

Freimuth, M., Moniz, S., & Kim, S. R. (2011). Clarifying exercise addiction: Differential diagnosis, co-occurring disorders, and phases of addiction. *International Journal of Environmental Research and Public Health, 8*(10), 4069–4081.

Furst, D. M., & Germone, K. (1993). Negative addiction in male and female runners and exercisers. *Perceptual and Motor Skills,* 77(1), 192–194.

Glasser, W. (1976). *Positive addiction.* New York: Harper & Row.

Goldberg, A. (1988). *The sports mind: A workbook of mental skills for athletes.* Northampton, MA: Competitive Advantage.

Goldfarb, A. H., & Jamurtas, A. Z. (1997). Beta-endorphin response to exercise. An update. *Sports Medicine, 24*(1), 8–16.

Griffiths, M. D. (1996). Behavioural addictions: An issue for everybody? *Journal of Workplace Learning, 8*(3), 19–25.

Griffiths, M. D. (1997). Exercise addiction: A case study. *Addiction Research, 5,* 161–168.

Griffiths, M. D. (2005). A 'components' model of addiction within a biopsychosocial framework. *Journal of Substance Use, 10,* 191–197.

Griffiths, M. D., Szabo, A., & Terry, A. (2005). The exercise addiction inventory: A quick and easy screening tool for health practitioners. *British Journal of Sports Medicine, 39*(6), e30.

Hailey, B. J., & Bailey, L. A. (1982). Negative addiction in runners: A quantitative approach. *Journal of Sport Behavior*, *5*(3), 150–154.
Hamer, M., & Karageorghis, C. I. (2007). Psychobiological mechanisms of exercise dependence. *Sports Medicine*, *37*(6), 477–484.
Hausenblas, H. A., & Symons Downs, D. (2002a). Exercise dependence: A systematic review. *Psychology of Sport and Exercise*, *3*(2), 89–123.
Hausenblas, H. A., & Symons Downs, D. (2002b). How much is too much? The development and validation of the Exercise Dependence Scale. *Psychology & Health*, *17*, 387–404.
Hay, P. J., & Bacaltchuk, J. (2001). Bulimia nervosa. *BMJ (Clinical Research Ed.)*, *323*(7), 33–37.
Johnston, O., Reilly, J., & Kremer, J. (2011). Excessive exercise: From quantitative categorisation to a qualitative continuum approach. *European Eating Disorders Review*, *19*(3), 237–248.
Kjaer, M., & Dela, F. (1996). Endocrine response to exercise. In L. Hoffman-Goetz (Ed.), *Exercise and immune function* (pp. 6–8). Boca Raton, FL: CRC.
Klein, D. A., Bennett, A. S., Schebendach, J., Foltin, R. W., Devlin, M. J., & Walsh, B. T. (2004). Exercise "addiction" in anorexia nervosa: Model development and pilot data. *CNS Spectr*, *9*(7), 531–537.
Kurimay, T., Griffiths, M. D., Berczik, K., & Demetrovics, Z. (2013). Exercise addiction: The dark side of sports and exercise. In D. A. Baron, C. L. Reardon & S. H. Baron (Eds.), *Clinical sports psychiatry: An international perspective* (pp. 33–43). West Sussex, UK: Wiley-Blackwell.
Lamb, K. L., Roberts, K., & Brodie, D. A. (1990). Self-perceived health among sports participants and non-sports participants. *Social Science and Medicine*, *31*(9), 963–969.
Lejoyeux, M., Avril, M., Richoux, C., Embouazza, H., & Nivoli, F. (2008). Prevalence of exercise dependence and other behavioral addictions among clients of a Parisian fitness room. *Comprehensive Psychiatry*, *49*(4), 353–358.
Lejoyeux, M., Guillot, C., Chalvin, F., Petit, A., & Lequen, V. (2012). Exercise dependence among customers from a Parisian sport shop. *Journal of Behavioral Addictions*, *1*, 28–34.
Lotan, M., Merrick, J., & Carmeli, E. (2005). Physical activity in adolescence. A review with clinical suggestions. *International Journal of Adolescent Medicine and Health*, *17*(1), 13–21.
Loumidisa, K. S., & Wells, A. (1998). Assessment of beliefs in exercise dependence: The development and preliminary validation of the exercise beliefs questionnaire. *Personality and Individual Differences*, *25*(3), 553–567.
Lyons, H. A., & Cromey, R. (1989). Compulsive jogging: Exercise dependence and associated disorder of eating. *Ulster Medical Journal*, *58*(1), 100–102.
Miller, W. R., & Rollnick, S. (2002). *Motivational interviewing: Preparing people for change*. New York: Guilford Press.
Mónok, K., Berczik, K., Urbán, R., Szabó, A., Griffiths, M. D., Farkas, J., et al. (2012). Psychometric properties and concurrent validity of two exercise addiction measures. *A population wide study*, *13*(6), 739–746.
Morgan, W. P. (1979). Negative addiction in runners. *The Physician and Sportsmedicine*, 7, 57–70.
Morgan, W. P., & O'Connor, P. J. (1988). Exercise and mental health. In R. K. Dishman (Ed.), *Exercise adherence: Its impact on public health* (pp. 91–121). Champaign, IL: Human Kinetics.
Morris, M. (1989). Running round the clock. *Running*, *104*, 44–45.
Ogden, J., Veale, D. M., & Summers, Z. (1997). The development and validation of the Exercise Dependence Questionnaire. *Addiction Research*, *5*(4), 343–355.
Paffenbarger, R. S., Jr., Hyde, R. T., Wing, A. L., & Hsieh, C. C. (1986). Physical activity, all-cause mortality, and longevity of college alumni. *New England Journal of Medicine*, *314*(10), 605–613.
Pasman, L. N., & Thompson, J. K. (1988). Body image and eating disturbance in obligatory runners, obligatory weightlifters, and sedentary individuals. *International Journal of Eating Disorders*, 7(6), 759–769.
Pierce, E. F., Eastman, N. W., Tripathi, H. L., Olson, K. G., & Dewey, W. L. (1993). Beta-endorphin response to endurance exercise: Relationship to exercise dependence. *Perceptual and Motor Skills*, 77(3, Pt 1), 767–770.

Piko, B. F. (2000). Health-related predictors of self-perceived health in a student population: The importance of physical activity. *Journal of Community Health, 25*(2), 125–137.

Piko, B. F., & Keresztes, N. (2006). Physical activity, psychosocial health, and life goals among youth. *Journal of Community Health, 31*(2), 136–145.

Royal College of Physicians. (1991). *Medical aspects of exercise. Risks and benefits*. London: Royal College of Physicians.

Sachs, M. L. (1981). Running addiction. In M. Sacks & M. Sachs (Eds.), *Psychology of Running* (pp. 116–126). Champaign, ILL: Human Kinetics.

Sachs, M. L., & Pargman, D. (1984). Running addiction. In M. L. Sachs & G. W. Buffone (Eds.), *Running as therapy: An integrated approach* (pp. 231–252). Lincoln, NE: University of Nebraska Press.

Sforzo, G. A. (1988). Opioids and exercise: An update. *Sports Medicine*, 7, 109–124.

Sforzo, G. A., Seeger, T. F., Pert, C. B., Pert, A., & Dotson, C. O. (1986). *In vivo* opioid receptor occupation in the rat brain following exercise. *Medicine and Science in Sports and Exercise, 18*(4), 380–384.

Slay, H. A., Hayaki, J., Napolitano, M. A., & Brownell, K. D. (1998). Motivations for running and eating attitudes in obligatory versus nonobligatory runners. *International Journal of Eating Disorders, 23*(3), 267–275.

Smith, D. K., & Hale, B. D. (2005). Exercise-dependence in bodybuilders: Antecedents and reliability of measurement. *Journal of Sports Medicine and Physical Fitness, 45*(3), 401–408.

Smith, D. K., Hale, B. D., & Collins, D. (1998). Measurement of exercise dependence in bodybuilders. *Journal of Sports Medicine and Physical Fitness, 38*(1), 66–74.

Steffen, J. J., & Brehm, B. J. (1999). The dimensions of obligatory exercise. *Eating Disorders*, 7, 219–226.

Stephens, T. (1988). Physical activity and mental health in the United States and Canada: Evidence from four population surveys. *Preventive Medicine*, 17(1), 35–47.

Sundgot-Borgen, J. (1994). Eating disorders in female athletes. *Sports Medicine, 17*(3), 176–188.

Sussman, S., Lisha, N., & Griffiths, M. (2011). Prevalence of the addictions: A problem of the majority or the minority? *Evaluation and the Health Professions, 34*(1), 3–56.

Symons Downs, D., Hausenblas, H. A., & Nigg, C. R. (2004). Factorial validity and psychometric examination of the Exercise Dependence Scale-Revised. *Measurement in Physical Education and Exercise Science, 8*(4), 183–201.

Szabo, A. (1995). The impact of exercise deprivation on well-being of habitual exercisers. *Australian Journal of Science and Medicine in Sport, 27*, 68–75.

Szabo, A. (2000). Physical activity as a source of psychological dysfunction. In S. J. Biddle, K. R. Fox & S. H. Boutcher (Eds.), *Physical activity and psychological well-being* (pp. 130–153). London: Routledge.

Szabo, A. (2010). *Addiction to exercise: A symptom or a disorder?* New York: Nova Science Publishers Inc.

Szabo, A., Frenkl, R., & Caputo, A. (1996). Deprivation feelings, anxiety, and commitment to various forms of physical activity: A cross-sectional study on the Internet. *Psychologia, 39*, 223–230.

Szabo, A., Frenkl, R., & Caputo, A. (1997). Relationships between addiction to running, commitment to running, and deprivation from running. *European Yearbook of Sport Psychology, 1*, 130–147.

Szabo, A., & Griffiths, M. D. (2007). Exercise addiction in British sport science students. *International Journal of Mental Health and Addiction, 5*(1), 25–28.

Terry, A., Szabo, A., & Griffiths, M. D. (2004). The exercise addiction inventory: A new brief screening tool. *Addiction Research and Theory, 12*(5), 489–499.

Thompson, J. K., & Blanton, P. (1987). Energy conservation and exercise dependence: A sympathetic arousal hypothesis. *Medicine and Science in Sports and Exercise, 19*(2), 91–99.

United States Department of Health and Human Services. (1996). *Physical Activity and Health. A Report of the Surgeon General*. Atlanta, GA: U.S. Department of Health and Human Services Centers for Disease Control and Prevention, National Center for Chronic Disease Prevention and Health Promotion, The President's Council on Physical Fitness and Sports.

Waddington, I. (2000). *Sport, Health, and Drugs: A Critical Sociological Perspective*. London: Spoon Press.

Warburton, D. E., Nicol, C. W., & Bredin, S. S. (2006). Health benefits of physical activity: The evidence. *CMAJ*, *174*(6), 801–809.

Wilson, G. T., Fairburn, C. G., & Agras, W. S. (1997). Cognitive-behavioral therapy for bulimia nervosa. In D. M. Garner & P. E. Garfinkel (Eds.), *Handbook of treatment for eating disorders* (pp. 67–93). New York: Guilford Press.

Yates, A., Edman, J. D., Crago, M., & Crowell, D. (2001). Using an exercise-based instrument to detect signs of an eating disorder. *Psychiatry Research*, *105*(3), 231–241.

Yates, A., Leehey, K., & Shisslak, C. M. (1983). Running—An analogue of anorexia? *New England Journal of Medicine*, *308*(5), 251–255.

APPENDIX 13-1 EXERCISE ADDICTION ASSESSMENT MEASURES

Exercise Addiction Inventory (EAI)

	Strongly Disagree	Disagree	Neither Agree nor Disagree	Agree	Strongly Agree
Exercise is the most important thing in my life.	1	2	3	4	5
Conflicts have arisen between me and my family and/or my partner about the amount of exercise I do.	1	2	3	4	5
I use exercise as a way of changing my mood (e.g., to get a buzz, to escape, etc.).	1	2	3	4	5
Over time I have increased the amount of exercise I do in a day.	1	2	3	4	5
If I have to miss an exercise session, I feel moody and irritable.	1	2	3	4	5
If I cut down the amount of exercise I do, and then start again, I always end up exercising as often as I did before.	1	2	3	4	5

Note: Details on scoring and interpretation can be found in Terry et al. (2004) and Mónok et al. (2012).

EXERCISE DEPENDENCE SCALE

Using the scale provided below, please complete the following questions as honestly as possible. The questions refer to current exercise beliefs and behaviors that have occurred in the past 3 months. Please place your answer in the blank space provided after each statement.

1 Never	2	3	4	5	6 Always

1. I exercise to avoid feeling irritable.______
2. I exercise despite recurring physical problems.______
3. I continually increase my exercise intensity to achieve the desired effects/benefits.______
4. I am unable to reduce how long I exercise.______
5. I would rather exercise than spend time with family/friends.______
6. I spend a lot of time exercising.______
7. I exercise longer than I intend.______
8. I exercise to avoid feeling anxious.______
9. I exercise when injured.______
10. I continually increase my exercise frequency to achieve the desired effects/benefits.______
11. I am unable to reduce how often I exercise.______
12. I think about exercise when I should be concentrating on school/work.______
13. I spend most of my free time exercising.______
14. I exercise longer than I expect.______
15. I exercise to avoid feeling tense.______
16. I exercise despite persistent physical problems.______
17. I continually increase my exercise duration to achieve the desired effects/benefits.______
18. I am unable to reduce how intense I exercise.______
19. I choose to exercise so that I can get out of spending time with family/friends.______
20. A great deal of my time is spent exercising._____
21. I exercise longer than I plan.______

SCORING

Component	Item Numbers
Withdrawal effects	1, 8, 15
Continuance	2, 9, 16
Tolerance	3, 10, 17
Lack of control	4, 11, 18
Reduction in other activities	5, 12, 19
Time	6, 13, 20
Intention effects	7, 14, 21

Note: More details on scoring and interpretation can be found in Hausenblas and Symons Downs (2002b) and Mónok et al. (2012).

CHAPTER 14

Meditation and Spirituality-Based Approaches for Addiction

Sri Sri Ravi Shankar[1], Kenneth Paul Rosenberg[2], Anju Dhawan[3], Achar Vedamurthachar[4]

[1]The Art of Living Foundation, Ved Vignan Mahavidyapeeth, Bangalore, Karnataka, India, [2]Cornell University Medical Center, Psychiatry Department, New York, NY, USA and UpperEastHealth.com, [3]National Drug Dependence Treatment Centre, AIIMS, New Delhi, India, [4]Centre for Addiction Medicine, National Institute of Mental Health and Neuro Sciences, Bangalore, Karnataka, India

INTRODUCTION

Addiction is among the most vexing social and medical problems of our era. Medications are effective, although access, costs, stigma, side effects, and health risks may deter utilization. Likewise, professional psychotherapy helps yet is unaffordable and unavailable to most. And, even when empirically based treatments can be accessed, relapse, mortality, and morbidity are the rule with addictive disorders. Therefore, there is an urgent need for new, affordable, and accessible treatment options.

"Alternative" or complementary medical and spiritual approaches are promising and are associated with excellent patient acceptance. A 2001 study of the American population revealed that the majority of the respondents (67.7%) had used some sort of alternative medical approach in their lifetime (Kessler et al., 2001). There appears to be an upward trend toward acceptance and utilization (Frass et al., 2012). This chapter addresses 12-step programs and then yoga and meditation, an alternative or complementary form of mind-body medicine, to (1) examine the evidence for utilizing yoga and meditation, (2) encourage further research, (3) integrate practices that are found to be effective, and (4) provide informed choices to practitioners and patients based on the clinical consensus and research.

LESSONS FROM ALCOHOLICS ANONYMOUS AND 12-STEP FACILITATION

Since psychologist William James (1929) wrote his landmark *The Varieties of Religious Experience*, experts have championed the utility of spiritually based approaches. Chitwood, Weiss, and Leukefeld (2008) completed a systematic

Behavioral Addictions
http://dx.doi.org/10.1016/B978-0-12-407724-9.00014-8

review of the articles that were published from 1997 to 2006 and found higher levels of religiosity and spirituality are associated with decreased substance use. Research on religiosity and general health has shown a relationship with positive health outcomes. Mind-body medicine specialist Herbert Benson, M.D., and others believe that our brains are hard-wired for God (Benson, 1996; Fingelkurts & Fingelkurts, 2009), and therefore, spiritual approaches can exploit our natural predispositions. A review of the research in the field of mental health showed that higher levels of religious involvement may be positively associated with indicators of psychological well-being, evidenced, in part, by reductions in depression, suicidal thoughts, and drug and alcohol use or abuse (Moreira-Almeida, Neto, & Koenig, 2006). Attention to assessment of spirituality is now required by certain bodies such as the Joint Commission on Accreditation of Healthcare Organizations (JCAHO) and has also been added to the training requirements of psychiatric residencies (Galanter, 2008).

Psychiatrist Marc Galanter studied the spiritually based 12-step programs that are based on the model of Alcoholics Anonymous (AA) founded by Bill Wilson and Dr. Bob Smith in 1935. AA views recovery as "spiritual awakening" and has been reconfigured for numerous behavioral and chemical addictions, which are collectively known as Twelve-Step Facilitation (TSF). These fellowships now include groups for behavioral addictions, such as Gambler's Anonymous, Sex Addict's Anonymous, Overeaters Anonymous, and Recovering Couples Anonymous (for Sex Addiction). Galanter views TSF as a category of complementary medicine, alternative medicine, and/or "spiritual fellowships" (Galanter, 2008).

Does TSF makes a difference? The answer depends on what is being measured. Project MATCH found that TSF produced an outcome comparable to cognitive behavioral therapy and motivation enhancement (Tonigan, Miller, & Connors, 2000). A review by Kaskutas (2009) found that higher levels of TSF attendance were related to higher rates of abstinence. In contrast, a Cochrane review of eight trials involving 3,417 people concluded that no experimental studies unequivocally demonstrated the effectiveness of AA or TSF approaches for reducing alcohol dependence or associated problems, although AA may help patients to accept the general need for treatment (Ferri, Amato, & Davoli, 2009). Other studies have found that AA also leads to better outcomes through increasing spirituality/religiosity and by reducing negative affect (Kelly, Hoeppner, Stout, & Pagano, 2012). A qualitative study with AA attendees using in-depth interviews found that the role of religion and spirituality was important

(Morjaria & Orford, 2002). The research may be summed up in one of the more popular AA slogans "It works if you work it." In other words, those who go to AA meetings more often seem to do better.

Most importantly, regardless of the uncertainties about efficacy, most physicians and addiction experts regard AA as an important part of treatment for alcoholism and related addictions based on their clinical experience. Aside from the spiritual teachings, experts find the social support and therapeutic milieu TSF can provide to be very helpful. While a belief in and a reliance on a "higher power" (e.g., God) is the core of TSF, many other factors may account for TSF's popularity and utility. TSF offers daily support, mentorship or sponsorship, and provides workbooks and a considerable amount of literature. The groups offer mantra-like sayings and slogans that can be extremely useful during recovery and provide patients with cognitive restructuring for cravings and life challenges. Strict rules for recovery, mentorship, and anonymity are key ingredients of the fellowships. AA provides a large network of sponsors and supporters for fellow travelers on the road to recovery that can be self-regulated according to need (Kelly & Magill, 2009). Groups are accessible in most major cities and towns in the United States on a daily, and sometimes hourly, basis. Another factor contributing to TSF's accessibility is that it is free of charge. Although some TSF groups may oppose medical and professional approaches, generally speaking, TSF groups are very supportive of the medical (or disease) model of addiction and support contemporary medical treatments. Hence, accessibility, affordability, altruism, fellowship, peer support, destigmatization, an organized philosophy, an inclusive approach that allows for other forms of therapy, and a spiritual foundation appear to be the key elements of TSF.

YOGA AND ADDICTION

Yoga is a spiritual discipline that originated in India more than 5,000 years ago; it aims to unite one with the core of one's being. Although many texts explain yoga, the earliest known on the subject are Patanjali's *Yoga Sutras,* which describes various stages on the way to realizing this union in terse aphorisms. Yoga today is largely understood to be a set of physical stretches, which are commonly practiced in U.S. gyms and fitness centers, but the ancient classical texts available on the subject indicate that it is much more. According to Patanjali, yoga is the cessation of the distortions or modulations of the mind. Another well-known text, the *Bhagavad Gita* (1966; Woods, 1914) defines yoga as complete equanimity of the mind.

Patanjali describes eight "limbs" of yoga, which include preparing the body through the practice of posture and physical stretches (*asana*), directing life force energy by control of breath (*pranayama*), and meditation (*dhyana*). According to Patanjali, deep states of meditation are sometimes marked by heightened clarity of mind, while at some other times, there is an experience of bliss and ecstasy. Sometimes, there are moments of thoughtlessness in meditation, and one does not know who, what, or where one is but just has a faint awareness of "I am" (Ravi Shankar, 2010).

Being a sort of a map of the states that the mind travels through, yoga also recognizes the condition of obsession or addiction of any kind. According to yogis, all experiences are stored as impressions in the mind, including stimuli due to addictive substances. Craving for the same impression with repeated stimulus leads to addiction. Although an ancient postulate, this belief is in keeping with the current neurobiological constructs for addiction discussed in the introductory chapter of this book, particularly the PKM Zeta long-term potentiation of memories (Sacktor, 2011; Xue et al., 2012) and reward/executive function of addictive cycle learning (O'Brien, Volkow, & Li, 2006.).

Breathing techniques such as Sudarshan Kriya (described later) are said to take the practitioner into a state of deep relaxation and meditation. This state is often described by practitioners as a "high" and acts as a substitute for the "high" that comes from addictive substances (see the description of Patients 2 and 6 later). Patanjali states that the impression of the higher states of meditation erases all other unwanted impressions from the mind (Ravi Shankar, 2010). The authors believe that regular practice of these techniques may gradually reduce cravings in the case of recovery from addiction.

The various techniques of yoga and meditation that have been studied in the field of addiction include mindfulness-based meditation, transcendental meditation (TM), and Sudarshan Kriya yoga (SKY). The mindfulness-based technique is a more recent derivation of ancient meditation techniques for use in clinical practice. As described by Kabat-Zinn (1982), meditation focuses on the present moment with the goal of dispassionate self-observation. Hölzel et al. (2011) note that mindfulness is a concept stemming from ancient Buddhist practice, and is practiced to achieve enduring happiness and to gain insight into a view of the true nature of existence. This concept is also similarly described in the ancient practice of meditation based on the Hindu Vedic philosophy.

MINDFULNESS-BASED MEDITATION

In their review of yoga and mindfulness as complementary therapies for addiction, Khanna and Greeson (2013) noted a small but growing number of well-designed clinical trials and experimental laboratory studies on smoking, alcohol dependence, and illicit substance use support the clinical effectiveness of mindfulness-based interventions for treating addiction. Mindfulness meditation, in addiction, is aimed at reducing cravings or the urge to engage in the addictive cycle.

In 1979, Kabat-Zinn developed the Mindfulness-Based Stress Reduction (MBSR) program in which patients are taught relaxation/meditation techniques and counseled to accept their problems rather than to modify or suppress them. The MBSR program targets cravings and negative affect and their role in the relapse process (Witkiewitz, Lustyk, & Bowen, 2012). It combines Marlatt's cognitive-behavioral relapse prevention program (e.g., identifying high-risk situations, coping skills training) with mindfulness practice, providing skills in cognitive-behavioral relapse prevention and mindfulness meditation. Clients meditate for 30–45 minutes in session and are assigned approximately 45 minutes of daily meditation, using audio-recorded instructions. The mindfulness practices are intended to increase awareness and acceptance, teaching clients to observe physical, cognitive, emotional, and/or craving states without reacting (Witkiewitz & Bowen, 2010).

In 1982, Kabat-Zinn published findings that MBSR significantly improved chronic pain among 51 refractory patients in an uncontrolled study. After 10 weeks of MBSR, 50% of patients had a 50% or greater level of pain relief and 65% had a 33% or greater level of pain relief. Subsequent researchers adapted MBSR for cigarette and substance abuse, developing a program called Mindfulness Based Relapse Prevention (MBRP), which is an 8-week, group-based, psychoeducational intervention that is based on a similar paradigm as used for MBSR for chronic pain.

Four studies have evaluated the effectiveness of MBRP in the treatment of substance use disorders. In a controlled pilot-study, Bowen and colleagues (2009) studied 165 individuals with substance abuse disorders who recently completed outpatient or/and inpatient treatment. They received MBRP sessions that began with a 20- to 30-minute guided meditation and involved a variety of experiential exercises, interspersed with discussions of the role of mindfulness in relapse prevention and review of homework assignments. Participants were assigned daily exercises to practice between sessions and were provided with a meditation CD for practice outside group sessions. The MBRP group reported significantly lower levels of craving following treatment, in comparison to a treatment-as-usual control group, which mediated subsequent substance use outcomes. The retention rates were similar in the study and control arm, while alcohol and drug use in the experimental group were five times lower than in the control group. The study had serious flaws—in particular, that there was no blood or urine toxicology that could confirm abstinence, and no differentiation between alcohol and other substances of abuse.

Davis, Fleming, Bonus, and Baker (2007) reported 56% abstinence in smokers (confirmed biologically) after 6 weeks of an MBSR course for smokers. Brewer et al. (2011) completed a controlled, randomized study on 88 smokers and found that eight sessions of mindfulness training over 4 weeks resulted in greater reduction in smoking than the American Lung Association Freedom from Smoking program and had significantly better abstinence at 17 weeks after the training.

A 10-session group-based psycho-educational intervention called MORE was designed by Garland, Gaylord, Boettiger, and Howard (2010) and Garland (2013). It has been adapted from Mindfulness-based Cognitive Therapy (MBCT) for depression. It does not include yoga but includes mindful breathing, body scan, mindfulness of sensations, mindful walking, and compassionate meditation. MORE specifically addresses spirituality through discussion on interdependence, meaning, and spirituality. A pilot trial of 37 alcohol-dependent adults from a therapeutic community found that as compared to the control intervention (evidence-based support group), MORE reduced stress and thought suppression, increased physiological recovery from alcohol cues measured by heart rate variability in a laboratory setting, and decreased attention bias to alcohol (NIH, 2012).

This mindfulness construct has been incorporated into many contemporary psychotherapies, such as Dialectical Behavioral Therapy, a psychotherapy for patients with Borderline Personality Disorder (BPD) that has been shown to significantly reduce substance abuse in randomized trials with patients with comorbid substance abuse and BPD (Dimeff & Linehan, 2008).

TRANSCENDENTAL MEDITATION (TM)

Transcendental meditation is a mantra-based technique popularized by Maharishi Mahesh Yogi. It is an effortless procedure for allowing the excitation of the mind to settle down until a state of calmness is reached. This practice strives for a state of alertness with relaxation with no object of thought or perception. It has been described as a state in which the person is aware of his or her consciousness and its unbounded nature. It is called a state of transcendental consciousness, described as wholeness, devoid of differences of the division of subject and object (Orme-Johnson, 1994). It is practiced for 15–20 minutes, twice day, under the guidance and support of the TM community.

In a 1975 article published in the American Journal of Psychiatry, in a convenience sample, Shafil, Lavely, and Jaffe (1975) found that 40% of people who engaged in TM for 2 years reported discontinuation of beer and wine within the first 6 months. After 25–39 months of meditation, this figure increased to 60%. In addition, 54% of this group, versus 1% of the control group, had stopped drinking hard liquor. The authors suggested that TM could be an effective preventative tool in the area of alcohol abuse (Shafil et al., 1975.)

Studies on TM that were related to substance abuse were reviewed, and 19 studies were included in a meta-analysis based on the inclusion criteria by Alexander, Robinson, and Rainforth (1994). These included a total of 4,524 subjects, of which 3,249 were TM participants and the remainder were controls. These included a range of retrospective, cross-sectional, controlled, uncontrolled, and longitudinal studies in students, the general population, prisoners, Vietnam veterans, and Skid Row alcoholics, among others. Six studies used random assignment in their research design. The longitudinal studies included a follow-up of 3–20 months' duration. Some studies also compared long-term meditators with new meditators in an attempt to rule out self-selection as an important confounding factor. The authors noted that a summary of 14 studies found an effect size of 0.64 (moderate) in reducing negative psychological outcome among heavy abusers such as depression, anxiety, anger, and hostility. Ten of the TM studies reported positive psychological outcomes such as self-concept and internal locus of control, with an effect size of 0.51 (moderate) in enhancing positive psychological outcome. The effect size for reduction of cigarette, alcohol, and illicit drug use was 0.87, 0.55 and 0.83, respectively.

SUDARSHAN KRIYA YOGA (SKY)

Sudarshan Kriya yoga, or SKY, is a breathing technique that is said to help people slip into meditation effortlessly. It is taught at "Art of Living" Centers in the United States and around the world by, as of 2013, more than 10,000 trained teachers. SKY was developed by one of the authors, Sri Sri Ravi Shankar.

As described by Kjellgren, Bood, Axelsson, Norlander, and Saatcioglu (2007), SKY consists of (1) three-stage pranayama with ujjayi, (2) three sets of bhastrika, and (3) cyclical breathing. The breathing practices are done in a sitting posture, either in a chair or on the floor. Eyes are kept closed throughout the sessions. Normal breathing is at the rate of 14–16 breaths per minute. Ujjayi is a slow and deep breathing technique at 2–4 breaths per minute. Three-stage pranayama with ujjayi breath is an advanced form using a specific ratio of inhalation and exhalation, and breath-holds. Participants practice this component such that specific arm positions are held for approximately 10 minutes in total. The second breathing component is bhastrika, a vigorous and faster breathing technique with about 20–30 respiratory cycles per minute. Three approximately 1-minute rounds of bhastrika are followed by a few minutes of normal breathing. Arm movements and abdominal muscles are used to increase the force and depth of inhalation and exhalation. Practice of this component lasts for approximately 5 minutes. The central component of SKY is an advanced cyclical breathing exercise of slow, medium, and fast rates in succession. Slow breaths are about 20 respiratory cycles per minute, medium breaths are about 40–50 respiratory cycles per minute, and the fast breathing is about 60–80 cycles per minute. Despite the complexity of SKY, it is readily taught and easily remembered by participants for their daily practice, without any audio recordings or external guidance required.

SKY is taught in an atmosphere of belongingness and celebration for 5 days, which includes group techniques, singing and chanting, and discussion about healthy living and human values—all part of a spiritual program advanced by the Art of Living that is taught in a secular way.

In an open trial, Vedamurthachar et al. (2011) studied 102 healthy adult volunteers and found immediate beneficial effects of SKY. In Sweden, 55 healthy participants who received SKY course training were compared to 48 control subjects in a nonrandomized and uncontrolled trial. Participants in the SKY group experienced significant improvements in the scales of depression, anxiety, optimism, stress, and the experience of altered states of consciousness (which is associated with a daydreaming state of deep relaxation and stress release). In a controlled study of 183 subjects, Descilo et al. (2009) found tsunami survivors demonstrated significant improvements after SKY training. Hurricane Katrina refugees similarly demonstrated relief through yoga breath practices (Gerbarg & Brown, 2005).

SKY has been reported to be beneficial for diabetics with improved metabolic parameters (Vedamurthachar et al., 2011). Among smokers with cancer, Kochupillai et al. (2005) found that SKY was associated with significantly increased natural killer cells at 12 and 24 weeks of the practice compared to baseline, and associated with behavioral benefits that are comparable in efficacy to smoking cessation to bupropion, the Food and Drug Association–approved medication for smoking cessation.

Antidepressant efficacy of SKY has been demonstrated at The National Institute of Mental Health and Neuro Sciences (NIMHANS), Bangalore, through a number of studies (Janakiramaiah et al., 1998, 2000; Naga Venkatesha, Gangadhar, Janakiramaiah, & Subbakrishna, 1997; Naga Venkatesha, Janakiramaiah, Gangadhar, & Subbakrishna, 1998; Rohini, Pandey, Janakiramaiah, Gangadhar, & Vedamurthachar, 2000). An open trial demonstrated the efficacy of SKY as a sole treatment for dysthymia (Janakiramaiah et al., 1998). A randomized, but not double-blind, trial compared SKY to imipramine or electroconvulsive therapy (ECT) in 45 hospitalized patients with major depression, assessed by the Beck Depression Inventory (BDI) and Hamilton Rating Scales. SKY demonstrated a significant degree of efficacy, on par with imipramine but inferior to ECT.

In a randomized controlled trial of 60 alcoholics, when learning SKY over a 2-week period following detoxification, there was significant reduction in BDI scores and significant reductions in plasma cortisol and adrenocorticotropic hormone (Vedamurthachar et al., 2006). Yadav, Dhawan, and Chopra (2006) studied 15 participants in a community outreach clinic in North India for patients receiving buprenorphine (long-acting opiate) maintenance with a SKY course. Compared to 14 controls, the experimental group had significant improvement in their scores on the Addiction Severity Index (ASI) and WHO Quality of Life Scale (WHO QOL-BREF.).

In a randomized controlled trial of SKY as an adjunctive intervention to treatment as usual (opioid substitution treatment and psychosocial intervention) in comparison to the treatment as usual group, there was a significant difference in the quality of life indices in the patients who received SKY as well as a lower ASI score in the alcohol domain on follow-up (Dhawan et al., personal communication, 2013).

Community-based programs using SKY have been carried out in combination with detoxification in India in a camp-based approach. The entire village community becomes involved in the provision of services, providing free space and food for the participants, and creating awareness through the local religious institutions. The program resulted in a large community program attended by thousands of people from the village (Yadav & Dhawan, personal communication, 2009).

Clinical Examples

There are no published studies of SKY, mindfulness, or other meditative techniques or SKY with behavioral addictions per se, although a few reviews in the literature mention the likely useful role of meditation for the treatment of problem gambling (Alfonso, Caracuel, Delgado-Pastor, & Verdejo-García, 2011; Nespor, 1994). Since the authors of this chapter have experience in SKY training, several examples are presented in which SKY training was used as part of a comprehensive, multimodal addiction treatment program for patients with behavioral and/or chemical addictions.

Patient 1 is a 22-year-old woman who came to treatment for a combination of behavioral and chemical addictions: compulsive fatty food intake, anonymous sex, and marijuana abuse. The patient has Generalized Anxiety Disorder and a history of dysthymia. She had recently graduated from an undergraduate university with low grades, was unemployed, and had no significant romantic relationships. Within 3 months of initiating addiction-focused psychotherapy and bupropion treatment, the patient achieved abstinence in the areas of drug use and anonymous sex. Three months into treatment, she addressed compulsive eating with a dietitian, leading to a 50 lb. weight loss over the next 1-year period. At the suggestion of her therapist, the patient learned SKY in a 4-day course with five other patients who were also in recovery from chemical and behavioral addictions. The patient practiced on a daily basis and attended monthly booster sessions. At the time of writing, 2 years into treatment, the patient is involved in a 1-year monogamous relationship; is pursuing a master's degree; and has remained abstinent from substances, alcohol, and anonymous sex.

Patient 2 is a 34-year-old male economist who was referred by a local rehabilitation facility after a 30-day inpatient stay. The patient had a mild bipolar disorder and had abused oral opiates, benzodiazepines, and stimulants (amphetamine and dextroamphetamine), used in part, for self-medicating his depression and anxiety. His drug abuse prompted his detox and rehab. He was discharged on aripiprazole, lithium, and venlafaxine. During rehab, he was introduced to the concepts of mindfulness. As an outpatient, he engaged in group and individual psychotherapy and continued on appropriate medications. After several months of sobriety, he learned SKY with other patients in recovery and attended booster sessions. According to the patient, SKY focused his productivity, fostered positive thinking, and decreased stress. He noted that the feeling he got after SKY was "as good as my best opiate high"—of course, without the roller coaster of emotions and destructiveness of drug addiction.

Patient 3 is a 32-year-old heterosexual male, a successful screenwriter who self-referred to outpatient treatment after he found himself engaging in anonymous sex with a transvestite prostitute, at which point he realized that his compulsive sexual escapades, fueled by bouts of drunkenness, had progressed to the

Clinical Examples—cont'd

point of a sex addiction. After 2 years of therapy, he no longer engaged in sex compulsively and had a loving and appropriate marriage, yet continued to struggle with cravings for inappropriate sex, albeit without serious acting out. SKY and Art of Living participation became a regular part of his recovery regimen, and his thought and behavior improved. The patient terminated psychotherapy when it was no longer required but continued with daily SKY practice and engaged in group activities at the local Art of Living Centers.

Patient 4 was a 28-year-old computer programmer who self-referred for sex addiction. The patient reported that he compulsively masturbated to pornography with women wearing high-heeled shoes and sometimes masturbated with the actual shoes themselves. He gave a history of compulsive masturbation and depressive episodes. He was a successful intellectual technology expert working in finance, without significant problems at work; but his greatest challenge was maintaining significant relationships. The patient engaged in psychotherapy and tried a range of medications, of which the antipsychotic quetiapine fumarate was the most successful, particularly for calming him down at bedtime. The patient learned SKY and developed a daily practice. SKY reinforced his 12-step spiritual fellowship and provided a spiritual identity that he found compelling and therapeutic. After 4 years, the patient stopped psychotherapy and medication, and relied on a daily SKY practice to calm himself down at key times. He would practice SKY if he had trouble falling asleep or if he awoke in the middle of his sleep cycle and needed to go back to sleep. When he last came to see his therapist, he was engaged to be married and without any signs of psychiatric disturbances.

Patient 5 was a 55-year-old male accountant who was dependent on alcohol for the last 5 years; had a history suggestive of delusional disorder with delusions of infidelity in the past; and had prominent interpersonal problems with his spouse, children, and siblings due to his alcohol use. He was in treatment for the last 4 years with multiple relapses while in treatment. Treatment in the past had included detoxification, supervised disulfiram (a drug that makes people sick if they drink), and antipsychotics for the delusional disorder. He completed the SKY program and practiced regularly; in addition, he participated in a more advanced program at his local Art of Living Center that involved meditations and silence. He reported experiencing deep peace and is has been sober from alcohol for the last 10 years, and additionally reports several other positive lifestyle changes and improved relationships.

Patient 6 was a 40-year-old unemployed man who was dependent on heroin and was stabilized on buprenorphine for a few months when he completed a SKY program. He stated that the "high" he experienced with SKY was very similar to what he had experienced with heroin and felt that had he experienced this earlier, he would never have needed to rely on heroin. Soon after the program, he was gainfully employed as a result of his efforts to start working after being out

Continued

Clinical Examples—cont'd

of work for several years. Being part of a program that taught SKY in a community setting also altered the patients' relationship with the treatment team, as they facilitated his participation in the SKY program and he perceived the treatment team as more "caring."

These clinical examples demonstrate how SKY may be incorporated into clinical practice. Although some authors (Rao, Varambally, & Gangadhar, 2013) suggest adding yoga early in treatment, based on one of the author's (Rosenberg's) experience, intensive yoga-based techniques such as SKY should be offered only after patients are securely sober and seriously engaged in recovery, not while in the throes of addiction, as these techniques can be initially disorienting and are best practiced by a sober and stable mind and in the context of a overall commitment to recovery. In a few of the cases, additional benefits were derived from attending gatherings and groups associated with the meditation and spirituality-focused techniques.

SKY is not always met with success. The majority of patients offered SKY in one of the author's Manhattan practice declined training because of the time required to learn the techniques. The refusal rates may vary across different cultural settings. Of those who start the training, roughly 10% drop out because the training feels too uncomfortable, "New Agey," or "too touchy feely." Of those who have completed SKY training in the practice, the majority failed to maintain their daily or even weekly practice—not dissimilar to the large dropout rate in Twelve-Step Facilitation.

HOW DOES MEDITATION/SKY WORK?

Much of the literature on how meditation works comes from transcendental meditation or mindfulness meditation but may also be true for other meditation techniques. Evidence suggests that meditation practice is associated with neuroplastic changes in various regions of the brain such as the anterior cingulate cortex, insula, and temporo-parietal junction. Studies on long-term meditators suggest possible structural changes in the form of prefrontal differences as well as insular differences in the form of increased gray matter (Hölzel et al., 2008; Luders, Toga, Lepore, & Gaser, 2009). According to Hölzel et al. (2008), during meditation, experienced meditators show greater activation in the dorso-medial PFC and rostral ACC compared with nonmeditators. After participants completed an 8-week mindfulness-based stress-reduction course, Farb et al. (2007) found increased activity in participants' ventrolateral PFC, which the authors interpreted as evidence of augmented inhibitory control.

Witkiewitz et al. (2012) hypothesized the neurobiological mechanisms of mindfulness-based relapse prevention on presumed impairments in the addict's reward systems (ventral striatal), the habit circuitry (dorsal striatal), and the prefrontal executive control systems. The authors hypothesized that the neurobiological mechanism is probably due to both top-down and bottom-up action. Bottom-up mechanisms mean that greater present moment awareness leads to reduced emotional reactivity to craving cues, and top-down mechanisms mean that changes in the executive functioning, attention regulation, and cognition help modulate the anatomically and phylogenetically lower reward centers.

Westbrooke et al. (2011) studied the role of craving reduction using functional magnetic resonance imaging (fMRI) brain scans among tobacco smokers. Forty-seven meditation-naive treatment-seeking smokers viewed and rated smoking and neutral images while undergoing fMRI. Subjects viewed these images passively or with mindful attention. Participants, who smoked at least 10 cigarettes per day, were asked to abstain from smoking for at least 12 hours prior to fMRI. For the mindfully attending condition, participants were instructed to actively focus on their responses to the picture, including thoughts, feelings, memories, and bodily sensations, while maintaining a nonjudgmental attitude toward those responses. During mindful attention, subjects' self-reported craving to smoking images had significantly decreased. On fMRI scans, subjects had significantly reduced neural activity in a craving-related region of subgenual anterior cingulate cortex (sgACC.) There were many limitations to the study, as pointed out by Westbrooke et al. (2011), including an expectancy effect. Nonetheless, the findings are consistent with the notion that successful treatment for addiction must decouple the dysfunctional communications between the reward and reasoning pathways that have been hijacked by the addictive cycle.

A meta-analysis of 31 physiological studies found that TM significantly reduces physiological arousal as indicated by lower respiration rate, skin conductance level, and plasma lactate as compared to simply resting with eyes closed. TM subjects also show significantly lower baseline levels of arousal than controls, suggestive of a cumulative effect (Dillbeack & Orme-Johnson, 1987). TM claims to increase resistance to stress during daily activities by more rapid mobilization, habituation, and stability of autonomic response to stressful stimuli (Alexander et al., 1994). All these mechanisms may help patients with addiction. Brown and Gerbag (2005) speculated that SKY may improve the autonomic and stress response systems (Sharma et al., 2003), stimulate the parasympathetic system through vagal stimulation, balance cortical areas by thalamic nuclei, quiet cortical areas involved in executive function, activate the limbic system leading to stimulation of forebrain reward systems, and increase release of prolactin and oxytocin.

Alexander et al. (1994) reviewed studies on TM that showed reduced impulsive and rebellious behaviors in prison inmates as measured by reduced aggressiveness, hostility, and recidivism for up to 6 years after release. TM practitioners have shown improvements in cognitive flexibility, choice reaction time, learning and memory, creativity, and moral reasoning (Alexander et al., 1994).

Addiction has also been considered to be a dysfunctional means of dealing with negative emotions. In a meta-analysis of 146 meditation and relaxation treatment groups, Eppley, Abrams, and Shear (1989) showed that TM reduced trait anxiety significantly more than the other meditation or relaxation methods such as progressive muscle relaxation and EMG biofeedback. A meta-analysis by Alexander, Rainforth, and Gelderloos (1991) suggested that TM produced a significantly larger effect on the growth of positive affect than other forms of meditation and relaxation in the form of enhanced capacity for intimate contact, openness to one's feelings, and spontaneity. Controlled studies on TM suggest improvement in self-reliance, internal locus of control, and independence in TM practitioners.

As with AA and TSF, social factors in TM may influence the benefits. Galanter (2006) and others have commented that the social affiliations, particularly among members of religious, spiritual, or meditation groups, are generally beneficial given our evolutionary make-up and are known to buffer against depression, suicide, addiction, loneliness, and stress.

CONCLUSION

There is considerable evidence supporting the use of yoga-related spiritual approaches in improving mental health. In the 1970s, there was enthusiasm and research into the TM program. Currently, particularly in India, and increasingly in the United States, there is interest in SKY and techniques advanced by the Art of Living. As Khanna and Greeson (2013) note, mindfulness meditations are increasingly integrated into secular health care settings. The authors have the most extensive experience with SKY, but believe that the range of spirituality- and yoga-based techniques presented here are useful.

Overall, meditation and yoga have some cumulative effect with ongoing practice that should enhance the resilience to stress as well as initiation and relapse to behavioral and chemical addictions. Aside from demonstrating efficacy, future studies should address the efficacy of various techniques and specify which patient populations are best suited for yoga and meditation and how and when these approaches might be incorporated into routine clinical care.

REFERENCES

Alexander, C. N., Rainforth, M.V., & Gelderloos, P. (1991). Transcendental meditation, self actualization and psychological health: A conceptual overview and statistical metaanalysis. *Journal of Social Behavior and Personality*, *6*, 189–247.

Alexander, C. N., Robinson, P., & Rainforth, M. (1994). Treating and preventing alcohol, nicotine and drug abuse through transcendental meditation. *Alcoholism Treatment Quarterly*, *11*(1–2), 13–75.

Alfonso, J. P., Caracuel, A., Delgado-Pastor, L. C., & Verdejo-García, A. (2011). Combined goal management training and mindfulness meditation improve executive functions and decision-making performance in abstinent polysubstance abusers. *Drug Alcohol Dependence*, *117*(1), 78–81.

Anonymous. (1966). *The Bhagavad Gita*. Oxford, London, New York: Oxford University Press.

Benson, H. (1996). *Timeless healing: the power and biology of belief*. New York: Fireside.

Bowen, S., Chawla, N., Collins, S. E., Witkiewitz, K., Hsu, S., Grow, J., et al. (2009). Mindfulness-based relapse prevention for substance-use disorders: A pilot efficacy trial. *Substance Abuse*, *30*, 295–305.

Brewer, J. A., Mallik, S., Babuscio, T. A., Nich, C., Johnson, H. E., Deleone, C. M., et al. (2011). Mindfulness training for smoking cessation: results from a randomized controlled trial. *Drug and Alcohol Dependence*, *119*(1–2), 72–80.

Brown, R. P., & Gerbarg, P. L. (2005). Sudarshan kriya yogic breathing in the treatment of stress, anxiety, and depression: Part I—Neurophysiological model. *Journal of Alternative and Complementary Medicine*, *11*(1), 189–201.

Chitwood, D. D., Weiss, M. L., & Leukefeld, C. G. (2008). A systematic review of recent literature on religiosity and substance use. *Journal of Drug Issues*, 0022–0426 /0803, 653–688.

Davis, J. M., Fleming, M. F., Bonus, K. A., & Baker, T. B. (2007). A pilot study on mindfulness based stress reduction for smokers. *BMC Complement Alternative Medicine*, 7, 2.

Dimeff, L. A., & Linehan, M. M. (2008). Dialectical behavior therapy for substance abusers. *Addiction Science & Clinical Practice*, *4*(2), 39–47.

Descilo, T., Vedamurthachar, A., Gerbarg, P. L., Nagaraja, D., Gangadhar, B. N., Damodaran, B., et al. (2009). Effects of a yoga breath intervention alone and in combination with an exposure therapy for post traumatic stress disorder and depression in survivors of the 2004 South-East Asia tsunami. *Acta Psychiatrica Scandinavica*, *12*(4), 289–300.

Eppley, K., Abrams, A., & Shear, J. (1989). The differential effects of relaxation techniques on trait anxiety: a meta-analysis. *Journal of Clinical Psychology*, *45*, 957–974.

Ferri, M., Amato, L., & Davoli, M. (2009). Alcoholics Anonymous and other 12-step programmes for alcohol dependence (Review). *Cochrane Library*, *3*, 1–26.

Fingelkurts, A. A., & Fingelkurts, A. A. (2009). Is our brain hard-wired to produce God? *Cognitive Processing*, *10*(4), 293–326.

Frass, M., Strassl, R. P., Friehs, H., Mullner, M., Kundi, M., & Kaye, A. D. (2012). Use and acceptance of complementary and alternative medicine among the general population and medical personnel: a systematic review. *The Ochsner Journal*, *12*, 45–56.

Galanter, M. (2006). Spirituality and addiction: A research and clinical perspective. *American Journal of Addiction*, *15*(4), 286–292.

Galanter, M. (2008). Spirituality, evidence-based medicine and Alcoholics Anonymous. *American Journal of Psychiatry*, *165*(12), 1514.

Garland, E. L. (2013). *Mindfulness-oriented recovery enhancement*. Washington, DC: NASW Press.

Garland, E. L., Gaylord, S. A., Boettiger, C. A., & Howard, M. O. (2010). Mindfulness training modifies cognitive, affective, and physiological mechanisms implicated in alcohol dependence: Results of a randomized controlled pilot trial. *Journal of Psychoactive Drugs*, *42*(2), 177–192.

Gerbarg, P. L., & Bown, R. P. (2005). Yoga—A breath of relief for hurricane Katrina refugees. *Current Events*, *4*(10), 55–67.

Hölzel, B. K., Lazar, S. W., Gard, T., Schuman-Olivier, Z., Vago, D. R., & Ott, U. (2011). How does mindfulness meditation work? Proposing mechanisms of action from a conceptual and neural perspective. *Perspectives on Psychological Science*, *6*, 537–559.

Hölzel, B. K., Ott, U., Gard, T., Hempel, H., Weygandt, M., Morgen, K., et al. (2008). Investigation of mindfulness meditation practitioners with voxel-based morphometry. *Social Cognitive and Affective Neuroscience*, *3*, 55–61.

James, W. (1929). *The varieties of religious experience*. New York: Modern Library.

Janakiramaiah, N., Gangadhar, B. N., Naga Venkatesha Murthy, P. J., Harish, N. J., Subbakrishna, D. K., & Vedamurthachar, A. (2000). Antidepressant efficacy of Sudarshan Kriya Yoga (SKY) in melancholia: A randomized comparison with electroconvulsive therapy (ECT) and imipramine. *Journal of Affective Disorders*, *57*, 255–259.

Janakiramaiah, N., Gangadhar, B. N., Naga Venkatesha Murthy, P. J., Harish, M. J., Taranath Shetty, K., Subbakrishna, D. K., et al. (1998). Therapeutic efficacy of SKY in dysthymic disorders. *NIMHANS Journal*, *16*, 21–28.

Kabat-Zinn, J. (1982). An outpatient program in behavioral medicine for chronic pain patients based on the practice of mindfulness meditation: Theoretical considerations and preliminary results. *General Hospital Psychiatry*, *4*(1), 33–47.

Kaskutas, L. A. (2009). Alcoholics Anonymous effectiveness: Faith meets science. *Journal of Addictive Diseases*, *28*(2), 145–157.

Kelly, J. F., Hoeppner, B., Stout, R. L., & Pagano, M. (2012). Determining the relative importance of the mechanisms of behavior change within Alcoholics Anonymous: A multiple mediator analysis. *Addiction*, *107*(2), 289–299.

Kelly, J. F., & Magill, M. (2009). How do people recover from alcohol dependence? A systematic review of the research on mechanisms of behavior change in Alcoholics Anonymous. *Addiction Research and Theory*, *17*(3), 236–259.

Kessler, R. C., Davis, R. B., Foster, D. F., et al. (2001). Long term trends in the use of complementary and alternative medical therapies in the United States. *Annals of Internal Medicine*, *135*, 262–268.

Khanna, S., & Greeson, J. M. (2013). A narrative review of yoga and mindfulness as complementary therapies for addiction. *Complementary Therapies in Medicine*, http://dx.doi.org/10.1016/j.ctim.2013.01.008.

Kjellgren, A., Bood, S. A., Axelsson, K., Norlander, T., & Saatcioglu, F. (2007). Wellness through a comprehensive yogic breathing program—A controlled pilot trial. *BMC Complementary and Alternative Medicine*, 7, 43.

Kochupillai, V., Kumar, P., Singh, D., Aggarwal, D., Bhardwaj, N., Bhutani, M., et al. (2005). Effect of rhythmic breathing (Sudarshan Kriya and Pranayam) on immune functions and tobacco addiction. *Annals of the New York Academy of Science*, *1056*, 1–11.

Luders, E., Toga, A. W., Lepore, N., & Gaser, C. (2009). The underlying anatomical correlates of long-term meditation: Larger hippocampal and frontal volumes of gray matter. *NeuroImage*, *45*, 672–678.

Moreira-Almeida, A., Neto, F. L., & Koenig, H. G. (2006). Religiousness and mental health: A review. *Revista Brasileira de Psiquiatria*. *28*(3), http://dx.doi.org/10.1590/S1516-44462006005000006.

Morjaria, A., & Orford, J. (2002). The role of religion and spirituality in recovery from drink problems: A qualitative study of alcoholics anonymous members and South Asian men. *Addiction Research & Theory*, *10*(3), SJS 256.

Naga Venkatesha Murthy, P. J., Gangadhar, B. N., Janakiramaiah, N., & Subbakrishna, D. K. (1997). Normalization of P300 amplitude following treatment in dysthymia. *Biological Psychiatry*, *42*, 740–743.

Naga Venkatesha Murthy, P. J., Janakiramaiah, N., Gangadhar, B. N., & Subbakrishna, D. K. (1998). P300 amplitude and antidepressant response to sudarsha kriya yoga (SKY). *Journal of Affective Disorders*, *50*, 45–48.

National Institutes of Health Reporter. Retrieved from http://clinicaltrials. gov/ct2/show/NCT01505101.

Nespor, K. (1994). Approaches in the treatment of pathologic gambling. *Ceskoslovenska Psychologie*, *90*(3), 149–157.

O'Brien, C. P., Volkow, N., & Li, T.-K. (2006). What's in a word? Addiction versus dependence in DSM-V. *American Journal of Psychiatry*, *163*(5), 764–765.

Orme-Johnson, D. W. (1994). Transcendental meditation as an epidemiological approach to drug and alcohol abuse: Theory, research, and financial impact evaluation. In D. F. O'Connell & C. N. Alexander (Eds.), *Self recovery: treating addictions using transcendental meditation and Maharishi Ayur-Veda* (pp. 119–168). New York: The Haworth Press.

Rao, N. P., Varambally, S., & Gangadhar, B. N. (2013). Yoga school of thought and psychiatry: Therapeutic potential. *Indian Journal of Psychiatry*, *55*(Suppl 2), S145–S149.

Ravi Shankar, S. S. (2010). *Patanjali yoga sutras: A commentary by H.H. Sri Sri Ravi Shankar, Volume 1*. Bangalore, India: Sri Sri Publications Trust.

Rohini, V., Pandey, R. S., Janakiramaiah, N., Gangadhar, B. N., & Vedamurthachar, A. (2000). The role of Sudarshan Kriya on mental health. *NIMHANS Journal*, *18*(1&2), 53–57.

Sacktor, T. C. (2011). How does PKMzeta maintain long-term memory? *Nature Reviews Neuroscience*, *12*, 9–15.

Shafil, M., Lavely, R., & Jaffe, R. (1975). Meditation and the prevention of alcohol abuse. *American Journal of Psychiatry*, *132*(9), 942–945.

Sharma, H., Sen, S., Singh, A., Bhardwaj, N. K., Kochupillai, V., & Singh, N. (2003). Sudarshan Kriya practitioners exhibit better antioxidant status and lower blood lactate levels. *Biological Psychology*, *63*, 284–291.

Tonigan, J., Miller, W., & Connors, G. (2000). Project MATCH client impressions about Alcoholics Anonymous: Measurement issues and relationship to outcome. *Alcoholic Treatment Quarterly*, *18*, 25–41.

Vedamurthachar, A., Agte, V., Bijoor, A. R., Lakshmi, B., & Swathi, R. (2011). Sudarshan Kriya Yoga for improving health status and quality of life in adults. *Indian Journal of Health and Well Being*, *2*(4), 773–775.

Vedamurthachar, A., Anita, R., Dr, Bijoor, Vaishali, A., & Swathi Lakshmi, B. (2011). Short term effect of Sudarshan Kriya yoga on lipid and hormone profile of type 2 diabetic patients. *Research Journal of Chemical Sciences*, *1*(9), 1–7.

Vedamurthachar, A., Janakiramaiah, N., Hegde, J. M., Shetty, T. K., Subbakrishna, D. K., Sureshbabu, S. V., et al. (2006). Antidepressant efficacy and hormonal effects of sudarshana kriya yoga (SKY) in alcohol dependent individuals. *Journal of Affective Disorders*, *94*, 249–253.

Westbrook, C., Creswell, J. D., Tabibnia, G., Julson, E., Kober, H., & Tindle, H. A. (2011). Mindful attention reduces neural and self-reported cue-induced craving in smokers. *Social Cognitive and Affective Neuroscience*, *8*(1), 73–84.

Witkiewitz, K., Lustyk, M. K., & Bowen, S. (2012). Retraining the addicted brain: a review of hypothesized neurobiological mechanisms of mindfulness based relapse prevention. *Psychology of Addicted Behaviours*, *27*(2), 351–365.

Witkiewitz, K., & Bowen, S. (2010). Depression, craving and substance use following a randomized trial of mindfulness-based relapse prevention. *Journal of Consulting and Clinical Psychology*, *78*, 362–374.

Woods, J. H. (Ed.), (1914). *The Yoga Sutras of Patanjali*. Cambridge, MA: Harvard University Press.

Xue, Y. X., Luo, Y. X., Wu, P., Shi, H. S., Xue, L. F., Chen, C., et al. (2012). A memory retrieval-extinction procedure to prevent drug craving and relapse. *Science*, *336*, 241–254.

Yadav, S., Dhawan, A., & Chopra, A. (2006). Exploring: Breath, water and sound course as an adjunct intervention for opiate dependent patients. *World Conference-Expanding Paradigms: Science*, Consciousness and Spirituality, 2006; New Delhi, India.

CHAPTER 15

Behavioral Addiction in American Law: The Future and the Expert's Role

Daniel H. Willick
Los Angeles, CA, USA

INTRODUCTION

In American law, legal liability often may be excused or mitigated by a defendant's mental state or mental incapacity. Excuse or mitigation due to mental illness is common. It follows that the recognition by the *Diagnostic and Statistical Manual of Mental Disorders,* Fifth Edition (*DSM-5*) of the new diagnostic category of "behavioral addictions" will likely impact the legal process by creating new grounds for excuse and mitigation. It probably will increase the number of lawsuits in which a diagnosis that a party suffers from a behavioral addiction will become a material issue. Indeed, this has already been occurring in the absence of *DSM* recognition (Colasurdo, 2010). Behavioral addiction has been relevant to the outcome of lawsuits for more than a decade. This is illustrated by the decision of the United States Sixth Circuit Court of Appeals in *U.S. v. Sadolsky* (2000), where the court affirmed a U.S. District Court's sentence reduction based on a defendant's gambling addiction following the defendant's criminal conviction for fraud and theft. In another decade-old case, the Mississippi Supreme Court (*Bower v. Bower,* 2000) affirmed a lower court's refusal to award a mother child custody in a divorce proceeding because she was diagnosed with an Internet addiction and spent "enormous amounts of time on the Internet," which resulted in her "unstable behavior" of establishing physical relationships with men she met on the Internet. The Mississippi Supreme Court affirmed the lower court's conclusion that the mother's mental health diagnosis of depression and her excessive and unusual use of the Internet to establish relationships with men justified denying her custody of her children.

This chapter identifies existing law where behavioral addiction is relevant to court decisions. It is these areas of the law that are most likely to be impacted by the *DSM-5* recognition of behavioral addiction as a diagnostic

Behavioral Addictions
http://dx.doi.org/10.1016/B978-0-12-407724-9.00015-X

category. Although it is difficult to predict future legal developments or to harmonize the distinct bodies of American federal law and the laws of the 50 states, a discussion of the potential legal significance of behavioral addiction has value. Guidance is provided by reviewing existing law that has considered or may consider behavioral addiction as a relevant legal issue. Because the legal decisions to be discussed typically considered expert testimony by psychotherapists, the chapter concludes with a discussion of expert testimony in such cases.

BEHAVIORAL ADDICTION IN THE LAW OF THE UNITED STATES - LEGAL ISSUES IN WHICH BEHAVIORAL ADDICTION MAY BE CONSIDERED

Mitigation in Federal Criminal Sentencing

The area of the law in which behavioral addiction has had the greatest impact is federal criminal sentencing. Federal sentencing guidelines (United States Sentencing Guidelines Section 5K2.13) permit the sentencing judge to reduce the sentence of a defendant convicted of a federal crime if "the defendant committed the offense while suffering from a significantly reduced mental capacity...[which] contributed substantially to the commission of the offense."

Gambling Addiction

Defendants suffering from a gambling addiction may have their sentences reduced following conviction for fraud or theft under the standard cited in the preceding section (*U.S. v. Liu* 2003; *U.S. v. Sadolsky,* 2000). However, such a claim for a reduced sentence has also been rejected on a number of occasions (*U.S. v. Carucci,* 1999; *U.S. v. Miller,* 2006; *Venezia v. U.S.,* 1995).

Sexual Addiction

There has been one case permitting a downward sentencing adjustment based on a sexual addiction for a defendant convicted of possessing and distributing child pornography (*U.S. v. Lighthall,* 2004). This was based on a finding the defendant suffered from obsessive-compulsive disorder that compelled him to gather pornography. Other attempts to achieve downward sentencing based on sexual addiction have been rejected in cases involving child pornography or the interstate transportation of minors with the intent to engage in sex (*U.S. v. Brooks,* 2010; *U.S. v. Caro,* 2002; *U.S. v. Davis,* 2006; *U.S. v. Long,* 2001 *U.S. v. Romualdo,* 1996).

Shopping Addiction

Finally, a defendant's attempt to obtain a reduced sentence based on her shopping addiction was rejected after conviction of theft by wire fraud (*U.S. v. Roach,* 2002).

The Capacity to Contract

Many jurisdictions have a rule of law that a person lacks the legal capacity to enter into a contract if she or he is "mentally ill or defective" [*Restatement (2d) of Contracts* §12(2)]. In California, this rule finds expression in Civil Code §1556, which states in pertinent part "[a]ll persons are capable of contracting, except *persons of unsound mind...*" (emphasis added). It may be contended that a person is of unsound mind if she or he suffers from a mental deficit or a mental disorder. Additionally, the law may recognize that "a person who has a mental disorder...may still be capable of contracting" [California Probate Code §810, subd. (b)] unless the person "suffers from one or more mental deficits so substantial that, under the circumstances, the person" lacks the capacity to contract [California Probate Code §810, subd. (c)]. However, the requisite finding "should be based on evidence of a deficit in one or more of the person's mental functions rather than on a diagnosis of a person's mental or physical disorder" [California Probate Code §810, subd. (c)]. It is not difficult to envision a person suffering from a behavioral addiction seeking to invalidate a contract because of the addiction. For example, a person with a gambling addiction or a specific mental deficit that is part of or related to that addiction might seek to invalidate a gambling debt by arguing she or he was of unsound mind and did not have the capacity to agree when she or he entered a contract to pay the debt. Although no cases have been found that seek to invalidate a contract due to a party's behavioral addiction, it is not difficult to imagine such a legal theory being asserted.

Family Law Custody Issues

The mental illness of a parent may be grounds to deny or to limit that parent's child custody or visitation in a marital dissolution case. The child's best interests are usually the deciding factor in court determination of disputes in such cases. This means the behavioral addiction of a parent may cause a court-ordered loss or restriction of child custody or visitation rights.

It is not difficult to imagine a parent's manifestation of behavioral addiction, such as gambling, Internet, or sexual addiction, to be grounds for a loss of custody or visitation rights. This is illustrated by the Mississippi Supreme

Court case of *Bower v. Bower* (2000), which affirmed a lower court judgment awarding a divorce and child custody to a husband as being in the best interests of the two children from the marriage. The decision was substantially based on the wife's Internet addiction. The Mississippi Supreme Court affirmed the trial court's findings that the wife's parenting skills were inferior to her husband's because she "spent much of her time on the Internet" (*Bower v. Bower,* 2000, p. 411). The court also affirmed the trial court's negative evaluation of the mental health of the wife. The reason was that "she has spent enormous amounts of time on the Internet talking to strange men and has exhibited unstable behavior of meeting men and beginning physical relationships with those she has met on the Internet" (*Bower v. Bower,* 2000, p. 411). Interestingly, the Mississippi Supreme Court affirmed these findings while disapproving of the admission of testimony of a licensed professional counselor who opined that the wife had an Internet addiction (*Bower v. Bower,* 2000, pp. 412–414). The Supreme Court rejected the trial court's admission of testimony because the professional counselor was not properly qualified as an expert witness in Internet pornography or Internet addiction and was not properly qualified as a witness with first-hand knowledge of the wife's Internet usage. In other words, the Supreme Court affirmed the trial court's finding of the wife's excessive and unusual Internet usage based on the testimony of other witnesses with first-hand knowledge without reference to any purported expert testimony by the professional counselor. The trial court's admission of the testimony of the professional counselor was ruled to be harmless error that would not have changed the outcome of the case denying the wife child custody based on the finding of the wife's enormous Internet usage to establish physical relationships with men.

Strail ex rel. Strail v. Department of Children, Youth and Families of the State of Rhode Island (1999) was a decision in which the U.S. District Court for the District of Rhode Island did not approve a state agency's removal of a daughter from the custody of her mother based on allegations of the Internet sex addiction to pornography of the mother's live-in boyfriend.

Disability Rights Protection for Persons with a Behavioral Addiction

The Americans with Disabilities Act (the "ADA") is a federal law that protects individuals from discrimination based on a trait over which they have no control (42 U.S.C. §12101 et seq.). Protected persons include those suffering from "mental impairment" [42 U.S.C. §12102(1)(A)]. Protections extend to employment and public accommodations and services. Although the reference to mental impairment implies that persons with a behavioral addiction may be protected by the ADA, the law specifically exempts the following disorders from ADA protection (42 U.S.C. §12211):

> *sexual behavior disorders;…compulsive gambling, kleptomania,…pyromania [and]…psychoactive substance use disorder resulting from current illegal use of drugs.*

Legal research in the preparation of this chapter has not found any successful claim under the ADA based on a claimant's behavioral addiction. However, a number of states have enacted laws that are modeled on the ADA. Because state laws that provide protection equal to or greater than ADA protection are not pre-empted by the ADA [42 U.S.C. §12201(b), 29 C.F.R. §1630(d)], it is possible that state law may provide protection for persons with behavioral addiction.

A review of California's antidiscrimination law based on the ADA (California Civil Code §§51, 51.5) finds there is no protection for "sexual behavior disorders, compulsive gambling, kleptomania, pyromania or psychoactive substance abuse disorders resulting from the current use of controlled substances or other drugs" [California Government Code §12926, subd. (j)]. This exclusion is virtually identical to the exclusion in federal law (42 U.S.C. §12211) of many behavioral addictions from ADA protection. However, California's legislative declaration that its antidiscrimination law provides "broader coverage" than the ADA [California Government Code §12926.1, subd. (c)] opens the door for future coverage for behavioral addictions, such as Internet addiction, that are not specifically excluded from protection by either federal or California law.

Qualification for Benefits Pursuant to the Individuals with Disabilities Education Act (IDEA)

The IDEA (20 U.S.C. §§1400–1482) is a federal law which requires that a child with a serious emotional disturbance is entitled to public school special education and related services if the emotional disturbance adversely affects the child's educational performance (20 U.S.C. §1401). Emotional disturbance is defined as a condition exhibiting "[i]nappropriate types of behavior…under normal circumstances…" "…for a long period of time and to a marked degree that adversely affects…[the] child's educational performance" (34 C.F.R. §300.8(c)(4)). This seems to open the door for claims that a child's behavioral addiction is a proper basis to obtain IDEA protection. However, like some of the other areas of law discussed, there is a lack of precedent granting protection for behavioral addiction. Nevertheless,

IDEA claims based on students' behavioral addictions can be expected. For example, is a high school student suffering from an online gaming addiction entitled to IDEA protection that precludes enrollment of the student in any course involving required use of the Internet or a computer?

Loss of a Professional License

A behavioral addiction may be the basis for denial or loss of a professional license. *In re Menna* (1995) is such a case. The California Supreme Court affirmed the decision of the California State Bar denying an application to practice law by an applicant who had been disbarred in New Jersey based on his theft of client funds as a result of his gambling addiction. Although two psychologists who had counseled the applicant testified that he had fully recovered from his gambling addiction, the court ruled "we are nevertheless not persuaded he has demonstrated his overall rehabilitation by clear and convincing evidence.... Nor when weighed against the enormity of his previous misconduct, does applicant's recovery from a gambling addiction necessarily justify his admission" (*In re Menna,* 1995, 988).

Exclusion of Persons with Gambling Addictions from Casinos

A number of states enforce laws that allow persons who identify themselves as suffering from a gambling addiction to request exclusion from casinos. Such laws exist in Iowa [Iowa Admin. Code r. 491-5.4(12)], Louisiana [Title 42 La. Admin. Code §304(c)], and Missouri (Missouri Rules of Department of Public Safety Title 11, Chap. 17, 11 CSR 45-17.010). In *Borgman v. Kedley* (2011), the federal Eighth Circuit Court of Appeals ruled an Iowa casino was not required to pay a gambler a jackpot she won because she had signed a legally authorized exclusion request and also ruled the exclusion request justified her arrest at the casino by a state agent. In the case of *Caesar's Riverboat Casino, LLC v. Kephart* (2010), the Indiana Supreme Court ruled that Indiana's legislative scheme regulating casinos prohibited a gambler's damage claim to recover his gambling losses from a casino that knew of his gambling addiction and allegedly enticed him to gamble.

Conclusions

The *DSM-5* recognition of behavioral addiction as a category of disease is most likely of legal significance. Unfortunately, the specific implications of this development may not be predicted with precision. Nevertheless, this chapter's review of legal rules and court decisions recognizing the legal relevance of behavioral addiction before the *DSM-5* suggest some areas of probable legal impact. As discussed in the following sections, expert testimony will likely be important in legal cases involving behavioral addiction.

PITFALLS FOR THE EXPERT WITNESS

The Nature of Expert Testimony

With the recognition by the *DSM-5* of behavioral addiction as a diagnostic category, it is anticipated that the concept will become legally relevant in more lawsuits in which the mental state of a party is an issue. Expert testimony will be sought to establish or refute the contention that a party is suffering from a behavioral addiction that should excuse or mitigate the legal consequences of that party's acts or omissions. Hence, it is important to consider the role of psychotherapists who are contemplating or occupying the role of expert witness.

Expert testimony is offered to assist the trier of fact, which is often a jury, in resolving significant questions of fact at issue in a lawsuit. An expert is allowed to testify if she or he has special knowledge that will be of assistance to the trier of fact in deciding an issue of fact. Federal law (Federal Rule of Evidence 702) expresses the concept as follows:

> *A witness who is qualified as an expert by knowledge, skill, experience, training, or education may testify in the form of opinion or otherwise if:*
>
> *(a) the expert's scientific, technical, or other specialized knowledge will help the trier of fact to understand the evidence or to determine a fact in issue;*
> *(b) the testimony is based on sufficient facts or data;*
> *(c) the testimony is a product of reliable principles and methods; and*
> *(d) the expert has reliably applied the principles and methods to the facts of the case.*

State law may be more lenient than federal law in permitting expert testimony. For example, California courts have admitted expert testimony when it is "[r]elated to a subject that is sufficiently beyond common experience that the opinion of an expert would assist the trier of fact" [California Evidence Code §801, subd. (a)].

Expert testimony may be admitted in cases in which an issue is whether a party has a particular mental condition or diagnosis, such as a behavioral addiction, that is relevant to the issues in the lawsuit. Expert testimony may also be presented regarding what impact the mental condition has on the acts or omissions of the party. It is usual that a psychiatrist or a psychologist is designated as an expert to testify about whether or not a party has a particular mental condition and the consequences if the party has the mental condition. There are a number of legal issues and practical considerations that a psychotherapist designated as an expert should consider.

Considerations for a Psychotherapist Who Wishes to Testify as an Expert Witness

Qualifications and Expertise

A psychotherapist who wishes to be retained to provide expert advice or testimony on behavioral addiction should have requisite qualifications. This should include postgraduate training and degrees, licensure as a psychotherapist, board certification, experience in diagnosing and treating behavioral addiction, familiarity with the research literature on behavioral addiction and, if possible, participation in original research on the subject.

The Risk That the Expert's Opinion Will Not Support the Attorney Who Retains the Expert

Although experts often have the reputation of being "hired guns," it is always possible that the expert opinion rendered will not support the position of a party who retains the expert. Of course, this is not an issue where the expert is retained to provide a neutral opinion by the court or by stipulation between the contending parties to a lawsuit.

Protection of the independence of an expert retained by a contending party is possible when the expert is initially retained by the party's attorney as a consultant with the attorney having the option of turning the expert consultant into an expert witness. That way, if such a conversion does not occur, the expert consultant's opinion remains confidential and protected as attorney work product. However, should the attorney like the expert's opinion and designate the expert as an expert witness, the cloak of confidentiality is removed and communications between the expert and the attorney will be open to disclosure as relevant to the expert opinion to be offered in testimony by the expert witness.

The Risk the Court Will Exclude the Expert's Proposed Testimony

There is always the danger that the court will exclude an expert's testimony. This is particularly true in federal court where Federal Rule of Evidence 702 "specifies that a witness may provide expert opinion only if the testimony is based on sufficient facts or data, the testimony is the product of reliable principles and methods, and the witness has applied the principles and methods reliably to the facts of the case" (Witkin, 2012). This federal standard may be problematic when applied to opinions about the diagnosis and consequences of behavioral addiction. Specifically, the question is whether reliable and valid procedures were followed in coming to the opinions proffered (*Daubert v. Merrell Dow Pharms., Inc.*, 1993; *General Electric Co. v. Joiner*, 1997; *Kumho Tire Co. v. Carmichael*, 1999).

Some states use the more lenient standard for admissibility of expert testimony articulated in *Frye v. United States* (1923). This more lenient test makes expert testimony admissible where the opinion or the basis upon which the expert opinion is derived has gained general acceptance in the particular field of expertise. See California Evidence Code §802 and *The People v. Kelly* (1976) for examples. However, please note that a more recent California Supreme Court decision has moved California law toward the more restrictive federal rule (*Sargon v. Univ. of So. Calif.*, 2013).

A Treating Psychotherapist Should Not Be the Primary Expert Witness for Her or His Patient

Forensic ethics arguably preclude a treating psychotherapist from being the primary expert witness for her or his patient. (American Academy of Psychiatry and the Law, 2005, Ethical Guidelines adopted May 2005 at p. 3; www.aapl.org/pdf/ethicsgdlns.pdf; American Psychological Association, 2011, Specialty Guidelines for Forensic Psychology, Guidelines 4.02.01, 4.02.02). Furthermore, such a dual role may jeopardize the treatment relationship and waive the psychotherapist-patient privilege to the extent it has not already been waived by the patient's tendering her or his medical condition in the pending legal proceeding for which the expert testimony is sought.

The Expert Witness May Be Required to Comply with HIPAA

If the expert would otherwise be required to comply with the Health Insurance Portability and Accountability Act (HIPAA) as a health care provider, she or he will be required to comply with HIPAA when conducting a forensic examination or evaluation of a person for a possible diagnosis of behavioral addiction. HIPAA applies to any health care provider who transmits or uses protected health information in electronic form (45 C.F.R. §160.102). Protected health information includes information created or received by an HIPAA-covered health care provider or entity which is information that relates to the past, present, or future physical or mental health or condition of an individual (45 C.F.R. §160.103). This includes protected health information that describes or relates to the condition of the person being evaluated by the expert.

An expert subject to HIPAA must comply with each of the following requirements:

a. Adopt written privacy procedures specifying who has access to health information, how health information will be used and when information will be disclosed;

b. Adopt a written notice of privacy practices;
c. Have consent forms;
d. Have authorization forms;
e. Enter into written contracts with business associates protecting the confidentiality of protected health information;
f. Designate a privacy officer;
g. Train personnel; and
h. Have grievance procedures for patients or the person evaluated to inquire and complain about the use, disclosure, or privacy of their health care information.

Licensure as a Psychotherapist May Be Required in the State Where the Expert Examines a Person or Testifies

Some states prohibit a psychotherapist who is an expert from examining a person or offering an opinion as to that person's condition unless the psychotherapist is licensed to practice in that state (Simon & Shuman, 1999). Hence, the expert witness who is a psychotherapist may be required to be licensed in the state where her or his testimony will be presented in court.

An Expert May Be Sued and Should Have Liability Insurance to Protect Against This Possibility

An expert witness may be sued for damages or subject to disciplinary action allegedly caused by her or his work as an expert and may also be subject to prosecution or disciplinary proceedings for this work (Willick et al., 2002). For example, in *Budwin v. American Psychological Association* (1994), the California Court of Appeal ruled that a forensic witness in a child custody hearing may be subjected to prosecution for ethics violation by a professional society based on his in-court testimony as an expert. In another decision by a California Court of Appeal in *Susan A. v. County of Sonoma* (1991), the court ruled a forensic psychologist witness could be sued for defamation based on a press interview he gave about his in-court testimony in a juvenile criminal case.

It is important to note that not all psychotherapist liability insurance provides coverage for claims arising out of forensic testimony.

Prudence Suggests the Expert Enter into a Written Engagement Agreement with the Attorney Retaining the Expert

It is recommended that an expert enter into a written engagement agreement with any attorney retaining her or his services. The agreement should describe the terms of engagement including

a. Fees to be charged (a contingent fee is not proper and is unethical);
b. The status of the expert as a consultant who may be designated as an expert witness at the option of the retaining attorney;
c. The possibility that the expert's opinion may be adverse;
d. The possibility that the psychotherapist may not qualify as an expert and may not be allowed to testify;
e. The attorney retaining the expert is responsible for evaluating the relevance and admissibility of the work performed by the expert; and
f. The contract should be signed by both the attorney and the attorney's client and should state the terms of their obligation to pay the expert.

CONCLUSIONS

As discussed in the preceding sections, an expert in a case involving behavioral addictions should

1. Provide expert witness testimony only in a behavioral addictions case for which she or he has the requisite training and experience;
2. Make clear to any attorney retaining the expert that the expert's opinion may not support the position the attorney is advocating and, if possible, the expert should be retained as a consultant with the attorney having the option of whether or not to make the expert a witness;
3. Make clear that a court may choose to exclude the expert's proposed testimony;
4. Never act as the primary expert witness for a patient;
5. Comply with HIPAA, if she or he otherwise is required to do so;
6. Before taking an assignment in a jurisdiction where she or he is not licensed, confirm whether she or he must possess a license to practice in that state; and
7. Enter into a written agreement with appropriate provisions when retained by an attorney.

The issues confronted by a psychotherapist who wishes to provide expert advice in a legal proceeding concerning the diagnosis or consequences of behavioral addiction are complex and deserve thoughtful attention. A psychotherapist retained as an expert in a legal proceeding concerning behavioral addiction will be well advised to consider the points and guidelines outlined in this chapter concerning the current and evolving role of behavioral addictions in American law.

REFERENCES

American Academy of Psychiatry and the Law. (2005). Ethical Guidelines adopted May 2005, at p. 3, www.aapl.org/pdf/ethicsgdlns.pdf.
American Psychological Association. (2011). Specialty Guidelines for Forensic Psychology. *Guidelines*, 4.02.01, 4.02.02.
Borgman v. Kedley, 646 F.3d 518 (8th Cir. 2011).
Bower v. Bower, 758 So.2d 405 (Miss. 2000).
Budwin v. American Psychological Association, 24 Cal. App. 4th 875 (Ct. App. 1994).
Caesar's Riverboat Casino, LLC v. Kephart, 934 N.E. 2d 1120 (Ind. 2010).
Colasurdo, B. (2010). Behavioral addictions and the law. *Southern California Law Review, 84*, 161–199.
Daubert v. Merrell Dow Pharms., Inc., 509 U.S. 579 (1993).
Frye v. United States, 293 F.1013 (D.C. Cir. 1923).
General Electric Co. v. Joiner, 522 U.S. 136 (1997).
In re Menna, 11 Cal.4th 975 (1995).
Kumho Tire Co. v. Carmichael, 526 U.S. 137 (1999).
Sargon v. Univ. of So. Calif, 55 Cal.4th 747 (2013).
Simon, R. I., & Shuman, D. W. (1999). Conducting forensic examinations on the road: Are you practicing your profession without a license? *Journal of the American Academy of Psychiatry and the Law, 27*, 75–82.
Strail ex rel. Strail v. Department of Children, Youth and Families of the State of Rhode Island, 62 F.Supp.2d 519 (D.R.I. 1999).
Susan A. v. County of Sonoma, 2 Cal.App.4th 88 (Ct.App. 1991).
The People v. Kelly, 17 Cal.3d 24 (1976).
U.S. v. Brooks, 628 F.3d 79 (6th Cir. 2010).
U.S. v. Caro, 309 F.3d 1348 (11th Cir. 2002).
U.S. v. Carucci, 33 F.Supp.2d 302 (S.D.N.Y. 1999).
U.S. v. Davis, 182 Fed.Appx. 741 (9th Cir. 2006).
U.S. v. Lighthall, 389 F.3d 791 (8th Cir. 2004).
U.S. v. Liu, 267 F.Supp.2d 371 (E.D.N.Y 2003).
U.S. v. Long, 185 F.Supp.2d 30 (D.D.C. 2001).
U.S. v. Miller, 178 Fed.Appx. 70 (2d Cir. 2006).
U.S. v. Roach, 296 F.3d 565 (7th Cir. 2002).
U.S. v. Romualdo, 101 F.3d 971 (3d Cir. 1996).
U.S. v. Sadolsky, 234 F.3d 938 (6th Cir. 2000).
Venezia v. U.S., 884 F.Supp. 719 (Dist. N.J. 1995) affd. without opin., 77 F.3d 465 (3d Cir. 1995).
Willick, D., Weinstock, R., & Garrick, T. (2002). Liability of the forensic psychiatrist. In R. Rosner (Ed.), *Principles and Practice of Forensic Psychiatry (Chapter 9)*. London: Oxford University Press.
Witkin, B. E. (2012). *California Evidence* (5th ed.). San Francisco, CA: Witkin Legal Institute 637–638.

INDEX

Note: Page numbers followed by "f" denote figures; "t" tables.

D

E

F

G

H

I

K

L

R

S

T

W

Y

Z

Edwards Brothers Malloy
Thorofare, NJ USA
April 20, 2015